Molly Weir was born in Glasgow and spent her early years there – the background to this trilogy. She started writing at school and had her first article accepted, by the *Glasgow Evening Times*, at the age of fifteen. From then on she has freelanced 'as the mood takes her', for newspapers and magazines, among them the *People's Journal* and Canada's *The Scottish Banner*. In addition to her work as a writer, Molly Weir is well known as an actress on both television and on the radio, as well as films and the stage. Recent appearances include Victoria Wood's *As Seen on TV*, *Highway* (with Sir Harry Secombe) and *Why Don't You* (with Princess Diana).

By the same author

Molly Weir's Recipes
Stepping into the Spotlight
Walking into the Lyons' Den
One Small Footprint
Spinning Like a Peerie

MOLLY WEIR'S TRILOGY
OF SCOTTISH CHILDHOOD

Shoes were for Sunday
Best Foot Forward
A Toe on the Ladder

**LOMOND
BOOKS**

This edition published in 1995 for
Lomond Books Limited
36 West Shore Road
Granton, Edinburgh EH5 1QD
by Diamond Books
77–85 Fulham Palace Road
Hammersmith, London W6 8JB

Published by Grafton Books 1988

Shoes Were for Sunday first published in Great Britain by
Hutchinson & Co (Publishers) Ltd 1970
Best Foot Forward first published in Great Britain by
Hutchinson & Co (Publishers) Ltd 1972
A Toe on the Ladder first published in Great Britain by
Hutchinson & Co (Publishers) Ltd 1973

Contents

Shoes were for Sunday   7

Best Foot Forward   149

A Toe on the Ladder   359

Shoes were for Sunday

Dedicated to Grannie, and to her daughter,
who was my mother

'What strange, mysterious links enchain the heart,
to regions where the morn of life was spent.'

JAMES GRAHAME

1

Somehow I was never awake at the precise moment when Grannie came into bed. One minute I was drowsily gazing at the gas mantle, blinking my lashes against its soft radiance and making rainbows with my flickering eyelids and its glowing globe, and the next moment it was dark and Grannie was pulling the blankets round her, and easing herself into the hollow in front of me. As I cooried in closer, to keep my share of the bedclothes, she would reach out a hand to push my knees down. 'Your banes are like sticks,' she would complain. 'Streetch them doon noo. They're that sherp, they're cuttin' intae auld Grannie's back.' Sleepily, obediently, I would straighten out my legs, and I would drift off with a drowsy smile as I prodded with a small hand my offending knees. How could Grannie think they were sharp enough to hurt her? I wondered. They felt soft and ordinary enough to me. But then I was only three years old and Grannie was, oh maybe a hundred, for, after all, she was my mother's mother, and my mother was twenty-one, for she had told us so when we asked her.

I couldn't remember a time when I hadn't slept in the hurley bed with Grannie. This was a bed on casters, which 'hurled' under the big recess bed out of sight during the day, and was hidden tidily out of sight behind the bed-pawn, ready to be pulled out at a touch whenever it was my bedtime. It was only about a foot off the floor, so that it could be hurled away fully made up with its sheets and pillows and blankets, and was probably made by a neighbour who was a handyman joiner, and who grasped at once the necessity for using every inch of space in a room and kitchen which had to accommodate five people.

There was my grannie, my mother, my two brothers and myself. Away, way back I had a dream-like memory of a man who refused to pick me up and carry me when we had been out visiting one bitterly cold Sunday, and it was very late, and we couldn't find a tramcar. 'Give her a carry,' my mother's voice said. 'She's only a baby.' 'She can walk,' came the man's voice. 'There's nothing wrong with her legs.' There was no spoiling for me. That must have been my father. A father who lived only long enough to sire three children. Four if you count the little sister who died in infancy, and whom he quickly followed, leaving my mother to bring the three of us up without anybody's help except that given by Grannie. Grannie gave up her own wee single end, and came to live with us. I never missed my father. For, filling every corner of my world was Grannie. From the minute I opened my eyes in the hurley bed in the morning, she tormented me, disciplined me, taught me, laughed at me, loved me, and tied me to her forever, although I didn't know it at the time.

We called our room and kitchen a 'house', for we'd never heard the word 'flat' when I was a wee girl. It was in a red sandstone tenement, which we thought far nicer than the dull grey tenements farther up the road. In some mysterious way some closes were smarter than others. The Cooperative close at No. 290 was considered really classy. For one thing there were no children, and instead of painted dark green walls inside the close, like the other tenements, this one had tiles which were the envy of every other tenement wife, for they could be wiped clean at the touch of a cloth, and this sparkling cleanliness awed us with its rich look. This back court, too, was different from our ordinary earth one, for it was concreted all over, and the wall which divided it from our lesser courts was higher than ours, and not a railing was missing. This rigid iron barrier was useless in keeping out the rest of us children from the teeming tenements. Although we were fully aware it was forbidden territory, every now and then, just to test our courage, we would go tearing through the splendid tiled close and invade the concreted back court. We would stot our balls in an ecstasy of delight to see how high they would bounce off this marvellous concrete, then throw them against the walls of the posh tenement itself. Then, freedom from punishment going to our heads, we would go mad and start yelling at the tops of our voices, without rhyme or reason, 'Come up for yer dinner, ya red-heided sinner, cauld totties an' herrin'.'

At that a window would be thrown up, and an outraged face would appear. This was the policeman's house, and we shivered at our own daring in arousing his wife's wrath. 'Go back to your own back courts,' she called out furiously, in a much more polite accent than our own mother's, we noted, 'and stop yelling.' Yelling? Who was yelling? We were only singing. We were intensely curious about this woman, who had no children. We gazed at her, mesmerized, trying to imagine her quiet house with only herself and the policeman to keep her company.

I remember one day when I was about seven years old she actually called me up from where I was playing in the next back court and asked me to run to the butcher's and get half a pound of mince for her. I was startled to find she ate ordinary mince like us. When I went back to hand it over she asked me in, instead of keeping me on the doorstep like all the other mothers, who certainly didn't encourage us to race over their clean linoleum with our dirty feet. I stood stiffly in the middle of the floor, frightened to move in case I'd break anything, and astounded at the neatness and tidiness of it all. No toys. No papers. No shiny American cloth stretched over the table to keep it safe from spilt tea or gravy. Instead, unbelievably, a polished table with a vase of flowers on top. My eyes darted round the room, taking everything in, and I was quite dazzled by its splendour, and I felt a singing in my ears at its quietness. I'd never been in a house before which wasn't noisy with lively children. She gave me a piece of gingerbread which was so generously spread with salt butter that the richness was too much for me and I couldn't eat it. When half a pound of margarine had to last five of us as long as it could possibly be stretched, and the paper scraped to get the last tiny piece, you weren't used to your teeth meeting a thick layer of butter. But I wouldn't have dreamt of wasting it. I ran home with it to Grannie and she scraped off the thick top layer and prudently put it aside for her own tea later. She loved this butter, which she seldom got, but I, brought up on the cheaper margarine, thought it had a funny taste and gladly let Grannie enjoy this beanfeast.

Grannie could see I was full of my privileged peep at the inside of the policeman's house, and I daresay she was quite curious herself, for nobody else on our stair had ever got over the door. 'Grannie,' I said excitedly, 'she's got a house like a palace. Everything's shining! Dae ye know whit she was daein' when ah went in? She was polishin' the kettle, Grannie. The kettle! No' the brass kettle for the mantelpiece. The kettle that sits on the range. And it would juist get durty again as soon as she pit it oan the fire.' 'Och well, lassie,' said Grannie comfortably, 'she's got nae weans, you see, and she disnae ken whit to be at tae pass the time.'

Ever afterwards in my mind childlessness and sparkling tidiness went together, and when I passed the policeman's wife in the street after that she seemed to belong to another species, and I'd follow her in imagination into her quiet neat house, with never a raucous child to disturb its serenity. And I never made a noise in her back court again.

Old Grannie's down our stair was another house which fascinated me for much the same reason. Her children were all grown up long ago, and the silence and orderliness were such a contrast to our lively, bustling, noisy house that I needed no coaxing to go down to see if she needed any messages. She was a very old lady, even older than my grannie. She had a thin pink face, snow-white hair, was thin as a whippet, and she moved so slowly I felt sure she was frightened her bones would break if she hurried. She came from Ayrshire, and her accent was different from ours, and she called a saucer a 'flet', which I found highly diverting. She had photograph albums with pictures which went right back to her childhood, and it was my delight to pore over them by the hour asking, 'And was this your husband, Grannie,' for I knew it only needed that question for her to gaze dreamily into the coals and tell me about how she had gone to her first dance in the country at the age of fifteen, and how this handsome man with the moustache and side-whiskers had come over to her and asked her to dance. At the end of the reel he had thrown his bag of sweeties into her lap and said, 'You're for me,' and they were married when she was sixteen. The speed and directness of this courtship took my breath away. 'But did you *love* him, Grannie,' I would ask every time this story was told. I passionately wanted her to have some opinion on the matter. 'Aye, I suppose I did, lassie,' she would smile. 'But, you see, ah wis a ferm servant, and in those days you were only too pleased to get a guid man, and a hoose o' yer ain, so you didnae speir at yersel' too much aboot whether or no' ye liked him. And in oor village it was aye the man who did the seekin'.' As I gazed at the solemn bewhiskered face in the photograph I found it hard to imagine this dull man had ever done anything so romantic as sweep Grannie off her feet at the age of fifteen. Nevertheless, Grannie was only waiting now to join him in heaven, and under the bed she had a wooden chest containing her shroud and a cotton 'mutch', and even the pennies to cover her eyes, and a white bandage to tie round her mouth.

My mother was unwittingly roped in to help to fill this wooden burial chest with the final item. She had spent the whole of one precious lunch hour going into every haberdashery in Springburn searching for a cotton 'mutch', which this old grannie had asked her to buy for her, thinking the old lady was feeling the cold and wanted it there and then. When she dashed in in triumph, having found it in the very last shop, she was furious when Grannie pulled out the chest and said with satisfaction, 'Aye, that's the lot noo. I can go any time.' As my mother bolted her sausages before rushing back to her work in the Railways, she said to my grannie, 'Fancy that old rascal making me flee all over Springburn for something she'll no' want till she's deid. And here was me thinkin' ah wis doin' her a good turn, and keepin' her heid warm on these cauld nights.' My own grannie laughed, 'Weel, so you have done her a guid turn. She'll sleep faur better noo, kennin' her burial trousseau is complete.' In spite of herself, my mother had to laugh. But I didn't laugh. For I sometimes went down to sleep with this old lady to keep her company in the winter, and I didn't like the thought of sleeping on a bed with a shroud and burial garments in a fearsome box underneath.

All our neighbours were a source of great interest to me. I

didn't see them as an assortment of shabbily dressed women struggling against heavy odds to make ends meet, and keep dirt at bay. I was vividly aware of their peculiarities, and absorbed in their lives. There was our red-faced upstairs neighbour, with her five pale children and her dull quiet husband, who hardly opened his mouth. She was the terror of the stair. We could tell at a glance when she was in ferocious mood, as likely as not to give you a swipe in the passing just for staring at her. She was a huge woman, and I used to shiver with fright when the sound of yelling and screaming in her house above our heads told me she was giving the children another walloping. Her violence terrified me, and I never dreamed the day would dawn when she would become a semi-paralysed invalid, worn out by her own wild temper. Maybe she had high blood pressure or some awful secret illness, for we never associated health with behaviour. You were either a targe or you weren't, and there was an end of it.

There was a dirty woman in a nearby close, quiet and self-effacing, who stank to high heaven and we took the smell with the personality, but gave her a wide berth just the same. I was sternly forbidden ever to borrow a comb from any of her children in case I'd borrow a few beasts at the same time. My mother had vowed that when she had been speaking to her she'd been horrified to see the beasts running around the wool which tied this woman's specs to her ears! I made an excuse to go to her door, and, staring fixedly at the wool holding the specs, noted without as much as a shudder that my mother was right. It was no exaggeration.

I was usually far too wise to repeat any of the remarks overheard in our kitchen, but once I got carried away by what I thought was Grannie's praise of a chum's mother who had a particularly explosive laugh. I burst out admiringly, 'Oh, Mrs D., laugh like that again. My grannie says you've a laugh like a cackling hen.' Grannie seized me by the ear the minute I came in from play and demanded to know why I'd been so silly as to cause trouble like this, for of course Mrs D. had been furious. Somehow I just couldn't make Grannie understand that I thought it was a compliment. If I had been able to laugh like a hen cackling I'd have been delighted with my cleverness.

16

Grannie sighed, for she knew that one of my proudest party pieces was imitating a chimpanzee, walk, grimace, shrieks and all, and I had to be threatened with a walloping before I'd promise never to do it again.

There was even a dandy in the tenement, who donned yellow chamois gloves when he went out courting another woman, not his wife. She, poor thing, couldn't stop his amorous ways, but his mother-in-law told me fiercely, 'He's a rotter. He's lived on the steps o' the jile a' his life.' How could he live on the steps of the jail, I wondered, and still live up our stair? She also told me darkly that he'd even broken into a harem during the war, and had been lucky not to have been shot for it. A harem! What was so terrible about that? I would have liked to have seen inside a harem myself, and gazed upon all those concubines, a word which had intrigued me ever since I first read it in the Bible.

There was a wee skinny woman, so poor that she actually was glad to do our washing for us for half a crown, for my mother was too exhausted after her heavy work in the Railways to do this herself. This wee creature crept down to the warmth of our fire every single night in life. She never opened her mouth, but rocked silently back and forth, sipping the tea Grannie always had ready for her. Once when my auntie came to stay with us on a visit from Australia, and could stand this woman's silent presence not a minute longer, she jokingly sprang up and shouted to the wee washer-woman, 'What the devil are you making all the noise about?' The wee creature got such a shock she leaped to her feet, spilling tea all over the fireside, and rushed from the house, and never came back until Auntie had safely left for Australia again. My mother was mad, because we got no more washing done for us all the time Auntie was with us.

But our favourite neighbours, for us children I mean, were the newly married ones. When they came to our tenements they seemed so fresh, and lively, and young, after all the workworn mothers we knew. They sang at their work in their newly furnished kitchens. They didn't mind us perching on the window-ledges of their ground-floor tenement rooms and watching their every move. They showed off a bit as they worked, and we loved their exaggerated movements as they lifted kettles and polished their brasses. And they always had babies for us to take out in the big enveloping shawls which wrapped baby and baby-minder in a safe, warm cocoon. There were no prams in the tenements. A pram was as impossible in our economy as a Rolls-Royce. But if babies didn't always get enough to eat, they always had the warmth and comfort of being wrapped close to a loving body.

I was so small, nobody would entrust me to carry their baby in this way, although I was occasionally allowed to hold one on my lap. It was my life's ambition to be trusted to take one of those babies out in a shawl. At last one newly wed mother yielded to my non-stop coaxing. Trembling, I took the baby in my left arm, while the mother wrapped the big grey shawl firmly round the baby, then across my back, under my right arm, and tucked the ends safely below my right hand. Alas, she didn't notice she'd left an end of the shawl hanging down at the back, and I'd not walked a dozen yards into the back courts proudly carrying my precious burden when I tripped and went rolling over and over in the dirt. I never let go the baby, I'm proud to say, and it didn't seem unduly disturbed as it rolled over and over with me. But the mother nearly had a fit and came screaming from the house, seized the baby from me, and had a terrifying bout of hysterics with the sheer relief of finding it was still alive and no bones broken. That ended my career as a baby-minder. The whole back court had seen me, and I was disgraced. I rushed up to the swings at the top of Springburn to forget my misery, and was soon able to stop my trembling unhappiness as I flew round and round on the joy-wheel, and soared higher and higher on the big swings.

And yet, much as I enjoyed the excitement of the young neighbours, the face which comes and looks at me gravely through the years is the face of Mrs McCorbie.

How is this? I wonder. I've a feeling that some people have a quality about them which singles them out for attention wherever fate chooses to place them, and however humbly they work out their destinies. They're the sort of people whose lives fascinate novelists, for they've an out-of-the-ordinary ambience which makes their slightest action memorable.

Born into an artistic background, they'd attract painters and poets to sing their praises, but even when found among the working classes they somehow manage to triumph over the drabness of their surroundings and find a dignity which lifts them above the commonplace.

At least, that's how it strikes me. For why, among so many, should I remember Mrs McCorbie with such an anguished pang?

We were very proud that she should have singled us out for her friendship, because she had the stiff reserve of the very poor who can't mix freely for fear of getting caught up in an expenditure which was quite beyond her. There wasn't the tiniest margin in Mrs McCorbie's budget which she could spare for all the hundred and one little social occasions which made up our lives. A penny for the hospitals, a penny for a wreath, a penny towards a present for wee Cathie who was dying in hospital of tuberculosis, and so on, and so on. Each sum minute in itself, but quite beyond the reach of Mrs McCorbie, whose every penny was painfully earned and had to do the work of three.

She was only too aware of her poverty, and the easy-going ways of others in the same state were beyond her, and we were her only friends.

It was never mentioned, but years later I understood that her husband, who had brought Mrs McCorbie from the Highlands to the big city where work was plentiful, had later deserted her and their children for another woman. I don't suppose he'd ever seen blonde dyed hair or make-up before he came to Glasgow, or been aware that his own splendid physique was so attractive to women. Wife, children, responsibilities, were forgotten and he vanished to be seen no more.

Mrs McCorbie, stunned and bewildered, had been too proud to try to trace him to make him provide for the children. Instead, after the first numbness had worn off, she faced the grim necessity of providing food and clothing and, most urgent of all, of meeting the monthly demands for rent. They could survive most things if they could just keep the roof over their heads.

She couldn't leave home to look for work, for the children were still very young and needed constant attention and nobody in our tenements had time to take another family under their wing; they had children of their own which took all their energies and patience. No, it had to be something she could do within the four walls of her own living-room. Her eye, I imagine, fell on the sewing machine she had brought from her Highland home, and she had an inspiration. She would take in sewing. But not for the neighbours, oh no. She wouldn't be dependent on them for her livelihood. Anyway, she had to be paid as the work was done, and she knew she could never ask neighbours for payment if they were careless about their debts.

She had heard somewhere that factories sometimes employed home workers. So, dressing in her neat black coat, and pulling a felt hat over her mass of coiled black hair, she went to the only factory she knew, a large warehouse in the city where her husband had occasionally bought shirts. They were willing to let her stitch the collars and cuffs on their shirts for the handsome sum of a farthing per shirt. She was to collect a pile of unfinished shirts, loose collars and cuffs each morning, and return them the following morning, when she could collect a fresh batch. There was no limit to the amount she could have – it was entirely up to her how much she earned.

So her life of slavery to the machine began.

This all happened before I was born, and by the time I was toddling up and down the tenement stairs I accepted as part of the pattern of my life the whirring sound of the machine, like a gigantic bumble-bee, constantly buzzing in the house of Mrs McCorbie.

Her one treasured relaxation was the early-morning visit to our house to see my grannie. We lived immediately above her and it was my mother's furious denunciation of the scoundrelly Mr McCorbie that drew this wordlessly suffering woman to us in the first place. She herself didn't utter a word in self-pity or anger against her husband – her hurt went too deep for that – but in my mother's rage Mrs McCorbie sensed a warmth and a friendship for herself that she needed desperately at that time. Her reserve melted. She crept out from behind her shut front door and the morning visits helped her face her daily struggle. It was quite a little ritual. She would wait until the light tread of Grannie's footsteps overhead assured her that she wasn't too early, and her soft tap on the door was hospitably answered by Grannie's half-surprised, 'Oh come in, Mrs McCorbie,' as though the visit was a delightful impulse. She never accepted Grannie's invitation to sit down – that would have implied a real call – but always stood by the dresser, almost silent, listening with a quiet smile to Grannie's chatter and watching her brisk, busy movements as she made porridge for us children and set the table for breakfast. As she watched and listened, she subconsciously swung her house keys round her finger on a ring, and it's one of the most vivid memories of my early childhood, slowly emerging from sleep to the accompanying tinkle of Mrs McCorbie's keys, and then, as awareness grew, enjoying the steady murmur of the voices, pitched on a comforting low tone so that we might not be disturbed before it was necessary. I would glance through sleepy lashes, noting with pleasure the heavy coil of jet-black hair at the base of Mrs McCorbie's neck, the soft brown eyes and the pale skin, and become slightly hypnotized by the firelight winking and dancing in rosy reflection off the jingling keys she held.

By the time I was about six years old, her children were all out at work, but still she sewed eternally at those dreadful shirts. My mother was bitter in her denunciation of the three ingrate McCorbie children. 'Take after their father, every one of them,' she would exclaim. 'They're not fit to brush their mother's shoes, and look at them!' I looked, and saw two haughty girls and a strapping boy. Each went their separate ways, neither helping with the housework nor giving their mother enough money to make life easier for her. Now that they were grown up, all their meagre wages were required for dress and amusement.

As the whirr of the machine reached us during supper, my mother would start up in indignation. 'Listen to her, slaving away at that machine, and it's nearly ten o'clock at night.' I was startled by the word 'slaving', because Grannie was reading *Uncle Tom's Cabin* to me, and I thought slaves were all black. 'Maybe it's her black hair,' I thought to myself, 'that makes her a slave.'

Now that her family were out all day, Mrs McCorbie had nobody to run messages for her, and one day I heard her asking in her soft Highland voice if Grannie thought I might be willing to do this for her. 'Willing!' said Grannie at once. 'Of course she'll be willing.' There was no question of consulting me, for laziness was something which was simply not recognized in our family. The simple facts were that Mrs McCorbie needed a messenger, and I had plenty of free time after I'd got Grannie's messages in, so I might as well be useful as idle. Grannie knew that I was a bundle of energy, and if the energy could be used to help poor Mrs McCorbie, so much the better for everyone.

I presented myself at Mrs McCorbie's door after school, and we had a thrilling consultation about payment. It had never entered my head that I would be paid, but she gravely said she was willing to pay me a penny a day for full use of my shopping services when Grannie had finished with me. 'Full use' meant the shopping hours weren't to be confined to after four o'clock school, but I might be asked to go in the morning, or even at lunch-time in emergency. I eagerly accepted, and then there was the delicious choice of having my penny each day, or sixpence on a Saturday. I considered the matter carefully. There didn't seem much point in having a penny each day unless I were going to spend it, and that wasn't really fair to my other chums, for nobody else could afford sweeties during the week. The total wealth of the others seldom went beyond threepence or fourpence. If I took the whole sixpence on a Saturday, why I'd be able to save. I could put something past every week for Christmas and birthday presents and for the summer holidays. I felt dizzy with power. It was the start of a fortune. A silver sixpence weekly it was.

As my mother later said, I was Mrs McCorbie's body and soul for that sixpence. She used to knock on the ceiling when she wanted me, and even if I were raising the teacup to my lips I'd lay it down untasted when I heard the knock, and I would be at her door in a flash, ready to run the forgotten errand. Not that Mrs McCorbie wanted such instant obedience, but I had a high sense of responsibility towards my employer, and, with the wisdom of the poor, I knew what that sixpence meant to her.

We didn't speak very much to each other, I remember. Poor, over-worked people have little leisure for mere conversation, but I think she liked me coming to her door each day to see if I were wanted, and occasionally I was allowed to rummage through the drawers and play with the empty cotton reels, and to build lovely little houses with them. There was a silent companionship between us, and, of course, for me she had the added fascination of being 'a slave', for I never forgot my mother's description.

She saw less and less of her children. They'd come home from work, swallow their food, and be off again. One very hot summer night, when I was about ten, the youngest daughter came running into the back court where we were playing. She was white to the lips and trembling. 'My mother is dead,' she said. My heart gave a terrible lurch, for I had never met death until this time. I looked at the soft skies, and then at the bright eyes of my playmates and couldn't believe it wasn't some awful nightmare. The bigger girls crowded round me, for they knew our family were on intimate terms with Mrs McCorbie, but I crept away, dazed and shaken by the shock. I hadn't the usual childish sense of importance because I was close to the central figure in this drama – I felt sickened and wanted to go home.

I stole quietly past Mrs McCorbie's door, and it was terrible not to hear the whirr of the machine when it was still daylight, for she always worked until the last light faded from the sky. Now there was silence. They sent for my mother, and when she went down she found Mrs McCorbie slumped over her machine, her hands still holding shirt and collar, ready to join them under the needle. The pins had fallen from her hair, and it hung, long and black, to her knees and my mother told me later that she looked like some Highland heroine from a painting, with her pale face and flowing magnificent hair.

Nobody knew where to find the two older children. In their careless fashion they hadn't bothered to tell anyone where they were going. This seemed terrible to us, for, like most of the children in the tenements, we were never allowed out of the house without our mothers knowing exactly where we could be found. We were also left in no doubt as to the hour we were expected to be home.

But the McCorbie children came and went as they pleased. I wondered how long it had been since they had even noticed the little figure bent so uncomplainingly over the machine. I knew I was going to miss her much more than they would. She had been my first employer. Never again would I see the dark eyes approving my speed as I returned, panting, with a little bit of shopping. Never again experience the warm glow of the dignity of service, as she pressed the silver sixpence into my hand for a week's work well done.

I knew a stab of agony as I anticipated the quiet emptiness which would lie behind the McCorbie door from now on, as I passed it on my way up and downstairs. No more knocks on the ceiling for my services. And, worst of all, no more wakening to the firelight and the jingle of keys against the gentle murmur of a Highland voice mingling with Grannie's.

2

Like children the world over, we followed an unwritten pattern for our games. One minute we'd be playing peever, which was our name for hop-scotch, and the greatest thing in the world then was to hop skilfully from bed to bed without touching the chalked line, sending the marble disc or peever into the next bed with poised toe; and then, for no apparent reason, we were all hunting out our girds. The gird or hoop season was starting and we didn't want to miss a minute. I can still see my mother's wrath as her snowy bedspread was pushed aside, while we three children groped under the bed for our girds and cleeks. The cleeks were the metal batons we used to control the gird's movements. The pastime was one usually reserved for boys, but as a special concession to my enthusiasm and my flying limbs, I was allowed to join the runners.

There were usually about six of us setting off at one time. An assortment of metal circles leaned against our legs as we waited for the last one to arrive, and we dirled negligently with the cleeks as we listened to the leader outlining the course for that night.

'Noo, it's roon' the buildin' the night first of all. Then ower the park, doon past the power station, alang the canal bank, an' back by the road.'

'Right.'

With wild skirls and leapings we were off, girds spinning smoothly in front, eyes watchful for a break in the rhythm, cleek ready to administer sharp encouragement at the exact moment of metal wobbling, feet trotting in unbroken pattern as we raced along.

There were tricky moments with bumpy cobblestones, but we experts knew just when to apply the cleek to keep all steady and sweetly running. The menace of tramlines at a complex crossing would have to be met, and cleek, eyes, feet, and brain worked at lightning speed to manoeuvre the gird so that one would not fall behind the crowd.

The gird was a magic carpet carrying us into odd and sometimes forbidden corners of the town, and there was an unholy joy in speeding along the canal banks and over the bridges down into the heart of the city, where a tolerant policeman waved us through the busy crossings. We must have run miles on these races, and the exercise and caller air filled us with wild exhilaration.

I suppose traffic must have been lighter, for it's a fact that none of us met calamity on our wild outings, and the worst that befell any of us was a broken gird. When this happened the race was abandoned, and we all dawdled back together, to keep the unfortunate owner company, but we didn't really mind this, for a broken gird entailed a visit to the smiddy, and this was a never-palling thrill.

As we drew near the smiddy, we would break into a trot, clattering up the hill, swinging through the hole in the fence which took us slithering down the brae right to the smiddy door, there to cluster in an excited circle watching big Sanny pounding a live, glowing shoe into shape.

He made those horseshoes for stock-piling, but sometimes there would be a horse waiting to be shod, and we stood tense with admiration of Sanny's skill and daring as he hammered and pared, ignoring the wild gleam in the horse's eye as he drove the shoe home.

And then it would be our turn. With one mighty arm Sanny worked the bellows which transformed the smouldering glow of the furnace into a roaring inferno. The gird would be thrust in, heated, and laid on the anvil, and with a few tremendous smacks of the hammer which sent the sparks flying, the fracture was mended.

A quick plunge of the red-hot metal into a bucket of water, a hiss and a cloud of steam, and the job was finished. A penny changed hands, and surely better entertainment was never provided for such a trifling sum.

Trace-horses were a familiar sight in my childhood, and one

of the great dramas of our streets in winter-time was when one of those huge creatures slithered on the icy cobbles and went crashing to the ground. A silent crowd would gather round the still form as it lay inert, and I used to be stirred by the power that flowed from their watchfulness, heads bent forward, intent, willing the passive beast to rise.

A child's voice would query wonderingly, 'How can it no get up?', to be answered in deeper tones, 'It's feart it slips again, son. It makes them awfu' nervous once they slide an' clatter doon wi' the frost.'

The carter, cap pushed back to allow free movement for a perplexed scratch, would watch his charge anxiously. 'Come on, Jock,' he would cluck encouragingly. 'Come on noo, gi'es a good try. Up ye come.'

The beast would gather itself for a tremendous effort, and suddenly, every muscle springing to violent activity, eyes rolling and flashing wildly, it would rear in thunderous eruption, sending sparks flying as its hooves struck the cobbles, and the crowd would draw convulsively back in quick alarm in case it should fall among them.

With a slither and a crash it would fall down again in failure, quivering and quiet once more, only the fearful wildness in the eyes betraying the helpless fear that it was trapped and would never rise again.

'Nothing else fur it, mate,' somebody would shout, 'you'll have to loosen it oot o' the shafts.'

The carter had tried to avoid this labour, but he recognized the inevitable, and with elaborate ritual and willing hands to assist, every strap and buckle would be loosened till the animal lay free, only himself to raise now, and no shackling cart to impede his efforts.

A few men would place themselves at strategic points to lend a hand to steady the animal when at the next or the next attempt it had gained it's feet, and eager arms thrust forward to keep the beast erect and balanced, while they avoided the danger of plunging head and flying feet.

A cheer would rise from the rest of us as the drama drew to a close, and the huge trembling creature was harnessed to his cart once more.

The men would stroll off, pleased and satisfied at having helped at an event which needed their manhood and their strength, and we children would dash up to the high road to watch the horse clattering away into the distance, past Sanny's smiddy, away into the town.

The high road not only provided a marvellous grandstand view of everything going on underneath on the main thoroughfare, it was also our adventure playground. It provided games and contests of skill quite different from those to be found in the back courts, and we loved it.

On summer evenings as it grew cooler and we became tired of the joys of taking bottles of water and jeely pieces up to the public park, or satiated with the thrills of hunting for 'baggies' which disappointingly died almost as soon as they'd been fished from the pond, somebody would say, 'Whit aboot the high road?' We actually said 'hirode', for we didn't know it was two words and that it meant a road higher than the main road.

In swift consent we'd wheel in that direction, like migratory birds, each determined to be there first. The one to reach and touch the end pole first was the leader for the rest of the evening's playtime. Somehow it was always evening when we thought of pole slides. The leader, having established his right, was obeyed without question. His was the heady power which decided which poles we'd patronize, or whether we would do any sliding at all. We happily fell in with his most fantastic plans, made just as the spirit moved him.

The tall poles were spaced at regular intervals along the main road, and actually carried the overhead wires for the tramcar trolleys, but their tops towered challengingly near to the railings which topped the high wall behind them. These railings were really a safety barrier on the outside perimeter of the high road pavement to protect the heedless from toppling over into the street below. We thought they'd been placed there entirely for our delight, and to us they were the narrow entrance to our adventurous slides on the poles.

This road on such a high level excited us, and we would first of all peep down at the main road, shuddering with pleasurable fear. 'Whit a terrible depth up!' somebody would breathe, and we felt brave as any mountaineer scaling impossible heights.

Then, one at a time, the biggest going first to give the smaller ones courage, we'd squeeze our bodies through the narrow railings, reach out, clasp the narrow standard, and with an ecstatic rush slide down to the pavement so far below. A moment's pause to recover from the exhilaration of that breathless slide, then we'd tear round the foot of the hill, and back to the railings again, and so the game went on till bedtime. Sometimes a plump little tummy would stick for a second on its way through. 'Oh, gi'es a shove, ah'm *stuck*!', and the victim's eyes popped with terror. With a mighty shove from the rest of us queuing up behind, he would be released, and the following slide was all the sweeter for the risk that had been involved.

The first two poles were the only ones the younger children ventured to use, because as the gradient rose, the slide to the ground became longer. But when we were very small it was a thrilling occasion when some of the bigger boys joined us. We knew they'd only come to show off, but it was exciting all the same, and we would rush after them as though they were Pied Pipers. They'd swagger past our poles until they reached the very highest, which stood right at the crest of the road. With narrowed eyes they surveyed the hazards and then, because they were too large to squeeze through the railings, actually swung themselves over the top, paused for a second on the supporting stonework, launched themselves at the pole, and skimmed swiftly to the pavement. Timidly we would lean forward, noses pressed to the railings, and follow their rapid progress to the ground. How sickeningly far away it seemed.

They jeered at us, the bigger boys, but when one of our band looked as if he would attempt this death-defying slide there and then, a large hand would hold him back. 'Naw naw, son, look, your erms have to be as long as mine or you'd never be able to grab the pole when you jumped.' And he would hold out an arm and gravely measure the childish arm against it, and prove to us all that bravery wasn't enough. It seemed the wildest optimism to think *we* would ever be big enough or daring enough to attempt such hazardous heights, and with an envious sigh we'd return to our little poles until grannies and mothers called us all in for the night.

On winter days the best slides were on the pavement of the

high road. Somehow the ice was more slippery there, and, of course, the slope steep enough to satisfy the most speed-crazed heart. Arms outstretched to balance us, we'd skim along the silvery surface, cheeks and eyes glowing with joy, feeling we were almost flying. Our feet polished this strip of pavement to lethal slipperiness as far as the adults were concerned, and many a 'currant bun', which was our name for a crash, was suffered by the men next morning on their way to work, or the women with their shopping bags. I can't recall that any bones were broken, but I can remember the roars of fury: 'These weans and their damt slides – I'll belt the next yin I catch making slides on the pavement.' I could never understand their resentment. Surely they knew the pavement had just the right smoothness for slides, and anyway we wouldn't have minded them having a wee shot on our slide even though they hadn't helped to make it.

Sometimes, after our hilarious exercise on the slides, we'd make our way to the 'park', as we called the piece of waste ground behind the houses. We'd clamber up the 'mountains' to our rendezvous at the top, where somebody had run on ahead to start the fire. We were pretending we were gypsies, so we pitched our voices to a low whisper, in case the law was after us. 'Hiv ye brought yer totties?' a hoarse voice demanded. Silently we'd produce one or two potatoes, as many as we could sneak from the shopping, and lay them on the hot glowing embers. As we sat solemnly round in a ring gazing into the bright heart of the fire while the totties roasted, our eyes were wide and frightened. We dared not look at the darkness pressing at our backs. Oh, but how delicious it was to cup the burning potatoes in cold fingers, and stab with our sharp teeth the blackened curling skin to reach the soft, steaming flesh inside.

When we couldn't get potatoes we occasionally had an orgy with cinnamon stick. This had the very aroma of the sweet spices of the East, although I didn't really like it very much. But it felt so wicked to be sitting in the dark, round a fire, actually smoking this scented tube, that I fully expected the heavens to fall upon me for my wanton ways. I'd been very thoroughly warned, both at home by Grannie and at Sunday

School by my teachers, of the penalties of sin. To my amazement, the first time I indulged my baser instincts in this way the heavens stayed just where they were, quite indifferent to my evil behaviour. The absence of heavenly vengeance amazed me, and I wondered if maybe the angels were having a night off themselves.

Another fierce joy was to fill an old pierced tin with rags, set the rags ablaze, and run with this fiery torch into the 'forest', to help my master, Robin Hood. The smouldering rags gave off a fearful stench which clung to everything I wore, but which I didn't even notice, for I was far too busy robbing the rich and helping the poor. I was genuinely amazed when Grannie guessed the minute I came into the house exactly what I'd been up to. 'My heavens,' she'd exclaim, recoiling and seizing her nose, 'your claes are stinking! It's been thae burnt cloots again, you varmint. Into the sink wi' every one o' them. You're no' gaen into ma clean bed wi' a sark smellin' like an auld boot.'

She was deaf to the romance of Robin Hood and I was scrubbed into a state of scarlet cleanliness.

As she picked up the offending clothes she'd stripped off me, Grannie would sigh: 'My goad, we'll never get that smell oot. Ah doot if even the Candy Rock man wid tak' them.'

The Candy Rock man! How we loved him. We'd be in the midst of a game of peever, or ball-beds, or high-speewigh (our name for hide and seek), when some courier from another gang would come up panting, 'The Candy Rock man is in Bedlay Street.' Games were abandoned, with never a care as to who was 'het' or who was winning, and we'd stream towards the magic address with one thought in our minds – 'Candy Rock'. When we got there the barrow would be surrounded with wide-eyed children licking eager lips, ready to answer the chant rendered in a high falsetto by our benefactor: 'Who likes Candy Rock, Candy Rock, Candy Rock? Who likes Candy Rock?' Lungs bursting, we would answer with a long drawn-out 'Me-e-e-e-e-e-e-e' which he liked, and then there would be a waving sea of arms and legs as we scrambled for the thin strips of pink and white rock he scattered amongst us. One school of thought inclined to the view that by shouting 'Not me' they'd establish their characters as unselfish, and that this noble state would be rewarded by all the rock being scattered in their direction. But the other sweets-starved children, of whom I was one, couldn't believe he would think all that out, and we just *knew* he would scatter it in the direction of the loudest and most enthusiastic 'Me-e-e-e'. What fun it was, and what boasting there was afterwards as we compared notes on how many pieces we'd managed to grab and swallow in the short time the sport lasted. It was years, it seemed, before I realized that we were supposed to bring rags in exchange for this lovely striped rock. I had thought it an act of simple generosity, sent to us by the same mysterious Providence who had invented Father Christmas.

But we couldn't rely on getting our sweeties for nothing very often, for the Candy Rock man's visits weren't nearly frequent enough for our liking, and many a happy hour was spent gazing into the window of Mrs Frame's wee shop, spending our imaginary money. The variety, the colour, and selection of good things in those jars and boxes held us spellbound as we squashed our noses against the cold glass. There would be a sharp rat-tat from the inside of the shop, for Mrs Frame wouldn't stand for the steaming up of her spotless plate-glass window, so, reluctantly we'd draw back a little, and resume our discussion as to what we would buy if we had a ha'penny. Seriously we would scan the glittering jars with the boilings and the chocolates at the back of the window, then rake down to the front where sugar mice and dolly mixtures mingled with jelly babies and toffee balls, sherbet dabs and sugarally straps.

And when the time came for me to spend my ha'penny, given to me by Grannie as a reward for some task well done, such as cleaning shoes or drying dishes or sweeping the lobby, I never dreamt of spending all of it on one thing. My plans had been laid, and I sped down to Mrs Frame's on winged feet. 'A faurden's worth o' chewing nuts and a faurden sugarally strap,' I panted. The chewing nuts weren't nuts at all, which seemed perfectly logical to my childish mind, where everything masqueraded as something else and all was make-believe, and these 'nuts' were really tiny pale brown toffees, soft on the outside, with a delicious hard button of a centre, dusted gloriously with sugar and quite, quite irresistible to my palate. For a farthing I got three or four, screwed into a twist of paper, and they lasted me all the way to the grocer's where I was bent on earning my next ha'penny if I was lucky.

The sugarally strap at a farthing hadn't quite the rich quality of a ha'penny nailrod, but that was only just, for it was but half the price. Truly the nailrod was worth a ha'penny, for this piece of liquorice, with its four square sides, like a toothsome pencil, gave a lovely satisfying chew. It was thicker and firmer than the strap, but not so hard as the real liquorice. Still, for a farthing, the sugarally strap was quite good value and made the most satisfactory make-believe tobacco spit, which was always great fun, even if it outraged Grannie when she heard of it.

Speaking of tobacco, Wee Jeanie's, farther down the road, sold a specially luscious caramel at four a penny, and when the rare mood of luxury was upon me I would toddle into her shop with my farthing, ask for my single caramel, then politely request that she halve it with the tobacco knife so that I could make two bites of it. This knife, which was really intended to cut the men's thick black tabacco into ounce plugs, and half-ounce pieces, was a fascination in itself. I'd watch, spellbound, as Jeanie laid my toffee on the stained board, then brought it forward on its hinge in one swift stroke to smite the sweet exactly in half. My mother used to make a face when told of this transaction, and seemed to think there was something off-putting in mixing the flavours of tobacco and toffee, but if any tobacco was absorbed with the caramel I, in my blissful chewing, never noticed it.

What a choice of goods we had for our farthing! There were tiny sugarally pipes, with little scarlet dots inside the bowl, pretending they were burning tobacco. There were sweetie cigarettes at five for a penny, so naturally a farthing bought one, although it was a bitter disappointment to me that Jeanie wouldn't break the odd one into bits to give me exact justice for my farthing. I wasn't really convinced when she told me, 'Ye aye loss a wee bit, hen, when ye don't buy in bulk,' and I dreamed of the day when I would spend a whole penny and buy *five* cigarettes at once, ration myself carefully over a few days, and gain an extra sweet smoke.

Sweeties had been very expensive after war No. 1, and tumbling prices came along in the nick of time for me to enjoy them. Never will I forget the day when the number of aniseed balls went up to forty a penny. There were queues at the wee shop that day, and it was indeed a land of plenty to be given ten balls, hard as iron, for a farthing. I nearly sucked my tongue raw until, with dawning disbelief, I realized I'd have to leave some over for next day. For sweeties to last more than a few minutes was outside my experience until that moment, and it was a marvellous feeling to tuck that wee poke with the three remaining aniseed balls behind Grannie's hankies in the bottom of the chest of drawers, where my brothers couldn't make a raid without either Grannie or me spotting them.

My purchases were always made with farthings and ha'pennies, with maybe a penny when I was going to the Saturday matinée, but beyond those sums I never ventured to think. I never thought of my precious 'savings' as spending money. I put them away and they were as safe as if they were in the Bank of England. But one dizzy day when we were playing 'guesses' in front of Mrs Frame's window a drunk neighbour came up and surveyed us solemnly, blinking as he swayed, listening to our excited 'guesses' and stumbling in exasperation as we rushed past him across to the edge of the pavement when we had made our guess. The edge of the pavement was the finishing line for the winner. When we played guesses with shop goods like this we gave the initial letters of an article in the window, say JB for jelly babies, or WCB for whipped cream bon-bons, and the first to yell out the correct answer leaped for the pavement edge to win. A flight of fancy now made me give PARTW as mine, and when nobody guessed it, my triumphant yells of 'Putty all round the windows' brought a glimmer to the drunk man's face.

He fumbled in his pocket and brought out a handful of coppers. We stood silent, watching him. We were forbidden to talk to strangers, and certainly to drunk men, but we knew this one, alas, for he was a fairly new neighbour. 'Here's a ha'penny for each o' you,' he said ponderously. 'And you, the wee lassie that made the putty guess, here's tuppence for you.' *Tuppence!* For nothing! It was a miracle. It was a fortune.

As I looked at the two coppers, a daring thought sent my head spinning and twisted my stomach with excitement. This money had come for nothing. I hadn't earned it, so I needn't spend it carefully. It was riches galore. I determined to enjoy the thrill of real spending. I drew a deep breath. 'Can I spend it a' on one thing, mister?' I asked. 'On whit?' he said, puzzled. 'On one thing,' I repeated patiently. 'Instead of a faurden's worth of this and a ha'penny worth of that.'

'Spend it ony wey ye like,' he replied grandly as he turned unsteadily towards his house. 'Enjoy yersel', hen, ha'e a real burst.'

I turned to the window and examined every single thing slowly and deliberately. It must be something really wickedly extravagant. Something which wouldn't last, a luxury that would have to be eaten all at once if its flavour and filling were to be fully enjoyed. Suddenly I saw what I wanted.

The others had spent their ha'pennies by the time I went inside the shop, and were chewing happily, waiting for me. There was an awed silence as I demanded imperiously, 'A whipped cream walnut, please.' Mrs Frame smiled and turned to the box. A burst of excited whispering broke out from my chums. 'She's spendin' her hale tuppence on *one* thing.' 'Fancy buying a walnut, and it's that *wee*.' 'Don't buy it, Molly,' urged one chum. 'It'll a' burst when you bite it, an' ye'll no' be able to keep any till the morn.'

I smiled, deaf to reason, and my teeth fell exultantly on my whole tuppence-worth. It was a glorious moment. I enjoyed every extravagant bite, and I included that drunk man in my prayers for quite a while afterwards.

3

Even in our asphalt jungle, summer was very noticeable. Windows would be thrown up and left that way all day, instead of being closed tightly against damp and cold. Fires were kept just high enough to do the cooking, and the long days seemed always to be warm and golden. This was the time for our running games and our singing games. These songs were surely handed down from generation to generation, and we acted and chanted them, following a ritual which came from we didn't know where. But every movement and gesture was as exact as though it had been choreographed. It seemed as though we had always known words, tune and movement, and I only remember consciously learning one song during my entire childhood. This was 'Ah loast ma hurl on the barra'. It was after Sunday School when I learned it. The big boy and girl who lived in the next close took me home with them to get a taste of their mother's baking of pancakes. As we waited for the hot pancakes to be lifted off the girdle and spread with margarine, the boy started singing, 'Oh the bonnie wee barra's mine', and my ears pricked with interest. For ages I'd sung, 'The barra broke at ten o'clock an' ah loast ma hurl on the barra', and I thought that was the entire song. Now it seemed there was more. 'Sing it again, Henry,' I begged him with great excitement. 'Oh sing it again, I want to know the rest of it.' And by the time we'd finished our pancakes we were all three lustily singing:

> 'The barra broke at ten o'clock
> An' ah loast ma hurl on the barra.
> Aw the bonnie wee barra's mine,
> It disnae belong tae O'Hara,
> The fly wee bloke, stuck tae ma rock,
> But ah'm gonny stick tae his barra.'

I remember teaching a wee English boy, who was on a summer visit to his grannie, to sing:

> Missus MacLean had a wee wean
> She didnae know how to *nurse* it,
> She gi'ed it tae me, an' ah gi'ed it some tea,
> An' its wee belly *burstit*.

I was enchanted to hear this old Glasgow song rendered with a prissy English accent, and kept making him sing it for me. I was astounded one day when he refused. 'But why?' I asked him, 'I thought you liked that wee song.' 'My grannie says I'm not to sing it any more,' he said primly. 'She says it's vulgar.' Vulgar! I'd never heard the word before, and didn't know what it meant. When I asked my grannie, she laughed and said, 'Och well, you ken whit the English are like. Butter widnae melt in their mooths, to hear them. The word "belly" will likely be too coorse for them.' Belly too coarse! But it was in the Bible, and we called our navels our belly buttons without shame or thought. I wondered what else I said that was vulgar. I'd have to be careful. Maybe I was constantly being vulgar without knowing it. Grannie dismissed my fears, and said there was nothing wrong with the wee harmless songs we sang, and I was to go out and play and not to be so daft.

So we saw nothing to cause a raised eyebrow when we chanted as we ran through the closes:

> A hundred and ninety-nine,
> Ma faither fell in the bine,
> Ma mother came oot wi' the washin' cloot,
> An' skelped his bare behind!

One which caused us great hilarity because of the cheeky wee soldier's behaviour in church was:

> Ma wee laud's a sojer,
> He comes fae Maryhull,
> He gets his pey on Friday night,
> An' buys a hauf-a-jull.
> He goes tae church on Sundays,
> A hauf an 'oor late.

> He pulls the buttons aff his shirt,
> An' pits them in the plate!

And there was one we used to act, just showing our heads out of the staircase window, as though we weren't properly dressed and daren't lean out farther:

> Ah'm no' comin' oot the noo, the noo,
> Ah'm no' comin' oot the noo.
> Ah'm very sorry Lizzie MacKay, for disappointin' you.
> Ma mother's away wi' ma claes tae the pawn
> To raise a bob or two.
> An' ah've juist a fur aroon' ma neck,
> So ah'm no' comin' oot the noo.

In our songs it was the wives who left the husbands, for there was something funny in a man being left to look after the house.

There was a lilting one which went:

> Ma wife ran awa' an' left me,
> Left me a' ma lane.
> Ah'm a simple chap.
> Ah widnae care a rap,
> If she hadnae run awa' an' left the wean.

And a slower chant, which we sang in a slurred tone as if we'd had a wee bit too much to drink:

> Wha's comin' wi' me?
> Ah'm oot on the spree.
> Ma wife's awa' on the train,
> Ah hope ah niver see her again.
> Ah'm havin' the time of my life,
> Plenty of LSD,
> I'm off the teetotal,
> I've ta'en tae the bottle.
> So wha's comin' wi' me?

And a nice one for singing with a sob in the throat was:

> Ah've got the dishes tae wash,
> An' the flairs tae scrub.
> Nicht an' day ah'm niver away

Fae the washin' tub.
She does whitever she likes,
An' ah dae the best ah can.
Jimmy McPhee can easily see
Ah'm a mere, mere, man.

These were the Glasgow back-court songs which we added to our repertoire of the games played all over the country at their appropriate season. 'Queen Mary, Queen Mary my age is sixteen', 'Broken bridges falling down', 'The Bonnie bunch o' Roses', 'Down in yonder valley where the green grass grows', and 'Water water wallflower, growing up so high'. We moved delicately through the movements, oblivious of mothers and grannies who occasionally glanced our way from their tenement windows, self-absorbed and transported into a graceful mannered world.

We were merciless on those who couldn't or wouldn't learn the movements fast enough, and who spoilt the rhythm, and we'd pounce on the hapless novice and put her through it again and again until she got fed up. She'd stalk away from us and walk to the middle of the back court and address herself to an upper window, 'Mammy, throw us ower a piece.' We pretended to ignore her and our own dawning hunger, and she went on repeating her monotonous chant till a window was thrown up, a head appeared briefly, disappeared, and then a paper bag sailed earthwards, to land on the baked clay of the back court with a most satisfying smack. It was a lovely sound to our ears. A sound which meant cut fresh bread spread with margarine or, in odd moments of affluence, butter, or, favourite choice of the entire back court children, a delicious layer of home-made raspberry or strawberry jam.

When the hungry one returned to the group the sight of her drooling jaws sent several more strolling to the centre of the back court to take up the cry, and before long only the most dedicated girls were acting out their fantasies in the singing games – the others had abandoned themselves to the enjoyment of their jeely pieces.

I don't know what other mothers thought of this behaviour, but my grannie felt it was extremely vulgar (we both knew the word now, and it could be applied to many things). She sternly forbade me to indulge in it. Only if I could plead that I was actually starving, say on my return from the swimming baths, did I dare find the courage to raise my voice and give vent to the familiar cry.

Up would go the window, and Grannie's outraged face would appear between sill and sash. 'Wheest, you limmer, haud yer tongue. If you want a piece you'll have to come up an' get it.' And the window was slammed down. This was real strategy on her part, for she knew I'd have to be really hungry to climb four flights of stairs and face her irritation at being stopped in the middle of her housework. And nothing short of real hunger would let her encourage me to nibble between meals and put me off the real food she was preparing for my growth and enjoyment.

Usually her ruse worked, and I'd turn despondently away, kicking the stones and pretending I didn't care, while the others jeered at me, their mouths stuffed with bread.

Sometimes, however, when she was in an indulgent mood, Grannie would spread two pieces of thin white bread with fresh margarine or, if we were having an extravagant week with my mother's overtime money, a thin scraping of fresh butter which was as rare as caviare on our budget, wrap it in a white paper bag and send it plummeting towards me. The thrill of sharing a 'piece' with the other children invested the food with a sort of magic, and never did bread eaten at a prosaic table taste so satisfying or delicious. Like the 'chittering bite' eaten at the baths, the back-court piece had a flavour all its own, which was never recaptured elsewhere.

The height of luxury was reached when on rare occasions we were given two tea biscuits pressed together, with fresh butter squeezing through the tiny holes, making a most agreeable pattern. It was no trouble to climb the stairs for this treat, for if they broke in their flight from window to back court the artistic effect of the smooth disc of buttery points was lost, and I enjoyed looking at it nearly as much as eating it.

Once, in a flight of exotic fancy, somebody put half a bar of cream chocolate between the bread and butter, and we watched her with awe as she bit through this splendid mixture. I tried it myself at the very first opportunity, i.e., when I could bring myself to use fourpence from my savings as a birthday treat, and I shivered with delight at my extravagance rather than with pleasure at the flavour.

In the same field of gourmet experiment was 'a piece on chips'. Dieticians would have shuddered at all this starch, but to our palates there was something at once filling and exciting about the flavour of the deep fried potatoes which melted the butter as they were pressed between the slices of buttered bread.

Another great treat was 'a piece on condensed milk'. Sickly, sweet, but different in the most acceptable sense of the word. And of course, 'a piece on sugar' or 'sugar and oatmeal' was delicious, although some spoil-sports warned us that it would give us all worms! I never knew anybody who had worms, although I'd often seen worm-cakes in the chemist, and a spice of danger was added to enjoyment as we dipped buttered pieces into wee paper pokes of mixed meal and sugar.

'A piece on black treacle' was a rare delight, but this had to be eaten quickly, before the treacle seeped into the bread and turned it a horrible fawn colour which ruined the enjoyment. Golden syrup made a lovely piece, and caraway seeds a strange one which I tried hard to like because Grannie ate hers with such obvious relish.

We never aspired to a sandwich in the true sense. We never dreamt of meat, or cheese, or eggs, or fish. They were real meals, to be eaten at dinner-time or tea-time, and not lightly to be consumed for fun. No, for between meals it had to be sweet and simple spreads, and all that sugar and treacle and syrup seemed to give us boundless energy for dozens of thrilling, absorbing games which filled the endless leisure hours.

The Cooperative Store was the hub of our shopping activities. How else could working-class people shop on credit, and earn a little dividend at the same time? It always seemed to be packed with customers. In all the years I ran the messages for Grannie I never remember the shop being empty. Along one side ran the long mahogany counter, with female clerks perched on high stools, whose job it was to write down our orders in our 'store' books. Along the opposite side ran the long wooden counter, attended by the serving grocers, usually male. In the territory in between there was constant movement as customers moved over to be served, where boys barged back and forth with huge baskets balanced on their heads, filled with 'delivery orders', and men staggered in under heavy loads of steaming bread, and where customers finally tottered out with their filled shopping baskets.

When you arrived at the shop you dropped your 'book' in the slotted box at the end of the mahogany counter, and a quick glance showed if there would be time for a game of peever or ball-beds on the pavement outside before your name would be called. This risk had to be weighed very carefully, for if you missed your turn your book went to the end of the queue again. Ball-beds were a special temptation, as well as a time hazard, for the 'beds' had to be drawn on the pavement with chalk, the names of the players put in little artistically scalloped compartments at the top end of the beds, and then we took turns to bounce our ball in an intricate pattern from one bed to another according to the numbered squares, without touching a single line with either feet or ball. You could only chance this delightful time-consuming game if there was a huge stack of books in the box ahead of you. So sometimes it was safer to stay inside the shop and play at 'guesses', and as our Co-op only changed its display about once a month, the children playing 'guesses' knew the stock better than the grocer. It was well-nigh impossible to surprise an opponent with a new item, so you were reduced to tricks like 'SOTF' which meant 'sawdust on the floor' – technically this wasn't allowed, but such infringements of the rules were a great test of ingenuity, and the variations endless.

The grown-ups drove us to a frenzy with their endless chatter with the female clerks as they gave orders. There was an atmosphere in the Co-op unlike any other shop. With books having names and addresses clearly displayed, everyone was known by name, and it seemed to us that getting the messages entered in books and ledgers was the last thought in the minds of women on both sides of the counter. While we fidgeted, not daring to leave because it was getting near our turn, details would be exchanged of the latest wedding, or funeral, or Mrs So-an-So's operation, or the latest baby, etc, etc. We suffered in silence, for the slightest bit of cheek soon brought a clout on the ear from an outraged adult. All mothers were united in their treatment of impudent kids, and a skelp from a stranger was no novelty in our world. Wild as we were in many ways, we had to keep our place in the presence of grown-ups, and nobody thought we would come to any harm by repressing our impatience.

The only thing that made the gossiping women move, tut-tutting with annoyance, was when it drew near lunchtime or evening closing time, and the ritual of the sawdust-sweeping began. We children loved it, of course, if only as a diversion. Out from the back shop appeared the boy, importantly swinging a bottle full of water with a pierced cork stopper, and how we admired and envied him as he swung it expertly, scattering the clean shower over the sawdust floor. It was one of my fiercest ambitions to be allowed to wield that bottle, and watch the women jump as the splashes hit their solid legs. When I first saw this operation I imagined it was vinegar the boy was using, for my only other experience of a pierced cork stopper was in the fish-and-chip shop, but even the later discovery that it was only water didn't put me off.

Having laid the dust expertly, the boy then briskly swept up all the dirty sawdust, using a long-handled stiff broom, and customers who'd escaped the water leaped out of his way as his sweeps grew longer and wider. When all was clean, he reappeared with a square biscuit tin filled with clean sawdust which he deftly scattered over the entire floor. It was as good as a circus, and in our eyes he was the star turn.

When I first started shopping for Grannie I was so wee that I had to stand on my basket to see over the counter to make sure I wasn't being given short weight, hard bacon or outside loaves. As I grew a few inches, the basket turned over on its side was high enough, and then at long last the glorious day arrived, after a holiday at the seaside, when I found I could stand with my feet in the sawdust and rest my chin on the counter and see absolutely everything without any help at all. It was at the Co-op that I learned to accept teasing about my height and my name. 'Weir,' the assistant called out as my turn came to be served. Then, holding up two black puddings and winking all round, he would say, 'This is a wee-er black pudding than that one, so I think your grannie would like it better.' The laughter was good-natured and I enjoyed the joke too.

I loved seeing the new bread being delivered. It arrived in long rows, and as each two-pound loaf was sold, it was separated from its neighbours in most satisfactory clouds of steam.

In the back shop, potatoes were housed in a huge bunker which had a little sliding door in the front, near the bottom, just large enough for the 'tottie-boy' to push in his shovel and rattle down the necessary amount, which he'd toss on to a large scale standing beside the bunker. This was another enviable task performed by the sawdust boy. He seldom had to alter the weights, for nearly everybody in our tenements bought a quarter of a stone. If his sharp shovel was careless it would cut into a potato and savagely cut and blacken it, causing Grannie to tut-tut angrily if my watchful eye had missed it. I always enjoyed my glimpses of the back shop, for the bunker and the big shovel, the all-enveloping heavy apron worn by the boy, and the earthiness of the potatoes combined to create an atmosphere very different from the dull ordinariness of the rest of the shop.

Eggs were very precious when I was a wee girl. They were so scarce and so expensive that no grocer would guarantee to replace a bad egg without evidence that the egg hadn't been eaten. Like doubting Thomas, he had to *see* the offending egg, which often stank to high heaven. Many of the older women would reel back, holding their noses, and call appealingly to the grocer, 'For goodness' sake, Jimmy, let the wean take that egg roon' the back afore her turn, or ah'll be seeck!'

The rotten eggs had to be taken round to the midden in the backyard next to the shop, where a boy was stationed to make sure the eggs actually went into the foul-smelling bins. This was to make sure that no unscrupulous person would offer the same egg twice. It was my delight to volunteer to take the rotten eggs of the older women to this reeking depository, an offer which was thankfully accepted, and I enjoyed tossing the egg with unerring aim straight into the centre of the bin. No wonder I was so good at coconut shies when 'the shows' came round to our district – I'd had regular practice with rotten eggs.

Syrup and treacle, which we loved, weren't always easy to get, and I remember one day when we were all playing with our marbles on the pavement the cart arrived piled high with jams and jellies in their unmistakable boxes, and, at the side, two huge chests marked 'Syrup' and 'Treacle'. There was a wild scatter as we each reclaimed our store of 'bools' before we rushed home for the store books and the netbags, then out again to form a noisy, chattering queue. After at least a two-hour vigil, for the cart had to be unloaded and checked first, we had our reward. Black treacle was a passion with me at that time and I'd cheerfully have stood all day if at the end of it I could have had a piece on treacle. Well, this particular consignment had been delivered in cartons – not tins – and I laid mine carefully into my netbag. Alas, in my ignorance of the weakness of the new container, I put it at the bottom of the bag, upside down. And the tragedy was revealed only when I felt something warm and sticky running down my ankles.

The skelp I got from Grannie when she saw the mess and realized the waste, wasn't entirely responsible for my tears.

Everything that was bought at the Co-op was marked in the book, and no money changed hands until pay-day, when maybe a pound would be paid in towards the week's shopping, and the mothers usually attended to this payment themselves instead of leaving it to the children. On one bitter occasion, when I was entrusted with a pound, I put it into my coat pocket and stood quietly in the shop, not daring to go outside to play in case I'd lose it. And then, while I was waiting, I got so carried away with the new stock which had arrived, and with my stupendous success at 'guesses', that I didn't notice a thieving hand quietly rob me of the precious note. Only when I came to pay was the loss discovered, and we all searched the sawdust till our eyes and noses stung with the particles and the dust. But I knew with sickening certainty that we wouldn't find it. I knew I had been robbed. It was a terrible moment having to tell my mother, for she had just lost her job and only had ten shillings in the world after giving me that pound. It says much for her understanding that, in spite of her thin purse, one look at my stricken face told her I needed no other punishment. Tenement children didn't have to be told the value of money, we knew it only too well.

Two doors down from the grocery section of the Co-op was the drapery department, which also sold shoes. My grannie bought a pair of shoes every summer, before we went on our holidays, and I felt very important when I was sent down to bring several pairs 'on appro' so that she could try them on in the privacy of her own home. I never really knew what 'on appro' meant. I only knew they were magic words which, once uttered, entitled me to obtain three or four splendid cardboard boxes containing spanking new shoes, and that nothing was marked 'in the book' until we had made our decision. The excitement of trying to persuade Grannie to have the ones with the buckles, which she instantly dismissed as far too frivolous, and the responsibilility of taking back the ones she didn't want, and then, and only then, having the price marked in the book, had me fairly bursting with importance and a sense of occasion.

When it was our turn to have shoes bought for us, shoes which we wore only on Sundays, we were taken to the central branch, at the other end of Springburn, where there was a bigger selection. How proud we felt as we sat on squeaking chairs, only to be whisked out of them the moment an adult was seen to be standing. My mother stood no nonsense, but we didn't mind. Sitting or standing, we entered into the full drama of each stranger's purchase with as keen an interest as though the shoes were for our own feet. We criticized the quality, the colour, the price, the suitability of the shoe for its purpose. Nobody felt rushed, for we all knew that shoes had to last for a very long time, and money was scarce and we couldn't afford to make a mistake. When our turn came we tried to kick our battered and scuffed old boots under the chair out of sight. How shaming they seemed compared with the splendid new leather which now stiffly encased our feet. But their scuffed comfort lent wings to our feet as we ran home with our new shoe-box, and climbed on to a chair to lay the new shoes reverently on top of the wardrobe, out of harm's way until we drew them on on Sunday when we went to church.

There was a Co-op about every five hundred yards in our

district, but you got to know your own Co-op as though it were a club, and how alien other Co-ops seemed if you were sent there by a neighbour. But your own! Ah, that was different. So cosy. So chummy. The girl clerks in our Co-op lent me a new pen nib, shiny and smooth, for each school examination, and later for those I sat at college, and they rejoiced in my successes all the more because they had supplied the nibs which had written the answers.

They actually encouraged me to act my little stories as I waited my turn. This was amazing to me, for Grannie discouraged 'showing off' and described me as 'a Jezebel' if I dared imitate anything I had seen on the screen at Saturday matinées. And I found the packed Co-op a marvellous source of fun when I'd play practical jokes, the favourite being covering myself with sparkling frost and running in, panting, as though for shelter, pretending it was pelting with rain. This was especially mystifying when the sun was shining, but in our temperamental climate the trick worked every time, to my joy.

But for certain items my mother had her favourite shops, and I felt positively breathless with patronage as I went into those little specialized establishments. The one nearest our home was owned by a father and two daughters. The father was dark and saturnine, and the daughters placid, plump and fair. The father looked permanently in a seething temper. He probably had a bad stomach, but we took him as we four him and decided he was naturally bad-tempered. 'Mean as get ut,' my mother assured us. 'He'd take a currant off the scale to make sure you didn't get a skin over weight.' But his home-cooked boiled beef ham was her passion, and his spiced pork delicious. I was fascinated to watch him shake the spice from a canister with a pierced lid, and my mouth watered as I raced home, hardly able to wait to get my tiny portion spread on bread and margarine, and savour this aromatic food. I always liked it when the daughter with her hair done up in ear-phones served me. She was dreamy and far-away and quite capable of ignoring her father's sharp glance as the scale wavered past the quarter-pound to give me an extra half-slice with my order. Oh that was bliss indeed! The other daughter, though, hair done in a bun on top of her head, was her father's own child. Exact weight and no more, and I avoided her when I could, and gazed intently at the coloured boxes on the shelves until the ear-phoned goddess was free.

For home-cooked gammon we went to the little cooked meats shop at the top of the hill. It was always a pleasure to watch the owner-cum-cook slice the perfectly boiled gammon with his thin, viciously sharp knife, and lay it reverently, slice by mouth-watering slice, on the fine grease-proof paper, and then transfer the savoury load to the marble scale. This was a splendid character, rosy-cheeked, with a mop of wiry, curly black hair, a man who obviously enjoyed his work. Sometimes, to my joy, he passed over a sliver of the gammon on his knife, to let me drool over its flavour while he cut the quarter I'd ordered. Not every time, for this would have been spoiling indeed, but often enough to make an errand to his shop have all the excitement of a lucky dip.

We knew every mannerism of each assistant to the last nose-twitch. We had plenty of time to observe them, warts and all, in those busy shops in pre-refrigerator days, when shopping had to be done every day. One of my favourites was the man behind the cheese counter in a big store, privately owned of course, in the centre of Glasgow. He clearly loved his work. He reigned over the cheeses like a captain over his ship. He stood, white-aproned, behind his counter, and surveyed us all calmly, a brooding responsibility keeping his face very serious. Behind him, a vast range of swelling rounds of cheeses were arrayed. On the marble ledge in front of him smaller cuts rested, with wire-cutters neatly to hand. Each transaction was a little ritual. No plastic-wrapped portions for this expert. A gentleman in a trilby, inquiring about the merits of a particular cheese, would have a tiny portion removed by the wire-cutters and handed to him to savour. The cheese salesman would stand back, mouth pursed, eyes watchful, as the customer slowly chewed the morsel, while the rest of us awaited the result with keenest interest. We weren't impatient. This thoughtful consideration seemed absolutely right to us. At last the trilby-hatted gentleman would nod, 'Mmmm. Yes. Excellent. I'll take a pound, please.' A sigh from the cheese-man and from us, the audience. 'I thought you would like it, sir. A very mature cheese, and excellent with a drop of port.' Port! This was high living with a vengeance, and the humble purchaser of two ounces of Cheddar felt for a moment exalted to undreamt-of realms of luxury.

This cheese salesman was a wizard with the wire-cutters, and could cut a huge virgin cheese with the speed and accuracy of a circular saw, and extract an exact two ounces or four ounces to a milligram. He would have been chagrined beyond words to have to add the words: 'An extra ha'penny, or a penny under or over.' You asked for four ounces and you got four ounces. He was admired by all of us, for we knew an artist when we saw one.

Another exclusive grocer's in town was an Aladdin's cave to me. I loved going there with a chum, who collected a weekly box of special biscuits for the minister. There was a little stone bowl at the door, filled with clean drinking water so that customers' dogs might be refreshed. The mahogany and plate-glass doors had the weight and opulence of a bank entrance, and the well-polished counters were ranged with strange, exotic foods. Things I'd never heard of, much less eaten. Truffles. Foie gras. Peaches in brandy. Calves-foot jelly. This last particularly fascinated me, and I couldn't for the life of me decide when this should be eaten. 'It's invalid food,' somebody assured me when I whispered my puzzlement over this delicacy. But what was an invalid? I'd never heard this grand name used to describe somebody in poor health, and I continued to puzzle whether or not the invalid would spread the jelly on bread, as we did with my mother's home-made black currant, or whether she would sup it with her dinner; calf sounded like meat to me.

But I had no doubt whatever that the owner and his son were the two luckiest men in the world to be able to preside over this wonderland every working day of their lives. Fancy dealing with scented China tea, chicken in aspic, curries, spices, and even stem ginger! Father and son were immaculate in their dress, as befitted the stock they handled. Dark suits, sparkling white shirts, perfect bow ties, and gleaming shirt-cuffs. The food was parcelled in thick, expensive, crackling brown paper and fine strong string, and the son had a fascinating mannerism of shrugging his shoulders in sharp little movements as he deftly stroked down the corners of the paper to form a perfect seal to the package. I watched him with unwinking gaze, admiring every movement of those expressive shoulders, and envied him nearly as much as I did the Principal Boy in the pantomime, for it seemed to me they both lived in magic worlds.

And in our own much humbler district the shop we all loved best was owned by a somewhat frightening spinster lady always known as 'Miss P.' Nobody, not even the most chatty grown-up, ever called her by her Christian name, and nobody had ever seen her without a hat. She always dressed in black. Black silk blouse, held at the neck by a gold and Cairngorm brooch. Black, highly polished shoes and black lisle stockings. Surmounting a head of rusty auburn hair, she wore a black felt hat in winter and a black straw in summer. She had rosy cheeks and fierce black eyes, and knew her stock to the last shoelace. I liked her shop best of all in summer, with its rows and rows of sand-shoes hanging temptingly at the door-front, fastened to a long line of strong twine from top to bottom of the door hinges. I would stand mesmerized in front of them. White ones wooed my heart, but, of course, they'd never have kept clean enough to be practical. Navy ones would match my gym slip. Black ones looked exciting and grown-up, but the grey ones, with little speckles of black, looked most elegant and were my favourites. Oh the excitement when my mother would take us in on a chosen Saturday, to rig us out with our sand-shoes for summer holidays, and for running about at our games during the long long days of summer, to save our heavier more expensive boots and Sunday shoes. Although our sand-shoes cost only about two-and-eleven a pair, Miss P. treated us with the courtesy due to honoured clients. We were seated on brightly polished chairs, our noses filled with the delicious scent of the rubber soles carried to us by the breeze from the shoes by the door. She consulted my mother as to colour and size, then with unerring eye she would cut off a pair of shoes from the rows hanging at the door. The very stuff of summer holidays was in the sensation felt as those soft shoes encased the feet, so different from the rigid leather of the long-legged boots which were my workaday schoolday wear, or the formal splendour of my black patent lacing shoes for Sundays. A pair of new shoelaces would be threaded through, and I would stand before the little floor mirror, ready to leap into the air like a shorn lamb, drunk with the feeling of lightness in my feet. The shoelaces cost an extra penny, but sometimes Miss P. was in generous mood, no doubt realizing how precious every penny was to my hardworking mother, and she would present us with the laces free of charge. My mother's eyes would glow as brightly as Miss P.'s, at this generosity, and she would say, as we left with our parcel, 'Aye, a real lady, Miss P. It's a pleasure to be served by her.'

4

The first thing my mother examined when she was looking at any possible new house was the kitchen range. You could always disguise faulty windows with nice curtains, and put an extra shelf into a press that was too wee or awkward, but you were stuck with a range, and if it didn't 'draw' properly, or had been too neglected, it was a plague and a torment.

So we always made sure we had a good range. It was the centre of warmth and comfort, and the very hub of our busy kitchen. It stood along the dividing wall between us and the next-door neighbour, exactly halfway between the sink and the inset bed, spreading heat and cheer, and enjoyed by all of us from first light till bedtime, for the kitchen was bedroom, cooking place and living-room combined.

Its steely parts were burnished and its black parts blackleaded once a week, and a great ceremony that was. Grannie would spread newspapers out on the floor to protect linoleum and hearthrug. The long stool which usually held pride of place before the glowing coals would be pushed back out of the way, and the Zebo and cleaning cloths spread out in readiness.

All the movable steel parts were lifted aside – the 'winter', as Grannie called the steel piece which formed a small shelf in front of the glowing bars, the ashpan, the front barred section and the oven door.

Then slowly and methodically Grannie would Zebo the stripped monster that remained, making sure every bit of grease disappeared and every piece of cast iron got its black coating. I was never allowed to touch this part of the operation, for, as Grannie scathingly remarked, 'You'd have the hale kitchen covered in black'ning,' but I loved watching her, especially when it came to the polishing off of the Zebo. Huge cloths brought everything up to a gleaming ebony, and then when you felt it just couldn't shine any brighter the final touch was given with a soft polishing brush which reached every crevice, and the range gleamed like dusky satin.

But I *was* allowed to tackle the 'steels', as we called the other parts which had been laid aside. With emery paper and a judicious use of a little 'spit' on small rust spots these were burnished to a silvery glitter, and as I rubbed and panted I was urged on by Grannie to use 'plenty o' elbow grease'. A final polish with a soft duster to remove any lingering dust left by the emery paper, and I glowed nearly as brightly as the steels at Grannie's praise. 'Aye, ye've made a grand job o' them, lassie, they're like silver, juist like pure silver.'

The fire, of course, had been allowed to go out so that we could work at the range closely and comfortably, and now, when we had got everything shining and sparkling to Grannie's satisfaction, and the steels back in place, came the ceremony of lighting the fire. Screwed-up newspaper went in first, then the sticks were laid criss-cross to support the coal which was laid on top. Nothing must be packed too tightly or the air wouldn't get through and let it 'draw' – it was a great art, and a terrible disgrace if it didn't burn at first setting and had all to be taken apart, and laid all over again. Soon the flames were dancing and the fire roaring, and reflecting itself a dozen times on the black satin and silver glitter of our polished surfaces.

Once a month there was an additional ritual known fearsomely as 'cleaning the flues'. I didn't exactly know what a 'flue' was, but it obviously had to be treated with great caution and respect. Grannie would wrap her head in newspapers, looking like one of the mammies in *Uncle Tom's Cabin*, then she would take a long iron cleek in one hand, while with the other she would open a little sliding hatch above the empty fire, very very carefully.

A shovel and more paper were laid across the fire to catch any falling soot, and then, like an archaeologist after hidden treasure, Grannie would very gently poke the long cleek into the hidden cavern, exploring all the mysterious corners, to dislodge every lurking particle of soot.

We were in constant terror of the 'jeests', as Grannie called the joists, catching fire, for she assured us as she poked about the flues that if this happened then the whole building would blaze, and the next tenement as well, for those joists ran right up the height of the tenements inside the walls and could set flames roaring from close to top flat.

This was no exaggerated fear, for I remember one terrible night, when I was about four years old, wakening to see the kitchen full of fireman, who, under my dreamy gaze, broke the wall with their axes to get at the 'jeests', which had indeed caught fire in a flat below ours, and the flames roared into our kitchen the moment the wall was breached. While the tallest fireman fought the blaze, I inquired with interest, 'Are you Jack and the beanstalk?', and there was a cry of alarm as I was snatched from the bed, 'My Goad, I forgoat the wean was there.'

When the firemen were trying to trace the source of the fire my grannie enlightened them. 'It'll be thae dirty rascals doon below,' she said grimly. 'I ken fine that besom never touches her flues fae one year's end to the other.'

Every bit of our range was used for cooking. The kettle was always on the side of the hob and only needed moving over the flames at any time to bring it to full boiling point for cups of tea, or pease brose, or anything else we wanted. Beef tea sat simmering at the back of the hob when any of us needed this nourishing brew after illness. The big soup pot stood at the other side, slowly blending the good vegetables into a grand broth which, using a favourite phrase, Grannie declared, would 'stick to your ribs and see you through the winter'. The stew pot wasn't far away, and there was still plenty of room for the pot which held the potatoes.

A small hook at the side worked a grid which let the heat from the fire into the oven and Grannie was expert at knowing just how high the fire ought to be for scones and cakes, and how low it could go so the oven heat would be just right to finish off bread, or the roast at Christmas time.

When the top of the range was covered with pots, and Grannie wanted to make a bit of ham and eggs for my mother coming in from work, she would lay strips of ham in a shallow baking tin, carefully break an egg over them, and then prop the tin at just the correct angle in front of the glowing fire, to let everything grill gently and evenly. What a delicious smell would waft through the kitchen, and how fascinating we children found this method of cooking, watching with bated breath the tiny bubbles forming as the bacon took the heat of the fire, and the egg slowly firmed but never over-cooked. And, of course, we toasted our bread at the glowing bars, and were warmed through and through at the same time.

In bitter weather, the 'winter', that little steel shelf, was unhooked from the front bars of the fire, and a piece of flannel wrapped round it to protect our toes, and how comforting it was to put our stockinged feet against it as we supped our pease brose or hot gruel before we went to bed. Our Grannie found the wee 'winter' a great economy, for it heated itself at no cost at all, just by sitting in its place on the range and taking its warmth from the coals.

The long stool which ran the length of the range, standing on the hearth-rug, became our favourite dining place as children. We sat on the hearth-rug like worshippers before a shrine, gazing into the glowing heart of the flames, and watched with laughter our distorted reflection in the shining steels, while we sipped our tea or cocoa and munched our rolls before going to school or to bed.

The last sound I heard at night before falling asleep was made by the steel door being shut in front of the bars, to make sure no coal fell out during the night. The first sharp sound when I wakened was the ashpan being drawn out, and the ashes tipped into a bucket, ready to be taken down to the 'midden' when I went out for the breakfast rolls. There was a right and a wrong way to empty those ashes. 'Noo, stand close ower the pail, lassie,' Grannie would say, 'and tim it in quietly and slowly, so ye'll no' get the stour a' ower yer claes.'

Each range had its own personality and took a bit of knowing before one understood all its little ways, and I think the hardest thing to part from when we moved house was surely this beloved monster, the kitchen range.

Everything in the tenement kitchens was called into use by the children and used as equipment for games. Among all the kitchen fixtures I think our first favourite was the bunker. It was a plain modest thing of varnished wood with a hinged lid on top. A hinged flap on the front let down when the coal was getting near the bottom, so that we could reach down easily with the shovel and get at the last of 'the churlies', as Grannie called the small coal. To the right of it was the dresser, of the same varnished wood, its two top drawers filled to overflowing with dusters and tea-cloths and cutlery, plus all the paraphernalia of our games – our peeries, our peevers, our football cards, cigarette cards, skipping rope, bools (or marbles) and jawries. Under this dresser was a cupboard, where the pots and pans were stowed, the pipeclay for the stairs, the black-lead for the range, and the Angier's emulsion and Parish's chemical food, two great stand-bys against our winter colds and spring lassitude.

The whole arrangement seemed excellent to us, and we were aghast when we heard of some people who actually banished the bunker out to the stair landing so that the coalman needn't come into the house with his dirty boots. Fancy removing such a treasure from the warmth of the kitchen, we thought, and we felt sorry for the children of such finicky folk, being deprived of such a splendid plaything. For that was how we saw our bunker. It was *much* more than a mere receptacle for coal. It was our toy. Our play-pen. A permanent source of joy and entertainment and we never wearied of it all the days of our childhood.

On wet days, when we couldn't get out to play, the bunker was a favourite place to hide when we played hide-and-seek, although my heart was always in my mouth in case my brothers, in a fit of devilment, would fasten the wee sneck and keep me there against my will. But it was such an enchanted darkness that I suffered this fear willingly, for the fun of peeping through the line of daylight at the flap-hinge watching the chums trying to find me. Of course, once inside the bunker, you were stuck there until the searchers ran into the best front room or the lobby, and then what a scramble it was to get over the rocky coal, to clatter open the flap and leap out and race for the 'den' to announce myself uncaught, with another chance of hiding.

During spring-cleaning times my mother would have the fanciful idea of whitewashing the inside of the bunker, although

I can't think how she hoped to keep it clean for any length of time, considering it was usually full of black coal. Although Grannie and she cheerfully accepted the stour and dust on our clothes when we played in the bunker, they were both surprisingly furious when we appeared streaked with whitewash as well! I never could understand why the whitewash was worse than the coal dust, but I obligingly dusted myself down to please them.

Another favourite game was to lean a wooden plank against the bunker, climb on to the lid, and slide down this home-made chute, landing with a whoop on the kitchen floor. Our downstairs neighbour was most understanding, and accepted with placid grace the noise that surely must result from the playtime of three lively children when the weather kept them indoors. Mind you, she stood no nonsense when we ran about the house with our heavy boots, which was strictly forbidden by Grannie, and she'd knock the ceiling with her long wooden pole to let us know she was annoyed. When we heard this we'd gaze at one another with stricken eyes and change into our slippers without a word having to be said.

Sometimes the bunker was used by us for more serious things, and its lid became a desk when we spread it with our school books as we wrestled with homework, and pored over our jotters. Occasionally we had to make way for Grannie, so that she could use the top for cooling trays of toffee or pots of jam, and then we'd lean against it with covetous eyes, waiting for the toffee to cool and exasperating Grannie by poking with experimental fingers to see if the toffee was ready for breaking and eating.

About once in four weeks my mother, as she left for work in the morning would remind Grannie 'Oh, Grannie, don't forget to get the bunker ready – the coal's coming today.' There was a fierce scurry on our part to move our treasures out of harm's way so that the lid could be raised in readiness for the coalman. 'My drumsticks!' Tommy would cry, and move them carefully to the top of the dresser. 'My scraps!' I'd yell, and take my adored coloured angels and fairies, and lay them safely under the bed as a temporary refuge. 'My bools!' Willie would shout, and slide the saucer with his plunkers and jawries and glessies, the most prized marbles he possessed, to the far end of the dresser. Meantime Grannie took down the brass covers hanging along the back wall so that the lid could go right back unhindered.

Then the first faint cry would reach us, increasing in strength as the coalman mounted the stairs. 'Yeeee-how!', which we correctly translated as 'Coal', followed by 'WEEEEEEEE . . . R', delivered in a long drawn-out bellow which would have wakened the dead. At last he would stride into our kitchen, a gigantic figure in our eyes. Face blackened with coal dust, lips showing a rim of scarlet behind the black crust which had formed as he licked them, teeth startlingly white and gums gleaming pink as he grinned at us. This visitor in glorious Technicolor fascinated us. We admired the superb strength of him as he tossed the coal into the depths of the empty bunker, and appreciated his thoughtfulness as he smoothed out the bag deftly so that too much dust wouldn't rise to blacken Grannie's spotless shelves.

'How many bags are we gettin' the day, mister?' we would ask. 'Will it be right tae the top?' 'Right tae the top!' he would reply. 'Yer grannie'll hiv tae burn plenty o' fires afore there's room for you to play in the bunker.' He knew as well as we did that the bunker was more than just a thing for coal.

The tenements were all lit by gas, and on Fridays when Grannie and I were doing the cleaning of all the brasses in the house the mantle had to be removed from the thin brass gas bracket with its swan-like neck, and moved to safety, while we set to with busy polish and cloths and made the bracket and the band which ran round the mantelpiece sparkle like beaten gold.

Sometimes when handing the mantle back to Grannie for replacing on the bracket my fingers would grasp it too tightly and I'd hear a screech, 'My goodness, that's anither mantle awa'. Whit'll your mother say? How often have I to tell you that ye canna handle a mantle like a bool? Awa' doon to the store and get anither ane.'

The assistant would cock a quizzical eye as I asked, 'One inverted gas mantle please' 'Imphm! And who broke it this time, hen? You? Or yer grannie?' 'Me,' I had to confess. As he handed me the little square cardboard box, he'd say, 'Weel, don't run wi' it. Tak' yer time and walk, an' no break it afore ye get it hame.' So I'd walk very slowly, holding the box fearfully, and controlling my normal bouncing step in case I'd jiggle my frail cargo to destruction.

There was quite a ceremony as Grannie and I carefully raised the lid and gazed inside to confirm that all was well. And there, suspended by its four wee lugs, which hung from neat, cut-out projections of thin cardboard, was our 'inverted gas mantle'.

It looked incredibly fragile and white, with a frosted lacy texture which trembled at a breath, and the smooth chalky neck seemed too brittle for mortal hands.

A chair was brought forward for the hanging. I envied Grannie this part intensely, and it was many years before she listened to my plea of 'Och let me put the new mantle on, Grannie.'

'You!' she would snort. 'Dae ye want it broken to smithereens afore it's in the hoose a meenute?'

It was a delicate job and called for deft fingers to hang the wee lugs safely from the matching supports of the gas bracket, and we held our breaths as Grannie moved her fingers away, for the slightest misjudgement could send the mantle shattering to the floor.

Great care was taken when the match was applied to a new mantle. Some people, in fact, burnt the whole thing with a flaming match before letting the gas in, but we never did this. The gas tap was turned on just a little, so that only a small quantity of gas whispered into the tiny globe. The match was held at just the right distance to ignite the gas, but not so close as to endanger the new surface. There was a 'Plop' as the gas caught the flame, and the lowest tip of the globe sprang to brilliant life.

Cautiously the tap was turned up an up, until the whole mantle was pulsing with light. We let our held breaths go in a sigh of satisfaction. The new mantle had been successfully broken in.

But it took a long time for me to stop feeling guilty for having caused this needless expense. Poverty is a very exacting teacher, and I had been taught well. We learned never to waste a single thing during our childhood. We were generous with what we had – no beggar was ever turned away from our door, and we could always manage a welcome cup of tea for a visitor – but we wasted nothing. When I was old enough to be trusted to empty the sugar bags into the big glass jar, Grannie showed me how to fold back the corners, first at the top, and finally at the bottom, so that it was smooth and unwrinkled and not a grain of sugar lost in any tiny crevice. The same treatment was given to the tea packets, while the butter papers were carefully scraped with a knife before being folded and put away, and Grannie used them later to cover the rice pudding or grease the baking tins.

When my mother, visiting a neighbour, would see her transferring butter from paper to dish by tapping it out, before screwing up the paper and tossing it into the fire, she would shake her head, aghast at such waste. 'All that good butter into the fire,' she would say to us later; 'nae wonder they havenae a ha'penny to their name.'

It was years before I knew anybody actually *bought* string. When a rare parcel would arrive at our house Grannie and I would sit down at the table to open it. 'We'll just tak' time tae lowse the string,' she would say. 'Never waste a good bit o' string wi' shears, for you never ken when it'll come in useful.' With unhurried fingers she would undo every knot, until she had a smooth length of string, and then she would show me how to wind it into a neat figure of eight, and securely fasten it before popping it into the string bag which hung inside the cupboard door. The brown paper round the parcel was also smoothed and folded, and put away for later use, and, of course, every paper poke was smoothed and kept in a drawer for my mother's pieces for her work, or chittering bites and pieces for us.

We children of the tenements were aware of the economy of daily living. We knew food wasn't always there for the asking and we learned to know the price and value of everything. With a sixpence clutched in my hand, I would race down to the greengrocer's before breakfast. 'Sixpence-worth of vegetables for soup,' I would say, and I'd watch with eagle eye to make sure I got a wee bit of everything. Carrot, turnip, leek and some parsley. It was no use the greengrocer trying to tell me that parsley was too dear today to be included in the sixpence-worth. 'You need parsley for broth,' I would say stubbornly. 'And Grannie said I was to get it with my sixpence-worth.' I usually did.

An 'outside' loaf was a farthing cheaper than one baked in the middle of the row, for it had a hard shiny outside slice which was tough and indigestible. 'Will I get an outside one?' I'd ask Grannie eagerly when coppers were scarce and pay-day a long way off. 'They're a whole farthing cheaper.' 'Nae, naw lassie,' she would say, 'it's nae savin' at a', for naebody could eat it wi' pleasure, and that slice would be wasted,' and so I learned that a bargain wasn't always a bargain, even if the price-tag was lower.

I used to trot into town with the daughter of a neighbour, even poorer than we were, for there was a special shop which sold ham-bones for tuppence-ha'penny for two pairs, and that gave them two good pots of lentil soup, and a good picking at the bones with their boiled potatoes. It was a mile and a half each way, but we thought nothing of it, especially if it was the gird season, and we were there and back before we knew it.

I discovered gradually that a highly priced roast wasn't necessarily better than the delicious potted meats Grannie could make with the cheaper shin of beef. And I found too that boiling beef on the bone had a flavour all its own, and it didn't matter that it was a wee bit on the fat side, for that gave it added sweetness. 'Aye,' Grannie would nod approvingly, as she saw me waiting till there was just an inch of meat clinging all round before I'd hold out my plate, 'oor Molly kens what's guid for her. The sweeter the meat the nearer the bone.' And she showed me how to blow out the marrow to mix with my plain boiled potatoes, and we both remembered the words of the hymn, 'Even as with marrow and with fat my soul shall filled be'. I thoroughly agreed with hymns as practical as this.

By the time I was ten years old, Grannie could trust me to choose a piece of beef, knowing I'd bring back the very best value in the shop for the money I had to spend. I could shoulder this responsibility quite confidently when only one or two shillings were involved, but I remember one Christmas I was sent to get a piece of roast beef for our Christmas dinner, and when the butcher said 'Seven-and-six' I nearly choked in panic.

I didn't know so much about roasts. What if I chose wrongly and wasted my mother's precious money? So, oblivious of the other customers, and shaking with the weight of the decision, I asked the butcher to keep it aside while I ran home and described it to my grannie. 'It's like a great big chop, Grannie,' I told her breathlessly, 'with a wee bit of different colour in the middle, and a wee division of fat right here,' and I pointed to the place on the table where I was drawing it with my finger. 'And it's seven-and-six. Will I get it?'

She sat still, considering what I had said. 'Aye,' she said at last, 'get it. If it's like that, then it's sirloin, and it's a grand bit o' meat.' I flew back to the shop. 'I'll take it,' I said importantly, laying down my three half-crowns with a lordly air. It *was* sirloin. It was delicious, and Grannie gave me a special slice of the wee bit in the middle which was a different colour, and told me it was the fillet. That was a new word for me – I'd only heard of fillet fish – but I remembered it, and agreed with Grannie that it was the finest delicacy of all.

All the jam in our house was home-made. My mother's comment, 'She's the kind that aye has bought jam on the table', was enough to let us know the shiftlessness of the person she was describing. We'd watch the shop windows until the jam fruit was at its lowest price, then rush home with the news, 'Grannie, the man says the black currants 'll no' get ony cheaper', or 'The strawberries are goin' up again next week'. Out would come the big purse, and off we'd scamper to get the fruit and the preserving sugar, 'And mind ye get nice dry fruit noo,' Grannie would exhort. 'Nane o' his wet sleeshy stuff or the jam'll no' set.'

When a loved mother died in our tenements the tragedy was felt by us all. But the family was never broken up and scattered to different Council homes. The father went to his work as usual, but the children, skilled shoppers and well aware of the work every penny had to do, ran the house and bought the food, and would have been astounded if anybody had suggested it was too much for them. There was no mystery in housekeeping to them. They had done the shopping since they could toddle, and count up their change like adding machines. In our tenements it was never too early to learn to face up to life.

5

In winter-time the Angier's emulsion didn't always work its magic, and sometimes I'd have to be kept off school because of a bronchial cold or flu. We didn't bother to call the doctor, for we were used to this sort of illness. And I loved being lifted from the hurley bed into the cool vastness of the big recess bed where my mother usually slept, but she was now off to work. It was almost worth while being ill to lie there, snug and warm, with the stir and activity of the house around me.

What a lot of things Grannie had to do when we were out at school. There were all the vegetables to be washed and scraped or peeled, and cut into tiny squares for the soup. And I never knew she fried the onion and the floured meat when she was making stew. Mmm, what a good smell the frying onion had. And how pleasant it was to watch her get out the flour and the milk, and know that in a wee while I was going to be given a lovely pancake straight off the girdle, dripping with margarine. The wifie across the landing had smelt the pancakes too, it seemed, for she came in to ask the time, as her clock had stopped, and was just able to wait to have a cup of tea with us. And then the potatoes had to be peeled and put on to boil, to be ready in time for my mother coming in from work and the boys from school, for they all got home at dinner-time. I was only hungry for a wee bowl of soup, and a beggar who came to the door also got a bowlful, for Grannie said he looked more in need of a guid bowl of soup than a penny, which she couldn't spare anyway.

But when Grannie herself was ill, things were very different. She suffered from severe bronchitis, and every winter the doctor had to come to see her. I was usually kept off school to let him in, and the fuss that went on before his visit astonished me. The night before, my mother flew about laying out clean sheets and pillow-cases, and a clean nightie for Grannie. A fresh cloth was placed in readiness for the table. The range was polished, the floor swept, and the brass covers burnished till they hung in a gleaming row above the dresser, the coal fire reflected in every one of them.

The morning of the visit, my mother rose an hour earlier than she usually did. The bed was stripped, Grannie was put into the fresh nightie and laid gently against the splendid snowy pillow, hardly daring to breathe in case she'd crumple it before the doctor arrived. I sponged her face and hands while my mother put finishing touches to the bed-cover, and smoothed the gathers of the bed-pawn, and then, when she had made sure everything was really in mint condition, off went Mother to work. She was well satisfied the doctor wouldn't find a flaw anywhere, as far as material things went.

I busied myself getting the dinner ready under Grannie's sharp directions. She had small patience with slackness, sick-bed or no, and woe betide me if I used the wrong-sized spoon for anything, or stopped stirring till she told me the exact moment.

At last came the knock at the door. My heart in my mouth, I would gaze at Grannie.

'Will I open it?' I would whisper.

'Of course. Do you think you're going to keep him on the landing? Ask him to come in, and then don't open your mouth to say a word till he goes away.'

My cheeks flushed with nervousness, my mouth dry with fright, I'd turn the handle, and there on the landing was the doctor. A huge man carrying a wee black bag. 'Come in,' I would whisper, 'Grannie's in her bed in the kitchen.'

A pair of blue eyes would take in the neat, tidy, immaculate kitchen, and with a twinkling smile he would advance towards the bed and, to my horror, actually *sit* on my mother's good bed-cover. *Nobody* was allowed to sit on this! Grannie would flash me a warning glance when she heard my gasp of dismay. The doctor would speak. 'Now, now, Grannie, what have you been up to, eh?' I was sure Grannie would give him the rough edge of her tongue for daring to suggest she had been up to anything, but she was smiling and preening herself and, surprisingly, not the least bit angry.

Her chest was impressively sounded, and the wee black things he had worn in his ears were put away in the bag. A prescription was written out and left on the table and then, before I realized it, he had patted me on the head and was out of the door. The visit was over.

'Now,' Grannie would say, all satisfaction that everything had gone off so well, and I hadn't done anything to disgrace her, 'we'll hae a wee cup o' tea. A nice chiel yon, and real clever. I've never kent a doctor who gave a better bottle.'

'A chiel,' I'd repeat to myself, puzzled at such a description. He seemed like a very old man to me. He was strange and fierce, with his queer prescriptions written in an unknown hand, bold and free with his careless crumpling of my mother's best bed-cover, and greatly to be feared with his wee black bag. But Grannie was certainly right about the good bottles he prescribed, for it only needed one visit and one bottle to have Grannie on her feet again, and when Grannie was well we could all dare to be cheeky again, and I could get back to my rightful place in the hurley bed again, and coorie into her back.

But och I was glad that our Grannie only had bronchitis when she had to have the doctor, for there was another old lady in the tenements who was 'dotted' as we called the mentally ill, and the doctor had to prescribe a different sort of bottle to keep her safe and quiet.

She was very old – about eighty, Grannie said – with snow-white hair, a pink wrinkled skin, light blue eyes with an expression of bewildered innocence which made her look like an elderly baby, and a high sing-song voice. She was the mother of neighbours who used to live downstairs in our tenement, and Grannie had known her in her saner days. So when the family moved away, and nobody in the new tenement could be bothered with her, it was to our house she found her way almost daily.

I was about eleven years old at the time, and the number of times I had to take Grannie Mackay all the way back to her house were beyond counting. No question of riding on a tramcar or a bus either, for there was no money for such extras. Walk we must and walk we did.

How she found her way to our house without coming to grief in the heavy traffic was a mystery. When I would come home from school I would whisper to my grannie, 'Is she here?', and my heart would sink into a gloom of fear at the reply, 'Don't stand there on the mat – of course she's here, and she's lookin' furrit to seeing you.'

One of Grannie Mackay's more frightening habits was her inconsistency in the matter of sex. 'Here's Molly to see you,' my grannie would call out cheerfully. Old Mrs Mackay would fix me with a surprised blue eye, as though I didn't live in our house. 'Oh she's a fine boy, a fine boy,' she'd chant. 'I'm *not* a boy,' I'd mutter furiously, but this tactlessness was silenced by a quenching look from my grannie. 'Aye,' the chant would continue, 'a fine boy she is, a lovely boy she is, growing every day.'

My back would be pressed against the dresser to get as far away from the old lady as possible – her witlessness frightened me, but my grannie would have none of this timidity. 'Mrs Mackay wants you to comb her hair,' she'd say briskly. This was the thing I feared most. 'Oh, Grannie,' I'd whisper tearfully, 'I don't like combing her hair. It's cold, and it feels wet and her head's all pink.'

Grannie dismissed my distaste with 'What does it matter about *your* comfort? Doesn't Mrs Mackay need her hair combed? It's little enough she has to please her. She likes you to comb her hair, and at her age her feelings are far more important than yours.' So I would climb on to the back of the big chair and with trembling fingers undo the pins and quietly brush and comb the lank white hair. Old Mrs Mackay kept up a dreamy chant as I brushed, 'Och there is lovely, it is. Och she's a fine boy at the hairdressing. A fine boy.' This would irritate me so much I'd want to give the old head a smart tap with the brush, fear or no fear, but my grannie's watchfulness prevented any such tantrums. 'What does it matter whether she thinks you're a boy or not,' Grannie would say afterwards, 'you *ken* you're a lassie, and calling you a boy isn't going to turn you into one!'

At last the moment would arrive when Grannie would say 'Now, Mrs Mackay, your daughter will be wondering where you are, and your tea will be ready. Molly will take you home.' With great ceremony she would don her grey shawl, place her black 'mutch' over her carefully combed hair, and rise panting and grunting to her feet. Obeying a nod from Grannie, I'd draw old Mrs Mackay's arm through mine, and lead her slowly – oh, how slowly – out of the house, down the stairs, into the street and along the road through the traffic to her daughter's house. As often as not, I'd hardly be home again when she was back almost at my heels, having completely forgotten she'd just left us. Back we'd go again, and I'd whisper to her relatives that they must try to keep her in, because I'd homework to do and I couldn't be running back and forward all night. My grannie would have been furious had she heard me, but I felt I *had* to make a stand somewhere.

But if the clouded mind of the 'dotted' frightened me, the mere whisper of 'fever', that infant scourge, sent our mothers sick with dread. With twelve families to a close, infection could spread like wildfire, and the sight of the fever van struck a chill into our hearts. But curiosity amongst us children was always stronger than fear and we would gather on the pavement to catch a glimpse of a swathed figure on its way through the close to the ambulance, and shudder with relief that it wasn't us on the stretcher. Awed as we children were by the sight of our playmate magically transformed to a terrifying bundle, borne by two solemn ambulance-men, we realized that while we were lively and healthy we might as well enjoy ourselves, and give a bit of help at the same time. So we organized back-court concerts to raise money to buy presents for the hospital cases.

As soon as the ambulance had disappeared we'd race through the close to the back court and decide on our entertainment. We'd maybe arrange to do an imitation of the pantomime we'd seen from the gallery during the winter, or a cowboys and Indians episode from the latest film, and we had to decide whether our costumes would be made from crinkled paper or cast-offs begged from our mothers. We'd divide out the roles to be played, and we sewed and pinned and rehearsed for days, practically in a fever ourselves as we got everything ready for the performance. We never repeated a show. It had to be a full-scale new production for each victim, and we lived every minute of it.

We charged a ha'penny for children and a penny for adults, and the adults sat on the stone edging which ran round the back-court railings. The children sat on the ground or stood, just as they pleased. We generally gave two performances, and our audience usually stayed for both, and were highly critical if they didn't get an exact repeat performance at the second house, word for word, gesture for gesture. As nothing was written down and everything had been rehearsed on the principle of 'You say this' and 'I'll say that', this wasn't easy, but we pacified them by singing an extra verse of a favourite song if the mood turned too critical.

Although I was always very nervous, I was quite drunk with power when I discovered how easy it was to change the mood of an audience from one of enthusiastic noisy delight at my swash-buckling impersonation of a Principal Boy, to silent pathos at my rendering of 'Won't you buy my pretty flowers'. Heady stuff, and I quite forgot the victim in my enthusiastic production of my all-talking, all-singing, all-dancing extravaganzas.

We usually collected enough in pennies and ha'pennies to be able to offer the fever victim a huge box of chocolates and a bag of fruit, and the shopping expeditions were themselves a source of intense pleasure. We felt like millionaires as we crowded into the sweet-shop and selected, with great care, a box with a sympathetic dog on the lid, and then moved to the fruit-shop next door, where we spent the rest of the money on as many apples and oranges as the kitty would cover. No fanciful things like grapes or melons for us – oranges and apples were our limit and we knew they would be appreciated to the last bite.

Somehow one always assumed it would be somebody else who would be chosen for the victim, and the part of the entertainer would be filled by oneself.

And then, one year when we simply couldn't afford it to happen, the fever germ struck our house, and it struck me. My aunt was home on a visit from Australia on a specially reduced ticket which involved her travelling back by a certain date. If she went beyond this date an extra twenty pounds had to be paid, an enormous sum in our world, in fact an impossible sum for us to find. She had come to our house to have her last baby born in Scotland, and was within three weeks of her sailing date when I came in complaining of a sore throat and a throbbing head. I didn't know what those symptoms meant, but my mother and my grannie did. I caught the look of horror which passed between them and I was puzzled. They didn't speak, beyond handing me a glass, and pouring in some stuff and telling me to gargle. As I was tucked into bed, I heard Auntie whisper, 'We ought to send for the doctor.' My mother shushed her fiercely. 'We can't. You'd never be allowed to leave, and you must get that boat. Where could we get twenty pounds.' 'But, Jeanie,' my auntie urged, 'she should be in hospital.' Hospital! Ambulances! I was to be the next bundle carried through the awe-struck spectators! I felt tears sting my eyelids at the thought of it, but my mother would have none of it. 'I can do what's necessary,' she said.

Now at that time in our small room-and-kitchen tenement dwelling there were three adults, three children and an infant; an outside toilet had to be shared with two other families, so the risk of spreading infection was terrifying. But my mother faced it all, and took it in her stride. She was used to hardship, and to battling with difficulties, with poverty a powerful spur, and in this crisis she was magnificent.

She had her job in the big engineering works to attend to, but she saw that everything I touched or used was sterilized. She was so dramatic when she explained to my brothers about the dangers of using anything I had eaten from that for months afterwards they refused to drink from a cup if they'd seen it anywhere near my bed during my illness. Towels and face-flannel were kept scrupulously apart from the others, gargling routines punctiliously observed, light diet adhered to, and as I slept with Grannie we felt it wasn't very likely she would be infected at her age.

The worst part was trying to keep my school chums from visiting me. We couldn't and daren't tell them the real cause of my illness, but we couldn't risk suspicion and the dreaded 'sanitary' inspector descending upon us by refusing everyone admittance. So the one or two special chums who couldn't be kept out were made to sit at the other end of the kitchen, by the window, and yell their sympathy from there, on the excuse that I was very easily made sneeze, and the cold air they brought in with them sent me off on an attack if they sat too close to me. Strange to say, everybody believed this. We were a trusting community. Even I wasn't sure that it was fever I had, for the word was never mentioned, until the skin began to peel in strips from my hands. Then I wore little white silk gloves and pretended this was to keep my hands warm when I kept them outside the clothes, which I liked, for if they got cold it made me sneeze again. Once more, because I'd always been full of mad capers and loved dressing up, everybody believed us.

The new baby was kept in the other room, and I never saw her again, except held at a distance at the other end of the kitchen just before she left with Auntie for the boat. Auntie gazed at me compassionately and lovingly, but didn't dare come closer to say goodbye.

It was a miracle, of course, but nobody on the stair developed even the mildest symptom. I gradually found my strength, and at last was ready for school again. My absence had been explained as prolonged bronchitis, and as I was always top of the class and an enthusiastic pupil, nobody doubted us. But there was a terrible moment when I went back to school and the teacher looked up from the register as I answered 'Present, miss'. 'Oh, hullo. Are you better? Was it fever?'

I stared at her dumbly, the blood rushing to my pale cheeks. 'How had she guessed? What would I say?' It was one thing acting a lie, especially when I hadn't really known it was a lie for a long time. It was quite another thing putting it into words. Then she consulted the register again, with its marginal notes. 'Oh no, bronchitis, I see. Are you sure you're better? You look very congested to me.' Congested! I was on the point of fainting with fear, followed by relief.

So even into the school register our deception had succeeded. Succeeded so well, in fact, that I didn't have a single 'benefit' concert. No chocolates or fruit for bronchitis. Only for scarlet fever, and I hadn't had that. Or had I?

But if I hadn't had the chocolates, I hadn't had the ride in the dreaded 'fever van' either. Nor had anybody else in our house, or in our tenement during that epidemic anyway.

But that was a terrible risk my mother took.

Although we only had a room and a kitchen for the five of us, we never felt overcrowded, for our accommodation was palatial compared with many of the tenement families. There were several large families living in a single room in our neighbourhood, or at best a single room with a tiny apartment opening out of it, not much bigger than a pantry. This small box-like room was considered a luxury to be envied by those who had to crowd into a single room, and they dreamed of what good use they could put the extra space.

One family in our tenement had fourteen children and they all lived in one room with just this small box-like compartment leading out of it, and once they actually held a wedding reception there when the eldest daughter was married. As the younger children came in from play, they quietly crawled under the festive table and vanished into the smaller room, where bags of chips were handed through to them, and they boasted of this treat for weeks afterwards. Long experience of living in such cramped conditions had trained them to play noiselessly and happily, and they might have been a family of mice for all the noise they made. Indeed some of the wedding guests never even knew they were there.

In all the years of my childhood, I never knew that family's mother's voice raised in anger. And the wedding feast was the only occasion I ever saw her without her working apron. On this one glorious night her eyes could be lifted above the level of the kitchen sink, and the bridal pair were waved off in a shower of confetti to their own little single end, which they had miraculously found ten minutes away, so visiting mother and the thirteen brothers and sisters would be no problem.

Farther along the street, another family of fourteen had a room and kitchen like ours, separated by a lobby, and both rooms of equal size. They felt they were so rich in space that they added to their meagre income by taking in a lodger. This was a great source of interest and mystery to me. I'd never heard of a lodger before, and veiwed this man as somebody very special. He was on constant night-shift, which meant he slept during the day. None of us saw anything unusual in the fact that he slept in a bed which was used at night by several of the fourteen other occupants who, of course slept at the normal time during the night. I thought this a most resourceful arrangement, making a bed earn its keep in this convenient way.

As I was friendly with one of the daughters in this exciting household, I used to pay occasional visits there, and I must have embarrassed the lodger terribly, sitting staring at him with unwinking eye, noting every detail of his appearance, from his thick thatch of red hair to his heavy-soled tackety boots, careful to overlook nothing in the personality of this strange being, the first lodger I had ever seen.

The common factor to such large households was their quietness. This amazed me. I was too young to realize that where three children could be naturally exuberant, twelve or fourteen just had to be quiet and restrained or anarchy would have prevailed. And it was easy to see how fond they all were of each other. In the house where there were fourteen, the girl I was friendly with told me in all seriousness that when the oldest son was married they felt the house was empty. They missed him so much, they could hardly bear it. I'd have thought they would have been grateful for a little extra breathing space, but their minds didn't run that way.

With these examples of ingenuity all round us we didn't even stop to think twice where the wedding celebrations would be held when my mother's youngest sister got married. We'd have them in our house, of course, in the evening, after a five o'clock wedding so that all the men could be present. There was no question of anybody asking for time off work for anything so frivolous as a wedding, so the festive board would have to wait till they'd finished their day's work and changed out of their dungarees into their Sunday dark suits. My mother and her sister shared the costs, and of course it could all be supplied on credit on our Cooperative book, and the dividend on such a huge expense would be as good as winning a sweepstake. We knew about such things for my mother shared a sixpenny ticket with a workmate on Derby Day, and she had once won twenty-five shillings – a fortune.

Although my mother had thrown up her hands in amazement at the wedding which had been held in the close, with its slit of a boxroom for the children, she wasn't in the least daunted by the thought of having to arrange for all the eating, drinking and entertaining to take place in our one good room. Or of only having one wee kitchen for the coats, and the washing up and where Grannie and I would be sleeping. Or that the toilet arrangements were one flight of stairs down, and we were adding at least two dozen to the two families already sharing this amenity. She took such difficulties in her stride, and we all plunged into our various tasks with a will.

Everything that could be stowed out of sight was pushed under beds, or crammed into wardrobes and chests of drawers, and I may say we had a fine time afterwards trying to find clothes for bed that night and for school next morning.

About four o'clock in the afternoon, long trestle tables arrived and were set up, one along each side wall and one across the oriel window, and long benches were ranged behind each table to give seating accommodation to the greatest number that could be squeezed into the room. We had burst the bank and were having outside caterers, and we children rushed in and out among the workmen's feet, delirious with joy at the transformation scene which turned our one and only parlour into a little hall before our very eyes.

Long boards filled with crockery and glasses were brought in, and the places set on snowy white tablecloths, also supplied by the caterer. We'd never seen such vast pieces of linen, and shuddered with horror at the thought of tea being spilled on such dazzling cloths, for we couldn't imagine how long it must take to wash and dry cloths of that size, or how they could ever be ironed to such a state of smooth perfection. As we stared, fervently praying we wouldn't be the ones to disgrace ourselves with such a mishap, the next contingent were bustling in, carrying boards filled with plates of sliced bread, cakes and biscuits. These were ranged along the tables, and bottles of sauce and pickles placed at strategic intervals and, after a long critical survey to make sure nothing had been overlooked, vases of flowers were moved from the sideboard and laid exactly in the centre of each table.

Next came the drinks, which were left in a corner of the kitchen, ready to be opened at the appropriate moment.

As we lived two flights of stairs from the street, you can imagine the amount of tramping up and down that took place during this non-stop performance, but everybody loved a wedding and there wasn't a word of complaint from neighbours or workmen.

By five o'clock it was pandemonium, with my mother trying to get the three of us children dressed, not forgetting helping Grannie into her black silk blouse with the cameo brooch at the collar, and endeavouring to shake the creases out of her own lilac crêpe, which had been knocked off the hook at the back of the door three times by the men as they pushed past delivering another load of food.

We didn't go to the ceremony, as my mother was terrified to leave the house in case something calamitous would happen, so we had a little extra time for dressing. But the last button was barely done up when the bride and groom were with us, and guests pouring in behind them, shrugging out of coats and hats, and making their way to the room where the laden tables glittered and gleamed under the gas chandelier which was my mother's pride and joy.

There was much praise for the beauty of the arrangements, and a good deal of jostling and squeezing as people wriggled into their places. Then, with perfect timing, the waitresses arrived to serve the meal. Ahead of them four men strode in, bearing boards of steak pies and vegetables. We children yelled with delight. Never had we seen so many pies all at once, never such gigantic mounds of snowy mashed potatoes, never such tureens of peas, never such vast bowls of mashed swedes.

There was some slight embarrassment in having strange waitresses standing over us as we ate, but it was a bitterly cold night and we quickly forgot them as we tucked into our delicious meal, and soon toasts were being drunk to great bursts of laughter, much of which was beyond the children, and then the tables were dismantled and the floor cleared for singing, games and dancing.

The vocalists needed a bit of coaxing before they'd agree to sing us a favourite song, and my Uncle Johnnie was furious because his wife insisted on singing soulfully, 'The March of the Cameron Men'. He felt she was parading her pride in him too openly. This was because he had been a Cameron Highlander in the war!

Grannie sang, in imitation of Victorian music-hall ballad, 'Be kind to auld Grannie, for noo she is frail, like a time-shattered tree bending low in the Gale', and I wept copiously because I thought the words were so touching and so beautiful. Somebody else sang 'O' a' the airts the wind can blaw', and my mother wept, and we all had a lovely time.

We played forfeits, and bee baw babbity and games involving wee bits of paper and pencil. And then we had an eightsome reel, and quadrilles, and there wasn't a cheep of protest from the family living underneath.

The door of our house was wide open most of the evening, and anybody who felt like it was welcome to come in and see the bride and toast her health. The fun went on till midnight, and when at last they had all departed, our faces were flushed with triumph and happiness, for we had had a wonderful wedding. 'A great celebration, Jeanie,' they said to my mother as they left. 'A splendid repast and a grand wedding.'

Looking back, I realized all this must have involved an enormous amount of work for my mother, and it must have taken days to get cleared up in spite of help from caterers. But they were unsophisticated times, and a passionate belief in our ability to put on a show helped to make the work light. And for many moons afterwards, whenever anyone mentioned any grand occasion, I always countered with 'Just like my auntie's wedding, when we had real waitresses in our house and thousands of steak pies'.

6

When I was a wee girl if you said that something looked 'hand-made' it was the greatest insult you could hurl at the disparaged article. To be exactly the same as everyone else was the look that was coveted, and great was the anguish suffered by children whose mothers had to make do and mend from anything which came to hand.

Luckily I didn't mind a bit, which was just as well, for I don't think my mother was ever able to afford a single garment which the school required. Apart from my boots, which, of course, had to be bought because none of us had figured out how to make them from anything lying around the house, practically everything was hand-made and mostly out of things first worn by my mother or somebody else. The endless hours and patience which must have gone into fashioning my garments weren't met with a scowl by me, for I was well aware of the tightness of the family budget.

Grannie knitted my long black stockings, and I took as much pride as she did in the 'intakes' at the back, which made the shape and could truly be described as 'fully-fashioned'. How well they clung to my ankles, and rose long and snug right to the tops of my legs, where they met the buttons on my Liberty bodice.

When her tweed skirt was beyond hope for her own use, it was cunningly fashioned into a little pleated skirt for me, and we both thought I was elegance itself when this was topped with an exactly matching woollen jumper Grannie knitted. This wool we got from somebody who worked in a wool warehouse, and it was going practically free because it had become entangled, and the firm couldn't waste time rewinding it. A great bargain this. In fact I wore this particular jumper for years, with Grannie cleverly changing the collar each winter. One year it sported a grey angora collar, the next a red and white striped one, and latterly a white rabbit's wool one. I was elated when my school-teacher said in its final winter, 'Another new jumper from your grannie's clever needles?', and I was able to say demurely, but proudly, 'No, miss, just a new collar.' And I never forgot that lesson, that it is amazingly easy to ring the changes on an old garment by a new eye-catching accessory.

We saw nothing frumpty in wearing 'winter combs'. They were cosy and comforting in wintry weather, both indoors and out, for in spite of the coal fire in the range, it could be cold in the tenements. Grannie was able to knit us lovely cosy combs in pale grey or pale pink, buying the wool in bulk through that same good fairy in the wool warehouse. I don't think I ever saw Grannie without her steel needles flashing in her lap, summer or winter, for it was a constant task keeping us all clothed all year round.

She was an expert knitter, and I remember my mother being fascinated by a little waistcoat she saw in a pattern book, and beginning to knit this in brown and mustard shades. Grannie took one look at the size and said, 'That will fit oor Molly when it's feenished, but never you, it's far ower wee.' My mother was indignant for she had implicit faith that a book must be far more accurate than Grannie's invented patterns. Doggedly she followed the instructions, pressed out the finished garment and sewed it together. We all looked at each other, and my mother walked out of the kitchen without a word. I felt so sorry that it had turned out this way after all her hard work, for she wasn't a natural knitter like Grannie, but I must say that sporty little waistcoat kept my back snug and warm for a good few winters, and in the end my mother rejoiced that at least she had made a first-class job of this tiny garment. 'You'd think it had been bought in a shop,' she said proudly. 'You'd never think it had been hand-made.'

My summer ginghams were devised from about a yard of material at elevenpence ha'penny or one shilling and sixpence, and, of course, not a penny was spent on a pattern. My mother just copied whatever style took her fancy. Boys' clothes had to be bought, you see, for the first attempt to make a pair of trousers was so disastrous that a second was never even contemplated. The boys were far more conventional than I was, and utterly refused to be dressed differently from their fellows. But with a girl it was different – for I didn't mind my slightly unusual clothes. Mind you, dresses were easy, and with this girl it was certainly different, I'd been reading quite a lot about a little French girl who came to stay in Scotland, and who looked completely different from everyone else and went sobbing to bed each night because of this; but in the end she triumphed, because a rich lady came and instantly picked out this little oddity because she was elegant and *chic*, and not ordinary like the others, and she took her on a splendid holiday to the seaside. This story reinforced Grannie's teaching that it didn't matter if one looked different from other people, and in fact at times could be a positive advantage. Alas, no rich lady picked me out from the crowd, but the upstairs neighbours did take me with them when they went to the sea in the summer, after I'd had flu, and that was almost as good.

When the time came for me to move to the higher school we were at our wits' end, for now it was demanded that I wear a gym tunic with a blouse underneath. Where on earth could we find the money for a gym tunic? Even the coarsest serge was beyond my mother's pocket. She looked over her meagre wardrobe. She had a fine navy gaberdine jacket and skirt, and decided she'd sacrifice the skirt for me. This time I was in a panic, for I'd been told it *had* to be serge. How could gaberdine look like serge? It was much finer, and it was a slightly lighter shade of navy, and this time I just had to be the same as the rest of the class. It was a uniform. I was certain I wouldn't be allowed to study with the rest of the class, and would be condemned to the junior school for ever.

My mother ignored my anguished cries and sewed on. When I saw the finished result I sat down and wept. Not only was it a light navy, not only gaberdine, but with the curve of the skirt she hadn't been able to make a square yoke; and the pleats were hung on to a curved yoke, the square corners rounded instead of sharp. Added to this, my mother had decided the best value in blouses was Tussore silk, not white cotton. Not only was it cheap, but it wouldn't show the dirt, an important consideration. I crept to school that first day, hardly daring to take off my coat. To my amazement, half the girls in the new class had no gym tunics at all. The teacher cast an inquiring eye over us, and then asked me to come out to the front. My moment of shame was upon me. I could hardly see for threatening tears, and my face was red as a beetroot. My very ears were tingling. And through my confusion I heard her say, 'Now that's the sort of neat appearance I would like you all to achieve. You can have a choice of blouse, so long as the colours are pale, but you can see what a neat uniform appearance you will present when you're all dressed like this.' I went back to my seat in a dream. She hadn't minded at all about the gaberdine – or the curved yoke – or the Tussore silk blouse. My mother was delighted when I told her that I'd been brought out in front of the whole class to let everybody see the home-made gym tunic, which was an example of what the others should attempt. 'Aye,' she said happily, 'I'll bet she never realized it was home-made.'

Everyone else had satchels or leather cases, but not me. When the old satchel I'd inherited from somebody else at last fell to bits, just as I was transferring to the higher school, a man in my mother's workshop in the Railways made me a perfect little case of wood, and even added a little plate to it with my name. It was stained dark brown, and it seemed to me *far* better than leather, because I could stand on it in emergency without harming it a bit, and it could be buffed up with boot polish to a gleaming mahogany shade. I liked its originality and I liked its stout strength, and I loved its little name-plate.

For the final school party, when I was about to leave that school, Mother and I racked our brains to concoct something which would be worthy of the dux of the school. We were as hard up as ever, of course, so it would have to be something we could make from the simplest materials. A stroll past Margaret Hunter's, then the best children's shop in Glasgow, revealed a dream of a dress in the window, composed of yards and yards of narrow frilling and looking like the fairy on top of the Xmas tree. My mother stared at it intently, counting the rows, observing how the neckline was cut, how the sleeves fitted, where the waist was darted.

She counted the money in her purse, went next door to a big emporium stocking all sorts of materials, and came out with a huge parcel, bulky but very light to carry. 'Aye this will take me a' ma time,' she observed, 'for it will all have to be sewn in separate rows, but I think I can manage it for the party.' Every night when she came in from work she'd stitch those frills with tiny perfect strokes, and I'd hang over her, counting how many we still had to go before we could start shaping it into a dress. At last she had enough and we could pin it to its muslin base.

The night before the party I tried it on. It was perfect. My cheeks were flushed with pleasure, especially as my mother had somehow managed to add the last touch of elegance – a silver bow with narrow streamers fastening off the neckline. The party of course was a joy. Lots to eat, splendid games, prizes to be collected, and school holidays to follow. When I came home my mother was waiting. 'Well?' she asked 'Mother,' I burst out, 'my teacher asked me if you'd bought my dress from Margaret Hunter's.' We stared at each other. A great smile spread over my mother's tired face. 'Margaret Hunter's,' she said dreamily. 'Aye, I never thought in my wildest dreams my home-made dress would be mistaken for a shop one. It was well worth the effort, well worth it.'

All of us in the tenements took great care of our clothes. We knew how hard they were to come by, and we changed out of our school clothes the minute we reached home, without having to be told. We all had tough hand-knitted jerseys which the girls wore over tweed skirts, and the boys over old trousers for back-court games, while for Sundays and special visiting to relatives and friends we had a 'best' outfit, which we guarded and cared for like mink. How splendid those Sunday clothes seemed as we laid them out on the bed, before getting ready for church or Sunday School. The boys, in their dashing sailor suits, seemed entirely different creatures from their wild week-day selves, as they walked sedately on either side of me.

In summer I felt elegant beyond belief in a neat navy suit, Tussore silk blouse, little white socks and flat lacing shoes. Sometimes the shoes varied a little, and might have a strap across the instep, but whether strap or laces, they magically seemed to lend grace to my legs which, during the week, knew only the stout support of long lacing boots. Our mothers were firmly convinced that boots kept young ankles well shaped and supported, and who knows they may have been right, for certainly all of us seemed to have limbs like race-horses with trim, strong ankles.

In winter the suits were carefully brushed and put to the back of the wardrobe, and out came the heavy coats for the boys and myself. From the box on top of the wardrobe my black velour hat was brought out, and its elastic checked for strength and stretchiness, to make sure it would stay firmly anchored at all times. In church a favourite pastime during a dull sermon was to draw the elastic in a wide Vee out from the chin, and let it fly with a satisfactory 'ping' over the lips. We had to be careful though, for a too-loud twanging noise brought a sharp rap on the head from the nearest adult.

We didn't seem to grow very fast, for I remember wearing the same clothes year in, year out. Mind you, they had been prudently bought 'for growth', and were only replaced when the last inch of hem had been let down, and the last tuck removed from the sleeves.

Even in our frugal district, though, there were the feckless ones. There were also those so unskilled that they knew long stretches of unemployment. The children of such families wore their school clothes for back-court games, for they had no others to change into, and they gradually reached a state of shabbiness and tatters which were considered a disgrace by the teachers. At last the day arrived when the unkempt ones would be called out to the teacher's desk, and questions whispered about their financial position.

Poor as we all were, we were fiercely independent, and we others, sitting safely at our desks, decently clad in well-preserved school clothes, would lower our eyes in sympathy for our ragged playmates. We knew the teacher was going to offer a form of application for 'Parish clothes' and we shuddered. The Parish clothes were made from scratchy woollen material, with a built-in itchy quality which made them agony to wear, and the genius who thought up the dull grey porridgy colour should have had a medal for successful depression of the human spirit. These clothes were instantly recognizable by their ugliness and harsh durability, and anyone unfortunate enough to have to wear them avoided the rest of us in the playground, in case a tactless enemy might jeer the hated words 'Parish clothes'.

We each of us rejoiced that our own parents were thrifty and such good managers that we could wear our own clothes, washed and mended and let down though they often were, with pride and ownership. To have to be dependent on the Parish for clothes seemed to us a fate worse than death.

But if we liked to wear our own clothes and buy our own jotters we had no qualms about accepting the splendid slates which the school provided. There were slots at the back of our desks where we slid the slates when we'd finished with them, and an almighty clatter they made when we pushed them home at the end of the lesson.

An old slate pencil, broken into use, was a great joy, but a new one, light grey and chalky looking, didn't seem right at all until it had been wiped clean of its powdery bloom by our clutching fingers, and was smooth and black and shiny and entirely satisfactory as it skimmed over the slate.

Sometimes a piece of grit made the pencil squeak abominably, and my teeth would grate and my spine shudder at the piercing sound. A new one was hurriedly produced by the teacher, without even having to ask, for she was even more sensitive to this scraping than we were.

On wintry days the slate struck chill on the hand which leaned on it, and a jersey sleeve made a comforting layer between hand and slate when it was pulled down snugly over the fingers. In summer a moist palm left little shadows of steamy darkness on the slate, and made it difficult for us to write.

Unlike the teacher with her blackboard, we didn't have velvet pads for wiping the slate clean. Hideously smelling damp sponges or damp flannels were kept by each of us in little tin boxes, usually discarded tobacco or sweetie tins, depending on whether they'd been begged from dads or grannies. These cloths were supposed to be damped with water before we left home, but as often as not we forgot. Then there was many a surreptitious spit to get them wet enough to wipe our slates, and they must have harboured germs by the million. In the course of time the damp contents rusted the inside of the boxes, and the smell was awful. Somehow one grew used to the peculiar odour of one's own sponge when the lid was opened, and it was only when the nose twitched at the whiff of a neighbour's box that the pungent aroma seemed revolting. I remember my favourite tin box was a beautiful pale blue which had once held Grannie's Christmas butterscotch, and Grannie allowed me, as a special favour, to cut off a piece of our soft new sponge to match this splendid container, instead of the wee bit of flannel clout I usually carried. With what pride I flourished my box as I drew it from my desk each morning, and I was convinced it was the envy of the class.

I loved my slate. Compared with Vere Foster, with its ink and its ruled lines which allowed no mistake to go unnoticed, there was something almost light-hearted in working with materials which could so easily be corrected, with no trace left to tell the tale. Vere Foster had a perfection and a discipline which reduced the whole room to utter silence while we laboured to achieve the copper-plate writing it demanded. The top line showed a virtuous sentiment in perfect handwriting, 'Honesty is the best policy', 'A burnt child fears the fire', 'Virtue is its own reward', or 'Practice makes perfect'. On the ruled lines immediately below, we had to copy the sentence, using fine up-strokes and heavy down-strokes, and this exercise was to instruct us in the art of beautiful handwriting. There was no rubbing out tolerated, for we used ink, and you could have danced to the rhythm of our pounding hearts as we toiled, terrified to spoil this beautiful exercise book.

Slates were a blessed relief after such a strain. A wee bit of a spit, and who could guess that you'd had second thoughts about that sum, or this spelling? It was the perfect embodiment of the second chance, and it seemed to me wonderfully generous of the schools to lend us such an enjoyable instrument of learning.

We always had Bible teaching first thing in the morning at school, and one of the phrases which greatly puzzled me was 'entertaining angels unaware'. How could anybody be unaware of entertaining an angel, I thought? Surely they would be instantly recognizable by their beautiful white wings, and the clouds of glory round their heads? It never occurred to me that angelic qualities could be found in the most unlikely guises, hiding under very ordinary voices and in bustling everyday bodies.

My angel, as it turned out, hid inside the little figure of my school-teacher, Miss McKenzie. To me she was always a little old lady, with her roly-poly plumpness, her slightly bowed legs, grey hair framing a round rosy face and caught up in an old-fashioned bun on top of her head. Steady blue-grey eyes watched us all shrewdly from behind gold-rimmed spectacles, and although her voice was soft and seldom raised, she kept us all in firm control.

She seemed so ancient that I was astounded to hear her say one morning, in quiet explanation when she was a few minutes late, that she had been delayed waiting for the doctor to call to attend to her mother. Her mother! Surely she must be about a hundred! In my surprise at discovering such an old lady as my teacher could have a mother still alive, it never crossed my mind to wonder how she managed to look after such an ancient parent, and cope with the exhausting task of teaching every day. And a marvellous teacher she was. She had the gift of exciting us to desire knowledge for its own sake, quite apart from that needed for examinations, and our reading went far beyond the humdrum authors we'd have found for ourselves, if left to our own devices.

I, a natural born swot, was a great favourite of hers. This was a mixed blessing, which rather embarrassed me, for 'teacher's pet' was an insult in the tenements. Miss McKenzie refused to be kept at arm's length though, for she seemed to sense something in me which needed encouragement. She was greatly surprised to discover, when we acted out our little bits of Shakespeare, that I had a passionate interest in the theatre. She knew, of course, that my mother was a widow with few pennies to spare for theatres, so she it was who took me to a matinée one marvellous Saturday, to see Shakespeare performed as it ought to be, in a real theatre in the town.

It felt very strange to be meeting Miss McKenzie at the tram-stop, dressed in my best coat, and the tammy Grannie had knitted. I was terrified any of my school friends would see us and jeer 'Teacher's pet', which might put my teacher off the whole idea of taking me to the theatre, but mercifully they were all at the penny matinée, so we were safe. Although I felt a bit ill-at-ease sitting so close to her on the tram seat, I had to say something, so I launched into an account of how my mother had read my teacup the night before and had predicted a disappointment for me, and I'd prayed that the disappointment might not be that something would prevent us from seeing Shakespeare. Miss McKenzie seemed to have trouble with a cough just then, and even had to wipe her eyes, and I wondered if she was laughing at me. When I told Grannie about this later she was scandalized that I'd told my teacher about us believing in teacup fortunes. 'She'll think we're a lot o' heathens,' declared Grannie. 'When'll ye learn to haud yer tongue.'

Although I basked in Miss McKenzie's approval, I never really felt very close to her. We all held our teachers in some awe, and it never dawned on me to ask her advice as to what I should do when I left school. Surely there was only one thing to do? Get a job and earn money to add to the household purse as quickly as possible. What sort of job? Oh, if only I were lucky enough, it could be the Cooperative offices, a highly prized post in our district. I'd start as an office girl, and go to night classes to try to master the mysteries of office routine. If I couldn't get in there it would have to be a shop.

But Miss McKenzie had other ideas. We in our house knew nothing of scholarships for fatherless children. The idea of a child from a working-class household going to college was the very stuff of story-books, and had nothing to do with the business of living as we knew it.

Unknown to us, she bullied the headmaster into putting my name forward for a special scholarship open to children who showed some promise, and who would benefit from further education. As I was the school dux, he agreed, although he was a bit worried about the expense of keeping me at college for a whole year from my mother's point of view. No earnings from me, and fare and clothes to be covered, for, of course, only the fees would be paid if I won.

Miss McKenzie brushed all argument aside. She came herself with me to the interview with the scholarship board. My mother couldn't get time off work for such a wild-cat scheme, and in any case would have been far too frightened to have faced a board of men. To this day I can remember my utter astonishment when, on being asked if she felt I had any particular qualities, and would benefit from such a scholarship, this wee old-fashioned elderly teacher banged the desk with her clenched fist, sending the glasses rattling, and declared in an American idiom I never suspected she knew, 'I'd stake my bottom dollar on this girl.'

I trembled at the passion in her voice, and at her faith in me. 'What if I fail her?' I gasped to myself. 'What if she has to pay all the money back if I let her down?' I knew we hadn't a spare farthing to repay anybody, and I was sick with a sense of responsibility in case I ruined this new, violent Miss McKenzie.

As I've said, I was a natural swot, but even if I hadn't been, the memory of that indomitable little figure would have spurred me on when I felt like faltering.

At the end of my year at college I was able to lay before her the college gold medal as the year's top student, a bronze medal as a special prize in another subject, twenty pounds in prize money, and a whole sheaf of certificates.

And suddenly as I gazed at her, and saw her eyes sparkling with pride behind the gold-rimmed glasses, I realized how widely she had thrown open the door of opportunity for me. And I knew for the first time what the phrase 'entertaining angels unaware' meant. For there, standing before me in class, was my very own angel, Miss McKenzie.

But long before this, and before that visit to the theatre, when Shakespeare was revealed to me by real actors, one of the forms of our local entertainment which lured me like the candle to the moth was the annual kinderspiel put on by the Rechabites, a temperance society, commonly known as the Racky-bites. I joined this society purely and simply to get into the kinderspiel. Thoughts of temperance never entered into it, and one of my earliest attempts at being an entertainer took place at a Rechabite meeting. An important guest had failed to appear, and volunteers from the body of the hall were begged to step forward and provide the fun. I was about eight years old at the time and, swallowing nervously, but finding the call irresistible, I made my way to the platform and in a voice husky with emotion said I would dance the Highland Fling for them.

In full view of a highly diverted audience I first removed my tammy, then my coat, then a long string of 'amber' beads which were Grannie's and which hung to my waist, and might have banged back and forth as I danced, and lastly my cardigan. By this time the audience was convulsed. I was bewildered by their laughter, but quite undeterred. At last, having whetted their appetites with this innocent striptease, I plunged into my version of the Highland Fling, only narrowly avoiding leaping over the edge of the stage as I jerked forward a few dangerous paces with each step. Breathless and triumphant I finished to a round of warm applause and loud laughter. I then collected all my clothes and my beads and put them all on again to the mounting cheers, before descending to make room for the next performer.

My appetite was well and truly aroused, and I was in a fever of impatience for the kinderspiel. I went to Wednesday rehearsals, fairly jumping with excitement and anticipation, and I deaved Grannie for weeks with every chorus in which it was to be my privilege to take part. I was to be an angel, one of a host of about thirty, and my eyes grew wide with joy as I thought of the white dress I would wear, the little white lacy shawl which would cover my curls and keep them dry *en route* from house to hall and, the most exotic final touch, of the sparkling glitter frost which would be sprinkled over the shawl to simulate glittering sequins or rain-drops, I wasn't sure which. I couldn't wait for the transformation which would turn me from a wee lassie in a jersey and a skirt to a beautiful white glittering 'angel'.

Then tragedy fell. Three weeks before the show, on the very night the artists' tickets were to be given out, I fell a victim of the virulent influenza bug. The tickets had to be handed to each child personally. The organizers were all busy working men, who gave their precious time to the Rechabites free of charge, and they point-blank refused to deal with requests other than at the fixed hour on that fixed night, and nobody could collect a ticket for anyone else. 'Flu or no, I was determined to get that ticket, but Grannie was adamant and paid scant heed to my bitter tears. 'You'll not step a foot outside this door the nicht,' she said. 'Do you want to get yer daith.' Death at that black moment seemed a simple punishment beside the anguish of missing the kinderspiel. But she was grown-up and I was small, and stay in bed I must.

I lay there, numb with despair, and then resilience flooded back. I knew what I would do. I would simply get better. I would get better more quickly than I had ever done before from previous flus, and I would get an artist's ticket if I had to steal one. So I did everything I was told without a murmur, and three days before the kinderspiel I was allowed out to play again.

Without a word to anybody, I stalked the organizer from his work to his house. We all knew where everybody in the district worked, and it was easy to wait for the half past five horn and follow him home. My heart was thumping, but my mind was fixed on that ticket. It was against all the rules, but I was past caring about that.

I knocked at the door. It was opened, and the organizer stood regarding me. 'Please,' I whispered, 'I was off when you gave out the tickets, and I'm an angel in the chorus, and I *must* be at the kinderspiel.' My eyes fixed on his imploringly. 'I've got my dress, and my sparkling frost and everything.' The last words shamed me by breaking on a half-sob. Suddenly the man smiled. 'I remember you,' he said amazingly. 'You're the wee lass who did the Highland Fling, aren't you?' I stared at him, speechless, and nodded. I had expected aloofness, argument, maybe instant refusal, but never in my wildest dreams recognition.

He looked at me thoughtfully for a moment. 'Would you like to do your Highland Fling again for us, but this time at the kinderspiel?' he asked. I gulped, visions of myself in my white dress and sparkling frost fading. 'But I'm an angel,' I said. A 'single' turn made no impression on my young mind. To be one of the angels was the summit of my ambition just then.

'Well, that's all right,' he said, 'you can still be an angel, but one of our dancers has fallen ill and we need something to fill that space, and your Highland Fling would be just the thing.'

'But what will I put on. I havenae got a kilt.' Although I

didn't possess one myself, I well knew that all self-respecting Highland dancers wore kilts.

'You don't need a kilt,' he said surprisingly. 'Just you wear your wee jersey and skirt, and your long beads, and your cardigan and do it exactly as you did it before.' Something seemed to be amusing him, but I was in no mood to puzzle it out. The dazzling prospect of being at the kinderspiel at all was enough for me. When I ran home in triumph with the ticket Grannie said, 'Aye, I kent fine you'd get it, if you died in the attempt.' But she was smiling, not angry, although she had been aghast at hearing I'd followed the man home from his work.

There could never have been a happier angel than I was on the night of the kinderspiel. Never was sparkling frost more liberally sprinkled, and never did leading lady feel more glamorous than I as I adjusted my woollie shawl over my hair and stepped proudly from the close on my way to the show. I was the only angel who had to change back into everyday clothes in the middle of the performance, and I sighed regretfully as I laid my heavenly garments aside for a brief space.

The lilt of the dance introduction was heard, and I went forward, feeling miserably conscious of my workaday attire. I did my innocent striptease, the forerunner of all stripteases I believe, and then went into my Highland Fling. It brought the house down, although the only one who couldn't understand the reason was me. When I solemnly raised my arms to remove the amber beads there was such a roar of laughter I nearly forgot the opening steps of the dance. I needed all my concentration to stay on the platform, for I've never been able to dance on the one spot, and this time as I surged wildly towards the edge, there was a yell of apprehension, then a gasp of relief as I stayed trembling on the very brink for the final step. I took the warning shouts for granted. They were just the yelps of my grannie as I staggered towards the fireplace at home, multiplied in several hundred throats. Their laughter was beyond me, but their concern quite understandable. 'Naebody would want to see a wee lassie falling over that terribly high platform,' I thought comfortably, as I panted to a triumphant conclusion, and, the cheers still ringing in my ears, I hurried backstage to put on my beautiful angel's dress again.

What did it matter to me that my unorthodox Highland Fling had been the hit of the evening? I was too young to realize what a happy fate it is to be able to make people laugh, and too excited to resent their laughing at my honest efforts.

I took my place, with bursting heart, among the angels once more and bounced out with most unholy glee, to yell out the closing chorus which said goodnight to our audience, and to the kinderspiel for that year.

7

One of the most dramatic stories told to me by my mother was of an accident to me in babyhood, when a tramcar was pressed into the rescue operation. I was about nine months old at the time and my mother had stood me up on the sink-ledge by the window while she cleared up the bathing things before putting me to bed.

The china bath, washed and dried, was beside me on the draining board, and when I turned round at the sound of my father's key in the door, my foot went through one handle, and I crashed to the floor. The bath broke into a dozen pieces, and an edge cut through the bridge of my nose like a knife. My mother used to shudder as she described the blood as 'spurting up like a well', but my father quick as lightning, seized the two cut edges of my skin between his fingers, bade my mother throw a shawl round me, and before she knew what was happening had dashed down two flights of stairs, kicking over the basin of pipe-clay water and the stair-woman in his flight. He leaped on to the driver's platform of a passing tramcar.

'Don't stop till you get to the Royal Infirmary,' he ordered. The driver was so impressed with his urgency that he did exactly that, and all the passengers were carried willy-nilly to the doors of the infirmary. To me the most impressive part of the story was that the tramcar wasn't even going near the infirmary on its route. It should have turned at right angles at the points long before then. I was astounded that a tramcar should have been used in this way as an ambulance for me, and that the driver had dared vary the route from that marked on the destination board.

It was maybe this thrilling piece of Weir folklore which started my love affair with tramcars. When I was a little girl I only had the penny for the homeward tram journey, when my legs were tired after the long walk into the town for special messages. It would have been impossibly extravagant to ride both ways. That luxury was only indulged in when travelling with Grannie, and the journey to town then seemed so different from the top deck of the tram, the landmarks so swiftly passed compared with my usual walking pace.

Later, when I went to college and the novelty of gazing out of the window had worn off, I used the travelling time to catch up on my studies. I'd be so absorbed in the intricacies of book-keeping, or French, or drama projects that only the changing note of the tram, and the memorized lurching motion as it neared my stop, warned me that I was home and it was time to get off.

I was amazed one day when a conductor said to me, 'I've watched you for years, and in all the time you've travelled on my car I've never seen you read a book just for pleasure – you're a great wee worker.' We knew all the conductors and conductresses by sight, of course, but the notion that they saw us as other than a hand holding out a fare was a great surprise.

The most sought-after seating was in the front section of the upstairs deck. This was a favourite meeting place for the youngsters, for it felt just like being on the bridge of a ship, and it was cut off by a door from the main top deck. We could sing or tell stories if we felt like it and were sure we were disturbing nobody. The driver, whom we'd forgotten, could hear every word, for we were sitting directly above his platform with only an open staircase between us. He didn't mind the singing at all, but if a foot-thumper kept up a steady drumming in time to the rhythm of the ditty he'd shout up to us to be quiet, or he'd come up and throw the lot of us off. This was enough to silence us, for it would have been a terrible waste to have been thrown off before the stage we'd paid for had been reached. We all loved riding in trams and quite often went right to the terminus to get our money's worth, and walked back the odd quarter-mile to our homes.

At one time fares weren't paid for in cash, but in little bone tokens which were bought in bulk at the tramway offices in town. I don't know why this precaution was taken, unless it made the conductor's bag lighter, or foiled a would-be thief, or a dishonest employee. Their colours fascinated me and I longed to save them up and use them at playing shops, but the tram rides they bought excited me even more, so I never possessed more than one at a time.

When I was very small the routes were indicated by the colour of the trams. When colours were replaced by numbers we thought we'd never get used to them. How could we be expected to remember the No. 25 went to Springburn and Bishopbriggs when all our lives we'd travelled in a red car to our homes in these districts?

You could see colours a long way off, but you had to be fairly close to see a number, and the queues teetered uncertainly trying to decide which number suited them, and delayed the tram's departure. This infuriated the conductress, who would shout, 'Come on, youse. Whit are youse waitin' fur? The baund tae play?'

We could see no reason for this change, which confused us, unless the wild suggestion was true that it was because some people might be colour blind.

But we didn't resist for a single moment the arrival of the new tramcars. Such gleaming opulence, such luxurious chrome and glittering glass, such a richness of finish. We felt we were the envy of the entire country. We exclaimed over each splendid detail as though we had bought one privately. We used to wait for a new car, letting the shabby old faithfuls rattle past by the half-dozen, counting the time well spent to ride in such luxury.

This wasn't a habit indulged in by us alone. Some visiting relatives from America took me into town one day, and I heard the husband say to his wife that she must wait to travel in the newest tramcar, for they were the finest in the world. In the world! *We* thought they were, of course, but it was impressive to hear a visitor, and an American at that, agree with our opinion.

The new trams had a more sophisticated trolley arrangement than the old, so that hardly any skill or strength was required to swing it about for the return journey. With the older trams, the conductor had to exert some power and have a nice sense of accuracy to place the pulley against the overhead wire at the first attempt. We children used to cluster round the terminals, to assess the prowess of conductors, and we let them know in no uncertain terms just how good or bad they were.

Sometimes our mothers sent us to the terminus to get coppers for a sixpence, from the stock carried by the conductor. But, of course, if we'd been cheeky about his trolley attempts we could say goodbye to any thought of getting our money exchanged. There was nothing for it but to wait for the next tram, and stand admiringly by, hoping our compliments on the trolley finesse would soften the conductor and we'd get our coppers.

When the old cars were moving, these trolleys could be temperamental, especially if the driver was new. There would be a lurch, and the trolley would come bouncing off the overhead wire in a shower of sparks, and swing wildly back and forth as the car slithered to a halt. This was a nerve-racking experience for the timid, and there would be shouts, 'The trolley's off – the trolley's off', and all eyes would fasten anxiously on the conductor as he swung it towards the overhead wire again.

There was no danger, but it made us all uneasy to feel we were sitting there unconnected to that magic overhead wire. If this happened three or four times in the course of a journey, there would be alarmed tut-tutting from the women, and contemptuous opinions from the men that the driver had 'nae idea how to drive a caur'. 'Aye, he must be new,' somebody would murmur. 'He juist hasnae got the hang o' it.' Even with trams there were plenty of back-seat drivers.

When a ha'penny was laid on the tramlines it became a pretended penny after the tram had thundered over it and flattened it out most satisfactorily. To achieve this, we flirted under the wheels of the trams quite fearlessly, for we were so familiar with the sight of them rocketing past our windows we saw little danger. I never knew any child to be injured by a tram. We were as surefooted as mountain deer, and the drivers were quick to spot a faltering childish stumble on the rare occasion this happened, and to apply the brakes in good time. They'd all played on the tramlines themselves when children, and our games didn't make them turn a hair. If a child was occasionally scooped up in the 'cow-catcher' – a metal shovel arrangement worked by the driver to remove any obstacle in his path – well, that was all right. Wasn't that what the cow-catcher was there for? And it would be a good lesson to the youngster for the future.

But if we treated the dangers of being run down by a tramcar with contempt, there were plenty of other fears which shook us by the throat in our tenement games. There was the mysterious creature called 'Flannel Feet'. Nobody had ever actually seen him, but his nameless exploits filled us with such dread that it was a brave child who would go up a strange close in the dark. Even on our own familiar stair landings, a broken light would send us scurrying past the dark corners with pounding hearts, sure that this terrifying Flannel Feet would be lurking in the shadows. The fact that we never knew a single person who'd been attacked meant nothing. We frightened each other with stories which came from nowhere. A childish game called 'Robinson Crusoe' was the source of such a tale. In this game somebody had to hide, and we others rushed about, calling up closes and in alley-ways, with our hands cupped to our mouths to send our voices soaring:

> 'Robinson Crusoe give us a call,
> Give us an answer or nothing at all.'

The one hiding would call out in a high disguised voice 'Pee-wee' and we'd try to guess the direction of the sound and set off in pursuit. Then the victor would hide. Frightening tales were told of the answering 'Pee-wee' having been given by Flannel Feet, when the unsuspecting searcher fell straight into his clutches. Strangely enough, we never even asked for details of what the monster *did*. His mere existence brought terror to us.

The cemetery was another source of shivering fright. To pass its wall on a dark night was a dare few of us accepted, for didn't we all know that ghosts gathered behind the wall, ready to pounce on the unwary? Sometimes in winter, made brave by numbers after our slides on the ice, we'd perch on this wall and sing, 'I am a poor wee orphan, my mother she is dead', our eyes darting to the tombstones beyond. But one verse was enough, and we'd slither down, and race for home, glad to have escaped the clutch of ghostly fingers.

Living in our own world, as we children did, it never occurred to us that grown-ups could ever be nervous or frightened. We knew mothers and grannies were brave and strong, and weren't even afraid of the dark. You couldn't even scare them by jumping round a corner unexpectedly, and the last thing I dreamed of was that I, a particularly nervous wee creature, could instil real fear into anyone, least of all my beloved grannie. And yet I did it, all unknowingly, one terrible winter afternoon.

Grannie had slipped downstairs to visit a neighbour while we were at school, and when I came in at four o'clock I found the door 'off the sneck', and pushed it open. I was so entranced at the cosy warmth of the firelight that instead of going in search of her as I usually did, I curled up in the armchair to wait quietly till she came in to light the gas and maybe make a cup of tea. I was strictly forbidden to light the gas mantle anyway, which was out of reach unless I stood on a chair.

It grew darker and darker, and at last I heard Grannie's light footstep and the rustle of her long skirt as she pushed the door open. For some reason, which I can't explain to this day, instead of calling out, 'Is that you, Grannie?', I sat completely silent. She picked up the matches from the dresser, moved towards the gas mantle, and then stopped with a frightened intake of breath, sensing somebody was in the kitchen. By this time, the whole situation was so unreal, I was scared to open my mouth. Grannie's eyes searched the shadows, picking up the outline of a body in the chair, but instead of recognizing me, she gave a strangled cry, dropped the matches and rushed towards the door.

Now, thoroughly frightened at the effect I'd had on her, and terrified of retribution, I called out in a hysterical giggle, 'Grannie, it's me.' She stopped as if she had been shot, and turned back. 'You!' she cried, in such a tone of horror at my wickedness that I burst into tears. 'Why didn't you speak when I came in?' she demanded. 'I might have had a heart attack. Fancy thinking out such a cruel thing to do to your grannie.'

She sat down, trembling, too shocked even to light the gas.

I was in such a turmoil of confusion it was like a bad dream. Why had I done it? I didn't know. But fancy my brave grannie being frightened of me? Rushing to make amends, I leaped on a chair, seized a small glass from the shelf and poured a tot of our medicinal whisky into it and urged Grannie to drink it to steady her nerves. I'd seen my mother do this when a neighbour's little girl was run over by a push-bike, and it had magic properties then, and it would surely help Grannie at this moment. Grannie took one sip and let out a yell that scared me half out of my wits. In the dark I hadn't noticed that there was a sewing needle in the glass, put there out of harm's way, and Grannie had nearly swallowed it. Was there no end to the damage I was capable of on this black afternoon?

My mother, of course, was told of the whole wicked episode when she came in from work, and I was duly punished. As I lay crying in bed, I was bewildered and tried to understand how it had all happened. It seemed to me it all started because Grannie had been frightened by a shadow which she didn't know was me. I hadn't known till then that grown-ups could fear the unknown just as we children feared the invisible Flannel Feet. And for the first time I began to wonder if maybe even Flannel Feet wasn't a bogey-man at all, but just somebody like me who should have had the sense to open his mouth and speak, instead of creating an atmosphere of terror merely by keeping quiet at the wrong time.

But if we children hadn't actually met a bogey-man we knew everybody else within a radius of a quarter of a mile of our tenements. A stranger trying to lure any of us would have had a thin time. We knew the habits, good and bad, of the entire adult community. Our mothers and grannies saw no sense in hiding from us the evil effects of drink, and we saw enough drunkenness to make us teetotallers for life. We saw with horror how drink could turn a quiet father into a wild creature who could beat up his wife, and we saw ashamed women taking bundles to the pawn on Monday mornings to raise enough cash to carry them through the week, because earnings had been swallowed in weekend drinking.

With the harsh judgement of children we saw them all in black and white. Mr Grant was avoided because he drank.

We'd *seen* him on Saturday nights, so it was no good telling us he might be as docile as a lamb during the rest of the week, and maybe even a better husband and father than somebody else whose sins weren't so obvious and which we wouldn't have understood.

A puzzling figure in this assessment was that of Mr Carr. He was an old soldier, carried himself straight as a ramrod, and always looked, in my mother's words, 'as if he came out of a band-box'. Yet, according to my grannie, 'he drank like a fish'. How could Grannie, and other people too, say such a thing when I'd never seen him drunk? 'Aye ye widnae, lassie,' said old Mrs Peebles, his mother-in-law, when I asked her. 'He carries it weel, I'll say that, but he drinks away every penny just the same.' I knew she was a God-fearing truthful old lady, who was always reading her Bible when I went in to see if she wanted any messages, so I believed her; and Mr Carr joined the ranks of those who must be avoided, especially on Saturday nights.

And yet it was Mr Carr who taught me that there are many shades between black and white, and maybe even streaks of pure gold where they were least expected.

My brothers had been playing piggy-back on the staircase on the way up to our second-storey house, and when they reached our door the younger one had fallen with a terrible crash and hit his head on the sharp edge of the stair-rise. Grannie had no need to scold, for that still figure had quenched all argument on the part of my brother. By the time I arrived home from school, the doctor was busy at the bedside and my mother had been sent for from work. 'Severe concussion' was the verdict and my mother and Grannie were instructed what to do. Bottles of medicine were ranged along the dresser, but against all of them the small patient, with clenched teeth, rebelled and refused to swallow a drop. It had been impressed on us that the 'opening' medicine was vital, but, ill as he was, nothing would make the rebel swallow it. We tried everything. Even giving it to him as though he were a puppy, and holding his lips until he appeared to swallow. The minute the hand was taken away, he spat it up, or threw it up, and this seemed to go on for days.

I think everybody knew of our difficulties except the doctor. For some reason my mother and Grannie were frightened to admit no medicine had been swallowed, in case the wee chap would be removed to hospital. We had a terror of hospitals in the tenements, as so many who went there never seemed to come back. Or it could have been we just couldn't afford the fee for another visit from the doctor.

With the complete involvement of tenement neighbours, everybody on the stair and nearby had weighed in with ideas and suggestions. Old quarrels were forgotten as each rushed in with what seemed the perfect solution. No good. The patient grew more limp and exhausted, and we were desperate. It was Saturday night. My brother was afraid of only two things. Drunks and soldiers. In despair, my mother moved to the window, biting her lip to stop the tears, when suddenly she saw the upright figure of Mr Carr passing the close. She threw up the window, 'Mr Carr,' she called down, 'wait a minute. Can I speak to you?' I was horrified. Didn't my mother know he would be on his way to the pub to drink like a fish? How could a drunk man help us?

But my mother was inspired. She'd remembered my brother's fear. She'd remembered too that Mr Carr kept his sergeant's uniform well pressed for his territorial meetings. Hadn't she always said he looked as if he'd come out of a bandbox. She knew it was Saturday all right. But she also knew in our tenement world everybody shared the griefs and worries of the other, and it was certain Mr Carr, who only lived round the corner and whose mother-in-law often visited Grannie, was aware of the drama which had been going on with the small patient.

With zest he entered into the conspiracy. The pub was forgotten. Quickly he changed into his awe-inspiring uniform, and with cane under his arm, and peaked cap down on his nose, he thundered at the door. 'Where's this rebellious boy?' he demanded. 'Give me the medicine,' and he held out an imperious hand. My brother's lips parted in terror. The spoon was inserted. The medicine went down. 'Now,' said Mr Carr in a voice which shook the ornaments on the shelf, 'if you don't *keep* it down, you'll be sentenced to fourteen days in the guard-room.' Nobody knew what that meant, but it sounded terrible. Terrible enough for the patient to keep his lips tightly closed. Next day the medicine had done its work. From that moment my brother started on the long slow road to recovery. It was a miracle. But the greatest miracle, it seemed to me, was that we owed it all to a man who could drink like a fish. I never forgot Mr Carr. And, apart maybe from Hitler, from that day I never believed anyone was entirely bad.

In spite of Grannie's wizardry with cheap cuts of meat, and marrow bones, and food which would 'stick to wur ribs', as Grannie would say, there always seemed to be a space in our tummies which was never quite filled. And in summer-time one of the very nicest ways of trying to fill this space when we had a ha'penny to spare was at the Tallies. I don't suppose any of us suspected we were abbreviating the word 'Italians', as we raced from school to the Tallies in search of one of the many wonders within its small interior. At that time all the ice-cream in Glasgow seemed to be made by Italians. And I don't even suppose the lazily good-tempered proprietrix minded being called a Tally. She knew we loved her. She knew we were dazzled with admiration of the splendid marble counter, the glittering mirrors which lined the walls, the little round marble-topped tables, the neat chairs, all so different from the wooden fixtures in the old-fashioned shops which were her neighbours.

Her broken English was a constant fascination to our ears, and her unruly mop of crinkly black hair and brandy-ball brown eyes two more exotic signs that she came from a far-away country. Before I was big enough to toddle down to buy anything, the bigger girls would take me with them, and the large-hearted Tallie would lift me up on to the counter and break off pieces of thick slab chocolate from an open packet she'd been nibbling, and pop them into my all-too-willing mouth. I'd have to sing her a wee song afterwards, in payment, and of course I was certain I was getting the biggest bargain in Glasgow. She was never too busy to play this game. She was very fond of a wee poem too, which seemed to amuse her, coming from a two-year-old like me. It went:

A house to let, apply within.
A lady put out for drinking gin.
Gin you know is a very bad thing.
A house to let apply within.

I could almost measure my growing up against my purchases at the Tallies. When I was very small a ha'penny cone not much fatter than my thumb was as much as I could manage. Then, as I grew bigger and was able to earn some pocket money running messages, for the neighbours of course – I didn't get money for running our own messages – I moved on to penny cones, tuppenny wafers, three-penny sponges, single nougats, sugar wafers and, beyond these, oh unbelievable splendour, to such wondrous delights as a 98, which was a double sponge filled with ice-cream and a half-bar of cream chocolate. The first time my teeth plunged into this delicacy and met first sponge, then the chill of ice-cream, then the strange flavour of cold chocolate and its creamy centre, I thought experience could go no further.

In winter we didn't eat ice-cream at all. It was purely a summer delight. I had an aunt who was regarded as quite eccentric because she continued to indulge her passion for ice-cream beyond the summer season. She used to send us down for fourpence-worth in a jug, in the depths of winter, and we watched her curiously as she ate it, but refused to touch a spoonful ourselves, for there was something about wintry blasts and ice-cream which offended our sense of correctness.

In winter, our Tallie went over to hot peas, and no peas cooked at home ever tasted half as good as those bought in that wee shop. A penny bought a cup of 'pea brae', which was actually the thickened water in which the peas had been boiled, liberally seasoned with pepper and a good dash of vinegar. There was always the excitement of maybe finding a few squashed peas at the bottom of the cup, and we would feel about with our spoon, eyes lighting with joy if we found something solid and knew we had struck gold. How we dallied over each spoonful so that we could enjoy the warmth and camaraderie of the clean little shop as long as possible, for now it was cosy and heated, and steaming with cooking peas. The lordly ones seated at the tables consumed threepenny plates of peas, which made us sick with envy, but when the day arrived when we were big enough and rich enough to spend threepence in one go, I found to my surprise and disappointment that I preferred the penny 'pea brae'.

Alas, I lost my taste for hot peas and vinegar altogether the night I took scarlet fever, for I'd eaten this dish earlier in the evening, and the first sign that all was not well with me was the irritation the vinegar caused to my tender throat. Ever afterwards scarlet fever and hot peas were synonymous to me.

But before this disaster struck, that same aunt of the ice-cream orgies would occasionally take a fancy for peas. I was delighted when she'd send me down for sixpence-worth in the jug. Grannie snorted contemptuously at this extravagance. 'H'm, paying good money to get somebody else to do your cooking for you,' she'd say to my aunt, 'and peas biled awa' to nothing at that.' But that was precisely what our depraved tastes enjoyed, and there was a sort of wild indulgence in buying cooked food. We would sit round the fire, the sixpence-worth of peas divided out into saucers, the pepper and vinegar duly added, and our delightful, eccentric aunt would teach me to sing with her in harmony, in between sips and chewing of peas. There we would sit, singing soulfully 'Let the rest of the world go by', and she would make me switch from melody to harmony to make sure I knew what I was doing, until my brothers grew fed up and demanded to be told some jokes, and the evenings would end in a riot of laughter.

But Grannie didn't always object to buying food cooked by other folk, especially when it was fish and chips. Tenement families hadn't the space or the money to keep a pan of fat for deep frying, and that was where the chip-shops came into their own. They played a tremendously important part in our lives.

There were four fish-and-chip shops within ten minutes' walking distance of our house (or six minutes if we ran, as we usually did). Each had a subtle advantage over the others, which made choice agonizing when one's mother forgot to say which shop was to be patronized.

If it was your own pocket money, of course, the choice of shop was dictated by the amount of cash in hand. When it was a ha'penny, Jimmy's was the only possible choice, for he alone

102

understood infant economics, and he saved all the wee hard bits of potato which floated to the top of the fryer, and kept them in a separate partition, hot, crisp and greasy, ready to be served out by the fistful at a ha'penny a time, when we hungrily demanded, 'Ony crimps, Jimmy?' We were allowed to salt them, but no vinegar was provided. As he reasonably pointed out, he couldn't make any profit at all if he supplied vinegar on ha'penny sales, an argument which we felt was quite sound.

A penny in our pockets saw us deserting generous Jimmy for the shop at the bend of the road, where the marble counter reached to our noses, and where they sold the most mouth-watering potato fritters for three a penny. What pleasure to crunch through the thin layer of batter and reach the steaming potato in the centre.

When we had the rich sum of tuppence we went round the corner to the shop where they sold pies and black puddings. We had no intention of buying such delicacies ourselves – tuppence wouldn't have stretched so far – but we went for the sheer thrill of listening to the plutocrats who *could* order such foods, and for the pleasure we derived from watching the assistant lower pie or pudding into the hot fat. We admired his judgement in knowing the exact moment to whisk out pie or pudding, glistening and rich with fat. Sometimes a purchaser would grandly demand tuppence worth of pickles to enhance the feast, and we gazed at each other with smiles of delight that we were in the presence of such extravagant living.

Across the road and round the corner was the fourth shop, to which our mothers sent us when we could coax them to buy chips for supper. 'Very clean,' my mother would say, 'everything spotless.' We weren't all that impressed with this praise, because the bags in which the chips were daintily shovelled were scandalously small, but we daren't disobey and go where the helpings were bigger, because at that time this was the only shop using those wee bags.

Quality as opposed to quantity was an unknown factor in our voracious young lives, and we didn't trouble to hide our feelings as we watched the assistant blow out the diminutive bag in readiness for the disgustingly small helpings of chips. 'Humph!' we'd mutter audibly. 'Hauds practically nane! Some profit they must be makin'.' At that the assistant would fix us with steely blue eye and say, 'I've a good mind tae take aff a few, just fur yer cheek!' 'Aw don't dae that, Jessie,' we'd cry in anguish, 'we were just kiddin' ye. Pit oan a wee tait mair, go'n, Jessie, some fell aff yer shovel when ye were liftin' them oot.' And because she was a good sort she would toss in maybe half a dozen on top of the bag, and we'd sneak out a couple on the way home, for, after all, they were a sort of bonus.

We didn't often have fish from these shops, for my mother's tightly stretched budget just wouldn't stretch to such extravagance. But on gala nights, such as when she was indulging her weakness for flitting, as she did five times in two years, my mother would acknowledge that willing helpers had to be fed after their labours, and there could only be one choice for the feast – fish and chips.

As the last piece of furniture was being dragged round the bend of the stair, and the helpers (all pals of my brothers and myself) panted and puffed to get it into the house unscathed, I was sent to the best chip-shop for three or four fish suppers, and an extra sixpence worth of chips. This was a far cry from a ha'penny worth of crimps at Jimmy's, and I hoped as many of my chums as possible would be there to hear me place this staggering order. This rich feast was wrapped in several thicknesses of newspaper to keep the grease from going through to my jersey, and I ran like the wind back to the new abode, hugging my steaming bundle to my bosom, to deliver it as hot as possible to the weary workers. When I arrived the party would be sitting round the freshly laid table, clean, and flushed with anticipation, empty plates in front of each. My mother carefully divided out the portions – the biggest helpings going to the biggest lads, for they'd done the heaviest work, right down to the smallest person in the house who had only run round with small items like shovels and brushes.

Piles of bread and butter and margarine and lashings of tea were provided, and our voices rose happily as the crisp batter and the golden chips disappeared down hungry throats.

Weirs' flittings were much sought-after social occasions among our crowd, for the fish and chip feast which ended the evening's labours was a golden bait which drew more volunteers than we could use.

These flittings were a miracle of neighbourly assistance and organization, for the only item which cost money was the horse and cart, and even that was only hired if the distance was just too far for the helpers to walk. They all took place after the day's work, for nobody dreamed of taking time off just to move house. After a quick tea, pals and neighbours rolled up, dressed in dungarees or peenies, and the tasks were handed out according to ability or nimbleness. The children ran about like ants with the small items from the fireplace, clearing the place so that the men could move the furniture more easily. Advice was shouted as tricky bends of the stair were negotiated. 'Aye, a wee bit your wey, Wullie, that's it!'. Or, 'Naw, naw, you'll hiv to go back – you're too tight roon' this corner, ye'll never dae it'. My mother's heart would be in her mouth during these operations, in case her precious wardrobe would get scratched, but these men were no amateurs. They'd helped at dozens of flittings and the furniture was in good hands. Meanwhile, another expert would be prising the linoleum up, and rolling it carefully so that it wouldn't crack. 'Aye,' my mother would say with satisfaction, 'that's the best of real inlaid linoleum, you can lift it and lay it a dizzen times and never a crack in it!' Willing hands were taking the big brass covers off the wall and wrapping them in newspaper, and piling them into an empty clothes basket, and other hands raced downstairs with it when it was full, tucked the covers safely beside the bedding, and raced back again with the empty basket, to have it filled again with the precious china, or 'cheenie' as everybody in our tenements called it. This was the women's work, and most tenderly each piece was wrapped in newspaper, and instructions called out to the couriers, 'Noo mind ye pit it a' on something soft, so that it'll no' shoogle in the kert. Pit the pillows roon' it noo, Jimmy, so it'll no' break.'

At the other end, another small army was waiting to unload the lorry, and everything sat on the pavement until the linoleum was re-laid in the new house, then more frantic activity to put everything in its new setting. How different everything looked, even if we'd only moved to the next close, which my mother did twice, for we knew our houses so intimately that the slightest variation in a lobby or a window frame, or the size of a fireplace, was of enormous significance. Everybody loved a flitting. Nobody minded the hard work. It was all fun, a real diversion, and it always ended up with a party, and who cared if it also ended up with an empty purse?

8

But however willingly shoulders were put to the wheel when they were needed, we weren't angels, and there were plenty of rows to whip up passions and cause the tongues to cluck in fury or sympathy. We lived so close to one another in the tenements, it would have been a wonder if there had been no clash of personalities, no misunderstandings which led to feuds which could last for weeks, until a common bond of suffering or hardship drew the rival factions together again.

One such feud went on for nearly six weeks between Mrs MacFarlane and Mrs Brown. The husbands didn't enter into it, and, ignoring their wives' temperaments, went on nodding to one another when they met as though they'd never heard of the word 'feud'. The two women had fallen out over an argument as to whose turn it was for the washing-house-key, and Mrs MacFarlane would pass Mrs Brown with lowered eyes, without a word of greeting. Their children were greatly irritated by this state of affairs. Their social system of bartering was ruined, and they found it maddening not to be able to exchange puzzles or 'bools' with each other, just because their mothers weren't on speaking terms.

Then one day of heart-stopping drama there was a squeal of brakes, and the cow-catcher of a tram swiftly and neatly scooped up little Annie Brown, who had fallen right across the path of the tram as she tried to retrieve her ball. Her mother had seen the whole thing from her top-floor kitchen window where she was performing her toilet. In her fright she dashed down and into the street, wearing no more than a camisole and skirt, to find that Mrs MacFarlane, her feuding neighbour, had already taken wee Annie into her house and was gently crooning and comforting the sobbing child. The whole street found the reunion most impressive, but almost greater than the relief that things were back to normal was our shocked amazement that Mrs Brown hadn't even realized she had been standing there in the middle of the main road in her camisole! Half-naked, for all to see!

Our own feud started when the neighbours across the landing acquired an Airedale dog. This beast had only to see a child and the staircase would echo with its furious barking and snarling, and the sight of its lip drawn back from long sharp teeth filled me with terror. It was no good Grannie telling me a barking dog couldn't bite at the same time. I didn't intend to give it the chance, and I'd run like the wind past their open door.

Neighbourly relations were undisturbed nevertheless, until the night I was sent down to the local fish-shop for fish and chips, a great treat which was provided by a visiting auntie. As I reached our landing, the Airedale, scenting the delicious aroma leaped at me. In spite of my terror, I clung to the precious parcel, but my screams opened every door on the stair. There was a furious row, for fright made me so sick that I couldn't touch food that night, or all next day, and Grannie had told Mrs Petrie, the dog's owner, that she would report her to the factor of the property for keeping a dangerous animal.

This was *far* worse than the wash-house-key rows. To be reported to the factor was as bad as being reported to the police. Worse, in fact, for the factor could turn you out of your house and could certainly make anyone get rid of a dangerous dog.

No word was exchanged between the families as they passed on the stair. The Petries' door was kept closed at all times, so the Airedale was heard but not seen, thank goodness.

When it was their turn for the washing-house the key was slipped through the letter-box, not handed over as was usually the case. When it came round to paying their share for washing the staircase window their few pence were wrapped in a twist of paper and put through our letter-box. Goodness knows how long this feud would have lasted, but I took a very bad dose of gastric flu, and my appetite vanished completely for nearly a fortnight. Grannie and my mother tried to tempt me with everything within their modest means, but listlessly I refused the lot. I grew thinner and whiter and they were at their wits' end. Then one day a delicious smell of chicken broth drifted across the landing. We all knew that the Petries were quite well off, for weren't they all out working, with four pay-packets coming into the house? We only saw chicken soup at Christmas, and not always then, so my passion for it could only be satisfied once a year at the very most. When Grannie came over to the bed to ask, 'What would you like to eat?', I whispered, 'Some of Mrs Petrie's soup.'

Grannie stared at me. She was a marvellous cook, and at any other time would have felt outraged to go to anybody and confess I fancied something I couldn't find in her cooking. But now it was the first food I'd fancied for two whole weeks. And yet they weren't on speaking terms. It was impossible. My mother, who was in from her work for lunch, said, 'I'll go. I'll ask.'

Bravely she knocked at the Petries' door. She was met by and icy glare, and a dry 'Yes, Mrs Weir? What is it?'

My mother swallowed her pride. She explained how ill I'd been. That I'd eaten nothing sustaining for a fortnight, but today had smelt Mrs Petrie's soup, and if only she could spare a bowlful it might start my recovery. My mother told us later that Mrs Petrie's face broke into a smile as if she'd come into a fortune. In our poor community about the only thing anyone could afford to give away was a share of their food. But to be asked for soup by her feuding neighbour, when Grannie was herself known for her fine cooking, was the perfect compliment, and a sweet revenge.

Mrs Petrie brought in the bowl with her own hands, and watched me sup every drop of her fine soup. Later she claimed, 'It was my soup that saved Molly Weir's life.' We didn't argue about that exaggerated interpretation of the situation. We felt we had truly exchanged a feud for a mess of potage.

And we felt *our* feud had been on a far more dramatic scale than the usual petty squabbles over washing-house keys. The wash-house was in the back court, and each one served the twelve families in each tenement close, so a strict rota system operated for all the days of the week. As nobody wanted to wash at the weekends, each person's turn came round every twelve days. Domestic circumstances often led to the mothers swopping days with each other, and that was where the trouble started. If Mrs Brown swopped Tuesday for Thursday, then the woman who was entitled to the key after Mrs Brown had to be alerted, so *she* would know from whom to expect the key. But sometimes the woman who normally followed the exchanged day pretended she was entitled to the key following the swop day, and that was when the arguments started. With the meagre wardrobes we all possessed it must have been a nightmare trying to keep families in clean and dry clothes for twelve days between washing days, so an earlier washday was a blessing, and a wet day a tragedy. One couldn't blame them for trying a bit of cheating to get the key ahead of their turn.

There was never the same fierce competition to use the wash-house at night as there was in the daytime. Some of the night washers were younger women, daughters of those too old to do their washing during the day. They had the time, those elderly mothers, but not the strength, so the daughters had to tackle the household washing when they'd finished their day's work in shop or factory. Other women preferred to do their washing in the evenings for their own private reasons. My mother tut-tutted over this, for she felt washings ought properly to be done during the day when there was some chance of clothes being hung out in the fresh air and the wind, to dry, and acquire a fine fresh smell. Grannie would purse her lips and shake her head at the thought of pulleys in the kitchen, laden with steaming clothes, flapping in folks' faces as they moved back and forward to get the kettle from the range or put some coal on the fire. 'I don't like a hoose fu' o' wet cloots,' she'd say. 'It canna be good for thae lassies efter bein' oot at their work a' day.'

My mother would say of a neighbour who could easily have done the washing during the day, 'Aye, she must be awfu' glad to get away from her man and her weans when she'd put up with the damp cold of that wash-house instead of sitting at her own fireside.' And then she'd soften when Grannie would

110

reply, 'Och well, maybe she's better off at that, for her man's a surly blackguard and gey poor company.'

Grannie's use of the word blackguard, which she pronounced 'blaggard', always sent a shiver down my spine, and I thought she'd invented this damning description herself. I was astounded in later years when I came across the word again and again to describe the villains in the romances I devoured, and realized that Grannie's blackguard was a well-known character to many authors.

Far from sharing my mother's condemnation of the night washers, I used passionately to hope I could coax her to become one of them. There was a theatrical air about the whole scene which made a great appeal to me. The ordinary grey-stone wash-house of the daytime was transformed, as though at the wave of a magic wand, and I couldn't imagine that I had ever played shops on its window ledge, or jumped from its roof on to the wall which divided the back courts.

Guttering candles, stuck in the necks of bottles and ranged along the window-sill, provided the only illumination in what now seemed a vast cavern. Mysterious shadows flickered in the far corners, and the foaming suds in the tubs took on a romantic radiance. When the lid of the huge brick boiler was raised to see how the 'white things' were progressing (the 'white things' was our name for all the household linen), swirling steam filled the wash-house, the candles spat and flickered through illuminated clouds, and the scene became fearsome as pictures of hell. The washerwoman bending over her tub changed from her everyday self too. Hair curled round her ears with the damp, cheeks flushed with the heat and the work, and her eyes glowed in the candlelight, and she revealed a beauty I'd never noticed before.

Like animals attracted by the light, other women would drift from their tenements into the back court, and pause at the wash-house door. 'Are you nearly done noo?' was the usual greeting. The patient figure at the tubs, or 'bines' as we called them, would pause from her vigorous rubbing of the soiled clothes against the wash-board, charmed to be the centre of interest for once, and say cheerfully, 'Just aboot half-way through. I've juist the dungarees to dae, and then the white

111

things will be ready for "sihnin" oot.' I once asked my teacher how to spell this word 'sihnin' which we used when we meant rinsing, but she'd never heard of it, for she was from the north, so I just had to make a guess at the spelling and hope it was right.

At the word 'dungarees' the women would groan in sympathy. Washing dungarees was a job they all hated, and as ours was a Railway district, most husbands or brothers or sons worked with dirty machinery, and came home with grease-laden dungarees, so this was a task they all had to face. Our tenement women all had raw fingers from using the slimy black soap and soda which was the only way they knew for ridding the filthy overalls of their accumulated grease and workshop dirt.

The women's eye's would lazily follow the washer's movements as she scrubbed and rinsed, and put clothes through the wringer ready for the house pulleys, or maybe for the ropes next morning, if the next woman using the wash-house could be coaxed to let her put out a rope for a couple of hours before her own were ready to be hung out. But the ropes were only put outside if it promised to be a fine day, and the women were expert weather forecasters, for everybody detested getting their nicely wrung clothes wet again. The ultimate in disaster was reached when the weight of sodden clothes on the ropes was too much for the supporting clothes poles, and the whole lot came crashing among the dirt of the back court, and had to be taken in and rinsed through all over again.

I loved when the white things were judged to be ready, for then came the scene I liked best of all. The heavy boiler lid was lifted off, and leaned carefully against the back wall of the wash-house. Clouds of steam rushed everywhere. Up the chimney, out of the open door, into every corner. The washer, a long pole held in both hands, bent over the seething mass in the boiler, fished out a load, expertly twirling the steaming clothes to keep them safely balanced, and then ran with the laden pole across to the tub of clean water. Quickly and neatly a twist of the pole shot the clothes into the rinsing water. Back and forth, back and forth she went, her figure ghost-like in the rushing steam, until the boiler was empty. I longed to be allowed to help in this exciting operation, but met with scandalized refusal. 'Do you want to burn yoursel' to the bone?' the washerwoman would say in answer to my coaxing. 'You'll have this job to dae soon enough, hen, and then you'll no' be so pleased. Run away hame to your bed, or I'll tell your grannie on you!' But the women were more amused than angry at my interest in their activities, and they made sure I went nowhere near the steam.

When this final rinsing stage was reached the watching women lingering at the doors couldn't resist a bit of advice, especially if the washer was a younger unmarried woman. As the tub filled, they'd say, 'Take oot the plug, hen, and let the clean water run through the claes. You'll get rid o' a' the soap faur quicker that way.' Or, 'Jessie, you're just squeezin' the soap into them again – you'll ha'e tae gi'e them another water. You're putting them through the wringer too soon.'

They were all experts. This was their world. And the young washerwoman would listen to them all, glad of their company and of their advice, for it was a great source of pride to have someone say, 'Aye, she hangs out a lovely washing.' And the most disparaging thing a tenement woman could say of another's wash-house efforts were the damning words, 'She's hangin' oot her *grey* things!'

Another glimpse of the world of washing-day could be caught at the 'steamy', when we went to the baths. These were tubs and apparatus hired by women who had no proper wash-house in their tenement back courts, or who preferred the community atmosphere of the 'steamy' to a solitary session in their own wash-house. I used to pause in the open doorway, on my way out to the street, and watch the women at their work. It was like a scene from a play. The rising clouds of steam, the bare arms rhythmically rising and falling, the stately tread to the drying cupboards, and the measured walk back, bearing their washing gracefully before them, ready for packing into their prams or bogies for the homeward journey. Again I had a great longing to penetrate these mysteries and take part in the ritual myself, but I never did so, and these tantalizing glimpses were all I ever knew of this enchanting side of the baths.

When we children spoke of 'the baths' we meant the swimming pond, of course. Tuesdays were reserved for the girls, the other days for the boys, which seemed a bit unfair, but it was generally conceded that the boys seemed to enjoy the baths more than we did, and used them much oftener. We were quite happy, really, with our Tuesdays, and felt very privileged as we hurried up the road to make the most of 'our' day.

In summer, during school holidays, we met in the back court at half past seven in the morning, armed with our 'chittering bites'. Goodness knows how this habit arose, for nobody particularly liked early rising, but, once out of our cosy beds, there was something exciting and different about walking up Springburn Road when the streets were clean and quiet, and when the air had an unaccustomed freshness.

Some of the more opulent girls, who actually went to the seaside every summer, possessed their own bathing suits, but most of us hired a suit for a penny. The 'costumes', as we called them, were all the same size, and it depended on the size of the wearer whether the costume was short or long, tight or floppy. As one of the smallest girls in the neighbourhood, mine was held up in front by two huge safety pins on each shoulder, but even so the plunging neckline was all too revealing of my narrow chest, and the legs hung down unfashionably over my knees. But who cared? The laughter and derisive comments were all part of the fun. I had coaxed Grannie to buy me a natty black and white check rubber cap to protect my curls, and this sign of class earned me the greatest respect from my chums, and quenched their laughter over my floppy costume. *Their* caps were mere helmet affairs which pressed ears tightly to the scalp and almost completely deafened them, but mine had elastic round the edge and gave me the tremendous advantage, I thought, of missing *nothing* of the yelling and joyous joking which was the non-stop accompaniment of our visits to the baths.

Once stripped, some would jump in recklessly from the side of the pond without even testing the water with an exploratory toe. Others cautiously descended the three or four steps at the shallow end and then gently lowered themselves into the water. A few compromised, and stood on the top step at the shallow end and 'scooshed' forward, with tremendous squealing from everyone in their path as the water drenched them.

There were rings suspended from the ceiling on long ropes, from which we would swing like monkeys, high over the water. It was a great dare to use the rings over the deep end of the pond, for if the arms tired and we were forced to drop into the water, we'd have to be dragged gasping to the side by one of the bigger girls. Only a few could dive, and the rest would gaze awe-struck as some large girl self-consciously mounted the dale (our name for the high diving board) and stood poised, before leaping down in what, to us, was a magnificent dive and an inspiring deed of courage.

When we decided we had had enough of our water frolics, i.e., when our lips were blue with cold, what bliss to return to our boxes and scrub our shivering bodies with the hard towel we had been given with our entrance ticket, and to plunge chattering teeth into the crisp butteriness of the roll we'd brought with us as our 'chittering bite'. Nothing ever tasted quite so delicious as that roll, eaten in that particular atmosphere, and never was undervest so comforting to the skin as the one pulled over our heads in the dank air of the little boxes.

On the way home, the lucky ones with a ha'penny or a penny to spend, usually stopped at the little baker's shop on the corner, and the woman filled their outstretched jerseys, which they held out like a miniature tarpaulin, with broken biscuits. You didn't get a paper bag for a ha'penny or a penny purchase, and anyway we all felt it was *far* better value to get handfuls tossed into a baggy jersey, and there was always plenty for all of us. The biscuits were mostly plain, but what a find to discover a cream fragment among the digestives!

Later, when we had swimming lessons at school, the baths seemed quite different at three o'clock in the afternoon, and although we now had proper swimming instruction and learned to keep ourselves afloat, it lacked the magic of the morning visits.

Later still, as we grew older, we would go along in the evening, and again the atmosphere was entirely changed. Standing in the lamp-lit street, queueing to get in, we would hear the voices and shouts of those already in the pond, sounds

115

which echoed strangely into the glass roof. And when we finally got inside, the bath looked so different under artificial lighting that we wondered uneasily if it could indeed be the scene of our childish ploys.

It was about this time that we penetrated the mystery of the other side of the bath building. We were getting too big now for the zinc bath at home, and were given fourpence on Fridays to have a hot bath. This was indeed luxury. The fourpence admitted us to the delicious warmth of the cubicles, and provided a rough towel for drying. There were degrees of grandeur, and a first-class bath cost ninepence. But beyond seeing a softer, whiter, fluffier towel, I never discovered what other delights were in store. Spending more than fourpence on a bath was forever beyond both purse and imagination.

There was always a queue, and we sat on wooden benches alongside the cubicles and enjoyed watching the leisurely movements of the woman attendant as she swished water along the stone floors to keep them clean, and we listened dreamily as she bade slow bathers to 'Hurry up, there's mair than you wantin' in the night'.

There were no taps on the baths, only projecting pieces of metal which had to be turned with the attendant's iron key. This was no doubt to prevent extravagance and overflowing, but the result of having no control over the water could be agonizing. No matter how accurately one felt the temperature of the water had been judged, when one had been asked to 'See if this is aw right', the moment the attendant disappeared, and one submerged the body gingerly, it was only too painfully brought home that judgement had been badly at fault, and there would be a yell as the scalding water reached the tenderness of the waist, and an imploring screech, 'Oh come *back*, missus, ah'm bein' roastit.' The attendant, used to such behaviour, ignored the cries as long as possible, partly to teach us a lesson and partly because she had duties elsewhere, but when she could stand the shouting no longer she would return, fling open the door with her pass-key and stand glaring balefully in the doorway. A towel would be hastily draped round the scarlet torso, as she fiercely turned on a jet of cold water. 'Noo, pit yer feet in this time, you silly wee besom, and make sure it's cauld enough,' she commanded, adding: 'Fur ah'm no' comin' back *again*. Ah've the hale baths tae attend tae, an' ah'm no' dancin' attendance on you, so don't think it!'

Meekly a toe would be thrust from the folds of the towel, and the water tested. 'Oh aye, it's a' right this time', and she would depart, muttering, 'It better be!'

If a mistake had been made a second time, it just had to be endured. To face that woman's wrath twice was not to be contemplated. So if the water was still too hot, the only solution was to press the cold spray above the bath into service. This was infuriatingly slow and never seemed to make the least difference to the temperature of the water, and the moment those waiting outside heard the spray, they knew what had happened and there would be shouts, 'Hurry up you, are you in there fur the night!'

The soap was coarse and yellow, the floor was stone, and the towel was hard, but what luxury it seemed to be able to wallow in a long 'wally' bath, and feel a gentle sleepiness steal over one as familiar voices rose and fell on every side, and chums called to each other through the partitions.

There were squeals of mock terror when the final cold spray was applied to keep one from catching cold on the way home, and beatific smiles on our pink steamy faces when we at last emerged, scrubbed, rinsed and dried, and more than ready for a pennyworth of chips to eat as we walked home.

9

We didn't manage to have a holiday every year, but when my mother decided that, yes, she thought she could maybe afford one this year, we talked of nothing else for weeks beforehand. We'd sit round the table when my mother came in from work at night and pore over the seaside advertisements in the paper. The ones which drew us like magnets were usually worded, 'Room and kitchen to let, Fair Fortnight, no linen supplied, attendance if desired, Low door, own key'. The lure lay in the last words. Low door, own key. A low door which opened on to a little side street that ran down to the sea. To us, born and reared in tenements, used to climbing miles of stairs in the course of the year, the excitement of walking right from the street over a threshold which led straight to the living-room was a thrill of which we never tired. It was almost like living on the exciting bustling pavement itself, and for my mother and Grannie it seemed like playing at housekeeping.

The minute we got out of the train we would race along the street ahead of Mother and Grannie, searching for the number of our own particular low door. Once, to my joy, our low door was fronted by a *red* doorstep. This was pure fantasy. I didn't know it was achieved by the use of red pipe-clay, and I doubt if I would have believed it if anybody had told me. It was our magic seaside doorstep and I loved it. As soon as the door was opened, we children flew round the house, examining every drawer, every cupboard, the fancy taps on the sink, the fancy handles on the door. Everything was considered 'fancy' which differed from our own at home. While Mother and Grannie laid out our own clean linen and saw to the beds we were sent to the nearest shops to buy something for the tea.

Not for us the doubtful swank of sitting down to somebody

else's cooking. We liked to buy and cook our own food. Why, the day might have been blighted from the start if we had been forced to accept what somebody else considered a suitable breakfast, which could be *kippers*, or, worse, *steamed fish*! It was always eggs for us, lovely fresh country eggs, for the country was no further away than the end of the beach, and we could buy them from the farms any day. My mother had a whole egg, Grannie and I one between us, and the boys one between them, so half a dozen did us for two meals.

It was never any trouble to persuade us to run errands on holidays, for the shops were all so different from those at home. How absorbing it was to watch the man slice the bacon by hand instead of putting it into a machine. And didn't the milk taste more creamy and satisfying when it came out of a little tap on the side of a huge churn, carried on a cart, pulled by a donkey? Chips from a cart lit by paraffin flares were twice as good as those from a shop, and what a triumph to discover for ourselves a bakery which sold the crispest rolls in town, and which served them piping hot, in a bag with scarlet lettering, when we went down to buy them before breakfast each morning.

We worked cheerfully in the fields to help the farmer, regarding the whole thing as adventurous play, and were incredulous when we were given a bag of peas or strawberries as our reward. Our reward for what? For enjoying ourselves? This was paradise indeed. We were allowed by the farmer to go into the fields after the potato-pickers had finished, and keep for ourselves the tiny potatoes which had been left behind as too small to be worth lifting. With these my mother made chips for us, but we had to clean and scrape them ourselves, for she said they were far too fiddling for her. So the three of us would drape ourselves on top of sink and dresser, scraping and scrubbing the marble-sized potatoes, cutting them into minute slices, and at last, blissfully devour plates full of miniature fairy chips.

Seaside ice-cream had a taste all of its own too, served between wafers and biscuits intriguingly different from those at home. Some of the ice-cream may not even have been so good as our own Tallies in Glasgow, but it held fascination for us because it was different. Without ever being told, we knew it was the change which was the best part of our holiday.

The sea was a joy, of course, and distances so impossible to measure in that wide expanse of ocean that I caused great amusement by vowing, the first day we arrived in Girvan, that I was going to paddle out to Ailsa Craig the minute I'd swallowed my tea. I refused to believe it was all of thirteen miles! And it only a wee speck on the map too, and practically joined to the coast.

How golden the sands were, after the earth of our tenement back courts. We made forts, and castles, and leaped from the wall running alongside, and turned somersaults of sheer delight, and after our games, discovered that salt water was far more buoyant than the baths at home, and we could swim satisfying distances without putting our feet down. When we came out, teeth chattering and blue with cold, my mother shuddered and wondered how we could find pleasure in such icy waters. But to have gone to the seaside and *not* gone into the sea would have been unthinkable, and we pitied the grown-ups who wouldn't take off their clothes and join us in our Spartan splashing.

The pierrots at the end of the sands provided glamorous entertainment. We never went inside the railed-off enclosure, of course, but pressed against the railings and drank in every word and noted every gesture. We loved each member devotedly, but never dreamt of asking for autographs. To us they were beings from another world, and it was unimaginable that we could speak to them. We went to every performance, and knew the repertoire as well as they did, but the moment one of the company came round with the little box for contributions, we vanished. We had no money to give away to people who seemed to us so rich and prosperous, and anyway the 'toffs' sitting inside the enclosure must have contributed *hundreds* of sixpences.

We would have stayed at the seaside all day long, but my mother and Grannie grew tired of sitting there, and we were taken into the countryside on long walks. It seemed all wrong to be walking away from the sea, but soon we were climbing trees, and searching for wild flowers, and hoping Grannie would soon decide she must have a glass of milk and a wee rest. This meant the treat of a visit to a farmhouse, with milk 'straight from the cow' and, on very special occasions, cakes and scones to go with the milk. These treats usually came almost at the end of the holiday, when my mother would look into her purse, count up her money, and decide it was safe to have a little spree. We had already paid for our wee house, so all that was left in the purse was spending money.

And always, on the last day of the holiday, we went to one of the big local houses which had a card on the gate saying, 'Flowers for sale – a shilling a bunch.' We were allowed to stroll round the garden, and Grannie and I made a slow and careful selection of the beautiful, scented, old-fashioned cottage flowers to take back with us to our tenement, to remind us of the happy days spent in our own dear wee house, with its low door and its own key.

We always came home on a Saturday morning, to give us plenty of time to get in some food for the weekend, and to give my mother opportunity to get her dungarees ready for her work in the Railway wagon-shop on Monday morning.

Springburn, where I was born and brought up, depended for its existence on Railways and their equipment. We children were proud to think that our mothers and fathers had helped to build the wonderful engines we watched roaring away under bridges to far-away London, to Sheffield and to Aberdeen. There were other places too, places which were only names to us as we chanted the splendid titles of the engines and took note of their numbers in our little notebooks.

Widows deemed it the greatest good fortune to get a job as a carriage cleaner, and they devoted to the cleaning of the trains the same personal attention and thoroughness they showed in keeping their own spotless homes clean. They would stand back, affection in their eyes as they surveyed the sparkling train windows and well-brushed upholstery, and in their day there were no complaints of dirty trains.

As for the men, they never stopped discussing the finer points of engineering. It was their hobby as well as their bread and butter. They talked, breathed, ate and slept railways. My mother used to say scathingly that there were more engines

121

built over the counter of the local pub than were ever built in the sheds, for they talked of nothing else.

The Calley, Cowlairs, Hyde Park – magic names which spelled pay-packets to the fathers and even the mothers of all my chums. The 'horns', as we called the hooters, took the place of alarm clocks in our community. We wakened to the 'quarter to' horn, we stole an extra eight minutes, clinging fast to sleep before the 'seven minutes' horn had us tumbling out on to the cold linoleum; and by the time the eight o'clock horn had gone, we had plunged gaspingly into the cold water from the tap and were vigorously rubbing our frozen cheeks to life with a rough towel.

My mother had already left by the 'quarter to' horn, and was on her way to Cowlairs, where she painted railway wagons. Hard, heavy work for a slight little creature like her, but she was glad to get it, with three of us to feed and house, plus Grannie, of course.

We loved her tales of the railway shops, of the pranks they played on the 'gaffer', of how she and her chum Lizzie would hide underneath the wagons until he had gone past, so that they could indulge their passion for tea from the Thermos, and French cakes when they could afford them, consumed in the firm's time. There were no canteens in those days, and no 'breaks', and any nourishment was strictly unofficial. We shivered with fear as she told of near escapes, for we certainly thought discovery would have meant the sack – a dreaded word in the tenements.

She would describe in detail the vastness of the twelve-tonners and the sixteen-tonners, and the difference this made to the arm-stretching and reaching, and therefore to the speed of the work if they were given too many sixteen-tonners in proportion to the smaller wagons. I used to go along to the gate to meet her on pay nights, when the air was filled with chattering and laughing, as she and her workmates tumbled out, glad of the comfort of the pay packet safely tucked into the top pocket of their dungarees. On the way home, reckless with a week's pay, we all went into Charlie's the Italian shop on the corner, and tucked into the delights of sugar or nougat wafers. Nobody worried about spoiling the appetite for the meal awaiting them at home. It was the end of the week, they only had Saturday morning's work ahead of them, with maybe a dance on Saturday night and all day Sunday to relax. There was no hurry. They were all working. Life was good.

Sometimes my mother had to go on night-shift, and we grew used to seeing her come in at breakfast-time as we were getting ready for school. Her face and hands would be daubed with the paint she had been too tired to remove before she left the workshop, and her eyes closed with weariness as she sipped her tea.

Before taking this job in the paint-shop she had worked a machine at Hyde Park, where they made the big locomotives. She was very proud of her skill with the strong steel shapes, and sad when they had to sack all the women workers to make room for the men who needed the jobs. They made no fuss, the widows, at being ousted in this way. They accepted the fact that in normal conditions man was the bread-winner, and quietly looked elsewhere for work.

It was a tremendous excitement for us children when one of the big locomotives was ready for its journey through our streets to the docks, there to be shipped to China, or India, or some similar far-off land which knew, of course, that we made the best locomotives in the world. The huge iron gates of the works would swing open, and with the sure telepathy of children for knowing what was happening, we would be there clustered on the pavement, watching with bright-eyed interest and admiration as the gigantic locomotive was eased with deceptive skill in to its waiting trailer. It was a splendid thing of shining steel, beautiful in shape, and full of strength. The men who had fashioned her would spit casually to hide their pride in their workmanship, and the unemployed who joined us on the pavements would straighten their shoulders, for they believed and knew that they too were part of this great engineering tradition of Glasgow and Scotland.

Because of its weight and size, it had to travel very slowly over the cobbles, vibrating the dishes on our shelves, and we whooped and cheered every inch of the way, only turning back when we were frighteningly far from our own familiar streets.

At lunch-time the horns were the signal for our streets to be filled with the crunch of hundreds upon hundreds of tramping feet as the railway workers hurried home for their dinner. No canteen meals for them. They all worked within walking distance of a hot meal, and we ducked among them on our way home from school, avoiding many a half-hearted cuff on the ear as we nearly tripped them up. Wives had to have everything ready on time, and could tell to a second when their men would be turning in at the close, and mounting the stairs. Nobody used buses or trams, so there was no confusion over time-tables. Everybody walked, and dictated his own turn of speed.

After lunch, they didn't go in through the big gates until the final horn summoned them. It was their habit to squat down on their haunches along the walls flanking the works, smoking a final cigarette, studying their newspapers, or just enjoying a joke with each other, making the most of their last few minutes of leisure before the horn drew them to their feet and back to their machines.

They had skill in their hands, and the pride of the craftsman in their eyes, and my mother agreed with them when they declared that each steam loco had a personality of its own. Anyone who ever saw them taking the road out of our big works would know that. Each engine bearing its proud name, its boilers all ready to send sparks and smoke like a miniature volcano into the night, once its willing acolytes were in attendance. And we children felt a great sense of pride in these giants, for hadn't our mothers and fathers helped to create them?

The horns didn't sound on Sundays, and on that day we had to learn to look at the clock again. My mother had a long lie on Sunday mornings, for it was the one day of the week she hadn't to be up early for work. Grannie put on her white apron and got out the big bowl, and baked the most mouth-watering scones and pancakes in case anybody dropped in for tea. And we children played in bed till the baking was finished, and then fought and scrambled to get into the zinc bath in front of the fire, and enjoy splashing in the hot soapy water. We took it in turns to be bathed, and I was usually first, and my hair was washed too, and my brothers would lather it with soap until they could pull my front curls into a stiff point, like a rhinoceros horn, and I'd pretend to stab them as they drew a foot through the turbulent waters. Then I'd be whisked out, and more hot water was added for my brothers, from the kettles Grannie kept filled on top of the range. At the end of all this, the bath was rinsed and dried and put away for another week. In winter we dried our hair before the glowing fire in the range, but in summer we were sent down to the back court to let the sun adorn us with shining caps of curls. And afterwards, everything revolved round the church. What an enormous place this took in our lives.

As a four-year-old, I was trotted solemnly off to the morning service by the neighbours' older children, my penny or ha'penny clutched tightly in my hand. How important I felt as I dropped the coin into the plate when it came round, proud to be copying the actions of the big girls. I would gaze at the lofty ceiling, which I was sure reached right to heaven itself, then turn my fascinated stare to the stained glass windows, almost drowning in their rich jewel-like colours. The minister's voice rose and fell, but I heard nothing of the message. The atmosphere of church was soothing and mysterious, and I loved every minute of it.

Later, I went to Sunday School with my brothers, and this was a much more light-hearted affair. Each class occupied a portion of a pew, with the teacher perched on the desk facing us, and thrilling us with stories from the Bible. We had little coloured texts to memorize for each week, and we studied the catechism and the creed. I was very worried about having to say 'I believe in the Holy Catholic Church'. How could I believe in this, when I was a Protestant and a Presbyterian at that? I felt this was betrayal of the most terrifying order, and could never get a truly satisfying explanation which my conscience would accept.

The flowing language of the Bible stirred me, and it was no trouble to memorize whole passages. Indeed at one time I actually committed to memory the entire book of Luke in preparation for a special examination. It was like learning a play, and the answers fell into place so aptly I walked off with the prize, to Grannie's delight. She was sure I was going to be a minister, and I felt this was a splendid antidote to my passion for play-acting which could come to no good.

Later still, I was old enough to join the Bible Class, and at the same time I plunged into the activities of the Girl Guides, while my brothers were by this time in the Boys' Brigade. Getting the uniforms presented a bit of a problem, with our limited budget, but we made toffee apples and sold them to raise cash, and we found older boys and girls who were only too pleased to let us have their outgrown uniforms at bargain prices.

These uniforms were cleaned and polished to perfection for Church Parades, when the eyes of the entire congregation were on us as we formed into fours and then twos and marched down the centre aisle to fill almost the whole of the downstairs pews. There was no question of mothers or grannies helping us. It was all part of the discipline and the fun to wash and iron our ties, press the uniforms and polish belts and shoes, and Grannie watched this activity with a vigilant eye, amused at our industry, but full of encouragement of this excellent training in looking after ourselves. 'Aye, learn young, learn fair,' she would say, 'it's a grand thing to be independent.'

We weren't sure if Grannie and my mother would let us go with the Guides and the Boys' Brigade to summer camp. There would be billy-cans to buy, and mugs, and sand-shoes, and about a pound needed for the ten days' holiday, and the train fare. It seemed a fortune. 'Well, if you can each save up the pound you can go,' my mother at last announced. From that moment on we were in a whirl of excitement. We ran messages for neighbours, we gave special back-court concerts, we organized jumble-sales, and we made and sold trays and trays of tablet to those better off than ourselves. This delicious Scottish confection was a great favourite. Firmer than fudge, but not hard like toffee, it melted in the mouth. The piles of pennies grew and were changed to shillings, then into ten-shilling notes, and at last we had a whole pound each. The boys were going to Ayr and we were going to Berwick. We didn't need an alarm clock or a 'horn' to waken us on the morning of departure. We were up as soon as it was daylight. The sun was shining. We shivered with excitement. Grannie and my mother checked again and again that we had our pyjamas, a change of socks and underwear in our haversacks, and that our billy-cans and mugs were safely fastened to the outside strap. 'Noo mind and behave yersels,' they called after us as we clattered down the stairs, to meet with our companies outside the church. We were off. The officers had gone on ahead to see that the bell tents were erected, and we caught our breaths at the sight of those lofty tents spread over soft green grass, like a scene from Shakespeare's Agincourt we thought. We ate in one big marquee, and how good everything tasted eaten under canvas and in the company of our chums. It was a complete novelty to us to eat in company like this, outside our own homes, and our eyes met over the half-cold food, pleased with the strangeness of it all.

I was somewhat taken aback to find we had to take turns in the cook-house, and this meant not only cooking, but lighting the fire between an improvised fire-place of bricks. I trembled with fright at the responsibility of providing sustenance for all those hungry youngsters, *and* officers. I needn't have worried. Grannie's good teaching stood me in splendid stead, and once my cooking had been tasted, I was detailed to kitchen duties for the rest of the camping holiday. I didn't really mind. I was flattered that they should like my catering so much. Mass approval was more than I had ever expected, and I put it down to the fact that they couldn't all have grannies who were so expert as mine in giving us tasty and delicious food for next to nothing. And I had a few enviable privileges. All parcels sent down by more affluent mothers went straight to the kitchen. Oh the bliss of an unexpected pineapple tart sent down by a fond mamma and shared with me. This was a bonus to make the mouth water.

One of the surprising rules at this camp was that we must lie down on our sleeping mats and rest for an hour after lunch. This seemed to us quite hilarious. Big girls of twelve lying down during the day! We, who ran about from dawn till dusk at home, fitting in shopping, baby-minding, housework and a dozen other ploys between and after school, to need a rest on holiday! We couldn't lie still for laughing the first day, much to the officers' annoyance. But soon we grew quiet, and that lovely hour became something we looked forward to, and gave us a springboard for the rest of the day's activities.

When we came home from that first camp, a chum and I arranged a game of tennis for two o'clock the next day, for we were still in school holidays, and we couldn't understand why we were creeping about the courts yawning and half-dead. After a holiday too. There must be something wrong with us. And then it hit me with a blinding flash. This was the hour when we usually had our rest and already our bodies had formed the habit, and resented being asked to rush about. I was stunned at how quickly a habit, good or bad, can be formed.

As well as the Guides, we filled every seat at the Band of Hope and the Christian Endeavour meetings. The Band of Hope was splendid. We had lantern lectures, and learned the terrible dangers of picking up handkerchiefs in the street, which might be germ infested. We absorbed gravely the examples of the evils of strong drink. We could see this every Saturday in the tenements, but it drove the lesson home, seeing it up there on the slides, and noting with a shudder every detail of the poor wives and children being thrown into the street because the husband had drunk away the rent money.

In lighter mood we were entertained by visiting artists playing the violin with what seemed to us superb expertise, and singers who sang 'The Floral Dance' and 'The Bold Gendarmes' so beautifully, we made the rafters ring with our applause.

I can't remember much about Christian Endeavour meetings, except that we seemed to collect cash for every sick person in hospital, and I was sometimes thrillingly allowed to accompany the secretary with a basket of fruit or a box of sweets on the visit to the patient in hospital. I had to have a note to get off school for this journey, and I could never understand my teacher's barely suppressed smile when I said that we had raised the money through Christian Endeavour. It may have had something to do with the fact that I'd never seen the words written down and pronounced them 'Christian and ever'.

The church activities went on and on, catering for every age, and soon it was my turn to teach in Sunday School and perch on the pew and tell the little ones stories. They listened to me with wide eyes as I acted out the parables, and stammered and gulped with shyness when I made them tell me the stories in their own words. They were very poor, and I decided to save and give them a party in our house. They talked about this for weeks, and when I took them home after Sunday School on the day we'd arranged, their torn jerseys were washed and pressed, their hair slicked down with water, and their shabby boots shining with boot polish. It was the simplest fare, for I only had two shillings a week pocket money out of which I'd saved for this feast, but the table looked festive with my mother's china set out on a snowy cloth. These children only knew scrubbed tables or American cloth which could be wiped with a damp cloth, and were overawed at the sight of a real white tablecloth. We had salmon sandwiches, one tin eked out with lots of milk and margarine, but salmon was their favourite and a great luxury, and the mere smell of it set their mouths watering. We had jellies, and I'd baked apple tarts and a fruit cake. To finish up, we had a big dish of cheap sweeties and home-made tablet. When they'd finished the last conversation lozenge, one of the wee boys said it was just like the parable of the Prodigal Son – he'd never seen a fatted calf, but he was sure it was no better than my party.

My mother had been horrified at the idea of ten little boys stampeding the house, but when she saw their eager eyes, and their appreciation of our humble catering, her eyes filled with tears, 'God love them,' she said, 'they're that easily pleased. Aye, of course you can take them ben the room and play the gramophone for them.' This was the accolade, for only grown-ups were entertained in our 'room', which was kept like a shrine for special occasions, and I was as proud as if I'd been awarded the Victoria Cross. The 'room' made it a real Christmas party.

10

Time is very hard to measure when you are very young, and when we were children it was the windows of the big Cooperative up the road which told us that Christmas was near. Nobody at home mentioned it, for when you're working on a tight budget you don't go around encouraging your family to wild dreams of turkeys or extravagant toys and presents. You keep as quiet as possible, and try to forget the slimness of your purse, for however many letters are sent up the chimney to 'Santa', few are likely to find their way to your room and kitchen.

But the shops flashed the message from every window, and the news would quickly spread the moment the first spy noted that the blinds had been drawn on certain windows, to hide the activity going on behind. 'The Co's getting ready fur their Christmas windaes,' we chorused to each other. 'It must be gettin' near time to send a letter to Santa.' We wouldn't write a line, of course, until we'd seen what was newest in the way of toys and books. We were in a fever of impatience, and raced up the hill every half-hour to see if we could be the first to see the blinds go up.

I was never first to see the exciting display as the curtain rose, but I was certainly among the first in our tenement. One look at an excited face coming charging down the hill was enough. The blinds were up. I knew it. In a moment I was racing up Springburn Road on winged feet, like a Pied Piper, gathering children from every close as I ran. When we rounded the bend, and light from those magnificent windows spilled out on to the pavements, we automatically slowed down, the better to take in the general scene. It was a wild confusion to our eyes – colour, light, extravagant array of unbelievable toys – mountains of beautiful books – we drew a deep breath, and settled down to the bliss of examining each window item by item. Rapturous cries as we found the things we would love to have, if we were rich. 'Oh, isn't that doll *beautiful*!' I crouched low to the pavement, to make sure the enchanting creature had underclothes that I could take off and put on if she were mine. She had, and they were lace trimmed! And little socks. And shoes with buckles. Oh, and the bonnet came off too. I felt life could hold nothing better than the prospect of holding that perfect replica of a baby in my arms. But of course I knew it was impossible. Still, I could run up and admire her every single day until somebody bought her. It was always such a long time to Christmas and there would be plenty of time for this satisfying window courtship.

Each of us chose an impossible dream like the baby doll before we got down to the realistic level of things our mothers just might be able to afford. We pretended it was Santa, but we knew better than to wish for things of an extravagant nature. There were plenty of other delights, though, and in exuberant mood we'd choose about half a dozen each, and we always included a brand-new Children's Annual. I don't know who bought the new ones which were in the shop windows, but we always seemed to get one which had been passed down by somebody else, its covers printed by a variety of grubby fingers, and with rubbed-out scribbles down the sides of the pages. We shook our heads virtuously over this defacing of the Annual. If *we* had ever had the good fortune to have had a new book, we'd *never* have put a mark on it. *Never*. More, we'd have put brown paper covers on it to protect the lovely shiny outside binding.

So we chose our beautiful new Annual through the window, and added other coveted treasures, but always with a watchful eye on the price ticket so that we could throw out suitable hints for our mother's consideration. The sighing over the Meccano sets, the huge Teddy-bears, the life-like dolls, the boxing gloves, the football boots, the train-sets, the scooters, and the skates, whispered away. We concentrated now, with the realism of the tenement child, on modest desires. 'Oh yes, that wee box of paints at one-and-six, that would be great, and it would go into my stocking too.' My eyes moved along, 'Oh and maybe that wee sewing set – I could embroider a flooer on Grannie's apron.' How much was it? I nearly turned a somersault to see the upside-down ticket. 'Two shillings!' No, it was too much. What else was there for a shilling, or one-and-sixpence. 'Oh gosh, I nearly didn't see it! A pencil-box with a little painted flower on the lid, for one-and-nine.' It was empty of course, but I had plenty of wee bits of pencil and rubber to fill it, and a treasured bone pen with a Waverley nib given to me by a neighbour when I'd run her messages for a whole week.

Our final choices made, the letters to Santa started. Grannie was sure we'd set ourselves on fire as we leaned dangerously over the range and tried to float our little notes right up the chimney. It was terribly bad luck if it weren't wafted up first time, or fell downwards into the flames. Grannie scorned such superstitious ways. 'Do you think Santy Claus kens whether yer letter fell doon or no'?' she'd demand. 'Awa' tae yer beds, afore ye burn yourself.' And, as we protested and wanted to write just one more note, she'd threaten, 'Another word oot o' ye, and I'll write a note to Santy Claus masel' an' tell him no' to bother comin' near this hoose, for I'll no' clean the flues to be ready for him.' This was enough. We crept to bed. Och we could always write a wee letter tomorrow night. There was plenty of time.

And then suddenly it was Christmas Eve and time to hang up our stockings. We had been on the go all day. I'd been sent down to the butcher to collect Grannie's favourite piece of sirloin. We never had a turkey, or a goose, or any of the larger birds. They were as far beyond our reach as caviare or nightingale's tongues, and we were entirely satisfied with our sirloin. We never had mince pies either. The first time I tasted one, it was a bitter disappointment. I thought mince meant meat, and I couldn't believe it when my teeth met a fruity mixture when I'd expected mince and gravy. How could anybody write so glowingly about Christmas mince pies, I thought in disgust, they weren't even as good as Grannie's ordinary fruit tarts.

My mother was late coming home on Christmas Eve. She did the toy-shopping straight from work, and there would be an exciting rustling as she thrust her purchases into the press in the lobby before coming into the kitchen for her tea. We asked no questions, but nearly burst with delight as our eyes met each other's.

It was an eternity before morning came. The stockings were hung along the mantelpiece, my long-legged hand-knitted stockings made by Grannie, held down by the big darkie bank, that smiling Negro head and shoulders, with the moveable arm, and a hand which popped the pennies into his mouth. My brothers' stockings held down by the tea-caddy and the heavy alarm clock. I thought I hadn't been to sleep at all, but a movement in the kitchen as Grannie filled the kettle, sent my eyes flying open. It was still dark. 'Och light the gas, Grannie,' I pleaded. 'I'm waken.' 'It's only six o'clock,' she whispered back. 'I'm juist makin' a wee cup o' tea.' But she lit the gas, and handed my stocking into the bed. The boys heard us and came running through from their bed in the room. They climbed into the hurley bed beside me, and we all dived into the stockings. A wee toty doll for me, that I could make clothes for. Lovely! A wee sewing set for making the clothes – my eyes sparkled over the coloured threads. What was this now? Mmmm. A lovely big bar of chocolate, the sort I liked best. And pushed right into the toe of my stocking, a tangerine wrapped in silver paper. 'Noo, don't eat that chocolate afore yer breakfast,' Grannie warned, 'or you'll be sick.' As if I would! That was my treasure, to be broken off and eaten, piece by piece, during the day for as long as I could make it last. And I'd keep the tangerine for after my sirloin. The boys put their new cowboy belts on over their pyjamas, and fired their toy guns at Grannie and at me, and we all turned somersaults on the bed.

While we played, Grannie baked some scones and pancakes just as if it was Sunday, and we had them hot with our tea. Oh, Christmas morning was lovely. My mother wakened, and started to get ready for work, for there was no holiday on Christmas Day for her. Pointing to the mantelpiece, she said to me, 'Have you looked up there yet?' I gasped. There, quite unnoticed from the bed, was a luxury I'd never dreamed of owning. I'd put it on my wee letter to Santa, but only as a fantasy. A little toy piano. And my mother had somehow found the money for it. And beside it a set of toy soldiers for each of the boys. Now we knew the reason for all that overtime she'd worked. We could hardly speak for excitement. Carefully Grannie reached up and lifted the treasures down, and I tried to play 'God save the King' from the dozen notes of my piano. The boys ranged their soldiers in battle formation. Grannie sipped her tea and watched us, a twinkle in her eye. Oh, Christmas morning was more than lovely. It was perfect. We never had a tree, but we never missed it.

Everything was extra special to us at this splendid time of year. After our simple diet, everything provided over and above ordinary meals spelt luxury. The Sunday School party, with its bag of tea-bread, and maybe a prize here and there for musical chairs or races, was a treat we looked forward to for weeks. I remember one terrible time Grannie had bought us new tin mugs, and we had them tied round our necks with tapes and I was warned to see that we didn't lose them. When the hot tea was poured into them the handles became scalding hot, and we couldn't hold them. There they were, tied to our necks full of boiling tea, with us leaping back and kicking wildly to keep our legs from being scalded, while the tea cascaded to the floor. Oh, how ashamed we were, and it never occurred to us to take the tinnies off. So we lost our tea, and nobody thought to bring us a re-fill. And we didn't dare ask. 'Aye,' said Grannie, when she'd reassured herself we weren't burned, 'that's the way to learn – by your mistakes. You'll no' be so daft anither time.' But she gave us a cup of tea when we came home.

And one year I had to learn, the hard way, not to ask for things before I ought to have them. The Cooperative window held a John Bull printing outfit which I coveted above all else. I was terrified somebody would buy it before Christmas. 'Och, get it now, Mother,' I urged. 'I don't want anything else, if you'll just get it now.' My mother held out as long as she could, and then grew tired of my nagging persistence. 'If I buy it now,' she warned, 'you'll get nothing else at Christmas, for I haven't the money for two presents.' It had been a lean year and I knew she spoke the truth. Oh, I didn't want anything else, I assured her, only the John Bull outfit. So she got it for me.

And when Christmas came I'd used up the inked pad and all the special paper that came with it. And I didn't get anything else. That year the mantelpiece was bare of anything for me on Christmas morning.

Over the year we saved our precious pocket money to buy little things to give to Grannie and my mother. Acid drops for Grannie, or a wee bottle of Eau-de-Cologne. A quarter pound of chocolates for my mother or a hankie. One year I sent away to a magazine for a linen square about six inches by six inches, complete with transfer and coloured silks. The transfer was of a little crinolined figure, with a poke bonnet and curls, and I thought it exquisite. I sewed it up in the hot-houses of the public park, so nobody would know what I was doing. The materials cost two shillings – a fortune – and it took me months to finish it with its tiny stitching, for I had to do it so secretly and in my spare time after school. My mother was enchanted with this gift, especially when the park-keeper told her afterwards how it had been managed.

One useless gift, which I loved buying, but which cost me a whole year's savings, was a pale blue silk handkerchief sachet for my mother. I had to climb up on to the chair in the shop, so that I could gaze on the selection spread out for my inspection on the glass counter. I was dazed with the splendour laid before me, and refused to be persuaded to buy something more practical. I had run messages for a neighbour for a year to acquire this nest-egg, and I was determined that my mother should have something frivolous and beautiful. She didn't spoil it by telling me I had wasted my money, but somehow when I saw it in our tenement setting I knew I had, and I never saw her use it. It was kept in a drawer. The hankies my mother stowed in her dungarees' pocket were ill-suited to a pale blue silk sachet, and I know it now.

But if we didn't decorate the house for Christmas, we had a positive orgy of cleaning for Hogmanay. Grannie and I shone the steels on the range, the brass covers on the dresser, and the brass gas-bracket, door-knob and letter-box till they sparkled like gold. The flues were cleaned. The floor polished. My mother washed all the furniture in the room with vinegar water, polished the tiles on the fireplace till they looked like amber,

135

and rubbed the polished mantelpiece – solid mahogany she assured us – to a gleaming satin. The 'room' was the best room in the house, and it was in fact the only room apart from the kitchen where we ate, and lived, and where Grannie and I slept, and we were well disciplined to accept that in the 'room' we must not romp or play. We thought it beautiful, and it had for us the special air of a museum piece. We shared our mother's anxiety that it should be kept nice for 'folk coming' and for special occasions, and the most splendid of all occasions was Hogmanay. This was the only time food was brought into the room. At other times, nobody would have dared risk dropping food or drink on our best things. But at Hogmanay – ah! that was different. A table was set near the window, spread with our best white cloth, lace-trimmed, and on it was laid the best china. Plates were laden with Genoa cake (my mother's favourite), cherry cake, Dundee cake, a round cake of short-bread and shortbread fingers. There was a wee bit of black bun for those who liked it, but it was only the very oldest members of the company who seemed to enjoy nibbling it. We children never touched it. There was a tray with bottles of port, sherry and ginger wines. However poor the tenement people were, they could always manage a few bottles for Hogmanay. Glasses sat on another tray. On the sideboard the best crystal bowl was filled with oranges and tangerines for the Hogmanay visitors, and we gazed at them enviously, but would never have dreamt of touching them. I remember one Hogmanay a stray cat wandered into our best room just after my mother had arranged everything to her satisfaction, and when she went through later to have another peep to make sure she'd forgotten nothing, there was the brute sitting on the white tablecloth, clawing at the black bun! Her screech of horror brought us all running, and the cat disappeared in a streak of terror as we all leaped to rescue the rest of the food. Nobody got black bun that year.

When it grew dark my mother put a match to the fire in the grate, and soon the blaze was reflecting itself in the amber tiles, and everything was poised, in lovely cleanliness, waiting for the magic hour of midnight when the New Year would be ushered in.

We children were in our pyjamas by this time, and the minute the bells were announcing midnight, we were given a wee sip of home-made ginger wine and a bit of shortbread, then whisked off to bed in the kitchen. We would lie listening for the first-foots arriving, and we'd fall asleep to the sound of conversation and doors opening and shutting, and shouts of 'Happy New Year, an' mony o' them'. Occasionally a voice could be heard in the lobby, asking, 'Are the weans in their beds? Och here's something for their pocket. Gi'e it to them in the morning,' and sleepily we would wonder if it would be a threepenny bit or a sixpence that we'd have for our darkie bank when we wakened up.

On New Year morning I always took Grannie down to see her 'chum' a short tram ride away. But before we went, we made sure the room was tidied up, and the tables re-set with the food and the wines for the folk who would drop in during the day to wish us a Happy New Year. My mother would be at home to welcome them, for she didn't have to go to work on New Year's Day, which was always a holiday.

I helped Grannie to put on her good black shoes, and I fastened the pin of the black cameo she wore at the neck of her best black silk blouse, and saw that the blouse was tucked in right the way round inside the waist of her long dark grey skirt. Then on top went her dark coat, and last of all her hat with its winter trimming of cherries was set carefully on her silvery hair, at an angle which wouldn't disturb the wee bun at the back. She looked entirely different from our workaday grannie, and I was transformed from my schoolday self in my navy blue reefer coat, long black stockings and, best of all *shoes*, not boots. The shoes, I felt, gave me a most ladylike appearance. My black velour hat was held on with a good piece of elastic, which kept it firmly anchored at windy corners, and my curls were brushed neatly over my shoulders. When we reached the tram, where it stood waiting at the terminus, there always seemed to be a drunk man sitting inside, half-asleep, softly singing 'The Star o' Rabbie Burns', and for ever afterwards I always associated the name of Burns with New Year revelries. When she heard the man singing, Grannie would smile and sing herself, 'We'll a' be prood o' Robin'. The man's heavy lids would lift to Grannie, delighted by her approval, and he would be encouraged to break into a spirited rendering of 'Robin was a rovin' lad'. The variation in names, Rabbie, Robin, puzzled me, but Grannie assured me that both applied to our poet Burns, and she herself was gey fond of the name Robin for him, as she felt it suited him better.

We told the conductor where to let us off, and he stopped the tram long enough to let us get down without splashing our stockings or Grannie's skirt, and then we crossed the road to the tenement where Grannie's chum lived. We reached a beautifully polished door on the landing and rang the bell. A soft shuffle told us she was coming, and then I was being embraced in a flurry of soft arms and incredibly soft face and we were bustled into the kitchen. At this time Grannie was about sixty and her friend about seventy-five, so she seemed truly ancient to me. She wore a snowy white cap with a fluted frill, and her black dress was protected by a large white apron. When she spoke, her voice was so soft I had to lean right forward to hear what she said. She might have stepped straight out of the pages of *Little Red Riding Hood* and I was fascinated. She in her turn was filled with wonder over me, and how lively I was, and how quick, and she kept turning and looking at me again and again as she got out plates and glasses and wine.

The kitchen was full of knick-knacks and shining brass, and there were little lace covers on all her chairs. Occasionally, to Grannie's horror, I seized the poker as a prop when I sang them a song from a pantomime, but their favourite was 'Bonnie Mary of Argyle' which always brought a tear to their eyes, I never knew why.

There was an old-fashioned horn gramophone which wheezed out the songs of Harry Lauder, and I'd reduce the two old ladies to scandalized laughter when I imitated him afterwards. It must have been a long time since the old lady had entertained children, for she seemed to have no idea of what was suitable. I was handed a glass of port to sip when she poured out one for Grannie and herself. Grannie either didn't notice or was too polite to interfere, and I was forced to take tiny sips of this horrid-tasting liquid and pretend it was as nice as my mother's delicious ginger wine. Later, the strong tea nearly took the skin off my tongue, and Grannie frowned at me when I screwed up my nose. But the sandwiches and cakes were delicious, although the two old ladies didn't seem to have much interest in them. I was amazed that they seemed to get more pleasure from that terrible wine and the strong tea.

Afterwards, I brought Grannie home, taking great care to see that she got on and off the tramcars safely. She only went out twice a year, at the Fair and at Hogmanay, so she wasn't used to traffic. I nearly burst with pride at being her escort, and we had to stop every few yards for the neighbours to admire her outfit and to wish her 'Happy New Year'. When we got home her lovely shoes were put away in their cardboard box. Her coat was hung up and left to air before being stowed at the back of the wardrobe, where it would stay until it was brought out for her to wear at the Fair. Her skirt was folded over a hanger, the black silk blouse put away with tissue paper, and there was my dear familiar Grannie again, picking up her knitting needles and getting on with a sock while she told my mother all about our outing. When my mother asked if I'd behaved myself, I held my breath and wondered if Grannie would mention how free I had been with the poker, but she just glanced at me, and assured my mother, 'Oh aye, she did fine. She's quite gettin' to be the lady.' I gazed at her gratefully, but wondered if Grannie *really* believed I was getting to be a lady. I had heard her say often enough that folk were inclined to live up to the descriptions they heard of themselves, and maybe she hoped I'd try to be a lady, and leave other folks' pokers alone in future. Yes, that must be it.

The magic of the New Year lasted quite a long time, with even the postman being invited in for a glass of something and a piece of cake. But we knew it was over when one day we went into the room and the tablecloth and the food had vanished. It was back to school for us then, and back to the workaday world for the tenement, but our pleasure in the Hogmanay revels kept us warm for many a long winter day afterwards. In the tenements we accepted cheerfully that it had to be auld claes and parritch after the feasting.

11

I remember vividly my first deliberately social visit to 'the town', as we called the centre of Glasgow. Not for messages. Not with the gird. But just to be part of the grown-up world. Until that day, the boundaries of my world stretched from Bishopbriggs to Castle Street, with sometimes a dizzy venture to Campsie on holiday Mondays, when the route was filled with wonder. The long stretches of untenanted country, the wee row of miners' cottages, so different from our high tenements, the canal flowing placidly below fearfully averted eyes. We had been well warned to fear this canal. Terrible tales were told of disobedient children who had fallen in, never to be seen again. These stories of the dangers of water made such a strong impression on me that once, when crossing the 'steps of Kelvin', which were just large boulders to let us cross the river at that point, I took off my long-legged boots and slung them round my neck, so that if I did fall into the water, the weight of the boots wouldn't drag me down. As I stood on one of the boulders, it wobbled, and I shrieked and fell to my knees. To my horror, one of my new boots fell into the river, and floated away. I was about to leap after it, when a man on the bank shouted, 'Let it go, better a boot than a child.' These dramatic words shocked me back to my original terror of the water, and he had to wade out and guide me over to the bank. I raced down the path, and could see my boot, so near and yet so far, and I wept as I wondered what my mother would say. I was so distraught that instead of leaving both boots off, and going about in my bare feet till I could get home, I put on the one boot I had saved, and hopped about now on a bare foot, now on a boot, until my legs ached from the uneven progress. Later that night when I told my mother what had happened, she sighed, and weakly agreed it was better to have let the lost boot perish. She knew that a twenty-five and sixpenny pair of boots bought the previous day now had to be replaced from her two pounds ten a week pay, and maybe in her heart of hearts felt that in the interests of economy I might have attempted a brave little rescue of the boot, without too much danger to life and limb. I sensed her divided feelings when, on repeating the man's words, 'Better a boot than a child', for the third time, she cuffed me on the ear and said irritably, 'Oh, don't be so dramatic. Go to bed.' My poor mother. Half a week's wages lost because of my carelessness.

At the other end of my boundary was Castle Street, with its unknown back courts, and evil-smelling chimney dominating the chemical works. In between, lay romantic sounding Fountainwell Road, where I wept at an old lady's sink when I heard the story of how her only son had been killed on the very day of the Armistice of the First World War. This seemed to me a fate too cruel to be borne, and I wondered how she ever laughed again. Although I was a staunch Rechabite, I couldn't find it in my heart to condemn the old lady for seeking comfort in the 'bottle' when she thought of her poor son. My mother found out about those visits and stopped them at once. I was sorry, for I found the proximity of Fountainwell Road to the graveyard very mysterious, and somehow a fitting background to the sad story of the soldier son.

Nearby was another strange piece of territory known as the Hunts. The full name was Huntingdon Square, and this was a large square courtyard quite different from our oblong affairs, and providing limitless expanses of concrete for ball-beds, skipping ropes, peever, and all the childish games dear to my heart. And although we were timid about invading other back courts, the concrete courtyard of the Hunts was an irresistible temptation with its perfect surface for these games. Never was peever manipulated so skilfully, never ball stotted so high, as in the courtyard of the Hunts. It was worth the risk of being chased by the big boys and girls who rightfully played there, to know the fulfilment of such expert playing.

These then were my boundaries until the day of the students' collection for charity, when I suddenly stunned my two chums by suggesting we went into the town to see the start of the parade. I don't know where the idea came from. Perhaps the chrysalis was ready to burst its case, and the time was ripe for me to venture forth into a wider world. Until I actually said the words, I'd had no idea that I must subconsciously have been moving towards this moment. But, once uttered, we were all three passionately determined that the idea must be carried out.

We would walk, of course. The thought of spending money on fares was too ludicrous to be entertained. We would each save ninepence. That would allow threepence for a cup of coffee, and fourpence for two cakes. I knew these prices from my mother, who occasionally gave herself this treat with a fellow-worker. The remaining tuppence we'd give to the students for their charity.

At this time my pocket money for spending was threepence a week, and even with the odd ha'penny or penny earned from affluent adults for running down for a packet of cigarettes or a forgotten ounce of tobacco, it would take a few weeks to manage a clear ninepence. But I was in no hurry. This adventure to town was something to savour, and the brilliance of the idea of dining out was still so staggering I needed a bit of time to see myself actually doing it. I wanted to rehearse every move in my own mind.

I had never been inside a tearoom. My only experience of such things was on the screens of the cinema, where the heroine walked boldly in, accompanied by the man of her choice, sat down and ate large and wonderful meals. I shivered with apprehension and delight every time I thought of walking in and ordering coffee and cakes, but how actually to do it was beyond imagination.

When one of my chums told her mother of our plan, that good lady was horrified at my presumption. She was sure such grandiose ideas in one so young boded ill for my future. 'Who are you,' she demanded, 'to suppose grown women are there to attend to your wants?' But if they were waitresses, I thought, surely they must want customers. But, of course, I was much too confused to argue with her.

Still, she put a terrible doubt in my heart, and all the way on that walk to town I felt a sinking in my stomach when I thought a derisive waitress might refuse to serve me because I was too soon aspiring for attention. I need have had no such fears. I led the way and sat down at a table. 'Three cups of coffee,' I ordered huskily, 'and six French cakes.'

The waitress took us in at a glance. 'Imphm,' she said, 'I suppose you know they're tuppence each?' This was language we understood. 'Aye,' I assured her, 'we've each got sevenpence.' We'd never heard of tipping, and anyway would have considered it madness to give money to somebody who was clearly much better off than we were, and getting a good wage every week.

We had never tasted coffee before, and weren't sure if we would like it, but we could get tea at home and we felt this far too ordinary to choose in this magnificent glass-bedecked salon. We peeled the paper carefully off our French cakes, determined not to lose a morsel of the icing, which was apt to stick treacherously if treated too roughly.

When we had savoured the last crumb we leaned back, ecstatic and replete, and watched the students cavorting in the street below. Some gaudily clad males actually came into the tearoom and raced upstairs in search of us, lured by our eager faces at the windows. They were obviously disappointed to find gym slips and black lisle stockings. We each dropped our tuppence into the outstretched boxes with an air of abandon. It was a tremendous gesture to give tuppence away like this, for we longed for another French cake, and then we called for the bill. I collected the sevenpences from my chums and paid over the staggering sum of one and ninepence for our feast. We knew it would cost exactly this sum, but somehow when the moment came for handing it over, we felt we had spent a fortune.

Next moment we were in the street, ready for the walk home. We gazed at each other in triumph. We had done it. We had come to town. We had eaten and drunk at a famous restaurant, and we had each donated tuppence to charity. We had lived. We turned our footsteps towards home, and drew deep breaths of utter satisfaction. It had been a marvellous adventure.

That winter was the last I was to know as a child. Grannie took her usual dose of bronchitis at the end of November, but this time she seemed strangely listless. During previous attacks she ruled the house from her bed, and I had to follow her instructions to the letter. The soups were made, the vegetables prepared, the table laid, all under her vigilant eye, and she ate and drank her little meals with a critical palate. We talked and argued, and I was praised or scolded, and we didn't worry too much about bronchitis, for the only difference was that instead of sitting in the big chair with her knitting, Grannie was in bed. And I was doing the cooking.

Now she was very still, and my mother, who had stayed off work, kept glancing at her with a troubled frown. For some reason, it seemed we had to speak in whispers. 'Does Grannie want any dinner?' I asked, when my mother had poured the soup. 'You see if she wants any,' my mother said. I went over to the bed, and Grannie regarded me with frighteningly thoughtful eyes. When I asked if she wanted any soup she shook her head.

When I went over to the bed again, to see if maybe she would like a cup of tea and a biscuit, her eyes looked withdrawn, but she thought she could fancy a nice cup of tea. 'Nane o' yer sleesh,' she whispered. 'A guid strong cup noo.' That sounded more like my Grannie, and I quickly got it ready. But she was too weak to lift the cup to her lips and I, who was never allowed to help Grannie in this way, for she scorned softness, had to put my hand behind her shoulders, and take the cup to her mouth. This was surely a terrible dose of bronchitis, and I wished the doctor would come again.

He came in after lunch, and he sounded her chest and took her hand. 'Now, now, Grannie, what's this you've been up to? You'll have to take your soup, you know. You must have something to stick to your ribs.' She managed a smile for him, and I was shooed away from the bed. Surely he wouldn't talk to Grannie like that if she were really ill? She was just tired. That was it. How often had I heard her say, as she moved about our kitchen, doing a hundred and one different jobs, 'Aye, the willin' horse gets the heaviest burden to bear.' And she would laugh when I would say, 'Whit horse dae ye mean, Grannie? Is it Sanny the horse that helps at the smiddie?'

My mother decided to sit up all night, which made me tremble, for I knew people only did this when illnesses were serious. I was put into the big bed, in case I'd disturb Grannie in the hurley. I didn't go to the penny matinée that Saturday, for Grannie would only take her gruel or her tea if I gave it to her. It was a dream. Me ministering to Grannie instead of her doing it to me.

In the morning, Sunday morning, when I wakened and looked down at the hurley to see if she was any better, Grannie was lying, pale and remote, with her eyes shut and I knew that she was dead.

I was prostrate with grief that I was too young to express, and it was decided it would be easier for everyone if I were out of the way until after the funeral. It had to be somewhere not too far from school, for there was no spare cash for expensive tram or bus fares, and as we were in the grip of winter I couldn't walk far. And so, as Auntie Jeanie's house fulfilled these requirements, we accepted her offer to put me up. I could sleep with Betty and would be no trouble, she assured my mother.

I had never slept at anybody's house before, apart from holiday apartments, so I was quite unaware of the upset even one extra person can give to a household. In my numb misery I didn't even begin to appreciate Auntie Jeanie's generosity in offering to have me in addition to her own three children, and I went listlessly to the new address after school finished at four o'clock. I don't remember that first evening at all. I suppose I must have done some homework, have eaten something and finally gone to bed, but nothing of that remains in my memory. But the morning! Ah! that was different!

With Grannie I'd been accustomed to being roused almost as soon as she got up herself, and while the fire was being lit I was getting dressed, and swiftly off to the shops for the rolls for breakfast, and maybe some mince for our midday meal, which we called our dinner, and possibly whisking along to the fruit shop for some vegetables for soup.

I'd pull my hand-knitted jersey over my head, lace up my

145

long-legged boots, and at the same time reel off a list of the things I thought Grannie might want. I'd get the purse out of the kitchen drawer, seize the basket and be off, almost before Grannie had time to agree that I'd remembered everything. Sometimes, in winter, when I had chilblains, it took me an age to drag my aching heels to the shops and back, and I would stop at every iced puddle and splinter the mica-thin brittle surface with my boot. The fun of this nearly made me forget the agony of the chilblains, but then the pain would come flaming back and it would seem certain that I must be late for breakfast and for school.

Once the house was safely reached, I'd sit on the long stool and toast the rolls in front of the fire, which by now was blazing in the open range. One for Tommy, one for Willie, and a half each for Grannie and for me, which was all we wanted. As each was toasted, I would run to the scrubbed sink top with it, cut open the steaming centre, plop in a slice of margarine, and watch with pleasure as the yellow melting fat ran into the hot dough. A smart tap on the crisp top as I shut the roll cracked the surface satisfactorily in all directions, and it was popped on a plate on top of the range to keep warm while I toasted the others.

Grannie meanwhile had been making the porridge, and infusing the tea, and soon we three children were kneeling on the rug with our porridge bowls on top of the long stool which ran the length of the fireplace, the heat from the fire warming our faces and fingers as we supped the good meal. How cosy these winter breakfasts were, for we had all been out of doors to whet our appetites, the boys delivering their milk round, and of course me getting the messages in.

I had thought this routine would go on for ever, for I knew no other.

But now Grannie was dead, and here was I in a strange bed in a strange kitchen. I lay silent and still in my misery, waiting for a voice to tell me it was time to get up and go for the rolls. I wondered where Auntie Jeanie bought hers, and if I would be able to find the shop quickly, and get back in time to make my way to school before nine o'clock, for I would have farther to walk from this house.

I opened my eyes, and to my amazement Auntie Jeanie was standing by the bed with a tray. A tray! And on it was a cup of tea, a bowl of porridge and a buttered roll. I stared uncomprehendingly. 'Who's no' weel?' I asked. 'Is it Betty?' And I turned to the sleeping figure beside me to search for signs of flu or fever.

'No, no,' said Auntie Jeanie comfortably, 'it's for you, pet. It's your breakfast.' 'But there's naethin' wrang wi' me,' I said in bewilderment. 'And whit aboot the messages?' It was Auntie's turn to look surprised. 'What messages?' she asked.

When I explained that I always went for the shopping before breakfast, to make sure Grannie would have everything before I went to school, she looked round at her three children who were now awake and listening with interest to our conversation. 'Do you hear that?' she demanded. 'You three don't know you're born, that's clear.' Then, turning to me, she smiled, 'Well, no messages this morning, my lass. Eat your breakfast in bed, like the other three, and see if we can get some colour into those pale cheeks.'

I was dumbfounded. They had breakfast in bed *every morning*! So I was to have breakfast in bed too. And no messages. The fire was lit, the kitchen a picture of cosy comfort. I should have envied my cousins their life of ease, and yet I felt only contempt for them. I could hear Grannie's voice as though she were in the room, 'Bairns have to learn to stand up to life and work hard, for we never ken whit's in front o' them.' I knew what her verdict would be on my cousins, 'Spoiled, that lot – fair spoiled.'

I trembled. Maybe I was being spoiled too, now that Grannie wasn't there to keep me strong for the battle. Maybe I wouldn't be able to face up to life if I went soft this way.

But for one morning, in the strangeness of Auntie Jeanie's house, and under the numbing weight of my sense of loss, I allowed myself to savour, for the very first time, the experience of having breakfast in bed. I condemned myself for my weakness and I hoped it would do my character no harm.

I whispered to the shadows, 'Just for this one morning, Grannie. I'll get up for it tomorrow.' And I did.

Best Foot Forward

To my mother, and to all of that gallant
band who were sojer-clad, but major-minded

'How sweet to remember the trouble that is past.'

EURIPIDES

1

I can remember with particular exactness the day that I left childhood birthdays and went into my teens. 'Into my teens.' What a strange, grown-up sound that had. Nobody else seemed at all impressed by this milestone in my life. But I remember it. Because on the previous day, when I was jumping down the long school stairs two at a time, the eccentric Highland school-teacher had stopped me and had asked, 'How old are you now, Molly?' 'Twelve,' I replied. And I realized, with a surprising pang, that this was the last time I would be able to say that with truth. In school, people didn't usually go about asking your age. Your age-group dictated what class you were in, and everybody knew almost to the month what age everyone else was. I remember being very surprised that Mr McAllister didn't know how old I was, and thought maybe he had asked that question on that special day so that I should remember forever the last time I had told anybody I was twelve.

I was in no hurry to grow up. Schoolgirl heroines were far and away my favourites in the whole world of literature, which I explored to the full, and I had been haunted for months by the harrowing tales of a little girl who had died at the age of thirteen. She had been thrown from her horse, and knew she was mortally afflicted, and I could hear her rebellious cry, 'How would you like to die at thirteen?', ringing in my ears. The book ended with her sobbing, 'I don't want to die. I am only thirteen.' I was sure I was to share her fate, although the only horses I ever saw in Springburn were those which drew the milk-carts, or the coal-carts, or which thundered down West Nile Street between the Railway Station and the Post Office, with cheery wee trace-boys perched negligently on the animals' arched necks, caps pushed to the back their heads, monarchs of all they surveyed. I could possibly be knocked down by such a horse, but it was quite certain I would not fall off its back!

And yet I almost did share the fate of the little schoolgirl heroine with whom I had so closely identified. And it was from no outside danger that the hazard came, but from my own intense and emotional temperament. Grannie, who had shared and guided my every waking thought for as long as I could remember, had died, and my grief transformed me from a bright, eager, happy child, who had complete confidence that everything would go on forever, to a frightened, trembling wisp of a girl who jumped at every shadow, and who stood poised for terrified flight at every sound. When I came back with a message for my mother, instead of jumping up and down on the mat outside the door, as I used to do before diving instantly into the kitchen, I would post myself half-way across the landing, in case Grannie's ghost should leap out at me when the door opened. 'What are you standing away back there for?' my mother would ask irritably as I stared at her, not venturing a step forward until I'd made sure it was really my mother. 'Come in for goodness' sake, and keep the draughts out.' How could I tell her that it was Grannie's ghost I was frightened of? 'She looks haunted,' I heard a neighbour say to my mother, and I jumped in fright. Was Grannie haunting me? Grannie, who had left such a void in my life that I didn't know how to fill it?

Even worse to bear than the thought of her ghost was the awful emptiness of the house when I came home from school. My brothers and I would sit and stare at each other in the silence until it was time to set the table for my mother, so that it would all be ready when she came in from her work. She still seemed to be able to eat, and so did my brothers, but I had lost my appetite with my grannie and never felt hungry at all nowadays, not even for sweeties. With the habit of years, I would set the table for five, and then realize with a pang of anguish that the fifth place, Grannie's, would never be needed again. The terrible finality of it, the endless silence, nobody to tease and torment me and keep me right, all this I locked inside me. I dwindled, and grew thin, and was down to three stones and twelve pounds at the age of thirteen, and a terrible lassitude stole over me so that I seemed to be walking in a dream world where people walked and talked all round me, but left me isolated in this aching void of stillness.

One day a neighbour called, who hadn't seen me since Grannie died, and for whom I used to dance and recite whenever she asked me. She took one look at me, and, with the involvement we all felt for each other in the tenements, immediately tackled my mother. 'My Goad, Jeanie, that wean's away tae a shadow. Is she eatin'?' 'Nut a bite will she take!' said my mother, 'but she sleeps like a log, and sleep's life tae weans, you know.' 'It's no life at that age, Jeanie,' and she went on to whisper urgently to my mother and I caught the dramatic words 'fatal melancholy'. They had a great love for the dialogue from *My Weekly* in our tenements, and both women seemed almost overcome by the thrilling words 'fatal melancholy'. I began to be quite stirred myself, but I wasn't so pleased when my alarmed mother dragged me on unwilling feet along to the doctor's surgery the very next night. The surgery was packed, as usual, and there was the smell of wet clothes, and engine grease from the men's dungarees, and quite a sociable atmosphere as people recognized a neighbour and started a whispered conversation. The men disdained to talk, and picked up one of the dog-eared magazines and started to read, or turn the pages to look at the pictures, while the chairs squeaked as we each moved along one with the disappearance into the doctor's room of the next patient.

Children were 'shushed' to silence if they dared to make a noise, or attempted to crawl under the table to start a game of hide-and-seek. 'Whit?' an outraged mother would hiss. 'Ye don't play in the doactor's surgery, so ye don't. Ye sit still and behave yersel'.' My mother had found a listening ear, and settled down to explain that she wasn't here for herself, but it was Molly who wouldn't eat and couldn't get over losing her grannie. So that was why I couldn't eat, I thought in surprise, it was because Grannie wasn't there to tell me what to do. When I remembered how often I had said 'Och but, Grannie, I don't *want* gruel', and she had said 'Sup it up, for it'll gi'e ye strength', I wished, oh how I wished, that she could give me a plate of gruel now. Oh I'd take it, and never a word of argument out of me. My longing for my grannie was so intense that it completely exhausted me, and I sat down on the surgery floor -- for the seats were for the adults – and went to sleep.

'Come on, hen, it's oor turn,' and my mother pulled me up and took me into the surgery. The doctor drew me towards him, his eyes full of troubled sympathy, while I stared tiredly past him. 'My, my, Molly,' he teased gently, 'where's the wee girl who used to run to open the door to me when Grannie had one of her attacks of bronchitis, eh? And a fine cup of tea you used to make for me too.' At that memory of Grannie sitting up in bed, checking that I had everything in readiness for the visit, my lips trembled, but my grief was too deep to find words for it, and too paralysing to be endured. My mother was explaining that all I wanted to do was sleep, and she had thought that would be a fine cure, for didn't everybody know that sleep was life? 'But not this type of sleep, Mrs Weir,' said the doctor, just as that neighbour had said. 'She must be roused or she will simply slip away in her sleep.' My mother's eyes widened in fear. 'You see,' went on the doctor, 'for the moment, strange as it seems in such a wee lass, she has lost the will to live.' The words seemed to be coming from a long way off, and I listened with a sort of detached interest.

Exercise was prescribed. A walk to the park every day without fail, whatever the weather, so long as I was warmly wrapped. Red wine to stimulate my appetite and improve my blood condition. Brown wholemeal bread for nourishment. Liver and tripe for easy digestion, and to correct my anaemia. It would be a terrible struggle for my mother to provide such luxuries, he knew, but he was sure she would do her best for me.

From that minute I knew no peace. I was dragged, whimpering and miserable, from my warm bed, my only refuge from the world which was so empty for me without my grannie. Every day I was forced to walk up Springburn Road to the Public Park, my feet dragging at every step. If we met a neighbour I would stand in silence, tears trickling down my white face, until the cold forced me to whisper, 'Come on, Mother, come *on*!' The neighbour would look at me, baffled, wondering aloud where Grannie's wee girl Molly had gone, and then would whisper to my mother that she doubted I would make old bones. 'She looks as if she is going into a decline,' she would whisper to my mother, who by this time was distracted out of her mind at the change in me. 'People don't go into declines nowadays,' she would declare stoutly, more to comfort herself than in defiance, and I would be trailed round every path in the park, and in and out the hot-houses, and my face examined to see if the blood had whipped up some roses.

When we got back, frozen almost to the bone, for it was bitter January weather, I would crouch on the fender stool in front of the fire, and my mother would pour out a glass of that horrible red wine, which I sipped while I nibbled a thin tea biscuit, to ease the bitter taste. That wine was like poison to me. It was worse than the port Grannie's chum used to give me on New Year's Day, but it had been bought for my good and I forced it down my throat, knowing what a sacrifice it had been for my mother to buy it. My mother would watch me shudder at the bitter brew and would say sympathetically, 'I couldnae drink it masel', hen, but the doctor said you have to take it or ye'll no' get better.'

The slightest noise in the house became intolerable. I, who had raced, and leaped and sung with the children of the teeming tenements, regarding noise as the normal accompaniment of living, was driven to the edge of hysteria by every high laugh, by the noisy caperings of my brothers, by the chattering of the visiting neighbours who came in nightly for a cup of tea and all the latest news. In the end, to give everybody else peace, I was sent down to sleep in old Grannie's downstairs. The quietness of her single end was bliss. It faced the front too, whereas our kitchen looked into the back court, and I enjoyed the novelty of the big street-lights shining in the windows. There was just the one room, with a shining, immaculate range, which was kept as perfect as my grannie kept ours, a neat and tidy dresser with no toys or clutter like ours, which had to keep all the junk of five people, and a high double bed set into the recess, with curtains to screen it off during the day. Very posh, this last touch, and I admired it very much. The curtains were of gold-coloured chenille, and were looped back at night, and the matching gold-coloured chenille bedspread carefully folded and laid on top of the stool, before we climbed into bed.

This grannie slept at the front of the bed like my own grannie, and I at the back, but I couldn't coorie into her back, for she had high blood pressure and had been recommended to lie almost upright against banked pillows. When I would turn during the night I was terrified to see her sharp face in ancient profile against the ghostly light shining in from the street. Her breathing was so shallow I thought this was another grannie who had died, and if she was dead I would have to climb over her, and I knew I would never be able to do it, and I would be trapped beside a corpse until somebody thought to come to the door to see what had happened to me. Heart hammering with fright, I would tug at her flannel nightgown to make her start and mutter, just to reassure myself she was still alive, and oh the blessed relief when she told me to be at peace and lie still.

My teachers, those dedicated creatures who knew us as well as our own mothers did, were getting worried. What had happened, they wondered, to the industrious wee girl whose hand had always been the first to shoot up to answer their questions? Where was the mental alertness of yore? Worst of all, what business had a girl of my age to have such lack-lustre eyes and apathetic mien?

There was a consultation among themselves, and a note was sent to my mother, suggesting that they apply for a place for me in Kilmun Seaside Home, a convalescent home run by a temperance charitable organization. They were sure a holiday in the country was what I needed, a complete change from my usual surroundings, and a chance to build up my strength. My mother had a great respect for the wisdom of those in authority, and she certainly didn't know what else to do with me, and couldn't afford to give me a holiday or take time off work in the month of March, which was still regarded as winter in Glasgow. Nobody went for holidays at any other time than the Fair, everybody knew that. But we'd all heard of convalescent homes, and greatly envied those who belonged to the Masons, or to the Co-operative staff, and who were sometimes lucky to be nominated for such a holiday at no expense whatsoever. We'd never dreamed of such a thing for ourselves, and never imagined the directors of any holiday home would look sideways to help us, even if we'd dared to ask them. But an application went in signed by the headmaster, and in due course the Board were pleased to inform us that I would be granted two weeks' stay at Kilmun Seaside Home from 2nd March. At any other time the mere idea of a holiday by myself would have had me lost in delighted wonder, but not this time. It was all part of the nightmare I was going through. The seaside in March. There would be nobody there. It would be empty. There would be just me and the sea. I was still only thirteen. Maybe my fate was going to catch up with me there, and I would share my story-book heroine's early demise far, far from my home.

It was a peculiarly hard spring that year, and the loch was frozen over in a sheet of glittering silver when I got off the bus. I caught my breath. I had never seen the icy beauty of a winter landscape before, and in spite of the dull ache in my heart, and the strangeness of solitary travel, interest stirred. Bare trees cut from ice stood motionless. Grey skies were heavy with more snow to come. The Home stood by itself in a beautiful empty landscape, so different from the crowded silhouette of the tenements, and suddenly I felt for the first time for months that I could breathe. It was exactly three months since Grannie had died, three months since I had drawn a breath free from wretchedness.

I can't remember how I got there. I think I travelled alone, seen off by some official of the charity. Certainly no member of my family came with me, for who had money for fares for such coddling, and anyway I would come to no harm. I had taken my brief farewells of them at home, certain I would never see them again, and I wondered if they would miss me very much, and say to each other: 'She never made old bones. She was only thirteen.'

After our room and kitchen tenement house I had never seen such space. Fancy having rooms devoted entirely to *sleeping*? A huge room with four beds in it, with real wardrobes to hold our clothes, was shared with three women. I had always been used to sharing, so this was no hardship, and we had each a bed to ourselves! What a waste it seemed. Fancy a whole bed for each of us when we could easily have managed two in each bed. It would have been warmer too. I had always been used to the comfort of a warm body to coorie into in bed, and it seemed chill and strange to find only draughty spaces in front and behind me when I tried to go to sleep.

The three women with whom I shared were a bit taken aback to find a wee lassie in their midst. 'Whit wis wrang wi' ye, hen?' they asked sympathetically. When they heard it was just something vague like not being able to eat, tiredness, anaemia, all lumped into the term 'nervous debility', they lost interest. They had had far more interesting illnesses. They told terrible tales of operations, which fascinated and horrified me at the same time, and I had wild visions of adult life being a succession of near-fatal illnesses from which I would be lucky to be rescued in the nick of time, and certainly with some vital part of me missing after a butcher of a surgeon had done his dire work. I began to think my grannie and my mother had surely been exceptionally lucky to have gone through life with every bit of themselves complete, and nothing left of their precious insides in pickle jars in hospitals. I shuddered at the prospect of my own insides being on exhibition for students at some future date, for my companions assured me cheerfully, 'Och it happens to everybody at wan time or another.'

These morbid conversations did nothing for my mental state, but I thoroughly enjoyed their tales of their romances. This was even better than Grannie's *My Weekly*, for I was getting it at first hand, and no inhibitions about my being 'far too young to understand'. Two of the women were spinsters, a name which intrigued me very much, for I'd never heard the word before. The other was a widow. Both spinsters had been engaged to soldiers who had perished long years ago for king and country; how sad and how romantic they seemed, in spite of honest faces scrubbed clean with soap and water, metal curlers in their sparse hair, and pink flannelette nightgowns covering them modestly from neck to feet, and sleeves which came down to thin wrists. We speculated for hours on how many children they might have had their lost loves returned from Flanders field, and what sort of houses they might have lived in. It was all most thrilling and enjoyable until the widow, for some strange reason, would interrupt to say, 'Aye, they're the best kind o' weans to have, the wans that never made ye greet, even if they never made ye laugh.' This effectively quenched all conversation, the light was put out, and I fell asleep furnishing the never-never-land houses of the poor husbandless spinsters.

The Home took men as well as women, and there was strictly no integration. Two long tables ran the length of the dining room. This was another source of amazement to me. A whole big room devoted entirely to eating, and the tables standing there all the time just to hold our plates and food, and never cleared to play at cards, or for homework, or games. I felt I was in a castle when they could afford such a room to stand empty except at meal-times. I had never dreamed of such space or luxury. At one long table the women were ranged down both sides. At the other table two rows of men faced one another. I wasn't in the least interested in those dull men, and never even looked at them, for I thought the women were far more exciting, but I noticed some of the women seemed very curious, and kept stealing little glances across the no-man's-land between the tables. At the top of the room the matron and her assistants sat at a small separate table, keeping an eye on the proceedings, and two local women served the food.

I still had little appetite, and can't remember much about the food, except on one terrible night when the cook burnt the scrambled eggs, and the smell filled the whole house. We all came into the dining room holding our noses, but, burnt or not, the horrible mess was served up to us. I tried to swallow it, remembering Grannie's wrath if any food was left, but I just couldn't force it down. I may say it successfully put me off scrambled eggs for many a long day. The adults were loud in their condemnation of the cook, and furious at not being offered a substitute dish in place of the spoilt eggs, but I thought it quite reasonable, for, after all, on a Sunday night they wouldn't have been able to get anything from the shops, which in any case were miles away, and anyway no buses ran on Sundays from the Home.

The authorities must have been terrified there would be any fraternizing of the sexes, because for our morning walks the females turned left on leaving the Home, and followed the loch-side, while the men turned right and meandered towards the hills.

The afternoon walks saw the routes reversed, the men taking the loch walk, and the females the hill route.

Not a word was exchanged as the groups set off in opposite directions, but many a surreptitious glance was exchanged over a shoulder before the distance grew so far between them that it was no good hoping to discover whether somebody had found them interesting enough to become flirtatious, albeit in silence.

As for me, my appetite was returning with the caller air, and my meagre pocket money, scraped together by my mother, was enough to buy me ginger beer in a stone bottle from a wee shop half-way between the Home and the furthermost point of our walk. I had never tasted ginger beer from a stone bottle before and thought it absolutely delicious. And there was Cadbury's chocolate too, narrow thick bars all joined together in a row which had to be broken by the shopkeeper to detach my penny bar, and sometimes if she was clumsy I got a wee bit from the bar next in line. I never stopped to think of the sense of being cheated which must have been felt by the next purchaser, as I stood there silently willing the girl to break the chocolate in my favour. No gambler watched the turn of a roulette wheel more breathlessly than I watched the breaking of those chocolate bars. I was obviously getting better in health when I could turn my mind to such cunning, with my taste for sweeties coming back unimpaired. I never realized how lovely it could be to feel appetite for food – and for life – slowly steal back.

The stone monument at the end of our morning walk carried words which I carefully memorized, and used to chant to myself:

> 'Lives of great men all remind us
> We can make our lives sublime,
> And departing leave behind us,
> footprints on the sands of time.'

I puzzled and puzzled over the meaning. Why wasn't it 'footsteps'? I wondered. Well of course, you could *hear* footsteps, but the minute they were out of earshot they wouldn't be

160

left behind. That was it. But then footprints wouldn't stay on sand very long either. The next tide would wash them away. Departing must mean death. I was much preoccupied with death just then. Slowly I came to the conclusion that it must mean that whatever you did in life, even if you made it sublime, you wouldn't make more impression on the rest of the world than a footprint would make on wet sand. But even that was a lot when you thought of all the people there were hurrying about trying to be famous, who would leave no impression at all. That must be it. I determined to make that my goal, and leave a wee footprint of my own. I wasn't sure how. I'd always wanted to be an actress – maybe that would be it. Or a writer. My compositions usually met with approval. I wondered which it would be.

I had left footprints on the sand at Girvan. And my mind swooped back to those long golden days when I tumbled over my wilkies on the sands, and my mop of hair landed on a spot where a dog had visited shortly before, and I was yanked back to the lodgings to have my hair washed before I put everybody off their ice-cream. Grannie's voice rose again in my ears, 'Michty Goad, could you no' watch where you were pittin' yer head? I'll need a claes-pin for my nose before I get this mess oot o' yer hair.' And the sense of utter loss engulfed me once more. But such moments were becoming rarer, and seemed slightly easier to bear in this strange new world of adults, and fresh air, and frozen landscapes. It was a sort of limbo for me. No school, no other children. For the first time in my experience I was the only child in a world of adults, and also for the first time in my life I had no messages to go, either for Grannie, or anybody else. No duties of any kind. Just endless hours to fill with reading, or walking, or listening to folks' ailments, or dreamily staring out of the window.

After a week of this I felt as though I had been away from Springburn forever.

On Sundays we all marched to church, but this time they were not able to make men and women go in opposite directions, so the men set off first, then, after an approved interval, the females followed. And sometimes on the way home, if the matron or her assistant hadn't come with us, one or two of the males would dawdle, and some females put on a pretty turn of speed, until they were within casual chatting distance of one another, and could indulge in the delicious forbidden activity of actually *talking* to one another. The main body of us looked a bit shocked at the few who indulged in this dalliance, but the sight of the main gates brought everybody to their senses, and when we marched through we were in strictly separate groups once more, and the naughty ones demure, with eyes cast down as though butter wouldn't melt in their mouths. I was astonished at this behaviour, and noted that grown-ups could be just as devious as children when rules were broken.

And then, unbelievably, it was almost the end of my second week, and soon it would be time to go back to my old life.

Although I hadn't as much as looked at the men, one of the men had looked at me. I think he must have been a kindly, concerned creature, like one of our own neighbours, whose eyes didn't just skip past the rest of his fellow-creatures, but noted what they saw. He went to the matron and remarked that this wee lassie from the tenements had shown such startling improvements in the two weeks she had been in the Home that he thought it would be a splendid idea if Matron applied for an extension, and let another two weeks set the seal on good health. My three stones twelve pounds had crept up to nearly four stones, and he urged her to try for another two weeks for me in this wonderful fresh air, with lots of good healthy walking, before plunging back into the asphalt jungle again. He himself, he said, would like to take me on gentle hill-walking expeditions to strengthen my limbs and extend my walking range, but the matron pursed her lips and shook her head at the very idea. It was quite impossible, she said. I was in her care. Possibly his motives were of the best, she wasn't doubting him, but the rules of the Home had to be obeyed and she was answerable to the authorities herself. However, she *would* certainly consider his suggestion that she apply for an extension of my stay, for she agreed I was quite transformed from the wee white-faced ghost who had arrived a short few weeks ago.

I heard all this from the matron's assistant later, and I was amazed at the man wanting to take me for walks. Any of the men I had known of in Springburn would have died rather than be seen taking their own children, much less anybody else's, for a walk. Their idea of recreation and relaxation was the pub or a football match. This man sounded a bit daft to me. But fancy the matron not letting him take me, or even asking *me* if I wanted to go. I felt indignantly that I should at least have been given a choice. I couldn't see anything wrong with the man. Daft maybe, but not wrong. Maybe he was training to be a minister, I thought. Grannie always said you could trust folk who were open about what they did. It was the sleekit-pooches you had to watch. Anyway, the words of this good Samaritan did not fall on stony ears. The matron applied. It was very unusual, the authorities said, but obviously I was a special case. I got my extra two weeks, and I grew stronger and firmer as day followed day. The weather was still bitter, and now when I came home from the walks, my cheeks were glowing and rosy, and I was hungry for every meal, even for the lumpy porridge. My grannie would have had plenty to say to the cook in that Home. I had seen Grannie making our porridge every morning in life, and I knew fine that the cook hadn't had the water boiling, and that she hadn't sprinkled in the meal slowly enough, or kept stirring as she should. Grannie was scathing of people who wasted good food, and who were too lazy to do things properly. But fancy that big house, with its posh dining room, and its rooms devoted entirely to sleeping, not having such tasty food as we enjoyed in our wee room and kitchen in Springburn. I had thought that the richness of a house ran like a thread of pure gold through every part of it. But it seemed it could stop short of the kitchen, whereas our wee room and kitchen had had a treasure of pure gold in my grannie. I was pleased at the picture of my glittering grannie, and then laughed at the very idea. I was getting fanciful, and would have to be careful, for Grannie always said day-dreamers just wasted their lives, and the happiest folk in all the world were those who knew how to work for their living.

Because of the extra two weeks I was staying at the Home, I spent my fourteenth birthday there, and on that icy March morning I realized I was maybe going to make old bones, after all, for I had come through this dreaded thirteenth year and I hadn't followed my schoolgirl heroine to an early grave. Usually birthdays meant very little in our house, maybe a wee hankie, or toasted cheese for tea, but this time, because I had been away from home for such a long time, my mother must have rallied all my chums to mark the occasion, and I was almost overwhelmed by the letters and cards which tumbled in the letter box at the Home for me. A huge pile stood by my breakfast plate, and I flew to the lounge to open them all. How beautiful they were. Fairies with glitter on their wings, flowers in impossibly beautiful vases, bluebirds flitting through blossom, violets for March, and shamrocks because I was born on St Patrick's Day. And *all* the chums had told me the end of the 'following-up' serial which I had missed by being away. We had followed the heart-breaking adventures of our screen heroes and heroines for endless weeks, and I fell into a daydream of delight, imagining them walking together into a golden sunset at the end of all their sufferings, to 'live happily ever after'. Oh I wished I could have seen it all for myself, but the words in every letter, 'She gets him in the end', told me all.

Somehow my mother had managed to send me a box of chocolates, and I handed them round to my room-mates after our supper. We had a concert that night among ourselves, and because they knew it was my birthday, I sang for them 'I passed by your window' and for an encore 'Mother Machree'. Unaccompanied, of course, for nobody knew how to play those pieces on the piano. But I didn't care. I had sung them dozens of times at our back-court concerts, and knew every note, and how to start on a key which wouldn't be too high for me when I came to the top notes. In fact when one of the old ladies marvelled at my confidence, and had been afraid I'd never get up to the high 'Oh God Bless you and keep you, Mother Machree' phrase, I said, with shattering belief in myself, 'Och I *knew* I would get up, I've done it before.' I spoke in all innocence, not having learned that there are times when breathing and vocal chords don't always work in harmony, and when fear of an audience can do strange things to a performer.

We got a bedtime cup of tea on my last night, because so many of us were leaving in the morning, and even the staff stayed to sip theirs with us and nibble daintily at their biscuits.

I was coaxed to sing again, and gave them Grannie's chum's favourite, 'Bonnie Mary of Argyle'. I had started on it before I remembered that the last time I had sung it had been for Grannie and her chum on what was to be her last visit on New Year's Day the year before. Now I was singing it to a room full of strange old ladies, and my own grannie would never hear it again. My voice faltered. Grannie's voice was suddenly real to me, and I could hear her saying as she had said a hundred times when I was tackling a difficult task which had me pechin' with annoyance, 'Come on noo, hen, pit yer best foot furrit'. And, magically, I felt my voice strengthening and growing firm and clear, just to please her. I sat down to warm applause, and I heard the voices of my adult room companions saying, 'Ye got a rer clap, hen. That wis awfu' nice. By jings, ye fairly mind a' the words.' I paid no attention. I was absorbed, wondering if this was a new kind of haunting Grannie was going in for. A curious sort of peace stole over me. I wasn't frightened any more. I think it was at that moment I truly realized Grannie's spirit would never leave me.

2

It was marvellous to be home again, but how wee and neat and tidy our room and kitchen seemed after the vastness of the Home. My mother had put a clean tablecloth on the table, just as if I was a visitor, and there was home-made jam, and cakes from the City Bakeries, and a wee print of my favourite fresh butter and, unbelievably, even a wee drop of cream in the tiny jug with 'A present from Girvan' written on it in gold.

For some reason I felt strange and shy. Maybe it was the tablecloth, or maybe just the shock of seeing our house with new eyes after being away such a long long time. I sat with my feet neatly placed together under the big chair, where I was perched right on the very edge, my eyes running round taking everything in, from the flaming coals in the range to the reflections in the brilliantly polished brass kettle on the mantelpiece. It was just like the New Year. I was frightened to move in case I dirtied anything. Even my mother seemed different. Not tired. Not in dungarees, but in a nice white blouse (*white*, and it a week-day, and us not expecting company – what could it mean?). After being with the old ladies in the Home, and sharing life with my spinster room-mates and the elderly widow, I had forgotten how young my mother was. How bright and wavy her red hair, how clear her pink-and-white complexion, and how small and slim her build. I was puzzled why I had never noticed all this before, and wondered if it was because I had never taken time to sit and look at anybody very much in our house before I had gone to that Home, for I had always been too busy out playing, and in the rush and stir of our tenement life we never actually sat and *looked* at each other.

My mother was full of questions. 'Whit wis it like, hen?', 'Were the folk nice tae ye?', 'Did they gi'e ye enough to eat?'

She had heard it all from my letters, for I had written to her every week, but she wanted to hear it all over again. After all, it wasn't everybody's wean in the tenements who had been away in a great palatial Convalescent Home for a whole month. If it had been Buckingham Palace she couldn't have been prouder or more impressed. She hadn't even seen it, but she took my word for its size and its richness, and she even embroidered an extra here and there later when she was telling the neighbours about it. She kept exclaiming over my rosy cheeks, and how well I had filled out, and declared she was sure I had forgotten all about them I had been away such a long time.

It was said in jest, but I very nearly had. In fact I had almost forgotten I had two brothers until they came charging in for their tea, then stood staring at me, kicking their feet awkwardly. 'Hullo,' they said. 'Hullo,' I said. Then they took in the laden table. 'Ohhh! Cakes!' 'I want the Fern cake,' said Tommy. 'And I want the coconut one,' said Willie. 'You'll give Molly her pick first,' said my mother, 'for I bought them seeing it was her first night home.' They grinned, for they had seen the chocolate liqueur cake which they knew was my favourite, and they knew there was no competition for the cakes they preferred.

And then I remembered what was puzzling me. 'Why are ye no' at yer work, Mother?' I asked. She paused briefly as she poured boiling water into the teapot. 'Oh, the job feenished. They put a' the women off, even the widows, and took men on.' I stared at her. I knew this was serious, for we needed every penny she earned. 'Ur ye on the Buroo, then?' 'Juist for a wee while. I've been promised they'll take me on at the Co-operative offices, cleaning, as soon as there's a place.' I opened my mouth to say something, for I knew how proud she was of her skill as a fitter in the Railways, and as a machine operator in the big workshops. 'Come on, come on, sit doon to yer tea, and don't bother yer heid the night about jobs for me.'

It was like a party after all the solid food at the Home. It was the sort of tea we all loved. Lashings of bread and jam and cakes and biscuits, and the richness of cream to trickle on top of the tea, to form strange patterns and then transform the

167

brew to a satisfying fine beige colour. Neighbours knocked at the door and came in to see me, and to rejoice in the sight of rosy cheeks, a phenomenon in the tenements as far as the girls were concerned. The boys sometimes acquired this healthy glow, racing up and down stairs delivering milk on frosty mornings, but the girls were mostly pale and on the thin side, like me. One neighbour brought her wee boy, who had very bad rickets. My mother had told me that this was because wee Eck's mother had been too poor to give him real milk when he was an infant, and had given him weak tea in his bottle and his bone's hadn't developed. I gazed with interest at his wizened little face, and at his poor bent legs, and I wondered if it would straighten them out now, if he were to drink nothing but milk forever and ever. He saw me looking at his legs, and I quickly looked away, but I needn't have worried, for he wasn't self-conscious about them. I had just learned those finicky ways with all those adults at the Home, who seemed mad if their peculiarities were pointed out, whereas we saw nothing cruel about singing about a wee humpty-backed man who roamed our streets:

'Wee Johnnie Morrie,
Fell over three storey',

in explanation of his deformed back. Johnnie himself didn't mind, and seemed proud to be the subject of a song. But I had found out already that everybody wasn't like us.

It was great to be back to a world which held children and folk of all ages again, and I found myself slipping back into the easy acceptance of childhood with every passing minute.

Then it was bedtime and I lifted the bed-pawn to pull out the hurley bed, where I had slept all my life with Grannie. There was nothing there! Nothing but the clothes basket, and the bath, the zinc bath where we splashed on Sunday mornings in front of the fire, and which was usually stored by our next-door neighbour, who had the privilege of using it for her own four children for providing this service. 'Where's the bed?' I cried out in alarm. Was everything changing now Grannie had gone? I wanted things to be as I remembered them, especially my bed.

My mother laid down the paper she was reading. She loved reading the papers 'from batter to batter', as she graphically put it, and not even my homecoming interrupted this luxurious devouring of the world news. 'Oh we gave it to the McPhersons. They've a new wean, and they needed the extra bed.'

That awful empty sickness of thinking of the hurley without Grannie threatened to rise and engulf me again, but my mother was going on: 'Aye, you'll have to go along and see the new wean. You'd think it was the first wean that had ever been born. Mind you, it's nine years since she had Ella, and she's fairly taken on wi' hersel'.' My wise mother, knowing of my passionate interest in babies, held my attention. 'When was it born?' I demanded. I loved seeing infants practically as soon as the doctor left the house (or, more often than not, the midwife, for doctors were only brought in in our tenements if there were complications, which there seldom were). I loved their wee red crinkled faces, and the way they fastened on to their mothers, like kittens, when they were hungry. Bottle babies were practically unknown in our world, and seemed a terrible waste of money, when the mothers had all that good milk themselves and it not costing a penny. I thought that mothers had this magic milk supply all the time, and wondered why they didn't feed anybody else's baby when it screamed with hunger as they held it. I realized there might be a little mystery somewhere, for I had heard a neighbour say with a laugh, when holding a baby which butted her in search of food and comfort, 'Aw there's nothing there for you, hen.' 'Why wasn't there?' I wondered. 'She's got bumps the same as all the other mothers.' Something held me back from asking, though. But I kept a watchful eye afterwards and realized that only the ones with babies had milk. The others just had the bumps in readiness for when they were needed! The more I thought of it, the more sensible it seemed, for it could be very uncomfortable to have had pints of milk slurping about if no baby had come along to use it up. Yes, a very good idea, I decided. God knew all about it and had arranged it perfectly.

The McPherson baby had arrived ten days ago, I learned, and it was so tiny that Ella's doll's hat had fitted its head. I drew an ecstatic breath. As wee as all that! Just like a doll. I couldn't imagine anything more perfect, and couldn't wait for tomorrow to rush along to see it. The hurley was almost forgotten, and my mother was taking the cover off the big bed in the recess where she slept, and telling me to get in. So I was to coorie in at her back now, instead of Grannie's. How high the bed seemed, and what activity seemed to be going on in my sleeping quarters after the stillness of the Convalescent Home, where nothing went on in a bedroom but undressing, some quiet chatter and sleep. The boys were playing with their football cards, covering up the names of the teams at the foot of the painted cards, and guessing the number of letters which made up the title. A correct guess meant surrendering the card, and howls of anguish went up when a favourite card was lost. My mother was rinsing out some clothes. A neighbour popped a head in to borrow a cup of sugar. Another neighbour came in on her way home from the pictures, her eyes red with tears over Norma Talmadge's parting from her lover. My head was spinning. Had it always been like this? Would I ever be able to sleep in this kitchen, humming with life and excitement. Oh it was lovely to be home, but a treacherous corner of my heart yearned for the tranquillity of that still bedroom in Kilmun.

But the space below the bed, where the hurley used to be, provided marvellous extra storage and we felt a heady sense of tidiness at being able to lay our boots and shoes there in a neat row, hidden behind the bed-pawn. The dirty washing could be kept there too, and my skipping ropes, and the bools and the jawries we used for our games at moshie, and the big doll Auntie had sent from Australia, and the jeely pan, and the girdle. How had we ever managed without it? The dirty washing was stowed neatly in the bath, for we only used the bath on Sunday mornings. It was nice to have it in the house all the time, though, but I learned it had caused a great feud when my mother asked politely if she could have it back now as we had room to keep it ourselves. While the hurley had been used, our next-door neighbour had kept our bath under her bed, and she had grown so used to doing her washing in it, as she hated to use the wash-house, that she had come to think the bath was hers, and that *she* was lending it to *us* when we had it for our Sunday bathing. She had been astounded at being asked to return it, my mother told me, and had actually cast doubts as to who had bought it in the first place. 'My Goad,' said my mother, 'her that hisnae two pennies tae rub the-gither trying to tell me that she had ever bought a bath!' She sighed with righteous indignation. 'I've aye been feart she would try to pawn it, for as sure as daith she's pawned everything else in the hoose except the weans.' The mere idea of pawning her children sent me off into peals of frightened laughter, but my mother said sadly, 'Och that man never knows if he'll have tae staun' up for his dinner when he comes hame or if the table will be away at the pawn. Ah don't know whit she does wi' her money, and her wi' a man's wages comin' in.'

To my mother, a man's wages represented the peak of prosperity. She was horrified at the fecklessness of those who let all that easy money slip through their fingers, for she herself had had to work for every penny, and she would say, shaking her head at their foolishness, 'Aye, Mrs So-and-So's an awfu' bad manager.' To her it was crystal clear that money had to be managed wisely or it would be like fairy gold – gone when it was needed most.

.She had every sympathy for wives who were left staring at empty purses while their husbands squandered the best part of their wages over the pub counter, and she had not the slightest commiseration for the man compelled to drown his sorrows. One night we heard a terrible bang outside our door, and when we had all rushed out to see what had caused it, could hardly make out anything but a black shape on the landing and clouds of dust rising to choke us. 'My heavens,' gasped my mother, 'it's Mr Irvine. He's fallen ower the banisters.' Mr Irvine was a notorious drunkard, and my mother decided he'd taken a dive over the banisters, blinded by whisky. Then as the dust cleared we saw we were staring at the Irvines' bass mat and not the body of the drunkard. At that moment his daughter came down to recover the missile, which she had thrown at her father in fury because all they had to eat for their tea was bread and margarine, and her father had come staggering home from work drunk. 'You might have murdered him,' said my mother looking at the size and thickness of the mat, and judging the height from which it had been thrown, for by this time she had learned that the mat had been aimed at the vanishing figure of Mr Irvine as he'd reeled downstairs to get away from his family's wrath. 'A good thing if I had,' said his daughter through gritted teeth. We were very shocked at this savagery, but not really surprised. Far better to be without a man at all than to have one who thought his wage packet was to satisfy his own selfish drouth. But my mother sent me up afterwards with a pot of her home-made black-currant jam to add a wee bit of luxury to the bread and margarine.

Everybody envied the wife who enjoyed the rare novelty of having a pay packet handed to her, unopened, and whose husband meekly accepted a small portion of it as pocket money. We had one on our stair, and although she looked, as my mother described it, 'as if butter widnae melt in her mooth', she obviously held her pale husband in terrorized thrall. Whatever she spent her unopened pay packet on, it wasn't on food, for her four small children were thin and white and listless, and her husband much the same. She, however, continually sported new hats, and 'peerie heels' on her smart shoes. The tenement women may have envied the pay packet, but they clearly despised the husband. 'Nae spunk at a',' they declared. 'A moose!' And, final damning words, 'Of course he's English. Saft, that's whit he is. A damned good feed would dae him the world of good.' I would have thought a soft Englishman who handed in every penny of his pay was a far better bargain than a Scotsman who drank away half his earnings, but the women seemed to find something in their own dour men which satisfied them. I decided adults were sometimes hard to fathom.

And one of the strangest things to understand about adults was how difficult it seemed to be for them to write a letter. I was always scribbling. I even made up the words on my Christmas cards, and I wrote the words for our children's concerts in the back courts, and anybody would have thought I was doing something special the way the neighbours respected this trick with the pen, for it was to our door they came if they wanted a letter of importance sent or read.

Even at the age of ten I was asked by an aunt to write a letter for her to a lawyer. A lawyer! I was terrified, but most impressed. She told me the gist of what she wanted to say, I phrased it in what I decided was formal language, she was delighted, and the lawyer apparently never raised an eyebrow. That, maybe, laid the foundations of my career as the tenement scribe.

When unemployment was rife in my native city, shabby boys and men would come to our door, and would sit in pathetic humbleness while I wrote out cogent reasons why their unemployment pay should be continued. I'd drum up proof of having 'genuinely sought employment', giving names, addresses and times of application. Great was the mutual rejoicing when it was agreed the few shillings a week would continue to be paid, and the children could eat a sausage with their stark diet of potatoes and bread.

For another I'd make earnest application for a job at sea, with recommendations from the Minister, and from our local JP as to the character of the man sitting so bright-eyed and hopeful watching me writing. I'd copy out references in my best handwriting, in ink, of course, with a brand new pen-nib given to me by the girl in the Co-operative – a nib which helped to make my childish hand seem more impressive and grown-up looking.

When a letter was required to impress upon the factor the urgency of a particular claim to have a sink repaired, or a leaky pipe mended, or a new pane put in a draughty window, the irate tenant came to me first, so that I could put it as forcefully and yet cunningly as possible. What the factor must have thought at receiving so many letters of complaint in the same handwriting, nobody stopped to think. It was enough if we could frighten him into doing the repairs, for we felt he would be far more likely to remember to alert plumber or glazier if a complaint was made to him in writing than if it were given verbally when he was collecting the rents.

I was so successful in getting pipes mended and the communal lavatories unstopped that I was in danger of getting no homework done at all, with the stampede of tenants eager to make use of me as a scribe. Nobody cared a scrap that it was my time they were using. What was time to a wee girl? And if I had the ability it was only correct I should use it to help them.

The Scots are great settlers, and everybody in our tenements had relatives in all parts of the globe. Many a letter I'd pen to cousins in Canada, or New Zealand or Australia, telling them that John, or Helen, or Nessie would soon be joining them, travelling on the SS so-and-so, and arriving on such-and-such a date, and would look forward to the reunion at the port of arrival. I even wrote letters for the emigrants to take with them, to be handed to their new employers, and copies by the dozen of the appropriate character references. I sometimes felt I was sending the whole of Scotland's young manhood and womanhood overseas on a tide of my letters.

And when we went down to the quay-side to wave them off, and enjoy a last eightsome reel before the tearful singing of 'Will ye' no' come back again', as often as not they'd pat an inside pocket and say, 'Aye, we've got yer references here, hen, you're a rare wee writer, so ye are.' I just hoped they would find somebody in Australia or New Zealand or Canada who would be able to write for them, or we'd never hear if they prospered or failed in those far-away places which held out such high hopes for them.

We seldom did hear. The usual dramatic intimation of prosperity was when we found them in our midst, dressed up to the nines in light-coloured clothes which would have dirtied in five minutes in the smoke of Springburn, eyes filled with wonder that they could ever have lived among us. This laconic habit of just getting on to a boat and heading for Scotland without so much as a letter was carried to extremes by an aunt and uncle of mine. He had landed in Australia at the end of the first world war, my mother told me, and kept promising to send for his wife as soon as he had gathered enough money for the fares. This went on for a year or so, until she became thoroughly fed up, and went down to consult the authorities as to how she could join him. To her delight, she was able to get a passage for herself and the three children under a special ex-servicemen's scheme, the small amount charged to be repayable by her husband from Australia. No sooner the word than the blow. Without a word to him, she packed up and set off for Sydney. He for his part had decided to give her a wonderful surprise and come home and take them all back to Australia.

He never dreamed of sending a letter, for where else would a wife and three children be but at home?

My mother told me she had nearly collapsed with shock when she met him walking up Springburn Road. 'Whit are you daein' here?' she screamed when she was assured he wasn't a ghost. 'Jessie and the weans will be in Australia by this time.' Now it was his turn to lean on the shop door to steady himself. As my mother told me dramatically, 'They had passed each other on the way.' I had a vivid mental picture of their ships barely grazing one another and couldn't understand why they couldn't have *seen* one another, and joined parties in mid-ocean.

I wasn't a bit interested in a distraught auntie arriving in a strange country with three children and no home or husband to go to, or hearing how the ex-service association cared for her in a hostel until her husband joined her. He, fortunately, had taken a round ticket, so there was no problem of finding his fare to get back to Sydney.

No, what thrilled me was the drama of those ships passing each other, and later when I heard the expression 'like ships that pass in the night', I felt it was surely invented to fit the story of my auntie and uncle who could have saved themselves a whole lot of trouble if only they'd written a wee letter to each other, telling of their intentions.

We thrived on drama in the tenements, where each knew everybody else's business, and another sea adventure we all sighed and thrilled over was that of the girl in the next close who went out to join the lad who had emigrated to Australia a few years earlier. She was only nineteen, had never been away from home before, and was put in the care of an emigrating couple, middle-aged, who had promised to keep an eye on her. Marion and Peter were to be married as soon as the ship docked, and we nearly swooned with delight as she described to us, before she left, how Peter would come rushing up the gangway with his best man and the bridesmaid, and they would go straight to the church and be married. He had a house for her, was in a marvellous job, and they would live happily ever after. She could see it all, and so could we. It was far better than the pictures, for it was happening to us.

We all went down to the Broomielaw to see the ship off. Melodeons played while we danced the reels, bagpipes droned sadly, 'Will ye' no' come back again', but this time it was all excitement, for it was a wedding celebration we all dreamed of, and the elderly couple were caught up in all the joy, and felt it was their own daughter who was the centre of all this attraction.

We heard nothing for months. Then Marion's parents had a letter from the elderly couple. This was a letter which had to be written, and it told how the atmosphere of the ship had completely turned Marion's head, and they had been able to do nothing with her. She'd been the maid-of-all-work at home, while her older sisters went out to work, and she'd never been used to being dressed in nice clothes every single day and to living what seemed to her the life of a millionairess. She was only travelling steerage, but it was all unbelievable bliss.

The Australian accent was glamorous as Hollywood to her simple ears, and she'd fallen madly in love with one of the ship's officers. She refused to listen to the old couple's advice to wait till she got to Australia, for the man might be a married man, and not to do anything she'd regret. We heard all the full details later when the old couple came home for a holiday. When they had got to the port where Peter was to meet them he'd rushed up the gangway, just as we'd imagined he would, with his best man and his bridesmaid, and Marion had drawn aside and said, 'I'm not getting off, Peter. I'm not getting married.' The old lady who was telling the story said he turned white as a sheet, and begged her to come off and at least talk it over. She wouldn't. Peter left the ship. They sailed on to Sydney. And, in the end, the ship's officer did turn out to be married. The old lady said he had been as dismayed as Peter at this turn of events, for, of course, it had only been a ship's flirtation to him and he didn't dream Marion would expect him to marry her.

My mother was on night-shift when this old lady had called to tell us all this, and she was nearly late for her work following all the details of the broken romance. 'What happened to Marion?' she asked as she scrambled into her dungarees. 'Did she stay in Sydney?' 'No,' said the old lady, 'I think she was too ashamed. She went up country and worked in a fruit farm, and she ate so much fruit she got a sort of blood disease and had to be taken to hospital. And, believe it or not, she married one of the doctors.'

'My goodness,' I thought. 'Marion, who used to take me down to the Tally's for a pokey hat. Who used to sing to me when I sat on the dresser and watched her scrub the kitchen floor. Abandoning Peter. Falling in love with a married ship's officer. Getting poisoned. And then marrying a doctor!'

Gosh, the penny matinée would have to be good on Saturday to beat all this.

3

The only time we ever went to the pictures was on Saturday afternoons. The evenings were totally undreamt of by us, for who could possibly have afforded sixpence or more to see the same show at night that we could see for a penny on a Saturday? It cost tuppence for the balcony, but I only knew of this from the prices written on the ticket window – I never had tuppence to patronize this exclusive part of the cinema, nor had anyone else I knew. Downstairs was good enough for us, and we queued patiently the moment we had swallowed our dinner, which was our name for the glorious feast of ham and a shared fried egg which we always had on Saturdays, and which represented for us the tastiest and best dinner we could imagine. What a marvellous day Saturday was. No school for a start, and even when Grannie was alive, hardly any messages, for all the week-end food was laid in by Friday afternoon when I came home from school, and the only thing I was likely to be sent for on Saturday were some mutton pies from Torrance's the bakers, if there was enough money for them, after I came home from the pictures.

We didn't even play in the back courts on Saturday mornings. Those with enough pennies tore along to the newspaper shops to make careful selection of their favourite comics, and the rest of us breathed down their necks to follow the adventures of colourful boys and girls who led such stirring lives compared with ours. The purchasers of the comic papers were cocks of the walk on Saturday mornings, and would often be carried to the shops shoulder high by some penniless volunteer who would cry, 'Gi'e ye a cerry-coad doon to the shop, if I get first read of your comic efter you've read it yoursel'.' This offer was often taken up, and it was like some Eastern ceremony, with the rich one perched high above the head of his human beast of burden, arms held out to balance himself, fists gripped securely by the trotting boy, the rest of us racing alongside to take part in the thrilling purchase, and enjoy the sight of a brand-new clean comic. Comics changed hands again and again from one Saturday to the next, their value going steadily down with each exchange, and their colours getting grubbier and grubbier, as unwashed hands smoothed them out and drooled over their contents. Once read, they could be exchanged for another second-hand comic, and in this way we all managed to read every comic published, although the original purchasers were a mere one apiece.

Sometimes I helped a chum deliver greengroceries. She had left school and landed an enviable job as message girl in a greengrocer's shop for the splendid salary of nine shillings a week. It seemed an odd sum to me, somehow. Why not ten shillings, I wondered? That was a nice round sum. My chum was indignant when I mentioned this. 'Well, it's more than the seven-and-six Nellie is getting in the dairy,' she exploded, 'but if you think nine shillings is so funny, then you needn't bother to come and help me deliver the baskets on Saturday.' 'Oh I don't think it's funny,' I assured her, seeing my treasured peep at the 'toff's houses' vanishing under her rage. 'It's just that I thought you were worth ten shillings.' Oh! cunning one that I was. It worked, as I hoped it would. And I was instructed to wait up the road, out of sight of the shop, for she didn't want her boss to think she couldn't manage the heavy baskets herself. That nine shillings meant potatoes and cabbage and ham for their Saturday dinner, for her mother, unemployed dad, and three brothers and sisters, instead of potatoes and oatmeal and a bit of margarine. Besides many a wee 'extra' for their teas during the week.

So I would hide in the doorway of the Maypole Dairy until I saw Maggie stagger up the road, the big brown shiny basket grasped tightly in both hands. It was a grand basket, and we both approved and admired its fine quality, even if it was a ton weight to carry. We balanced it methodically between our crossed hands, and headed for Balgray Hill and the houses of people who seemed to us rich beyond the dreams of avarice. I had often run along the narrow alleyways between those big houses, on my way to the Public Park, and had never dreamed that those brick walls actually represented the ends of gardens, and that once through the little door in the wall, one found real green grass, and flowers, and *back doors* to the houses. I had once heard a man in the butcher's, ordering two chops, say to the assistant, 'Tell the boy the back door', and wondered what he could have meant. Now I knew. Deliveries were made at the back doors, straight into the kitchens, so that the posh fronts of the houses wouldn't be dirtied or made untidy. I was very impressed. Maggie and I would lug the big basket into back porches, bang the knocker and wait until we heard a voice say 'Come in', or have the door opened to us. We would tip the potatoes into big boxes, lift out tomatoes and fruit carefully, stand by patiently until everything was checked to make sure the greengrocer had sent only goods of perfect quality, and, if we were lucky, be given a biscuit at some houses, or even a ha'penny. But we hardly ever got money, for these posh people settled their accounts monthly, and so didn't have to hand money over to the delivery girls. We were especially fond of one house which employed a cook – fancy, a cook! – and if this large-hearted creature had time, she'd make us a cup of tea, or, better still, some hot cocoa if it was a chilly morning. She made delicious rock cakes, and it was a field day for us if we were given one of those to nibble with our hot cocoa. Then we had to run the rest of the way to catch up, for Maggie's boss knew practically to the minute how long she should take to return with an empty basket. I thoroughly enjoyed this glimpse of how the other half lived, and my mother and Grannie seemed highly amused at my descriptions of the fine kitchens, and gratified that I found no cooking range which was as shining as our own. It was a sad day for me when Maggie was promoted to serving behind the counter and my Saturday morning deliveries to Balgray Hill came to an end.

While the job lasted, though, these deliveries filled my Saturday mornings, and then it was a sprint home for my dinner, then out to queue for the pictures. We had a grand choice. The Princes was my favourite. Clean and comfortable, and just out of the wind for queueing. The wee Ideal was favoured by a lot of other children, especially as there was a well-tried method for 'skipping-in' without paying. An unguarded door was stealthily opened by the one who had paid, and his pals slipped through for nothing. It was a terrible risk, and an awful showing up if you were caught, and I never knew any girls who did this. Only the boys had the daring, or the cheek, depending on how you looked at it. Anyway, as I was an ardent member of the Church, Sunday School, Bible Class, Guides and Band of Hope, I was sure God would have struck me dead if I had tried it!

The Kinema, or the 'Coffin', as it was called because of its shape, was up the High Road, but was not among the favourites of the children. It was a concrete building, cold and cheerless, and far too near the cemetery for comfort, although the grown-ups didn't seem to mind, and it was usually packed in the evenings.

The Public Hall had pictures too, strange films with French actors with dead-white faces and black lips, and frightening films about monsters, but they also had marvellous 'following-ups', as we called the serials, and once you'd seen the first episode you just *had* to go back for the whole twelve weeks.

Also, they had a rare wee man called Dougie who told us all what we could expect to see the following Saturday. He was a great character, loved by us all.

The lights would go up after the big picture, and wee Dougie, the projectionist, would make his stately way from the magic room where he worked the projectors, round the gallery, thence down a flight of steep stairs to the stage. We children waited in a state of eager anticipation – eager, but far from silent. At the first sound of his footsteps, we chanted in unison 'Here's Dougie, here's Dougie', a noisy chorus which may be thought to have been some embarrassment to the man. Not a bit of it. He was quite unmoved, and neither speeded his footsteps nor slackened his pace. He chewed rhythmically on a piece of tobacco and ignored our cries. He may even have enjoyed being the centre of attraction for this brief moment each Saturday matinée, for we were certainly never told to shut up.

Having reached the centre of the stage, he would hold up a

hand for silence. He obtained instant obedience. You could have heard a pin fall. For weren't we to hear of splendours and thrills in store for us next Saturday? And on those special occasions, when the current serial had finished, wouldn't we be told what hair-raising adventures were to be ours for the next twelve weeks? Tucking the tobacco safely into a spare corner of his cheek, and in a voice which reached every corner of the cinema, he would give us a word picture of the attractions for the coming week. Names of our favourites were greeted with yells and cheers. The announcement of a lovey-dovey picture met with groans and cat-calls. He had us in the palm of his hands, and we responded vociferously to each announcement.

His brief moment of glory over, he took the long walk back to the projection room, accompanied this time by our chanting 'Good auld Dougie: good auld Dougie'. He would disappear through the little door at the back of the gallery, the lights would go out with a blinding suddenness which plunged us into dramatic darkness and made us catch our breaths almost in fear. Then the screen would spring to life, usually after a false start which we basely jeered. Dougie was in command of the projectors, and we were lost in the life pulsing on the screen for the next hour.

We were all very docile in this cinema, apart from our noisy reception of wee Dougie, maybe because it was the Public Hall during the weekdays. But in the Princes we always seemed to go wild with an excess of energy before the pictures started, and raced up and down the passages downstairs in the stalls, throwing oranges or apples to one another, and changing comics.

The plutocrats upstairs, though, enjoyed the luxury of fighting to place themselves within spitting distance of the wide beam of silvery light which shone from the window of the projection room to the screen. Within a certain strategic range they could send showers of quicksilver through that magic ray, never pausing to wonder what happened to their transformed spittle when it reached the heads of the unfortunates sitting underneath. I don't suppose I'd have given it a thought myself had I been lucky enough to be able to penetrate the mystery of the posh seats in the balcony. They didn't follow such actions to their conclusion. It was joy enough to be able to make silver showers with their saliva, and how I envied those who could perform this miracle, even if it was often my luckless head which received the shower once it had gone through its silver beam. It was much better than sparkling frost, for it cost nothing, but my mother would wrinkle her nose in disgust when I came home bearing only too obviously the evidence of the pastimes of the upstairs spitters, and my head would be plunged beneath the cold tap to rinse it clean, my yells of anguish completely ignored as the icy water hit my warm scalp. Sunday morning was for hair-washing, and I needn't think I was having kettles boiled up specially for me on Saturday at tea-time if I was silly enough to sit underneath people who had such bad habits. Bad habits! I kept quiet about my secret longing to be able to indulge in such things myself.

When the cinemas emptied after the matinées, the boys, like the innocent, unconscious animals they were, immediately relieved themselves. Now that *was* a bad habit, I quite agreed. We girls turned our faces away delicately, and pretended we were unaware of the fierce jets battering the corrugated fence which lined the side exits. If the male and female adults in Kilmun were forbidden to mix, we needed no such embargo. We didn't choose to mix. Girls went with girls, and boys enjoyed the company of boys. When boys were very small they were looked after by older sisters or bigger girls, but the moment they realized that boys had far more exciting games like 'buckety-buck-buck-buck' played with a tin can, and involving fast races through the closes, and back courts, and that boys had far higher jumps from the dykes than mere girls, they were off. They would have been regarded as Jessies if they had behaved otherwise, and even mothers and sisters accepted this, though sometimes with sighs of misgiving when the toddlers were very wee.

We hated having to take any of the wee boys with us to the matinées, for they often became frightened, and started to yell, and an attendant would race down the passage, jerk a thumb in the direction of the screaming boy and shout, 'Who's wi' this wean? You? Right, oot wi' him.' There was no possibility of argument. If you dared protest he simply charged along the row, lifted both noisy child and his accompanying sister or bigger girl bodily, and put both outside the door. Nobody came to the rescue, for one word from anyone only resulted in him or her being hauled from the seat and pushed outside with the others. And, of course, we all wanted to see the end of the big picture.

When I came home I used to re-enact every bit of the fantasy I'd seen on the screen for my grannie, or my mother, and later for any neighbours who came in for their bedtime cup of tea with us. Old Mrs Peebles used to declare, 'My Goad, it's as guid as being there masel'.' Grannie and my mother would frown at her, for they felt I needed no encouragement in this direction, since I play-acted far too much as it was. Mrs Peebles had been frightened off the cinema for life because one night, years before, she had gone when there was a film showing a terrible storm of rain, thunder and lightning. She had jumped to her feet and shouted, 'My Goad and I've left ma washin' oot.' She'd run from the pictures, only to find the streets outside bone dry, for, of course, the storm had been on the screen. Not only had she made a perfect fool of herself in front of everybody, but she didn't even get back inside again to see the end of the picture. If you wanted to go out for any reason you had to obtain a 'pass-out' ticket, and Mrs Peebles in her passionate rush to rescue her washing had no such thought in her head. So, no pass-out ticket, no re-entry. How unjust that seemed to her, and to us when she'd told her story for the hundredth time. But her dramatic rush from the 'Coffin' cinema passed into Springburn lore, and was related with tears of laughter to every newcomer to the tenements. But the cinema never got another penny of her money as long as she lived. She learned of all the plots and dramas through me, and in her I had my perfect audience. If it was a comedy, I was 'faur better than wee MacGreegor'. If it was a drama, I was 'faur before yon Garbo wumman'. She heard of every single episode of the serials from me, and was just as eager to hear how the heroine or hero had been rescued as I was to tell it. I hadn't realized I was maybe beginning to feel superior to this simple woman until I came in from Sunday School one day and began memorizing the text we'd been given. Mrs Peebles was in having a cup of tea when I came home from Sunday School. 'How beautiful upon the mountain,' I intoned, and then stuck. To my amazement Mrs Peebles continued: 'Are the feet of them that trespass not.' I stared at her open-mouthed. 'Do you know that, Mrs Peebles?' I asked. 'How do you know that? We just got it in the Sunday School the day.' Her eyes twinkled at me knowingly. 'Aye, I know it weel, lassie,' she said. 'Ah'm no' juist a heathen, ye know, even if I don't gang tae the pictures.' I could feel my face getting scarlet. 'Och, I didnae think ye were a heathen, Mrs Peebles,' I protested. 'It was just . . .' and my voice trailed away. 'Aye, it was just ye didnae think I wid ken a thing like that.' I was thankful when my mother said, 'Don't scuff your good shoes. Put on your slippers and sit doon at the fire.' But I looked at Mrs Peebles with new eyes after that, and I realized it wasn't only my teachers who knew far more than I did, but the tenement women knew a thing or two as well.

They took note of every change in our appearance, those neighbours of ours, and when I came back from Kilmun they noted with pleasure that I had grown rounded and healthy, and that I had a 'fine fresh colour'. They weren't the only ones who noticed me. To my annoyance and slight dismay, the boys began taking an interest too. I had absolutely no interest in *them*. I was astounded when a chum's brother slid a little note into my hand as I stood on the mat outside their house waiting for Lizzie to join me. When I opened it I read: 'Dear Molly, I was asking for you.' I screwed it up and threw it back at him. 'What a stupid thing to write,' I thought, angrily. And then, at the very idea of his regarding this as a letter, I began to laugh. His face grew scarlet, and then in mounting amazement I noticed him mouthing something. What was he trying to say? I stared at his contorted lips. 'Give us a kiss,' he was miming. I pretended I couldn't understand his fierce grimacing and mouthing, and marched out of the close. 'I'm not coming for you again, Lizzie,' I informed his surprised sister. 'You'll just have to climb the stairs and come up for me.' 'But why?' she protested. 'It's easier for you to come for me, because I live in the close and you've to come downstairs anyway.' 'I don't care,' I said. 'Your brother's daft, and I'm not coming to your door again.'

And I didn't. Every time I saw him afterwards I burst out laughing to cover my embarrassment at the mere thought of kissing that contorted mouth. I was probably influenced by Grannie's short sharp treatment of one schoolboy who had tried to make me a present of a puppy. He had brought it to our door, and Grannie had seized the broom and swept him from the mat, puppy and all. Poor David. I didn't dare look at him in school after that. He was English, his father having been transferred to our Railways, and he didn't realize it was soft to carry on like this, especially as I was about ten at the time. I didn't reason that Grannie wanted no truck with a puppy which would have to be fed and exercised and which would add to her work. I just took it that I was not to bother my head with boys, who were only a nuisance anyway, so Lizzie's brother received only scorn from me. I didn't even like being teased about boys. One sure way of rousing me to fury, as he well knew, was for a neighbour of ours to pretend he had seen me from his kitchen window playing in the playground at school with a wee bandy-legged boy. 'Aye,' he would say dreamily, 'I saw ye tak' yer cheuch Jean from yer mooth, and gi'e him a wee sook at it, and then take it back again.' 'I did *not*,' I would shout angrily. 'I widnae dae any such thing.' 'Och aye, I saw ye a' right,' the old man would say, 'and a bonnie sicht it wis. He's a nice wee fella in spite o' his bandy legs.' I would be near to tears by this time, and baffled by the impossibility of making anybody believe me when an adult said such untrue things. Then he would relent and say, 'Och weel, maybe it wisnae you efter a', maybe it wis Ellie Cairns.' As Ellie Cairns was about six inches taller than I was, and twice as fat, I felt everybody would think the old man was just letting me down lightly, pretending to mistake some-body so different for me, and that in the end they *would* believe I'd been playing with the bandy-legged Joe, and sharing my toffee ball with him. When I complained about this to my mother, protesting, 'But, Mother, it's such *lies* Mr Simpson tells,' she just laughed. 'Och it's only his fun. What does it matter. You should just laugh at him and he would soon stop tormenting you. It's because he kens you'll get your dander up that he does it.' But her words fell on deaf ears. I wasn't wise enough to pretend I didn't care, and had to content myself with dodging Mr Simpson when I could.

How betrayed I felt one night when I came in from playing up the High Road, when Grannie was still alive, and had found Mr Simpson actually sitting in our house chatting to her. He'd called on somebody upstairs with a message, and Grannie had been at the door when he was on his way down again. He had marched in and sat himself down at the fire, and produced his whisky bottle and poured a glass out for Grannie. When I appeared she handed it to me, with a whispered, 'Put it in the press, hen, I canna drink a' this whisky.' I, as a Rechabite, was horrified at the idea of my grannie sitting consuming whisky with this torment of an old man, and neither of them ill, for the fiery spirit was only consumed in our house in case of ill-health. 'Will I pour it doon the sink, Grannie,' I asked eagerly, seizing the glass from her hand. 'You'll dae nothing o' the kind,' she'd answered fiercely, forgetting to whisper. 'Pit it in the press as ye're tellt, and it'll dae us as medicine for the rest o' the winter.' I wanted to pour the hated Mr Simpson's whisky down the sink in front of his very eyes, but I didn't dare rebel against Grannie's wishes, so I put it in the press beside the sugar, and hoped somebody would knock it over when they went in to get the things to set the table.

I felt there was no end to the mischief this wicked old man could make, what with tormenting me and then encouraging my own grannie to indulge in the evils of strong drink. I couldn't think of a single way of getting my own back, unless maybe I wouldn't go to see him when he was dead and lying in his coffin.

4

In our childhood, death wasn't hidden away as an obscenity from which we must all be protected. It was on calling terms in the tenements, and came at any age and at any time, and not just in old age. It was always good for a bit of drama to brighten up all our lives, not least being the details of how the loved one had passed away.

We would listen, enthralled, to tales of 'She sat up and gazed at the ceiling, as if she was seeing something we couldn't see, and then she gave a beautiful smile and breathed her last.' Oh how marvellous, we felt, how peaceful! We hoped we would be lucky enough to pass to the other side with such a welcome smile on our own lips. When wee bedridden Donald had died his mother told us he had looked up over the top of the wardrobe and cried, 'Mammy, Mammy, I can see the children playing in the sky and they've all got wings. Oh I'm so tired, Mammy, it will be lovely to have wings to lift me up and take me everywhere without walking,' and then he had held out his arms and laughed, and passed away. How could we be sad at wee Donald's release when he had been able to pass on to us what heaven was like before he had joined the angels?

I couldn't reconcile those stories with the sight of a neighbour's dying husband whom I had seen when I went in to deliver some messages for her, and which had so unnerved me that I had been unable to eat for days afterwards. That was an exception, I decided, the ones who happily left for heaven must be the rule.

We all believed with utter conviction that we would all meet again in heaven afterwards, and we were only too willing to be convinced by the dying visions that the happy land truly existed, and the sight of it to glazing eyes would make the prospect of leaving home and family very easy to bear. This familiarity with the grim reaper who visited the tenements so frequently, and our trust and confidence in life after death, armed us against a too-consuming grief. Death seldom came as a bolt from the blue, to find us unprepared, so we were able to cope with it. And the rituals we followed helped the bereaved to get over their grief. Mourning neighbours would have been very hurt if we had shown no interest in the corpse which lay coffined on the big table in the best room, where no fire burned during the three days of lying in state, and where the chill air struck to the heart as we entered to pay our respects, especially in winter. Bodies were not hidden away in chapels of rest in our childhood. They were on view for everyone to visit, and we went to see every corpse in our tenement, from babies to old men, and nobody thought it might be unseemly for children to have to face such things in the midst of play. Life had to be faced, and death too, and we thought it right that our loved ones stayed under our roof until the moment came for burial, and that everyone should want to gaze on their faces for the last time before they went from us to the cemetery. The quality of the coffins was a subject of much comment, and the women would agree that 'she had given him a beautiful send-off, with that polished mahogany coffin with the lovely handles and pure silk cords'. Penny a week insurance policies were taken out even before a birth certificate was obtained, to make certain of a proper burial. To have to be buried on the parish was felt to be a great disgrace. The women pursed their lips over one old woman, too poor or feckless even to afford the penny insurance. 'Ah well,' she would say cheerfully, 'if they don't bury me for decency they'll bury me for stink.' This was a dreadful attitude, everyone said, and the remarks on beautiful coffins were very pointed when she was in the company. For didn't everyone know parish coffins were made from orange boxes? One of the famous phrases of our childhood, often used by music-hall comics in lighter mood, was, 'Wid onybody like a last look at the corpse before he's screwed doon?' We saw nothing funny in these words used by the undertaker before the final solemn carrying out of the body, but could recognize the humour of the situation, of course, when applied to a drunk man on the stage.

I was always struck with the chill dignity of people in death. Their remote calm completely transformed them from the flesh-and-blood people I had known and perhaps played with. Adults liftcd us children up to place a hand on the brow of the corpse, because this was said to prevent nightmares afterwards, but in my case it induced them, and I used to shudder with fear at actually making physical contact with those waxen faces. 'No, no,' I would whimper, 'I don't want to touch wee Jimmy's forehead. No, I don't care if I get nightmares. No, no, no.' If I were forced to lay a hand on a clammy brow I felt haunted for weeks afterwards. It was considered a terrible disgrace to be so reluctant to touch anybody's loved one, and nobody else seemed to mind. I couldn't understand myself why I didn't mind looking at corpses, but yet couldn't bear to touch them.

The Irish Catholics held wakes, which struck us as being very heathenish. Fancy sitting up all night, all those men and women and children, drinking and carousing as if it was a party! It was even hinted that bottles of whisky were put in beside the corpse in case he was buried alive, and he'd have a wee drop to comfort him when he found himself under the cold clay. 'Buried alive'! That haunted many of us, and we listened, trembling, to stories of coffins having been dug up and the corpses turned over on their faces, or eyes staring with terror, and clawed marks on the coffin lid where they had scrabbled to get out. Cremation was practically unknown in my childhood, and certainly unthinkable for working-class people, but those stories of people being buried alive so tormented me that I made everybody promise, especially during the period following Grannie's death when it was predicted I 'wouldn't make old bones', that when I died they would see to it, 'cross their hearts and hope to die', that I was well and truly cremated. Of course they all promised, and although I felt sure they wouldn't have the least idea how to go about it, I was reasonably comforted. Nobody had to invent terrors for us, we invented them for ourselves, and not a soul worried about the effect on our young minds of all those macabre tales. And they were right. For as time wore on we forgot them, and, apart from the Irish wakes, accepted all the rituals of the next funeral with undiminished zeal.

We had a lot of Irish people beside us, who had come over to work in Glasgow, and my mother always described them as coming 'from the bog'. I used to picture them walking with feet sucking at wet peat to get to us. They greatly amused us by taking a long time to get accustomed to tenement life, and it used to be many months before they realized they were walking on good linoleum, and that they mustn't just chuck down their tea-leaves on the kitchen floor to empty the pot, for there was no turf floor in Springburn to soak all the lees up.

Their vocabulary was a source of entertainment too. One of the mothers came charging into the back court one day and demanded, 'Hiv ye seen John's faddle?' 'His whit?' we asked. 'His faddle. He had it not ten minits ago, and one of you spalpeens has taken it, so ye have.' We stared at each other in perplexity. What could a faddle be? 'Whit is it like?' I asked her, inspired, for a description seemed the only way we could find out. 'It's a wee thing, made o' silver, and ye blow it like this,' and she stuck her comb into her mouth and blew out and sucked in. We rocked with laughter. 'Ye mean a mooth-organ,' we gasped. Oh these Irish were comics and no mistake. Fancy calling a moothie a faddle! And then I laughed even harder, for as I said the word, it dawned on me she was saying 'fiddle' with her Irish accent. She thought a mouth-organ was a fiddle. Aye, my mother was right, they came from the bog, all right, but you had to like them, they were so funny. They didn't even go down on their knees to wash out the closes, as the other women did, they stood upright, then bent over double from the waist so that we could all see their bloomers as they swished back and forth with a soaking wet cloth. 'My heavens, you could swim through the close when thae Irish have washed it,' the women would tut-tut in vexation, 'and the weans tramp a' that water right up to the top flat.' However often they were told, they refused to get down on their knees, for the cold stone struck them as hard and unyielding compared with the soft earth they had come from in Ireland. So we sighed and put up with it, glad that ours weren't the 'dirty Irish' and at least knew the value of soap and water.

We always thought we knew the best way of doing everything, from washing closes with well-wrung-out cloths, to making briquettes to stoke the fire from sugar bags filled with dampened coal-dust. But if there was one field where we felt we excelled above all others it was in the matter of home cures. Doctors were only called in when all else had failed. Apart from the cost, we had great faith in the folk medicine which had been handed down to us from one generation to the next.

For whooping cough the favourite cure was to suspend the victim over a tar-boiler, or 'torry-biler', as we called them. During an epidemic of the 'whoop' it only needed a whiff of the boiling tar to send us rushing home. 'Mammy,' we would pant, 'the torry-biler's here. Do you want to haud Willie ower it to cure his whoop?'

Mothers would seize unwilling victims and drag them from the house – no one was keen on having this cure himself, but all thoroughly enjoyed the sight of others getting it. Soon there would be a procession of mothers, patiently queuing to hold the spluttering child over the boiling, bubbling inferno, smoking like hell itself.

'Take big breaths, son,' they would urge. 'Draw it right doon into yer chest, and you'll no' cough any mair.' The victim, gasping at the sudden rush of tarry smoke which threatened to choke him, would cease coughing from sheer fright. Mothers would nod with triumphant smiles at each other, well satisfied that this free cure had worked once more.

Mind you, there were terrible tales of butter-fingered mothers who had allowed wriggling children to fall right into the bubbling pitch, later to be extricated coated forever in a deadly black embalming jacket. We'd never actually *known* anyone to whom this had happened, but the mere thought that it *might* have happened, and could do so again, was enough to make us stifle the slightest cough whenever we had occasion to pass the tar-boiler in company with an adult.

It was this added risk which made the sight of other children held high over the tar take on the excitement of a horror film. We would watch them with our breaths held in suspense until each little victim had feet planted safely on the pavement again. Only then would we resume our play, finding some of the soft tar to make 'torry-balls', which we rolled between our palms. Hardened in cold water, we used them like marbles for our games.

Some more fanciful mothers, with influential relatives, managed to get a card which admitted them to the gasworks, and swore by the effectiveness of the fumes there. The children were marched into the retort chamber, then instructed to climb upstairs and inhale deeply, to allow the gas fumes to circulate in their wheezing chests. It seemed to work, too, in spite of the envious sneers of those who couldn't get cards to take them inside the gasworks, and who declared it was just the diversion of the journey and the excitement of getting inside this impressive building which cured the weans.

One horrible scourge in our tenements was ringworm. I caught it myself, because a wee girl in my class at school fancied the tammy knitted for me by Grannie. She snatched it off my peg and pranced around the playground with it the whole of playtime one day, before I could grab it back. I jammed it firmly over my own curls and wore it in school the rest of the morning in case she would run away with it, for I knew Grannie would be mad if I lost it. What I didn't know was that the cheeky wee girl had ringworm and the infection had found a new home in my scalp! Home cures were no good this time and I was hauled off to the doctor, where every curl was cut off, then my head was shaved, and a bottle of iodine poured over it. I was taken to that surgery every Sunday, which was the one day my mother could spare from work, and more iodine poured over until the infection was killed. Oh the shame and misery of that shaved head! To be a skinhead in our tenements meant only one thing – ringworm! It shouted aloud as though I had carried a bell, and intoned 'Unclean, unclean', and left such a mark on my mind that I could never again be persuaded to let anybody try on my hats, nor would I even try one on in a shop afterwards, in case anybody with ringworm had been there before me.

Another head invasion, almost impossible to avoid in the tenements, was nits and head lice. The sight of fingers scratching at our heads was the signal for my mother to send us down without delay to the chemist for some quassia chips. These wee wood-shaving-like things were boiled up in water and the liquor strained off, and then a comb was dipped in the brew and drawn from root to tip of our hair. This went on for days, till all the eggs were tracked down, but unlike the iodine, which was drastic on hair roots, the quassia chips brew gave the hair a lovely gloss.

Borrowed combs were said to be the cause of spreading nits from one to another, and for a while we'd remember never to lend anybody our comb, then freedom from itch would make us careless – we'd lend our comb, and the quassia chips went on to boil again.

Worms was another affliction of our infants. It was quite usual to hear big brothers or sisters asking the chemist for a 'worm powder for my wee sister'. 'How old is she?' the chemist would inquire, unmoved at the thought of a human being having worms. I used to shudder at the thought of those wriggly things in anybody's inside, and wondered how they got in there in the first place. It was whispered that pieces spread with oatmeal and sugar resulted in worms, but I liked this concoction so much I refused to believe such a tale.

We all believed implicitly that the huge jars on the chemist's shelves, filled with orange or royal-blue liquid, held the unborn babies till the mothers came into the shop to buy them. We'd stare intently at those bottles, imagining we could see the tiny infant shape swimming about in this glamorous liquid.

We were most interested in each other's purchases and could diagnose each ailment from the goods bought. Gregory's Mixture, declared by my mother as a marvellous cure-all, meant somebody's stomach was out of order. 'Enough to cover a sixpence' was the recognized dose. This was stirred in cold water and swallowed as rapidly as possible, for the smell was awful, and it helped to keep it down if the nose was held firmly as the nauseous drink was imbibed.

If the stomach wasn't too badly upset, and the discomfort could merely have been a touch of wind, then a pinch of baking soda in water was highly favoured by all of us. I quite liked this. It had a sort of flavour of puff candy, and the ensuing belches or 'rifts' were warmly encouraged, instead of being frowned upon as downright bad manners if heard at any other time.

For lazy bowels, my mother's favourite cure was senna pods, or 'seenie pods' as we called them. I liked to be allowed to float the flat dry shapes in the tumbler of water, and was fascinated to find it transformed to a nice tea-coloured mixture next day. And it took no coaxing at all to get us to take sugarally water. This was made by putting a wee piece of jet-black Spanish liquorice in the bottom of a medicine bottle, topping it up with water, and a spoonful of sugar, and shaking it for hours until the brew turned dark brown. We used to chant a wee rhyme as we shook the bottle:

'Sugar-ally waater,
As black as the Lum,
Gether up peens,
An' ye'll a' get some.'

Sometimes we sat it on top of the range to let the warmth draw out the flavour more quickly. A lovely fine froth formed on the top, and we sucked the sweet black liquor through this. Mmmm, it was delicious, and it seemed impossible to believe it could be doing us good at the same time.

Castor oil was used only as a last desperate remedy, for we all hated it. Everybody had patent ideas as to how to make it more palatable. Some swore by a wee drop of milk sipped just before and after the oil, making a sort of buffer sandwich which would disguise the foul taste. The magic didn't work for me. I still 'reached' and 'boked' in misery. Others favoured disguising it in orange juice, but in my opinion the oil wasn't disguised by the juice, but the juice entirely ruined by the smelly oil, and a good orange was never sacrificed in this way in our house.

The only way I could stomach it was to hold my nose in a pincer-like grip, swallow it down, and then lie flat and avoid any unnecessary movement for about ten minutes. Grannie thought this excellent behaviour, especially as it ensured the oil staying down and not having to go through the whole drama again, as well as being a saving of a second lot of oil.

But I never minded the magic of castor oil in getting grit out of the eye. I'd be playing with my gird, or my peever, and whoosh! a lump which felt as big as a marble would land in my eye. I'd drop everything in my anguish, and, eye red and puffy, sniffing and squinting, run upstairs. Grannie would take one look at me and reach for the castor oil and one of her steel knitting needlcs. I'd lie back in the big chair, head tilted over the side of it. 'Noo don't move,' Grannie would command me, 'or you'll get the needle in yer eye.'

Still as a mouse I'd crouch, while Grannie inserted the knitting needle in the castor-oil bottle. Then, holding the needle above my eye, which I was holding open as wide as I could, the drop of that blessed oil would be skilfully guided by Grannie's steady hand right under the lid, and in a second came relief. The rock had floated out, the raw eyelid was soothed, and I was ready for play again.

Sometimes it was my turn to administer our home cures to Grannie. When bronchitis threatened, I'd warm my hands at the fire and then smooth warmed camphorated oil gently over her wheezy chest. 'No' too hard noo,' she'd gasp. 'Just rub it weel in, but dinna scart me wi' yer claws.'

'Claws, Grannie!' I'd say indignantly. 'Ah hivnae got claws.' But I'd be careful, and then I'd put a layer of lovely pink Thermogene on top. This was an airy-fairy material which seemed to do Grannie a lot of good, but it was terribly wasteful and had to be burned when it had done its magic, for it couldn't be washed.

We knew Grannie was gey bad when she wanted Thermogene, for that was the last resort before we sent for the doctor. At three-and-six a visit this was delayed until the last possible moment, and often the camphorated oil and Thermogene saved us sending for him, for it did the trick, and Grannie would be breathing easily in no time at all.

For the wee tickly cough she sometimes got she liked Victory Vee lozenges. These fiery cough sweeties were reasonably safe from marauding small fingers, but we loved her other favourite cough-soother, acid drops. We were always coaxing her for one when we thought my mother was out of earshot.

For our own coughs, my mother pinned her faith on emulsion. To me it tasted like Brasso, but we had to swallow a spoonful every day in winter to prevent colds. I didn't demur, though, when it came to the spring tonic and her other standby, Parrish's Chemical Food. Sweet and sticky, and a lovely red colour, I could hardly credit such a pleasant-tasting beverage could possibly do me all the good my mother swore it would.

For that other scourge of winter, chilblains, everybody had a different cure. The Spartans among us declared that to run barefoot in the snow shocked the fiery chilblains into submission and, what was more, kept them at bay for the rest of the winter. Others thought a plaster of mustard and paraffin most efficacious, and gladly endured the smell of paraffin which clung to socks and bedclothes for ages.

One old woman in the next close declared there was nothing better than the inside of a banana skin laid coolly on the chilblain to draw out the heat and effect a miraculous cure. My mother preferred Snowfire, that nice inexpensive green block, shiny and greasy, which was also a certain cure for the hacks we got on knees and knuckles on dank wintry days. Oh the agony of my serge skirt slapping round my hacked knees to the point of rawness and bleeding, and then the blessed relief of that healing Snowfire. I shuddered with sympathy for the children who had hacks on their heels, for these were most difficult to close. Everybody agreed goose-fat was the best remedy for this painful condition, but as hardly anybody in the tenements had ever seen a goose, much less eaten one, ordinary lard had to do.

We all shared the nightmare of toothache, and agreed with Rabbie Burns, strong language and all, that it was 'the hell o' a' diseases'. Apart from the fact that it cost two-and-six to have a tooth extracted, we were all terrified of the dentist, and only the punishing agony of a tooth rotten beyond the solace of our home-made remedies would drive us to his chamber of horrors. I quite enjoyed oil of cloves, the flavour strongly reminding me of Grannie's delicious apple tarts, but Sloan's Liniment had a heat and bite when rubbed inside and outside my cheek which brought tears to my eyes.

Adults swore to the relief afforded by a tiny drop of whisky dropped into the throbbing cavity, and once, when my own toothache had reached the unendurable stage, I was permitted a tiny drop of the golden brew. Not nearly so nice as cloves or myrrh, in my opinion, but strangely effective.

If the toothache developed into a gumboil, a favourite cure was heated salt inside an old sock laid gently against the swollen cheek. This was the cure, too, for a sore throat, and it was quite a performance heating the salt on a shovel, then guiding it into the sock with the aid of a big spoon, making all possible speed before the salt cooled. It was slapped against the sufferer's throat, and yells of 'It's too *hoat!*' met with the invariable reply, 'It *has* to be hoat to do ye ony good.' A scarlet neck, stiffly held away from a chafing collar, was mute testimony next day that the victim had been right. It *had* been too hot.

It was seldom that the hot-salt-sock cure was required a second night. When asked how the throat fared the reply usually came surprisingly swiftly, 'Ma throat's fine noo.' It seemed to me marvellous how one hot sock was such a powerful cure.

Hiccups, which my mother for some reason called 'hippocs', while they could be painful, were always regarded as something of a joke. A fright was considered the best cure, but as we always frightened each other anyway with our tales of Flannel Feet, and the Cowlairs Swifts, it was difficult to think up anything which could take a sufferer by surprise.

'Hold your nose,' we'd urge the sufferer, 'and drink a cup of water upside down.' The contortions which followed before it was realized that what was meant was simply drinking from the opposite side of the glass had the amateur doctors in hysterics, sometimes to the point of taking hiccups themselves. Some set great store by pinching the ear-lobe while drinking water, but others favoured pinching the very tip of the nose.

When the nose itself gave trouble and blood poured forth dramatically there was only one cure – the wash-house key, ice-cold, pushed down the back of the patient's neck.

You could always borrow a wee rub of wintergreen from any of our tenement houses, for it was considered effective against all winter's aches and pains. We had read in books about iodine and camphor lockets for chest ailments and rheumatism, but this struck us as very fanciful, and we were more inclined to believe the testimony of the old folks, who swore to the effectiveness of a piece of raw potato carried in the pocket. Raw potato was also good against warts, as was the fasting spittle.

Rheumatism was an old people's disease, and anaemia a young one's trouble. Sometimes, when I was a bit anaemic after 'flu, I'd have to take Blaud's Pills. I found these so difficult to swallow that my mother was driven to try to break them on the kitchen table, using the poker as a cleaver. Those attempts dented our table for all time, and when the question of pills was raised as a cure for anything she would stare accusingly at the marks, and tell the story all over again of how thrawn I was at refusing to gulp down such a wee pill. But an uncle gave us a good laugh by coming to my defence with the suggestion that maybe I had a wee throat like a whale, which balked even at a tomato skin. 'She's certainly got a memory like an elephant,' retorted my mother, 'so maybe she's got a throat like a whale. Onywey, she's ruined my good table.'

For her own persistent affliction, blinding headaches, my mother found nothing better than a cloth dipped in vinegar, which I placed over her eyes as she stretched out on the bed. As the cloth dried, I'd dip it again and again in the saucer of vinegar, and soon she would drift off to sleep, soothed by this pungent bandage.

One old lady told me that when she was a wee girl her mother's cure for all the ills that God could send was the 'traycle' tin. This was a tin filled nearly to the top with black treacle, and it was put on top of the range to make it warm and runny. Into it went a big spoonful of Epsom salts, one of senna powder, one of Gregory's powder, and a pinch of sulphur. Then the lot was well stirred, round and round, and the whole family had a teaspoonful every night till the tin was empty. The taste was horrible, she told me, and the grit stuck to their teeth, but not a lad in the family ever suffered from pimples, and they all had clear and smooth skins, and required no other medicine throughout the year.

5

It was great to be back at school again. I could never understand why some of my chums hated it, for I enjoyed every moment, marching upstairs to the rollicking tunes pounded out on the piano by the youngest schoolteacher, wheeling off to our separate classrooms, and starting off the day with a hymn 'Jesus loves me', or 'Who is on the Lord's side?', or 'Dare to be a Daniel', roared out with enthusiasm.

Our school was a red sandstone building, new and modern in its day, with handsome heavy gates and matching railings, and a lovely big playground. A huge drill-hall filled the centre of the ground floor, and all the classrooms branched off this to house the younger schoolchildren. A gallery ran right round the upper floor, and the classrooms of the bigger children led off this gallery. At one end, high in the wall, was the big clock which kept perfect time. This clock was the pride and joy of the 'Jannie', as we called the school janitor. Not only did he keep it well oiled and correct to a second, but it was his duty to ring the bell underneath the clock to announce playtimes and lunchtimes.

When the morning seemed interminable, and one had to 'leave the room', it was a reassuring sight to see the janitor standing by the clock, poised in readiness for the exact minute to sound the bell, and to know that release was near.

I don't think I ever put my hand up to utter the parrot sentence 'Please may I leave the room?' to indicate urgent need to go out to the toilet, all the time I was at school. For one thing, I wouldn't have missed a second of my lessons, and for another I was curiously shy about letting anybody know that the lavatory was my goal. We had one boy in our class who loathed history lessons, and as soon as the teacher announced that we could put away our jotters and take out our history books his hand shot up. The entire class knew he was only going to race round the playground for the next half-hour, but the teacher never tumbled to it, and I expect he went through his whole school life without knowing a thing that happened before the first world war. We used to catch one another's eyes as he sauntered towards the door, and we'd press our lips together to keep from giggling, for we wouldn't give him away, but we were baffled that the teacher could have been so blind as not to notice that Billy never reappeared until he had heard us safely finish our chanting 'The Battle of Bannockburn was fought in 1314', 'The battle of Flodden was fought in 1513', and 'The battle of Waterloo was fought in 1815'. As the last echoes of long-forgotten battles died away, Billy slipped through the door and took his place in class once more, ready to continue his education.

The mid-morning playtime was, I suppose, really to allow us to make ourselves comfortable, but we wouldn't have dreamed of wasting valuable time on mere toilets. Those who had 'left the room' in school-time were already comfortable, and few of the others gave such matters a thought. Our minds were on the opportunity for a quick game of skipping ropes, or high and low water on the low school wall, or chases, or the forbidden unholy joy of sliding down the coal-bunkers. The rusty hinges were a terrible hazard to school bloomers, and Grannie used to be mystified as to how I could cause such ragged tears in mine if I was behaving myself as I ought. I never dared tell her of the coal-bunker games or she'd have warmed my ears for me.

Apart from those of us who threw ourselves energetically into the games, there were the handful whom I secretly despised, and called under my breath 'tumphies'. Their mothers were ranged outside the school gates, and they fed and nourished the 'tumphies' through the bars as though they were animals in a zoo. I shuddered at the mere idea of such mollycoddling and was glad my own mother was safely at work and couldn't be tempted to such outrages. These cosseted ones usually had scarves tied over their school caps, or their tammies, to give extra warmth, a fashion I wouldn't have been seen dead in, and I'd snort contemptuously as I saw little cans of tea or cocoa passed through the bars, followed by buttered rolls, or toast, or slices of cake.

It was due to Grannie that I was so disapproving of such goings-on, for when I had told her about the mothers outside the railings she had snorted, 'Spoilt, fair spoilt. It's a wonder their mothers havenae anything better tae dae than tae waste their time putting their weans off their dinners. Just making them soft, that's all.'

I was so sure Grannie was right that I wouldn't even take a play-piece with me and eat it during games, as most of my chums did. My appetite was undimmed by any mid-morning indulgence, and I flew home at lunchtime ravenous. Grannie knew I wouldn't loiter on the way, hunger lending speed to my legs, and she'd have the mince and tatties on the table, or the soup, good broth, followed by the beef the soup had been made with, and mashed tatties and turnip. Sometimes it was sausages, and sometimes it was tripe, but it was always good, and always eaten with enthusiasm. Nothing had crossed my lips since my early-morning roll at breakfast-time, and I was more than ready for whatever was put before me.

Because my hands and face weren't sticky or dirty with playtime pieces, my adored Miss Oliver selected me to take the attendance figures of the entire school each morning at eleven o'clock playtime, and again in the afternoon at the three o'clock playtime break. I felt like bursting with importance as I raced round from class to class, a stiff-backed folder under one arm, and the teacher's beautifully sharpened pencil lent to me to mark down the numbers there were in each class. These attendance figures were chalked on a small blackboard outside each room, so that I needn't disturb anyone if I were a few minutes early or late and the teacher busy with her class. I would then swiftly add up all the numbers, and arrive at the total number of children at school that morning, and then again that afternoon, and absentees were checked against the figures when I took my folder to the staff-room for safe keeping in the file there. It was strange to see all the teachers there, drinking tea and nibbling at biscuits. Tea! Fancy having time to make tea at playtime. It always seemed far too short when we were tearing about at our games, for it to have been possible to have brought a kettle to the boil and infused tea, and poured it out, but they had managed it somehow. My eyes darted about, trying to solve this mystery, and then I spied a gas-ring roaring away at full pelt under a kettle, no doubt for washing up their dirty cups, and realized that of course that was why they could have tea so quickly. They didn't have to wait for water to heat over the coal in the range, as we did at home. Schools had tons of money and it would be nothing to them to pay for that expensive roaring gas which provided the boiling water for their tea.

I was never offered as much as a sip of their tea, and would have been horrified if I had been. Teachers were teachers, and pupils were pupils, and a wide gulf yawned between. I was uneasy to see them at such unguarded moments, drinking and eating, and was glad to be dismissed with an 'All right, Molly, back to your room now.' I never followed those attendance figures to their conclusion, when they eventually reached the headmaster's desk, and the truants were reported to the 'School Board'. I was in great awe of male authority, and shuddered at the mere idea of 'plunking' school and having one of those dread creatures come to the house to demand what was keeping me from my education. But many others had no such scruples, and cheerfully accepted the wallopings they received from mothers or fathers who had had to face the 'School Board', as we called the truant officer, and try to explain why their boy or girl hadn't been at school.

Only dire necessity ever kept me at home, either my own illness or Grannie's, and then I would return with a wee note; 'Please excuse Molly, but she was required at home', or 'Please excuse Molly but she was in bed with a severe cold'. This was accepted without argument, because everybody knew that books and learning were meat and drink to me. Not so some of the others, poor things, who were known as regular defaulters, and whose notes were perused with a quizzical eye, and doubts cast as to who had actually written them. We all felt sorry for the boy or girl as the teacher's eye mercilessly scanned the note, for a lie on top of absenteeism could only end in the strap, and crossed hands at that to make it sting even more. Some of the teachers were suspected of dipping their leather tawse in whisky to make them bite with a fiery fury, but I could never imagine any teacher wasting expensive whisky in this way when the leather strap was quite painful enough without a thing being added to it. I only ever had the strap once, and I was deeply ashamed, so vexed indeed that I never breathed a word of it at home to let them know I had fallen from grace. The teacher had gone out during a drawing lesson, and left us to continue with our crayoned attempts to copy an orange. The girl next to me had a tiny glass tube filled with 'hundreds and thousands', those little coloured sugar dots no bigger than a pinhead, which had clogged together and refused to come out, however hard she sucked. Trying to help her, I hit the bottom of the tube sharply, and the whole lot shot out in a wet blob, soaked with her saliva, and landed right in the middle of her drawing, exactly at the point where the orange stalk had been. Under our horrified gaze, the coloured sugar began to run, and in a minute the orange looked as if it were affected by a horrible scabby disease. We dared not touch it in case we got it all over our clothes, and we knew the teacher would be furious with us for spoiling the precious sheet in our drawing book. Fear made us hysterical, and as we caught one another's eye, we burst into peals of laughter which we simply couldn't control. The girls in the back row crowded round to see what we were laughing at. We held our sides, and gasped out an explanation between bursts of giggles. It was infectious and soon the entire class was shouting with abandoned laughter.

The door opened, and the teacher walked in. 'What is the meaning of this?' she demanded. The rest of the class fell silent, but my neighbour and I were well beyond control now. Tears of laughter poured down our cheeks. We shook, and our voices squeaked as we tried to speak. The teacher walked slowly up to us, her eyes disbelieving that I, her pet, had actually been the cause of this unseemly noise. She looked at the drawing, tightened her lips, and bade us both come out to the front of the class. There was not a sound in the room now. Nobody had ever seen me get the strap, and I felt sick and bewildered that I could have got myself into this terrible situation. How would I stand up to it? I wondered. Suppose I shamed myself by bursting into tears in front of the whole class? The tears threatened to come even before the strap was drawn from the desk, and I opened my eyes as wide as possible to stop them from forming in a humiliating shower. Oh how I envied those who were able to swagger out and hold out their hands, with an arrogant wink to the rest of us. I prayed soundlessly, 'Oh God, please let me not cry. Please let me not cry in front of everybody.' The teacher was drawing the tawse through her hands and looking at me. 'I had expected better of you, Molly,' she said. 'I expected you, as top of the class, to know better. What do you suppose would have happened if the inspector had been coming today, instead of tomorrow? He'd have thought I had a class of hyenas!' The rest of the class, sitting safely in their seats, ventured a little giggle at this witticism. She turned on them sharply. 'You were all just as bad, so be quiet, and let this be a lesson to you.' She raised the strap, I held out a shaking hand and shut my eyes. The strap fell gently on to my rigid palm. I had heard if you held your hand as stiffly as possible it didn't hurt so badly. I didn't feel anything. I was still praying. Quietly the teacher said, 'Go back to your seat now.' I opened my eyes and stared at her. Only one stroke of the strap. Sometimes she gave as many as six. I looked at my hand. There wasn't a mark on it, not so much as a pink flush where the strap had fallen, no hurt at all. Only my pride had been bruised and splintered. But my prayers had been answered. I hadn't cried.

When we had settled down to our drawings again the teacher began walking round behind the desks to see how we were getting on, and when she reached us she showed Margaret how to blot off the worst of the sticky mess and cover in the rest with shading, and in the end the inspector seemed to notice nothing when he came to inspect our work next day. When she looked at my work she laid a hand on my shoulder and pressed it comfortingly, and the hard knot in my stomach warmed and loosened, and the blackness of my disgrace lightened a little. And the tears which I had conquered so successfully now burst their dyke, but nobody could see them as I bent lower and lower over my page and filled in the shadows round the orange with delicate little strokes.

The inspector who examined our general work was bad

enough, but the one I dreaded most was the music inspector. He had been in the war, and wounds had left him with one side of his face twisted, and the lower lid of his eye was pulled down in such a way that he looked as if he was permanently leering. For some reason he liked my husky voice, and after we had sung our class songs, 'I saw three ships a-sailing', 'She left her baby lying there', 'When I'm lonely dear white heart', he would tell us to sit down. Then, tapping his tuning fork against his other hand, he would say 'What about Molly Weir singing "Robin Adair" for us?' 'I've got a sore throat,' I would whisper. Terror had so gripped me that I indeed sounded as if I were in the throes of a bout of laryngitis. But he knew perfectly well that it was sheer fright which was making me hoarse, and he ignored my excuses. 'We'll find the right key for you, eh?' he would say, striking the tuning fork against the desk, and making me forget my fears in the magic of this little instrument which could produce such a sweet note when it was laid gently upended on the desk as now. Sweetly the note sounded, he'd raise his hands, and I would keep my eyes firmly fixed on my music book, pretending I didn't know the words, so that I needn't look at his and be reminded that I was standing up all by myself in class singing a solo. He also liked me to sing 'Jock o' Hazeldene' and Grannie's favourite, 'The Rowan Tree'. The rest of the class were sympathetic, and used to commiserate with me afterwards. 'Aye, he's got it in fur you a' right, Molly,' they would say. 'Thank goodness it's no' us he asks to staun up an' sing. Jeez, it must be terrible.' And it was. Nobody, least of all me, regarded it as a compliment that a music inspector should request a solo – I regarded it as a punishment and I spent anguished hours wondering what I could possibly have done to make him torture me like this.

We never sang the class songs outside the classroom but we had a fund of little songs which pleased us because of their funny words or comical rhymes. We would join hands in a circle in the playground and chant, giggling foolishly at the end,

'S-O, so, ma big toe,
Fell in the sugar-bowl,
And Ah didnae know.'

This was followed by:

> 'Sent fur the doctor, he widnae come,
> Sent fur the ambulance, pum, pum, pum.'

One day we were so carried away with ourselves we sang the words louder and louder, and faster and faster, as we raced round in our circle, until a classroom window was thrown up and Mr McAllister's furious face appeared. 'Be quiet, you big girls,' he yelled in a frenzy, 'or move to another playground.' We were stunned into complete silence that he had heard us yelling such idiotic words, and crept away to the other end of the sheds where we could intone, without bothering anybody,

> 'Come a riddle, come a riddle, come a roat, toat, toat,
> A wee wee man, wi' a rid, rid coat.
> A stave in his haun' an' a stane in his throat,
> Come a riddle, come a riddle, come a roat, toat, toat.'

We had some that we sang far from school ears, because we knew the teachers frowned on our dialect, and we were never absolutely sure what they regarded as vulgar. So we kept for the back courts or Paddy Oar's park such ditties as:

> 'Ma Maw's a millionaire,
> Blue eyes and curly hair,
> Hokey, pokey, penny a lump,
> That's the stuff tae make ye jump,
> Ma Maw's a millionaire.'

And when we followed the watering cart, with its lovely spraying jets to lay the dust, we burst into:

> 'Ah'm gaun doon the toon,
> Ah know wha's gaun wi' me,
> Ah've a wee laud o' ma ain,
> An' they ca' him Bonnie Jimmy.
> He took me to a soirée,
> He took me to a supper,
> Him an' I fell oot,
> An' ah dipped his nose in the butter.'

And there was a marvellous bit of rhyming selling which we all learnt by heart from a man who used to sell things at the

corner of Vulcan Street, by the marble fountain, every Friday
night:

> 'For you've all seen a cork in a bottle,
> But you've never seen a bottle in a cork.
> Anything with a hard, smooth surface.
> A billiard ball, a button or a coin.'

We would repeat this until we could rattle it off like an
auctioneer, vying with each other to get it as crisp and expert
as the man on the soap box by the fountain. We hadn't the
faintest idea what he was selling, but we were certainly sold on
the hypnotic effect of his swiftly delivered patter. We used to
stand on the fringe of the crowd, lips parted with expectation,
and the moment he came to 'For you've all seen a cork in a
bottle', we joined in the chorus with him, word for word, and
the men standing round would give an ironic cheer, while the
man on the soap box would shout: 'You weans should be in yer
beds. Scram.'

When we watched rival schools playing football we enjoyed
bursting into song, both schools taking it up, and yelling out
the name of their own school at the appropriate line:

> 'Hyde Park, Hyde Park, as it used to be,
> The best wee school that ever ye did see.
> For when they score, you'll hear a mighty roar,
> Hurrah for good old Hyde Park.'

While we were shouting 'Hyde Park', the other school would
be trying to drown us out with 'Albert', or 'Petershill', and the
noise was deafening.

We felt unbelievably daring when school holidays
approached and we'd rush around singing:

> 'Only one more day, and then we shall be free.
> No more English, no more French,
> No more sitting on a hard wooden bench,
> When the Jannie rings the bell,
> Out the gates we'll rush . . .'

and, depending on who was within earshot, we'd finish 'pell-
mell', nice and douce-like, or, if it was younger ones we wished

208

to impress with our grown-up abandon, we'd substitute the words 'like hell'. 'Hell' was a terrible word to sing out loud in a song like that, and we shivered at our own daring. Our mothers would have cuffed our ears for us if they'd heard us, but we made very sure they never did.

We felt we were terribly lucky in having Paddy Oar's park immediately behind our school. We never knew who Paddy Oar was or when it had been his park, but my mother had some vague idea that it had once been grazing fields which Paddy had let out to farmers as summer quarters for their animals. No cow or horse lent a rural air to the landscape even in our day, but the park was a gold-mine for our raw materials when we played at sand shops. During school holidays we would stream towards Paddy Oar's park as soon as we'd swallowed our breakfasts, and we'd spend the entire morning collecting bits of stone. We had brought old chisels or bits of tin for digging up specially coloured pieces, and we jealously kept our best finds to ourselves, so that we would have something exclusive to sell when the time came to open shop. We'd run panting back to our back courts old aprons bulging with our prized materials, and after our dinner we settled down on the hard surfaces of the back courts to champ the stones into beautiful heaps of powdery stuff, some fine for flour and icing sugar and spices, others coarse for sugar, rice, barley and semolina. The special pieces were greatly coveted, for they had a deep rich colour just right for curry powders and ginger and cinnamon, and there was a lovely whitish stone which ground down perfectly to a fine rice flour.

We were as busy as bees, silent and absorbed in the preparation of our stock for our little shops. We would pile our wares in neat little heaps on the window-sills of the wash-houses, or the ledges of the kitchen windows of the houses at ground level. We would arrange a sheet of stiff cardboard so that it stuck out at right angles like a weighing scale, with a heavy stone to keep it in place, and a variety of little stones to act as weights ranged alongside. Then we flew about the earthy back courts, digging out old pieces of broken dishes, of which there seemed to be an endless supply, to form 'wally money'. The pieces with a tiny chip of gold still visible were 'sovereigns' and the others were graded in value according to size, from pennies to half-crowns. An old sweetie tin was our money till, and we drooled over our 'sovereigns' like any miser.

We drew lots to see who would start selling first, for, of course, the whole joy was in selling, but if you didn't buy, then you didn't sell, for your customers boycotted you. So the first 'in', as it were, would yell, 'Shop open, come and buy, ready-money buyers.' We had no idea what 'rea . . . dy-mo . . . ney buy . . . ers' meant, and that it had come down to us from the shopkeepers who refused to give customers 'tick' and demanded payment on the nail.

As soon as the first notes of 'Shop open' sounded, the other shopkeepers would leave wee sisters or brothers in charge of their stalls, with instructions to yell the alarm if the boys appeared and threatened to wreck the place. They would stroll over and critically survey the rival stall, make a few leisurely purchases which they promptly threw away, filled with envy of the shopkeeper and the fun she was having weighing out minute quantities of 'flour' or 'sugar', and the fussy altering of the weights which preceeded 'I'm sorry, that's a ha'penny over, will I leave it on?' The saleswoman was longing, of course, to be told, 'No, that's too much, take it off', so that she could enjoy juggling with weights and scoop, but the purchaser was keen to start her own selling and usually said, with a lordly air, 'No leave it on, I've plenty of money in my purse', and she would hand over the correct amount of 'wally' money, so that at least there could be no prolonging the transaction with having to wait for change.

It didn't take long for the person next in line to get fed up with being a mere customer, and she'd rush back and set up the rival cry 'Shop open', but all too soon her turn was over, and with a sigh she'd join the ranks of the customers once more. I used to take my shop up to the house when the day's selling was over, and many a clout I got from Grannie when she found herself crunching horrible sand under her feet and taking it all over the kitchen floor in her slippers. 'Whit's a' this dirt?' she'd demand furiously as she scattered it over the floor, and I'd shriek with dismay and rush to rescue my dispersed treasure.

There was a special part of the park which had gorgeous

sticky clay which we used for our clay shops. It was cold and wet and heavy to dig out, but we lugged back great dods of it, and, using flat pieces of wood begged from the fruit shops, who always had plenty of orange boxes, we battered it into various shapes. With what patience we designed boats, houses, saucers, blocks of butter, pieces of cheese, marzipan potatoes and pounds of margarine. The wash-house ledges weren't so desirable for clay shops, for the boys congregated on top of the roofs and pelted the shopkeepers with ferocious aim, with wet clay stolen from the stock. Not only did those boys rouse us to spitting fury, but they incensed the washerwomen too, for while they were up there they took the opportunity to stuff the chimneys with old rags and when the women lit the boiler fire next wash-day, smoke and soot would come pouring into the wash-house and spoil the good clean washing which was ready for the boiler.

With our clay models the salesmanship was different. We all created our own shapes, and we dispensed with wally money on this occasion, and went in for barter. It was a thrilling decision to have to weigh up the splendour of an offered miniature Clyde steamer for a submarine which one had designed with loving care.

And even when it wasn't providing stock for our shops Paddy Oar's park had yet another joy for winter fun. The slopes round the highest part, behind our school sheds, were satisfyingly steep, and formed into deep furrows, and with borrowed draining boards and old trays we would toboggan from what seemed incredible heights right down to the back school wall. How swift the descent was, and how long the toil upwards to begin all over again, but our legs were strong and sturdy and we accepted the hard slog uphill for the sake of the wild whoosh down again, when we seemed almost to be flying.

We saw no danger in this until one day a big girl in my class, heavier than the rest of us, couldn't stop her tray when she got to the bottom of the run, and banged her head right into the school wall with a thump that stopped the rest of us, who were toiling uphill, dead in our tracks. She lay at the bottom so still and silent that we thought she was killed. Her forehead was gashed open, and blood poured from it. We stared at her, frightened to move, then somebody ran for the janitor and he came and she was carried into his wee house in the playground. We'd never been inside his house, and in spite of the drama of the accident we were curious to notice that he had a range exactly like our own, with a cosy glowing fire burning, and a brass kettle on the mantelpiece. A doctor was sent for, and Dorothy had four stitches put in her forehead, and that was the end of our mountaineering. The headmaster came to the drill-hall next day, and lectured us about such dangerous play, and made us all solemnly promise that we would not attempt to take part in any such games at that particular part of the park. Och it was a shame, but the sight of that still figure, forehead dripping blood, had frightened us enough, and we kept our promise, and sadly put away our draining boards and trays. But we couldn't get over the fact that we hadn't even *known* it was dangerous until one of us had been hurt. How hard it was to know when you were being good and when you were being bad, even if you went to Sunday School and Church and everything.

6

As well as the big Church, where we went to Sunday School, and Bible Class, and had our church parades of Girl Guides and the Boys' Brigade, we had the excitement in summertime of tent missions coming to Springburn to convert us. We didn't know we were being converted from heathenish ways, we just enjoyed the sight of a huge tent being erected on the piece of waste ground at the end of Gourlay Street, and we begged to be allowed to help to hand out the little leaflets telling all that Jock Troup would be preaching and saving souls that night and all week from 7.30 P.M. As soon as our tea was swallowed, we raced back to get front seats, and the adults crowded in at our backs, greatly entertained to be having hellfire preached at them inside a tent. Jock was great value, and we all imitated him afterwards, not in any spirit of derision, but in profound admiration. He could make the flames of hell so real, we felt them licking round our feet, and the prospect of heaven so alluring we often stood up to be saved several times during the week, just to see him fall on his knees in thankfulness at having plucked so many brands from the burning. His hymns were different from those in Sunday School and had a sort of music-hall ring to them which we all enjoyed.

One obviously designed to appeal to our Scottish sense of economy, went:

> 'Nothing to pay, no, nothing to pay,
> Straight is the gate, and narrow the way,
> Look unto Jesus, start right away,
> From Springburn to glory, and nothing to pay.'

We particularly liked 'Springburn' coming into the hymn, not realizing that he just substituted whatever district he happened

213

to be visiting, and we felt he had composed this hymn specially for Springburn sinners.

Another rollicking hymn Jock honestly and freely confessed he had obtained from another hot gospeller, who had written it especially for us children, went like this:

'Zaccheus was a very little man,
And a very little man was he,
He climbed into the sycamore tree
For he wanted the Lord to see.
And as the Saviour passed that way
He looked up in the tree
And said, "Zaccheus, you come down,
For I'm coming to your house for tea."'

I thought that was a marvellous hymn, and it bore out my mother's wisdom in always having a wee something in the tins in case anybody came in unexpectedly, and could be offered a biscuit or a piece of shortbread and not just plain bread and margarine. Fancy if it had been the Saviour dropping in with a reformed sinner and you'd had nothing special to give them! That would have been just terrible. After I'd learnt that hymn I always made sure that our tins held at least four abernethy biscuits, just in case.

We attended Jock's services every night, and I used to come home and act them all over again to Grannie, and when she told me to be quiet she was fair deaved with my shouting, I would say, 'Well, Jock Troup said the streets of the New Jerusalem would be filled with the voices of little children,' and Grannie would say, holding her hand to her head, 'Weel if their voices are like yours, folk'll wish they had gaun someplace else for a bit o' peace.' 'All right then, Grannie Weir,' I would say huffily, 'the man's come all this way to show us how to be saved, but if you don't want to be saved, I'll just tell him tomorrow night and he'll come and pluck you from the burning himself.' 'My Goad,' Grannie would say, 'that wean's gaun to be a meenister, I'm mair shair o' it than ever,' and for some reason she seemed to be trying to stop herself laughing. How could she be so calm when Jock Troup told us we had but little time to repent, and she was far nearer to Judgment Day than I was!

After a whole week of Jock it was quite peaceful to awaken the next Sunday morning to the lovely sound of the Salvation Army silver band which played at the end of Gourlay Street before moving up Springburn Road to the Salvation Army Hall and its morning service.They were splendid musicians, and the silvery notes were welcomed by everyone within earshot as a most fitting way to start our Sundays. They just played tunes at that time of day, but later on in the evening they had an outdoor service and we all went along to hear them and to join in the singing. My auntie was a Salvationist and it was a proud day for her when she 'got the bonnet', which was only awarded after a qualifying period. We liked the way the officer who took the service shouted, with a high clear voice, so different from the soft tones of our minister. We didn't reason it was because he had to make himself heard above the traffic, but thought he was shouting straight up to heaven, so that God could hear what a good job he was making of it. After the outdoor service we marched up Springburn Road behind the band, and went into their hall, to listen to another short service, and discover how many sinners felt they now wanted to be saved. There was a long bench at the front, called the Penitents' Bench, where those wishing to be saved knelt and were received by the officer who had taken the service. I found this all very moving, and was saved twice, once for myself and once for Grannie, since she wouldn't budge outside the house to make sure of salvation in person.

But neither Jock Troup nor the Salvation Army had Sunday School picnics, and we felt Church Sunday Schools had a great advantage in this respect. Some of our chums went to every Sunday School in the district whenever the time drew near for the trips, as we called the picnics, and actually went to the Protestant, the Catholic and the Methodist churches just because one gave tattie scones, the next gave sausage rolls and the other gave pies. I thought this was a terrible thing to do, and felt that God must have been very confused wondering how to treat people of such fickle faith. At least all our religious tastes were Protestant, and we didn't go to the Tent Mission or the Salvation Army for anything but the sheer enjoyment, although I daresay if a trip had also been included we wouldn't have said no.

The trips were always on a Saturday, and the sun always seemed to be shining. There were carts drawn by fine Clydesdale horses, and these were used to take the older people and the youngest children, whose legs weren't so strong as ours were. We all met at two o'clock in the street outside the Church, and with our tinnies tied round our necks with tape, and wearing our best summer clothes, we marched behind the Boys' Brigade band up to Springburn Park, or out to Auchinairn to a field kindly lent by one of the farmers or the gentry.

As soon as we arrived, we tore one end of our ticket off at the perforated edge, where it said 'Cakes' and handed it to one of the ladies who stood behind a huge hamper, and she gave us a poke of pastry. I loved those pokes we got at the trips, and I looked inside them right away. I just had to check what was inside, although I knew the contents never varied. Always exactly the same things, and I was always delighted. A round thick high sponge cake, with pieces of sugar on top and a strip of paper round the outside, which we called 'a sair heidie', because the paper reminded us of the hankies our mothers tied round their foreheads when they had a headache. Two squares of pastry with a layer of bashed fruit in between, with sometimes a few stones from fruit which had been incautiously cleaned, and this we called a fly cemetery. I always swopped this one, for I hated the name 'fly cemetery' and wouldn't have been surprised if there had indeed been some flies in among that funny-looking fruit. Strangely enough there was always somebody who actually liked fly cemeteries and there was no difficulty in getting another coffee bun in exchange. Mmmm I loved a coffee bun. Sort of biscuity, dark brown and crumbly, and mysterious too, for it didn't taste of coffee and it didn't look like a bun, and I didn't know how it could have got its name. And a fern cake, with white icing on top, and a dark brown chocolate fern traced over the white. I usually took this home for Grannie, so I couldn't blow up my poke and burst it as many of the others did when they'd eaten all their cakes. The other end of the entrance ticket had a perforated slip with the word 'Milk' written on it ('Tea' for adults) and it was a great novelty to have our tinnies filled with creamy milk straight from the churns which lined the refreshment corner of the field.

After the food we had the games and the races. What an excitement to see the men stretching the rope across the end of the measured distance, and we'd stand panting with nerves waiting for our age-group to be announced. 'The hundred yards will now be raced by the under tens.' We gave our ages to the men in charge of the start of the race, and the entrants who were younger than ten got a starting point nearer the winning tape, according to age, right down to the age of five. The five-year-olds were half-way to the post, but then their wee legs weren't as strong or as fleet as the older ones, and they needed this encouragement to get them to race at all. 'Noo watch me,' the man at our end of the 100 yards would say, 'and as soon as I drap ma hankie, off youse go.' Parents and school pals were ranged the whole length of the sidelines between starting and winning posts, cheering the contestants on. Every eye was on the starter's hankie, and the minute he dropped his hand, we were off, arms flailing and legs going like pistons, and hearts pounding as if they'd jump out of our chests. Och what a distance the finishing tape seemed to be, however hard one ran! It was easy to pass the wee five-year-olds who toddled happily at their own pace, lost interest, and started playing among the daisies, but completely impossible to catch up the fleetest of foot, who had breasted the tape almost before my legs, at any rate, had got into their stride. And then the winners proudly panted out their names and their ages, and were given their prizes. I never won that sort of race, but I came into my own at the 'fancy' races – the three legged, where two of us tied inner legs together with a big hankie, and trotted up the field in harness. This needed a bit of manœuvring, and identical rhythm, and we used to trot about practising until we'd developed what we thought was an unbeatable style. There was generally a prize for me for that race. And the thread-the-needle race. I had eyes like a hawk, and always threaded Grannie's needle, so was experienced at sucking the end of the thread into a sharp fine point, ready to be jabbed through the eye of the needle at the proper moment. This speed with the needle helped to compensate for the lack of top speed in my legs, and I usually got a lucky bag for this race too.

But the races we all enjoyed best were those run by the fathers and mothers. It was hilarious to see mothers running up the measured distance, fat ones puffing and blowing, thin ones recovering their youthful zest as they raced out in fine style. Hair-pins fell out of buns, and blouses came adrift from skirts, and it was highly comical to see the mothers trying to stuff their blouses back to hide their camisoles, while racing along the slippery grass. I loved the sight of their rippling hair flying unbound in the breeze, and was delighted at how young they looked when they were pink-cheeked and dishevelled like this. There was much giggling and panting as they bound up their hair into douce buns again, but I couldn't help noticing they were not in the same hurry to do this as they had been to tidy up their blouses, and I had a notion they quite enjoyed the free feeling of their hair tumbling down their backs, and the admiring comments made by the men on the 'fine heids o' hair' they had.

The men were almost as funny when it came to their races. They took off their jackets and handed them to the women to look after them. They rolled up their trousers, revealing long socks above their sand-shoes, and sometimes long combinations. They adjusted their 'galluses', as we called their braces, to let their chests take in great gulps of air. They did impressive 'knees-bends' to loosen their muscles. Meantime the wives stood by, eyes amused or critical, holding the coats over their arms, while the children whooped and cheered on the sidelines. Somehow the sight of men running sent us off into peals of laughter, and I remember being so surprised during one race when Mr McCarthy's galluses burst and his trousers threatened to tangle up his legs, his wife calling out: 'Wid ye look at Wullie McCarthy! I knew fine that button widnae haud, but wid he take time to let me sew it on for him! Not him!' The other women tut-tutted sympathetically while shouting with laughter at the sight of Mr McCarthy trying to rescue his breeks, but what amazed me was that his wife had called him 'Wullie McCarthy', just as if he was a stranger. I had never heard women describe their husbands as anything other than 'ma man' or 'ma Hughie' or whatever their Christian name was, and it was the first time it had struck me that once upon a time misters and missuses had been separate human beings, with separate names; and always after this revelation I tormented the lives out of everybody by asking them: 'Whit was your name afore ye were Missus Brown?' I was fascinated by this knowledge that women had a different name before they married, and that there was a time in the distant past when their own husbands' names had been quite strange to them. I decided that I really didn't want to change my surname, and I thought maybe I would be an old maid, for I had learned you kept your own name forever if you stayed a 'miss'. Or maybe the minister would let me keep my own name if I asked him, if I decided, after all, I would like to be married.

The Sunday School trips put us in the mood for picnics, and the next Saturday saw us setting off for Springburn Park with borrowed lemonade bottles filled with water. We used to pretend we could detect the faint sweetness of long-vanished lemonade or Iron Brew, and wondered that anybody could have been so careless as to leave the precious drops which flavoured our picnic water. That water tasted so different drunk from a bottle, we could deceive ourselves it had a far better taste than the stuff straight from the tap, for it surely borrowed a wee bit of the magic of the lovely fizzy sweet stuff we all loved. Our bread and margarine, with sometimes a wee bit of corn mutton, tasted all the better too, washed down by this enriched water. We had all learned at Sunday School about the wedding party where the Saviour turned the water into wine, and who knew but that something special had happened to our bottled water for our picnics in the park. We spent hours of blissful play in the park, sustained by our simple picnic fare, and how good it all was after the back courts because we had real grass and warm sunshine. We all had empty jam-jars and wee 'nets' made out of old hankies fastened to pieces of thin wood. We fished for baggies, our name for baggie-minnows, and transferred them to our glass jam-jars, and felt drunk with success as we watched our catch swimming round and round in their glass-walled prison. We'd take them home, with slimy green stuff in the bottom of the jar, which was supposed to keep them alive, but which so disgusted our grannies or our mothers that they quietly poured the lot down the sink, ignoring our wailing cries. We were forbidden to paddle in the park pond, in case we'd 'catch our death', for who in our tenements had towels to spare for weans to take with them to dry themselves? Those who fell into the water, through over-enthusiasm, just had to run home to get a change of clothes and a walloping, and they ran home alone, for the park was a good twenty minutes' walk from our houses, and the rest of us weren't going to cut short our play because somebody else had been daft enough to fall in the pond. I remember one time my brother Tommy fell in, and nothing would persuade him to go home and leave the exciting fishing contest, so he took off all his clothes and lay on the bank to dry himself in the sun. Grannie was scandalized when she heard the story, for, of course, his clothes were still damp when he came to be undressed to go to bed, and she was sure he would get pneumonia. She refused to be convinced that the sun had been 'rer and hoat', even if his jersey and trousers hadn't dried so quickly as his skin, and he was dosed with a big spoonful of emulsion that night, although it was high summer and not our usual season for staving off the ills which stalked us on dank winter days.

My mother was never a natural picnicker. She had a finicky preference for eating at a table, and a timidity about insects and wet ground. But sometimes we managed to coax her to take us on picnics, and we always wanted to go to Rouken Glen, because it was the longest tram ride from Springburn. She couldn't be bothered with the fag of taking three excitable children all that way every time, and occasionally she would fob us off with taking us out to Auchinairn. We'd troop out of the tramcar take one look round, and shout accusingly in one voice: 'This is no' Rouken Glen.' 'How do you know?' my mother would counter defensively. 'Because we just do.' We'd stand mulishly and repeat annoyingly: 'This is just no' Rouken Glen.' 'Well, it's every bit as good,' my mother would parry. 'And if the rain comes on, we're far nearer home, and we'll be home quicker.' We were furious at the weather coming into it, for we didn't examine the sky for rain-clouds. And then the sight of a very climbable tree would divert us, and soon we were shinning up it, playing Tarzan, or cowboys and Indians finding another even more exciting tree, with thick branches where we could actually sit down, and frightening the birds with our yells. We'd cut weeds for Mrs McGregor's canary, and grasses and wild flowers for Grannie, who never came on picnics, however hard we tried to persuade her.

Once, after Grannie died, my mother took us on a picnic to Rouken Glen, and to our delight she provided no dull bread at all. The entire meal was made up of thin Scottish crumpets and potato scones, spread with fresh butter, which we all loved and which was a marvellous treat, washed down with water from the lemonade bottle. The 'toffs' had tea in the lovely Mansion House in Rouken Glen, and we peeped in the door to watch them sitting at their tables, spread with cakes and scones, and decided they must all be 'gaffers' and their families, to have so much money that they could afford to buy a real tea instead of bringing food from home. But we didn't envy them that day, for we hadn't even had to eat bread and margarine before our crumpets and tattie scones, and we had had real fresh butter. 'Aye, ah'll bet ye they didnae get *that* in the Mansion House,' we told each other happily. That was a perfect day out of doors with our mother. It was pleasing to see her sitting among the flowers, undistracted by any sort of work, and feel she was admiring our prowess as we climbed the trees and played races with one another in a wild corner of the park. She didn't have many days when she could afford to 'stand and stare'.

We didn't take a picnic when we went to the bluebell woods, for we only went there in high summer, and there was plenty of daylight for us to come home from Sunday School, change into our everyday clothes, have a jeely piece, and set off for the walk over Crowhill Road and out to Bishopbriggs, and on to the bluebell woods. We were always told by Grannie and my mother not to pull the flowers out by the roots – or there would be none for another year, and we did our best to be careful. We were full of glee and excitement, for nobody was allowed to pick the flowers in the Public Park, and this seemed a wonderful bounty from nature supplying us with all those thousands of bluebells which were there for the picking. Hours later we would come trailing towards the car terminus at Bishopbriggs, with arms full of wilting bluebells, heels blistered and sore, and queue up patiently for a tramcar, for it was too far to walk both ways from home and back, and we had kept a penny from our Saturday pocket money for the tram ride home. Many a precious bluebell was trampled underfoot as we battled to get on to those overflowing tramcars, and many more perished against our hot jerseys before we reached home. I remember once we found wild raspberries in a corner of the woods, and they were a gift straight from heaven, for it was one of my favourite fruits, and to get them for nothing, without committing the crime of pinching them from somebody's garden, seemed sensational.

For in spite of all our bible teaching, holidays in the country, which Grannie loved, were a terrible temptation to us. We were entranced to see fruit growing on bushes in country gardens, quite unprotected by any sort of fencing, and it didn't need much egging on on the part of the local children to help ourselves. They knew perfectly well we weren't supposed to do this, and no doubt were delighted to see how credulous city children could be. We must have been condemned by the garden-owners as city vandals when they saw us dart in and out of their gardens, mouths crammed with fruit, but maybe there was such an abundance that they didn't worry overmuch, for we only took what we could swallow, and we were so choked with guilt as we chewed, our terrified eyes never moving from the windows, that it was pilfering on a very tiny scale. I used to be sick with fright and guilt in case anybody would tell Grannie or my mother, but somehow we were never found out, and that made it seem worse because we *should* have had some sort of punishment for our sins. And yet maybe my punishment came at night when I had to leave the cosy lamplight of the kitchen and go through the garden to the wee hoosie at the far end to use the toilet, for the bushes were full of dark shadows and strange shapes, and my heart went skittering to my mouth at every rustle which shook the leaves. I was sure the devil was lurking there, ready to pounce and take me away with him to the bad fire. It was then that the fruits of conscience were tasted to the full, and oh how I regretted those mouthsful of stolen gooseberries or raspberries.

Grannie usually took us down to the country in advance for my mother was generally working and she joined us only at week-ends. We used to dash up to the station on a Saturday afternoon to meet her train, and chanted from the advertisement stretching along the wall in front of us:

'They come as a boon and a blessing to men,
The Pickwick, the Owl, and the Waverley pen.'

We also memorized a horrible advert for Keating's powder:

'Big fleas have little fleas upon their backs to bite 'em,
The little fleas have lesser fleas, and so ad infinitum
– Kill the lot with Keating's Powder.'

We all knew about fleas, and it was something to be ashamed of, and not talked about, and we were amazed at the cheek of those Keatings' people putting it up on a huge board for all the world to see. We didn't know what 'ad infinitum' meant, and anyway we caught ours by putting down a basin of cold water as we undressed, and the fleas headed straight for the water and drowning. Who needed Keating's powder?

There was an even stranger advertisement in the station, which puzzled me for years, which read:

'If it hurts you to laugh,
Don't read London Opinion.'

I thought that was a gey queer way to sell papers, warning people off them. Nobody I asked could work it out either, and I never ever saw anybody reading this paper, and I decided it served them right that nobody bought their old paper when it was advertised in such a daft way.

During one of those country holidays there was great excitement, for the little town had a visit from a member of the Royal Family. The streets were crammed with sightseers, but my brothers and I became tired of waiting for the royal personage and the procession of dignitaries to arrive, and we wandered to the back of the crowds and peeked over a bridge where a river sluggishly wound its way. Suddenly, to our horrified interest, we saw a huge water rat swimming from one bank to the other, and we became so engrossed in its progress that the royal person, procession and all, had passed by the time we turned round. I had a vague feeling that we had missed something important, but my brothers stoutly voted in favour of the rat. 'Faur better fun,' they assured me. 'You've missed nothing.'

On one holiday, when my mother had managed to accumulate a rare healthy divi from the Co-operative, she had the fanciful notion of taking rooms 'with attendance'. We were very curious as to what this meant, and she told us impressively that it meant that we would just have to do the shopping and the cooking ourselves, and the landlady would keep the rooms clean, and clear the table, and do all the dishes for us. No dishes to wash or dry – oh that was a great idea, we thought. But it didn't work out that way. My mother, never having been used to anyone working after her, became embarrassed at the thought of our landlady having everything to do, although she was being paid for it, and she made us volunteer to do the washing up, a job we hated. 'She's getting peyed fur it!' we would hiss rebelliously, as my mother pushed us out behind the landlady's retreating back and the tray of dirty dishes, with the instruction that we were to offer our services. My mother ignored our unwillingness, and shut the door on us. To our increased fury, the landlady generally accepted our muttered offer, and the boys would stand scowling with the tea towels, while I banged the dishes into the bowl of soapy water, and washed them as fast as I could. We longed to rush out, for we hated wasting a precious minute of the holiday, and then when the job was completed, and everything put away, we were ashamed at the landlady's praise of us and how well my mother had brought us up, to be such rare wee helps. 'Rare wee helps' indeed, when we had been press-ganged into doing those hated dishes. So we scuffed our feet, torn between shame at the undeserved praise, and annoyance that our mother's hard-won money was being taken for attendance that wasn't real attendance at all in our childish eyes. We felt the least that woman could have done was to have given us a rebate. My mother was quite serenely indifferent to our miserly reasonings, and was clearly enjoying the novelty of being somebody of substance in the eyes of our landlady, somebody with enough 'roughness' in her purse to be able to afford the delightful extra of 'attendance'.

7

My mother hated being out of work. Apart from the loss to us of the pay packet, her restricted budget was felt right down the line by everybody who was just that much worse off than we were. The wee washerwoman who did our washings for half a crown was the first to go, but because it was unthinkable to deprive her of her entire livelihood, my mother would rush round all the neighbours in our close, and ask if they would let the washerwoman wash the stairs for them at fourpence a landing. 'Och aye,' they agreed. 'It'll only be for a wee while, for a smert wee wumman like you is sure to get another job soon, Jeanie, and we'll manage fourpence till she gets daein' your washings again.' So that was one-and-fourpence to help out the wee washerwoman during this lean period. But the man who did the staircase window for fourpence had to be refused for a while, and my mother took out the steps and did this large grimy window herself, awaiting better times.

When at last she obtained the coveted job in Cowlairs we were all in seventh heaven. She had gone along to the gates every Friday, trying to catch the eye of the foreman to see if she would get first chance painting the big wagons. At first he was dubious, for she was very tiny and very slim, but she was so eager, and so desperate, he decided to give her a chance. It was only on a temporary basis, at first, to see how she would manage such heavy work, but what she lacked in strength she more than made up in energy, and for those first few weeks while she was on probation we grew used to seeing her come in from work, take her tea in a dream, and then push aside the plates and drop her head on her arms on the table and fall sound asleep. We'd stare at each other, and wonder if we should disturb her by clearing the dishes and getting them washed, or if we should just leave them and let her sleep, and risk her wrath at all the washing up still lying about at bedtime.

And then one Friday night she came in, eyes shining, and not tired at all. 'I've been taken on,' she announced. 'It's permanent.'

After her spell of unemployment this prosperity went to her head, and my mother celebrated it by the wildest burst of extravagance we had ever known. She bought a piano on the pay-up! A piano! And on the pay-up! We caught our breaths in frightened admiration. What would Grannie have said, Grannie who frowned on buying anything unless she had the money in her hand, and who considered any form of hire purchase was the road to ruin. But my mother reasoned that if we waited until we had all the money which the piano cost we would never get one in this life, for there would always be something more pressing. Och, and anyway it would be marvellous to have a piano for parties, and she knew I had always longed to learn to play this instrument. It would give us some real music, and would help to drown the clatter of Tommy's drum-sticks on top of the rubber practice-pad. He was learning to be a drummer at the Boys' Brigade and drove us all frantic with his endless 'para-diddles' on the dresser-top, for our ears could find no tune at all in this noisy hammering.

My mother revelled in this purchase. She didn't waste a second on mere tone when she bought it. It was the beautiful black polished case which entranced her. The sideboard was pushed to the end of the room where it squeaked tightly against the sofa, and the piano was installed, magnificent and shining, along the wall opposite the fireplace. We all stood silent, drinking in its splendour, while my mother flicked off imaginary specks with a duster. She would work overtime, she told us, and what with that money and her good weekly wage she would never even feel the instalments. If only *one* of us could have sat down and played a tune of triumph at this splendid moment her cup would have been full. But she was determined to give me every chance to develop a talent, and she arranged for me to have lessons at sixpence a week from a wee man who worked beside her. Somebody had told her he was a dab hand at the piano, and when she had approached him to see if he would consider teaching me he had said at once, 'Of coorse ah'll learn the wean: ah've still goat the books ah hid when ah wis a wee fulla, an' she'll easy pick up hoo tae use her fingers on the right keys.'

He was a widower, and lived alone, and his dank fusty single apartment fascinated me. The first thing I noticed was the smell. A compound of dungarees, tobacco and airlessness. I felt sure the window was never opened from one week's end to the next. A hook which wouldn't have disgraced a crane stuck out from the back of the door, and on this hung his wardrobe. Raincoat, heavy coat, jacket, bunnet, and sundry odds and ends. The room was crammed with furniture. Two big chairs with newspapers stuck down the arms, two kitchen chairs and a big table of heavy mahogany, like the ones normally used in our tenements for supporting coffins. Surely he didn't take his meals off that? But he did, as I had plenty of opportunity to discover during later lessons, for he walked about making his tea, peeling his tatties and frying his sausages while I stumbled through scales and fingering exercises. The frying pan was never off the hob, and it was clear to me he lived on nothing but 'fries'. Grannie would never have approved. I imagined I could hear her say, 'Dear to buy, hard on the stomach, and no' nearly as nourishing as guid stews, cooked long and slowly to draw oot every bit of good from the meat.' But of course Mr Patterson would never have had time for all this, and him at his work all day. I had never met a widower before, and accepted this strangely smelly room as part of the aroma of a house without a woman. His dresser was covered with dishes, and books, and a draught-board, and dominoes, and at the end a fascinating object which I discovered was a pipe-rack. He arranged all his pipes on it for me to see the complete effect. I'd not seen such a thing before, and decided it was a lovely tidy idea to store all those pipes so neatly together, but they smelt to high heaven. I could never see my mother letting them sit so near the frying pan, but he didn't seem to mind. It dawned on me that men weren't nearly as fussy as women in these matters, for when I asked him how he cleaned them he said, 'I don't. The tobacco tastes faur better frae a weel-used pipe.' No wonder they smelt. Apart from the food we ate, there wasn't a thing in our house that wasn't cleaned at some time.

At the end of the lesson he would wipe his hands and sit down at the piano and thunder out 'Scots wha ha'e' and 'Bonnie Dundee' until the dishes danced on the dresser and the smelly pipes accompanied them in a gentle jig. I thought he was a marvellous player, and with all the noise he was making I didn't mind raising my voice in song, and the concert only ended when the sausages in the pan were in danger of burning or the potatoes boiling over. He told my mother I was 'a wee warmer', but he decided I had learnt enough and he couldn't conscientiously take my mother's hard-earned sixpence any longer when I knew how to run up a few scales and pick out carefully the tune of 'The Bluebells of Scotland'. 'The rest is nae bother,' he assured me. 'Ye'll easy pick oot a' the other tunes for yersel' noo ye know the ropes.'

But I never did. We had no money for sheet music, and this slight knowledge of reading music ruined any ability I might have had to play by ear, so I badgered my mother to try another teacher, the father of a school chum who charged seven-and-sixpence a quarter. That seemed a fortune, until we worked it out and found it was only three-halfpence a week more than Mr Patterson. But this was a dull, dour man who took not the slightest interest in me. The room was cold and clean, with a flickering gas mantle which gave out a cheerless light, and there was a damp feeling as though the fireplace had never known the blaze of comforting coal. Mr Torrance held open the door for me, sat me down at the piano in front of a sheet of music, retired behind his newspaper and never uttered a single word during the entire lesson. If I asked a question he just cleared his throat, raised his eyebrows, and either shook or nodded his head. I had dark suspicions he was only wasting my mother's good money, and felt there must surely be more to teaching than this. We'd be far better off spending the seven-and-sixpence on music books ourselves, and my mother would get the pleasure of hearing me actually learning! So one night I announced to the silent Mr Torrance as he rose to show me to the door, 'Ah'm no' comin' back. Cheerio.' And that was the end of that. I don't know whether he was shocked, or disappointed, for his face registered nothing, but I knew a small sense of triumph that he wasn't going to escape into the room away from his family to enjoy a good read of the paper at my mother's expense any more. I might not be able to play the piano, but I wisnae daft, thought I, as I skipped home to the warmth of our own fireside, and to my mother's laughter when I told her what I had done.

So we bought a book of Harry Lauder's songs, and I sat down confidently, armed with my knowledge of all those scales which I had mastered, using all the right fingers, and found my progress went at a snail's pace. Far from enjoying hearing me learning, my mother wondered audibly when that wean was ever gaun tae play onything that sounded like a tune. I *longed* to be able to sit down and rattle off 'Will ye' no come back again', which she loved, or 'I Love a Lassie' from Lauder's repertoire, but although the tunes dirled in my head, my fingers just refused to echo this smart tempo. I could only manage dirges which gave plenty of time to read and find the notes.

'Gi'e Tommy a wee shot,' she would say, and Tommy, to my shame, would sit down, without the benefit of instruction from any music maestro, and rattle off tune after tune by ear. All that money wasted on me, and every note of every tune had to be wrestled for, while he sat down and pounded notes by the dozen and a tune emerged. And he didn't know a crotchet from a semi-breve. It was maddening. But it made a welcome change from those drum tattoos, and it was grand to sing out a rousing chorus accompanied by our fine piano, even if mine weren't the fingers which drew the tune from the instrument.

But Tommy and I did manage one hilarious duet, me doing scales, and him battering away with his drum-sticks, at the end of one of our flittings. We hadn't moved house for at least a year, and my mother was getting restless. We knew this when we saw her begin to look round the house with a critical eye. The range wasn't drawing properly, and she knew fine that the factor would do nothing about renewing vital parts. The room windows let in a terrible draught – the frames were old, so nothing could be done. She was sure the woodwork on the kitchen sink was rotten.

Then one night after tea she announced casually that she had heard of a rare house in Millarbank Street, which wasn't only half-way to Cowlairs and would mean less walking for her, but it actually boasted a bathroom! The property had originally been intended for the higher-paid employees of the works, and had been good once upon a time, but had come down a wee bit socially, and the rents were reasonable. We were all getting too big for baths in the zinc bath in front of the fire, anyway, she told us. We hadn't noticed this but she said she had. To us this was just another excuse for flitting, which we cheerfully accepted.

This move was too far for us to be able to indulge in the economy of running round with most of our household stuff, so we had a horse and cart, kindly supplied to us by the coalman. My mother rushed out and swept off the coal-dust from the cart before our furniture and effects were loaded, and the horse trotted off with a nice turn of speed, our stuff swaying perilously as it turned off Springburn Road, but kept in check by the boys who sat beside the driver, urging the horse to 'Gee up' while they held on to stools and chairs which threatened to crash to the ground.

We no longer had Grannie to examine the flues for dangerous soot, and my mother had rashly accepted the word of the out-going tenant that the chimney had recently been swept. It was a bitterly cold night, and as she got the room to rights she piled masses of flitting junk into the fireplace, for the double purpose of getting rid of it and heating the icy room. She heaped on old rotten linoleum she had found lining a press, old wallpaper, boxes, junk of every description, making a grand clearance while she was at it. There came an ominous rushing noise in the chimney, and we knew the worst had happened even before the hot soot began falling in the hearth.

'Heavens, the chimney's on fire,' my mother called out in anguished tones, as though we weren't all fully aware of the fact. She felt it was in the worst possible taste to introduce herself like this to her new neighbours. It would be a terrible start to life in our new house if we set the joists of the whole building on fire.

Suddenly I had an inspiration. As there were twelve families in the tenement, it was almost impossible to tell from the blazing chimney seen from the street which tenant was the offender, so I leaped into the front room, sat down at the piano, and raced up and down the scales like mad. My mother thought I had gone off my head until I explained my craftiness.

'You see,' I shouted above the din of the piano, 'if they hear us playing they'll never think it can be our chimney. Who would suspect us of fiddling while Rome burns?' We'd just heard about Nero in school.

My mother began to laugh helplessly, and Tommy, infected by the spirit of the thing, seized his drum-sticks and beat out a rhythmic accompaniment to my scales, while Willie and my mother threw salt on the fire to put the flames out. The strategy worked. We were never found out. As my mother said afterwards, 'That piano ferry earned its keep, and a' thae piano lessons werenae wasted, efter all.'

The roaring fire in the chimney had done one good thing, though. It had heated the water, and for the first time in our lives we were able to turn on a hot-water tap and fill a basin with beautiful, piping hot water. I was all for taking a bath, for the sheer joy of lying down in a full bath in our very own house, but my mother decided against this. The bath needed painting, she said, and she'd read of a new paint which was guaranteed to be perfect for baths and to be unaffected by the temperature of even the hottest water. She decided green would be ideal, for it would look like the sea when the bath was filled, and she followed the maker's instructions to the letter, letting each coat dry thoroughly before applying the next. Then after three coats had been lovingly applied, the bath was filled with cold water so that the whole surface could harden. We hung breathlessly over the shimmering water, and pressed surreptitious finger-tips against the side to see if the paint was drying properly, and longed for the moment when the time would be ripe for the first bath. On a Saturday afternoon, when everyone was out, I decided if the paint was ever going to harden it must have done it by this time, and I let the cold water out, replaced the plug, and turned on the hot tap. I was determined to be the first to sample this wonderful new luxury. I carefully measured in a tablespoonful of Woolworth's bath salts – pink and scented – and sniffed rapturously as the perfumed steam rose and swirled about the room. Gently I lowered myself into the water, and lay back, rejoicing in the novelty of a bath at home, with no shouts from the cubicles next door, and no watchful attendant to curtail the length of time as I wallowed in sleepy bliss. I sat up and began to scrub myself with the loofah and found I couldn't move my bottom. I had stuck to the bath! I shot to my feet in alarm and found that my nether regions were thickly coated with green paint! Frantically I began to scrape it off with the blunt side of an old knife my mother had left on the ledge. Then I felt my feet sticking to the paint. I moved to another part of the bath, thinking it was maybe only in the centre that the paint hadn't dried. As I walked from one part to another, the paint lifted off in layers, each one acting like a sucker to pull off the one beneath. First green paint, then white paint, right down to the rusty metal of the bath itself, stripped of all its top coatings. I was hysterical by this time, partly with terror at having ruined the bath and all my mother's good painting, and partly because the sight of paint festooning my feet like thick-soled sandals convinced me that nothing short of burning would ever get it off. I couldn't even get out of the bath, for in the excitement of getting into it, I hadn't put a towel down, and I daren't walk over the floor to look for turpentine or a sharper knife. At that moment my mother walked in, smelt the bath salts and threw open the bathroom door. She took one look at me, covered in paint, at her fine bath stripped of its lovely sea-green surface, cuffed me over the ear, and disappeared. 'Mother,' I yelled after her, 'come back. I couldnae help it. The paint just melted wi' the hoat water. It couldnae have been the right stuff ye used.' This infuriated her even more, for she prided herself on her knowledge of paint. Didn't she use paint every working day, and weren't the gaffers expert at giving advice on the right quality to use for a bath? By this time she was scraping paint off my feet, and rubbing vigorously with an old piece of towel dipped in turpentine. It sent me off into paroxysms of laughter, for apart from being agony, it was also tickly. She began to laugh herself. 'Och I'm glad it was you, and no' me,' she said at last. 'I'd never have got it off in time for the dance the night if I'd had the first bath.' Then she sighed. 'And right enough, if it hasnae dried in a hale week, it couldnae have been the right stuff for baths.' Oh how I admired her generosity in admitting it, for I knew she was heart-sick at the rusty mess which her grand bath had become, and I promised to help her to rub it all down with sandpaper, and take a shot at applying the next lot of paint, and this time we'd go up to the drysalters and get expert advice, and not *dream* of putting hot water near new paint for *weeks* after the last coat had dried. By that time, surely, the fires in the soles of my feet would have cooled, and the blisters on my bottom healed. But I'd let one of the boys have the first bath next time, just in case.

When we first moved into this house we had noticed, as a sort of bonus, that it was above a fish-and-chip shop. This, we thought, was great. We wouldn't have far to go for our favourite treat of shop chips, and the occasional luxury of fish for special occasions. We hadn't the least suspicion that there might be hazards in living above such pungent smells. As the weather grew warmer, everything in the house smelt of fat. The blue smoke from boiling vats of dripping drifted upstairs and filled our rooms. Worse was to come. The fat which was so nice to sniff when passing a chip-shop door on a cold night was now nauseating us, for it clung to our jerseys, our coats and our bedclothes, and filled our noses as we dressed and undressed, or pulled the blankets up round our chins in bed. And we discovered, to our horror, that this penetrating fat was a perfect Pied Piper to every mouse for miles. When we turned out the gas at night the patter of their scurryings was as insistent as Tommy's drum-sticks. My mother was terrified of them. She began to jump at every shadow. One morning, as she put her foot into her slipper when she jumped out of bed, a startled mouse leaped out before she could squash it. Her screams wakened the whole stair. That was the end, and we knew it. She went shuddering off to work, vowing she wouldn't stay another night in this infested building. It was impossible to keep that vow, of course, but by the end of the week she had found another house, in Keppochhill Road, two stairs up. There was no bathroom, but there were no fumes from fish and chips, and no attraction for mice. There was, though, an inside toilet. On balance, we decided this amenity was the best possible exchange for a rusty old bath, for it wasn't absolutely necessary to have a bath too often, whereas the toilet was in use all the time. Oh and what a luxury not to have to share with any other family. A whole toilet for the four of us. Dreams of comfort could envisage nothing finer.

This move was one of the most enjoyable of all the Weir flittings, but the fish and chips for the party afterwards did not come from the shop below the house we were so thankfully leaving. We decided to patronize the newest shop off Keppochhill Road, whose white tiles, and the immaculate overalls of the lady behind the counter, ensured absolute cleanliness. The quantities were tiny, compared with other slapdash shops, but we could be sure the fat hadn't been shared by a colony of mice. Maybe it was the grandeur of having a bath and a piano at the same time, but we seemed to be getting pernickity in our ways, or giving more thought to cause and effect, for up till that time we'd never concerned ourselves with the possibility of mice thriving where chip fat was plentiful. Certainly other folk didn't seem so finicky, for there was no shortage of takers for the houses situated above all the fish-and-chip shops in Springburn. And the family who took the place we left were delighted to get it, rusty bath and all, especially when we could assure them, hand on heart, that there wasn't a bit of dirty soot in the chimney.

Mind you, we couldn't really be surprised at mice enjoying chips, for I was sure it was the chips they went for, and not the fat. Even Bruce, the little Highland collie Tommy had brought home from one of his long walks into the country, loved our fish-and-chip shops. In fact, when he ran away for a few days, leaving us all heartbroken, the first places we looked were the fish-and-chip shops. When the ones in our immediate neighbourhood yielded nothing we scoured back courts as far down as the Moss-House on our way to the next cluster of chip shops there, and in the other direction we went as far as the Low Road, nearly to Bishopbriggs. Nothing. Oh and how empty the house seemed without him. We had grown used to being greeted with a rushing, welcoming licking, and an eager wagging tail every time we opened the door. I had spent hours training him to be obedient. I refused to pick him up, even when he ran after every passer-by in the street as a puppy, for he had to learn to follow me when I called, and to use his own legs to get about, just as I had learned. How proud I was when he came to heel at a word from me. Even my mother missed him, although he nearly drove her mad by eating any food she thoughtlessly left within his reach.

Then one night I was sent to deliver a message to an auntie who lived about a mile from us. It started to rain when I left her house, and she insisted on treating me to a penny ride on the tramcar, so I wouldn't get soaked. As I sat on the top deck, enjoying this unaccustomed treat in the middle of the week, my gaze fell on the open doorway of a chip shop a full three stops before the fare stage for our house. There, standing with his paws on the counter, an ingratiating tongue lolling, was our Bruce! In one bound I was at the top of the stairs. I clattered down, and threw myself off the platform recklessly, although the tram was fairly tearing along between the stops. I was terrified Bruce would take off again and we would never find him. I had only a passing swift regret for the lost three tram stops for which I'd paid and not enjoyed.

I panted into the shop. 'Bruce Weir,' I thundered as severely as my relieved heart would allow, 'where have you been?' The girl laughed when she heard me. 'My,' she said, 'I've never heard onybody crying their dug wi' a second name. Whit's up? Wis he lost?' 'For four whole days,' I said tremulously, relief at the sight of Bruce standing there, safe and sound, threatening to dissolve in tears. 'Four days,' she said wonderingly. 'Jings, nae wunner he was dyin' fur a chip!' I allowed him to eat just one, and then ordered him out of the shop. He slunk out ahead of me, with guilty backward glances, a furtive sort of lope quite different from his usual eager gait. When we reached home Tommy walloped him so that he would know it was wrong to run away, and that he must never do it again. I held his collar while Tommy smacked his bottom, and I couldn't see for tears, because while he was being punished, Bruce was licking my hand. I supposed he had to be punished for his own good, but I couldn't bear this humble acceptance and loving forgiveness. I would far rather he had bitten both of us.

236

8

When I was a wee girl in Glasgow, Hallowe'en was celebrated by all of us with keenest enjoyment. The weather always seemed clear and frosty, the skies filled with stars, and there was the exhilaration of dressing up in strange garments, with the added tension and nervousness of a performance about to begin. I usually wore Grannie's old hat, when it had got beyond the stage when a bunch of cherries or a spray of flowers could rejuvenate it, and I sat it on top of my head at a rakish angle, over my blackened face. A long skirt of my mother's, and Grannie's tartan shawl completed the disguise, but I wasn't able to round off the effect with my mother's high-heeled shoes because I couldn't even hobble in them, so my long-legged boots and black woollen stockings just had to be worn, even though they were completely out of character. This was a terrible disappointment, for I longed to prance about in elegant high heels, but for running out and in closes and up and down dozens of stairs sure footing was vital, and boots it had to be.

There was much giggling and mutual admiration when we all met after tea, and set out on the rounds of all the neighbours' houses. Sometimes, greatly daring, we went beyond our own district, and we shivered with excitement and a little dread at the thought of knocking at such strange doors. We were very critical of the brasses, and surprised to find that in some posh closes the name-plates weren't a patch on the glittering gold polish our own mothers managed. We each carried a little bag, home-made from an old petticoat or blouse, with a draw-string top, to hold the expected apples and nuts and sweets we hoped we would collect, and we prepared our acts as we raced along from close to close. We never expected to be handed our Hallowe'en gifts just for knocking on a door and chanting, 'Please gi'e us wur Hallowe'en!' We knew we were expected to do a turn to entertain our benefactors.

We would be invited into the house, and the family would sit round in lively anticipation as we went into our performances. I usually sang the latest popular song, and I particularly liked one requiring the use of my hostess's flue-brush, which I stuck over my shoulder and used as a bayonet. Very dashing I thought this, and so did my audience! There were recitations and ballads, and we generally finished with all of us doing a Highland Fling. We received our applause with flushed and happy faces, and we opened our draw-string bags to receive the apples, and the nuts, with maybe a piece of puff candy or some home-made tablet. Tablet was a great treat and so tempting that it was devoured on the spot, and seldom rested in the bag for a second. A turnip lantern lit our way and we went bobbing through the darkness like glow-worms. The preparation of those magic lanterns was a great ploy. We hollowed out swede turnips skilfully, made two slits for the eyes and a perpendicular line for the nose. A curved slit made a smiling mouth. A little hollow in the bottom held our candle, and the complete effect was golden and delightful. I may say everybody in our district ate mashed swedes for days afterwards, using up the discarded inside of our lanterns.

A party was a great excitement at Hallowe'en, and everyone went in fancy dress. Home-made, of course, for these were unsophisticated as well as hard-up days, and only 'toffs' would have known about hiring clothes. Angels and fairies, their wings fashioned from cardboard boxes coaxed from the Co-operative, and covered with coloured crinkled paper, were ten a penny, for the girls. The boys favoured pirates and cowboys, which were easily fashioned from old hats, and their father's leather belts, and toy guns. All this helped to break down the shyness we would have felt in ordinary clothes, although Hallowe'en fun was so different from any other form of merriment there was never a minute of sitting still wondering what you were expected to do. After the tea, with its salmon sandwiches if we were lucky, or corn mutton if money was tight, followed by the jellies, the games started. The big zinc bath was pulled from under the bed and filled with cold water, then rosy-cheeked apples were tumbled in in a colourful shower. A chair was placed with its back to the bath, the apples and water given a vigorous stir to send them bobbing as wildly as possible and make a difficult target, and we would each kneel, one at a time, on the chair, head sticking out over the top edge just as though we were about to be guillotined. A fork was held between clenched teeth, and we'd gaze at the bobbing fruit below us, waiting for the moment when the biggest and reddest apple was exactly placed for our aim, then *plonk*, down went the fork, usually to slither off between the bouncing apples. There would be howls of glee from the onlookers, and gulping disappointment from the unlucky contestant as he or she climbed down from the chair to go to the end of the queue again. Not till everybody had speared an apple would the next game start, and, of course, it became harder and harder to succeed as the numbers of apples grew fewer and fewer with each win, and the final apple had the whole room shouting opposite advice. 'Drap yer fork noo. *Noo*, Wullie. Ach missed it', 'Gi'e the watter a steer, it's easier when it's movin'', or 'Don't steer it noo, gi'e 'im a chance seein' there's only wan'. And from the faint-hearted, or those who wanted to go on to another game, 'Ach just gi'e 'im it, and let's get on wi' the party.'

There was a lovely game, unpopular with parents but beloved by us children, where a huge home-baked soda scone was covered in treacle and suspended on a string from the centre gas bracket, or hung from a string stretched across the room. It was sent spinning by the leader, and then, with hands clasped behind our backs, we would leap into the air and try to snatch a bite. What a glorious mess we were in at the end of this caper, hair, eyes, cheeks and neck covered in treacle. Mothers and aunties and uncles urged us instantly towards the kitchen sink, 'Go and dight yer faces noo, we don't want treacle a' ower the hoose,' and what a splashing there was under the cold tap, and a battle for the solitary towel as we removed the mess.

And, of course, we loved the trinkets which were buried in a mound of creamy mashed potatoes. Even the poorest family could afford tatties, so everybody could enjoy this traditional bit of fun. The quantities of potatoes we consumed in search of our favourite ring or threepenny piece must have saved many an anxious hostess from worrying how she was going to fill us up.

The older girls were full of romantic notions concerning apples. They'd try to take off the peel in one continuous strand, which they threw over their left shoulder, and whichever initial it formed was supposed to be that of the lad they would marry. Oh the teasing and the blushing if by chance the initial formed was that of their current heart-throb. The boys pretended they had no interest in this performance, but there was plenty of jeering and pushing when the initial fitted, and a casual pairing off when the game had finished. Especially if the next game was the one where an apple was placed on the top edge of a door, with a chair placed on either side, a boy on one chair and a girl on the other. They each ate towards the core, and the winners were the couple who reached the core – and a kiss – in the shortest possible time.

We children thought the swinging apple game was far better, and it was funnier too. There were up to six contestants at a time required for this game, which made it rare and noisy and exciting. They had to stand in line, in front of six apples suspended on cords from a string stretched across the room. The apples were set swinging, and the point of the game was that, without using hands to help, the contestants had to bite the fruit right down to the core. The winner, of course, was the one who finished first. The apple could be manœuvred on to one shoulder only *once* during the game to assist the eating, but otherwise everybody leaped and bit like hungry birds, and a most comical sight it was for the onlookers. It was especially funny when the grown-ups took their turn, and we held our sides with laughter when specs slithered down perspiring noses, when braces parted from buttons, and when false teeth were dislodged on hitting an apple too suddenly. We could have played this game all night, but all at once the apples were finished, and it was time to go home, this time without lanterns to light our way, for, of course, we didn't take them to parties, only when we went out chanting 'Please gi'e us wur Hallowe'en'.

What a long time it seemed between Hallowe'en and Christmas. The nights were dark, but they didn't keep us in, and we flew out and in the closes following our usual games of High-Spee-Wigh, and Buckety-Buck-Buck, and the boys had their own back courts and we had ours, for we wouldn't have dreamed of mixing. The boys had another game, which was fiercely condemned by the grown-ups and was always guaranteed either to irritate or frighten the victims half out of their wits. This was called 'clockwork'. A button or a lead washer was threaded on to a long piece of black cotton or thin string, on the pulley principle. The terminal point was fixed with a pin to the wooden sash of the kitchen window, and then the boys stole through the back court, carefully paying out the string. Silently they climbed on top of the wash-house, to give them the necessary height and keep them out of sight, and for the next hour they rocked with laughter as they tormented the occupants of the chosen house. They'd give the thread a little jerk, the button or washer would run down, knock against the window-pane, tap, tap, before being eased back. Inside the house, where folk sat quietly reading or talking, for there was no radio to make a noise, the tap on the window was like ghostly fingers. 'Who's that?' a voice would call out. 'It's somebody at the door,' a dull-of-hearing grannie might answer. 'It's no' the door, it's the windae.' 'My Goad, wha would be at the window at this time o' night?' The curtains would be parted and a face would peer out into the darkness. The boys, convulsed with giggles from their hiding place behind the chimneys on the wash-house, would wait till everything was quiet again, and start off their tapping once more. You would have thought the neighbours would have suspected 'clockwork' instantly when they heard a tapping at the window, but we were all brought up on a diet of ghosts and Flannel Feet, and the first thing anybody thought of was the supernatural or some unnamed horror. It was bad enough when this game was played on the people who occupied the houses in the close, for their windows were at ground level and it might just have been a friend knocking, but when some daring boys climbed the rhone-pipe and fastened the string and button contraption to a house one storey from the ground, they even had the added success of a few screams from the mothers, who were convinced it must be a descendant of Jack the Ripper at the very least. But when the tapping went on, and nobody launched himself over the window-sill into the room, the truth dawned. Windows would be thrown up, and groping hands would seek the string and the pin fastening it there, and a furious tug from the irritated occupant of the house ended the game for that night. Sometimes a ground-floor husband, who no doubt had played the game many times as a wee boy, would steal through the back close and slip through the shadows to the wash-house. With a roar, he would vault among the boys, and send them scattering in terror as he tried to cuff as many ears as possible in the dark. This successful turning of the tables generally put the husband in a great good humour, but so scared the boys that clockwork got a very long rest, and other livelier games took over, with no risks of a thumping involved.

Our mothers were always warning us about the dangers of jumping off the wash-house dykes, or playing near the broken railings which divided the back courts, but these were our playing fields and we accepted the cut knees and bruised heads as part of the added spice. Once, when I was very small, I had a passionate urge to climb right to the top of the railings, and as I clung with fingers and toes to the rusty iron, I turned round and urged a chum to 'Push me up, ach goan, juist a wee push and I can hing on to the top bar'. As I turned my head, she obligingly pushed, my head fell back and the spikes went right through the skin. I jumped down, put a hand to my curls, and drew it away dripping with blood. With shaking legs I ran up the two double flights of stairs to the house, where my mother was just changing out of her dungarees. She took one look at me, and moved the kettle over the fire to get hot. The news went round the stair like wildfire, and in two minutes our kitchen was like a first-aid station. 'Have you got sherp shears, Jeanie?' demanded one. 'You'll hiv tae cut away her hair.' 'Oh don't cut ma hair,' I wailed, 'I don't want to be baldy.' 'Ye'll no' be baldy,' said Mrs Sampson soothingly. 'It'll grow in again, but ye don't want it a' stickin' tae the bluid, dae ye?' Mrs Sampson had a bandage and Mrs Dalrymple had some sticking plaster. My mother had now filled the white enamel basin with warm water, and was urged to add salt to clean the wound. Nobody had cotton wool, so she used an old clean hankie to dab off the blood, and carefully she snipped away at my curl. It stung like fury, but she had gripped me between her knees and I couldn't move. 'Get a' the roost washed off, Jeanie,' the women urged, 'or it'll fester.' Oblivious to my cries, my mother washed and rubbed until I was sure she was right through to the bone. Plaster was applied, then, for good measure, some boracic lint, then a bandage, and then I got a skelp across the legs for having given everybody such a fright. There were no cuddles for weans in our tenements when they played at such dangerously daft games.

Even more serious was the fall suffered by one of Tommy's chums who lived in the next close. He was a quiet, very thin boy, who never seemed to get enough to eat. His father always seemed to be out of work, and once when my auntie went to visit them when the mother was ill she saw the father mixing flour and water and frying it in the pan, pretending this paste mixture was pancakes. Auntie had cried when she told us, but we thought it was quite clever of him thinking of such a thing, for we weren't used to menfolks taking the slightest interest in cooking. It must have been this sort of diet, though, which made the boy Alan so pimply and listless, and yet when the boys went exploring over the roof-tops of a workshop at the Railways one summer night it was Alan who got the devil into him and accepted the dare to jump from one wooden roof-frame to the next without touching the glass. He hadn't the energy for such leaps, and the next moment had crashed through the glass to the floor beneath. Luckily, a policeman had seen them, and when he heard the crashing glass, phoned immediately for an ambulance. He took little notice of the other terrified boys, and sat by Alan until the ambulance arrived to take him to hospital.

Few of us got any sleep that night. It seemed terrible that a summer game could end in such disaster. Our mothers told us that Alan had had to have dozens of stitches in his cuts, and his blood was so poor, if he were to raise his arms above his head, he could die! Raised arms would draw the blood away from his heart, it seemed. 'But how'll they stoap him fae pittin' his arms above his heid, Mother?' I asked. I always put my arms on top of my head when I went to sleep, and I didn't see how Alan would know what he was doing if he were sound asleep. 'Oh a nurse will sit beside him to make sure he disnae,' my mother said. We all prayed for him when we went to bed, and I lay and tried to pretend I was the one who mustn't move my arms or I would die, and I found it was torture to stop them creeping up to the top of my head. Oh I was so glad it wasn't me in that hospital. Oh this proved that our mothers knew best. Oh how good we would be if only Alan got better. It was touch and go for a week, for his constitution wasn't good. All the years of poor feeding had taken their toll, but he was a bonnie fighter when it came to it, and maybe our prayers helped, for he confounded the doctors and got better. We had a marvellous party when he came home. We didn't have it in his house, for five of them lived in a single-end with hardly a stick of furniture, so we had it in the back court, on pay-day. We had bottles of Iron Brew, and, when that was finished, wee pokes of health salts to make fizzy drinks, and Torrance's pies (one between two), and biscuits. And we drew chalk stumps on the wall connecting our wash-house and the one in the next back court, and played cricket, using an old tennis ball and a bat Alan's father had made from an old piece of orange box, and it was great fun seeing all the mothers down in the back court with us. Alan looked quite different. The food in the hospital must have been a wonderful surprise to his stomach, for he had filled out, and his thin cheeks were rounded and pink, and, best of all, he hadn't a single pimple. When I asked him if it was terrible not having been able to put his arms above his head, he stared at me. 'I never pit ma erms above ma heid in bed,' he said. 'I coorie doon and put them roon' ma shoulders to keep warm.' I decided the doctors must have been daft not to have asked him that, instead of making a poor nurse sit up all night making sure he didn't do something he wouldn't have thought of doing anyway. I thought if ever I had to go to hospital I would tell them everything I did and didn't do, so nobody's time would be wasted.

Alan's mother, with her sad face, red nose and pimply complexion, looked absolutely bewildered with all the excitement over her son's recovery, and I felt she must have something else to look forward to, so on an impulse I asked her to come along to our very next Guide concert. 'You don't have to take off yer coat,' I assured her, thinking I was being tactful, for I knew she didn't have a good dress for Sundays which she could reveal at a concert, but she needn't feel self-conscious in her brown tweed coat. 'I'm allowed to take somebody in for nothing,' I told her happily, 'because I'm producing one of the wee plays, and I'm helping to make the cakes.' This wasn't really true, but I knew I could easily make some tablet and sell it and raise the threepence to buy her a ticket. 'Whit about yer mother?' she asked me. 'Does she no' want to go?' 'Och naw,' I said. 'She's been umpteen times and she's going to a dance anyway that night.' That part was true, and Mrs Dalrymple's eyes brightened as I described the lovely tea she would get, with home-made cakes and scones which we would bring round in the interval. These concerts were very popular with the mothers, and we did everything ourselves. They were held in the church hall, and the church officer rigged up a real curtain for the occasion, which we thought was very professional. For weeks beforehand we rehearsed our little plays and sketches, and I rejoiced in the heady power of producing several of them, ordering my cast about ruthlessly, and even replacing them if they hadn't learnt their words well enough. The captain and the lieutenant subcontracted the cooking chores. One batch of us was detailed to make scones, another to make pancakes, a third lot to make apple tarts or sponge cakes, and the money for the ingredients came out of the funds. On the night of the concert we streamed from our closes bearing large plates of home-baking, which we laid triumphantly in the church kitchen where a few mothers had been roped in to help set out trays of cups and saucers, fill sugar bowls and cream jugs, and see that the tea urn was working all right. This was put on at a wee peep of gas as soon as the concert started, so that the water would be boiling at the precise moment the curtain closed at the end of the first half of the concert. Having attended to the domestic side of the affair, we flew backstage to change into our acting clothes, and shivered with nervous delight as we heard chairs scraping and our audience filling the hall. They were out to enjoy themselves, were uncritical and easy to please, and they greeted our sketches and recitations and songs with enthusiastic applause, and we believed them when they told us we were 'as guid as a pantomime'.

At the end of the first half, eyes shining with delight that we'd all remembered our words, and drunk with power at our ability to send them all off into hilarious laughter, we raced to the kitchen for the plates of scones and cakes, and became waitresses handing out all the melting home-baking to our audience, who had now pushed their chairs round the walls of the hall to give us plenty of room to attend to them. The mothers came from the kitchen with teapots, for we weren't to be entrusted with hot tea in case we'd skail it over good coats, and soon everybody was sipping and munching to their hearts' content. 'Hiv wan o' thae scones,' they'd recommend a neighbour. 'Wan fae Jessie's plate, fur Mrs Grant makes a scone as light as an angel's wing.' Pursed lips from a mother indicated she too had made scones, and was furious at somebody else's being preferred. We'd been well warned by our officers not to indicate the bakers of any of our proffered goodies, but old customers among our audience easily recognized tried and trusted pastry and were not to be fobbed off with just anything stuck under their noses. One fat lady sent me into hysterics when she tried to pop a piece of apple tart into her mouth, and it disintegrated and scattered over her ample chest. Rescuing the pieces, she said with a wink, 'Missing the rosebud every time.' This description of her large laughing mouth struck me as being so funny that I couldn't wait to get home and tell my mother about it. Every time I saw that big fat woman in the street afterwards I daringly called her 'Rosebud' under my breath, and enjoyed the incongruous description all over again.

Wee Mrs Dalrymple was enchanted with everything. As my mother would have said, she fairly 'came oot her shell', and laughed and clapped, and drank tea, and devoured everything that was offered to her, whether it be entertainment or food. I nearly burst with pleasure when at the end, as I was on my way to the kitchen to help stack away the dishes and collect my scone plate, she caught my arm and said, 'My, that's the best night I've had for years, hen. Wait till I get hame and tell

Erchie a' aboot it, he'll hardly believe whit rer wee turns youse a' are.' Her face was so flushed, her nose didn't look red at all, and the pimples were invisible, and I was amazed to discover she was quite nice-looking. What a transformation for threepence!

I wasn't sure whether I liked the concerts in the winter or the evening picnics in the summer best, for the Guides taught us to indulge in the exciting luxury of cooked food after an evening walking or trekking in the country. No dry or soggy sandwiches for us then. We'd saved up for weeks and bought little flat frying pans with folding handles which served both as cooking utensil and plate. We were shown how to make a fire from the paper we'd taken with us, and twigs we gathered on our walk. Stones were cunningly positioned to provide protection and a strategic draught, and we'd crouch over damp twigs and paper until a glow told us the fire had caught, and then it was turn and turn about to make cheese dreams or sausages. Another fire was started a little way off and this was for our tea, and what a lovely smoky taste it had. I was charmed with how easily an ordinary cheese sandwich could be transformed into a delicious gooey delight by the simple process of turning it over and over in hot dripping or margarine until it was crisp and brown on the outside and running with soft melting cheese in the centre. Not that we often managed to achieve such perfection, for we were all thrusting our frying pans over the rim of the spluttering fire at the same time as the girl who was supposed to be having sole use of it, and we were far too impatient to wait for a golden outside and a soft centre. A prodding finger would tell us our sandwich was warm and we'd shout, 'Oh, mine's ready', and the sight of our rolling eyes and munching jaws would be too much for the steadier types, and soon they were eating their half-cooked sandwiches too. I only really learned what it ought to look and taste like when I made some one night for my mother's tea at home, and after that I took time to wait and achieve proper results on our Guide picnics. Nobody had to tell us about litter, for we burned all our papers in the fires to help the cooking, and we ate every single bit of food we brought. If one couldn't finish what she had cooked there were plenty of eager takers to snap up the leftovers. In fact, some of the girls brought nothing, and, as I primly quoted from the Bible to them, depended on 'the crumbs from the rich man's table'. 'Ach you and your bible,' they'd retort, 'there's aye plenty left, and onywey we helped to blaw into the fire tae get it gaun.' That was true enough, but still I felt if other folk could take the trouble to provide a sandwich, however small, so could they. I was a great one for fairness, and scornful of lazy ways, and anyway Grannie had taught me to despise mooching.

It was strange how the language of the Bible always sprang so readily to my lips. I loved its rolling phrases, and used to race along to school chanting, 'Tell it not in Gath, publish it not in the streets of Askelon, lest the daughters of the Philistines rejoice, lest the daughters of the uncircumcised triumph.' And as I turned the corner, I wailed, 'Ye daughters of Israel, weep over Saul, who clothed you in scarlet, and other delights, who put on ornaments of gold upon your apparel.' What marvellous sounds they were. And yet when we went into the playground I could also chant with the others,

> 'The Lord said unto Moses,
> The Jews have a' big noses.'

And when we played a running game I could sing with the rest, 'Matthew, Mark, Luke, John, hold the cuddy till I get on.'

I saw no difference between this doggerel and the back-court chant of

> 'Dan, Dan the funny wee man,
> Washed his face in the fryin' pan.
> Combed his hair wi' the leg o' the chair.
> Dan, Dan the funny wee man.'

They were just daft rhyming sounds, but ah, the language of the Holy Bible was quite different and stirred me to the heart. There was a special prize given at our Sunday School, and seeing my interest in the Bible's teachings and my ability to memorize, the superintendent gave another girl and me special coaching up at his house every Friday night for the six weeks before the examination. We'd trot away up Balgray Hill after our tea, and I drank in the splendour of the fine red sandstone terrace house, with its stained-glass windows in the hall. Stained glass! I'd never seen that anywhere else but in Church, but maybe he got it specially because he was a church superintendent and they'd had a few bits left over when they'd put in our stained-glass window in the Church. We wiped our feet carefully on the bass mat inside the front door, and tiptoed through the tiled lobby to the big room at the back. There our teacher sat at a desk spread with papers of old examinations and proceeded to question us on our bible knowledge. He seemed smaller in his own house somehow, and different wearing his working jacket and not the black one he usually wore on Sundays. But he soon stopped my mesmerized staring by thrusting an examination paper into my hands and bidding me sit down and answer the written paper now. He recommended we study the book of Luke for the main part of the exam and I committed the entire book to memory, striding up and down our kitchen every night at home until I had got it all off by heart. That was that, I thought, they wouldn't catch me out now, for I knew it word for word. What a boon this was later on in my school exams when bible knowledge was one of the subjects, and I could choose the New Testament. With St Luke's help I flew through the paper, and made sure of good marks for at least one subject. And the dedicated little superintendent's coaching paid off too for I was dazed and honoured to be presented with the special John Brown prize with the best marks for all the churches in Springburn. My goodness, maybe my grannie was right, maybe I was going to be a minister! I was sorry for my fellow-student, though, who had taken the special coaching with me each Friday. 'Ach I didnae want tae go to thae lessons,' she said stoutly. 'Ma daddy made me go, but ah knew I wisnae in the hunt.' I hoped she meant it, for I was beginning to realize that when one wins, another has to lose, for this was the first time I had been taught in a class of two people, when I could see the loser had worked too but had not met success. When a youngster was immodestly boastful of triumphs, and somebody else criticized this, we used to say in the tenements, 'Ach well, if ye don't blaw yer ain trumpet, naebody else will blaw it fur ye.' But I knew this was no time

for blowing trumpets and I kept very quiet about my John
Brown prize, and put the special bible on the shelf without
showing it to anybody. I was surprised to find all these mixed
feelings in myself. Was it possible I was learning sense, as
Grannie had always predicted I might some day?

9

I hadn't much sense, though, the day the teacher finished up an English lesson by instructing us to see for ourselves how widespread was the habit of bad spelling, by taking a look at the big signboard on the rag store opposite the school. The rag store was the mecca of all who were short of a few pennies to tide them over till pay-day, but were without anything which would be acceptable to the pawnshop. Old fenders were lugged round and put on the big scale, and the heavy weights adjusted to find an exact balance so that justice could be seen to be done. Prices were chalked on a board inside the shop. Woollens tuppence a pound, iron a penny a pound. We watched like hawks to make sure we weren't being done, for we regarded the old man as our natural enemy, who would short-change us if he could get away with it. It seemed to take a mountain of old woollens to make up a pound, and, of course, only jerseys or skirts or trousers torn beyond redemption found their way there. Great gaping sacks of old clothes were ranged all round the tiny shop, and there was a mound of old fire-irons, ashpan fronts, pokers, kettles with the bottoms burnt out, which compounded to make a curious smell which made us catch our breath when we came out of the fresh air. Grannie or my mother seldom had anything for me to take there, for everything in our house was either unpicked and used again, or washed and hemmed and turned into dusters or polishing cloths. But often my chums' mothers were pleased to exchange their old bundles for welcome coppers to buy chips or Lorne sausage for their tea, and I went with a chum and thoroughly enjoyed my peep inside this ragged emporium. We had paid no attention to the big hand-printed sign above the door, for we knew exactly what went on inside the shop and that the old man wanted our rags and our old iron. Fancy the teacher reading the sign though, and what could she have found? We could hardly wait for four o'clock, and raced across to the rag store, wondering what we had missed. It was as good as playing guesses in the sweetie-shop windows. There were so many spelling mistakes, we sat down on our school-bags or our cases, whipped out our jotters and pencils and started writing them all down. 'Will bye anithing.' Giggles from all of us. 'Oh there's another one,' and we laughed triumphantly, 'only one l in woollens.' 'Och, look how he's spelt cardigan, with a "k".' 'And trousers with two oo's.' This was great fun, we thought. Wondering what all the commotion was about, the old man came out, looked at our convulsed faces and the signboard above his shop. 'Whit ur youse daein'?' he demanded. 'Whit's up?' In perfect truth and innocence I piped up, 'We're writing down all your spelling errors – the teacher told us.' The teacher no doubt had merely intended we silently note the inaccuracies and take a lesson from them that we must be more careful in our own writings. She certainly couldn't have intended this open assessment of the old man's poor spelling.

After I'd spoken there was silence. He didn't chase us away as we'd thought, for we'd half-risen from the pavement ready for flight. Instead his face slowly crimsoned, and he turned back and went into the shop without a word. I felt sick. I suddenly realized how terrible this was, giving somebody such a showing up in front of everybody. And maybe he hadn't had a good teacher like ours to teach him his spelling when he was a wee boy. How could I have *done* such a hurtful thing, and me with the John Brown prize for bible knowledge. 'Tell it not in Gath,' I cried to myself as I ran home. 'Publish it not in the streets of Askelon.' For a long time I couldn't face that old man, but one day when I went in with a chum to help her carry a clothes-basket full of rags I gave him a wee gollywog Grannie had made before she died, for good luck. He took it and pinned it on his skimpy cardigan, and I knew I was forgiven.

But who could have dreamed a wee lassie like me could hurt a grown man, and who could have thought anything I said could bring a shamed blush to the cheeks of somebody I'd always thought of as an old skinflint. Oh when would I ever learn!

It was around this time that I plunged into the mysterious world of domestic science at school. I, who was a natural swot, who loved books and learning, now found myself in a strange practical world where I had no great natural aptitude (apart from cooking) and where my tiny build was a positive handicap. We marched round Springburn Road to Petershill School because Hyde Park, our own school, had no domestic equipment. This was a great novelty in itself, and I was prepared to enjoy everything. For laundry lessons we went down to a dark, damp, steamy basement. Little tubs were filled with soapy water and we were shown how to scrub the garments we'd been asked to bring. A soiled pillow-case one week, a dirty jersey the next, some tea-towels another week, socks, and so on. Mothers were highly amused at this tiny washing, but we took it all very seriously. Hot stoves were ranged along one wall, and their fierce heat soon dried our washings, while we listened to the teacher tell us how we must scrub some materials gently, and that we must never rub woollens, and how socks and handkerchiefs had to be washed separately. Little flat-irons were neatly ranged against the hot stoves and were heating while we absorbed all this information. We'd never realized there was so much to getting clothes clean. Our mothers just went to the wash-house, and seemed to manage everything quite naturally. We felt sure they'd never get through their work if they were as finicky as this teacher.

Then came the ironing. Our linen was laid smoothly on the ironing board, and damped with tiny sprinkles of water if it was too dry. The iron had to be picked up just so, and given a tiny spark of the cold water from the cup, to make sure it was the right heat. If it bounced off in a fiery spark, that was perfect. We must on *no* account use spit! But there was only one cup and we grew tired of waiting our turn. Everybody we knew used spit, and so we did too, and many a burnt wrist we got in consequence, for we jerked the iron back to apply the saliva surreptitiously and if the wrist was too small, as mine was, the weight of the iron tipped it back just that fraction too much and it stung the wrist with a fiery tongue. Then it was a rush back to the stove to get rid of the iron, and a war-dance of agony till the burn stopped stinging. We soon learnt, though, that the pain stopped if we plunged the burnt place in water at once, but, of course, if the teacher saw us racing for the sink and the cold tap she knew what had happened and we were sent to the end of the queue, and had to miss our rightful turn at the ironing board. What with the heat of the stoves, the steam, the weight of the irons, the burns, I felt I was in hell. One day the teacher said to me with a sigh, after inspecting a half-washed tea-towel, 'I'm afraid you'll never make a washer-woman, Molly.' I looked round this inferno and muttered, 'I've no intention of being a washer-woman.' I waited for the heavens to fall, but she actually laughed. It was much better after that, but I only got through this course with the skin of my teeth, with exam marks that made me grit my teeth in despair.

The cookery classes had been started earlier and were great fun, and no trouble to me, thanks to Grannie's good teaching. And then it was my turn to be amazed at how difficult some of the girls found these lessons. Where they were neat and quick and enviably professional with washing tub and iron, and I was all thumbs, the moment it came to weighing out ingredients and rubbing fat into flour, or beating and sugar, they were in agonies of indecision. They'd race round behind the big scrubbed tables and show each other their mixing bowls, while the teacher was busy. 'Is that a' right?' they would ask. 'Ah don't know whit she means when she says it should be like fine breadcrumbs', or 'Oh gosh, I'll *never* get this bloomin' margarine and sugar to look like cream'. And I, who was a dead loss with the smoothing iron, would have my cake, or scones, in the oven, and was able to spare a hand to get their baking ready for the oven.

But when it came to the sewing machine I was back once more to bewilderment and misery. I hadn't even dreamed I could be so thowless, for I loved the ordinary sewing classes. With enjoyment and great care I did tiny gathers on a little piece of flannel, and the result was like a dainty Lilliputian bedspread. Buttonholes on linen looked flatteringly professional. My hems, which took hours, showed not the faintest stitch through to the right side of the material. I did cross-stitch, and I even managed blanket-stitch and honeycombing, and I had actually looked forward with keenest anticipation to the day when I would reach the stage when I'd be introduced to the joys of the sewing machine. Fancy being able to whizz along seams in seconds, where hand sewing would take hours. I was dazzled at the prospect, and could see myself making all my mother's curtains, and running up wee pieces of gingham into summer dresses for myself. Maybe even managing a blouse for my mother. At last after the Easter holidays wee Mrs McKenzie took the cover off the old-fashioned machine, told us to gather round while she explained the various parts to us, and our eyes sparkled with joy at having the luck to learn to be dressmakers in the school's time. In my innocence I had imagined all I needed to know was how to get the material to hold still while my feet pumped the treadle, and the magic union of thread and material would follow. I was soon to learn otherwise. There were terrible hurdles to be overcome first. There was a shuttle which had to be threaded, and before even *that* could be done a wheel had to be loosened, another little gadget brought down to hold the shuttle, and the final snapped off thread brought through a slanting slot which, as far as I was concerned, gripped the thread in a steely jaw and refused to release it. Then came the battle to insert the shuttle, and bring the thread out of a little central hole. This completely baffled me. The other girls could sit down, hold top thread gently but firmly in steady fingers, give a quiet pressure on the treadle, and up popped the thread for them, like magic, without the faintest sign of a tangle. Never for me. With a sigh Mrs McKenzie would show me over and over again, while the others got on with the finishing touches to their garments.

Threading the needle was just as bad. My tummy turned somersaults of mingled eagerness and dread as the moment approached for me to step forward, perch nervously on the chair, and try to copy the teacher's instructions. Heart pounding, I'd put the reel on top of the little spindle upside down. Gently Mrs McKenzie would turn it right way up, while the rest of the class sniggered into their sewing. I'd attempt to wind the spool without first slackening the wheel at the side. Snap would go the thread. Red-faced, my eyes smarting with tears of shame, I'd correct this mistake, only to overfill the spool and have the extra thread whirl round like a dervish, while my feet, which ought to have stopped by this time, still threshed round with wild abandon.

I begged Mrs McKenzie to allow me to do all my sewing by hand, but it was no good. She was being paid to teach me to familiarize myself with the use of the sewing machine, and teach me she would or die in the attempt. Well, she never died, indeed if anybody was going to die it looked more like being me, for the nervous tension of every sewing lesson was now enough to bring on a heart attack. I never did learn to familiarize myself to anybody's satisfaction, least of all my mother's.

We had a drop-head sewing machine at home which was my mother's pride and joy, and which stood like an ornament in the corner of the kitchen. My mother had bought it second-hand, because nearly everybody in the tenements felt this item was an essential part of household equipment. Think of the money that could be saved by turning sheets sides to middle, by giving a new lease of life to pillow-cases, or turning ones past repair into hankies. Of the curtains which could be run up from sale material. Oh a machine was a godsend to anybody. But somehow it didn't work that way in our house. In fact I basely thought I must have inherited my ineptitude from my mother, for she was always on the point of going to use it for one of those many marvellous savings, but somehow she never did. I began to feel she was as frightened of a sewing machine as I was. She'd encourage a neighbour to try it, and to show her how to do this splendid bit of renewing of worn sheets.

So warm was her admiration, as feet flew up and down on the treadle, and sheets gained new life before her very eyes, that the neighbour carried on and completed the job, basking in the warmth of my mother's genuine praise. While all this was going on, I'd stand by, sucking in my cheeks in concentration, trying to watch every single movement of the expert.

When the neighbour left, an old piece of material was coaxed out of my mother, and I'd sit down at the machine, sure that *this* time I had the measure of it. I would place material carefully under the lever, just as the neighbour had done, I would check the size of stitch, tautness of thread in needle, make sure the side-wheel was properly tightened, and balance my feet on the treadle in readiness for the tattoo to follow. In about thirty seconds the needle was back-firing, then plunging up and down on the same spot. Panic filled my breast and my feet forgot their rhythm. The wheel flew backwards and the thread broke. Seething with fury and frustration, I'd leap to my feet, kick the machine for a stubborn brute, and head for Springburn Park and the road leading to the Campsies. Only a good long walk could calm me down. Those attempts to familiarize myself with that unconquerable machine were the starting gun for many a marathon hike towards the hills, and maybe even the basis of my reputation as one of the best walkers for miles around.

And I never did get making my mother's curtains. On the one occasion when she had rashly entrusted a piece of precious curtain material to me I'd had to unpick every single stitch because the stuff had somehow got itself puckered and wouldn't lie flat. We both stared at the rows of wee holes bizarrely flanking the re-sewn seam, and my mother declared she could never hold her head up again if folk saw such a mess at her windows. Ruining my wee bits of cloth was one thing. Sabotaging her treasured window-drapes was quite another and she wasn't having it, not even to spare my feelings. I couldn't blame her. I sighed gustily, and I had to agree in my heart with my school-mates who told me, 'Aye, ye can maybe pass exams, hen, but you're rotten at the sewin' machine.'

And then thankfully we went to embroidery, both with silk and beads, and this was much more to my taste. We had the excitement of ironing transfers on to our garments, and following the design of little flowers and scrolls with all the traditional stitches passed on to us by clever Mrs McKenzie. My mother picked up a bit of brown serge at a sale, which I made into a dress at school, and I decided to embroider a scroll design round the neck in tiny brown beads. The other girls thought I was mad, risking ruining a dress in this way, for our other transfers had been stamped on to pillow-cases, or hankies, or nightgowns. But Mrs McKenzie approved this flight of fancy, which she flatteringly said was how dress designers worked to achieve originality, and she helped me to iron the transfer on to the serge without scorching the material. I think she felt I needed some encouragement after my disastrous attempts with the sewing machine. I was allowed to take my dress home to work on this bead embroidery, for there wouldn't have been time to do it in class if it was to be ready for the school concert, and I curled up in the big chair every night after I'd done my homework, fascinated to see the flowers and curves take substance as each bead was carefully stitched into place. The neighbours followed the progress of this embroidery with keen interest. With their practical approach, they'd never heard of anybody putting beads on clothes, which would make both washing and pressing difficult, but we all enjoyed a touch of luxury, especially when it cost nothing but a packet of beads at sixpence, and they were forecasting a future for me as a finisher in some swanky dressmaking establishment. They were sure the toffs would love to have beads on all their clothes and would be glad to let me work for them. I was so surprised and flattered by all this praise that I instantly saw myself top embroideress in a posh dressmaker's, then realized how long it was taking me to get round that wee neckline. 'Naebody could afford to pay good wages to somebody who took hours and hours and hours to do one neckline,' I thought. Anyway, could I be bothered to sit still for all that length of time, just sewing? Reluctantly I put the dream aside. There were far too many exciting things to be done to spend my life sitting sewing.

And then, suddenly it seemed, I was within three months of leaving school. Exams followed fast upon one another, and the whole tempo of schooldays changed, for now we were having all our teachers' good work put to the test, and writing down answers which would decide what sort of leaving certificate we would have to present to future employers. The girls in the Co-operative again gave me special pen-nibs to flatter my hand-writing, and I used an old ivory pen-handle, a treasured favourite, which I thought brought me good luck. I cleaned my ruler to make sure there wasn't a speck of grease on it, and a rare wee pencil-sharpener brought all my pencils to a fine neat sharpness. The teachers provided clean sheets of blotting paper. The answers were to be unlocked from head, heart and memory. There wasn't a sound to be heard in the room but the scratching of pens and the rustling of leaves as we turned over our papers to finish our questions. It was a strange feeling, just seeing the teacher sitting quietly behind her desk, nothing written on the blackboard, and not a word to say to us after the opening advice to read through the question, make sure we understood it, and answer to the best of our ability. She was only to be consulted in emergency, if a question wasn't entirely clear. The only respite from study during this time of concentration and decision were the hours spent finishing the dresses we were all making for the prize-giving on our very last day. My mother had bought a little remnant of pale green sponge-cloth for a few shillings, and this was not only to be my exam entry for the dressmaking class, but was also to be worn on my very last day as a schoolgirl. Mrs McKenzie helped us to cut out our dresses, and supervised every move, and as a great favour I was allowed to make the whole thing by hand, as I was terrified to trust the pale purity of this material to the devilish whims of the sewing machine. This concession was granted, because I promised on my part that I'd make and embroider the white collar which was to finish the neckline, instead of buying one at the wee shop up Springburn Road for 6½d. Mrs McKenzie said that as I wanted to spurn the machine, I should go the whole way and make the entire dress by hand, collar and all, and prove that all I needed was patience and sewing cotton. And anyway, she was always keen to see us master the art of embroidery.

The dress pattern was of the simplest. High round neckline, short sleeves, skirt gathered with little stitches on to a longish bodice, and the white collar was made from a left-over piece of material from another girl's blouse. Round the edge of this collar I worked little blanket stitches in pale green, the exact shade of the dress, and as a final touch I worked small clusters of French knots in the corner of each front scalloped edge.

The night before prize-giving we had a concert for our parents, and for this I wore the brown serge with the beads round the neck. Fancy having *two* new dresses at once! I kept running to the wardrobe and looking at them, hardly able to believe that they were mine, and that I had made them all myself. I thought it was truly marvellous of the school to let us sew like this, for I never regarded sewing lessons as lessons at all, but just a sort of playtime between the serious stuff of learning. A great chum Maggie called round to collect me for this concert. She had grown to alarming proportions during the previous year, and her mother had decided that for the school concert she must wear what we called 'stiff stays', and what the shops called whalebone corsets. She was only fourteen with a large sad face, and lank greasy dark hair, but she was clever in class, and she held for me the fascination of having a father who kept a fruit barrow, and who always had a barrel of rotting apples in the lobby, to which the family could help themselves. These were apples 'touched' with the weather and so not perfect enough to sell, but good enough for the children to munch for nothing. I found this fruity smell entrancing and a great change from the usual house smells of soap and dunga-rees. I didn't much like the apples themselves, for they were usually cookers and far too sour for my taste, but Maggie munched them with noisy enjoyment, finishing them right down to the smallest core before she would throw the stump away. She ought to have been slim as a willow, and have had a complexion of milk and roses with all this fruit, but alas her face was sallow and heavy, and her figure definitely in need of something. I was horrified, though, to find that it was to be stiff stays for her at such a tender age. 'But, Maggie,' I said, shocked when she told me, 'how will ye breathe?' After the freedom of a Liberty bodice I felt such constriction would be like a strait-jacket. 'I don't know,' she said mournfully, 'especially when it comes to the high notes of yon songs we're to sing.'

When she arrived to collect me we all stared at her curiously, as she perched herself stiffly on the edge of the chair. I'd told my mother and my brothers of Maggie's stiff stays as I couldn't keep such interesting news to myself. Poor Maggie. She couldn't bend, and she might have been wearing armour-plate below her blue taffetas, she looked so rigid. We didn't say a word, of course, for we didn't want her to know that we were all aware of her corsets, and then to my fury and embarrassment Tommy, who had been sitting chortling over a piece of paper and pencil since she came in, thrust the paper under my nose and there, large as life, he had drawn a congested Maggie seated perilously on a collapsing chair, and underneath in large letters he'd written : 'Maggie Gourlay in her stiff steys!' I burst out laughing before I could stop myself, and delighted with his success, he stuck it under Willie's nose, then my mother's, and there was poor Maggie looking from one struggling laughing face to the other, murmuring 'Whit is it? Can ah get seein' it?' 'Naw naw, Maggie,' said my mother at last. 'It's juist a daft family thing ah'd be affrontit to let onybody clse see.' I seized the paper and threw it on the fire, ashamed of our laughter, and gave Tommy a skite on the ear in passing for his cheek. It would have been awful if, on top of the misery of her armour-plating, Maggie had realized she had been the subject of that unexpected cartoon.

When we got outside I tentatively touched her back with an exploratory finger to see how the stays felt. It was like touching a brick wall. 'Oh, Maggie,' I cried, 'I hope I never get fat! I hope I never have to wear these things. I'd *die*. It must be like being suffocated.' 'Och I expect I'll get used to them,' said Maggie gloomily. 'But right enough, they're murder. You'll have to sing twice as lood when we come to the high notes, for I know fine ah'll never get them oot.' But the funny thing was when we got to the concert, the teachers complimented her so heartily on her trim figure, so nicely encased in whale bone, that she forgot her discomfort and sang as blithely and bonnily as any lintie. It was splendid to hear her, and to be reassured so convincingly that she could breathe after all. I was so happy for her, and I wanted to make up for our family laughter and that comical drawing, so I went and collected the tea and the cakes for both of us, and left Maggie purring to the praise of the mothers who told her she had a rer wee wasp-waist noo, and was a fine figure of a wumman. I go back in time too to hear them say that they'd never heard 'The Eriskay Love Lilt' and 'The Tangle o' the Isles' sung better. Maggie's cup was full. For those were the songs our class had sung on its own, and Maggie had taken a solo verse in each. So her stiff stays hadn't handicapped her the least little bit. She drank her tea and ate her cakes with zest, and told me all about the job her father had found for her and which she was starting the week after she left school. Her dad knew the fruit and flower trade, even though he only had a barrow himself, and Maggie was going to work in a posh florist's shop, and would learn to make bouquets, and wreaths, and deliver flowers and plants to the big houses out Great Western Road. We both thought this was a marvellous job, for we both loved flowers, and had once been so carried away by our passion for the scented delicacy of pansies in the Public Park that we had picked two purple ones each, and had hidden them in the elastic of our school bloomers before we ran home to put them in water. The poor, crumpled things had refused to revive in water, and we had learnt our bitter lesson that not only could we not enjoy them, but neither could anyone else. Oh just fancy having all the flowers in season to play with, and to be taught such an artistic trade.

I, to my amazement, was going to college. My mother had hoped for a job for me behind one of the impressive mahogany desks in the Co-operative offices. This was the summit of her ambition for me. To her, the Co-operative had the all-embracing security of a merciful God. It provided the food we ate. It provided us, through its rare dividends, with savings for holidays, for blankets, and all special occasions. It gave jobs to my brothers, delivering milk, and actually gave them woollen gloves in the winter to stop the cold of the can handles biting through to their fingers. And surely, she thought, if only they could be persuaded to give me a job as a clerkess, we would be set up for life. She actually persuaded Tommy to start there as a message boy and go on to being a grocer behind the counter. When at last the light dawned, and he realized he was the squarest of square pegs in a round hole, and that he wanted to write and explore the world, she nearly broke her heart, certain that he would die a pauper, but not before he had lived to regret giving up such a splendid job. If he'd abdicated from the throne of England she couldn't have been more shocked or grieved. However, as I have told elsewhere,* my head teacher had other ideas, and somehow she got my mother's permission

* See *Shoes were for Sunday*

262

to let me try for a scholarship to a business college, pleading that this year without earning would be well spent and would be the rock on which I could build my future. My mother and I bleakly knew that the fees weren't the only obstacle – where could we find the money to dress me suitably to fit into such a background? The other girls would be from moneyed homes and we never had a spare sixpence. But my teacher's eloquence won the day, and my mother reluctantly gave up her dreams of seeing me take my place among the lucky ones to be privileged to sit behind one of those prized mahogany desks in the offices of the Co-operative.

So my schooldays weren't finished, after all. After the prize-giving there would be a year, a whole year, of college. It was the very stuff of fairy tales, for I'd never known anyone outside story books who had gone to such a place.

But first there was the prize-giving and my last day at my own school, which I had known and loved forever it seemed.

10

The sun shone down from a cloudless blue sky on my very last day as a pupil at Hyde Park School. We had gone home at lunchtime to change into our best clothes for the prize-giving, and I felt I had never looked so clean or, to use my mother's words, as if 'I had just stepped out a band-box'. My hair had been washed for the concert, of course, and was shining and clean, and I had pushed the waves up with my hand, as my mother did with her own red hair, to make them fall deep and furrowed over my ears. My pale green sponge-cloth home-made dress was so impossibly elegant that I held my hands stiffly away from my sides, in case the smallest trace of human moisture should sully its perfection. My mother had allowed me to wear my Sunday shoes for this special occasion, and I gazed happily at my feet encased in what the box described as 'champagne fine leather'. We'd never seen or tasted champagne, so took the shop's word for it that it looked like my shoes. Oh how dainty this impractical light leather seemed to me over my white socks, and such an exciting change from my long-legged black lacing boots and hand-knitted black stockings. I stood in line, still as any mouse, savouring the bliss of shoes on my feet on a Friday. The pebbles which I'd have normally used as miniature peevers to while away the time were ignored today, in case I'd scuff my toes and damage the splendour of my Sunday feet. I would have to walk up in front of the whole school to receive my prizes, and I wanted to be worthy of the honours I was receiving. For not only was I getting my leaving certificate, and books for English and bible knowledge and arithmetic, but I was also getting a silver watch from all the teachers because I was dux of the school. A silver watch! For me! I couldn't believe it. It was the first time such a thing had been done at our school, and they told me it was to mark the special privilege of my having been accepted at college, and because my work had shown such promise. They had actually asked if they could keep my school essays and had said something daft about the writing demonstrating to future pupils how imagination could bloom in unlikely surroundings. Of course they could keep them, I said. I'd never expected to have them back anyway. What did I want with them now that they were finished. I had loved writing them and used to go into a hypnotic dream over them, but they were only composition, after all, and I didn't see anything special about them. So while everybody else had their work returned to them, the school kept mine.

My mother was agog to hear all about it when I came home later that afternoon. What had the headmaster said? Did my teacher like my dress? She hoped I had been told how many turns to wind the wee knob at the top of the watch, so I wouldn't burst the main spring. This was a terrible risk, it seemed, and it was vital to know exactly how many turns to give. And I must *never* turn the hands backwards, if it stopped, for that would be the end of my watch. I nearly disgraced myself in her eyes, though, when I told her about the concert which had followed the prize-giving, when we had all been given sweets from a huge box handed round by the teachers, and then had been asked to recite or sing our favourite pieces. We had returned to our separate classrooms for this treat, and when we had exhausted our repertoire there were still about fifteen minutes to go before the teacher could decently dismiss us, so to fill in the time she had asked what we would like to do. For my first command performance I responded enthusiast-ically to the class yells of 'Molly Weir doing Malvolio's speech from *Twelfth Night*', followed by 'Molly Weir doing the snake dance'. My mother declared that Shakespeare, even if she didn't understand a word of it, was all right, but to do a snake dance in front of the class *and* the teacher was in the worst possible taste. 'Well, they wanted me tae dae it,' I protested feebly. I had felt in my bones I shouldn't have done it, but I'd been carried away by the shouts of my class-mates. My mother shuddered and cast her eyes heavenwards. 'Whit must have the teacher have thought o' you, and efter them gi'en ye a silver watch.' I had copied this dance from the performance of one of the adored film stars of the penny matinées; she was a slinky siren clothed in floating veils, who writhed and waved her sinuous arms under the hero's nose, and inflamed him to nose-flaring passion. It must have looked quite different performed by a wee panting school lassie in home-made apple-green sponge-cloth dress, waving her sinuous arms under the nose of a small elderly schoolteacher, whose gold glasses pinched her little button nose. But my mother's condemnation made me feel ashamed, and robbed the prizes slightly of their fine taste. Was I never going to learn to be a lady? I wondered. It was very difficult to know when I was behaving badly, for the teacher had been startled at first, which had alarmed me, but then she had laughed till her eyes all misted up and she had had to take off her gold-rimmed glasses to wipe them. She hadn't seemed annoyed, but maybe they weren't tears of laughter at all. Maybe I had disappointed her, just as I had my mother, this little teacher who was my good angel and to whom I owed the chance of going to college and getting a good start in life. I would never know, but oh I would work, how I would work when I went to that college, and I'd make her proud of me, for surely at the end of a year studying alongside the children of the gentry I'd know the difference between the beauty of Shakespeare and the vulgarity of a penny matinée dance. Oh I hoped so. I hoped so very much indeed.

How strange it felt not to have any school to attend on Monday. My mother was out working, of course, so my first taste of being a lady of leisure was looking after the house. I did the shopping and the cooking, but my mother emphasized I wasn't to do much housework, for she was sure I would breenge about and knock things down in my zeal. I could be trusted to set the fire, for I'd seen Grannie do this hundreds of times, and I could make the beds and sweep the floor, but I was to leave everything else until she came home at night. Our wee washer-woman was with us again, so the washing was taken care of, and we just had to do the ironing at night, and the brasses on a Friday or a Saturday. My mother scrubbed the floor, and I liked going down to the back court with her while the floor dried, and shaking the mats, and brushing them against the tenement wall. But I didn't think I liked this domestic life as a full-time job. It was too quiet with no Grannie to tell me what to do, and the fun vanished when you were doing housework all by yourself. I began to understand why those young housewives who moved into our tenements enjoyed our admiring glances and comments as we perched on their window-ledges in the close and watched them at their household tasks. How lonely it must have been for them, transplanted from the camaraderie of the shop or the factory to the emptiness of a room and kitchen.

Ah but it wouldn't be for long as far as I was concerned, I told myself, for we were all going on holiday with my mother when she had her ten days off at the Fair, and then in August I would go to college. As I peeled potatoes for our dinner, I tried to imagine myself at this strange place. Would I be able to do the lessons? I would have to travel on a tramcar down into the town every single day, once in the morning, and again home at dinner-time. I'd walk back after my dinner to save the fares, and I'd walk home at five o'clock, for there was no hurry then and my legs were strong and willing. I could work out the time-table, but try as I might, I simply couldn't *see* the setting. Och well, there was plenty of time to think about it before August. But first there was the holiday. We pored over the advertisements in the 'holiday' column of the newspaper. We wanted the seaside. My mother said she preferred the country. Then we spied an address in Perth. We looked it up on the map, to make sure my mother was right when she told us it wasn't too far from Crieff, Grannie's birthplace, and it looked a splendid choice. The best of both worlds, really, for although it wasn't a seaside place, it had a grand river, and two Inches – what a funny name Inches – what could it mean? Best of all it was cheap. It sounded just fine for us. 'Room and kitchen with two beds, convenient for station and river. All linen supplied.' This last was a great boon, for it meant we could travel nice and light. No need for a hamper. This was far better than attendance, especially when we knew from bitter experience that my mother would never have taken advantage of attendance anyway.

It was a lovely holiday. A special sort of holiday. My mother was with us right from the start of the holiday for the very first time, and she came everywhere with us. I was in a sort of limbo, poised on the brink of the adventure of college, a prospect which half delighted and half terrified me, and the strange newness of my mother being with us all the time was all part of the flavour. It seemed very strange at first. We were so used to seeing her like this only at week-ends, when she was busy catching up on all the arrears of home tasks, and then she often brought home a workmate for company, that to have her all to ourselves made us a bit shy. We weren't used to having her listening to us all day either, or to have to slow down our pace to suit hers, and we kicked our feet and wondered if she would mind if we raced on in front. She didn't mind a bit. She was quite happy to sit reading her paper or a magazine, while we played all over the Inches. These, we discovered to our delight, were huge stretches of grassy territory at either end of the town, one of them flanking the river, and on that bonnie river there were rowing boats which we could hire. We didn't go out on them very often, for my mother had a horror of wee boats, as she called them, for they were far too easy to coup, and she just knew we would start changing places when one of us grew tired of rowing, and everybody knew that if you stood up in a wee boat it couped and a 'body landed in the water. She told us dire tales of it being a bottomless river, and if we fell in it would probably take days, if not weeks, to recover our bodies. All my mother's rivers were bottomless. Her favourite description was 'They juist don't know hoo deep it is, naebody's ever been able to fin' oot'. The boys jeered at this, but they didn't have enough money to defy her wishes, so we mostly enjoyed the boats from the safety of the river-bank.

The ice-cream was delicious, and the shops as usual were great fun, especially the bakers, which had all sorts of different bread and rolls and tea bread from the ones we were used to at home. We looked after ourselves, of course, but the landlady was very good at putting a light under the potatoes and the mince about half an hour before we were due home for our dinner, so we didn't have to waste too much time indoors bothering about cooking.

It was during this holiday we experienced our first electric storm and a terrifying thing it was. We had been coming home over the Inch when great brilliant flashes of light had broken across the sky. We raced home, and threw ourselves under the big table in our landlady's room, the one where she told us her husband's corpse had been laid out the year before. We had shuddered when she had told us this, but we had no thought of a corpse as we crouched under the thick mahogany top. We only felt it was a wonderful protection against the wrath of the heavens. To our amazement, my mother stood chatting with the landlady, in front of the window, ignoring the fiery flashes which lit the room. I was amazed at her courage. How could she be frightened of a bottomless river, which flowed quietly and innocently, and unmoved by the visible sign of heavenly upheavals? I wanted to be as brave myself, and tried to stand up beside her, but my legs wouldn't let me, and I cowered cravenly under the table with my brothers, until all was quiet.

And I was plagued by a wee ginger-headed lad whom Tommy had picked up one day at play, who gazed at me with such dumb wonder that I could have slapped him. I had no pity for his feelings. He used to leave bunches of wilting wild flowers outside the landlady's front door, and whisper through the letter box hoarsely, 'Floo'ers for the Glesca lassie.' My mother thought this a great joke, and said we must invite him to go with us to the Inch to play. I utterly refused. 'He's no' comin',' I said obstinately. 'Ah don't want him. He's daft, the wey he carries oan.' 'Och poor Sammy,' my mother sighed, 'he's just tryin' tae be nice tae ye.' He walked behind us at a few yards' distance, like a faithful hound, never taking his eyes off me, so I joined up with my mother and pretended an interest in her magazine and let him play football with my brothers, and he showed off abominably, under the delusion that we were watching him. I was mad, because I wanted to kick the ball myself but refused to join in the game in case it encouraged Sammy to believe I was interested in him. I had no time for such things when I was girding my loins and concentrating all my energies for the adventures which lay ahead, in gathering courage to face the ordeal of the strange new world of college.

As soon as we came home from Perth, we had to start

thinking about clothes for me, for there was only a fortnight till the beginning of my first term. Thank goodness it was summer, and the one or two gingham dresses my mother had concocted from sale remnants would see me through the first few weeks, so I needn't be ashamed among all those girls who could afford to pay their own fees. But we had to think of coats and warmer things for the winter, and on the Saturday my mother vanished for hours. When I asked her where she was going, she answered vaguely, 'Doon the toon.' There was a conspiracy of silence about the names of the shops where my mother bought my clothes now. She didn't want me to know that she had a marvellous source of second-hand clothes at a wee shop near the Barrows, and delicacy forbade me to hint that I had guessed as much. There was a woman, I know, with whom she had an understanding, who kept a stall near the market, and this good soul kept aside specially good items bought from one of the big houses beyond Botanic Gardens. I had good cause to bless the well-lined girl who must have grown like Jack's magic beanstalk to be finished with her lovely clothes so quickly, for I couldn't believe anyone could have shown such a wanton lack of fondness for such expensive garments merely out of a desire for change. They looked so new that it was easy for me to pretend to my mother that I believed they came straight from an ordinary shop, and weren't the cast-offs of some 'toff's' daughter. What did it matter to me, anyway? The quality was staggering, and the cost out of my mother's hard-earned wages only a few shillings. Thanks to this unknown rich girl, so providentially one or two sizes bigger than me, I had a beautifully cut navy gaberdine raincoat for autumn days, and a heavy navy-blue reefer coat with matching navy velour hat for the coldest of wintry days, and those, with her navy gym slip, and my own jerseys and school blouses, which mercifully still fitted me, would see me through my year. 'Aye,' said my mother happily, when we'd tried on everything for fit, 'ye can haud up yer heid onywhere. Noo pit them away, and if ye can juist manage no' tae kick the toes oot yer boots, we'll dae fine.'

On the Sunday night before my first day at college I laid out my clothes for the morning. The weather was warm, so we decided my brown and white check gingham would be neat and cool, and my brown sand-shoes and white socks would be a douce respectable match. Books had already been listed and provided out of the scholarship, and I packed these in my school-case.

I could hardly sleep for sick excitement and when morning came I couldn't even swallow the roll I'd halved with my mother. How strange it felt to be waiting for a tramcar at half past eight in the morning. I'd never queued up for a tram with people setting off for work, and I hadn't realized how many folk slept in, and came dashing out of closes signalling furiously to the tram-driver to slow down so that they could jump on and not have the frustration of waiting for another car to come along. When my car came I clattered upstairs as usual, but at this time of the day it was packed mostly with men, and they were smoking, and I could feel my eyes begin to water with the heat and the smoke-haze. Oh goodness, I'd have to travel downstairs in future, for I didn't like this. That first morning I took the car right round to Bath Street, and walked along to the front entrance of the college, but later on I was brave enough and knowledgeable enough to come off at West Nile Street and cut through the lane, which saved a good two or three minutes while the tram was held up at the lights. I felt terribly self-conscious as I walked in those doors and up to the first landing, where the details of the classes were posted. I was far too early, and there was hardly anyone else there, so I stood and read the notice-board, trying hard to look as if I belonged. 'Secretarial Course' – ah that was mine! 'Shorthand, typing, arithmetic, bookkeeping, English, French, amanuensis, business methods, preparation for Royal Society of Arts examinations.' My stomach turned over at the strangeness of the subjects. English, French and arithmetic I knew, but what of the others? To take my mind off all this newness which I'd have to absorb, I turned to the other list. 'Civil Service Course'. What a rotten name. Civil Service. It sounded a bit like Domestic Service. I didn't think I would fancy that. I was glad nobody had thought of giving me a scholarship for *that*. Suddenly I was aware that the landing had filled with movement, and when I turned round I was surrounded by men and women. Not boys and girls. Men and women. How tall they were, and how old! Oh help, I'd never be able to study with such grown-up people. And what would they think of somebody as wee and as young as me daring to suppose I was in the same class as them? They were more like schoolteachers than pupils.

It was worse when I got into my first class, for I found that when I sat on my seat I couldn't reach the desk, so I had to sit on my feet, and there was an amused giggle from everyone, including the teacher, when I asked if I was allowed to do this. I didn't speak to a soul, apart from that teacher, on my first day. We changed rooms for each subject, and this was entirely new to me. We'd never done that at Hyde Park, apart from going away to another school for the domestic science subjects during our final years. What a clatter there was as we charged along corridors to the next class, and I was amazed that we weren't told to be quiet. Our Mrs McKenzie would never have tolerated such a row. Maybe the teachers were frightened to tell those big men and women to hold their tongues. That must be it. I was dazed with the noise which ricocheted off the narrow corridor walls and went echoing up to the high ceilings. We seemed to do nothing but rush from class to class that first morning, and register with each teacher. I was glad to get out into the air at lunchtime, and join the queues waiting for the cars which would take us home for our dinner break. Hardly anybody ate in town in those days, and the cars were packed to bursting point. 'Full up inside,' sang the conductor as I leaped on to the step of the first red tram that came along. Oh well, I'd just have to thole all that smoke again. But to my surprise the air on the top deck was quite clear. Nobody, it seemed, was going to waste money smoking at this time of day, or maybe they didn't want to spoil the taste of their good dinner. Oh this was great. I could travel home on the top deck, after all, and have a good look out of the window. The shops were shutting for their dinner hour, and I was interested to see the assistants or the owners all dressed for the street, locking the doors after they'd pulled down the blinds. I hadn't realized how wee some of them were, having only seen them behind their counters, and some of the fierce ones looked quite ordinary with their hats on. One baldy-headed old man who kept a second-hand bookshop looked startlingly important with a dark Homburg on his head and a silver-knobbed cane in his hand. Mind you, we'd always suspected he was different from the rest of us, for he put hilarious notices in his windows when he went on holiday. One year it was 'Escaped – till 14th August' and another year it was 'Gone from the haunts of men – till 15th September'.

By the time we reached the Cally, the men were teeming out of the big railway workshop exits, and they marched alongside the tramcars, like an escorting army. I'd never realized how they filled the pavements as far as the eye could see, until this moment when I was able to look down on their heads from my seat aloft. Black faces above dark dungarees moved like a dark tide, with here and there a flash of amazingly white teeth as somebody laughed in response to a mate's comment. How quiet and purposeful they seemed, and although I had never heard the words then, I was conscious I was looking at the living embodiment of the dignity of labour. My mother had no time for conversation, for she was only in for her dinner too, and she was dishing out the broth for the four of us when I arrived. My brothers were also hurrying, for nobody had time to dally when the lunch period lasted only an hour. We had the boiling beef the soup had been cooked with, plus some potatoes my mother had heated through with the soup, and a bit of turnip to mash with them, and then it was time to clear the table, wash the dishes, and scatter to our various jobs. 'You go on,' said my mother to me. 'You'll need a' yer time if you're to walk back to the toon.' So the boys helped her with the dishes, and off I went, on foot this time, to complete this bewildering day. Some of the Cally men had already drifted back to the work gates, and were sitting on their hunkers against the low wall opposite, chatting, or reading their newspapers. They wouldn't budge till the horn blew, I knew, but they liked to be within strolling distance so that they were ready to start work when the second horn went.

The shopkeepers, too, were opening up their shops, and pulling up their blinds, in readiness for the afternoon's business. I realized I would be able to follow this pattern every day, now I was to be walking and travelling at regular times myself, and a sort of simmering excitement began to bubble up inside me that I was becoming a part of the busy life of Glasgow, and would be able to observe all sorts of exciting things on my way to and from college. I wasn't terribly sure whether or not I was going to enjoy being a student, but I was certainly going to enjoy two tram rides a day, and two rare walks to and from the town through interesting, teeming streets.

When I got home at half past five that first day I quickly changed into my old serge skirt and my weekday jumper, and ran down to the back court to tell my chums all about the vast difference between a college and school. They were in the middle of a game of 'statues', when a pose was struck and frozen at the command of the leader. This was one of my favourite games, and I especially loved to call out the commands. As I ran to join them, the leader waved me away. 'Ye canny jine in, we've got enough.' My stomach lurched even more wretchedly than it had done on arriving at the college. I felt the hostility. I was different from them now. I was a college girl. It was as though a gulf had suddenly yawned wide between us. I didn't know what to do. These were my chums. I didn't want to be different from them. Suddenly I remembered Grannie's voice when I'd been left out of a back-court concert given by the big girls. And I'd stood dejectedly beside them, miserable at not being allowed to join in the songs and dances. She'd thrown up the window and called me upstairs, and when I got into the kitchen she had said, 'Whaur's yer pride? Dinna staun' there and let them see you're hurt. You're faur better than ony o' them onywey.' I'd been so astounded by her support, for normally I was never encouraged to believe I was any better than anyone at play-acting, that I'd forgotten my misery, and hugged to myself the fact that Grannie thought I was good.

Now I looked at my chums, and I realized I mustn't say a word about college. I had just wanted to share the strangeness with them, but it might look like crowing. So I just called out with what I hoped sounded like a cheery indifference, 'Och it disnae maitter, I've to get the tea ready onywey,' and I skipped through the back court and up the stairs to the house. It was all right after that. I never brought home tales of student life, and when they did ask me anything I made it sound just like the schooldays we had all shared at Hyde Park, so we were friends again, but I felt I was leading a double life, where the inhabitants of one half were completely uninterested in the activities of the other half.

After about a week or so I settled down to the new routine, and began to enjoy myself. Everything was a challenge, and of all the subjects embraced in this secretarial course, shorthand was my true love. I honestly can't explain just *why* shorthand should have held such an attraction for me, but from the age of nine the very word 'shorthand' fascinated me. Perhaps it was because even then I knew I wanted to write, and as my thoughts and words always tumbled out at lightning speed, it seemed to me marvellous that a system had been devised where I could write everything down with the minimum of delay.

I can remember at this early age tricking my chums one day by announcing proudly, 'I can write backhand.' I knew with childish cunning that they would think I meant 'shorthand', for I was always talking about this magic writing, and when they clamoured round me eagerly, I began writing carefully on the wall with chalk. They looked at my writing, which differed from the normal only in that it sloped backwards instead of forwards, and they fell upon me with disgust and disappointment, so that I had to run as fast as my laughter would allow to avoid a hefty bumping.

One night, not long afterwards, I was coming home in the tramcar from an annual visit to the Kelvin Hall Carnival, and I was sitting with my chums in the wide-open portion at the back of the tram where we could all crowd together in comfort. Somebody had dropped a leaflet from the current business exhibition, and I dived and rescued it from under a passenger's feet. I had spied the enticing word 'shorthand'. The leaflet gave the first elementary lesson in shorthand, and I began tracing the outlines with my finger and memorizing the rules there and then. A gentleman who had been watching me leaned forward, 'Don't worry about that sort of shorthand,' he said. 'You wait till you're older and try learning Pitman's. It's understood all over the country and most business offices prefer it.'

I, of course, didn't know one form of shorthand from another but I was always willing to take advice. I threw away the leaflet, and made a mental note that if ever I had the luck to be able to study this subject it would be Pitmans for me.

And now I had my chance. I was starry-eyed as I opened the manual and was given the first lesson in the subject which was to be a much-loved asset for the rest of my life. From the first moment, I took to it like a duck to water. It had a logic which appealed to me, and which made understanding very simple. The flowing nature of the outlines were absolutely designed for speed, and the system of inserting vowels made reading back no problem. I found, though, that mere love of a subject wasn't enough. It also needed complete concentration to master every intricacy of the system, but this was no obstacle when the exercise was as attractive as shorthand was to me. I was like a race-horse who'd been waiting for years to have a shot at the Derby.

I carried my shorthand manual with me everywhere, except to church, I studied it in the bus, in the trams, queuing for the pictures and while waiting to have my hair trimmed. There was no more gazing out of the windows on the trams. My nose was buried in my manual. Grammalogues and phraseograms filled pages and pages of my notebooks, until they practically wrote themselves.

I was possessed. I'm sure of it. When people talked to me, I'd develop a glazed look in my eye, for I'd be writing down every word of the conversation in shorthand, in my head. At dances I drove partners mad by tracing the conversation on their backs with my fingers. 'Is that you writing shorthand again,' they'd demand irritably. It was. It took *years* to break that habit.

After six months' study I'd won a bronze medal for having made the most rapid advancement of any student of my year. I couldn't understand why they felt they had to give me a medal, on top of the boon of teaching me something I was passionately eager to learn. It seemed to me a daft way to throw away their money, but of course I accepted it and my mother was very proud, and hoped I'd stop working ower thae books so much and go oot and enjoy masel' a bit for a change.

11

I still hardly knew a soul at the college, for as well as being frighteningly grown-up, those big students spoke 'pan-loaf', and my ear was sharp enough to detect a vast difference between their accents and mine. It wasn't necessary to speak very much, anyway, apart from reading back our dictation in the shorthand class, and that didn't come at the beginning, and I was so busy drinking in all my new lessons, so that I shouldn't waste a minute in making Mrs McKenzie's belief in me come true, that I didn't really see my fellow-students as individuals.

One day our shorthand teacher asked if any of us would like to visit a Business Efficiency Exhibition at the Kelvin Hall, as he had one or two free tickets. I peeped cautiously round the class, for if it had been Hyde Park and something had been going for nothing a forest of hands would have shot up. To my amazement, not a hand was raised. Fancy none of those big folk wanting to go to the Kelvin Hall. Well, I'd given them their chance. Up shot my hand. 'You'd like to go, Molly?' the teacher enquired. I nodded and whispered, 'Yes sir.' 'One or two tickets?' he enquired. Oh! I could take somebody. 'Two, please, sir,' I said huskily. I felt this was generosity beyond belief. My tickets were for the following Friday, and my chum and I walked down after our tea. I'd already walked down to college after my dinner that day and home again at five o'clock, but we were so used to having no money for such luxuries as fares that another walk to the town didn't give us a thought. Our legs were strong and it was marvellous to have free tickets for an exhibition. We'd have walked to the Campsie Hills and back for such a treat.

Lizzie, the chum I took with me, was fascinated to have a peep at this amazing world of typewriters, shorthand machines

– yes, they actually had a machine with shorthand characters on it – comptometers, even dictaphones which did away with the use of shorthand altogether, for the boss spoke into a wee gadget, and the typist wore earphones and listened to his voice as she typed. I thought this must be terribly confusing, and I wasn't too keen on anything which ruled out the use of my beloved shorthand. We played with envelope-addressing machines, and we shot a pile of envelopes through an automatic stamping fitment. When we came to the typewriters, I showed Lizzie how fast I could type 'Now is the time for all good men to come to the aid of the party', which Lizzie thought was a daft thing to type, and then I typed out her name and address and she thought this was wonderful. She'd never seen her name in print before, and was most impressed, especially as I had lengthened it to Elizabeth. In fact, she was so pleased that, without realizing it, I had rechristened her, for from that moment onwards she insisted on everyone calling her Elizabeth, and skelped her brothers on the ear when they forgot. On the way out, a man handed me a little printed slip. We took everything that was given to us for nothing when I was a wee girl, and we read every leaflet that came our way, for we felt that it was only right if folk went to the trouble to write something and give it to us, then we must show some appreciation and read what they had to say. This leaflet told us that there was to be an essay competition open to all the business colleges in Glasgow and district, and three prizes would be given for the three best compositions describing the attractions of the exhibition. Closing date was the following Friday.

I had masses of homework to do, for each teacher piled on the work irrespective of the demands of the others, and the only night in the week I went out now was a Saturday, while the only day I didn't work was a Sunday. But I loved writing, and it seemed forever since I had written an essay. So I sat down at the kitchen table the minute I got home and started to write. I was still writing at 1 A.M. when my mother came in from one of her much-loved dances at the Highlander's Institute. 'You're no daein' mair hame lessons?' she said, aghast to find me up at that hour. 'Och it's fur a competition,' I said, 'but I don't think it's good enough. Ah'm no' gaun tae send it in.'

'You'll send it in,' said my mother decisively, 'efter burnin' ma
gas till this time o' the mornin' and your face as white as a dish-
cloot.' So we found an envelope and addressed it, and folded
up my sheets of writing, for posting next day. And then we had
a cosy cup of tea together, and I ate the gorgeous marzipan
walnut she'd brought me home from the dance. They always
seemed to get delicious food at those dances which were such a
relaxation for my mother after her hard work in the Railways.
Petty foors, they were called, which was a gey funny name for
such lovely sweeties. (It was only after some time at French
lessons I realized I was giving the Glasgow pronunciation of
petits fours.) There were sometimes little toffee biscuits, luscious black grapes coated in transparent brittle toffee, slices of
oranges treated the same way, glacé pineapple, wee bits of
fudge, and even tiny chocolate biscuits. My mother would save
one or two for me, for I always wakened when she came home,
and she would have them wrapped in some tissue paper to keep
them from making the inside of her evening purse sticky. They
didn't have such luxury items at every dance, just the special
ones at Christmas, or Hallowe'en, or St Andrew's Night, and
they were a wonderful treat for me.

I'd almost forgotten the essay competition, in spite of my
misgivings at having posted it, in case the college would get a
bad name if my work wasn't judged very good, when I came
out of class one day and found a crowd clustered round the
noticeboard. The names of the winners were posted up, and at
the top was my name, sole winner from my college. 'Who's
Molly Weir?' I heard them ask each other. 'I don't know do
you?' 'Oh, wait a minute. It's not that wee thing who sits up on
her feet to reach her desk, is it?' 'Yes, I believe it is. I didn't
even know she'd entered. I never heard her consult the teacher
about it.' As if I would! If they were surprised, it was nothing
to the astonishment of my English teacher, and the college
principal. 'You entered for this competition without asking for
any help, Molly?' said my teacher. 'Without mentioning it to
anybody?' 'I didn't know I had to,' I whispered back, nearly in
tears, for it suddenly occurred to me that maybe I should have
asked permission before going in for the competition, seeing I
had had to put down the name of the college. 'Oh you didn't

have to,' laughed the teacher, 'but I should have thought you might have wished for some help from me.' I stared back at him. Surely that would have been cheating? Getting somebody to help me with work which was supposed to be all my own? I would never have dreamt of doing such a thing, but I didn't know how to say it without sounding ungrateful, so I didn't say anything. The college principal was delighted. 'Well done, well done,' he beamed. 'We'll have to keep an eye on you, young lady. It's a great honour for the college.' The blood rushed to my face. He had called me a young lady! Oh if Grannie could only have heard him.

And suddenly after that I seemed to know everybody and everybody seemed to know me. They laughed at my eagerness to study, and called me 'the mighty atom', and I listened to the way they spoke and tried, without getting pan-loaf, to tone down my broad accents a little. My mother helped, for somebody had heard me describe lovely brittle toffee as 'glessie toaffie', and had said to her, 'I'm surprised that yon college your Molly gangs tae his nae taught her to speak a bit better than that.' Actually we all had two languages, one broad and comfortable that we children spoke to each other, and another which we used in school. I'd been sharing my 'glessie toaffie' with a chum when this neighbour had overheard us giggling about it. 'Oh, Molly knows how to speak when she needs to,' my mother had said loyally. 'The weans a' speak like that to one another.' Fancy my mother knowing that we did, and fancy her also knowing that I could speak properly if I wished. I'd been shy of doing this at home, afraid that they would think I was going all uppity because I was at college and I didn't want to emphasize any difference they might have noticed. And yet it was very difficult to speak correctly not only to the teachers but to all the other students in an acceptable accent, and change back to the broader vowels of Springburn at home. So, with my mother's encouragement, and a nervous ear for jeering always on the alert, I began to speak 'teacher's language' everywhere, and to my surprise, after a few laconic 'Swallied a dictionary?' queries, nobody seemed to take a bit of notice.

My prize for the essay was a fountain pen, and it was presented to me by the Lord Provost, no less, in a vast assembly hall off Sauchiehall Street. To my surprise, my mother decided to come with me. She usually kept away from prize-givings or any public appearances where she might have to speak to officials, but she couldn't resist a peep at the Lord Provost, and she wanted to see me march up and receive my fountain pen dressed in my navy-blue reefer coat and velour hat. It was a golden opportunity for her to check that I was as well turned out as other college students, and have a look at the fashionable outfits worn by their mothers. 'Aye,' she nodded sagely as she took the scene in, 'you can see they're a' gentry.' Her green eyes sparkled with pleasure when she noted that my navy reefer equalled the quiet quality of the clothes worn by most of the girls, but she was a bit disappointed that the Lord Provost only wore an ordinary dark suit and there wasn't a sign of a gold chain. Still, he had shaken hands with me, and had commented on my extreme youth, and she felt we ought to celebrate this honour by having coffee and cakes in M & A Brown's, the tearoom, when we came out. We never had coffee at home. This was a treat specially reserved for enjoyment in tearooms, and my mother radiated rich enjoyment as she ordered 'Two cups of white coffee, please, and some cakes'. She took the waitress into her confidence, to my embarrassment, and insisted on my showing her my newly presented fountain pen. 'My, a gold nib and everything,' said the elderly waitress admiringly, 'and ye goat it fae the Lord Provost, did ye, hen? That wis rer.' She brought us double sponge cakes filled with cream, liqueurs and meringues, and gave us an agonizing choice, for we could only afford one cake each, so I chose a double sponge and my mother chose a meringue, and we halved them, so we each got a taste of both cakes. The waitress flashed chummy smiles at us as she served the other tables, for she knew as well as we did that this was a very special occasion for us, and that we didn't have coffee and cakes in a posh tearoom on many Saturdays of the year.

As we walked over Sauchiehall Street, gazing our fill at all the shop windows, my mother kept patting herself on the back. 'Aye, if it hidnae been for me, you widnae have posted that composition,' she kept saying. 'Noo maybe you'll believe what I say and you'll listen to me when I tell you you should get oot mair and enjoy yersel'. It's no good for you sittin' in like that every night. I'm sure nane o' thae other lassies dae it.' My mother was so certain by this time that I had found the secret of successfully passing examinations that she thought I was being unnecessarily cautious in going over and over my lessons every night. What with her confidence in me, and Mrs McKenzie's faith, I was in a fever every time I looked at that pile of books whose secrets had to be mastered. How could she encourage me to go out to enjoy myself with so much work waiting to be done?

In fact the only week night I went out during that whole year of the scholarship was the following Friday, when an old school chum knocked at the door to see if I'd go with her to a Scout Concert being held in the church up Springburn Road. Her mother had bought two tickets, for Ada and her sister, but the sister had gone down with a heavy cold, and Mrs Paterson thought I might enjoy a night out, as my mother had told her I never put a foot over the door at night from one Saturday to the next. 'Go on,' urged my mother. 'It's Friday and you've nae college tomorrow, so you can dae yer lessons before your dinner.'

I hesitated. I had dedicated myself to study, but it was Friday, as my mother said, and I was well ahead with my shorthand exercises, my arithmetic paper was finished, I'd polished off the bookkeeping homework and the wee bit of French, so all that was left was a précis for the English teacher and I knew I could easily do that in the morning if I really felt I might allow myself to go out. But was I weakening my character, yielding so easily to temptation? 'Och come oan, Molly,' said Ada, 'I don't want to go masel', and ye get tea and cakes, and the ticket would just be wasted noo.' That settled it. I couldn't let Mrs Paterson's ticket go to waste, so I went.

The church hall was ablaze with lights, which fairly dazzled me. I had forgotten people still went out enjoying themselves. It seemed almost bewildering to be with so many pleasure-seekers, and I could feel my head swimming with the buzz of conversations going on all round me as friends greeted each other, and I sat quite dazed by all this commotion after months of quiet concentration on my books in the comparative calm of our room and kitchen. I was glad when the noise simmered down and the concert started, and the strange, disorientated feeling vanished as I watched the Scouts drilling, and competing with one another in raising a tent as fast as possible, and listened to musical items which struck me as being very expert. There was an interval half-way through, and we were given a bag of cakes, and tea in cups, not tinnies. I'd never been to an adult affair like this before, and hadn't realized it was only at children's concerts the tea or milk had to go into tinnies provided by ourselves. What a rich church this was, though, for the cakes were from Torrance the bakers, and there was even a sausage roll as well as four delicious pastries. I kept a cake for my mother, a wee chocolate one, which I knew she liked. After the interval there were comedy sketches, and a comic who led us all in singing the choruses, and it was all thrilling and marvellous and I was enjoying myself 'up to the nines', as my mother would say. And then suddenly it felt all wrong to be sitting there among that audience who maybe had no responsibilities to work hard, as I had. I felt miles away from my books. When the concert ended, I told Ada that it had been great, but if she got any more free tickets, would she please not offer one to me, for while one night off wouldn't do much harm, two might lead me down the slippery slope to slothfulness, and it would be sheer treachery to the people who had got me my scholarship. She was a big girl, Ada, who was studying to be a nurse and she laughed at me, but kindly. 'All right, Molly,' she said, 'I won't tempt you again. But you're a gift to the comics, for you've got a rare hearty laugh when you let yourself go, and forget how wicked you are in skipping your homework.' I felt a great rush of affection for this understanding, kindly girl. Poor Ada, at the end of all her years of study, she had to give up nursing, for she possessed every quality except one. She could build up no immunity to germs, and fell a victim to every germ and virus, and, worse than that, she was a carrier. It was a cruel shame, for all her dreams were of curing the sick and caring for them in every way. But she was a good loser, and turned to nursery-school work instead, and the hospitals' loss was surely the children's gain.

Sundays were a great oasis in the working week, and I felt no sense of guilt in not opening a single college book the entire day. How enjoyable it felt to be getting ready for the church in my best clothes and my polished shoes. It made Sunday *feel* special to be so differently dressed. It induced a feeling of leisure, and people seemed to put on quite a different personality. The pavements between our house and the church took on a different look too, as though the very paving stones knew they were being lightly trodden on by the fine Sunday boots of the men and the patent or kid shoes of the women and children, and the rhythm was different from that made by the tramp of working feet or the busy skipping weekday steps of hurrying schoolchildren. Everybody strolled, the better to take in what everyone else was wearing. Not so much as a new pair of gloves went unobserved as we made our way from close to church, but not a word of this was spoken until after the service when we all gathered in groups on the pavement outside. We were supposed to be thinking of higher things on our way to church, and it would have been considered in very bad taste to mention fashion at that moment. I remember the older sister of one of my chums being severely upbraided by her parents because she had thoughtlessly confided that she had been thinking of the carpet for her new house while she was singing the hymns in church. She was shortly to be married and hadn't been able to keep her mind from straying, but she was told in no uncertain tones that she had taken all the good of the service away by furnishing her house in the Lord's time. Her mother and father felt no good could come of such behaviour and if that was the way she was starting out her married life, well she mustn't be surprised if God, in His own good time, didn't remember it and hold it against her. Even her sister said to me it wasn't much good Phemie taking her body to church when her mind wasn't also in attendance! Secretly I felt if I were getting married and getting a brand-new house and spanking new furniture and curtains I'd have found it just as hard to stop mentally placing all my beautiful things in their place, even in the Lord's House.

We were released from this pious attitude, though, the minute we streamed down the church steps, and formed our little groups according to age and inclination. We who were in the Guides and taught at Sunday School swooped on each other, and admired our new hats, or freshly pressed coats, or new umbrellas. Long umbrellas had come in again, and as one of the chums had a job in a shop specializing in these elegant accessories, we were all saving every penny to take advantage of her offer to get one for each of us 'wholesale'. The lucky ones who had already got theirs were the envy of the rest of us who were still struggling. We admired every detail of each handle, how neatly it fitted over the arm, how fine the quality. The silk tassel came in for its share of attention – how perfectly it took up the tone of the silk cover. We shared the owners' fervent hopes that it wouldn't rain too soon, for how would they ever restore the slim folds to their original perfection.

Meanwhile the mothers were complimenting each other on their own outfits and how well the weans were turned out. 'My, you've goat her just lovely,' one would say to another, eyeing a child in new summer or winter outfit. The men looked very impressive out of dungarees, in dark coats or suits, with hats having snap brims for the younger ones and heavier Homburgs for the older men, plus a bowler here and there worn by the dashing lads who had had the good fortune to land a job in an office in the city. The boys were very aware of their manhood and of the fine figures they cut in their Sunday best, and a few shy smiles were exchanged with the girls who stole glances at them under their eyelashes, before all went their separate ways for their dinner.

All our romantic attachments were formed with these boys whom we met through the church. Our religious observance, which played so large a part in our lives, became more thrilling and exciting when we could peep across at the lads under cover of our hymn-singing, and later we might join up with them for a few delicious moments on our demure walks over Crowhill Road after evening service.

One of these boys appointed himself to be my permanent escort. Not only did he race after me on my way home between church and Sunday School, he also accompanied me on my walks to and from college and back and forth to the office. He adapted his tastes and time-tables to mine and after he met me seldom spent money on fares.

From such small economies were our life-savings begun, for although we didn't realize it then, we were forming the habit of saving, a habit which never afterwards deserted us.

We saved against every hazard life had to offer, and our clothes were specially guarded against premature shabbiness, or 'Tashing', as we called it. I always changed out of my good clothes into my school pinny or my dressing gown the minute I got home from morning service for it would have been awful to have spotted my Sunday garments with soup or gravy, or even dish-water while I was doing the dishes. Then it was on with my finery again, and away to Sunday School, and my class of wee boys. They too wore their decentest clothes, often shabby and sometimes darned and patched, but their boots shone, and their hair was slicked down in wet spikes with cold water from the tap. Their faces shone from recent washing, and they settled down with much pushing and jostling to sit beside favourite chums, then to listen with great attention to the stories of the Bible. They collected the little coloured text-cards, which they had to memorize, like football cards, and if any were left over due to an absentee there was always an eager claimant ready to deliver the card to the missing pupil. They had so few presents in their lives that even a text-card was a covetable item, and they chanted off the message as though it were a popular song. They each had a ha'penny for the collection bag, which they proudly produced at the right moment, and they vied with one another to answer questions at the end of story-time. They called me 'miss' when they answered, just as though I were a real school-teacher, but they clearly knew that I wasn't one, for they always insisted on telling me the latest episode of the 'following-up' film, in their own words, if they decided the bible story hadn't been exciting enough to provide colourful answers from them. I enjoyed my elevation to the teaching profession, and the boys were happy in the warm companionship and ritual of Sunday School, and if it wasn't exactly a quiet reverent class, somehow it all added up to a satisfying hour in each other's company.

After Sunday School there was time for a walk up to Springburn Park before tea would be ready, and we admired all the flower-beds, and strolled through the hot-houses, and in high summer listened to the music from a brass band from the bandstand. We wandered up to the flagstaff, and gazed with passionate envy at people rich enough to possess cameras, who posed their families artistically against railings or leaning against bridges, to make a collection of snapshots for the family album. We thought it would have been marvellous to have had a record of ourselves in our best hats, carrying our splendid new umbrellas, to keep such elegant moments forever. To cushion our disappointment, we would say to one another, 'Och they'll no' likely come oot anyway, it's no' sunny enough', and we'd run home for our tea, for there was still the evening service to attend. I loved the evening service in our church, which had a small enough congregation to let us sit in any seat we fancied and not to be confined to our own pew, and my chums and I always sped upstairs to the gallery. The altered angle of the pulpit and the choir and the stained-glass window made it all so different we could hardly believe we were in the same church. Even our voices sounded different when we sang the hymns, and the lighting at eye-level dazzled us and made it all seem like a dream. I had a hard job not to be like Phemie, the bride-to-be, whose mind wandered, but just when I found myself beginning to think of my lessons, and start tracing the sermon in shorthand outlines on the ledge in front of me, it was the final hymn and there was time for a last stroll out Bishopbriggs before bedtime.

Sometimes, though, the evening was devoted to family visiting, especially if we had a relative home from abroad. This was especially exciting if it involved a tram journey, for Glasgow Sunday trams would be packed to bursting point with couples coping with excited vociferous children, clutching their toys, and maybe a wee present for their auntie or their grannie. Go-carts were manœuvred good-temperedly by conductors, and the air was lively with young voices, as children were handed down to parents at each stop the car made. It looked and felt like a holiday, as sons and daughters went to pay their filial respects.

And much much later that night, returning from visiting our own relatives, the tram would again be filled, but this time with silent, exhausted young parents, their white-faced weary children lying with heavy heads against drooping shoulders. There would be a whimper as a stop was reached, and a sleeping child had to be roused, and a go-cart handed down, and then once more a heavy weary silence which almost lulled the rest of us off to sleep. I was always struck with the contrast of the two journeys, and of the toll an evening's visiting could take out of people. And I never ceased to marvel at the heavy stupor of a child in deep slumber, or the pale exhaustion of parents. Sunday, the rich interval in the working life, was almost over, and maybe our tiredness came from knowing that the next day was Monday.

Our Sunday clothes were hung on the hook at the back of the kitchen door to air, before being transferred to the wardrobe in the lobby, where they would stay until the next Sunday and never see the light of a working day. Many of our neighbours, in fact, knowing such clothes wouldn't be needed from one week-end to the next, pawned them on a Monday morning and redeemed them at the end of the week, and so had use of the extra money the clothes earned. This meant they didn't even need a wardrobe, but my mother shuddered at the idea of living 'on the steps of the pawn' as she described it, and would have scrubbed pavements before she would have entrusted our hard-won best clothes to the care of a pawnbroker. The men in the tenements seemed to remain in ignorance that their Sunday best provided many a wee extra titbit for their teas during the week, for when a death occurred and the funeral required their dark Sunday clothes before Sunday the wives who patronized the pawn flew round the closes in a panic, trying to borrow money 'right, left and centre', as my mother said, to redeem the clothes before their husbands could discover the truth. 'Aye,' my mother would say, as she handed over a precious two shillings to help a distraught wife build up the necessary sum, 'there would be murder if your Jimmy found oot his suit was in the pawn every week.' 'Oh I know, Jeanie, I know,' would come back the answer. 'Oh it's awfu' good o' you. I'll pey ye back on Friday. Noo if I can just get another two bob from your neebor, I'll be a'right. He'll no' look for his suit till he comes hame fae his work the night, and I'll have it oot hingin' on the back o' the door by then.' The women seemed to thrive on such dramas, and the threat of an unexpected funeral didn't stop them making their usual trip to the pawnshop the following Monday morning. The funny thing was that nobody ever acknowledged that they themselves pawned clothes, until death struck and the urgent need for cash revealed all. They followed the most elaborate pretence in getting the Sunday clothes to the pawn on Mondays. Some went first thing after breakfast, the clothes concealed in the middle of a bundle of washing, as though the bearer were on her way to the public wash-house. Another would hide a suit in a big carrier bag, under the 'empties' being taken back to the licensed grocers, and this trip of course, was at a very innocent time of day when people would be doing their ordinary shopping, and the bottles lulled all suspicion, or so the owner thought. Yet another would use a go-cart, with the suit carefully hidden under the baby's feet. They all knew each other's routine, and they staggered their visits to the pawnbroker, so they never actually saw one another while the business was being transacted, and they could all pretend quite happily that it never happened at all. But everybody knew. And nobody said a word. Live and let live was the tenement motto, and if that was the way some folk liked to live, well naebody was hurt by it, and the women enjoyed a conspiracy, even a conspiracy of silence, especially if it meant the men remained 'nane the wiser' of what actually went on.

12

After the refreshing break of the week-end I was ready once more to plunge into the working week of lessons, walking back and forth to college, and homework at night. Because of my high speeds in shorthand and typing, I was now having separate lessons after the others had finished, for I was already writing shorthand at one hundred and forty words per minute, and being coached for even higher speeds so that I could demonstrate high-speed writing for the college in public. My typing speed too was well beyond the class norm, and I was breezing along at speeds varying from sixty to seventy-five words a minute, depending on the subject-matter. I thought it a great privilege to be allowed to use the college typewriters to practise on, and I moved from one make of machine to another, graduating to the lightest weights so that nothing would put a brake on my flying fingers.

Because of this special coaching, I grew to know the assistant head of the teaching staff very well indeed, because he was the only one whose tongue could get round dictation fast enough to equal my speedy fingers. At Christmas, as he knew my mother was a widow and had little money to give us children many extras, he and his wife invited me to have high tea with them. They lived in a very posh district on the other side of Glasgow, and my mother saw to it that my shoes were polished until you could have seen your face in them, that my skirt and jumper were pressed neatly, and my navy velour hat as perfect as brush could make it. I was going home first to change, after college, so all my clothes were laid out neatly, ready to be put on the minute I reached home. I didn't know anything about taking presents to my host, but fate took a hand and atoned for my ignorance. I had to change tramcars in the centre of the city, and as I sped across the road from one tram to the other. I noticed a beautiful spray of mimosa lying practically under the wheels of the oncoming tram. Somebody had obviously dropped it as they crossed the road from Malcolm Campbell's big shop on the corner. I've always loved flowers, and I couldn't bear the thought of those lovely things being crushed, and anyway it would have been a terrible waste. I swooped down, practically under the wheels of the moving tramcar, and rescued the precious blossom, marvelling at the little furry velvety pom-poms against the dark stem. What could I do with it, though? It was far too big to put in my button-hole and there was no paper round it. Och well, even if it seemed a bit daft, I would just ask my hostess if she would put it in water, for I couldn't bear to have it die. This was December, and although I didn't know it, mimosa was prohibitively expensive and would have graced only the wealthiest tables in Glasgow. I reached the address, and was nervously preparing my speech about putting the flowers in water for me, when the stained-glass door opened. Before I had time to take in a thing, or even open my mouth, my hostess fell on me with such cries of rapturous astonishment at my good taste, at my extravagance, as she buried her nose in the yellow pom-poms, that I simply hadn't the heart to explain that I had found the spray. How could I confess that spending money on flowers, apart from a shilling bunch at the Fair after our holiday, was something quite outside my experience. Wisely I kept silent, and sent up a prayer to heaven for so inexpensively teaching me the social graces.

My mother had to hear every detail of the visit. She wanted to know if they had a cakestand, and if they went in for a white tablecloth or a coloured one. When she heard that the cloth was not only white, but had white lace embroidery, *and* matching napkins, she decided they must surely have a firstclass washer-woman and plenty of money, for such a cloth would have to be washed by hand every time it was used. She was very interested to know I was the only visitor, and that this childless couple had entertained me by playing gramophone records. I had heard a woman called Gally-coorchy, it sounded like, singing like a canary. It was years before I realized I had been listening to a very famous record by a world-famous

Italian soprano, whose coloratura was internationally renowned. My mother approved my having refused sherry on the grounds that I was a Rechabite, although my host and hostess seemed to think it was quite a joke. When I told her about the mimosa my mother said, 'Och whit a loss for whoever droppcd it. I'm pleased you never let on you found it in the street, although mind you, they must have wondered whaur ye got the money to buy such a thing.' And then she laughed. 'By jings, it must have very nearly peyed fur your tea!'

One of the things I learned over tea was that as well as certificates for the end-of-year examinations the college gave money prizes for every subject which gained over ninety per cent in marks. I learned that the strange subject 'amanuensis' also carried this prize, and this was simply taking dictation in shorthand, and typing it out in a given time. What a bonus this seemed to me. For surely if you could take down shorthand at speed, and type at speed, this was putting icing on the cake to give you yet another prize for combining both and calling it amanuensis? My host and teacher laughed and said it didn't always work out that way, for sometimes students became so nervous they couldn't type back their notes, although they could maybe write them out in longhand if they could take their time to do this. It was the typing from shorthand which foxed them. Yes, I could see that now, for we'd only typed from the printed page to teach our fingers to touch type, and had never tried to translate our shorthand notes straight on to the machine. Oh, but I'd have a try at it, especially for a two-guinea prize. I wanted to use any prize money to come back to college for night classes, for apart from now realizing I had still so much to learn about everything, I knew I couldn't sit my shorthand teacher's exam till I was eighteen, and I'd have to continue studying to keep my work up to scratch for that frightening examination.

There was no time to go out to play even when the nights grew lighter, for this commercial course ended up in a perfect frenzy of examinations. The results for each subject were posted up on the board in the hall within a few days of each examination. I was terrified to look at the arithmetic passes, for although this was one of my best subjects, the paper had seemed so straightforward I was sure I must have missed the trickery behind the questions. I'd perched up on my feet as usual at the desk, read through the questions, found nothing particularly worrying and had finished the paper in just about half the allotted time. I looked up enquiringly at the teacher, and he looked back in surprise at me. 'Is there something you don't understand?' he asked. I shook my head. I went through the paper and the answers again. I couldn't see a thing to add. If I started looking too intently for tricks, I might feel I ought to change everything. I couldn't risk it. Early or no, I'd hand it in. The teacher and the class looked up as I walked to the front of the class, and handed in the paper. 'You're sure you are finished, Molly?' he asked. 'You've read it through again?' I nodded and left the class, and those big men and women sitting writing stared after me as I shut the door quietly, sure I must be out of my mind not to use up the time available for checking and correcting. However, the results sent my heart skittering into my throat. The first prize of one guinea was mine. Arithmetic – ninety-eight per cent. After that I trusted my own judgement. I was always nervous before each paper, of course, but once I started writing, or typing, I forgot my fears and concentrated on proving that I hadn't wasted my time during all those months of study. Shorthand brought two guineas, typing two, and that comically named amanuensis another two. Altogether the cash prizes came to eleven guineas, a fortune, and there was a further shorthand medal, for the long test piece at one hundred and forty words per minute, and a solid gold medal for being best student of my year. Oh I hadn't let Mrs McKenzie down. Nor the scholarship people. But it was agony to have to walk forward in front of all those big students and take my prizes and my certificates. Instead of the principal reading them all out at once, each was announced and awarded separately and I had to go forward again and again, and I became so self-conscious I could hardly see for embarrassment. The principal was in highly waggish mood, and when my arms were piled high with certificates he called out, 'Some gallant will have to escort Miss Weir home. I'm sure she will have plenty of volunteers.' That was what he thought! I was only a baby to most of them, and my brown and white check gingham dress, made by my mother from a remnant, must have looked very unalluring to those grown-up young men. Anyway, not a gallant moved a muscle in my direction. It was just as well, for I wouldn't have known what to say to them if they had. I ran like the wind when the prize-giving was over, because my mother, who was on the night-shift that week, was meeting me outside the college. We were going to celebrate by having coffee and a cake in Craig's, but to my surprise she took me into Watt Brothers first. I thought we had only been window-shopping on the way to Craig's, but she had been noting my enthusiasm for a dark red knitted suit, and she insisted we went in so that I could try it on. 'But, Mother, it's far too dear. And I don't *need* it. Wait till I get a job.' She brushed my objections aside. She was determined to celebrate my release from study (she thought I'd finished!) and the winning of all those prizes. She must have been saving for ages and she hadn't told me. I was so thrilled and touched that she should have thought of such a thing, especially with me earning nothing while all my chums were out working. I tried on the suit. It was lovely. We bought it, and I treasured and wore it for years.

I was now equipped and ready to be somebody's secretary, but in spite of my speeds and qualifications, nobody was at all interested in me. The college sent me for many interviews, and I was absolutely furious to be turned down again and again because I was judged too young or too wee. 'But I can *do* the work,' I'd argue rebelliously. 'Just give me a test.' A smile and a shake of the head. 'I'm sorry, we wanted somebody older, who could take responsibility.' I ground my teeth in a rage. I'd been taking responsibility since the day I was born, but how to make those snooty employers realize it? And after all the work I'd put in during all the previous year, and me with a gold medal in my drawer to prove it. It was being brought home to me the hard way that the most difficult prize of all to win was that of a pay packet. I felt so ashamed, and I could hardly bear the puzzled disappointment in my mother's face as I'd come back yet again from an interview, without a job.

And then one day I came home dizzy with triumph. My mother knew the moment she looked at my face that I'd landed a job. With a lawyer too – a most respected profession. I was engaged as a typist at the breathtaking sum of fifteen shillings a week, a shilling for every year of my age. My mother could now sit back and take it easy, I told her, her daughter was entering the world of commerce.

It was a very old-fashioned office, but it was my first sight of the business world, and I loved every single article with a passionate loyalty. There was a high desk, where the other female member of the staff and I coped with the books. Two small tables held our typewriters, and a tiny grate had a coal fire to warm our toes. There was a long mahogany counter where clients enquired for the lawyer, and the end of this was partitioned off from the public gaze. I used to disappear behind this screened-off portion when somebody came in whose solemn appearance gave me a fit of the giggles. I was too young to disguise my feelings, but too polite to let them see me laughing. I began to realize why those other employers had judged me too young to take responsibility. No wonder they couldn't trust me when I couldn't trust myself to keep a straight face when somebody talked too pan-loaf or raised a solemn hat two feet in the air when I approached the counter.

The ribbon in the office machine was indelible, so that letters could be copied in an ancient press with the aid of damp sheets and a heavy weight. Our old-fashioned employer was a splendid character, but he didn't believe in carbons, and I'm sure this copying press went back to the days of Dickens. I'd been used to modern ribbons in the machines at college, where if a mistake was made one just rubbed it out, but with this new horror of a ribbon it was impossible to erase an error. A horrible stain, a real give-away, just spread all over the letter and it had to be re-typed. On top of this, the ancient keyboard was different from the ones I'd trained on, and I made such a mess of the first letters I typed that I was sure I would be sacked. I was appalled at the amount of paper I wasted, but the other girl was quite unconcerned, and kept telling me not to worry, and anyway there was no hurry, for it didn't matter how long I took to get the letters done. The old boy wasn't used to speed! This to me, with a drawer full of certificates for speed and efficiency! The waste she took for granted, but it was a knife in my heart, and I felt Grannie would never have approved this easy-going attitude on the part of my colleague.

I was ashamed of my slowness and I felt I'd never master this strange machine with its dreadful ribbon. Instead of screwing up spoilt sheets and throwing them in the basket, I'd use the backs to practise my altered fingering, and then suddenly I found myself using the heavy old monster quite effortlessly, and that was a happy day indeed. With that worry removed, I was in seventh heaven and enjoyed every moment of my working day

Although I was so young, I was sent out to collect rents in a very rough district. As I had neither a shawl nor a baby, I was the object of much attention, and it soon became evident to the whole district that I was from the factor's office. The only tenant who frightened me was a man who was slightly unbalanced, and who was convinced the entries weren't being properly made in his rent-book and that he would be thrown into the street any day for defaulting. Everybody dreaded being put out by the factor, and I knew this was a real fear. I had to explain every time I went into his kitchen that the rent-book was absolutely up to date, and I ticked off each entry while he gazed at me with wild, uncomprehending eyes. Poor soul, these rent days were a source of terror for him, and as for me I was always glad to get out of his wee, spotlessly clean kitchen.

But I was a great success with the other tenants, because I was so sympathetic to their requests for repairs. Coming from a tenement myself, and knowing how often my mother denounced the meanness of the factor when there were plumbing or joinery repairs to be done in our house, I sent off the repair cards to our workmen as soon as I got back to the office.

My employer was aghast at the money which was now being spent on keeping the property in good shape, but he couldn't deny I was right when I said, 'But the repairs had to be done, sir. The pipes were leaking', or, 'The window-ledges let in rain'. What good was it trying to explain to me that money couldn't be spent so freely on this work? I had brought money back for rents, and it was only right that the people paying these rents should have good homes to live in. My boss shook his head and retired to his room, despairing of making me see

296

his point of view, so I had my way, and the tenants declared I was a wee warmer, and they'd never kent a better collector. It was a pleasure to see me each month, so it wis, and they didnae grudge a penny o' their rents nooadays.

I learned what a true gentleman was in working for this dear old lawyer. He was always polite, always courteous and he trusted us implicitly. In the bottom compartment of the petty cash box one day I found about a dozen golden sovereigns, which he hadn't even known were there. I used to love to play with them, for they were bright and shiny like jewellery. One day when he found me making a long golden bridge with them he was astonished to discover that they were his, but he just left them with me, for he saw that I liked playing with them, and he knew I would as soon have thought of them as my own as I would have thought of carrying the typewriter home. We both took honesty for granted, and not even worth mentioning.

In another office along the corridor an elderly lady worked for her father. Well, she seemed elderly to me, with her old-fashioned mousey hair done up in a bun, her long thin hands and feet, and her black blouse and skirt. She always tut-tutted over my thinness, and was sure I burned up whatever food I ate long before it could build any flesh on me. She used to bring me slabs of home-made cake on Monday mornings, the left-overs of her week-end entertaining. When I'd ask her if she didn't want to keep it in the tins at home for a wee 'roughness' in case visitors called, she made a face and said it would be stale by that time. Stale! I'd never heard anybody describing *cake* as stale, for it would certainly never have lasted long enough in our tenements for such a thing to happen. This cake was a great treat in the office, though, especially when she also found time to bring a little brown pot of tea with her, and we had quite a party behind the glass partition. There was no recognized mid-morning break when I was in an office, so we had to be very quiet about our orgies, and we hid everything behind a ledger if the boss appeared. I don't suppose for a moment he would have minded, for we on our part never worried about staying a bit later without payment if it were necessary, but the feeling that we were indulging in a forbidden picnic added to our enjoyment, and the spice of danger made us feel very wicked.

The boss went away for the entire summer with his wife and family, leaving the other girl and me in charge of the office. The law courts were in recess, I think, and I was worried because we had nothing to do. I was desperately anxious to earn my fifteen shillings, but the other girl just laughed and produced her knitting, so we sat up on the window-ledges to catch the sunshine, knitting and chatting, or reading all day long, and answering the telephone when it gave the occasional ring. The older girl had window flirtations with a fellow in an office a few yards up the street, on the opposite side, and giggled and blushed when he would wave across to her. Sometimes they even spoke to each other on the telephone, but it went no further. I couldn't see how she could possibly be interested in this vague face, for it wasn't easy to see what he really looked like at that distance, and I privately thought they were both a bit soft in the head. Still, she helped me with my knitting pattern, and she was a nice girl otherwise, and if she wanted to make a fool of herself waving across the width of the street to a man, then it was none of my business. It wasn't as if we were neglecting our work.

When she went on holiday I was left in sole charge. As my brother wasn't working just then, I invited him to come and share my caretaker's duties. He was delighted to accept, and we used to stroll down to the office every day, both in plimsolls and bare legs, with a shilling between us for our lunch. By walking to and from the office, we added another sixpence to our spending money. This was no hardship, for we liked walking, and we were at an age where everything on the road was interesting.

My brother was very impressed with the office, and spent hours playing with the machine for copying the letters, whirling the press at terrific speed and pretending his victim was lying underneath, ready to be crushed to death.

Then there was the fun of the internal telephone, where I stayed in the outer office and he went into the boss's room, and we spoke to each other after much feverish turning of the handle to make the bell ring. We were helpless with laughter during this escapade and couldn't talk for giggles, and of course being so young we couldn't think of a thing to say once we could control ourselves. When we grew tired of this we ventured one day to use the outside telephone to ring up an older friend who worked in an office in town, and he was furious and told us never to do it again or we would get him the sack.

Somewhat subdued, we wondered what we could do next, for the day seemed endless when we could only go outside for lunch. Suddenly my brother decided to climb up on top of the safe. It was covered in dust, and his plimsolls made most satisfactory prints all over the top. This was too enticing, and in a minute I was beside him, and we played at jumping off the safe on to the floor, in a lovely flying motion. What the people below must have thought, I never stopped to think.

Just as we were in the throes of this fascinating game, whooping with laughter as we leaped from safe to floor, a startled face appeared round the door of the office and a gloved hand went to a mouth open with dismay. There was an instant of terrified silence which I couldn't break and then the lady enquired in amazed tones, 'What are you children doing here?'

Children! The very idea. I was restored to my dignity as caretaker and typist immediately.

'I am in charge of the office,' I said as coldly as my breathlessness would allow. 'Mr Gardner is on holiday. Can I help you?'

Her eyes went from me to my brother, who was trying to hide behind the safe. 'And who is this?' the lady asked.

'He's my brother,' I explained. 'He's come to keep me company.'

'Oh! I see. Then I suggest you keep each other company a little more quietly. When will Mr Gardner be back?'

I gave her the date and took her name, and she went. My brother and I were left, appalled, wondering if I would be sacked the moment my boss returned from holiday.

I don't know whether she ever told him and he forgave the whole episode on account of my youth, or whether she maintained a discreet silence, but I kept my job. My lovely job and my wonderful fifteen shillings a week.

Sometimes on a Saturday morning the boss's wife would call

with her little boy, and I had to keep him amused. He loved the typewriters, and I used to make rows and rows of little soldiers for him, using the % sign, and then using the backspacing stop to superimpose a / over the shoulder as a gun, plus a 7 sign underneath, and a few other signs to make it all look real. We filled sheets of paper with those troops, and the wee boy carried them carefully home with him in an envelope. I was always fascinated with the boss's elegant wife, who had a high, carrying voice. 'Darling,' she would call out, 'can you let me have some money – I seem to be a bit short and I want to go to the shops.' I noted that he never once refused her, and just smiled with the greatest good nature and gave her what she asked. I could just see the tenement husbands if their wives dared to ask for cash so lightheartedly. They wouldn't have parted with as much as a curdy, for what was left in their pockets after handing over the housekeeping was strictly their own, and not to be shared. The rich must live very differently, I decided, when the husband kept the money, and the wives just asked for whatever they wanted, and were sure of getting it without an argument. I wondered if our tenement wives would like that, though, for they seemed to enjoy handling money, and wouldn't have trusted their husbands not to spend the rent money or the money for the store book on drink.

But oh how glad Mr Gardner must have been that he was so good and generous and kind to this lovely lady, because one day, not long after they'd returned from their holiday, I heard him speaking to the doctor on the telephone while I was taking notes. Mrs Gardner had a very sore throat, and the doctor was worried because she had a soaring temperature. He thought they ought to have a nurse in, and he was going to send a swab for analysis to the hospital. Mr Gardner put down the telephone, stared into space, and then with an effort came back to the notes and finished his dictation. 'I'm going home,' he called out to us a few minutes later. 'I'll sign the letters in the morning. There's nothing urgent that can't wait till then.'

Next day he didn't come in. He rang us to say his wife was worse, and we were not to make any appointments for him for the rest of the week. My colleague and I were quite distracted. We couldn't work. My mother tried to reassure me when I told her of Mrs Gardner's illness at lunchtime. 'Oh they'll have the best of doctors, and they'll do everything for her,' she said. 'She'll aye have the best of food and that stands onybody in good stead at a time like this.' I knew my mother was very wise and I tried to believe her, but a sick feeling in my stomach told me this was a very serious illness, and yet I wanted so much to have confidence that a rich lovely lady like that couldn't die of a sore throat. But she did. Infection from a tooth had added to the quinsy throat, and there was an unsuspected TB gland which also flared up – or at least that was what we understood – and she was dead within forty-eight hours. I sat at my dinner at home, the tears pouring down my face, unable to eat a bite. That wee boy, for whom I'd made the typed soldiers, left without a mother. That fine man left without a wife. Not all his money had been able to save her. I laid my head on the table and cried more bitterly than I had been able to do when I lost my own grannie. I was grieving for all of us in that office, which would never be the same again.

I watched Mr Gardner when he came back after the funeral, and he now looked a really old man. His shoulders sagged, his eyes were blank, and he lapsed into long silences in the midst of dictation. It was terrible. I was too young to be able to say a word in sympathy and left it to my older colleague, and I could only whisper in reply if he asked me a question, because I was frightened I would burst into tears.

I don't know how long it would have taken us all to get over this shock had it not been for the young client who got herself into the most terrible mess with an unwise marriage. She'd secretly married a chauffeur, and later found out what a mistake she had made, for she came from a very wealthy family and had been educated abroad, with every advantage money could buy. Then, of course, she'd met somebody from her own background, of whom her parents thoroughly approved, and with whom she'd fallen really in love. How could Mr Gardner get her out of it? We were all plunged into this business up to our ears. The new young fiancé had to be told, for his co-operation was essential. He seemed to be able to forgive the girl quite easily, for she had only been seventeen when she'd married the chauffeur. Anyway, what with her having married without consent, and having been so young, Mr Gardner managed to have the marriage ended, and the whole thing was accomplished in complete secrecy, without the girl's parents knowing a thing. We were all sworn to keep quiet, of course, as we signed papers and witnessed this, that and the other document untangling the mess. This had Ethel M. Dell beaten into a cocked hat, for it was real, and it was happening in our very own office. I was so sorry I couldn't tell my mother, or anybody at all, for I had given my solemn word. I don't know what they did about the marriage certificate, but it all ended with the girl getting married to the man approved by her parents, and they never knew to the end of their lives that their only daughter had been married and divorced before she had married the man they so approved as their son-in-law. Oh what an exciting chapter that was in our old-fashioned office. It was marvellous to be able to say, inside my head, 'And they lived happily ever after', and know we had helped to write those words. It all came at just the right time too to get us over our grief for poor Mrs Gardner, and although we still missed her and spoke of her a great deal, the worst was over. Only when the little boy came to the office on a Saturday with a nannie did the ache start again, but it grew less and less, and by the time I decided I ought to try for a better-paid job I could think of her without tears.

13

Actually it was Mr Gardner who put the idea into my head that it was time to move on. I'd never have dreamt of seeming disloyal by suggesting I would leave him. But he called me in one day and said that now I had had a year of good training in his office, with its demands of absolute accuracy, and its discipline with legal documents, I could do better for myself in a larger office. He could give me a tip-top reference, he told me, and he would be sorry to see me go, but with experience now added to those top speeds, it was a shame to keep me when he couldn't afford to pay me any more money. He told me, truly, that a year in a law office was the finest training anyone could have, and that if he hadn't given me a great deal of cash he had been able to give me an excellent start, and a good foundation on which to build.

My mother and I were quite happy with our fifteen shillings a week, but we were always willing to take advice, especially from a man who showed such interest in my welfare and whom we trusted completely. I didn't think of going back to college for help in finding this new job, but we all pored over the 'situations vacant' at home, and I sent off applications in my best handwriting, and promised that if accepted I would endeavour to serve their interests to the best of my ability. I was very pleased with such flowing phrases, and amazed that I didn't have a reply from every single advertiser. I had several, though, and turned down the ones in tiny offices, however tempting the salary offered, for my boss had impressed on me that I needed the competition of a larger establishment now. Eventually I settled on one with a very grand title and which I vaguely thought had something to do with insurance. Compared with our Dickensian setting, with shelves filled with big tin deed boxes, all cosy and old-fashioned, this new office was the epitome of sparkling modernity. Huge plate-glass windows, overlooking Renfield Street, let in every fleeting ray of sunshine. The desks were light oak, the chairs were padded, and the typewriters were all brand new. Best of all, it seemed to me, there were about twenty people in the office, whose ages varied from mine at sixteen to quite middle-aged men and women. The boss was foreign, and quite quite different from Mr Gardner, who, although kind and thoughtful, had only seemed vaguely aware of us as females. This one darted about staring intently into our eyes and, to my surprise, insisted on all of us using Christian names. By Mr Gardner, young as I was, I had been addressed as Miss Weir. To this restless new boss I was Molly. It didn't seem right somehow. I didn't like him very much, but I liked the office and I thoroughly enjoyed all the chatter and the romances of the older typists, especially the one who wore her engagement ring on a ribbon round her neck because her people would have thrown her out if she had dared to hint that she was getting married. I found this very thrilling, and quite up to the standards of the stories in *My Weekly*. Another girl had been persuaded to 'go steady' with a young man whose name was McGinty, but she told me that every time she visited his mother's house her heart turned over when she looked at the name on the name-plate, for she knew that she would never never marry a man with a name like that and find herself called Mrs McGinty for the rest of her life. As my feelings were not involved, I urged her to give him up, for there was absolutely no use encouraging him if she didn't intend to marry him. But, she told me, 'I *like* him so much. It's just his name I can't stand.' And then a terrible thing happened. He was involved in a serious accident with his motor-bike and they sent to our office for May, the girl whose confidences I'd shared, to go to his bedside. He asked her to marry him, and there at the hospital bedside she said 'Yes'. When she told me this I could hardly breathe for emotion, it was such a drama. It was the very stuff of story-books. 'But, May,' I said, 'I thought you would never never be called Mrs McGinty, what if he gets better?' She shook her head and her eyes filled with tears. 'He won't,' she said, 'I never will be Mrs McGinty. The hospital told me there was no hope, and that's the only reason I said yes.' The hospital spoke the truth, but for a long time afterwards I worried and fretted over what she would have done if the young man *had* recovered. Strangely enough, she didn't marry anyone, and I often thought it would have been far nicer to have had McGinty on the letter box than to have had no letter box at all, or the door, or her very own wee house.

We mostly shared these tales while we were working late. We had to work for a whole week till 9.30, once every three months. It seemed to have something to do with interests and dividends or some figures having to be made up at such intervals, and we were paid two shillings per night, which was supposed to be our tea money. I'd never have dreamed of wasting whole two shillings on such a thing, for my mother and I decided it was a marvellous opportunity to do a solid bit of saving. Just fancy ten shillings for the bank in one short week, when normally it would have taken us months to put by such a sum. I brought a piece from home, and I was given a few chips from the other girls, who sent me up to the Savoy fish-and-chip shop at the corner of Renfrew Street for the fish or pie suppers they loved for their tea. We used to order them in advance, for we knew exactly when we would be working late, and that it would go on for the whole week, and I sped like the wind up Hope Street, collected my delicious-smelling parcel and raced back to the office before it could get cold. It was great fun eating our meal in the office like this, but the hours seemed to crawl so slowly afterwards that I often couldn't believe it was only half past seven when I'd look up at the big clock. Nobody bothered to sympathize that it was a very long day from 9 A.M. till 9.30 P.M. for a sixteen-year-old. The work had to be done, and I was glad of the chance to earn an extra ten shillings, and would have rebelled at the very idea that it was too much work for me.

The boss had a canary in a cage, and it was my job to clean out the cage regularly, and to see that the little songster had fresh seed and water every morning. One of the older girls had shown me how to do this the first day I arrived and she seemed glad to be rid of this task, but I quite enjoyed it, and it made an interesting start to the day, attending to this bonnie whistler.

305

Another funny job we had to do in this office was to make up siphons of soda water for the boss. It was the first time I'd seen such a thing done, and I was fascinated. There was a siphon with a sort of wire netting all over it, which they told me was to prevent it exploding in a million pieces if anything went wrong, and we fitted a little metallic bullet into a slot, pressed down the trigger, and fired it into the water-filled decanter, instantly transforming it into fizzy soda water. I thought the whole performance was magic, but I was always a wee bit nervous of firing the bullet myself, and contented myself with standing by, waiting for the moment when water became fizz. My mother would have loved one of those, for she enjoyed, above all things, a wee drink of 'sody watter and milk' when she had a headache, or an upset stomach, but those special siphons were terribly expensive and far beyond our reach. But my mother liked hearing about such things, and thought it must be a marvellous convenience not to have to run down to the shops every time you needed a bottle of soda water.

One night the boss decided to stay on late at the office, with a client who'd come from abroad and seemed to have a lot to discuss which could only be done that evening. When he rang to tell his wife this, she said that somebody would have to be sent out to their home then, to deliver the meat he was bringing home for dinner. People were coming for a meal and it was too late for her now to go to the shops. It was about five o'clock, so I was told to get my hat and coat on and take the parcel. I was quite pleased to get away half an hour before the usual time, and I looked forward to the novelty of exploring unknown territory on the other side of Glasgow, and having my fares paid into the bargain. How strange it seemed to be taking a tramcar away out 'the other way' from Springburn, right beyond the Plaza, to the wilds of Clarkston eventually. The fog was drifting down when I handed over the parcel, and the boss's wife graciously handed me another – a box of chocolate truffles. Unopened. An entire half-pound. For me!

I hugged them to my jersey and raced for the homeward tram, pelted upstairs, darted along the top deck and made for my favourite seat right out at the front in the wee compartment above the driver's head. The fog had slowed everything down, and our driver was obviously impatient at proceeding in fits and starts, and when he could see a clear run he whirled the levers and sent the tram rocking like a roller-coaster along squealing yards of track. He was indulging in one of these wild bursts of speed when the fog obliterated everything in one of those blankets of patchy blackness which had irritated him all the way. It cleared just as suddenly, to reveal a tramcar only a yard or so ahead of us on the track, but too late for him to apply his brakes with any effect. It's the only time I hated my ringside view on a tramcar. I watched with horror the faces staring back at me from the back compartment of the other car, saw them rise to run back to avoid the worst of the impact, rose to my feet with a piercing shriek, and then bounced unharmed into the air as we crashed into each other with a sickening splintering of glass. Amazingly, nobody was injured, but both trams took a battering and we had to sit for nearly an hour while the police were contacted and all details noted. To calm my nerves – and my hunger – I ate every single chocolate truffle. I, who hoarded even a fourpenny bar of chocolate to make it spin out as long as possible, devoured an entire half-pound box, getting sicker by the minute but unable to stop this orgy. I was white as a sheet when I tottered into the house, hours past my usual time. My mother was equally white, but her pallor came from fright, for she thought I'd been run over at the very least, if not abducted! We never knew a soul who had come to the slightest harm from attack, or who was in the least danger of being kidnapped, but this didn't stop my mother fearing the worst if we were late in coming home.

I didn't dare tell her about all the chocolates I'd eaten, for even in her relief from anxiety she'd have condemned such greed and extravagance. She was sure I must be starving, and rushed to get my tea ready. I took one look at the warmed-up pie she had kept for me, heaved convulsively and left the table at top speed. She put it down to the shock of the tram crash. But to this day I've never been able to eat a chocolate truffle with any enthusiasm.

Next day they were agog to hear all about my tram adventure when I got to the office, but some of the older ones were a bit critical of the boss for sending me away out to the other side of Glasgow in the fog. 'Well, what do you expect,' Mr Mac, the oldest man said, 'moneylenders have to have hides like rhinoceros or they'd never be in this business.' I stopped as if I'd been shot. Moneylenders! Who was a moneylender? Not the boss, surely? I surely wasn't working for a moneylender! It was an insurance company – that's what it said in the letter headings. I rushed and seized a letter sheet, and carefully read the wording. There, it did say insurance, but what was this other word, 'Investors', could that mean moneylending? Suddenly I remembered my lawyer boss's face when I'd told him where I was going to work. He had wrinkled his nose and said, 'I could have wished it was some other type of business.' I hadn't known what he meant and just thought he would have preferred me to choose another, bigger, law office where I could carry on getting experience with more advanced documents. He must have guessed what investors meant. This was terrible. All the story-books I'd read condemned moneylenders. From *My Weekly* to Somerset Maugham I'd learned to what depths of despair the hero or heroine could be plunged, once they got into the clutches of moneylenders, and here was I, a member of the Church and a Sunday School teacher, actually helping one to make his fortune! I stared round the office, and wondered if they all knew. And if they did, how could they go on working there?

I didn't tell my mother of my discovery, in case she would feel too shocked by such a revelation, but I announced I was going to look for another job, maybe back to a smaller office again, which, after all, was nice and cosy and gave me a lot of responsibility. In a big office all the duties were apportioned according to age, but in a small office you had a chance of doing any mortal thing that needed doing, and this was far more interesting. This made such good sense to my mother, who knew my busy lively nature, that she didn't stop me studying the 'situations vacant' columns once more, and in a matter of weeks I had shaken the dust of the money-lenders' office off my shoes, and could hold up my head once more.

This new office promised to test my speeds all right, for there were three bosses from whom I had to take dictation, and an office girl whose business it was to do the filing, attend to the mail and look after the petty cash. The first morning I was bursting with curiosity to clap eyes on my very first office girl, for as I was the only typist, she was junior to me. I was far too early, and when the door opened, I nearly fell off my stool. In walked a female who looked far older than I did, who was head and shoulders above me in height, and who was dressed like a fashion model. She had sleek black hair, and a pale face, and actually wore make-up! How would I ever be able to send such an elegant creature for stamps? Or tell her to get on with the filing? With a brief 'Good morning', she started to open the mail, still wearing her coat. And what a posh coat to wear to work. A dark coppery-red fine tweed, with a natty shoulder cape, and a little matching cap. Shoes of fine kid exactly to match and – I couldn't believe my eyes – long kid gloves! She must have tons of money and only be working for fun. Fancy such a vision only being an office girl.

I was just recovering from this shock when the bosses walked in, one after another. Two big fair men over six feet in height, and a wee dark man like Charlie Chaplin. It was the wee man who had engaged me, and if I got a shock at sight of my office girl the two big blond men were equally surprised at my appearance. 'But she's a child!' I heard one say to the other. 'I can't believe she's seventeen.'

It was a hectically busy little office, and I flew from one desk to another, taking dictation all morning, and typed out all the stuff in the afternoon. Patsy, the office girl, had a grand appetite and was always willing to run round to the shops for a pie or a cake for our mid-morning break. I don't know if this was an official break, but she assured me she'd always done it, and she often 'stood' the cakes or pies. I was quite willing to believe her. I think she must have been allowed to keep all her salary, for she had plenty of cash to spare and never seemed to have to save for anything. I took my turn with the cake purchases as long as my pocket money allowed this, but even when it was finished Patsy insisted on sharing. She was a most generous girl, and didn't have a care in the world. The filing was in the most chaotic mess, but she seemed to have a sort of Pelmanism which told her where everything was. During her few odd free moments I'd beg her to put it in alphabetical order, or at least in order of dates, but she'd just laugh and say she couldn't be bothered, and anyway she could always find what she wanted. 'Yes, that's all right while you're here, Patsy,' I cried, 'but what if you're out and they ask for something. I can't find a *thing* in those drawers.' Patsy's method of filing was simply to thrust everything in every available drawer, not even in folders, with a corner stuck up here, a corner folded down there, to indicate to her the various weeks or months when they'd arrived and been dealt with. I shuddered with dread that one day she'd be found out and sacked. And then one day the worst happened. She fell ill with 'flu, and was off. An important client arrived from the Midlands, where the head works were, and wee Mr Brown rang the bell for me. When I went in he said, 'Oh, Miss Weir' (I was back to Miss again) 'will you just bring me in Patent and Grant's file.' I turned white, I'm sure I did, for my stomach certainly gave such a convulsive heave of fear that I felt sick. I stood in the middle of the outer office and closed my eyes in panic. Where would I look first? I opened a drawer, and papers burst out in every direction. I shut it hastily, and decided I'd start at the top drawer and work my way down, on the theory that the latest correspondence would maybe be right at the top.

The top drawer was packed so tightly with letters that I couldn't even get my wee finger in to check the dates, and when I pulled up the first lot of papers, the others closed behind them in serried ranks. Feverishly I turned over dozens of letters. Not one in alphabetical order, and all about six months old. I stuffed them back and opened another drawer. The same chaos there, but this time only about a month old. But *where* had Patsy put the most recent ones. I ran about the office opening drawers and slamming them shut again, frightened out of my wits, picturing the two men sitting in the private office waiting for me to reappear. As I didn't, Mr Brown himself strolled in. 'Having trouble finding the letter?' he said pleasantly. 'It can't be far away – it just came in last week. Where's the file?' 'There are no files.' I blurted out miserably. I didn't want to give Patsy away, but there was no way of disguising the truth. 'No files,' he said with slight irritation.

'Don't be silly, girl, of course there are files,' and he pulled open a drawer. 'Good God!' he said, as letters sprang up in dozens, all bunched together just any old way. He pulled open every drawer in the office, and his face twitched, in fury as I thought, but suddenly to my amazement he burst out laughing. I decided he'd gone mad from the shock. But no. 'Well,' he said at last, wiping his eyes, 'like the bloke who's fiddling the books, if you have a system like this, you just must never be ill, that's all.' He patted my arm kindly and told me not to bother looking, for it was like looking for a needle in a haystack. He gave me a conspiratorial wink. 'Don't tell the others,' he said, 'and we'll straighten it all out when Patsy comes back.' He was Scots, and the other two big blond men were English, and I think he felt we Scots must stick together. I thankfully agreed, and just prayed they wouldn't ask me to find a letter while she was away from work. When Patsy came back that kind Mr Brown had a little talk with her, and between them they started a real filing system. He made her tackle one drawer at a time, told her it would probably take her some months, but if she wanted to keep her job, and let him keep his sanity, then it would just have to be done. And I was to see that she spent at least two hours every morning and afternoon on it. Poor Patsy, I was a hard taskmistress. By this time I'd long forgotten my awe of her smart clothes and her ladylike appearance. Deeds, not looks, were what counted in the long run, and I was determined she would repay Mr Brown's confidence in both of us, and show a proper gratitude for not losing her job. There were no more pies or cakes for many a long day, for I just wouldn't let her go out, not even to buy stamps. I did that in my dinner-hour. We did the mail between us at night, and by Christmas we could look with pride on a really efficient filing system where even I could find a letter at a moment's notice.

I was so glad we had worked so hard, because one day during Christmas week our doorbell rang at home, when I was home for my dinner, and a delivery boy handed us in an enormous parcel. It was addressed to me. 'Are you sure it's not a mistake?' I said. 'Are you sure it's for us?' 'Oh aye,' he responded cheerfully, 'It's your name and it's your address so it must be for you. It was sent from England.' 'From England,'

I said. 'I don't know anybody in England.' 'Well, somebody knows you,' he said. 'Come on, ah've no' got a' day. Sign for it and ah'll be on ma way.' When we opened it, it was from the head office of my firm, and it was the biggest bird we'd ever had inside our house. It was a goose, and it was so huge it wouldn't go inside the oven. 'Oh my,' said my mother, 'wisn't that lovely of them? They must think a lot o' you to send such a grand present. It wid feed the hale o' Springburn.' I was sent up to the big Co-operative bakers, and they promised to bake it in their big oven and we were to collect it on Christmas Eve. We had often done this with big steak pies if we were having a special celebration, but this was the first time we had had the pleasure of presenting a magnificent fowl to be cooked. 'By jings,' said the boy who took it from me in the Co-operative, 'it's nearly as big as you, hen. Whit a tightner you'll have aff that. It'll dae ye for a week.'

When my mother and I went to collect it, the baker had to lend us one of his big baking trays to carry home the delicious fat. 'Just the stuff for a tight chest, Mrs Weir,' he assured my mother. 'Pit it in a big jeely jar and keep it – it's faur before ony o' yer embrocation.' And so we were able to prove for ourselves, after all, that goose fat was the very dab for winter ailments. What a beautiful bird it was. It lasted right through to Hogmanay, and filled the tastiest sandwiches for our Ne'er-day visitors that any of us could have imagined. And to think it had cost us nothing, and had been a gift from a firm for whom I'd only worked for a few months. And that wasn't all, for the three bosses had clubbed together and given Patsy and myself a pair of silk stockings each, and a wee box of chocolates for the office. 'What a marvellous firm,' I thought, it was nearly as good as the Cratchit's Christmas from Scrooge, all those gifts landed in our laps so unexpectedly, and allowing us to spread our bounty so widely among our own friends because of the size of that enormous bird. I wrote to the head office, urged to do so by my mother, although my bosses said it wasn't necessary, and I told them that thanks to them we had now all tasted goose, and we had a big jelly jar full of the fat to see us through our winter colds, and they sent a very nice letter in return saying how pleased they were with my work, and thanking me for taking the trouble to write. Trouble! It was nae bother at a'. I'd have written a hundred letters for such a Christmas.

One day, when the spring sunshine transformed the dusty streets of Glasgow, and sent little motes shimmering into every bright ray, I went into the boss's sanctum to leave some letters for signing. To my dismay, for I had thought the room was empty, the younger of the two tall blond Englishmen was sitting with his arms spread over the desk, and his head sunk in them, groaning. I stood there, biting my lip, not knowing what to do. Should I say something? But what? Should I just tiptoe out and hope he hadn't heard me come in? I had no social graces at all to equip me for such a situation. I decided to retreat, and was just creeping quietly to the door, when his voice stopped me. 'No, don't go,' a strangely muffled voice said, 'I've got to talk to someone.' My heart gave a jump and I stopped, but I didn't turn round. I didn't like the sound of that voice. Could he be crying? I'd never thought a grown man could cry, and I didn't want to be proved wrong, especially by my boss, and him with such an English voice that it had taken me weeks to get used to him, and of whom I was very shy. 'Come and sit down,' he said. I kept my head down and sidled into a chair, my eyes on the floor. There was no sound now except the ticking of the wee clock on the mantelpiece. I bit my lips, and held my breath, and was terrified my stomach would make a noise, for I'd hurried all the way down Parliamentary Road, and we'd had lentil soup for our dinner, a windy food even when you took your time over it.

At last the silence was unbearable and I was forced to look up. He *had* been crying! Even now a big tear rolled down his cheek. What could be the matter? I was suffocating with embarrassment. 'Oh I'm sorry to make such an ass of myself,' he said, and then gave another frightening gulp, 'but my fiancée has just broken off our engagement.' I let out my breath, in a long sighing sound. The novels were all true. When they said, thrillingly, 'Such emotion was strong enough to make a grown man cry', I hadn't believed them, but it was all *true*! Here was a grown man crying because he had been crossed in love, and I was privileged to see it. Oh I was on familiar territory now, all

313

right, and I sat back, as receptive and willing an ear as he could have hoped to find. I made him describe her in detail, not realizing the possible anguish I might be inflicting. 'Was she tall, like you?' I asked. 'Was she English, like you?' Yes, to both questions, and that had been the trouble. They had been too much apart, with him being posted to the Glasgow office, and she had found someone else. I closed my eyes with the sheer rightness of the words. 'She had found someone else.' How often had the final words of a *My Weekly* story ended on that very sentence. There was no doubt about it, grown-ups got into the most terrible messes with their romances, and nothing was safe when not even the beautiful diamond ring he had given her had kept her faithful to his memory.

I was glad to see, though, he had stopped crying and actually seemed to have found a grain of comfort in remembering how he had never liked her parents very much. 'Oh that's terrible,' I said, 'for if you don't get on with your in-laws, it's murder. You're maybe just as well without her.' I was aghast at my own daring, when I'd uttered this so impulsively, but he didn't seem to mind. In fact with a bewildering change of mood he leaned his elbows on the desk, stared at me and said, 'Do you know, I never noticed before that you have a black spot under the pupil of your eye, like a beauty spot in the wrong place.' I jumped with embarrassment, suddenly remembering that he was my boss, and I didn't much fancy him gazing into my eyes like this. Especially when he'd just lost a fiancée. It wasn't seemly. Not seemly at all. As I sat there, hypnotized like a rabbit, not knowing what to do next, the door opened, and it was wee Mr Brown. Oh what a relief. I leaped to my feet, pointed to the letters I'd laid on Mr Brown's desk (how many hours ago it seemed!), and escaped to the outer office. Gosh what a strange lot the English were. I couldn't imagine a Scotsman behaving like that, whatever the novels said, but it had all been very exciting, and I couldn't wait to get home and tell my mother all about it. Strangely enough her reaction was 'Hoo auld did ye say this man wis?' 'Och I don't know,' I said, impatient at this flat response to such a dramatic tale. 'About thirty-five maybe. He's quite old.' My mother laughed. 'Aye, too old to be greetin' in the office like that – he must be a bit soft.' 'Oh, Mother,' I said reproachfully, 'he was heartbroken, so he was.' Mind you, I came to the conclusion myself he really was a bit soft, for after that when I went in for notes I'd find him staring at my eyes, as if he couldn't keep his mind off that wee black spot in the iris. It was terribly rude of him, and I wished I had the courage to tell him to get on with his dictation. That broken engagement seemed to make him go daft, right enough, for one day he actually picked me up and sat me on top of the big corner cupboard and I couldn't get down. I was scared out of my wits, because I couldn't move in case I'd crash to the floor, and he was such a tall man he could put his arms on either side of the cupboard wall and keep me trapped there. I squeaked feebly in protest, 'Please let me down, sir, oh *please*!' He didn't take a blind bit of notice, but just laughed. I could have hit him, if he hadn't been my boss. He strolled away towards the door, pretending to leave me there marooned, and when I let out a scream of fright I lost my balance and slipped forward. One bound, and he'd caught me in his arms. The next minute, Patsy had arrived and was staring as if her eyes were going to fall out. Aye, it was high time I looked for another job.

Wee Mr Brown, my Scots boss, helped me in this decision, because, like my nice lawyer boss, he had my interests at heart. 'I don't know why you stay in a pokey place like this,' he kept telling me, 'with your speeds you could be earning twice what we are able to pay you. Why don't you try for one of the really important firms in Glasgow.'

I decided to take his advice, but I'd wait a wee while. After that generous treatment at Christmas I felt it would be most ungrateful of me to desert them so soon. I just couldn't decently hand in my notice before the Fair. By that time I'd have been with them a year, and my mother too would take it quite naturally that I wanted to move on. She'd never suspect the middle-aged English boss had helped to drive me out, because he showed every sign of going wrong in the mind.

14

The summers were periods of blessed release from learning, for I had used my prize money, as planned, to go back to college for night classes, and the winter months were devoted entirely to study. Three nights a week at classes, one night at the Guides, choir practice, and homework filled every week from September right through to the end of May. I discovered what a marvellous help to study walking was. I walked to the office in the morning, back to it again at lunchtime, home at night, back to college, and home again after classes. The only time I rode in a tram, unless it was absolutely torrential rain, was home for my dinner. I'd never have dreamt of spending money on fares for all that travelling, and the movement of my feet and legs seemed to increase my thoughts. I did trial balances in my head for the business methods class, I translated my French exercises, I wrote every word of every shop advert in shorthand as I passed the windows, and I wrote little stories for *The Times* and for *The Citizen* and *The Bulletin*, describing all the humorous things I observed in my daily marches to and from Springburn. I had discovered also, to my surprise, that newspapers liked what I wrote and actually paid me. *The Times* gave me first encouragement. I was so inexperienced that I didn't even know I ought to enclose a stamped addressed envelope if I wanted my article returned, and nobody was more surprised than I when my brother picked up the paper one night and cried, 'Hey, is this you?', pointing to the initials M.W.W. at the foot of an article about Glasgow trams. 'Oh, they've printed it,' I shouted, and seized the paper from him. The family were stunned. I had told nobody. Tommy was particularly amazed, for he was already trying his hand at the writing game, with mixed success, and he was full of encouragement that I had hit the jackpot with my very first piece. They paid me fifteen shillings. The equivalent of a whole week's wages from the law office. I hoped I would get some more good ideas, for this seemed a great way of adding to my savings and enjoying myself at the same time, since writing was always a wonderful respite from all the hard grind of lessons and homework.

I even enjoyed taking the minutes for the Guide meetings for not only was it good practice for my shorthand, but I could write out a précis of our discussions in my own words. The Guides were a great source of pleasure, and provided a fine outlet for my energies after nights of quiet study during the rest of the week. I was now a patrol leader, and chose the swallow for my emblem. I admired the dark blue and white of the embroidered badge, and I loved its swift darting movements in flight, and the way it never seemed to keep still. As my mother always said of me, because I never 'warmed a chair', 'it's a pity oor Molly hisnae a pair of wings', I thought the swallow particularly appropriate, and so did she. We had a great time marching up and down in our church hall, playing racing games, learning country dancing, and studying for our various badges. All my earlier childhood activities were a great help in acquiring those coveted badges. Needlework just meant doing a piece of simple sewing, and a few pieces of knitting, plus a crochet edging, all of which I had done either at home or at school. Grannie had taught me to knit before I went to school, and although I could never hope to work as fast as she did, I could turn the heel of a sock well enough to please her before I was ten years old. The cookery badge didn't give me a minute's worry, for again I had cooked with and for Grannie since I could toddle, and I felt the few things I'd been asked to do for the badge hadn't really earned me that beautifully embroidered emblem to put on my sleeve. The first-aid one was harder, though, and we had special classes from some of the big boys from the Boys' Brigade, and learned all about splints and slings, and how to cope with fainting and nose-bleeding, and such minor disasters. There were dozens of tricky questions we could be asked about the various bones of the body, not to mention the parts of the brain, and the differences between veins and arteries, and the composition of the blood. Oh how we groaned and worried over our first-aid book, and trembled in case we'd be asked something we knew absolutely nothing about. We could hardly believe it when we all got through, and we felt that that was one badge we had well and truly earned.

Our company was particularly good at maze marching, and for the big combined display at St Andrew's Hall we were chosen to do this intricate form of marching to represent Springburn. Our captain was a really fine pianist, and we rehearsed to the splendid tunes she chose, until we knew every turn and twist and wheeling movement and could have performed in our sleep.

I washed my hair the night before the display, for an abiding passion with me has been soft, clean, silky hair. The only time any of us visited a hairdresser was to have our hair trimmed, and the very idea of paying somebody to set it in smooth neat waves round our heads was beyond imagination. We just washed it, pressed wee combs in to form some sort of wave, and let it go its own sweet way, which in my case was to stand up in a great fluffy mop which added a few satisfying inches to my small stature. I've always walked with a spring in my step, a sort of bouncing rhythm, or, as my mother tactfully put it, 'as though I were dancing'. I just couldn't walk any other way, and so I was quite unconscious of the fact that when we went into our maze marching on the stage of St Andrew's Hall before a packed audience I presented a very comical figure, my mop bouncing in time to my springy steps. As we twisted in and out, arms swinging, heads up, forming intricate patterns for the admiration of our audience, a slight ripple of laughter started, and grew and grew. None of us could understand it. The whole audience were soon convulsed. 'What is the matter?' we wondered in panic. We couldn't utter a word of our dismay, of course, for we were too busy following our long-rehearsed movements, but we had done this marching so often that we could allow ourselves to steal glances at one another as we passed and repassed. Every eye became riveted to the hem of the opposite number, to see if anybody's knickers were falling down. No, not a bloomer leg in sight. What could it be? We were scarlet with shame and confusion, and when we came off the stage we gazed at one another in bewilderment, deaf to the applause which followed our exit. And then a patrol leader who had been watching from the audience came in, gasping with laughter. 'It was Molly Weir's bouncing walk and her hair going up and down that looked so funny,' she said. 'It was like a hairy-jock in the wind.' I blushed with mortification till the tears came to my eyes, and the others were furious that I had spoiled the effect of their neat marching. Fancy making such a fool of myself up there in front of everybody. Oh how glad I was that my mother hadn't come to see us. And then at the thought of my mother I laughed, for I remembered one of her favourite stories was of the country lassie who had gone out with the farmer's son, and during the course of the evening he had rifted right out loud in the pictures. She had laughed and laughed, for, as my mother had said, she hadn't enough gumption to hide her feelings and spare those of the young man. At last he had said, sarcastically, 'I won't bother to take you to the pictures again, since you're so easily entertained with a mere rift.' We all thought this a great joke, and a fine bit of repartee, and I suddenly thought it was equally hilarious that a whole audience could be so easily amused by a clean head of hair. If they were as daft as all that, why should I let it bother me? But I never forgot, all the same, how easily one could become a figure of fun through something in one's appearance, and how ignorant one could be of the effect of such a thing on the rest of the world. I wondered if the time would ever come when I would feel calmly sure of everything, like my mother and the minister and the Guide captain, and I longed to look into the future and see how I would turn out.

We were all getting to the age, my chums and I, and the girls I met in offices, where the future tantalized us with its mystery, and one of the great excitements of those days was having our fortune told. We knew well enough it would be *years* before any of us could afford to think of getting married. Oh we were romantic, all right, but we had first-hand evidence all round us that marriage involved rent, insurance, clothes, and that a house had to be furnished before you could live in it, and furnished from savings at that.

Everybody was far too poor to be able to count on such

munificent presents as suites, or indeed any sort of furniture, and hire purchase was regarded with horror in the community where I lived. The nearest we ever got to H.P., apart from my mother's mad flight of fancy with the piano, was 'the Menage', or 'the Minodge', as we pronounced it, to which working-class wives belonged because it meant being able to buy sheets and blankets and towels when they were needed, all essential items if the decencies were to be preserved, and which could be paid off at the rate of a sixpence or a shilling a week over what seemed like an eternity of time.

Even this mild form of H.P. was frowned on by my mother and my grannie, and we saved up and had the money in our hand, or at any rate covered by the Co-op dividend before we bought a single item.

We were prepared for the long legendary Scottish courtship, and saw nothing odd in courtships which lasted for ten or fifteen years. One enterprising couple delayed the wedding day until they had won their household equipment by their skill at local whist drives, and we all knew that they were just waiting to win the bed, and then the great day could be named. Eventually the nuptial couch was won, they were wed, and seemed none the worse for the waiting. The whole district followed those whist drives, and the couple themselves rejoiced no more with each prize than we did, watching on the sidelines.

So with such examples to keep us with a proper sense of perspective and stifle any thoughts of indecent haste in such matters, we followed the thrifty ways of our elders, but nobody could stop us from dreaming, or from seeking occult help in trying to penetrate the mysterious future which lay so far ahead. The clap-trap of the spae-wives was drunk in with almost swooning eagerness, in spite of the fact that we were all respectable attenders of Sunday School, Church and Bible Class. We saw no contradiction in believing in both, and news of a new spae-wife flashed through the young community with the speed of bush telegraph, just as it had with the advent of a new church mission bent on saving our souls. The very word 'fortune-teller' held magic for us and we clamoured to be taken to the new oracle. 'How much is it?' we demanded. If it were sixpence, we decided she couldn't be much good. Anybody with the real second sight would put a far higher value on her gift, for she would be in great demand. A shilling was more like the thing, we felt, and could be scraped together now that we were working, without too much sacrifice. We'd put the money we saved on fares towards the shilling, and we'd cut out sweeties entirely – well, except maybe for one or two Imperials to suck in church on Sunday. A spae-wife at two shillings, though, had us searching the corners of our purses, and doing frantic calculations to try to meet this enormous sum. 'She must be good,' we'd think excitedly, 'if people pay her two whole shillings.'

The spae-wives generally lived in the South Side of Glasgow, or the 'Soo-side', as it was known, alien territory to most of us. We shivered with nervous delight as we bowled along in strange, different-coloured tramcars through unfamiliar streets. We tried to keep these excursions from our mothers, but somehow they sensed that something was going on. They'd have had to have been deaf and blind not to have noticed, for we rushed about to each other's houses in frantic activity, and in a hiss of whispers, for days before the actual spae-wife visit took place. My mother was so sure we'd be murdered, or at the very least 'set upon' and left for dead in those darkly suspect districts, that she reduced me to a state of fear where I could scarcely take in my fortune when it was told to me.

The fortune-tellers were, almost without exception, Irish, with vast bosoms, over which were stretched tight handknitted jumpers. We talked to each other in whispers as we waited in dingy lobbies for our turn to go in, and, once confronted with the oracle, could hardly breathe as fear blended with desperation that having come this far we couldn't turn back. The rooms always seemed strangely dark, with a queer smell which I realized later was compounded of dust and sooty chimneys and drying clothes. Sometimes they read the cards, but sometimes they peered into the lines of our hands, and the heavy scent of their bodies came suffocatingly close. We chattered non-stop on the way home, like birds released from a cage, glad to be in the open air again, with safe, familiar faces round us. We compared notes on what we'd been told. Each and every one of us were told we would cross the water, but as we'd already crossed the Clyde to reach the fortune teller, we felt this was a pretty safe prediction. Secretly we were terribly disappointed at having to share even this one forecast with each other. We wanted to be unique, but, of course, as the spae-wives were Irish and had migrated themselves, they doubtless felt this was the most important thing that could happen to anyone. However, the rest of our fortune had a satisfying variety. One was to marry a tall dark stranger. Another a short, thick-set fair man. A third would be widowed early in life, which we felt was thrillingly romantic. Even the future widow liked this, and was glad she was fair, because everybody knew that widows' weeds looked far nicer on fair-haired people. None of us had even seen widows' weeds, but we'd heard our mothers and grannies speak of them, and the description sounded beautifully dramatic and tragic.

Some would have three children, some five, some were guaranteed twins, and none would be childless. We were so sure that spae-wives were right, we almost started knitting our layettes to be well prepared for our broods. Only a lack of money, and the impossibility of truly seeing ourselves as mothers, stopped us buying the wool.

We never suspected that they were frauds, every single one of them. We wanted so desperately to believe that they knew what lay ahead that we pretended to ourselves that the things they told us were coming true one by one.

All except one of my chums, who had complete faith in my mother's ability to read fortunes from tea-leaves. 'She's *faur* better than yon spae-wives,' she'd declare, 'and she doesn't charge you anything.' My mother only did this for fun, and had started it just to prove anybody could make up a fortune if she put her mind to it, and to try to stop us wasting our money on 'thae Jezebels ower at the Soo-side'. Strangely enough, many of the things she said did come true, and what had started out as a joke became her party piece, and she was in great demand by all my friends. In fact she became quite fed up with the whole business, and made every excuse to go out when she knew my chums were coming to do their sewing, or wash their hair, for she knew she wouldn't get a minute's peace until she'd read their fortunes in the tea-leaves.

We were becoming very absorbed with our grooming now, and stayed in at least two evenings a week for the sole purpose of washing our hair, doing our nails, going over our clothes and mending any straps or stockings which needed attention. We shared breathless ideas for making our hair or skin more dazzling, and these usually had to be concocted from household items, for none of us wore make-up, apart from a little daring use of lipstick. One chum with beautiful hair swore by an egg-yolk mixed in with liquid green soap as *the* perfect shampoo. Another urged that oatmeal mixed with egg made a terrific face-pack and gave you rosy cheeks. My mother's scorn at this waste of good food had me rushing through the lobby to hide my meal-covered features, for I would defeat the whole purpose if I let the stuff crack by arguing. However rosy my cheeks were when I went to bed after such beautifying treatments, they wore their usual Glasgow pallor in the morning, and justified my mother's wrath at the waste of a good egg. We spent hours tidying out the solitary drawer we were allowed to use in the big chest of drawers, and checking over all our treasures. I once found tenpence stowed away in a typewriter-ribbon box, where I'd stored it for safe keeping for my holidays and then forgotten where I'd hidden it, and if I had inherited a fortune, I couldn't have been more elated.

I don't know how many times I'd lifted out that box during the many tidyings I'd done, but the pennies were packed so tightly they hadn't rattled, and the treasure within had lain unnoticed all that time. Oh I could now appreciate to the full the story in the Bible of the rejoicing which took place when that which was lost was found again. Whole tenpence! And just in the nick of time for the hat sale.

As far as we were concerned there was only one hat sale and we waited for it every summer. What the Queen's milliner was to London, Annette was to Glasgow. We could never have afforded her hats at ordinary prices during the year, and contented ourselves with mere window-gazing until sale time rolled round. She had a routine which never varied, so you knew exactly where you were.

As soon as Glasgow Fair was on, and those with money to burn had equipped themselves with their holiday and summer hats, a huge notice would appear in the window of her exclusive little shop in Sauchiehall Street. 'SALE – HATS TODAY £1.' So those with a pound to spend got the pick of the stock. Then, a few days later, when Annette felt the hats were getting a bit too battered to ask a pound for them, the second notice went up. 'SALE – HATS TODAY 10/-.' None of your gentle reductions for Annette. Prices were slashed dramatically or not at all. The exciting thing was that you didn't know just *when* she'd reduce her prices. You knew it would happen, but whether days or merely hours would elapse between one reduction and the next, only Annette herself knew. And she gave no hint. So you had to flee up to the shop every lunch-hour from office or college to check how the odds were being reduced. If you saw a hat for which your heart panted, you had to weigh the risk of it surviving the ten-shilling customers, and oh the agony of trying to decide whether to splash your savings at this stage and make sure of it, or chance it not attracting anyone and getting it for five shillings later.

If you were a gambler you waited. Inevitably, the next notice was 'SALE – HATS TODAY 5/-', to be followed a few days later by 'SALE – HATS TODAY 2/6d'. But madness really took over among the youngest fry when somebody came rushing into the cloak-room with the news 'They're down to sixpence tomorrow.' At that stage Annette put the notice in the window the afternoon before, so we had advance warning.

There was no time for leisurely eating that day. We'd snatch a sandwich on the wing, wouldn't even stop to walk, but raced up to the shop as fast as our excellently trained legs would carry us. It was like a football scrum. Sharp elbows working over-time, we dived into the centre of a milling mass of teenagers. Nobody wore a hat, for if you'd gone in wearing one, you'd never have recovered it again. Ten to one somebody would have plonked down sixpence for it and vanished before you could have protested. We had a hilarious time. Hats with veils were tried on to shrieks of laughter. Anybody with a sense of comedy paraded round in feathers, reducing the others to hysteria. But when it came to actually choosing something for our sixpence we became deadly serious and called all our chums to give an opinion.

How Annette could have allowed us to invade her shop like this I simply don't know. Maybe it made a change from the usual quiet elegance of her surroundings, and she may even have enjoyed the rapturous appreciation we gave to all her battered sales models. She stood at the back of the shop, smiling, and only volunteered a quiet word of advice when the agony of indecision was almost reducing a customer to tears. We had a glorious hour, and at the end of it each and every one of us bore off in triumph a sixpenny hat in a brown-paper bag. This would be the last hat purchase for many of us until the notice went up next year: 'SALE – HATS TODAY SIXPENCE'.

My best sixpenny bargain was a pale pink straw boater trimmed with black veiling, which was an exact match for a pink linen dress I made. I felt so grown-up I almost choked with my own importance, and my mother was amazed at the transformation it wrought. We all helped each other with our home dressmaking, and I had the great benefit of being close chums with a girl who had obtained a job with one of the top dress houses in Glasgow. She used to be allowed to bring home cuttings from the posh dresses made for the aristocracy of Glasgow and Renfrewshire, and from these she showed us how to cut leaves and petals, and stitch them into lifelike chrysanthemums and spring bouquets which we pinned to the neckline or shoulder of our home-made garments. This added a most elegant touch to our bargain remnants, and we spent hours stitching and trying on and pressing to pass the critical eye of our dressmaking chum. She also showed us how to make little crêpe-de-Chine garters, again from exquisite material obtained from her employers, and all of us eventually sported silken garters which exactly toned in with our outfits, so we didn't mind a bit when our skirts were whirled up during the active birlings of the eightsome reels and quadrilles at the church dances. Our garters were part of our outfit, after all, and it would have been a shame if nobody had caught a glimpse of them and appreciated all our hard work and dainty stitching.

Those church dances were great fun, and our mothers served behind the scenes and kept an eye on us at the same time. Instead of bags of cookies and cakes we had boxes handed out to us at the interval, and this seemed so opulent and grown-up.

There would be a salmon sandwich, moist and delicious, and usually a Paris bun and one or two dainty little cakes. The mothers came round with steaming cups of tea, and we all sat round the hall, and ate every scrap. We couldn't rush back to the cloakroom to save anything to take home, and we wouldn't have dreamt of leaving anything when we'd paid for it, so there wasn't a crumb left.

The boys sat along one side of the hall, and the girls along the other wall, and the minute the orchestra struck up, there was a dash for the girl of the moment. Paul Jones' foxtrots took care of the wallflowers, and gave everybody a chance, and ladies' choice sent us off shyly to choose the boy who found favour in our eyes. At the first of these dances my mother who had romantic ideas of daintiness, had made my heart turn over with dismay by buying me a little pair of pale blue dancing pumps, dead flat like ballet shoes, to match a pale blue chiffon dress she had found in one of her mysterious sorties down by the Barrows. I hadn't the heart to disappoint her by telling her how I longed for higher heels, and how much I needed them to boost my miserably small size, and I tried to hide my feet under my chair in case nobody would dance with me because I was so wee. A few of the girls were scathing and said they weren't proper dance shoes, but the boys didn't seem to mind, and once my embarrassment was forgotten those flat shoes were marvellous for scooshing up and down the hall during the quadrilles, and for leaping round the hall dancing the Dashing White Sergeant.

For a special Christmas dance my mother had managed to find some floral ninon dress material and some matching net, and although it was inexpensive sale material, we decided we couldn't manage such flimsy stuff ourselves and would have it made by a real dressmaker. It would have to be somebody cheap, of course, but there were plenty of seamstresses in Springburn at that time who were glad to earn a few shillings by taking orders for dressmaking. We heard of a wee woman out the Low Road, as we called the road between Balgrayhill and Auchinairn, and one foggy Friday night after my mother came home from work, and I had done my homework after my office job, we set off for the dressmaker's house. I had a picture from a newspaper which I wanted her to copy, for to me the mere word 'dressmaker' invested this unknown lady with all the qualities of *haute couture*. It was a dark wee close, with a gas-lamp which flickered from a broken mantle, and I was glad my mother was with me. We climbed the stairs and peered at all the name-plates and found the name we sought on the second floor. We rang the bell and waited. Not a murmur. We rang again, 'Maybe she's no' in,' my mother said, 'but where could she be on a night like this?' She didn't stop to reason that she and I were out on such a night, and not in our own house. I wouldn't give in, for I was dying to get my beautiful ninon and net into the hands of this expert. 'Ring again, Mother,' I urged. So we gave another yank at the bell-knob and sent a wild jingle of sound echoing down the lobby which was assuredly on the other side of the door.

We heard footsteps, the door opened, and a frightened face peered round the frame. 'Who is it?' she demanded, in a high, shrill voice. I couldn't answer, for I was too busy taking in her appearance. She looked about a hundred, and nothing like my mental picture of a dressmaker at all. We followed her through the lobby, to an ice-cold front room where she lit the gas. We hadn't managed to speak a word so far, for she had spied the parcel we were carrying and had obviously assumed we wanted her services to make a dress. 'Who is it for?' she asked, looking from my mother to me. While my mother opened the parcel I spread out the newspaper picture and started to explain that I wanted her to copy it, but she seized my arm abruptly and called, 'Wait a minute.' She disappeared, and came back almost at once carrying something which glittered in the gas-light. 'Now,' she said, 'what is it you want?' and, so saying, she raised her arm and smartly put an ear trumpet to her ear. My mother and I stared at each other, and I could feel the laughter bubbling from the pit of my stomach, up through my chest and over the top of my head. My mother shook her head reprovingly, and pushed me towards the trumpet. I opened my mouth, placed it to the mouth of that trumpet and tried to speak. Instead of words, out came a strangled shriek of laughter which nearly blasted the poor wee woman to the other side of the room. At her look of reproach, tears of laughter and embarrassment ran down my cheeks. 'I can't, Mother,' I gasped. 'You'll have to tell her.' 'Indeed I will not,' said my mother sharply. 'You'll just control yourself and tell her yourself. I never saw such bad manners.' I gulped, put my mouth to the trumpet, tried to speak, shrieked again with hysterical laughter, then turned and ran down the stairs into the fog, leaving my mother, the dressmaker and the ear trumpet. I leaned against the wall of the close, aware of my terrible behaviour, but unable to stop laughing. At last it all ended in a bout of most uncomfortable hiccups, and still there was no sign of my mother. I *couldn't* go in and face that poor wee deaf woman again, but now I was frightened of the dark close and the flickering gas-light. I crept upstairs again and listened outside the door which I had left wide open in my flight. To my amazement my mother and the dressmaker were chatting quite amiably, and the wee dressmaker was telling all about her days as a court dressmaker to which she had been apprenticed at the age of fourteen and had only left to nurse her mother a few years back. Her mother! How could anybody so old have a mother? I wondered The type of work she was doing now, I heard her say, was a far cry from what she had been used to, but sewing was all she knew and she had just to take whatever offered in the district. Oh how ashamed I felt, but I couldn't have returned to that room if I'd been shot for not doing so. When my mother eventually came out, carrying my dress material, I couldn't meet her eyes. When I tried to take her arm she shook me off. 'I was black affrontit,' she said. 'Fancy laughing like that, and you supposed to be a lady. I don't know what you learned in that college, but it certainly wasn't manners.'

My heart felt like lead. How could I explain to my mother that I wasn't laughing at the poor deaf woman, that it was self-consciousness at having to speak down a trumpet that had been my undoing. Miserably I realized that I was no lady. I was just like the farm servant who had laughed because somebody had rifted. No, I was far far worse, because she had just been a simple girl, whereas I at least had had the advantage of a good education. Would I ever learn to be a lady? I doubted it very much, especially after this black black episode.

My mother broke the silence. 'Well,' she said at last, 'you'll come oot o' this worst anyway, for you'll sew every stitch of that dress yourself, and then maybe you'll be sorry you lost the chance of that clever wee woman doing it for you.' She was right, of course. It was ghastly material for an amateur to work with, and many salt tears were shed over puckered neckline, stretched sleeve-seam, and uneven hem before I could wear that dress to the church dance, and every time I wore it I could see that ear trumpet, and remember my undisciplined behaviour. In the end I gave it away long before its usefulness was ended. I couldn't bear the sight of it. It was a bitter lesson.

15

At the end of that winter term of night classes the college principal asked if I would stay on for a few weeks to be coached in special high shorthand speeds in short bursts, for they wanted to arrange public demonstrations of my skill and at the same time give the college a boost. I was delighted to do this, for I owed them so much. The head teacher whose house I had visited was still the only one who could rattle off the test pieces at breakneck speed, so he and I stayed on for an hour every night, when his day classes were over and I came from the office, and soon we were zooming along at the dazzling speed of 300 words per minute. It didn't seem possible. It was comparatively easy to get up to 200, then 220, but every 20 words per minute on top became progressively difficult. I still had to perch up on my feet on the seat, and I used to feel a bit like a jockey, crouching over my book and desk, hand racing along like lightning. By this time, I didn't even have to think of an outline. I had been going over and over the teacher's course at night classes, to keep me in training for the exam, which I couldn't take till I was eighteen, and I must have drilled every outline, every grammalogue and phrase a million times since I was fourteen. In fact, I was greatly encouraged one night when, after I'd done my oral stint at the blackboard, my teacher said laughingly, 'If you give them this sort of example when you go for your exam, they'll hand you your teaching certificate as you walk out of the door!' I may say when the exam did come I was just as terrified as if I'd never looked at a book. And when the results came out, and I knew I'd passed, I was so exhilarated I could have done cart-wheels all over Glasgow.

My high-speed demonstrations to parents and would-be students were part of a campaign to boost the numbers enrolling at the college, and as an added personal draw I came in for a week of my holidays and enrolled the students who were to start after the summer term. How business-like I felt, standing behind the counter on the first floor, welcoming each new arrival, taking details of name, address, previous school, what subjects they would study, and finally their payment for the course. I whirled round date-stamps with great authority, signed with a flourish the copperplate receipts given to me by the principal, and handed over with fitting solemnity a folder giving all details of the books required. The principal christened me Peter Pan, as I flew from desk to counter, back to desk again, round to his office to hand over the money, and back to the desk again to take care of the next student. I thoroughly enjoyed this taste of officialdom, and was astounded when at the end of the week the old man pressed a ten-shilling note into my hand. For what? For being allowed to play at running the whole college? Fancy getting money as well as such fun. Whole ten shillings too, to add to my savings.

Although they were very pleased with my speeds and were frighteningly certain I'd get through the teacher's exam with flying colours, the college heads took another look at me and came to the conclusion that with my tiny proportions of 4 ft. 11½ in. height and a weight of under seven stones I'd need some backing to give me authority over heavy-weight pupils. They decided that the thing for me to do was to have professional voice coaching. I didn't even begin to suspect that it might also be to iron out the broad Springburn accent, which I was hardly aware of now, for I was using my posh office voice all the time, being careful not to be too lah-di-dah, of course. It was almost worse being too 'pan-loaf' than being too rough in accent.

By a strange coincidence, I had actually heard of the voice teacher whom the college suggested. Months before this, Patsy, my sophisticated office girl, had come in one morning full of enthusiasm for a concert she'd enjoyed the previous evening. With my interest in everything to do with acting, I drank in every word, and before the morning was over she had taught me two poems by A.A. Milne which she'd heard at the concert. If she was terrible at filing, she had a wonderful memory for words. The performers had all been pupils of this marvellous teacher. I envied them from the bottom of my heart. And now, to my delight, the college were suggesting I take lessons from this very teacher. It was too good to be true. And then the harsh facts of life brought me back to earth. How would my mother and I pay for the lessons? Although we weren't quite so hard up, I still had only thirty shillings a week, and there were books, and clothes, and fares, and Guide subscriptions, and a dozen other calls on my pocket money of five shillings a week.

My mother thought I was daft enough paying to join the Scottish Clerks' Association, just to get my teeth looked after, in case I would one day be an actress and need a perfect smile – she herself would have run a mile from any dentist – so how could I ask her to pay for voice lessons? The very idea of paying to learn how to *speak*, when she thought I was a lovely speaker, would have seemed like throwing good money down the drain.

I was still very shy of those elderly college men, and didn't know how to tell them that I had no money to help me to follow their lovely suggestion, but they sensed the difficulty and said they would put in a word and see that I had specially advantageous terms. They might seem especially advantageous to the college, I thought, but any charge at all would seem impossible to us, who hadn't a penny left over for such frivolities.

Suddenly I saw a possibility. This was maybe the right moment to look for a new job with better money. I'd promised myself I'd only stay where I was till the Fair anyway, and if I got one right away, I'd have from the Fair till September to save, for there was no hurry to start the voice coaching until the autumn term. It would be perfect timing, for I'd also be into the final winter session before the shorthand teacher's examination, and I'd be able to make immediate use of my voice training. I began looking at the advertisements in the newspapers that very night, as soon as my mother had finished with *The Times*. There were several which took my fancy, but the most interesting one was for a shorthand typist required by a huge steel company's head office in Oswald Street. They asked for 'exceptionally good speeds in shorthand and typing.

Must be over eighteen. Good salary to right applicant.' I knew I had exceptional speeds in both shorthand and typing, but I wasn't even eighteen, much less *over* eighteen. I ground my teeth in frustration. Should I have a try anyway? I wondered. What was age, if I had the speeds? It was a good thing they hadn't put 'must be over five feet,' for I certainly couldn't have done anything about my height. I could grow older, but I seemed to have stuck in height and was still far too small to impress anybody with my office efficiency. Ah well, nothing beats a good try, I said to myself, and I wrote out the application. To be on the safe side, I also wrote to several other firms, and I begged all of them the favour of an interview.

Every night when I came home I flew to the chest of drawers to see if there was a letter for me lying on the top, beside the wee dish with the buttons in it and my mother's best brooch.'There's been nae post the day,' my mother would say irritatingly. She wasn't at all sympathetic to my wish to change offices. She hadn't forgotten that beautiful goose they'd given us for Christmas, and she had a great loyalty to those who were 'good to us'. I hadn't breathed a word about my crazy, lovelorn boss, but I had told her that the college felt I should have voice lessons to 'hold my own' with the big boys I might find in my classes when I taught shorthand, and that I'd have to find the money for such lessons. 'Well, maybe they'll give you a rise where you are,' my mother suggested. 'Och, Mother,' I said, 'it's *time* I moved to a bigger office. Anyway, they can't afford to pay any more where I am, so if I want to better myself I'll just have to move.' My mother pursed her lips. 'You've hardly been wi' thae nice folk ony time at a', and here you are wantin' tae shift. Well, you'll no' find onybody that'll think ony mair o' ye than they dae.' My mother had a great desire to be thought well of. This was far more important to her than money, and she couldn't understand why I couldn't be content to remain where I was, happily basking in approval and popularity. She was nervous of my ambition, but she respected the advice I obtained from the college heads, and she knew if voice lessons had been suggested for me I'd move heaven and earth to try to get them.

A week passed, and I decided the steel firm didn't want

anybody so young as myself. I had had two interviews with smaller firms, but I explained that I wanted the experience of a large company and the chance of promotion and a good salary. And then one morning, by the first post, a letter arrived from the steel company offices. Beautiful thick, crackling notepaper. They would be pleased to see me at three o'clock the following afternoon. I'd have to ask time off for the interview, but I knew wee Mr Brown was on my side, for he had told me often enough I was wasted where I was. I showed him the letter as soon as he came in that morning, and he was enthusiastic. 'A marvellous firm,' he assured me, 'you will do well there.' 'But they'll maybe not have me,' I said, 'for they wanted somebody of eighteen.' 'Well,' he laughed, 'they'll be mad if they don't take you on. I'll give you a letter if you like, and tell them I can thoroughly recommend the employment of this mighty atom!' He was a bit of a coughdrop, I decided, but I refused the letter. I didn't want my prospective employer to think I had been working for lunatics. Fancy handing anybody such an unbusiness-like note! Anyway, you didn't receive a reference until after you left your job.

I was glad it was summer for this interview, for it was so much easier to look nice and neat and tidy in a striped cotton dress than in a well-worn winter coat and maybe stockings splashed with rain. It was a lovely warm sunny day, and I checked the appearance of my blue and white 'Kodak' dress in each shop window that I passed between our office and Argyle Street. I wore a little white jockey cap and my best Sunday shoes, and I decided I must look pretty grown-up because I got a few encouraging whistles from the lorry-drivers as I bounced down Hope Street.

The offices were huge. Red sandstone rose to a height of three storeys, and they actually had a lift entirely for themselves. In fact the whole building was theirs. I was to go to the second floor, to the office of the company secretary. A middle-aged lady in the outer office bade me wait, as Mr Stewart wasn't quite free. I sat with my feet tucked neatly under the chair, not moving a muscle, but my eyes darting round this splendid office. Beautiful panelling half-way up would have pleased my mother with its quality, and above the panels ran opaque glass, giving a pleasant light look to the place. The door fittings were all of the best, and the typewriter, files and paper were everything that I could have desired. No shortage of anything, I decided. A very rich company.

Then the door leading to the inner office opened, and a very tall elderly gentleman beckoned me through. He looked surprised at my appearance, checked that I really was as much as seventeen, said I was younger than they had wanted, but in view of my speeds they had decided to see me, and give me a test. My heart warmed to him. This was the sort of reasoning I liked. I simply hated being dismissed as 'too young' before being given a chance to prove that I could do the work. He handed me a shorthand notebook, dictated three letters of varying lengths, and asked me to go outside and type them. The elderly lady showed me where paper and carbons were, and I sat down at the machine and polished them off, returned to the inner office, and handed them over. Mr Stewart seemed to be concealing a smile as I bounded back to his side with the letters. 'Well, that's an impressive display of speed,' he said. 'Let me just see how you've set the letters out.' He put his head on one side. 'Well, young lady' (lady! my heart gave a bound), 'I don't think we can let you go. I also think we'll have to make an exception in your case about salary. We normally pay according to age, and at seventeen you'd only be entitled to thirty shillings a week. Clearly you're not going to change jobs for the same money, and clearly such speeds merit a special reward. You will start at the rate for a twenty-one-year-old, but you must not tell anyone of this, or it will create discontent. You will start at two pounds a week, with a yearly rise in salary in line with our policy.' Two pounds a week! Ten shillings more than I was getting. Och it would easily be enough to give my mother a bit extra, and leave me something to put towards my voice lessons. I ran back to the office on air, gave Mr Brown my notice, and felt I couldn't wait for the summer to be over to begin my voice lessons and to meet my very first elocution teacher.

The new office was bewilderingly different from anything I had known. I was attached to the export department on the third floor, and the men and women worked strictly separately, apart from the actual time taken for dictation. The men worked at desks in a large open-plan room, and the typists were placed in a narrow room leading off this main office. It was panelled up to eye-level, and had glass above this height, so that one could see into the main office when one stood up. Two typists were allocated to each section, and whoever was free answered the summoning bell. In case of emergency, or extra pressure of work, we all worked for anyone. There were about ten of us in each typing room, and the combined clatter of the machines in that narrow space was terrible. I'd never worked in such close proximity with other machines, and wondered if I would ever get used to the din. The head typist handed me a list of branch offices, and foreign offices, and details of the category of letter which would require three carbon copies, or four carbon copies or even six carbon copies, and I had to learn these by heart so that I would know at once how many copies were required. I could ask at first, of course, until I got used to things. I was shown where to get supplies of paper, and carbons, and ribbons, and pencils and rubbers. It was like a wee shop. It even had a lady in charge, who handed you out the materials you needed, and for which you signed a chit. Fancy an office doing so much work that there was a constant job just handing out materials! And office girls were kept busy all day long, emptying our baskets of finished work and taking them to the section heads for signing and despatch. Commissionaires dealt with them at this stage, and they were in constant touch with the postal department. I was fascinated. All the jobs Patsy and I used to do between us were handled by separate departments in this office, and some of those grand typists with whom I now worked had never filed a letter or done a trial balance. They knew nothing but their own little cog in this vast machine. I began to realize what a splendid experience a small office was, when you just had to know how to do everything if the wheels were to turn smoothly. In spite of their poshness, I comforted myself that I knew a whole lot more about office routine than those fashionable typists. And I began to feel it was just possible that I was even worth my two pounds a week. I didn't let on, of course, that that was what I was earning, and I took my place as the most junior of junior typists, for I was by far the youngest in the typing room. Although I had been told to ask anything I wished to know for the first few weeks, I soon realized that those elegant young ladies didn't mean a word of it. Each time I queried a foreign market, or an Asiatic spelling, eyes would be cast heavenwards, and a voice dripping sweet-sour tones would say, 'You don't mind asking a great many questions, do you, Miss Weir?' I didn't recognize the sarcasm at first and replied innocently, 'Oh no, for you told me to ask.' But after I'd intercepted a few amused glances I shut my mouth, and asked the bosses instead, and they didn't mind telling me anything I wanted to know, for they were charmed with the speed with which I rattled off their letters and specifications. In fact, I soon earned another nickname from them, and was known throughout the building as 'The Flying Scotswoman'.

Oh but I longed to be as assured and sophisticated as my typing companions. I had thought my accent was pretty acceptable until I went into this office and listened to the voices of girls who had been educated at the best schools, and for whom the expressions of workaday Glasgow were a source of rippling amusement. They would send each other into shouts of laughter by parodying their 'dailies', and saying, 'I was *that* annoyed', or 'Oh she was *that* nice'. How could I laugh when I lived among people who spoke like that every day of their lives, and when I wasn't above saying such things myself? Feeling I was speaking a foreign language, I began forcing myself to say, even at home, 'Oh it was *so* nice, Mother,' and to my surprise the heavens didn't fall, and nobody seemed to notice. I had been afraid people at home would think I was stressing inadequacies in their own speech, but my altered vocabulary went right over their heads. I was so glad. I'd have hated to have hurt them, but I did want to fit into my new smart office background. Other expressions culled from those oft-quoted dailies were 'I'm a done day this wumman', and if they were in a rush in the afternoons they'd exclaim, to peals of laughter, 'Two o'clock and no' a peenie on the wean', or 'Two o'clock and no' a wean washed'. I hadn't realized such expressions were comical; to me they were quite normal, for I'd heard the women in the back courts use them all my life. I was base enough to curry favour by adding one of my own, which I'd heard from my brother, and which even struck us as being funny, although we knew perfectly well what was meant. Our typists had to have it translated. Describing a bus conductor who'd infuriated him, one of my brother's mates had said, 'He wis wan o' thae fullas wi' eyes a' sewn wi' rid worset.' When I translated this as 'One of those fellows whose eyes were all sewn with red wool', a perfect description of red-rimmed eyes, the typists fell about holding their sides, and making such a noise with their gasping laughter that the boss on the other side of the glass rapped it to make them be quiet. But on that warm gale of laughter I was admitted to their friendship. I was accepted as one of them. I knew I wasn't, and I hoped they would never think of coming to Springburn, where nobody knew what a 'daily' was, and where they said without a blush, 'Oh I'm *that* hoat', or 'I'm fair sweetin'.'

There were some in that fine office, though, who knew coarse Springburn words. I was walking along the corridor with an old commissionaire one day, to recover something from Postal Department, and he said, observing a plump young girl walking ahead of us, 'My the young lassies nooadays have awfu' big bums!' I jumped in fright. I was absolutely scandalized. Fancy hearing such a word in the office. I pretended I hadn't heard him. But my heart sank. I betted to myself he would never have used such a coarse word in front of any of the other typists in my room. He obviously knew I was from the tenements, like himself, and that he needn't choose his words, as he'd have to have done if I had been a lady. Just wait till I had my elocution lessons, though, he'd soon change his tune.

By the time September came, I had saved enough for my first quarter with the elocution teacher. I raced home from the office, swallowed my tea, and walked back the mile and a half to her house 'down the town', in a very swanky area. To my surprise the first thing I had to do was to learn to breathe. I thought everybody breathed as a matter of course, but it was a highly complicated performance, with ribs having to be held out, diaphragm allowed to extend, and stomach gently lowered. All this without raising the shoulders. I got into a terrible fankle, and was sure the talented elocution teacher would give me up as a bad job. I thought she was quite quite perfect. Beautifully dressed, with soft brown wavy hair, rosy cheeks, good teeth, and, best of all, a lovely voice. I had expected a good voice, of course, but this was a deep, warm, carrying voice which sent tingles down my spine. I had always had a husky voice, and because it was so different from the voices of my chums, I was inclined to whisper when I was with grown-ups. Miss Mitchell changed all that. She taught me to recognize the different qualities of my voice – to use middle register, lower register, and top register, and said I was very lucky to have such a wide range. We did 'Mee, moh, mah', and 'Mah, may, mee', and I breathed out and in till I was dizzy and had to hold on to the chair. Far too soon the hour was up, and I was to go home and practise all she had told me, and see how improved I would be the next week.

I danced up the road on air. It was difficult. It was strange to have to begin to examine so intensely something I had taken for granted all my life, like breathing and speaking. But instinctively I knew that this was going to be a great asset to me in my future life, and not only for the teaching of shorthand. Oh if only I could learn to speak like Miss Mitchell I would be indistinguishable from all those posh typists, and I would be able to speak out loud in public just as they did, with the confidence bestowed by an impeccable accent. I hoped I wasn't getting too big for my boots, but I had a passionate desire to 'fit' wherever I was.

I rushed home and showed my mother and my brothers how to breathe, and walked about the kitchen shouting 'Mee, moh, mah', and they thought that teacher earned her money gey easy if that was what elocution meant. 'Ye canny go aboot sayin' thae things,' my mother said, 'I hope she knows whit she's daein'. I wouldnae like tae think ye were wastin' yer two pound twelve-and-sixpence.' My mother still hadn't got over spending this fortune on a quarter's lessons, paid in advance. She kept equating it with all the useful things we could have bought with it. A new pair of blankets for the bed. A pair of shoes and a hat maybe. A winter's coat, or at least a good bit towards one. But she began to think I might be getting a bit of value for my money when I started reciting poems instead of making unintelligible 'Maw, moh, moos'. I hadn't imagined for a moment that this bonus would be added to the vocal exercises, and when Miss Mitchell handed me a book one night, and asked me to read a poem, I thought she was just giving me a break from the monotony of all those sounds. Instead it was the start of drama coaching for me. Rudyard Kipling was followed by W. D. Cocker, and then Walter Wingate, and de la Mare, and, to my joy, A. A. Milne. We found that the light range of my voice was just like a little boy's, and Miss Mitchell decided I was going to be Christopher Robin at her annual performance by her pupils. The shorthand goal was forgotten, and as the performance date drew near, I was introduced to the other pupils and plunged into the dizzy excitement of plays and sketches. These rehearsals were pure joy, and a perfect relief from the monotony of the shorthand studies which occupied my other evenings, but I had to discipline myself to stick rigidly to my little time-table pinned up beside the kitchen range, and devote the proper time to my shorthand theory, including psychology, or it would have been only too easy to spend every free moment learning my poems and my part in the sketches and plays.

We were to perform in a real concert hall, with proper footlights and curtains, and Miss Mitchell arranged all our costumes, partly from our own clothes, and partly from a huge trunk of 'props' she possessed. I'd never heard the word used before, and I thought it held the very savour of the theatre. She decided my own little red-and-white gingham dress would do for Christopher Robin, plus a floppy straw hat to hide my hair, to pretend I was a boy, and little white socks and plimsolls would complete the childlike effect. For once my tiny build was going to be a positive asset. She even had a backcloth painted with all the A. A. Milne characters, and I was to do the whole thing as a solo performance, starting off with 'Where am I going, I don't quite know', and finishing up with 'In the dark', where the poem ends in sleep.

All this rehearsing and reciting had robbed me of my diffidence when speaking to this beloved teacher, and one night when I was chattering away she startled me by asking me if I had no father. When I said I hadn't, she exclaimed, 'I knew it!' How did she know it? I wondered. 'Well, you have an unusual independence and vigour, and I just felt you had always had to stand on your own two feet. You've had very little cosseting, and that always shows.' Fancy all Grannie's teaching being so obvious to this clear-sighted teacher. For Grannie had always said, 'Bairns have to learn to stand on their own two feet, for they never ken whit's in front o' them.' Wouldn't Grannie have been pleased to know this teacher had used her very own words, and had seemed to approve of my independence? Mind you, clever as my grannie was, I doubt if she would have known what an elocution teacher was. After all, I'd hardly have got within spitting distance of one myself if I hadn't wanted to teach shorthand.

During the final rehearsals before the concert Miss Mitchell again surprised me by saying, 'Can I ask you something?' My heart always gave a lurch at such questions, for I never knew what was coming next, and I hoped Christopher Robin wasn't going to be taken away from me, or that I'd be asked to pay an impossible subscription to help finance the concert. To my utter astonishment, all she wanted to ask me was to remove a ring from my middle finger and transfer it to my fourth finger! With great delicacy she explained that it looked rather unladylike where it was, and it lent a grace to the hands if worn on the fourth finger. I was most impressed with this tender care for my feelings, and I realized there was far more to being a lady than I had ever dreamed. I began to respect my mother's values when she used the words 'She's a real lady', and I knew this was a true accolade to somebody very different from me.

On the night of the concert I was absolutely sick with nerves. How I worked in the office during the day I simply don't know. The hours at work passed like a dream, and I have no recollection of taking a single note or typing a single letter that day. My entire imagination was pinned on the concert, and my first appearance on a real stage. I didn't recognize it as just an end-of-season display of pupil's work. This was the stage, the theatre, and we'd be acting for an audience. Friends of Miss Mitchell made up our faces, and I had mine creamed and powdered and coloured by the famous Scottish character actress Miss Elliot Mason. I didn't know her then, but later hugged to my heart her praise for my performance.

My first appearance was to be in the Christopher Robin characterization, and while I was waiting back-stage with Miss Mitchell we both paced up and down in complete silence. At last she turned to me. 'Do you know, Molly, this is a sign of true artistic temperament – this silent tension – I think you may have your future in the theatre, and not in the schoolroom.' And then she groaned, 'Mind you, it's a terrible price to pay – it's so much easier if you can take it all in your stride, and be more light-hearted about it, but I'm afraid you're stuck with this sort of artistic temperament, just as I am.'

So that was why I felt so sick! It wasn't because I had been too excited to take my tea, to my mother's annoyance, and whose dire predictions that I'd upset my stomach had followed me all the way down the stairs and through the close to the street.

Everyone had a programme, so there was no announcement before the items. Just a programme note: 'Molly Weir as Christopher Robin'. The curtain rose, the footlights were blinding, and my heart raced so hard I thought I'd never get a word out. And then suddenly I was hopping across the stage and my mouth was opening and shutting, and I could hear A. A. Milne's words and knew I must be saying them. The first ripple of laughter took me by surprise, for I hadn't thought of A. A. Milne's poems as being very funny, just deliciously childish and true. It couldn't be the St Andrew's Hall and the maze marching all over again, could it? It *couldn't* be something in my appearance that made them laugh? No, it was the words, for here it came again, and this time I saw what had amused them. Oh the sweet sense of power in finding myself able to make an audience laugh because of my acting.

This new awareness was my undoing later in the evening, alas. We had a little one-act play about a grandmother taking a crowd of youngsters to the theatre, and as they perch in the gallery waiting for the performance to begin, Grannie's comments and the children's behaviour form the play. The girl who was playing Grannie was marvellous, and she had us all in hysterics at rehearsals. We were just to do anything irritating or appropriately childish between our brief bits of dialogue, and show enough animation to make us look naturally obstreperous. During the performance I found, to my delight, that Grannie had a lipstick in her handbag, a hangover from her private life, and I was inspired to draw a cupid's bow on myself, then squiggles and scrolls all over my face. The audience were convulsed. They were riveted, wondering what I'd do next. Not a word of Grannie's rehearsed dialogue was heard. All her subtleties drowned out on gales of laughter. We exited to warm, strong applause, and I was fairly carried away with excitement in discovering I was a comic. I thought Miss Mitchell would have been delighted with our success. Instead she looked at me thoughtfully, and told me, oh so tactfully, that I had done a most unprofessional thing. That I had, by my 'business', diverted attention from the dialogue and had changed the entire nature of the play. That all our rehearsing had been for nothing, rendered ineffective by my broad comedy. That 'the play was the thing'. I could feel the colour drain from my cheeks, and the shaming tears rise to my eyes. I hadn't known! I had thought I was pleasing her, and that it was a good thing to make an audience laugh. But I had been wrong, it seemed. I had been carried away with my own power. It was at this black moment that Elliot Mason came to wipe off my make-up and mop up a few tears at the same time. 'You have a real gift for comedy, Molly,' she told me cheerfully, 'you just have to learn to keep it under control. That's not hard to learn, you'll find. The main thing is that you *have* it, and it's not a bad thing to make people laugh.' I gulped gratefully, as she went on: 'You must just remember there are other people on the stage with you, and it's also a gift to know when to be quiet.' I never forgot that lesson, a lesson which was to stand me in great stead in later years when I was privileged to work with some of the greatest comics in this country.

16

It had been a hectically busy year, culminating in the two-day shorthand teachers' examination which would decide whether or not I would be able to add the initials P.C.T. after my name. I had to have two days off work for this marathon, and it seemed so strange to be back at a school desk in the daytime again. Thank goodness the desks were lower in the huge rooms where the examination was held, so I didn't have to sit up on my feet. In spite of four years' preparation the concentration demanded by the stiff papers was terrific, and my head was throbbing when I went out at lunchtime to eat my piece. I didn't speak to anybody, for they all seemed quite old to me, and many of them seemed to have enough money and enough light-heartedness to go and actually drink coffee before the afternoon session. I wandered about the streets until it was time to go back again, and didn't even look in the shop windows, for I didn't want to divert my mind from thoughts of the exam.

It was the oral next day, plus one other paper, and I was thankful for the elocution lessons when I came to give my lesson in front of the blackboard, for the examiner walked about the floor, sometimes facing me, sometimes with his back to me, and I had to be very clear and loud and interesting to hold his attention. I finished by the middle of the afternoon, and nobody had given a sign as to whether or not I had done well, not even the man who took the oral exam. He had just asked a few questions, nodded curtly, and dismissed me. What if I failed, after all this hard work, and all the money we'd spent on my lessons? I had a terrible sense of anticlimax and a great tiredness in every limb. I seemed to have been running forever. All that winter and spring whenever I'd come home from the office I'd swallow a meal and walk back to the town for my classes or rehearsals. My brothers used to say, 'How can you bear to race home from work and rush out again like this every night? You never sit down.' As my mother watched me darting about collecting my tammy and my satchel, she'd say, for the thousandth time, 'Aye, it's a peety she hisnae a pair o' wings. She hisnae got time tae live, that yin.' I had just laughed, because I hadn't recognized the existence of weariness in my eager pursuit of all the new and marvellous things I was learning.

How was it then, when both the concert and the exam were over, I could feel so tired? I couldn't even sleep when I went to bed at night, and even if I went to bed early there was no peace, with my brothers and their friends playing the radio or having endless discussions on politics long after midnight. People in the tenements were so used to all activities being carried on in the warm kitchen that it wouldn't have crossed anybody's mind to go through to the cold room, the best room, for amusement or discussion, especially just because somebody wanted to go to bed. What a daft idea.

I drooped and grew pale, and when my 'peelie-walliness', as we called my wan looks, could no longer be ignored, we visited the doctor. We hadn't really wanted to go, but again, just as they had done after Grannie's death, the neighbours kept saying, 'My, I hope Molly's no' gaun into bad health' – this was their polite understatement for consumption, a disease which hadn't been conquered when I was a young girl, and which had taken off the wee chum in the next close. That was enough. 'We'll just go along and see the doctor on Sunday,' my mother said. 'Maybe ye need a wee tonic efter a' that night school on top of your job.'

The doctor never even mentioned a tonic. What he did say sent us into a flurry of amazement. We were so open-mouthed that he said it again, watching our astonished faces, 'Yes, she must have some place where she can be quiet and sleep, without disturbance from the rest of the household. She needs a room of her own.'

These were revolutionary words, and seemed to us as fantastic as though he had recommended regular rides in our own

Rolls-Royce! But the seed was sown in my mind. A room of my own. 'What bliss, oh what bliss,' I thought.

To be able to go to bed and put out the light when I wished. To end the pressing weariness of trying to shut out the lively noise of the kitchen as I tried in vain to sleep. To be able to read in peace. The doctor's words revealed unsuspected currents, for I had had no idea I longed for privacy with such intensity.

Although we were a happy family, this craving for solitude must have been there all the time. I realized it now. The doctor was suggesting a reprieve from having to live in the constant whirl of family life in our wee room and kitchen, which he said was slowly undermining my nervous health. I hadn't known what I needed until I heard those words, and I knew now I'd never rest until I had that room.

But how would I set about it? We hadn't a hope of the only sort of accommodation we could afford, a Council house, roomy and cheap. With only four of us the Corporation would laugh in our faces, for we certainly didn't qualify on the grounds of hardship. We had two rooms, hadn't we, and according to the standards of our neighbourhood, this was verging on the luxurious. If fourteen folk could live in a boxroom and kitchen in the close, we hadn't a case, so we could save our breath to cool our porridge and not bother the Corporation with trifles.

All this was going on inside my head, for my mother had listened to the doctor's advice without having the slightest intention of doing anything about it. She was astounded when I started to coax her to 'ask the factor' if he could find us a bigger house, one with two rooms and a kitchen. 'A two-room-and-kitchen,' she echoed. 'Hiv ye ony idea whit the rents are for a hoose of that size?' She banged down the kettle in irritation. 'I wish I'd never taken you near that doctor. There's many a family twice oor size would be glad of the chance of oor room and kitchen.'

'But, Mother, the doctor *said* I needed peace and quiet, and I would help with the extra rent. I won't have so many classes next winter, so my fees will be lower, and that will leave a few spare shillings I could give you to help pay for my room.'

'I ken somebody who's no' gaun tae get ony peace and quiet and that's me,' said my mother grimly. She had no idea of the fire that had been kindled in my mind by the mere possibility of privacy, and she was truly bewildered by what seemed a sudden desire for a bigger house, just because of a few words spoken by the doctor because he couldn't find anything wrong with me for which a tonic could be prescribed.

We both set the cups and saucers on the table in silence, but I could see she was thinking about what we'd said. 'And where would we get the extra furniture for a bigger hoose?' she said, playing her trump card. I felt this was no time for argument, but for cunning and coaxing. 'Och we'll get a wee bit of furniture here and there,' I said vaguely. 'And,' I swallowed desperately, carried away by my own boldness, 'I'll pay for the decorating myself. I'll save up.'

So now, as well as saving for Christmas, birthdays, holidays, insurance, elocution fees, fares, clothes, and my precious Scottish Clerks' Association. I would just have to start saving for paper and paint for my dream room and for some wee bits of furniture to fill it.

I took out a ruler and drew an extra column in the book where my savings were zealously noted. I headed it 'For my room' and noted down 'two shillings', the first instalment towards paradise.

I wouldn't be able to save much on fares, for I walked practically everywhere. Still, I could save the odd ha'penny by walking to the fare stage even when it poured with rain. I could let my hair grow, and the one-and-six saved on cutting would go into the column 'for my room'.

I changed my mind about going to Aberdeen and tasting the splendour of a boarding house for my summer holidays, and decided to go to the cheaper Girl Guide camp instead. That would be a terrific saving.

And I had a marvellous piece of luck when a neighbour asked me if I would teach her daughter shorthand as a private pupil, and she would pay me half a crown for each lesson of an hour. I practically danced down Parliamentary Road to the office that day. A whole half-crown! My shorthand teaching was proving its worth at just the right moment. It would be sheer profit, for I'd never expected a pupil to land in my lap like this. And if I had my own room I could teach my pupil there, and we could be utterly quiet on our own away from the rest of the house. Even my mother saw the extra room as a source of profit if I could get shorthand pupils, and best of all she was getting used to the idea that it might be possible after all.

At last, one never-to-be-forgotten day, the factor told us he had a flat he thought might do for us, and I rushed my mother round to see it in my lunch hour. There was a large kitchen, a really fine sitting room, a lovely square hall, a *bathroom*, and – the best point of the flat as far as I was concerned – a long, narrow bedroom with a lofty window.

My mother had only gone along to see the flat to humour me, but I could see the extra space everywhere was having a telling effect, and she fell in love at first sight with the scullery, an amenity she'd never enjoyed before. 'Where's the sink?' she'd asked the factor, as she looked round the big kitchen with its high wide windows. He flung open a door dramatically, revealing a neat little scullery with white sink, well-scrubbed draining boards, and useful, roomy dresser. My mother gave a gasp, and turned to me, starry-eyed. 'Oh whit a handy wee place,' she enthused. 'Just fancy, if onybody came in and ye hidnae done the dishes, you could just shut that door and naebody would be ony the wiser.'

The factor looked out the window, whistling, while we anxiously worked out whether we could afford the extra rent. I'd just had a five shillings rise from the office, and that, plus the two shillings I had been putting away for furnishing the room, plus the half-crown from my shorthand pupil, would just about cover it. This flat wasn't far from our present house, so we'd be able to carry the small items round ourselves, and just have to hire a van for about an hour. That wouldn't cost much, and my mother thought she could manage it. She'd forgotten all her opposition to a two-room-and-kitchen and I laughed to think how she had gradually come round to my point of view without even knowing it.

We took the flat. 'Oh my, ye could haud a dance in that big lobby,' my mother said happily, and did a little 'Pride of Erin' step as we moved to the front door.

Now it was up to me to see about the decorator, for much as

I loved my room, I wasn't blind to the fact that it was dull and dark and dingy with its scuffed brown paint. A friend heard of a decorator who was starting his own business and who was looking for work, and I felt very excited and grown-up when I took him round and showed him the room and discussed colour schemes. I'd never dealt with a real tradesman before, and it was most thrilling. My nest-egg was very small, and my heart thumped as he narrowed his eyes, looked round the walls, totted up the amount of paper and paint we'd need, and quoted me £2 10s. for papering and painting. I hadn't counted on paying so much, for I hadn't any idea how much these things cost. My mother usually just had a neighbour in to help her when she papered our kitchen, and as they did it in their spare time, we seemed to be in a mess of paper and paste for weeks. I couldn't ask her to tackle the lofty walls of this room, and anyway I had said I would pay for it, and pay for it I would.

But £2 10s. – it was an awful lot of money. I bit my lip, and then I remembered that hardly anyone in our tenements paid outright in cash. Young as I was, I knew the value of a lump sum.

'Two pounds in cash outright,' I said, my heart hammering at daring to bargain with a big grown man. He looked at me, and made up his mind. 'Done,' he said. There need be no delay in starting, for the house was already empty.

I chose pale yellow wallpaper, and duck-egg blue for the paintwork, this at a time when colour schemes everywhere in our Glasgow tenements were fawns and browns and strong dark greens. Everyone dismissed this flight of fancy as sheer madness, but the pastel effect in that murky atmosphere was charming and those who came to scoff stayed to admire when the painter had finished, I kept running in and gazing round the room, almost swooning with pleasure. The bright colours had made it all look so *big*, and it was twice as bright with all the reflected light.

But I still had to face the problem of furnishing the room. My little nest-egg consisted of about six pounds now, and I was furiously puzzling how best to allocate it when I had another piece of luck, although it was a sad occasion for my benefactor. One of the older women in the office lost her mother, and as her only brother lived in England she decided to move there to set up house with him and share his expenses, so a lot of her mother's old stuff was superfluous. This was a gift straight from heaven, and I wasted no time.

I was invited out to her house in the South Side of Glasgow, and it was an Aladdin's cave of treasures for me. My office friend kept apologizing because everything was fairly shabby, for it had all been used for years and years in their kitchen, but what did I care? I could see my room filling before my very eyes, and the bargains I was getting seemed to me beyond the dreams of avarice. Fancy having all this stuff to sell, at practically give-away prices. My goodness, they must have been very rich. You could have furnished three Springburn tenements with the things they described as odds and ends.

The old kitchen chest of drawers was mine for five shillings, and with a coat of duck-egg-blue paint became my dressing chest. The marble-topped washstand which they'd used for a baking top, changed hands at three-and-six, and you'd never have recognized it when it too received its transforming coat of duck-egg-blue paint and was tastefully draped with a matching cotton frill, to become my dressing-table. What a marvellous sound that was – a dressing-table, I who had never owned more than one drawer in the family chest of drawers. This was opulence indeed. A small very shabby plush-covered chair changed hands for two shillings, and a little rug was valued at seven-and-six. An upholsterer friend of my mother re-covered the wee chair in brown velvet for us for nothing, using a piece of velvet left over from another job, and my mother was loud in her praise of the chair. 'My word, it's as nice as yon wee chairs you see in the good antique shops,' she enthused. And so it was. Its shape was delightful, and I used plenty of elbow grease to give the wooden edging a satin gleam, and the quiet browns made a soft focal point against the pale walls and paintwork.

My mother vanished towards the Barrows just before we flitted, and returned to announce that she had managed to get a bed for two pounds, and as she had always been prudent and kept a good stock of bed linen, this was no problem. There would be sheets and blankets galore for my two-pound bed.

There was still the floor to cover, though. We decided to have a wander round Bows Emporium – 'Bows Implore 'em', my mother called it – and to our delight, although there wasn't a sale on at the time, they did have one blue linoleum square 'slightly off-pattern' which had been reduced to a pound. This was a marvellous buy, for it was real linoleum, and as my mother said, could be lifted again and again without cracking, for future flittings. Future flittings! And we weren't even into our two room and kitchen yet! But I knew what she meant. It was the quality which impressed her, and even if it was never moved from my room, the fact that it *could* be lifted was a great comfort. Fancy getting such a reduction in price just because a flower was out of place, and it would be hidden under the two-pound bed anyway. How lucky we were. We celebrated this victory, as usual, with a coffee and a cake, this time in the D. & F. Stores at Glasgow cross, before walking home on air.

Hoeys in Springburn yielded a little imitation copper kerb for the fireplace, and a glass-fibre-top stool in blue for fifteen shillings the two. I was so excited about these that I wouldn't let them deliver, but carried them across Springburn Road myself, in case they would come to any harm in the van.

My mother unearthed a pair of curtains which, with a little alteration, fitted my window. A tremendous excitement filled me as I ticked off the items in my mind's eye. I had done it! I was furnished!

I gave my mother what was left of my six pounds to help with the flitting, and I forced myself to help with the dull ordinary arrangements for the rest of the house.

It was a great flitting. Great.

It was quite different from all the other Weir flittings. For one thing, the outgoing tenants had departed weeks before, and the house had lain empty, because of the poor demand for a house of that size, with its comparatively high rent. People in tenements were so used to being crowded together that there seemed no advantage to be gained from paying good money which was needed elsewhere for the mere luxury of a bit more room to spread out. This vacancy allowed us the unaccustomed treat of being able to go round there at every spare moment to clean the house in readiness for the flitting. And to be able to place her things in a house which had been cleaned and scrubbed from end to end was unalloyed bliss for my mother.

The normal practice was for outgoing and incoming tenants to move practically in unison, and my mother used to be in a frenzy, overseeing the packing of her precious 'cheenie' and ornaments at the house she was leaving, and, if the new house wasn't clean enough for her liking, racing like the wind ahead of the cart carrying the furniture, and trying to fit in a frenzied bit of cleaning before the linoleum could be laid down or the furniture set in place. As soon as this was done, she'd race back to the original house again, and lend a hand to the women who had remained there, to make sure of a spotless house for the incoming tenant. The highest praise which fell on the ears of a departing tenant was 'Aye, she left a hoose that clean, you could have ta'en yer tea off the floor.' And my mother made sure those words were spoken of her after all our many flittings. This frantic activity completely exhausted her, but we didn't know any other way, and took it all as part of the fever of changing house.

If the new address was too far away for my mother to find time or opportunity to achieve a spotless background, then when we moved everything was kept in boxes or cartons until the place was properly scrubbed. My strongest recollections of such occasions were of wakening in the morning after the flitting, to a tug on my arm and a hoarse voice whispering in my ear, 'Where's my galluses?' My brother would be standing by my bed, holding up his trousers and urging me awake. 'In the button box,' I would answer automatically, 'in the top drawer of the chest of drawers.' I had been the winner of so many 'Kim's games', where articles have to be memorized in one minute, that my photographic memory was relied upon by every member of our family. I would be falling asleep again when my other brother tugged me awake. 'Where's ma bunnet?' 'In the jelly pan under the bed,' and a triumphant 'Goat it' would assure me that was just where it had been stowed. And then it would be my mother's turn, 'Molly, waken up, do you know where I put the store book.' 'Aye, it's in the darning basket in the lobby.' By this time I would be thoroughly awake, and staring with dismay at the chaos which faced us, and which would only be cleared up when my mother had made certain that not a speck of dirt left behind by the old tenant remained.

This time there would be no such awakening, for we had all made sure the new house was as clean as soap, scrubbing brushes, and elbow grease could make it. The flues of every chimney had been cleaned. The windows sparkled. We had laid the new bargain linoleum square in my room, and covered it with papers in readiness for my second-hand furniture, which was to arrive ahead of the main flitting. When I had been knitting my brows, wondering how I would get this furniture from the South Side to Springburn, my goodhearted office colleague had come to the rescue. She knew a friend who had a van, and as she was giving him so much work in connection with her move to England, he would move my stuff without extra charge. I think she was so staggered at my elation over her mother's old furniture, and so infected by my enthusiasm, she wanted to make her own contribution to this room of mine. So, a whole week before our actual flitting from the old house, my second-hand bargains were transferred from the grandeur of their bungalow setting to our Springburn tenement. Help was freely given by male friends, and as freely accepted, to rub down this old furniture with wire wool, to apply undercoats and topcoats of paint, and never a minute wasted, to make sure it would be completely dry by the end of the week. While the boys were painting, I stitched three yards of blue-and-white gingham at sixpence a yard into a petticoat which would be draped round the marble-top washstand. When at last the curtain wire was slipped through the top hem, and snapped into place, held by two screws on the back legs of the wash-stand, the frill cunningly concealing the fact that there was no linoleum underneath, I was quite dazzled by the effect. Oh it was so feminine and dainty, and so unlike the usual bed-pawn that I could have sung an anthem in praise of it. 'Don't craw sae crouse,' I could hear Grannie's voice admonish me. 'Don't craw sae crouse.' But it was no good. I had to exult over my good fortune or I would burst!

When the last paintbrush had been cleaned in turpentine we

removed the papers from the linoleum square, and pushed the pale blue painted furniture into place.

The little blue stool from Hoeys stood snugly beside the imitation copper kerb. The newly upholstered brown velvet chair repeated the warm tone of the kerb, and looked almost elegant against the pale wallpaper. The chest of drawers and the marble-top dressing-table gleamed like pale blue satin, and nobody but us knew that the drawers had sprung a little with the years of standing in a steamy kitchen far from Springburn.

All was now in readiness for the big flitting.

It was a lovely dry evening for it, and as soon as I got home from the office I joined the usual army of helpers who attended the Weir flittings, and packed china in newspapers, wrapped blankets and sheets round the crystal bowl and the overmantle, to cushion them against damage, then raced round with the others with fire-irons, pots and pans, wee stools, and other small items which were light enough to be carried by hand. We were like a colony of ants as we passed and re-passed one another, shouting instructions and checking everything as we ran. All the pals joined in, willing as ever to enjoy the bustle and fun of a flitting, with all the time in the world to lend a hand where needed.

What a difference it made, though, moving to a bigger house. There seemed to be tons of room, and our helpers were loud in their appreciation of 'how rer and easy it wis' with space to move freely and no banging into one another, and, best of all, no awkward corners or tight bends to negotiate when handling the wardrobe and the big mahogany chest of drawers. And, of course, this house had the great advantage of being in the close, which meant no tricky stairs to worry about either. We'd never lived in a close before, in fact we'd never been nearer the ground than two storeys up, and we hoped we would like it. Still, there were half a dozen steps up to the close from the pavement, so folk passing along wouldn't be able to look into the rooms. We wouldn't have relished being continually over-looked by every passer-by, having always lived so high above the streets.

The van was loaded and unloaded in record time, the old house swept and tidied, and I laid the rest of my personal possessions on my newly installed bed. I didn't want to arrange them just then. I wanted to take my time, to enjoy every second of the completion of my room.

I would stop now and give my attention to the feasting. There were at least eight hungry helpers waiting for the fish-and-chip party which was the only reward they expected or were given for having lent their brawn and advice in effecting this successful flitting. While they were washing themselves in the much praised little scullery, and having great fun shutting the door between that and the kitchen, pretending they required complete privacy, I ran round to the special fish-and-chip shop off Keppochhill Road, the one with the clean tiled walls which my mother favoured, although they weren't too generous with their helpings. I waited patiently in the queue for my huge order. 'Oh, have you been flitting again?' enquired the big pleasant woman behind the marble counter. She knew as well as everyone else that nobody bought that amount of fish and chips unless a flitting had taken place. 'Imphm,' I nodded happily. 'We've just moved into a two-room-and-kitchen and I've got my own room now.' Her eyes widened. 'My,' she said, 'you're ferrly comin' oot yer shell.' Then, as she handed me my parcel, 'You're no' lookin' for a lodger, are you?' The very idea. 'No fear,' I said, and ran home with the large, savoury-smelling parcel. My mother had spread the big white cloth over the kitchen table, and had cut a whole square loaf for the hungry helpers who sat round, faces shining with soap, waiting for their reward. Only then did I realize that I was starving, and we all fell on those delicious fish and chips as if we'd not seen food for a month. We even had two kinds of sauce, a fitting touch of luxury to celebrate our elevation to a two-room-and-kitchen. I chose tomato, which I'd learned to like on my infrequent visits to city tearooms, but the boys were happy with H.P., and my mother had to make two lots of tea to quench everybody's thirst.

At last they all went and the flitting was over. I was free to attend to the rest of my tidying. Oh the joy of arranging my little possessions. Reverently I laid jerseys, undies, hankies, poems, plays, shorthand books and Girl Guide treasures in the capacious drawers of my beautiful five-shilling chest. My hairbrush and comb seemed absolutely at home on top of the pale blue marble top. My shoes were hidden behind the sixpence-a-yard frill. I had thought this move was special because of the extra room, but it was special in another way I could never have dreamed. It was to be the last flitting we would ever do as a complete family. From this house, two of us would be married. I would become a stage and radio actress, and I would hear the sound of bombs dropping and witness the break-up of the world as we had known it. But all that was hidden in the future and not even the most expensive spae-wife could have foretold it.

But I had no notion of any of this as I gazed round my room on that first night. I had done it! The doctor had applied the spur and I had galloped into action. It had taken a lot of planning and saving, but it had been done. In less than a year.

I wondered what Grannie would say if she could see those yellow walls. Would she say, as I'd heard her say so many times, in scathing comment of some high-falutin' finicky notion of mine, 'Aye, that yin should ha'e been born wi' a silver spoon in her mooth.' What a long, long way I seemed to have come since I cooried into her back in the hurley bed. I wished I could tell her that I could now write the initials P.C.T. after my name. But I knew my grannie well enough to appreciate she wouldn't give a 'thank you' for the initials themselves. It would be the hard work which went into getting them which would always earn her praise. I wondered, if she could see me now lying in a whole bed all to myself, if she would be pleased with me. I remembered reading that Barrie's mother never envied the wife of a great man, but always said, in praise of a special quality, 'Oh I'd love to have been that man's mother.' We knew our mothers felt like that too, and our pride would have known no bounds if somebody had wanted to be our mother.

My grannie would never have said it in so many words, but it would have been a crowning joy to have seen it in her eyes. 'I'm pleased to be that bairn's grannie the night.'

I put out the light – my light – and felt the peace and quietness gradually steal away the excitement which twitched at my toes. I grew drowsy, and at last fell into the first of the deep sleeps which were to restore me to full health and vitality in that delightful room of my very own.

Peace and privacy, those desirable twins whose company I was always to cherish, were mine at last.

A Toe on the Ladder

For Sandy
Ever faithful, ever ready to help me
Watchootfurrastanks

Earning recognition without getting it is better than getting it without earning it.

We Scots have learned the lesson of poverty, that nothing comes without effort, and that we value most what costs us most.

JOHN BUCHAN

1

My mother told me I sang before I spoke, and I danced before I walked, but in spite of such early signs that I might have a talent for the theatre, nobody, least of all me, could have foreseen that with my unlikely background my dreams of becoming an actress could ever come true. But I had taken careful note of the story of the ten talents in the bible, and I was determined that not a single talent of mine was going to wither and die in the ground. I'd develop every single one of them, as the good Lord God instructed, and see where they led me.

The sheer excitement of pursuing all my ambitions was so heady, that I felt drunk as I raced back and forth between my office job and the college, for now I was taking evening classes again at the invitation of the college, to see just how fast my shorthand speeds could reach. Fancy all this happening to me! Special classes of one, with the assistant head doing the dictating, for only his tongue could get round the sentences fast enough and still remain intelligible. It felt a bit daft to be sitting there in a large classroom, all alone, perched up on my feet as usual, for I still hadn't grown enough to let my feet touch the ground if I sat on the seat properly like everybody else, with Mr McLeod standing in front of me, stop-watch in hand, breathing deeply as though in training for a racing sprint.

But it was exciting. I had practised shorthand so lovingly and assiduously that I could have written the characters backward if asked to do so, and there was nothing which came between hearing the words and sending the pen skimming over the note-book. Not a second had to be wasted in fumbling for an outline. Each one was there with the speed of sound. We easily passed the 200 words per minute mark, and grinned at each other with approval. Then 250 words. After that, it was a struggle all the way to add each extra ten words per minute. There were no grins now. My hand perspired, and the pen shook with tension as my fingers gripped it like a vice. My heart thumped as I pressed against the desk, and I had to lean back and readjust my seat or the beating would have slowed my speeding hand. Each night I sped up Renfield Street after my day's work was finished, and perched myself like a jockey in the echoing classroom, determined that tonight, yes tonight, I'd go every bit as fast with my pen as that man could go with his voice. It never occurred to me to feel that all this could be thought of as dull hard work after a day's stint in an office, where I was also writing shorthand and typing all day. But my mother was utterly bewildered. 'Whit dae ye have to go tae that college every night fur?' she'd demand. 'And without a bite to eat either'. For of course there was no question of dining out either before or after such speed practices. Tearooms were for celebrations, not for ordinary eating. When I tried to explain that the college were trying to find out just how fast I could write, because they wanted me to demonstrate high-speed writing as a 'star' pupil, she shook her head disbelievingly. 'You've goat a medal a'ready,', she said. 'Can they no' just show folk yer medal?'. 'Mother', I said, 'it's like doubting Thomas in the bible. Folk'll no' believe what high speeds are, just from looking at a medal. They have to SEE me actually writing, and hear the rate Mr McLeod gabbles oot his words!' Although I was ladylike in speech in the office, it was comfortable and restful to revert to Springburn usage when I was arguing at home. With typical contrariness, my mother pounced on my speech. 'Aye, it's a good job Mr McLeod disnae hear ye talking aboot him gabbling', she said primly, 'and him daein' his best to improve you every night'.

But although I could talk so glibly to my mother about people having to see me demonstrating high-speed writing, I was absolutely terrified at the thought of having to do it. I knew I had the speed in my fingers all right, but I also knew what tension and nerves could do, for we'd had a few trial runs with one or two of the teachers present, and I had shaken so badly that my speeds flew down by a good ten words each time. I knew I wasn't ready for the public and I felt sick at the thought.

But training was telling. After about a week when we stuck at 270 words per minute, and couldn't get a syllable faster, we had a marvellous session when everything went like clockwork. It had started badly, with Mr McLeod struggling through a bad cold, and me using so much pressure on the pen that the ink splattered and the nib scratched the page.

Then we settled down. Mr McLeod cleared his throat, nodded to me, pressed the stop watch and we were off! At the end of the fastest piece of dictation I'd ever heard, he pressed the watch again, and his cheeks were tinged with bright pink. Without a word, he nodded to me to read back my notes. His excitement was infectious, and my voice trembled as I read the dictated piece. Not a single mistake or omission. He took off his glasses and wiped them. 'Molly', he said solemnly, after clearing his voice once or twice, for cold or emotion seemed threatening to choke him, 'that was three hundred words a minute'. I stared at him, speechless. We had done it. We hadn't actually admitted that this was the speed we were after, but we both knew it. A tremendous exultation filled me. I had done it once, and I'd do it again. And again. And again! Oh how *marvellous!*

And then came the quenching thought that now I'd have no excuse. We'd have to do it in public. Before an audience.

But first I would have to celebrate in some way. I must mark this historic landmark in a fashion I would never forget. What would it be? Suddenly I remembered that that day I had held the earring of an office colleague against my ear, and had been filled with the daring idea that I might one day wear earrings myself. But not screw ones. Oh no. For if ever I became an actress, and had to dance, I didn't want my earrings to fly off and spoil my concentration, much less that of my public. Now that I could write 300 words a minute, there didn't seem any reason why I couldn't also reach my other goal and go on the stage some time. So, without a word to my mother, I went into a top-class jeweller in Buchanan Street on my way to the office next morning, and made an appointment to have my ears pierced that night. It was expensive. Seven and sixpence, which was a fortune, and which would have to be taken from my holiday fund at lunch-time. But I couldn't risk less than the best with my precious ears, for everybody knew quacks were notoriously unreliable for cleanliness. And I needed good healthy ears for shorthand demonstrating and for acting.

Every time I thought of the evening appointment while taking notes in the office during the day, my stomach turned over. It was almost as bad as going to the dentist. I hadn't realized I could be so nervous over such a little thing. Why, thousands of women wore earrings and they had all had their ears pierced if they wore expensive earrings. Everybody knew that screw ones were not to be trusted, because they were always at risk with their insecure fastenings.

Trembling, I climbed the stairs to the room above the shop. It was after closing time, and the place was hushed, like a surgery. There was a wash-hand basin, and a sparkling clean white towel, and a few little instruments lying on a small table. The elderly man in the black jacket and striped trousers looked at me enquiringly. 'Now you're sure your mother approves of your having your ears pierced?', he asked me. My mother knew nothing about it, so I felt I could truthfully inform him that my mother had always wanted to have her own ears pierced but had never had the courage. Which was true, if slightly evasive as far as his question was concerned. If he saw through this, he said nothing.

He showed me a little spring, with a gold needle fixed to the end of it, and told me he was going to put a cork on the other side of my ear, spring the little needle through, and catch it on the cork, and then immediately slip a little gold 'sleeper' through the pierced hole. I shut my eyes. In spite of his assurances that I would feel no pain, I yelped like a dog whose paw has been squashed by a large foot, when I felt a stab through my ear lobe. The tears rushed to my eyes. It wasn't so much agony, as pain in a place where one had never felt anything until now. Like somebody pinching the tip of your nose in sharp talons. How would I ever let him do the other ear, I thought wildly. I'd have to go through life with one earring, like a gypsy.

I gulped, preparing to tell him this, while he was extracting the little needle from the cork with a tiny pair of elegant pliers. Before I could open my mouth he said, 'Do you know, I've pierced thousands of ears and I've never felt a thing.' I felt there was something strange about this sentence, and said wonderingly, 'Have you not?', and while I was trying to work out what he meant, he'd shot the gold needle through my other ear, and the deed was done!

Oh! the cunning of the brute, I thought. Still, it was just as well I'd been so stupid about comprehending his words, or I'd never have managed to get both ears done. I was instructed to bathe my ears with boracic and warm water, and to turn the little 'sleepers' regularly to prevent the skin adhering to them, and in a week or two my lobes would sport smooth round holes, all ready to receive the fancy earrings of my choice. Blood dripping gently on to my coat, I left him for the walk home to Springburn, and my mother's wrath.

The minute I walked in the door, my mother said, 'What's that on the shoulder of your coat? Hoo did ye get ink away up there?', then her eyes travelled upwards and she gasped, 'It's no' ink, it's blood!'. She couldn't take her eyes off the wee gold sleepers, for in spite of her outrage that I could have done such a tremendous thing without a word to her, I could see there was a slight envy that I had found the courage to submit my ears to this torture, while she herself had got no further than talking about it. As she flitted about the kitchen making the tea, she muttered to herself and to the heavens, 'Seven-and-sixpence, nae less. Seven-and-sixpence off her holiday fund. And nut a word to onybody! And here's me has wanted to have ma ears pierced a' ma life, and never managed it.' But we both knew it wasn't the seven-and-sixpence, fortune though it was, which had stopped her. It was fear.

But in the weeks that followed, she had good cause for rejoicing that she had kept her ears intact, for in spite of that posh jeweller and his little wash-hand basin and his strippit trousers, my ears became infected, and festered, and it was agony to have to turn the gold sleepers, which I forced myself to do every day, for I was absolutely sure the flesh would grow on to them if I didn't follow the man's instructions to the letter. 'Don't *touch* them', my mother would implore, as my hands would steal up to wrench them round their sticky home, 'Leave them alone till the holes heal'. And she'd pour more warm water on to some boracic powder, and tear off a wee tuft of cotton wool, so that I could bathe them for the twentieth time since I came home from the office.

As if the infection wasn't scourge enough, I simply couldn't get used to having things impaled through my ears, and when I was running a comb through my hair I'd forget to be careful, and the teeth of the comb would catch in the sleeper and yank it out, and there would be howls of anguish as I threaded it back yet again through the once-more bleeding orifice.

'Aye, ye wid have yer ears pierced', my mother would say, with what sounded suspiciously like smugness, 'If you'd asked me first, I could have warned ye.' And I could see she'd already come to believe she hadn't been frightened at all to have holes put in her ears, it was simply that she'd had the foresight to know it was a mug's game, and not worth all the pain and misery which would follow.

I was so absorbed in the drama of my oozing ear-lobes that I quite forgot why I'd had them pierced in the first place. But Mr McLeod and the college hadn't, and without a word to me they had arranged the date for the first demonstration of high-speed shorthand writing before a tolerant public. It was held in the prize-giving room of the college, and he and I sat up on a platform, me at a little single desk, with the audience seated all round us. He dictated at varying speeds, starting at 140 words per minute, and going forward in 20-word-per-minute leaps until we had reached 300. After each piece of dictation, I rose and read back my notes. For the first time since those wee gold nails had gone through them, I forgot my ears, and they became once more just a part of me without nerves or feeling. The rest of me quivered like a jelly. My face burned, my palms sweated, and when I stood up to read, my legs shook so much I had to press them against my chair to steady them. It never occurred to me that, as far as our audience was concerned, it could all have been a trick. I'm sure none of them cared a jot about shorthand, and nobody was concerned enough about the accuracy of speed to have attempted to check our boasts with a stop-watch. It was a night out. It was buckshee, and they were seeing inside a college, a place they'd never have had the nerve to put a foot inside at any other time. They seemed amused by my tiny build when I stood up, and by my husky voice when I read back from my notes, but it might as well have been Chinese, for what did they know or care of Directors' reports and statements from Company Chairmen, which was what the dictation was all about. But they applauded generously, and happily accepted brochures for the coming term, and drifted out in search of fish and chips and a tramcar home.

And that was the start of our 'double-act' as I later called it to myself, for I was still very much in awe of Mr McLeod, in spite of the fact that we travelled the country together, to the various cities and towns where the college or Pitmans had an interest. My mother was amazed at the amount of money they must have spent on train fares, and we neither of us stopped to consider that if the railways made a tiny profit out of it, we ourselves made nothing, for of course nobody dreamed of paying me for those exhibition bouts. I was only too delighted to get free travel. Fancy riding all those hundreds of miles on trains, and not having to fork out a curdy. And staying in hotels, and having a bedroom all to myself in such posh places, and ham and egg breakfasts if I wanted them. It was just like the pictures, with crusty, elderly gentlemen walking silently to the sideboard in the mornings, lifting the silver covers from tureens and helping themselves to kidneys, or kedgeree, and once actually to roast beef. At nine o'clock in the morning! I'd never realized that anybody's stomach could be ready for dinner at breakfast time. And I'd never come across so many people eating in such a profound silence. Once, when we were joined at breakfast time by the wife of one of the college principals, I was so pleased to see another female that I chattered non-stop to her in the way I usually did at home. Suddenly I was aware that all knives and forks were suspended, and every head was turned my way, as outraged as though I had started doing cart-wheels in church. The words died on my lips, and I bent my head over my toast. It was made very obvious that I'd done the unforgivable thing. I'd broken the morning calm. I was no lady.

My mother was entranced to listen to all the details of the

journeys and hotels, and what sort of sheets and blankets they had on the beds, and whether I'd been warm enough. For of course I only had one outfit for such public appearances, and that was my navy reefer coat and good velour hat for the train, and my red knitted suit from Watt Brothers which she had bought for me to celebrate my college prizes. So whatever the temperatures, these clothes were my uniform and I merely added or subtracted a semmit to raise or reduce my temperature.

If I am now legendary for keeping a firm track of all my possessions under all circumstances, this is entirely due to my observation of Mr McLeod's methods during those exciting journeys. He was a man of very correct habits, and the moment we entered the train he counted each item as he removed it, and named it aloud. Thus, removing his Homburg, and placing it on the rack. 'One – a hat,' he would say. Then came his overcoat. 'Two – one overcoat', and this was placed alongside the hat. 'Three – one pair of gloves', and they were tucked inside his sleeve. 'Four – one umbrella', which took its place at the back of the rack. 'Five – one briefcase', which he tucked carefully behind him on the seat. 'Six – newspaper', which he laid on his lap, ready for his enjoyment the moment we had ceased discussing the itinerary for next day. 'Seven – Molly'. 'Eight – Molly's hat', 'Nine – Molly's coat', 'Ten – Molly's case', 'Eleven – Molly's book'. It was always a book with me, either more shorthand tests, or a French grammar, or a poem which I was learning or a play. We indulged in no general conversation; I sat opposite him, and as soon as we'd checked on time of arrival, hotel, time of demonstration, etc. we both buried ourselves in our book and newspaper and didn't utter a word until five minutes before we were due at our destination. The newspaper was folded, and with a nod to me to close my book, he counted all our impedimenta once more, and when he was satisfied the numbers checked, then, and only then, did we leave the train.

I was always extremely nervous before a demonstration, and I became gradually aware how important a part good health played in giving of one's best before an audience. A heavy cold fogged the brain, and made the reactions so sluggish that there were times when I stood up to read and had to bite my lip with vexation because not all the outlines had been captured at the challenging top speed of 300 words per minute. Oh how ashamed I felt. And what a waste of the college's money to have brought me all those miles only to falter at the last hurdle. Not that the audience minded a missed word. But I did. And I couldn't meet Mr McLeod's eyes in case I would read in them the disappointment he must surely feel. I made no excuses for myself. I ought to have been perfect. I had practised often enough. I would simply have to have another 20 words per minute in hand to make up for the times when I had a cold, or that scourge of Western Scotland, catarrh. There were other times, too, when feminine tension screwed me into a trembling jelly, and my heart sank at the prospect of the testing time ahead. But my grannie's words echoed down the years and I could hear her say, 'The back was made for the burden', and I would shake my head to clear away the mist of fear, and remind myself that nothing that was worth doing was easy. Oh and what a marvellous preparation all this was to be for the much tougher life later in the theatre.

For I hadn't given up my dreams of the stage, and in a strange way those dreams were all intermingled with my shorthand. There was a tremendous challenge in plunging into all sorts of new activities, as well as keeping up with all my old ones, and there seemed aeons of time for all of them.

One of the girls in the office said to me one day, 'Here's an advert from the Pantheon Club which sounds just up your street, Molly. They want actors and actresses for their new season'. My heart jumped, and I eagerly read the little notice as I leaned over her shoulder, and jotted down the address in shorthand. All applicants were invited to go to their rehearsal room in a hall in the Charing Cross district the following Tuesday. That was the one night in the week which was free of nightschool, Guides, choir practice, and bible studies, and was usually devoted to going for a walk with my faithful 'steady', or clearing out my chest of drawers, or washing my hair, or learning my poems for my beloved Miss Mitchell, for I was still taking elocution lessons. So on this Tuesday my 'steady' fell into step with me as I trotted eagerly back to town after swallowing my tea, and tried to sound enthusiastic about my taking my first small step towards my never-far-out-of-mind goal, that of becoming an actress.

I had thought there would be some impossibly difficult entrance test piece. Not a bit of it. A selection committee took a casual glance over the hopeful applicants, and divided those who said they could sing from those who said they couldn't. I opted for being one of the non-singers. I hadn't forgotten that singing master at school who had made me stand up all by myself and sing solo for the whole class and I didn't fancy this happening among all those big men and women, so I was duly registered as a drama member. A drama member! How exciting the words sounded. My heart pounded as we were handed copies of a little play, and as I was by far the youngest and smallest of the group, I was assigned the part of the schoolgirl in 'Mrs Watson's Window', one of a group of one-act plays to be entered for the Drama Festival. It wasn't a very big part, but it was a good one, and to my secret joy I was rewarded by a few giggles when I rehearsed it over and over again in the weeks which elapsed before we played before an audience.

My 'steady' had grown so hungry waiting for me that he had indulged an irresistible desire for a Mars bar, and had kept a piece to share with me, and always for me the taste of that succulent sweet is intermingled with the excitement of my first drama part, the cool air of an October night as we walked up Parliamentary Road, and the heady feeling that everything was opening out before me. They hadn't turned a hair, those actor-folk, that I had wanted to be one of them. Nobody had said I was too wee, as those employers had said when I first looked for a job. Nobody had found my accent laughable. I hugged myself with delight. My feet scarcely touched the ground, and my steady gloomily decided he might as well enrol for the night-school at a Tuesday class, for he could see I was lost to him for the winter. He chose shorthand, to share another interest with me, and we had a rare time thereafter writing wee secret messages on our postcards to one another, and in our diaries, in our best shorthand. It was like a secret code, and greatly impressed, or infuriated, those who happened to catch sight of the mysterious characters we'd penned so lovingly.

To my surprise, as well as being in the drama section, I was roped into the musical section of the club. In my innocence, I had no idea that it was well-nigh impossible to get people to go through the monotonous chorus rehearsals for singing and dancing, without the final hope of playing a solo part in the limelight. I thought they had found such good theatre material in me, they just couldn't bear to waste the smallest portion of it.

I had always liked singing and dancing anyway, and once I was assured I would have the comfort of more than two dozen other voices to help drown mine, I was in seventh heaven. How light-hearted musicals seemed to me. There was freedom to move around, and do spontaneous little gestures, without disturbing the feeling of the story, and I positively revelled in being taught how to dance. My mother was a beautiful dancer, and indeed had won many prizes for old-fashioned ballroom dancing and I think we all inherited her natural feeling for rhythm. It seemed simply wonderful to me that the Pantheon Club were prepared to teach me how to tap dance, and do what was called 'personality' dancing for nothing. I had grown so used to paying for my elocution lessons, that I was astounded not to have to save for fees for this splendid bonus of developing any dancing talent I might have. I was so excited on the first night of the dancing class that I wouldn't even have listened if anybody had tried to tell me I would be using new and untried muscles, and that I ought to take it gently. I was determined to master the splits (I never did!), and launched myself to the floor again and again, furious that I couldn't collapse gracefully and effortlessly like the others in the class who had studied ballet and who seemed to have limbs made from India rubber. I kicked my height, forwards and backwards, sneakingly bringing my head back to meet my toe, and I whirled and bent and twisted like a Dervish.

Next day I tried to get out of bed when my mother called through that it was time to get up. I thought I'd damaged myself for life. A lightning pain zig-zagged to the top of my leg and shot through to my hip. I tottered on to the cold linoleum, and groaned with agony as I bent to pull on my slipper. The teenager of the evening before had been changed into an arthritic old lady overnight. My mother laughed when she saw me. 'Aye, ye'll know a' aboot it noo', she said. 'Gi'e me the Wintergreen oot the chest of drawers and I'll rub some in for you'. 'I canny go into the office stinking of Wintergreen', I wailed. 'I'll just have to wait till tonight'. 'Pride knows no pain', she sang, as Grannie used to do, and refused to believe I had broken anything. 'Ye'll soon get ower it', she said cheerfully, 'I tellt ye ye had done faur too much in one night. Once yer muscles get used to it, you'll no' feel a thing'.

I didn't believe her. I knew I had torn umpteen irreplaceable muscles and tendons and I'd never walk to the office again. But the thought of paying fares soon steadied me, and somehow I managed to crawl into the town, and as the day wore on, the pain abated slightly, and by the end of the week I hardly felt a thing. At the end of a month, I was dancing with enthusiasm and had learnt the traditional time-step, which my mother described, to my annoyance, as a 'rer clog-wallop'. The chorus rehearsed apart from the principals, and indeed I thought we were the whole show and when my mother asked who was our leading lady I said we didn't have one. We just had singers and dancers. She stared at me. 'Ye MUST hiv comics and leading ladies', she said. 'Naebody would pey good money just to look at chorus girls and fellows'. She was right too. One night we were told that the whole show would come together for a full rehearsal the following week. And I found that not only did we have a leading lady and gentleman, we had a soubrette and a juvenile comedy lead, and we had solo singers and dancers, and we hard-working bunch of choristers were only the tiniest and least significant part of the whole show. It was a shattering moment.

But the show was the greatest fun. It was far better than the Rechabite kinderspiels, although in a way not unlike. Ah! But we were in a real theatre, with footlights, and an orchestra, and the price of the top seats was five whole shillings. Oh we would have to be good to justify charging such a fortune.

We had no sparkling frost on our hair, which for me had been the greatest magic of the kinderspiels, but we had real dressing rooms, and we had people to make up our faces with grease-paints, although some of the others who had been in the

Club for a long time were trusted to make up their own faces. I determined to learn to do this as soon as possible, and watched carefully as No. 5 and No. 9 grease-sticks were blended into my skin, and a thin black stick dramatized my lightish eyebrows. Bright lipstick made my teeth very white by contrast, and little red dots in the corner of my eyes, and white ones on the outside corners, were said to be to give the eyes definition and sparkle. Sequin bodices topped blue fluffy skirts, and transformed a dozen wee Glasgow lassies into slinky houris, and we bounded on to the stage, sure that we were as good as anything to be seen in the pictures. 'Smile', hissed our director from the wings, and we discovered we were so intent on our feet that we had forgotten our faces, and were as grim-faced as though we were tramping blankets in the bath. Our lips burst into scarlet instant response, and there was a titter of laughter from the audience. What cheek! We weren't supposed to be funny. We finished at exactly the same moment as the orchestra, which was a minor triumph, for we'd never achieved this in rehearsal, and skipped off to a round of generous applause. We poured with perspiration, but we were delighted with ourselves as we raced upstairs to change our costumes for the next number. Oh it was great not to have to think of lines, but just to enjoy ourselves belting out choruses and dancing to lilting happy music.

That was my first and last year as a chorus girl. Willy-nilly I was roped into the musicals, but as a principal. I never saw the chorus line again, except when I was leading them in a comedy number. 'The Marriage Market', 'Belle of New York', 'Good News', 'Show Boat', and last but not least 'Desert Song' where I played Susan to Harry Welchman's Red Shadow. He was an old man by that time, but still had his own magic, and he it was who insisted that my right place was in London. I laughed at the very idea, thinking of my mother's reaction, but I didn't forget his words. And although it was all exciting and marvellous fun, the most annoying thing about those musicals was that everybody, without exception, found my singing voice had far more carrying power than my speaking one. And I'd spent *pounds* and *years* on elocution lessons, and hardly a sixpence on singing coaching. It wasn't fair.

2

And then, everything seemed to happen at once. There was to be an Exhibition at Bellahouston Park in Glasgow, the biggest show ever, with exhibits from all over the world it seemed, and our college was renting a stand. I was to do my high-speed demonstrating before the interested (we hoped!) visitors to the Exhibition.

As well as appearing in my capacity as high-speed merchant, the Pantheon were putting on a sort of historical pageant, and I found myself cast as a moaning Italian peasant, writhing, starving, on the ground while I clawed at the feet of some noble who, I was told to imagine, might be able to give me food and money. I was never really clear as to what it was all about, but I fairly enjoyed my rags and I rent the air with my foreign wails of 'Madre de Dios', as I clutched at a vaguely seen pair of trousered legs in the half-light. I knew perfectly well that Madre de Dios was Spanish, for my 'steady' was taking Spanish lessons from the Consul at that time and we each benefited from the other's studies, but this had a far more dramatic ring to my ears than the Italian 'Madre Mia' which I ought to have used as an Italian peasant. I thought it might give any Tally ice-cream vendors in the auditorium a good laugh, but I was fairly certain nobody else would turn a hair, or be at all surprised that a starving Italian had the gift of tongues and could moan in Spanish!

For some reason the lighting was very dim, which was just as well, for I had no time for a complete change of clothing. I used to tear up from the shorthand demonstrations, throw my ragged goonie over my jersey and skirt, trusting that nobody in all that gloom would guess that I wasn't fully dressed in character below my rags, and with an enjoyable agonized wail of 'Madre de Dios' I was into the play.

The best part of all this was that because I was appearing as an artist (how I loved that word), I had a free pass to enter the Exhibition grounds, and once my performances were over I was free to rush round the rest of the Exhibition and see everything that was to be seen without charge. All my office friends came to the demonstrations and to the play, and we met afterwards and ate hot doughnuts and visited the other stands and had a glorious time.

I felt slightly ashamed that the play made so little impact on my imagination, but pageants have never had much appeal for me, and my preference has always been for something with a good strong story. Still, it must have impressed at least one member of the audience, for the boy friend of an office colleague came up to me after the pageant one night and pressed something into my hand for my 'spirited performance as a foreign wumman'. When I examined it under the light at the exit door, I found it was a teaspoon with the head of Princess Elizabeth at the top. He'd pinched it from another stand, he confessed, and I was terrified we'd be searched on the way out and I would have stolen goods on my person. I was a great one for reading the news reports on crime, and knew all the jargon. However, John point blank refused to take the spoon back, for although his courage was equal to spoon-lifting after an unaccustomed pint of strong ale, it was not strong enough to face the ordeal of a public confession, and I have the spoon to this day, my first gift from a stage-door Johnny! And stolen at that!

It was small wonder that with all the late hours I was keeping, it became more and more difficult to reach the office in time to sign my name above the red line in the mornings. This line was drawn at ten past nine precisely, and the man who presided over the official book was as incorruptible as St Peter at the pearly gates. No amount of coaxing could persuade him to allow you to squeeze your name above it, once drawn. Even if you fell in at the door, breathless, as he was poised to draw his pen under the lucky last name, the red ink flowed remorselessly and he showed no mercy. More than three times in a month below the red line meant a visit to the boss's office, and a severe reprimand. The boss spoke quietly, but you were left in no doubt that it was desirable that you mend your ways, get to bed at a proper hour, and arrive in good time to attend to your duties, and refrain from robbing the firm of all that precious time for which you were being paid.

We all hated being summoned to this austere man's room, and it was even worse for me, because I now worked for him, and had to face his frowning disappointment as he studied the attendance book and found my name there far too often these days. It made no difference that I could get through more work than most of the other girls, thanks to my speeds. Timekeeping was a discipline, and anyone who couldn't keep correct hours must have other unsuspected flaws which couldn't be tolerated.

Strangely enough, he wasn't nearly so critical of my late mornings after he'd come to see me acting in Show Boat. I had more singing and dancing in that musical than in any of the other big shows, and among the numbers was a hilarious cake-walk. My mother, always reliable as an expert source for any sort of dancing, taught me how to do a proper old-fashioned cake-walk, and I in turn taught it to Jack Laurie my partner. It was tremendously hard work, for we took it at a very fast tempo, with our backs bent down almost to the floor as we covered the stage. It brought the house down at every performance, and although the applause carried right through the following dialogue, Jack and I were thankful no encores were allowed to interrupt the flow of the story at this point, for we had neither breath nor strength to have given the audience any more.

This cake-walk fairly impressed my boss. He gazed at me next day, as I sat with bent head, eyes cast modestly down as I waited for my notes, regarding me as though I were the original model for Jekyll and Hyde. 'Can this be the same person I watched last night doing that energetic dance?' he murmured. 'No wonder you need a few extra minutes in the mornings.' I was delighted by this tolerance, but a bit surprised, for I never enquired of myself as to whether or not I was doing too much.

I even found time to run a wee sweetie shop in the office because once more I was raising funds for the Girl Guides. It never crossed my mind to drop one interest to make way for another. I kept them all on. The only thing I had to forgo during all this hectic period was choir practice for the church, and I wrote a little note to the organist explaining that because practice night now clashed with rehearsals for the Pantheon, I must regretfully give up the choir. He was entranced by my courtesy, because apparently everyone else simply ceased attending and he never knew whether or not it was his teaching which was at fault. I was very impressed by this reaction, for it hadn't occurred to me that such a confident clever man could have any doubts about himself or his music, especially when he had the courage and originality to play 'Moonlight and Roses' and 'In a monastery garden' as voluntaries instead of the usual religious pieces in church. It was now borne upon me that even older people could feel just as uncertain as youngsters like myself. It was a disconcerting discovery, for I had been so looking forward to being absolutely sure of everything once I was fully grown up. It was shattering to discover that utter certainty would always be elusive.

My sweetie shop was a tremendous boon for everyone, for we didn't have canteens in those days, and people either brought a biscuit or an apple to eat during a furtive visit to the toilets during the forenoon, or starved till lunch-time. But my shop changed the habits of the entire office. I had thought I'd have to advertise my wares, albeit secretly, for we weren't allowed to waste time chatting or doing anything other than work during our employer's time. In a day, it seemed, the whole building was aware that Weir's sweetie shop had opened. Two office drawers had been emptied, and my chocolate bars ranged neatly inside, with an empty typing ribbon tin serving as my cash box. I'd scarcely sat down before the first customer drifted over, demanding sustenance to keep her going till lunch-time as she hadn't had time to eat any breakfast. I'd imagined I'd find business brisk around 10.30 to 11 in the forenoons, and around 3 o'clock in the afternoons. Not a bit of it. Those who resisted temptation all morning, found the smell of chocolate irresistible each time they came to get some work done, and with lunch-time seeming more and more distant, they would succumb and start wolfing chocolate after 12 o'clock in the day, successfully destroying their appetite for their proper meal. It was the same in the afternoon. Long past normal nibbling time men would come in, stop dead in their tracks and sniff the air, decide they were starving and buy a bar of chocolate. Although I wanted to make a profit for the Guides, I was concerned that their wives would be furious if they couldn't eat their tea, but it was no good trying to dissuade them. I had created the need by supplying the goods. My boss must have wondered what was going on, especially when everybody could be seen leaving my desk chewing happily, but if he smelt the chocolate he said nothing. I think he had learned by this time that whatever extra activities I was indulging in, I'd still get through my work, and the memory of the cake-walk seemed to throw a haze over his judgement of me.

I did such a roaring trade with my hungry colleagues that I had to race over the High Road to the Guide Captain's house at lunch-time for replenishment of my stock, and stagger down to the office carrying whole boxes of chocolate bars which then had to be smuggled into my office drawers without the boss catching me. Tolerant he might be, but I couldn't tempt providence by carrying in the goods too openly. This commerce lasted for three months and I was glad when it came to an end, for the cloak and dagger subterfuge was wearing me down, not to mention the weight of those boxes. I think my arms grew a good three inches during this period! However, I was able to hand over £20 to the Captain, which went a long way towards extras for our summer holiday camp that year.

But summer camp was a long way off, and I was very busy with rehearsals for the one-act play with which the Pantheon was sure that this year would bring them triumph as winners of the Drama Festival. The play was 'The Pagans' and I had a lovely part as the wee servant girl. I was servant to two artists, one played by Alan McKill, who himself produced many excellent dramas for the club, and the other by a fine actor called David Baxter. I had almost no contact with them at all on a social level at that time, for I regarded them as towering above me in every sense – grown men, with no interest whatever in wee lassies like me. But I poured it all out to my 'steady' as we walked back and forth to rehearsals, and he shared all my hopes that this play would bring the top Festival prize to the Pantheon and that I'd share in the glory. Four one-act plays were done each evening, and adjudicated by a professional judge at the end of the evening's performances. This public assessment of the plays was the highlight for audience and actors alike. The audience wanted to see if their opinion coincided with that of the judge, and we actors rejoiced if praised, and groaned if adversely criticized. Our Pagans was well received by a packed house, and the adjudicator was loud in his praise of the play. Of my performance he was almost at a loss for words, he said. I held my breath. Did he mean good or bad? The audience was very still. Then he continued, 'If C.B. Cochran saw this girl, he would take her to London at once.' I was stunned. I was also puzzled by this reference to C.B. Cochran, for all I knew of him was that he employed dazzlingly tall young ladies, and I couldn't by any stretch of the imagination fall into that category. But the audience found no such confusion. They broke into enthusiastic agreement and applause, and the next day the *Daily Express* had banner headlines, 'Call for Cochran at Drama Festival'.

My office colleagues were as excited as though Garbo herself had landed in the export department, and everybody vowed to be present at the finals on the Saturday night. There had been such enthusiasm from press and public that everyone felt that it was a foregone conclusion that the Pantheon would walk away with the top prize. But it was a different adjudicator for the finals, and this man took a very cool view of 'The Pagans'. He picked faults in the construction line. He wasn't overkeen on the production. He thought the wee servant girl gave the best performance (I hid my face. I couldn't bear to think what the grown-up men actors were thinking), and in short he could not award us a place. Consternation! Pandemonium! And such a stushie, indeed, that Jack House, then a radio reporter as well as a newsman with the *Citizen,* rushed to Broadcasting House to announce to a largely indifferent Scotland that he had come hot-foot from the Festival where the shock of the evening had been the Pantheon's defeat with what everyone had judged to be the best play to be seen at any Festival for years. And he was kind enough to add that the only point of agreement the adjudicator could find with previous judgements had been over my performance.

This defeat in the face of general acclaim had one good result though. It was so manifestly unfair that that was the last Festival where the awards were left to the taste of one man. From then on, a panel sat in judgement. So 'The Pagans' made history in its own small way.

My 'steady' and I had intended having a special celebration feast in the Royal Restaurant, whose menus we often studied on our way to and from night classes, but whose prices were away beyond our normal egg and chip treats in Reids. Now there was nothing to celebrate, so we just walked home, and tried to forgive that black-hearted adjudicator who had not only robbed the Pantheon of victory, but had deprived us of our victory supper.

However, one night when we couldn't get into the pictures because it was too cold to stand in the endless queue which twined right round the side alley at the Regent, where a lethal East wind bit through the thickest coat, we decided we would enjoy our delayed celebration treat, and have a wee hot meal in the famous restaurant in St Vincent Street. We smiled to give each other confidence as we tip-toed through the heavy doors, assuming an ease we were far from feeling, and the sound of our footsteps was swallowed up by the rich carpeting. It seemed palatial to us. And we didn't even have on our best clothes, for we hadn't prepared for this, and had just acted on impulse.

How quiet the restaurant seemed, and how posh, with its dark panelling, and with waiters who stood with eyes gazing towards the ceiling while we studied the menu. We looked for the cheapest item, for we could only afford something which cost the same price as the pictures would have done – 1/6d each. We could only see one item anywhere near that price, and that was roes on toast for 1/4d. With a threepenny cup of tea, that came to 1/7d altogether. Just an extra penny apiece. That would do. So we gave our order to the waiter and sat back to watch with interest, tinged with great envy, the plates covered with rich mixed grills, the chops and chips, the large Dover soles.

'They'll be up a' night', we whispered to one another. We were too overawed to speak out loud in such surroundings. 'Fancy eatin' a tight'ner like that at 9 o'clock at night'. Privately I was making up my mind that if ever I had the luck to celebrate anything else in the future, I was going to have a mixed grill, and enjoy the opulence of eating three dinners in one, for that's what chop, sausage, kidney, bacon, tomato and chips meant to me.

When the bill came for our insipid roes on toast, whose only appeal had been its price, we were appalled to find that the total came to five shillings and not the 3/2d we'd expected, including our two threepenny cups of tea. With beating heart we called the waiter over, and pointed out the price for roes on toast on the menu. With a lofty arrogance he explained that there was a minimum charge of half-a-crown per person, no matter what was ordered below that sum, in order to discourage people making use of the restaurant for mere cups of tea.

We were absolutely outraged. Why couldn't the rotter have *told* us that, when he'd seen us studying the menu so intently. He must have *known* we could have eaten a mixed grill, given half a chance, and that we'd only taken their miserable old roes on toast because that was all we could afford, and because there wasn't anything cheaper on the menu. I ground my teeth in rage when I saw all the things I could have had for half-a-crown. Fish and chips. Sausage, bacon and chips. 'Don't gi'e him a tip', I hissed in a stage whisper, which I fully intended should reach this supercilious waiter's ears. My timidity in the rich surroundings had given way to seething fury at having been done, and I gave him a baleful glare as he held the door open for us.

Standing outside on the pavement we read the menu framed in the window to attract passing trade. There, in tiny print, at the very bottom, we found the words we'd missed in our excitement at actually being inside such an establishment, 'Minimum charge 2/6d.' Ever after, when I heard people say, 'always read the small print', I thought of that menu, and our disappointment at not having chosen something to the full value of our bill, and I may say that nothing written in small print has escaped my attention since then. I learned my lesson well.

As we walked home, we spoke of the day when we'd walk in with a swagger, wearing our best Sunday clothes, and order a mixed grill in that restaurant, but it would have to be something really marvellous we'd be celebrating, to justify spending all that money – whole three-and-sixpence on the grill alone, without tea, or bread and butter, or anything.

The celebration came sooner than we could have dreamed.

My brother Tommy had always been tremendously keen on playing the drums. As described elsewhere,* he drove us all mad practising his 'para-diddles' in a fast tattoo on the dresser, and on the rubber pad he'd saved to buy when he was promoted to the side drum in the Boy's Brigade. He was always interested in music and, like me, always singing. The neighbours were very tolerant of our rhythmic choruses, unselfconsciously warbled as we kept time with our feet when we trudged up our two flights of stairs for our dinner when we were children. I rather fancied what I regarded as posh songs, like 'In my sweet little Alice blue gown', or 'She left her baby lying there', but Tommy would thunder out:

Dae ye ken Elsie Marleyhoney,
The wife that mak's the barley honey,
THE WIFE, THE WIFE, THE WIFE that mak's the barley,

with a fine heavy thump to each 'THE WIFE' which shook the stair. But the one which made my mother laugh, for no good reason that we could fathom was when he used to chant with great vigour:

Lordy, Lordy, Lordy *how* I *loved* her!
The birds were singing in the wild wood,
My happy childhood comes back once more.
My heart is sore.

Probably the fact that he was about eight years old at the time may have had something to do with her mirth.

Now his singing had given way to drum-beats, and after he discovered the world of Nat Gonella, Red Nicholls and his Five Pennies, and Joe Venuti, he was afire to start a wee dance band of his own. The B.B. had given him the necessary training with

* *Best Foot Forward*

the drum-sticks, and Glasgow, which has always been a dancing city, provided endless opportunity for anyone willing and able to play at local dances for a few shillings' reward. So the dance band was formed. Tommy was on the drums of course, Dougie on the fiddle and tenor saxophone, and Jimmy on accordian and piano. Jimmy was a versatile instrumentalist, and free-lanced with other bands on the string bass. My mother was a great help with the tunes dancers liked, for she always found the energy to go out dancing fairly regularly, however tiring her job might be. The Highlanders' Institute was greatly favoured, and the Lesser Public Hall, while the Guild dances in Angus Street were a regular source of pleasure. With her increasing deafness, other forms of entertainment were becom-ing more and more difficult for her, but the rhythm of the dance could be felt through her feet, and the note of a violin sang for her and penetrated the fog of her partial deafness. Her eyes would grow misty as she recalled the talents of one, The Great Tucker, who apparently was a wizard on the fiddle. And she was in no doubt at all as to the tunes the boys ought to play for old-time dances like Pride of Erin, Military Two-step, The Valeta, St Bernard's Waltz and the Lancers. For the quicksteps, slow fox-trots and modern waltzes they stuck to the tunes of their gods, Red Nicholls and Joe Venuti, and they soon acquired a reputation as a 'rer wee dance band' whose tempo was really strict, and whose musical sense was first-class. Dougie was a hot favourite, with his accurate ear for the styles of the musical giants of the day. His fiddling was modelled on Venuti, his tenor sax on Benny Carter, and in his singing he was a dead ringer for the immensely popular Fats Waller.

When they started this venture, they earned the handsome sum of seven and sixpence each for an evening stint which could last from 7.30 till 1 A.M., and naturally they preferred halls within walking distance, to which they could hump their instruments without having to pay fares out of their profits. Such was their popularity locally that it didn't take too long before this figure had doubled to fifteen shillings a night, and they felt their fortunes were made. But the true accolade came when they became resident dance band at Morrin Street dancing establishment every Saturday night. Tommy was torn between triumph over this regular Saturday engagement, and dismay that his climbing week-end was to be disastrously shortened. He was now playing the drums several nights a week after his day's work at the Co-operative, playing each Saturday night at Morrin Street, and up at crack of dawn on Sunday mornings to enjoy a day on the hills he loved. The hills were as necessary to him as breathing, and he never dreamt of giving up this form of relaxation and refreshment, however tempting the bed might seem after the Saturday dance sessions. Not for nothing had Grannie taught us to use to the full every minute of our lives, and to waste nothing.

In their initial enthusiasm, the boys threw themselves into the evening's work with scarcely a pause between the numbers to wipe the perspiration from their brows. Then, as they grew more experienced, and before exhaustion completely overtook them, they began to realize that a proper vocalist might be a good idea. It would give them a rest, would allow Dougie some welcome respite between his scat numbers, and would also add a sophisticated touch to their outfit. So a swooning crooner was found, but he very soon refused to continue with them unless he had a microphone. He hinted it was an insult to his status as a dance-band singer, and anyway soft murmurings into mikes were the latest thing and he was determined to follow the current trend. Already the boys had begun to appreciate the restfulness of the moments when this warbler was charming the dancers, so they made the big decision – they would invest in a microphone. And it was this acquisition which led my footsteps in a direction I could never have dreamed.

The night it arrived, they were having their band practice in our house. Sometimes they went to Dougie's and sometimes to ours, to divide the racket fairly between the neighbours of both families. The tenement walls, thick though they were, couldn't baffle all sound, and both mothers were terrified of being reported to the factor for the noise the 'jam sessions' caused. Actually nobody complained that we knew of, although the noise inside the kitchen itself was earsplitting at times. I didn't blame Jimmy's mother for dissociating herself completely from such sessions, and refusing to let the trio set foot inside the door.

I was trying to study through the arguments which accompanied the setting up of the mike, but at last it was accomplished, with much racing back and forth between the room and the kitchen, and great experimenting as one sang a few notes while the other two listened. Suddenly Tommy said to me, 'You go through to the room and test it, and we can all listen in the kitchen and decide if it's working properly.' I raised my head from my book of poems 'What will I do?' I asked, giggling with nervous pleasure at being asked to co-operate. 'Och some of thae wee daft poems you're aye reciting', Tommy replied. So I pretended I was at my elocution class and launched into a little item which involved the use of several accents, and which was a sure-fire winner at concerts, as well as being a real bit of showing-off of anyone's skill with other voices. 'Dae something else', came Tommy's voice commandingly from the kitchen. I grew bold, as they hadn't laughed my efforts away in jeering scorn. I was generally told to 'shut up, I'm trying to read' when I went about the house doing my impersonations. This was a great chance to do the lot before anybody could stop me.

I was passionately devoted to Garbo, and I did the little scene where Basil Rathbone's dog discovers her in a barn. Not a sound from the kitchen. I followed this with Gracie Fields singing 'Sally'. I listened intently for any reaction, waiting to be yanked away from the mike. Nothing. So Dietrich's 'Falling in love again' was purred into the mike, then a bit of Zazu Pitts, and finally, as a raucous curtain piece, a chunk of Tommy Morgan. There was complete silence while I waited to be told if they wanted any more, or if they were satisfied that the mike was to their liking. Then Tommy came through to me in the room and stood gazing with amazement in his eyes. He wasn't exactly eulogistic, but he *was* impressed I could see. 'Here, you sound just like thae folk through the mike', he said, and walked back to join his pals. I was elated. I was as complimented as though I'd just been awarded a Royal Command performance. This to be said to me by a brother who had, up till then, dismissed my impressions as so much noise. I went back to the study of my poems like the cat who'd swallowed the cream.

And then, the next week Carroll Levis came to Glasgow.

It was Tommy who saw the paragraph in the newspaper. 'Here', he said to me as I sat doing my homework after tea, 'there's a man asking folk to apply to the Savoy if they want an audition to be considered for the stage. He's looking for discoveries'.

I seized the paper from him. 'Och it's for variety turns', I said, 'I'm not a variety turn'. I was busy with my elocution lessons, and my Pantheon rehearsals, and was in training to become a real actress, not a 'turn'. But it was tempting all the same, if only I could do a 'turn'. 'Yon wee things you did for oor mike would make a turn', said Tommy. 'What did I say?', I asked, knitting my brows, for I'd just made it all up as I went along. So we all sat round the table, and when they came in Dougie and Jimmy joined us, and we each remembered what I'd said as Garbo, a sentence here, a word there, until I'd jotted the whole performance down in shorthand. Thus armed with an 'act', I sent in my application in my best hand-writing penned with one of the special pen-knibs hoarded from the ones given to me for exams by my friendly girl clerks in the Co-operative, and I waited for a reply, half-filled with hope, half with dread as I thought of having actually to perform that made-up act before grown up people.

'There's a letter for you on the dresser', my mother said when I came in from the office, a good week after the application had been sent. 'Dear Miss Weir', it said, 'If you will present yourself at the New Savoy at 10.30 P.M. next Friday, at the close of the final performance, you will be given an audition to consider your suitability as an aspiring discovery in the Carroll Levis show.' Sick excitement and cold terror struggled within me as my mother echoed 'Hauf-past-ten at night. My Goad, fancy expectin' folk tae start acting at that 'oor. There'll be naebody there.'

'Well there canny be many folk wanting to be discovered when they're asking me to come so late', I said, 'so I'll no' likely be very long'. I wasn't so worried about the time of night as I was at the thought of getting up on the stage of the New Savoy and saying lines I'd written by myself, and pretending this was good enough to be described as an 'act'. Everything else I'd ever done had been originated by somebody else, and I shivered at my own daring and cheek at attempting to say my own words, and in competition with other folk at that.

In my innocence I had expected about a dozen people to be there at such a late hour. I walked from home, as usual, but it felt very strange to be walking towards the town at what was normally nearly my bed-time. When I reached the Savoy, I thought there had been an accident, or the place was on fire. It was seething with HUNDREDS of would-be discoveries. Carroll Levis hadn't just replied to those who had written neat, well-penned letters. He had written to every single person who had applied, and it seemed that Glasgow teemed with embryo performers. I could hardly get inside, although I was early, and I was right at the back of the stalls. And then, as I gazed in dismay at the jostling throng, somebody climbed up on to the stage and said that in fairness to us all, we would be taken in alphabetical order. And my name was, as it is now, Weir. Practically the end of the alphabet.

I felt as though I were in a dream as I watched jugglers, acrobatic dancers, Highland dancers, impersonators, singers, duettists, ventriloquists, appear and perform, in a never-ending stream. My stomach grew emptier and emptier, and the sleep which had threatened to engulf me at one point, now disappeared and left instead an icy nervousness which induced a feeling of nightmare. I had nothing to do with any of this. What was I doing here at all?

Then suddenly, when I had decided it really *was* all a dream, I heard my name being called. It was 1.45 A.M. My legs jerked into action and I walked quickly down the side passage, up through the pass door, and on to the stage. It was the first time I'd heard the proper name for the little door which divided audience from backstage, and even in my extremity I noted it, and was stirred. There were about six people in the audience. Carroll Levis, the Savoy manager, and one or two friends. Everyone else had gone home. In a husky voice I gave my name and my age. Levis laughed and said I looked about twelve. They themselves must have been punch drunk by this time, having watched hundreds of acts, and I could see from their tired postures that they were lolling in their seats, not paying much attention. When I had impersonated the well-known film stars of my choice, I announced 'This could be any British film star', and I assumed the high-pitched starlet voice which we in Glasgow despised, and laced the dialogue with the upper-class blasphemies very popular in British films at that time. The figures in the stalls jerked to attention and there was a ripple of surprised laughter. 'Who suggested that item?', somebody called up to me. 'Nobody', I was roused to answer indignantly, 'I made it up myself.'

When I had finished, they checked my name and address, said I would hear from them if I was successful, and the next moment I was out in Hope Street, facing the long walk back to Springburn, wide awake now and hoping I could creep in without disturbing my mother. The minute I put the key in the door, she was up, 'My Goad, you've a sin tae answer fur', she said. 'I was sure you'd been murdered. How did ye get oan?'. She was reassured when she heard there had been hundreds there, and not just one wicked impresario, and she had to be told everything over a cup of tea. It was quite like New Year, sitting there drinking tea in the middle of the night, especially when the boys wakened up and had to be given some too.

3

I didn't tell a soul outside the family, and my 'steady', that I'd
gone along to that audition, partly because I wasn't really sure
if I wanted to become a 'turn', but more strongly because I felt
that anything I had made up couldn't possibly be considered as
a real 'act'. When four days went by and no letter arrived,
although the boys and my mother said nothing, I could see they
felt I was out of the running. But on the Thursday morning, the
first post brought an invitation to take part in the eliminating
round on the following Tuesday evening at the New Savoy. I
was to be there at 8 P.M., with my music if required (I had
none), and I was informed that one winner would be chosen on
each of the week nights, which meant that five finalists would
be judged by public applause on the Saturday night, to decide
who would be No. 1 discovery for Glasgow. There would be a
second and third prize for the runners-up. And all three would
be invited to take part in the National broadcast from London
at the end of the country-wide contests. First prize carried a
prize of three guineas, second of two guineas, and third of a
guinea. All would be judged by volume of public response in
the cinema, which would be measured by a special machine.

Between Thursday morning when that letter was delivered,
and Tuesday evening when I walked into the Savoy, I suppose
I must have gone through the motions of eating and sleeping
and working, but I seemed to be moving on another plane of
existence altogether. I could hear myself talking and laughing,
and I could see myself walking down to the office and taking
notes, and typing them out, but it wasn't me at all. The real me
was muttering those impersonations over and over again, and
trying to project myself in time to the moment when I would
walk on to the Savoy stage and stand out there in front of

hundreds of folk, and try to hypnotize them into believing I was a real talent awaiting discovery by them. I didn't even have a sheet of music to help me. Not even a roll of drums. Just me. And a microphone.

Everybody in the office knew by this time. I had blurted it out when somebody who had been reading about the Carroll Levis show asked why I hadn't entered for it. My stage aspirations were common knowledge, and many had already seen me with the Pantheon. I hadn't meant to tell them, for I didn't want to broadcast my disgrace if I failed, but the truth just leaped out when I was asked point blank why I wasn't among the contestants. To my amazement, they were all agog with interest, and even a few of the men decided to rush home for tea and get back in time for the Levis show that Tuesday night. I felt sicker than ever, but it never crossed my mind not to turn up. If anybody asked me to do anything in those days, I did it, and indeed I'm pretty much the same today. My mother couldn't face the prospect of my getting 'the bird', and decided to stay at home. The boys didn't come either. Tommy had a band engagement, and Willie was going out. So at least the family wouldn't have to share any public odium if I were a flop. I didn't even want my 'steady' to be there, but he went anyway.

I walked home from the office as usual, but beyond sipping a cup of tea could eat nothing. My innards had suddenly turned to jelly, and I leaped out and in the toilet (thankfully indoors and not on the stair in this good house), until I thought I'd never have the strength to get to the Savoy in time for the performance. When people remarked on my confidence at later public appearances, my mother would echo, to my dismay, 'Confidence! My Goad, naebody can get near the lavy, when she's to go oot daein' onything. Ma life's no worth a ha'penny, for she's juist a bundle o' nerves.'

She was right too. For the butterflies which attended that Levis performance took up permanent residence with me and have never left me since. But I wasn't to know that then, and I thought it was just because this was a special sort of competition, and all the office would be there.

There were no dressing rooms in the cinema, so we all huddled in the wings and at the back of the curtain. Levis was a jolly plump fair-haired man, with twinkling blue eyes, in immaculate dinner-suit, who bounded about back-stage like an India-rubber ball. My mother always said fat men made the lightest dancers, and certainly Carroll Levis amply demonstrated this as he leaped around, checking everything, and deciding the order in which we would appear. He and the manager had assorted the acts, which must have made it pretty difficult for the audience to decide between a man with a concertina and a tap dancer, but they were intent on providing balanced entertainment and in catering for all tastes. It wasn't an examination after all, but a gigantic variety show.

My five fellow-competitors consisted of a pianist, a girl singer, a tap dancer, a boy with a melodeon, and a crooner. Everybody had music but me. Which, in my eyes, made them real variety turns. I was to be last. The discoveries came on at the end of the big picture, and for this special week there was only one main feature instead of the usual two, to keep within the regulation cinema hours. And to let people get home to their beds at a reasonable hour. They couldn't risk the audience deciding against losing their sleep over a bunch of amateurs and walking out if the show went on too long.

Even as it was, it would be 10 o'clock before I would go on, and I doubted I would survive until that hour, for now my heart was beating so loudly it could only be a matter of time before I dropped dead before their very eyes. There was a glass of water in the wings, which rattled against my teeth as I sipped it, for my throat felt so dry I could hardly swallow. I listened to the other acts, and how good they seemed. The audience fairly thundered out their applause, it seemed to me, and I was certain that they too would have no strength left for a good clap by the time my turn came up.

And then I heard Carroll Levis say, 'And now, ladies and gentlemen, give a warm welcome to a wee Glasgow lassie who is going to entertain you with some impressions'. Somebody pushed me on to the stage, and under the blaze of blinding lights and a soft spatter of applause I walked to the mike. Levis asked me my name, 'Molly Weir', I replied huskily, and heard this reply booming round the building. 'And what do you do for a living?' he asked me. 'I'm a shorthand typist'. Unconsciously I had stepped back from the mike a little for the second reply, and this time the sound seemed much more natural. There was a bit of clapping from my office friends up in the gods, which was instantly 'shushed', and suddenly I was in control and determined to be as good a 'turn' as it was in my power to be. The film star impressions were well received, the Gracie Fields one and the Dietrich one with ripples of surprise, but it was the Tommy Morgan one which brought the house down. I had only put this one in at all to demonstrate the real broad Glasgow accent against my 'posh' office voice, and not only was the contrast very effective, but at that time no female had ever thought of impersonating a man, and the sheer surprise sent the place into an uproar. It was pandemonium as they demanded an encore of the Tommy Morgan piece, so I just had to do the same bit again, for I had no more patter, and after that reception even I knew that it was a foregone conclusion that I was winner for Tuesday and would go on to the heat the following Saturday.

Tommy appeared not to be surprised when he heard of my victory. 'Tellt ye they were juist like they stars, didn't I?' he said. My mother was less enthusiastic. 'My Goad, have we to go through a' this again on Setterday night?', she demanded. 'Then I'm gaun oot afore ye, and ye can have the hale hoose tae yersel' to march up and doon, and go through to the toilet as often as you like'.

The office were wildly enthusiastic and kept asking me to 'do' Tommy Morgan for those who hadn't been able to be at the Savoy. Always willing, I must have gone through Tommy's throat-searing voice a dozen times until I was in danger of losing my own voice, and there was Saturday still to come.

The Savoy was packed. For everybody wanted to be in at the death, and the queues had stretched right round Renfrew Street on one side, and right round the lane on the other side, hours before the doors opened. They had added another act from the closely fought tie of Friday, so that made six of us in the running for the first three places. It was better than the originally planned five, I thought, for it would be rotten to be left one of a losing pair, whereas half winners and half losers didn't seem nearly so terrible.

Everybody seemed very sure that I would win it, but I shook my head and refused to believe anything was a foregone conclusion. And it wasn't. The first prize was taken by a bus conductor who did great whistling sounds with his larynx and his cupped hands, and whose Corporation pals nearly lifted the roof when he won. I was voted second, and a singer was third. We were all presented with our cheques – which was the first time I'd ever had a cheque in my own name – and we all made a little speech. I thought I'd make them laugh by using the voice of Tommy Morgan, which turned out to be a terrible faux pas. As an experienced performer told me afterwards, 'Don't you see, you should have used your own nice, well-modulated voice, which naturally makes the Morgan accent all the more impressive. Now they will all think that Tommy Morgan's voice was a natural for you, because you speak like that yourself.' I did see. And it was too late. Oh there was a tremendous lot to learn about show business. I blushed with shame that I could have been so stupid and the thought of the London broadcast couldn't comfort me for the flat response to my little speech.

By the time the summons came to go to London I had worked myself into such a state of nerves that the doctor had to supply me with a bromide to make me sleep and comfort my stomach. With the memory of the Savoy speech vivid in my mind, I dreaded to think what other awful pitfalls might await me in a broadcasting studio. My mother was quite stunned that I was making such a long and fearful journey all by myself. She had never been further than Crieff and Stonehaven in her life, and to go south over the border into England was to vanish into alien territory. But she checked that I had a nice clean nightgown, and had put in the wee Japanese kimono auntie had brought for me when she came from Australia and which was nice and light for packing, and my slippers, and brush and comb. The green dress with the green and white striped top which I wore for the shorthand demonstrations would be fine for the show, which was to have an audience. I didn't then know that a lot of broadcasting was done without an audience, so I accepted it as perfectly natural that the studio at St George's Hall in London would be filled with people. I was so frightened of getting lost that I sat in my hotel almost the whole day, just contenting myself with a walk along Oxford Street and keeping the hotel within sight. I couldn't resist a visit tc Selfridges, which was a magic name to us in Glasgow, and which stunned me by being as big as Copland & Lye, Pettigrew & Stephens and Hendersons, all rolled in one. I felt I had walked miles in the hour I had allowed myself, and even then I hadn't seen all the counters or been in the basement. I bought a pair of gloves and a vest with the money I had brought with me, and a truly glamorous nightdress in another little shop, which was destined for my bottom drawer, for who knew when I would ever have the chance again of shopping in England's capital, where the King and Queen and all the Royal family lived.

Before the broadcast that evening, I seemed to be in even more desperate need of finding the nearest toilet than ever before. I was also growing sleepier and sleepier, and my eyelids felt so heavy I could hardly raise them. The broadcast itself passed in a dream, and I went straight back to the hotel afterwards, fell into bed and knew nothing until thunderous knocking on my door warned me I'd have to hurry for breakfast if I was catching the 10 A.M. train to Glasgow. This was so unlike me, for I am not a good sleeper at the best of times, and certainly not after such an exciting experience as a first broadcast, that I began to suspect that I was ill. A glance at the mirror showed me with blackened swollen eyelids, and my eyes felt so strange that I could scarcely read a word all the way to Glasgow. Next day when I saw the doctor, he pursed his lips. 'Mmmm', he grunted, 'let me see that bottle'. He put a tiny drop to his lips. 'Well, young lady', he said, 'don't let anybody ever think they can give you arsenic poisoning and get away with it, for there are signs of this substance in your finger nails and your hair.' I jumped with fright. It appeared the chemist had mistaken the tiny quantity of arsenic prescribed, and although the dose included wasn't lethal, it was pretty dire in its effect on me as I happened to be one of the people whose bodies absorb arsenic instantly. That was certainly an unforgettable lesson to me for the future, and taught me to look after my own nerves, and not to rely on any old bromide. Fancy spoiling my first visit to London in such a way! I could have had *hours* in Selfridges instead of sitting in my hotel, and I might even have managed a quick shoosh round the zoo before

my train if only I'd been more wide awake. I didn't even ṇ
thought as to how my broadcast might have been affecṭ
Frozen terror had obviously numbed my brain, for I found ị
couldn't remember a thing about my performance. I sighed
regretfully and decided that that was probably the end of my
broadcasting career.

But Jack House changed all that. During this eventful year
when so much was happening to me, Jack was keeping a
weather eye on this lass with the assorted talents. He was also
in charge of a BBC programme called 'Who's Here', which
brought visiting celebrities to the mike in Glasgow after the 6
o'clock news, following a fast sprint round Bellahouston Park
where that Empire Exhibition was held, plus, if time permitted,
a speedy tour of Loch Lomond. The celebrity of the evening
then told us all what he thought of us, of the Exhibition and
our beautiful countryside. They had recruited some very big
names, all from show-biz and many from Hollywood, and most
of them were flown from London to take part in the programme. One night, due to a tangle of mishaps and bad flying
conditions, they were left with no celebrity. What to do?
Suddenly Jack said, 'What about having a local celebrity.
There's this wee girl who combines the oddest interests. She
writes shorthand at 300 words per minute. She has been named
as the most promising young actress at the Drama Festival.
And now she's just won a place in the Carroll Levis Contest.
What about having her as our celebrity?'

With the reporter's zeal it didn't take him long to find out
where I worked. My boss was telephoned, and although it was
strictly against the rules that we took private calls in the firm's
time and on the firm's telephone, he handed the instrument to
me. He was impressed by the words, 'This is the British
Broadcasting Corporation'. Could I come straight to the BBC
as soon as I finished work at five-thirty? I would be on the air
just after the 6 o'clock news so I mustn't delay. The tram
passed the Botanic Gardens, and I was to waste no time.
Nobody suggested I should take a taxi, and I of course would
never have dreamed of such extravagance. Luckily there wasn't
enough time to get palsied with fear, and this time I was simply
burning with excitement. The entire office flew home on the

dot of 5.30 to listen to what was going to happen to me at the hands of experienced broadcasters. With a panel of newsmen to see that it was genuine, I took down a dictated piece at 300 words per minute from Mr McLeod, whom they'd lassooed from his college duties, and then I read them back. Next I did a short scene from the play, the part where it was virtually a monologue, and lastly I did a couple of impersonations from the Levis show, finishing with Tommy Morgan. Then I was asked a few questions about my interests, and that was that. Thinking it over later, probably the most striking tribute to the absolute confidence held by everyone in the integrity of the BBC was the fact that there wasn't a single suggestion from any quarter that the high-speed writing wasn't genuine. It *could* have been faked, after all. On a radio show, who could prove that speeds and shorthand were authentic? We could merely have said that the newsmen were there. Of course we knew it was truly all open and above-board and honest, but for all anyone really knew I could have been reading from the printed page.

This trust in the BBC was shared throughout the civilized world, and in later years when so much lying propaganda came from Germany, we were all certain that if the BBC said it was so, then it was indeed so.

The whole thing had gone off splendidly and my steady was waiting for me when I came out. Now we *really* had something to celebrate – a broadcast from London and one from Glasgow. This was the moment to knock the supercilious smile off that waiter's face in the posh restaurant. We'd march in like lords, and order a mixed grill.

We went to the same table, to make sure the same waiter would take our opulence in, and after a perfunctory glance at the menu to make sure the prices hadn't gone up, we ordered two mixed grills, and sat back to wait, gazing expansively round the dining room, bubbling with excitement and anticipation, but trying to look as though we were quite at home in such an establishment. When the food came, we gave ourselves up to the pleasure of just looking at it for a minute before spoiling its perfection with rude assault by knife and fork.

A beautiful lamb chop, two sausages, a succulent looking kidney split open to look like a flower, two rashers of bacon, a grilled tomato, and perfectly cooked fresh dry chips. A little piece of watercress adorned the picture. It was magnificent.

We'd often eaten a chop at home, we'd also had sausages, and bacon, but never all at once. And we'd never tasted grilled kidney or tomato before. The kidney was delicious, but the tomato seemed wet and squashy compared with the firm flesh of a fresh one and we left ours. I could hardly finish this huge meal, in spite of my ready appetite, and wished I could have spied a bottle of sauce to help the last mouthfuls down, but there was no sauce to be seen on any of those beautifully laid tables, or on the waiter's side table either.

I was thankful we hadn't marred the bliss of this triumph over the snooty waiter by asking for sauce, because next day at the office when they all wanted to hear every detail of the feast, one of the accountants, whose gentlemanly style had always impressed me, shook his head smilingly when I mentioned sauce and said it would have been criminal to have spoilt such perfectly cooked food with bottled sauce. Such condiments killed real flavour, he said, and were only used to disguise poor taste. Besides, they ruined the palate. What a lot there was to learn about eating expensive food, I thought! We had never had any carry-on like this with our egg and chips in Reids. He was also sad that we hadn't eaten the grilled tomato. 'The best part', he declared, 'succulent and juicy and a perfect complement to the meat'.

Thanks to my belief in this colleague's judgement, I persevered with grilled tomatoes, and learned to enjoy their succulence with the same enthusiasm once reserved for tomato sauce. Incidentally I was glad when I outgrew my need for tomato sauce, because one of Tommy's pals always drowned his chips in my sauce when he came to our house. It was a constant irritation to see his extravagance when I had bought it specially for my own use, for nobody else in our house liked it. Now he would just have to eat the HP sauce the others liked, or go without. If only I could stop him devouring my brown bread, leaving me none for the morning, I might quite like him again.

One day in the office the little gentlemanly accountant who'd unconsciously taught me to develop a discriminating palate, asked my great office chum Rita and myself to help him with some work which was urgently required by the director. It made a nice change for us from the eternal tenders and letters we had to type, and as we folded and added, we chatted, which wasn't normally possible over the clatter of our machines. Donald Thrush, the little chap, told us with a sigh that he had hoped to go to a hockey club meeting that evening but he was afraid he wouldn't be able to get along because there were so many black currants in his garden he *must* lend a hand to his sister and pull them, or they'd go to waste. We had always thought hockey was a girl's game, but not the way those posh West End men played it, as we discovered when we went to a match one Saturday afternoon. We knew he lived in a large house somewhere in the Pollokshields area, territory as far removed socially from Springburn as the University was from a Board school. 'Fancy complaining about having to pick black currants from your very own garden', I said enviously. 'We all love black currant jam, and we have to buy our berries.' Donald looked at me thoughtfully, 'Well, if you and Rita would like to come out tonight and pick the fruit, you can keep it, and I'll get to my hockey club meeting. Besides, it will be company for my sister, and it will be nice to know the fruit will be used.'

So after our tea, Rita and I took the tramcar away out to Pollokshields, counting the fares well spent for a keek at one of the posh houses, and knowing there would also be free fruit for our mothers to turn into delicious black currant jam. It was a large grey stone house, with wide front steps, and pillars either side of a beautifully polished mahogany door, but we were taken round the side entrance, straight into the garden and shown the fruit bushes, for Donald was in a hurry to be off to his meeting. The garden seemed huge to our eyes, and we were directed to the part known as 'the kitchen garden' where the fruit and vegetables were grown. The part nearer the house was laid out in beautiful flower beds, and all down the border were what I described to my mother later as big bushes, but which I later learned were called shrubs. Donald's sister, a rather shy plump little roly-poly of a lady, told us we could pick all the berries we could manage, for she had taken all that they needed for their own use. But we weren't to work too hard and we must stop when we were tired. She gave us each a large basket and left us. We giggled to each other. 'Fancy anybody getting tired picking black currants for nothing!', and we set to with a will and steadily stripped the bushes. Robyna, the sister, had to come out to rescue us when it was dark, astounded that we had worked so late. Little did she know that we were so elated with this bounty, we'd have worked through the darkness if she had offered to supply us with torches. When the fruit was weighed, I had gathered just on 6½ pounds, and Rita just over 5.

When we came indoors, I caught my breath at the richness of the furnishings. Dark velvet curtains hung to the floor of the large drawing room window, a matching velvet suite glowed against a pale green carpet. *Pale green!* For a carpet! I had never seen a fitted carpet before, and wondered how she could possibly keep it clean, or how she dared to let dirty shoes walk on it. A roaster of a fire blazed in the fireplace, and was reflected in beautiful little porcelain figures on the mantelpiece, and, sitting on the tiled hearth was a bonnie green and white china plate piled high with buttered toast. And it *was buttered* toast. The very words had a sort of magic for me, ever since I'd read H. G. Wells, *The History of Mr Polly,* when the hero asks his young love what they will have for tea, and she replies, in her comical accent 'Buttud Toas'.' At home, we all enjoyed toast, but would have considered it a wicked extravagance to have spread it with butter, for everybody knew how much fat the hot toast soaked up, and we and all the folk we visited used margarine. We thought it was just as good. Who could tell the difference on toast? Now, when my teeth met hot toast dripping with real butter, I knew why Mr Polly's love had thought buttud toas' a special treat. It was *scrumptious!* It was even better than cake. Especially on a cold night, after hours of berry-picking out of doors. And we drank tea out of matching pale green and white china cups, and Robyna told us it was China tea, which seemed scented to my palate, as though she'd washed the cups in scented soap and not rinsed them properly, but remembering my ignorance on the subject of grilled tomato I held my tongue, and told myself it was delicious and far before your ordinary Co-operative Ceylon tea.

We were just finishing our tea when Donald came in from

his meeting, and because our baskets were so heavy, he insisted on running us back to the tram-stop. He had a car! No wonder he knew all about grilled tomatoes, and drank China tea out of china cups. He must be rolling in money. We wondered why he could be bothered coming in to our office, but we were very glad that he liked working, or we'd never have been privileged to share this rich life for one evening.

My mother was entranced with my descriptions, but shook her head at such an impractical item as a pale green carpet. 'Aye, she'll have her hands full keeping *that* clean', she flatly declared. 'I widnae exchange my good linoleum and my rugs for all the pale green carpets in Templetons.' Templetons, in my mother's vocabulary, was synonymous with carpets. When Hoeys received their new stock, she drooled over the window display for hours. I could see she was horrified and yet fascinated by the idea of a pale green carpet, and wouldn't rest until she had seen something in Hoeys' window which would give her a true estimate of the nightmare of keeping it clean.

But she was overjoyed by the beautiful black currants I'd picked. 'Lovely big dry berries', she gloated, 'not a squashed one among them. They'll make lovely jam, and be nae bother to set.' My mother made the best black currant jam in our tenement, and a pot of her famous preserve was greatly prized by any neighbour lucky enough to receive one. Pieces on jam were still greatly favoured by all of us, from the youngest to the oldest, for diets were unheard of and we cheerfully filled up with bread, and the home-made jam was a great source of sweetness and vitamins. My mother made the most of all the fruits in season, and although we seldom had money for luxuries, we always had a shelf filled with home-made jams and jellies. The very idea of having only one pot of bought jam in the house would have filled us with dismay, for as long as you had plenty of preserves in the press, you needn't be found wanting when the unexpected visitor came to your door.

My mother was always interested in our stories from our places of work, and she followed all the sporting activities and romances of our workmates as though it were a long-running serial. She particularly enjoyed hearing all about my posh fellow-typists, but was dismayed at the number of times I had to fork out a shilling or two shillings, depending on the closeness of the working relationship, for the weddings of the girls who left to be married. Fortunately I didn't know any of these older girls well enough to feel obliged to give a personal present, but I was expected to contribute to the office tribute. The sight of a girl entering our typing room, a long stiff sheet and a pen at the ready, sent me into frantic calculations about my spare money. 'Another bob off my clothing account', I'd groan to myself, as I smilingly wrote down my name and 'one shilling' against it. But we had the fun and excitement of the 'show of presents' at the house of the bride-to-be's parents. We usually went in a body, straight from the office, in our best Sunday clothes, and after gazing enviously at the array of gifts all laid out like a shop counter in the sitting room, we were regaled with a splendid tea. All the mothers tried to outdo one another in hospitality, and we feasted ourselves right royally in exchange for our modest contributions to the wedding gifts.

One mother, far from feeling ruined by all the expense of her daughter's wedding, had actually been so infected by the sight of the new furnishings for the bride's home, that she had completely re-furnished her own. We'd never heard of such a thing. By the time families were old enough to be married in Springburn, parents felt their time on this earth was far too short to have wasted good money on replacing their worn-out furniture. But this well-lined lady clearly felt she was entitled to just the same new setting as her daughter. After looking at the presents, we were shown into a room so splendidly decorated in pale colours that we were frightened to sit down, much less gorge ourselves on tea and sandwiches and cakes. Rita and I, balancing our cups on our knees, gazed fearfully at one another. We were the youngest, and we were very overawed. The mother encouraged us each to take a fragile cream meringue, but just as we laid the cakes on our plates on our knees, somebody squeezed past us, the plates slithered down our sloping legs, and the meringues burst open with a horrifying splashing of inches of rich cream all over the brand new carpet. We daren't look at one another as we fell to our knees and started to scrape the mess up. Hot cloths were brought, knives came into play, while tears of mortification sprang to our eyes.

We were only saved from howling with shame when the sister of the bride was hurriedly asked to oblige with a song to cover the embarrassing situation, and sent us into suppressed hysterics by screaming out 'One fine day' so stridently that the very ornaments on top of the piano rattled.

What with the meringues and the need to keep a straight face through that aria, we were shaking wrecks when we emerged into the street. We both decided that there was a lot to be said for a nice shabby house, where you could be at your ease, and that it was simply asking for trouble to serve sticky food in a room so perfect that you became a bundle of nerves and were practically hypnotized into dropping things.

The fathers usually kept well out of sight during the shows of presents, which didn't surprise me at all, for Springburn husbands would have been seen dead before attending such feminine affairs. However, at one show, held in a very grand house which seemed a fitting background for the bride-to-be whose rich clothes we all envied, her father, loud and gross, was present.

As we typists sat in a circle, sipping our tea, and nibbling at dainty sandwiches, he went round inspecting us all, as though judging a beauty contest, and said, 'Now, I wonder who will be next to follow my Jeannette to the altar?'. Pausing briefly before a rather elderly, but very ladylike member of the typing pool he said, to my horror, 'Not you anyway'. I gasped, and choked over my sandwich. How could anyone be so destructive of an elderly spinster's serenity? Poor Miss Parkinson flushed and bent her head over her tea-plate, while I broke into a torrent of chatter to drown the embarrassment which threatened to choke me. This vulgarian's coarse insensitivity was proof positive, if ever I needed it, that money did not necessarily confer gentility on its possessor. No wonder my mother laid such stress on gentleness and put it far above mere money. And I agreed wholeheartedly with the little elderly typist when, on the tram going back to town, she said to me, 'How could such a sweet girl have such a pig for a father?' We weren't really supposed to call people pigs, but I had to admit to myself that it was the exact word on this occasion. We maybe had boozers in Springburn, but, as my mother said when I told her of the incident, 'They widnae hurt your feelings for the world'. Exactly.

It was a change to hear about Willie's work-mates for he worked with men in a machine shop, and he had a lively eye for their idiosyncrasies. The man we liked best was the one who took mince and tatties every single day of his life for his lunch. The works' canteen provided quite a wide choice of dishes, which we enjoyed hearing described, but this man told Willie that he had lived so long in digs where all he had was tatties and margarine, or tatties and Lorne sausage, that mince represented for him all that he could desire for his dinner. 'Aye', said my mother, pointedly looking at me, 'some folk's easy pleased. You widnae get him spending a fortune on a mixed grill'. She hadn't forgotten my extravagant nerve in dining so richly in that swell restaurant, although she herself dearly loved a visit to the La Scala.

4

What the Royal Restaurant was to me, the La Scala Cinema restaurant was to my mother. It was absolutely unique, and she adored it. This was a little restaurant laid out inside the cinema itself. Tables were ranged on a raised dais to the right of the stalls, which brought them a little below the level of the circle, so obstructed nobody's view, and the diners could enjoy the luxury of eating and watching the performance at the same time. Discreet lighting illuminated the food they ate, but didn't distract the main body of cinema-goers. It seemed to my mother a marvellous arrangement, and to the Glaswegians in general it combined the best in the way of their preferred entertainment – dining out and going to the pictures.

For any special treat, my mother chose the La Scala. She was vivacious and she was a lively red-head, so she wasn't short of escorts to provide such entertainment on birthdays or at Christmas, but she didn't go often enough for it to become an everyday thing. It was very special, and had for her the glamour that the Ritz might have for a Londoner, or Maxims for the Parisienne. I rather fancied the idea myself, but I didn't want to rob her of her triumph that this experience was unique to her, and only went once to celebrate when the BBC followed that first Who's Here appearance with a small part in their Radio Cartoon series which Robin Russell and Jack House were producing.

They had apparently regarded my Who's Here engagement, when I did the high-speed writing and the impersonations, as a sort of unofficial audition, and it wasn't too long afterwards that they asked me to come along for a small part in Radio Cartoon. The neighbours were very excited that wee Molly was going to be heard over the wireless, and they were all determined to listen, for this time they had plenty of notice. They had been very disappointed because the Who's Here programme had been a last-minute engagement and they were too busy getting the tea ready to keep listening when the news had finished, and so had missed me. This time, they would all be listening, to hear me put Springburn on the map. Mrs McFarlane down the stair didn't own a radio, having continually put off such an expensive purchase until she won the Irish sweep. However, this was different, and she sent up to the Co operative, and had the man deliver one and put in an electric point and the whole thing cost her eleven pounds, a vast sum for an elderly widow. A waste of money, she declared to all who would listen, for she hadn't even recognized my voice! And no wonder. I was playing a little boy, and I had exactly five words to say. 'Hullo daddy'. 'Kazoo'. 'Londonderry Air'. But I was acting with real radio actors, and although I didn't know it at the time, they were among the 'greats' of Scottish radio. There was Jimmy McKechnie, later to be recognized as one of the most accomplished broadcasters in the country and with whom I worked often in London in after years, Ian Sadier of the many voices, dear Meg Buchanan one of Scotland's finest actresses and destined to be my beloved antagonist in 'The McFlannels' where she was of course Sarah, lovely Grace McChlery later Mrs McCotton of the McFlannels, and splendid Jean Taylor Smith, a contemporary of Meg's, and a fine actress when she wasn't busily engaged in her career as a dentist.

I was handed a script, given no instruction of any kind beyond being told that I was playing a wee boy, so I just watched the others like a hawk. I noted where they stood, how they held their scripts, and hoped my heart beats wouldn't be heard by every listener in the land. I was far too shy to speak to anyone, and too terrified to ask questions. There were three lights, like little traffic lights, high up on the studio wall, and I wondered what they could be for. Radio was done 'live' in those days, and when it came near zero hour, the red flashed on, so I guessed this was a warning light. Then the green flashed, and it now made sense to me that when, during rehearsal, the director had said 'On a green', he meant that when the green light flashed we would speak. The last light was a white one, and it was ten years before I learned that this was the silent indication that the telephone was ringing for someone in the studio! Nobody told me, and I never asked.

When I came home, my mother said 'Don't tell onybody the next time you're oan the wireless. I was black affrontit. Fancy Mrs McFarlane gaun tae a' that expense for nothing. Naebody knew who you were.' The office were similarly disenchanted. After my solo performance in Who's Here, they imagined I would be playing the lead. After all, I'd been on once – surely the BBC knew by this time I could do it! Little did they or I know that progress would normally go at a snail's pace, with a sentence more here, a little scene added there, as producers learned to trust the performer's reliability to perform coolly under the tension of live broadcasting.

None of us outside the BBC took into consideration the fact that my five little words had gone out to the widest audience any of us could have envisaged. It just all seemed disappointingly feeble, measured against the strong comedy parts I played for the Pantheon, and the solo performances I was also giving now on the concert platform. Temperance Associations, church concerts, Guides, all provided audiences eager to be entertained by my elocution pieces, and I could have been out doing concerts every night in the week if I had said 'yes' to all of them. I even took part in cabaret at some of the dances, but I detested this, because I felt nobody really wanted to listen. They liked watching a line of chorus girls, because they could sip their drinks and chat without concentrating, but who wanted to listen to an elocution piece in the middle of an evening's dancing?

The first time the Pantheon provided a cabaret for a big affair at the Central Hotel in Glasgow was when I was in the dancing chorus and, having danced that particular routine in the musical for a whole week, not to mention having rehearsed it for over three months, we were reasonably certain we could provide a lively, smart dancing programme. But pride went before a fall. We had never danced on a polished floor before. And, to our utter shame and confusion, we went down one after another like ninepins! The audience was in an uproar by

406

the end of the first chorus, and we were in a tangled heap on the floor. When we got to our feet, we were so nervous of the floor surface, we daren't let ourselves go and kept our legs as stiff as pokers, and made our exit to tepid applause. We suffered less from the bruises to our legs than the hurt to our conceit. *How* could we have been such idiots as not to have foreseen what a polished floor would do to our tap shoes! We were very ashamed, and felt we could never hold our heads up again.

Another Pantheon dancing chorus was provided for a special occasion at the Odeon cinema. We came on in the interval, clad in heavy sequin trousers, bare midriffs, and little chiffon tops, as houris from the harem. As we danced, the weight of the sequins pulled my trousers lower and lower, and during the dance I glanced down and to my horror saw the elastic top of my bloomers clamped firmly about two inches above the trouser band, adorning what was supposed to be my bare midriff. I prayed that the strong pink light would disguise my shame from the audience, but a growing ripple of laughter confirmed my worst fears that my bloomers had caught every eye, and I finished the dance with jaw muscles which ached from trying to disguise the tears of mortification behind a wide professional smile. Oh there were terrible hazards in appearing before the public, and I was learning new ones every day. The other girls were mad that I had ruined the seductive effect of the dance with my schoolgirl underwear, and the memory of this incident gave true sincerity to their congratulations when I was promoted out of their ranks to become the company soubrette.

Somebody who wore school bloomers with harem trousers was clearly not going to be missed too much. Who would have thought it would have been necessary to explain to any self-respecting chorus girl the sort of undies to be worn in a harem? It just showed them, you couldn't be too careful. In short, they were delighted to be rid of me.

The part which lifted me out of the chorus was that of Susan in 'Desert Song', playing opposite Eddie Fraser in the part of Benny. Eddie was later to be head of Light Entertainment at the BBC, but even in the Pantheon he seemed frighteningly professional to me. He had done a lot of musical comedy, and had a name in Glasgow as an outstandingly good light comedian. I was very shy of him at first, for I had done no solo dancing since I was at school, but he was enthusiastic that I had the makings of a good 'hoofer', and we rehearsed every spare second we could get away from the 'book' rehearsals. This was a very exciting production, for the Pantheon had, with great imagination and daring, decided that as we were now all regarded as practically of professional status by the Glasgow public, we would engage a real full-time actor as the Red Shadow, and we would go for the one who had created the role many years before, Harry Welchman.

It didn't mean so much to me as it did to some of the older members of the company, for I had never seen him, and when he did turn up a week before the show, I was dismayed to find that he seemed quite an old man. I was also perplexed to find he didn't seem all that sure of his words, for I had been told he had played the part for years and years all over the country and abroad. I was far too inexperienced to appreciate that a professional actor can get inside the skin of a performance very easily, if it is one he has established, and that the words themselves aren't important until the moves have been settled. And so it proved with the lovable and delightful Harry Welchman. He was delicately built, but his voice was still sweet and thrilling, and in his Red Shadow robes he looked romantic and handsome, and quite unlike the rather fragile old man who had walked into rehearsals. Watching from the wings one night during a performance, I was stunned to find he could sing romantically to the heroine and give us in the wings a saucy wink. Fancy being able to be so detached! Oh would I ever be other than in a fever of excitement or fear when I was on the stage? I doubted it. And would I ever learn to know what was the right thing to do on all occasions? Sadly and with some cause, I also doubted it. Because I had done a terrible thing, quite unwittingly. In one scene, where the Red Shadow's Riffs captured me and blindfolded me, I was carried, screaming, to his hide-out. While he sang one of the show's big numbers, the blindfold was removed from my eyes, and I had merely to register bewilderment at my surroundings and remain silent till the end of the song. When it came to the performance before the first-night audience, it seemed to me quite unnatural that a young girl would find herself in the unexpected presence of such a romantic figure as the Red Shadow and not register something, so I rolled my eyes flirtatiously, and puffed up the sleeves of my dress in feminine vanity, to demonstrate the fluffy female in Susan's skittish character. Never for a moment did I think an audience would look at me with any attention when Harry Welchman was singing. But they did. And my actions sent waves of amusement from stalls to gallery. I froze with horror, but it was too late. They were watching my every move. It was my elocution teacher's play all over again, when my comedy had spoilt the older girl's dialogue. I felt sick. Like the gentleman he was, Harry Welchman realized it was sheer inexperience which had led me to spoil his number. He told me with great gentleness, and after tactfully complimenting me first that I was the best Susan he'd ever played opposite, that it was absolutely essential *not* to move on the stage when the spotlight was supposed to be on someone else.

When I tried to explain that I hadn't realized the audience would bother to look at me when *he* was singing, he smiled sadly. 'An audience will always look at a pretty girl in preference to an old man'. I could have wept for my stupidity. But the lesson burned itself into my heart. And I can truthfully say that never since that occasion have I twitched so much as a muscle when any other character is speaking or singing.

I didn't tell my mother how badly I'd behaved, and she couldn't understand why I wasn't more pleased about the nice things the press had to say about my performance. 'By jings', she said, 'it wis worth a' thae weeks and weeks o' rehearsals. Fancy them takin' a' that notice o' you when Harry Welchman was on the same bill'. I gave a jump, for she was using practically my own words of the night before. 'Aye', she went on, 'I'm gled he's gettin' such praise for his Red Shadow. He must be gettin' on, but he's a real gentleman, and that aye tells.'

I gave a gulp. Would anybody ever say I was a lady? Would I ever achieve what Grannie and my mother desired for me above all else, to be really genteel? Or would it always be obvious that I was no such thing?

My mother's favourite word, in fact, tenderly spoken in

praise of someone whom she admired, was 'gentle'. 'She's that *gentle*', she would say, fixing me with an accusing eye, because we were both aware that that was the last word anyone would use to describe me. I was always puzzled that she found this quality so admirable, for she was no more gentle than I was, with her fiery red hair, and her tough independent spirit. Although she had a natural timidity in the face of authority, she was the opposite of gentle. She told us hilarious tales of her various jobs, in the sweetie factory where she ate herself sick in the first two days and then never touched another chocolate; in the pottery, where she painted exquisite designs on the china; in the machine shops where she and Lizzie, her partner in crime, seemed to spend half their time dodging the foreman and breaking all the rules. And although she herself had had innumerable jobs, she invariably reacted with emotion, as in the bible, 'Oh sharper than the serpent's tooth' was my ingratitude when I wanted to change my job. I suppose there was a difference. She changed jobs because she was 'laid off' and had to seek work elsewhere, but she had never handed in her notice to an employer in her life. Whereas, skipping nimbly up the business ladder, and remaining in each job only long enough to acquire more experience or skill, I had no qualms about announcing that I was leaving to find a better situation. I think she was terrified that I would walk in one day and announce that I was giving up my job in the big city office, and would live to regret such folly. She need have had no such fear. I was ecstatically happy. There were enough departments and opportunities to satisfy the most ambitious shorthand typist (we did not call ourselves secretaries then, until we truly reached that exalted post), and when I compared it with the strange little job which had occupied one trance-like month during one restless period, I hugged myself with delight that I had fallen on my feet.

That little job was a mistake in every way. Not that there was anything wrong with the company or with the people with whom I shared the office. They were kindness itself. The entire set-up was just wrong for me. For a start, instead of being in the centre of Glasgow, it was out in the country, near Bishopbriggs, territory which I associated with Sunday walks after church and not with earning my daily bread. My sense of propriety was further confounded by discovering that the little factory, in whose office I was to work, was in the middle of a field. Offices, I felt, to be real offices should not stand in green fields, they should be on concrete. Four other females shared the office, two who appeared to me very old indeed, and even the youngest member was about twenty years older than myself. The factory produced baby food, and my first task in the morning was to perch myself at a high desk, go through the births' columns in all the morning papers, type out on labels the names and addresses of newly blessed parents, and then tie up little bunches of heather with ribbons, which I finally enclosed in a box with a sample of our baby food, leaflets explaining its virtues, and a little card of congratulation, before transferring the box with its label to the post basket. White heather with a green ribbon was considered tasteful for baby girls, purple heather with red ribbon for baby boys.

The first morning, I had thought this little game with heather and ribbons was merely the prelude to more serious work, but to my dismay nobody all day rang a bell to summon me for notes. When I asked the older ladies what I ought to do, they sent me out for hot pies from the home bakery nearby. These were consumed with great gusto at 11 A.M. and we didn't even require to hide the teapot, for nobody bothered to enquire whether or not we had enough work to do. At three in the afternoon, I was sent out again for cream cakes. They were delighted to have a young pair of legs not unwilling to run messages for them. When I asked where the boss was, I was informed he was out of town on business, so I breathed a little more easily, and decided this lack of work was just because of his absence.

After the second day's pies, the older ladies looked a bit more closely at my small proportions and decided they were all too fat and would I show them some exercises. Thankful to have something to do, I bade them clear the middle of the office, and drilled them in bending and stretching and high kicking until they fell, panting against the desks, exhausted. So, each day afterwards, before their orgy of pies and cakes, they lined up in front of me and I led them in a knees-bend, knees-stretch, arm-flinging and toe-touching routine, ending up with them all lying on the floor doing imaginary bicycling. At the close of each session, they fell on the pies and cakes with a will, sure that they had earned them after all those exercises, and certain that they would not gain an inch.

It was all so different from any work I'd ever done that I felt I was living in a dream, and I was fretting because I wasn't earning my salary. One day, gazing out of the window, I was astounded to see a group of men rolling up turf in the specially green field next door. Each roll was laid aside like a carpet. 'What do they *do* with grass rolls?', I asked in great surprise, for I'd never thought of grass being transportable. 'Oh it's sold for bowling greens', was the reply. And so it was. No wonder my mother described bowling greens as 'like a velvet carpet', for that was exactly how they were bought. This was the most interesting discovery I'd made since working in this strange organization, and I longed to be able to cut a swathe myself, and to examine how it was possible to cut grass in ribbons like this, without it all breaking up into pieces. But it was a skilled job, and I wasn't allowed near the cutting spades. I was very impressed, though, that anybody could have thought up such a brilliant idea, and could make a profit out of selling God's green grass.

The boss returned before the end of the week, and at once I sat poised, ready to run the moment a bell rang. On Friday he dictated half a dozen letters, and the rest of the day was mine. On Saturday morning, he didn't come in at all, and after the heather ceremony and the pie buying, plus some token exercises, I had nothing to do. I ground my teeth in frustration. It was playing at work. I felt I was wasting away. Me, with a speed in shorthand of 300 words a minute, and secure in typing with my place among the top three in the country. It was ridiculous. And yet, they were all so nice.

I stuck it for an interminable three weeks, then without a word to my mother, marched in to my employer and handed in a week's notice. 'But why, Molly?', he asked me in some bewilderment. 'Aren't you happy with us?' His use of the word 'happy' made me gulp with embarrassment, at the thought that I might be hurting anyone's feelings. But I just *couldn't* let my talents wither away in this backwater. With my eyes on his polished shoes I said flatly, 'I haven't enough to do'. He shook his head in perplexity and said it was the strangest reason he'd ever heard for giving up a job. My eyes flew to his face, and I could see he was genuinely puzzled, so I forced myself to say that I was nervous that my speeds might vanish like fairy gold if they weren't used, and that it was a terrible waste of somebody like me to employ me to sit tying up wee bunches of heather. A smile crept round his lips, 'Yes, I can see you wouldn't want anything wasted', he said. With a sigh, he added 'Of course you do need a bigger office, I can quite see that. But it's a pity, all the same. It was nice to see a bit of young life about the place.' He accepted my notice and at the end of the week we bade each other farewell. I shook hands with all the rest of the staff, told them to keep on with the exercises, and sped home on wings of joy, filled with relief that it was all over. I could begin to live again.

After this experience, it was no wonder I loved my large busy office with passionate zeal. I soon became known as the Flying Scotswoman, because when any of the girls fell ill, in any department in the building, and there were urgent left-over notes in their books requiring transcription, these were given to me for deciphering and typing. I thoroughly enjoyed my visits to unfamiliar strange departments, and soon got to know everyone in the building. I wasn't yet eighteen, which was the earliest I was allowed to sit my shorthand teacher's examination, and I gloried in the challenge to achieve a correct transcription of notes which hadn't always stuck strictly to the rules. This was part of our study at college anyway, for it was necessary not only to know the correct use of the rules, but also the incorrect use so that one could teach properly, and diagnose where a pupil was failing to understand the logical progress of the system. What with the college training and the extra experience gained through reading other girls' notes in the office, I grew to anticipate every possible deviation of outline a careless writer could commit. The worst shorthand was an open book to me, and years later I astounded the caretaker at Ayot St Lawrence by being able to read George Bernard Shaw's diaries, written in his own individual style of shorthand.

In my previous jobs in little offices, I had had to look after my own typewriter, and used to spend every spare moment cleaning it, brushing the keys with specially provided tools, and extracting stubborn ink accumulation from e's and p's and o's with a nice smelly putty ball which was pressed into each key and drew out the blob like a blackhead. I dropped oil into the right holes, used a special spirit to clean the little rubber caps protecting the keyboard, and used a duster over the rest of the machine until it shone. I looked after it as lovingly as a boy with his first new bicycle. To my surprise, in the large office, they didn't trust us to do this, but they shrewdly valued the efficiency to be obtained from machines kept at full concert pitch, and so the representatives of a typewriter company appeared once a month and serviced all the machines in the building. I couldn't lose the habit of keeping my beloved typewriter in immaculate condition, and the rep constantly praised me for the cleanliness of my machine. He actually tuned it up to take my specially high speeds, rather like a racing car, just to please me. He would nod approvingly at the absence of eraser droppings from the oiled works. He would note the smoothness of the patten roller, unsullied by any tell-tale pattern which would have told him that a careless operator had not used the all-important protective backing sheet when working without carbons. In short, his arrival at my desk was the signal for a nice quiet interval for him, thanks to the immaculate condition of my machine. But, alas, all this loving attention to my typewriter was my undoing. For, when at the end of my service in that office I wanted to buy it second-hand, that ungrateful wretch of a rep told the firm that he couldn't in all honesty place a second-hand value on it, for it had been kept in such excellent condition that it was actually probably a better, smoother-running machine than when it had been sold, and would have to be charged at the full price! It was a bitter blow. I told myself that in future I would be more careful, and, like the Chinese, would not over-praise something of which I was fond. But I never did learn the ways of China. I could never hide my enthusiasms. And I found I preferred to go along with Shakespeare's Polonius, 'This above all, to thine own self be true'.

My life was falling into a most delightful pattern. The office provided non-stop opportunities for advancement, and at the same time the behaviour of my fellow-typists was teaching me genteel and refined ways, for I observed their every move and was determined to stamp out any sign of vulgarity in my own behaviour. But I was constantly amazed at the numerous ways which could give offence to those thin-skinned creatures. There was a terrible row one day because the director's secretary had come into our cloakroom and had apparently been nauseated by the sight of grubby soap bubbles drying inside the wash-hand basin instead of having been properly rinsed away. She questioned everyone until she had found out who the culprit was, and the word 'SLUT' was hissed across the typing room with such venom, that we all shook with fright. The protagonists didn't speak to one another for days, and I used gallons of clean water for weeks afterwards, to make sure I for one wouldn't sin in this way. I hadn't even known it *was* an awful thing to have done until that terrible afternoon.

Another newcomer drew gasps of horror when she dabbed at her perspiring under-arms with the towel we all had to use for drying faces and hands. The wordy battle over what was and was not good taste waged furiously, ending with 'It's easily seen you have had *no* upbringing.' If I had given the matter any thought at all, I just might have brought myself to a fine sense of outrage over drawing a perspiration-stained towel over my face, but, coming from a tenement where five of us shared a towel until it was considered fit for the washing-tub, I wasn't so easily moved to shouts of horror over such a trifle. I'd have to be careful though. Who knew what terrible thing I was capable of, which would cancel out in a minute my newly acquired acceptance by those delicate creatures?

From two sisters in the office, I learned that middle-class, sophisticated mockery could be far more effective than callow jeering in taking somebody down a peg. The younger one had once had the conceit to enter a beauty competition, and the family had found out. She had lost, but instead of the sympathy or laughter she would have met in Springburn, this 'good' family called her 'Our Beauty' ever afterwards. And when anybody asked why they used this expression, the whole story was told all over again. She was never allowed to forget her vanity. Not as long as she lived. I decided such polite sarcasm was far more deadly than our rough and ready reactions, and that Springburn could maybe even teach those refined ladies a thing or two about letting sleeping dogs lie. For although I was now speaking with greater care than most of my Springburn friends, none of them bothered to remind me any more that I had swallowed a dictionary. And at least one mother decided that the road to success might be achieved through shorthand and asked me if I would teach her daughter. I was elated. We fixed a sum of half-a-crown an hour, and I walked down Parliamentary Road on air. This was far better than class teaching. There was something special about private coaching, and I would pour all my knowledge into this girl who had come to me unsought. She proved an apt pupil, and when she had gained her essential speed certificates, I further gladdened her widowed mother's heart by finding a job for her in my own splendid office. They took her on my recommendation, for I knew she was good, and she never looked back and stayed with the firm until she married. And I derived a wonderful bonus from this friendship. Jeanie's mother proved to be a marvellous dressmaker, and turned all my bargain remnants into stunning outfits. We plotted and planned together to transform odd pieces of material into works of art, and when customers disappeared during the various Glasgow depressions, I somehow contrived to pick up little pieces of material to keep her busy, and the few shillings which changed hands kept her afloat. She seemed to enjoy my enthusiastic co-operation, and my appreciation of her skills, and one day, when funds were very low and I had insisted on giving her an extra shilling on her bill, she said to me, with tears in her eyes, that if ever she left her tenement and went as a 'living-in' housekeeper to remove the worry of the weekly rental, I would have first chance to buy her beautiful mahogany sideboard. She had been much amused that anyone so young as I should appreciate its beauty, but I wasn't my mother's daughter for nothing. My mother had taught me to appreciate the quality of fine wood and expert workmanship, and although I hadn't known the sideboard was a relic of richer days and a family heirloom, I was aware of its beauty.

True to her promise, she broke the news to me one night when I went up to have a dress fitted, that she was leaving Springburn, and did I want to buy the sideboard? I had to ask my mother if she would find space for it until I married and had a house of my own, but I had no doubts in my mind that I would treasure this fine piece of furniture if only it could be mine. When I went back and said yes, I would have it, this dear little dressmaker told me that both the doctor and the minister, the only two professional men who ever entered a working class tenement, had asked if they could buy it. This exciting news set the seal on my good taste! 'What did you say?', I asked her curiously, for I couldn't imagine myself saying no to such exalted characters. 'I said Molly Weir was getting it, because she was the only one who had ever given me a helping hand and a word of encouragement when I needed it.' I gasped. 'Och but I didn't!' I protested. 'You paid for Jeanie's lessons, and look at all the lovely clothes you made for me at such modest charges'. 'I know what you did', she said quietly, 'and I'm glad your mother is going to keep the sideboard until you need it for yourself. I like to think of it being in your house.' I had often wondered what the bible saying meant, 'Cast thy bread upon the waters, and it shall return to thee after many days'. Now I knew. I have the sideboard still, and every time I polish it I think of my fine little widowed dressmaker, her industrious serious little daughter, and of days when half-a-crown meant so much to all of us.

5

Now that I had passed my teacher's examination for shorthand, I had a glorious amount of free time for other activities. I decided I'd take some cookery classes, for although I had acquired my cookery badge in the Guides so easily, because of Grannie's good teaching in the kitchen, I felt there were a lot of refinements I could profitably achieve. The classes were great fun, and as I provided the ingredients from home I was allowed to bring the finished results back with me at the end of the evening. My brother Willie and his pals soon decided that their Friday outings would end up in Weir's house, and when I arrived home from my class I would find them sitting up licking their lips, ready and eager to sample the results of my cooking experiments.

I was highly flattered by their appreciation of my apple pies, and sausage rolls, soups and cakes. But my mother grew increasingly annoyed when, if she happened to be a little late in getting home, both brothers would say, 'Och, let Molly make the tea.' There were some dishes she made superbly, but, truth to tell, she wasn't really a dedicated cook, whereas I had inherited Grannie's interest in this art. They say it often skips a generation, and the daughter of a splendid cook has little interest because the competition is too close, but in the granddaughter the enthusiasm surges up again. So it proved in our family.

Anyway, at this time my mother had the fanciful notion of trying her hand at golf. Some man in the works had offered to teach her, and as she had always enjoyed a round of putting, she thought this a great idea. One round of golf with this workmate convinced her that this was her sport, and the very next week she acquired a set of clubs at the Barrows. She had no idea of numbers of irons or the finer points to study when buying such things. The man at the stall kept her right, and she was well pleased with her natty bag and few clubs, which she purchased for a pound. She can have had little competition, I feel, from other tenement females for such equipment. When I asked her, with some amusement, if it was difficult to play golf, for I simply couldn't imagine her playing the game so glamorized by Bobby Jones, she said in genuine surprise, 'Whit's difficult aboot it? It's juist the same as putting, only you hit the ba' faurder.'

I joined the YWCA for the sake of its verse-speaking classes, and I went to the University for German, and for drama classes under Parry Gunn. Although I was acting for the Pantheon and reciting at concerts, I wanted time to study drama in a detailed way, and to analyze the whys and wherefores, and Parry Gunn's classes were a revelation. I learned the difference between conveying distant memory and recent memory, and how to express by the tilt of my head and the stillness of my body that a noise had disturbed concentration. I was taught how to convey by my use of body muscles, a feeling of weight and strain in picking up a heavy suitcase or parcel. I was encouraged to observe and utilize characteristics in others to create a rounded personality, and to use every experience in my own life, good or bad, to help me to be a better actress.

I absolutely adored those classes, and they were a marvellous light relief after the concentrated work in the German class. But German, I found, was amazingly akin to broad Scots as far as pronunciation went, and the reading of it much simpler for me than French. I didn't acquire an impressive vocabulary, but I did achieve a good accent which, in later years, brought quite a few compliments when I travelled abroad and which enabled me too, to my surprise, to chat in German to Lilli Palmer's mother when she preferred her own language on the 'phone.

The office friend who had encouraged me to join the Pantheon had a beautiful contralto voice, and was a member of the Orpheus choir, and we used to have long talks about the speaker's art and the singer's skills. She knew how frightened I was of solo singing, although I loved all singing, and now that I had been roped into the Pantheon musical shows as soubrette I had to face the nightmare of solo stage numbers in real theatres. So she took me along to her singing teacher Ian MacPherson, a noted Scottish baritone, and I enrolled with him for a winter's work, and had lessons one night a week, which was all I could afford. Thanks to all my elocution coaching, he was delighted with my diction, and declared that in his opinion all singers could profitably study elocution, and all speakers study singing. In later years, I found that all American drama students followed this practice, so Mr MacPherson was ahead of his time.

He knew I had no aspirations to the Orpheus choir or anything so musically exalted, but that I merely wanted to make the most of what I had in the way of a voice. Soon I was warbling to him, 'Wild strawberries', and 'Hey ho, come to the Fair', and feeling exceedingly hilarious inside as I aped all the gestures of a real soprano.

Between whiles, I took another class for dancing lessons, but this again was sheer fun, just to keep me up to the minute with tap steps, and so that I would be upsides with my male partner in the next musical for the Pantheon. This turned out to be 'The Belle of New York', and, backed by the confidence the singing lessons had given me, I sang out the numbers like a lintie and enjoyed it from beginning to end. Jack Laurie was my co-comic, and I was flattered beyond words when he told me he would leave the precision dancing to me and he would just go through the motions, as I was so expert! By jove, all those lessons had paid off. With Eddie Fraser, I was the pupil, with Jack the teacher, and with both their humble slave, for they had much to teach me in the way of timing laughs and 'business'. My dear ma-in-law-to-be always declared my partner and I were 'just as good as Fred Astaire and Ginger Rogers', and while we didn't believe a word of it, for we had enough sense to know that amateurs always think they are up to professional standard, it was nice all the same to hear such encouraging words.

I hadn't heard from the BBC for ages, and then one day I had a letter from Robin Russell asking if I would come along after work the following night, as he was doing a recording of a series called 'The McFlannels', and he was considering me for the part of Mrs McLeather. When I arrived I found that Meg

Buchanan, (whom I had met on my very first broadcast for Robin that radio cartoon item where I had the five words), was in the studio. She greeted me coolly but kindly, and I discovered she was playing Mrs McFlannel, while the other lady whom I recognized from that first broadcast, Grace McChlery, was playing Mrs McCotton. I didn't know anybody else, but I was later to get to know them all intimately, after I met the brilliant writer and creator of the series, Helen Pryde, and she wrote for me the part which made me a radio name in Scotland, the gallus Ivy McTweed. But all that was to come. As all Scotland who heard the series will know, the characters were named after materials, prefaced with Mc. So we had McVelvet, as well as the others I've mentioned, and I thought these invented names a stroke of genius, quite apart from the hilarious comedy of the show itself. I wasn't greatly excited over Mrs McLeather, who was a fairly lugubrious character, but it was great to be in a studio again and working for the BBC.

This engagement was followed by a part in 'Wee McGreegor', again with Meg Buchanan as the mother, and almost immediately afterwards I was booked by the schools' department to play the part of a little boy. I was destined to play boys' voices for quite a long time after this, for my husky quality was considered just right, and I was quite a 'find' apparently, as such parts were fairly difficult to cast satisfactorily. Incidentally, one of the best little boy voices I ever heard on radio, on either side of the border, was that of Elsie Payne as Ian in 'The McFlannels'. Meg Buchanan and I used to be wide-eyed with admiration of Elsie, and shaking with laughter over the perfection of her maddening mimicry as the wee pest.

My 'steady' and I now had plenty to celebrate, but we weren't spending money too freely, for we were saving up for an engagement ring. I wasn't in any hurry to be married. Oh I knew the happiness of having someone in my life who could make my heart turn over, and for whom I seemed to make the sun shine, but I had no great desire to shut myself away in a wee house all by myself just yet. It had its attractions of course. I remember my mother sending me round to collect a package from a friend's house. This girl had been one of the big girls at school when I was in the baby class, but she lived round the corner from us and I knew her quite well by sight. It was the first time I'd visited a house where the lady was somebody I'd known as a schoolgirl, and I was very curious to see what it was like. It was a bitterly cold winter day, and I was instantly struck by the warmth and the quietness of her kitchen. A coal fire glowed brightly from the shining kitchen range, her little boy played quietly with some drawing paper and crayons at the table, and Pansy was washing out some things at the sink. The picture etched itself on my retina. It was a scene of complete domestic cosiness, and yet I was aware of a sense of loneliness. It seemed so cut off from the bustle and excitement of everyday living. I gazed at Pansy with some curiosity for signs that this was what was meant by being 'married and living happily ever after'. Yes, I had to admit it. She seemed quietly content, and hardly aware of what she must surely be missing. When I saw her eyes when she looked at the little boy, I knew this was the source of her greatest joy. But oh! how soon it seemed to me that she had retreated from the stir and competition of the world outside. It was beautiful in a way. But it was not for me. Not yet.

But getting engaged was something else again. For months, our favourite pastime when we were out walking, or coming from rehearsals or classes, was poring over the ring trays in the jewellers. My mother used to say, observing the stir round such windows, 'Isn't it a funny thing, hooever poor folk are, they aye like looking at jewellery.' It was true at any time, but especially exciting when one was actually contemplating a purchase. I went through agonies of indecision as to what sort of ring I would have. The number of diamonds all carried their own special meaning. Five denoted 'Will you be my wife', one word for each diamond. Three meant 'I love you'. A solitaire uttered the dramatic 'Mine', and the old fashioned REGARD was depicted by a ruby, an emerald, a garnet, amethyst, ruby and diamond. A cluster ominously reminded the fiancé she was possibly only one of a crowd! Not for me that one. The solitaire was my true choice, and I just hoped there would be enough money, without going mad, to get one of respectable size. When the final weeks came round, we haunted the Argyle Arcade, running from one shop to the next, to see which gave the best value, for all Glasgow knows that the Arcade was like Aladdin's cave with expensive jewellers' shops, and the choice was wide. We eventually settled on the shop of our choice, and the ring of our choice, and, with beating hearts, walked in one Saturday afternoon and asked to see their diamond engagement rings. We knew exactly the one we wanted, for we had studied it in the window for weeks, but I wasn't going to miss this glorious opportunity of trying on an assortment of classy diamond rings. After all, it was the one and only time we'd be in the market for diamonds and I was determined to make the most of it. I had a half-hour's pure fantasy, slipping diamond rings of every style and degree of magnificence on to my engagement finger, holding my hand up to the light, and studying the effect with affected seriousness. The salesman seemed to be stifling a smile, and I had a feeling he knew exactly what I was up to. At last we asked for the solitaire tray in the window. He brought it in. I went very still. There was no excited playing at buying now. Suppose I didn't like it on my finger after all? I'd maybe have to buy one of those I'd already tried on, and I hadn't even properly noticed whether or not they suited my hand. I'd have to buy this most important jewel in a hurry. I held my breath as the salesman extracted my ring from the tray and slipped it over my knuckle. It was *gorgeous*. It was *perfect*. Well, it was maybe a wee bit on the loose side, but that could easily be adjusted, he assured us. Ah, but I could wear it over the week-end if I liked, because it wouldn't go to the workshop until Monday. If I liked! Of course I liked! I could hardly bear to have him take it off to get the number and all the other details.

My fiancé was far more easily pleased when it came to buying his gold signet ring. I was amazed at how easily a man could forgo the fun of trying on everything in the shop. He even left his ring to have his initials and the date engraved, instead of wearing it for the week-end, like me.

I danced up Buchanan Street on air, terrified to take off my glove in case the ring would come off with it, since it was just that shade too large for my finger. But when we reached the Ca'doro and ordered our 2/3d. high tea in celebration of this milestone in our lives, I flashed the ring all round the tearoom, as I gesticulated and acted the whole purchase all over again while we waited for our fish and chips.

The Scottish National Players were doing a play at the Lyric and my friend Meg Buchanan was in it. The only seats we could get at the last minute were in the sixpenny gallery. We were delighted with our bargain seats, for we were by this time a trifle scared with our extravagance that day, and sixpenny seats were more than welcome. And when I held up my ring in the rays of the beaming light which shone down on to the stage, it glittered far more magnificently than it would have done down there in the dull stalls.

We walked home afterwards and my fiancé came in for supper. My mother, always a reliable and shrewd assessor of values, was warm-hearted and satisfyingly enthusiastic over the beauty of my ring. It had been a marvellous day.

It isn't my intention in this book to delve too deeply into the strong personal happiness I've known with my 'steady' down the years. Incidentally, my mother always described him as 'As steady as the rock of Gibraltar', and in her and in my eyes he truly deserved her favourite description, 'gentle'. I always remember reading in Winston Churchill's autobiography, 'We married and lived happily ever afterwards'. I thought that was a marvellous and economic sentence to use, to describe the happiness of a lifetime. He said not a word more, implying that the rest was their own private concern. So it is with us. I am the extrovert. My husband the quiet one. In deference to his feelings, and because this book pursues the course followed from Springburn to the bright lights in search of a career, I am confident the reader will understand why I choose simply to borrow the words of the great man, and echo his telling phrase with joyous sincerity, 'We married and lived happily ever afterwards.'

I'm telling you this now, so that you won't be disappointed in finding no minute details of wedding bells, orange blossom, and the rest!

Even if I hadn't been guided in my feelings about such private matters by the great Churchill, I would have been influenced by a holiday in Girvan after Grannie died when some neighbours took me with them for a fortnight, to bring the roses back to my cheeks. I had to share a bed with one of the daughters, who was in the throes of wedding plans, and full of romantic tales of her best beloved. At first I was thrilled to the marrow to be the confidante of her whispered secrets as soon as the light went out, but as night followed night and her enthusiasm showed no signs of flagging, right into the wee sma' 'oors, I had to seek refuge in snoring to nip the flow of words in the bud! I had had no idea love could be so tedious in all its wearisome details. That experience undoubtedly gave me a preference for the Churchillian way of dealing with romance.

I had almost forgotten that the Carroll Levis contest win also carried with it the promise of a stage show at some future date, when a letter arrived informing me that the Discovery Show would be going on at Glasgow Empire twice nightly, for a week, and as one of the Glasgow winners I would be added to the company's strength. I was going to be a 'turn' in Glasgow's biggest variety theatre! Excitement, fright, and stunned surprise that my made-up 'act' could be accepted in a professional theatre fought for supremacy. But everything now had a sort of inevitability, as though I were following a selected path and had no alternative but to do as I was told.

The first half of the bill was to be composed of established variety acts, and we Discoveries would occupy the entire second half of the programme. We were called to attend the theatre on the Sunday to go through the running order of the show, and when I arrived I found that the bill-boards were being pasted up, telling all Glasgow that we would be appearing that week. I noted with interest that there would be jugglers, a dancing act, Jimmy James with his drunk sketch, and a ventriloquist. Then, in huge letters, in flaming scarlet, came the words 'CARROLL LEVIS WITH HIS DISCOVERIES, INCLUDING GLASGOW'S OWN MOLLY WEIR'. There it was. Up on the bills. And for the first time, I was 'Glasgow's own'. Nerves crawled up and down my spine, and there was a taste in my mouth like metal polish at the mere thought of having to live up to that description. But what had happened to the first and third prize winners? Oh yes, their names were there too – thank goodness the Glasgow public wouldn't be coming just to see me.

Inside, there was the strangely familiar smell of all back-stage theatres. A sort of compound of heat and dust and greasepaint which grips an actor by the throat and is more potent than drink or the finest perfume. I drank it in, and found it so heady that I was off in a day-dream of bringing the house down with my performance and heading straight for Hollywood. I was brought down to earth by being asked to attend the 'band call' on the Monday morning, for I knew my boss would have a fit if I asked off work again. I assured Carroll Levis that I didn't need any music, and that for the closing music and the song 'Stardust', which the entire company was required to sing, I was word and note perfect and needed no rehearsing. He enquired when my lunch-hour was, and suggested I look in then, and I would get an idea of the final line-up, and where my dressing room would be. I was to share with one of the Discoveries who was doing the tour of the entire country with him and she would show me the ropes. Fancy! A real dressing room for just the two of us. Marvellous.

On the Monday when I reached the Empire at lunch-time, having run all the way from Argyle Street, the queue for tickets was right into the street. Discoveries were a great novelty, and of course for Glasgow there was the added attraction of three examples of their own talent being on the bill. This, I discovered later, happened in each town the Levis discoveries visited. The local prize-winners were added to the company's strength, and so whipped up local fervour, and made sure of good houses. A very shrewd arrangement, I had to admit. But at the time I thought it was the simple honouring of a promise made to us as prize-winners – I didn't see it as a business move at all.

The people in the queue paid not the slightest attention to me as I made my way round to the stage door. But I looked at them. They were my public. They were a true variety audience. They were used to real acts, for at that time the cream of the variety world visited Glasgow. Florence Desmond was their idea of an impersonator. Layton & Johnson had sung for them, Leslie Henson clowned for them. And the big bands filled their ears with music. How would they react to a bunch of amateurs?

Back-stage, a group clustered round the pianist, running over the words and the key for 'Stardust'. I was just in time. Levis, genial as ever, without a care in the world apparently, went through each entrance and exit with us, placed us for the final chorus of 'Stardust', and told us to sing out and smile radiantly when the moment came at the end of the performance. In the empty theatre you could hardly have heard our voices behind a car ticket, but nobody seemed worried, and I hadn't even time to see my dressing room, for my whole lunch-hour had been swallowed up and I had to run like the wind to get to my desk for 2 o'clock. I nipped into Fergusons in passing and snatched up two Bourbon biscuits, and that was my lunch.

At half-past-five I left the office, carrying my little case with my make-up box and my knitting. Thanks to my work with the Pantheon, I knew to store my grease-paints in the traditional cigar-box, for no self-respecting aspirant to the theatre would have been seen dead using anything else. I had a tin of Cremine, big enough to have removed the make-up of the entire cast, bought through a colleague who could get it wholesale, and which lasted me for about fifteen years. The larger the tin, the greater the economy, I was told, and in the following years when such pure fats were impossible to buy, many an actress rejoiced in my prudence as she enjoyed the smooth efficiency of that Cremine in removing her make-up. A box of powder, cotton wool, and talcum completed my equipment. Unlike the Pantheon, which was all chatter and running about backstage before a performance, the Empire was strangely muted. This was the normal working background for most of them. The musicians were tuning up their instruments. Two men chatted quietly outside a dressing room door. A woman came from wardrobe with a freshly-pressed dress over her arm. I seemed to be the only one who had any nerves about the evening ahead. The girl with whom I was sharing the dressing room was very blasé about the whole thing. She was sitting filing her nails and reading a paper when I arrived. Fancy being able to read a paper at such a moment! I spread my freshly ironed towel on the dressing table, and laid out my things. How professional it all looked. The row of greasepaints inside the cigar-box. (I hoped the girl realized I knew about such things.) The huge box of Cremine to the right. The powder box and talcum, with the cotton wool to the left. My brush and comb dead centre. One of the things I can't remember at all is what I wore. Nowadays it would be almost my first concern, but with my limited wardrobe I expect I just wore my best dress, and, secure in the knowledge that it *was* my best, never gave it another thought. I know my hair was clean and shining, for I washed it once a week, and I had done this as soon as I had reached home after the Sunday rehearsal. It was naturally curly, and bounced round my head in finger-pressed waves.

The other girl seemed in no hurry to apply her make-up, but I always liked to get dressed and made up first, and then have all the time left to do as I wished, so that if some unforeseen disaster struck everybody on the stage and I had to go on early, I would be ready to face the public.

The other girl, Jessica her name was, lifted an amused eyebrow as she watched me. She had been doing the show twice nightly since they had left the London area weeks ago and regarded the whole thing as a slightly boring job of work. Boring! 'Calm down', she said, observing my excitement. 'You'll have nothing left for the performance.' She was aghast to discover I worked at an office desk from 9 till 5.30. She herself never rose much before noon, now that she was working in the theatre. 'Och but it's only for a week', I told her, 'and it's only a wee turn. Not nearly so hard as doing a whole musical after my work'. She stared at me. 'You do whole musicals as well as a day in the office?', she gasped. 'Good grief, you must be as strong as a horse, for all your small size.'

Oh I was glad I had brought my knitting with me, for it was going to be an endless wait till the second half of the programme came on. I was too nervous to watch any of the show from the wings for this first performance, and there would be another long wait between the houses and before our second appearance. So my knitting would keep me quiet and stop me running about demented. I have always found the therapy of the hands has a calming effect on me. Nowadays the house is full of fire-screens embroidered by me during the long hours and days of waiting in rehearsal rooms and dressing rooms. It's not only Satan who is kept at bay by busy hands. Nervous tensions are effectively chased off too. Well, up to a point anyway.

Jessica wrote letters while I knitted, and then all at once it was time for our part of the show. A call-boy knocked at the door. 'Curtain up – your call ladies'. The nation-wide winners went on first. Jessica, who had seemed such a friendly simple ordinary girl in the dressing room, was transformed into a striking and dramatic soprano, elegant in black evening dress, and with a voice like an angel. I watched her from the wings, and applauded enthusiastically with the audience at the end of her Grace Moore selection, and was equally delighted with her encore rendering of a Strauss waltz. She was good, oh she was better than good, she was terrific. In fact they were all terrific. They were the pick of the contests after all, and I trembled at the thought of being judged alongside such performers. Levis bounded on after each act, and described where each performer had been found, asked a few questions, and then galloped back beside us back-stage, checking that we were all where we should be.

And then I heard him say, 'And now, give a big hand to a wee lassie from Glasgow – your very own, Molly Weir'. And I found myself walking on shaking legs towards the mike. The theatre seemed enormous, with as many faces as on the terraces at Hampden Park! The applause took me right to the micro-phone, and only died down when Levis started his questions. I had been praying hard for the last five minutes. 'Oh God, let me be as good as it is possible for me to be. Not necessarily a genius, just let me do my best.' I had to stop praying now, and tell Levis and the audience that I was Molly Weir from Springburn, and that I was a typist in an office, and that I was going to do some impersonations for them. I stiffened my legs in a silent command to them to stop quivering, steadied my voice, and away I went into the 'act'. My mimicry was most cordially received, but as usual it was the Tommy Morgan one which brought the house down. After the experience of the Savoy demand for an encore, when I could give them none, I had written an extra little piece of typical Morgan patter, and so I was able to give this generous Empire audience a second good short punchy piece of characteristic Tommy Morgan comedy when they asked for it. My mother would be delighted to know I'd had an encore. No turn worth its salt got off without having to give an encore. I skipped happily off the stage to enthusiastic whistles from the gallery, solid applause from the other seats, and a beaming smile from Levis. My face was burning, but my heart bursting with joy. 'Thank you, God', I sang to myself in my head. 'Thank You for not letting me make a fool of myself out there. Oh Thank You!'

For the finale we all came on and sang the familiar theme song of the Levis show 'Stardust'. And then it was up to the dressing room and the long wait before we did it all over again for the second house. Some of the acts went out between the shows, indeed most of them did. But not me. I couldn't have left the atmosphere of the theatre. For me it would have destroyed all the magic of this never-to-be-forgotten evening when I had been accepted as a 'turn' with a professionally booked company in my native city.

A few nights later, Levis called us all together for a pep talk. He looked as stern as his merry face could manage and told us we weren't singing the words of Stardust enthusiastically or loudly enough, and it was vital not to leave it all to the orchestra. We must have verve, and sing and look as if we were enjoying ourselves. I was indignant. 'I was singing as hard as I could', I protested, my sense of injustice overcoming my shyness of him. He patted my arm reassuringly. 'Of course I didn't mean you, Molly', he said. 'You are always bursting with enthusiasm. It was some of the others.' The ones he stared at so pointedly now threw me derisive looks, and I heard one of them mutter 'For the peanuts we're being paid, why should we flog our guts out twice nightly'. I stared in absolute dismay. Fancy letting mere money dictate the integrity of the performance! In the Pantheon we got nothing, and it was far harder work. I was delighted to be paid anything at all – I would have done it for washers! In fact the only people who had paid me up till now had been the BBC, and I was quite surprised that they felt it necessary to pay me on top of letting me loose in their studios, and giving me the use of their microphones. £4 10s. for the Levis show seemed quite a lot of money to me. It was far more than I earned as a top typist, and I thought those other turns were very grasping, and it would serve them right if they came 'to want' some day. My mother and my grannie had taught me great respect for those who paid a steady wage, and although I later learned to discuss contracts and money with the best of them, I have never allowed my performance to be affected by the size of the fee. Whether a handshake or a cheque was handed out at the end of a show, I've always given of my best. Bebe Daniels was to say of me, much much later, 'That little Molly is always in there pitching!'

Before the end of that week in the Empire, I simmered down enough to be able to watch all the other acts in the first half from the wings. No wonder people say jugglers deserve better attention than they get from all those late-comers pushing their way to their seats. It is a very skilled act, and when one watches them so closely, admiration almost suffocates, for their concentration has to be absolute while at the same time they smile and skip and joke. Jimmy James was hilarious, and his lurching leering muddled delivery in complete contrast to the quiet man who stood so still while waiting for his cue in the wings.

But the act which I've never forgotten was the ventriloquist with his doll. Not the stage performance. That was good of course, but I felt my heart turn over when the curtain came down and the ventriloquist tossed the little man-doll on to a bench. There was something so life-like and so pathetic about that small still figure that I went over and took its hand to let it see it hadn't been entirely abandoned. I've been slightly frightened of those puppets ever since. And one of the films which scared the life out of me in later years was the story of the ventriloquist and his doll, where the doll absorbs all the man's life and takes control. It was brilliantly played by Michael Redgrave and was, for me, too much a reflection of my own feelings to be comfortable entertainment.

On the Saturday night, I had thought there would be a sort of 'end-of-term' feeling, with maybe even a wee party to celebrate the end of what had been, for me, a wonderfully exciting experience. Not a bit of it. The second-house curtain came down. Everybody disappeared to their dressing rooms. Jessica called 'Cheerio then', and vanished with her make-up box, and I was alone. It had been just another working week for them. That was my first experience of the sense of anti-climax which follows the excitement of sharing nerves, tension, happiness and success with a company which at once goes its own ways, and vanishes as unemotionally as though the whole thing had been a dream.

Maybe it was a dream.

But no, the posters were still there to reassure me it had actually happened. And my 'steady' and I walked home, and he wondered how I'd settle down again to 'auld claes and parritch'. I found I was starving, and somebody in the fish and chip shop recognized me and slapped me on the back for being such a 'rer wee turn', especially at good old Tommy Morgan. That, I think, was the first time I was genuinely recognized as a performer by someone who was a stranger to me. It was a pretty exciting moment.

6

Thanks to the Empire engagement, I was now becoming fairly well-known in Glasgow. Both the drama public and the variety audiences were mildly aware of my existence, and my 'turn' must have struck other critical ears as being reasonably good, for the next engagement I received for the Empire was from Jack Hylton. His was a legendary name to us in Glasgow. He was very much a star of the 'big band' era, and the sound of his opening music slowly swelling behind the closed curtain could send any variety audience wild with excitement. The applause would grow and grow, and every eye would be riveted on that curtain, which at last slowly parted and revealed his 'boys', ranged tier upon tier on stage, filling our eyes and ears with the magic of their presence.

And now this great man wanted me. At our first meeting on that Sunday morning (it always seemed to be Sundays for such work), he sent my heart skittering into my throat by saying to his musical director, 'Have you made sure she does that impression of Harry Gordon? That's the real kernel of her act.' 'I don't do Harry Gordon', I called out in alarm. Surely he hadn't engaged me in mistake for somebody else? It didn't dawn on me that possibly our Scots comics weren't such household words to him as they were to us. The ash dropped from his cigarette down his fine waistcoat, as he gazed at me enquiringly. 'I do Tommy Morgan', I gulped. 'Oh well, if that's the one you did for Levis, that's the one I want', he said. I was amazed. Fancy a famous band leader like him not knowing the difference between Aberdeen's own Harry Gordon, and Glasgow's own Tommy Morgan. I'd never have believed it if I hadn't heard it with my own ears. It was my first intimation that the great figures of stage and screen weren't gods after all.

433

My mother decided that this time she would risk coming to see me perform. She dearly loved a dance band, and she felt it was high time she saw for herself how I got on in front of such a big audience. Variety audiences were real audiences to her. She knew all about the big turns. Florrie Forde, Gertie Gitana, the Chocolate-Coloured Coon. She spoke of them as though she had been on intimate terms with them. She thought of herself as a shrewd critic, but she had adored them all and had nothing but praise for their beauty, their voices, their magic. She couldn't really believe anybody would judge me on that level, but she was curious to see how the rest of the audience would react. When I asked her afterwards if she had given me a good clap, she was aghast at the very idea. 'Of course I didnae', she said. 'Everybody would know I was your mother, and I would nae be seen clapping one of my ain family.'

My mother could never see us as anything but her own children, and couldn't hide her amazement that we could reach positions of importance in the world where we could be taken seriously by the adult population. When brother Tommy later became a mountaineer of International reputation, welcomed by the Alpine Society as a lecturer, not to mention the Geographical Society in London, and became a climbing colleague of Sir John Hunt on many hair-raising expeditions, he was seen in quite a different light by my mother. 'Back fae thae hills', she'd say in irritation. 'A sink-full of wet socks, and torn shirts', and then, warming to her theme, 'And his pick (her name for his ice-axe) and a' that rope falling oot the press every time I open the door'.

When she was sorting through his socks she would cluck despairingly, 'Look at that', she'd exclaim, 'all odd socks. A blue one a brown one a grey one and a heather mixture one – My Goad they must a' borrow each other's socks and they don't give a docken whether they're wearing the right ones or not'.

She had a strong sense of possession and was baffled by this sort of carelessness, and with his lack of regard for his other clothes. 'Pays a fortune for them', she'd tell me, 'and then catches his shirt in the middle of the back and pulls it over his head. And as for his tie – never loosens the knot – just pulls it wide enough to slip over his ears'.

Even when he was recognized as an authority as a writer when anything of particular reference to Scotland was required, she could never get over the fact that he didn't go out to do a daily job of work. It didn't feel right to her that he didn't don city clothes and catch a bus or a tram to a place of business, but merely wrote from a little room in the tenement house they shared. 'He goes into that room at the back o' nine o'clock', she'd say to me wonderingly, 'just as if he was going to his work, and he stops regular as clock-work for his morning coffee and his lunch'. 'But Mother', I'd say, laughingly, 'it is his work'. She'd give me a pitying look. 'Hoo can it be his work', she'd demand, 'when it's at hame, and naebody pays him a regular wage?'

The casual nature of his profession terrified her, and she could never believe he could earn enough by wee bits of scribbling to keep body and soul together. She was quite certain he would live 'to want' in his old age, and her not there to keep an eye on him.

Once when he was giving a lecture in Edinburgh to an audience of over 2,000 she was there, sitting in the front row, clearly baffled that all those people should have gathered to hear what he had to say, and had paid good money to look at his colour slides. He always used a long pointer to indicate the various interesting and focal spots of the climbs, and as the lecture was about to begin, she sensed at once from his frowning searching glance round the platform that he couldn't locate this vital prop. She was in an agony for him. He was her wee boy looking for his collar stud or his keys, notoriously careless as always in her eyes. All the audience were waiting. Suddenly her whisper went sibilantly round the auditorium, 'Tommy! It's in the corner behind you. At your back!' The audience rippled with laughter. Tommy turned – found it, picked it up, and the evening began. She sat back with a satisfied sigh. He might be the grand speaker, but it took her to keep him right.

She wasn't above teasing him either. She invariably infuriated him by pronouncing the Himalayas 'The Himullas', however much he corrected her. When a card arrived from him from India, she laughed as she described the pantomime of his packing to go off on that expedition. Then she added, 'I know fine Tommy gets mad at me saying the Himullas. Of coorse I know it's the Himalayas, but I *like* Himullas better'. I was astounded. I had always thought the mispronunciation accidental, but now I realized it was simply her way of asserting her independence. She wasn't going to conform just to please her own wee boy. Not she.

She hated it though when he was late in coming home at nights after climbing or lecturing to societies, for she felt his unworldly interests were no match for any possible thugs who might be lying in wait. She saw him an innocent abroad, and wasn't happy until he was safely home and the big outside door locked. This despite the fact that he travelled through Tibet and Morocco and in many wild territories where bandits were not unknown. 'I don't like it when he's oot so late', she'd confide in me. 'There's that many bad rascals hanging aboot, and oor Tommy would never see them, he's that busy thinkin' aboot his mountains and his birds'.

She was terribly proud that he had climbed with Sherpa Tensing, and delighted when they met again in Scotland, and she saw the Sherpa's 'lovely face and smile' in her very own kitchen. But lovely smile or not, she persisted in calling Tensing 'Tinsling'. She wasn't going to be overawed to the extent of giving the correct pronunciation!

But she showed no pride of any of us in public. She was much more likely to say of Tommy 'Fancy not waiting till I sewed that button on his shirt – I could see his semmit a' the time he was speaking up there on the platform,' and of me 'Aye, it's a peety you hadnae a pair o' wings, and then you could nearly be in two places at once'. Whatever the public eye saw in us, she made sure we understood we were her children, to be kept in order by her watchful criticism. There was no fear of any of us 'fancying our barrow' while my mother was there to impress a sense of reality and to make sure feet stayed firmly on the ground.

In spite of this attitude though, she grew so used to my ability to tackle anything I was asked to do, that it was less of a surprise to her than it was to me when my college telephoned one day and told me they'd recommended me to attend a great church debate in Renfield Street church, to take verbatim notes of the proceedings. I felt very honoured, but also very nervous of my responsibilities, because till then I had only done high speed demonstrating for comparatively short periods, and this was to occupy a whole evening and there would be proper names to cope with, religious sects, arguments, and there would certainly be no guaranteed evenly-paced delivery, but bursts of accelerated speed as tempers rose. Goodness, there might even be interruptions from the platform party, or from the body of the hall, and how would I ever know all their names? But I was to be paid a guinea for my services, and it was an irresistible challenge to try my hand at being a real shorthand reporter like the ones we saw in the pictures. I felt secretly rather elated. Nobody nowadays was telling me I was too wee for anything. I'd been accepted as a real theatre 'turn'. Now here I was being accepted as a real reporter. Life was so exciting that my feet scarcely seemed to touch the ground as I raced home on the night of the debate to collect pens and pencils, plus an extra notebook, before setting off again for the church.

I was led to a little table on the platform, at right angles to the main long table, and at 7.30 the debate began before a packed audience. As I was entirely unused to such work, I felt it essential to take down every single word, just as I did my pieces in college and in the office, and I thought my hand would drop off as page after page of notes were filled. Arguments raged back and forth for hours, with hardly a pause for breath. Everybody seemed to have lost all sense of time, and they certainly paid no attention to me sitting there frantically trying to get every impassioned word down. There weren't even refreshments, for it wasn't a social after all. It was a debate. I hadn't the slightest idea what it was all about. There wasn't time to think. The words hit my ears, and were transferred to the notebooks, with no comprehension on my part. I didn't even notice the audience thin out, as people must have left for their trains or cars or buses, but by the time those religious maniacs had finished their arguing, it was 1.30 A.M., the place was quarter filled, and I was absolutely exhausted. It was the

Carroll Levis audition all over again, with me walking home in the wee sma' hours, and my mother demanding to know this time, 'Whit kind o' folk are they church men then, to keep a young lassie oot o' her bed till this time in the morning?'. She took one look at my white face and put the kettle on, 'My Goad, your eyes are staunin' in yer heid', she said. 'It's a good thing the morn's your Setturday off, and you can have a long lie'. We had every fourth Saturday off in my fine big office job, and usually this was a treasured treat. But there would be no long lie for me this time. 'Oh I can't have a long lie, Mother', I said, as I began to riffle through the pages of notes, 'I've to take these down to the college and type them out, for they're wanted as soon as possible'. 'DON'T start looking at thae notes the night', my mother implored. 'Drink yer tea and get to your bed, or you'll no' be fit for anything in the morning. It's a good night's sleep you need.'

On the Saturday, I typed without pause till the college closed at 1 o'clock for the week-end. I went back every night after work the following week, and I thought I'd never come to the end of this nightmare task. When he saw the amount of work involved, my nice kind shorthand mentor pursed his lips and said one guinea was totally inadequate, and I must ask the church authorities to make it at least three. 'Och I could never ask them to do that, Mr McLeod', I protested. But when I added it all up, I realized there was as much work in that marathon as I did in a week at the office. And I had supplied all the paper and the carbons. So, when I handed the bundle of transcript over, I found courage to say, 'My college feels this work is worth at least three guineas'. I couldn't look the man in the face as I mentioned this enormous sum, and I felt a bit mean in case these church folk didn't have enough money. But some stubborn streak supported me and gave me strength to stand my ground. For good measure, I added, 'The bible says "The labourer is worthy of his hire", and my college says it's worth it'. The man's lips twitched when I raised my eyes to see how he was taking my bargaining. He weighed the paper in his hands and smiled, 'I'm sure it's a bargain. You've done a very conscientious job, young lady'. I must have been getting used to being called a young lady, or my bargaining had paralysed my emotions, for I never turned a hair at these once-surprising words he used to describe me. I got my three guineas, the first and only time I had ever earned extra cash solely from my shorthand speeds. 'By jings, I'm well away', I chortled to myself as I sped home to tell my mother of this bonanza.

Everything was possible. The story of the ten talents was absolutely right. As far as I knew, I hadn't allowed any of mine to be buried and go to waste, but had worked to develop and add to them and they were all gradually being used. There was no knowing where I would end up. There was plenty of time to find out.

It was the summer of 1939.

In spite of my preoccupation with my own absorbing affairs, two menacing figures strutted across the world's stage, and although it was easy and fashionable to laugh at the ranting Hitler and the buffoon Mussolini, I couldn't laugh. We all argued passionately about armaments. I can remember saying, with what I thought was deadly logic, 'You can't give a child toys and then tell him not to play with them. That's what we're doing with this man Hitler', and I was told to shut up. I was just being a scaremonger like that chap Churchill who was trying to frighten the daylights out of everybody. Nobody wanted war.

The war burst upon us, and the country was almost totally unprepared. My despair came from the sick feeling that all the wrong people were in charge. I remember sitting in a chum's garden one lovely sunny day and crying out against those in authority and their feeble decisions. My chum, exasperated by my attitude, said 'But what do you WANT then? What would make it better?' I drew a deep breath. 'That this lot be thrown out, or the whole Government work together with Churchill in charge', I said.

Somebody must have been listening! For the very next day after that conversation in my chum's garden, the papers and the wireless told us that a Coalition had been formed, and the man who would lead the nation to victory would be Winston Churchill. From that moment, and even through the darkest days which followed, I had absolutely no doubt whatever but that we would win the war. With God and Churchill on our side, victory was certain.

I kept waiting for the BBC to summon me to help them on the home front, but they seemed amazingly able to get on very well without me. I couldn't understand it. So I wrote to my first producer, Robin Russell, and told him so and he very kindly replied from his Air Force camp and advised that I write to the new head of drama, Moultrie Kelsall, and he also would drop a note in my favour. When the summons came to meet Moultrie, I found I had to sit absolutely silent while he corrected a batch of scripts. I felt petrified. I saw a lean stern face with a mane of silvered brown hair, and a complete indifference to my presence in the small room we now shared. I hardly dared breathe. At last he came to the end of his reading, and swung round on his chair to face me. 'Well', he said, after a minute or so's silent scrutiny, 'Robin Russell tells me I ought to be able to use you in my productions and that you're fairly versatile. What can you do?' This question is one which is absolutely guaranteed to make every fact fly straight out of your head. What could I do, I wondered. 'Come on, come on' he said impatiently, 'what did you do for Robin?' So, hesitantly, I told him about the 'McFlannels', and the Radio Cartoons, and the schools' programmes. 'Can you sing?', he said suddenly. Why was I always being asked this when I so wanted to be a dramatic actress? Cautiously I told him about the Pantheon, and the Carroll Levis show, and he jotted all the particulars down on a stiff card, and said I'd maybe hear from him when he'd considered his revue scripts.

Next minute I was out in the street, walking along by Botanic Gardens, and wondering if that fierce man would even remember my existence by the end of the day. But he did. And he became a much-loved colleague and taught me so much that I can never cease to be grateful for the trouble he took with me. It took me a long time to penetrate that apparently stern exterior, but when I really got to know him, it was his ability to make me laugh with his tantrums and theatrical scoldings which were most typical of our relationship. The first summons I received from him was to become one of half a dozen actors who were to sing and play all the characters between us in a

revue called 'Lights up'. There was Madeleine Christie, Charlie
Brookes, Janet Brown, Edith Stevenson, Moultrie's wife Ruby
Duncan (a brilliant pianist), and me. Ruby thrilled me to the
marrow the first time she heard me sing a solo piece, by
volunteering to transpose the number to a lower and more
suitable key. For *ages* I'd tried to have this done in the
Pantheon, and nobody would listen to me. Ruby, who read
music as easily as I read shorthand, actually transposed in her
head, even with five sharps! I breathed over her in ecstasy and
became her devoted slave. Those who have read elsewhere*
of my attempts to master the piano will realize how unstinted
was my admiration of this talented lady. And not merely
because, thanks to her true assessment of my vocal range, my
voice seemed better than it was, but because she was a musician
to her quicksilver finger tips. How lucky we were to have this
expertise at our service. It was all the greatest fun, in spite of
microphone nerves. We did burlesques of well-known numbers,
changing the words to our own comedy mood. We did little
black-out sketches. I sang duets and solos, and gradually lost
my fear of my own solo singing, and I played everything from
wee tough boys to elderly refined ladies.

We did all our own sound effects in the studio in those days,
gurgling water, marching up and down on gravel, banging
doors, rattling tea-cups, doing train-hooters with our throats,
and bleating like sheep. Later, when war was a memory, and
the sound effects were done from a separate studio, with only
a flashing light to indicate that the effect had taken place, it
seemed flat and unnatural and took a great deal of getting used
to. It was far more exciting to me to be dashing about the
studio and clattering things and then rushing back to the
microphone to fit in the dialogue.

This was the period known as 'the phoney war', for while we
were in a state of war, there was an uneasy lull when nothing
seemed to be happening. We had rationing, we had black-out,
and men drilled and practised Air Raid Precautions, and there
was a body of men called the Local Defence Volunteers who
were to deal with local situations as they occurred. I was
determined to go down fighting if the Germans parachuted
down, and I carried a pepper-pot to blind them if they got

* Best Foot Forward

441

within firing distance. For me the worst thing was the black-out, for I have always suffered from claustrophobia, and when the darkness closed down, I felt suffocated. I was certain if poison gas was used, I'd be the first casualty. I used to practise holding my breath as the tramcar passed the Chemical Works on my way to Springburn to see my mother, and I was always the first to cough. I just knew my lungs would never stand the test. In fact I volunteered to walk through a test caravan wearing a gas mask, not only to see if it would protect me against the tear-gas which had been sprayed in the test chamber, but to see whether my claustrophobia would allow me to keep the mask itself on. It didn't. I tore it off, and emerged into the street gasping and choking, blinded by the tear-gas, and made the family promise that if poison gas was ever used by those hellish Germans, they had my full permission to push my head in the oven and get it over with quickly.

There was very little entertainment in Glasgow at that time, and the soldiers were mooching around with nothing to do. Moultrie had the brainwave of putting on a revue in the Lyric, and as it was based to a large extent on our radio revue, I was invited to join the cast. The cast was augmented by the addition of Nan Scott, Willie Joss, Jimmy Urquhart (Glasgow's Jack Buchanan), Grace McChlery, and Alec Ross. Alec and I were the ingénues, and did all the romantic numbers, which sent me into ecstasies because for the first time I was able to wear floaty romantic dresses. Oh and Ian Sadler was with us, pretending to be a foreign soldier to my wee Glasgow hairie. While we were rehearsing, Willie Joss and Nan Scott decided that one of the sketches which had been written for them wasn't working as it ought to do, and Willie felt the part opposite Nan should be played by a girl. I didn't know the stage producer at all, and in fact I knew none of them well enough to be able to ask for the part, but oh how I coveted it. I started praying, always a positive help when I want to move mountains. 'Please God, let the man give it to me. Let him give it to me. Please God'. The producer looked round us all, and I suppose I gave God a helping hand by looking so eager and beseeching that the producer decided to take a chance. 'Would you like to try it, Molly?', he asked. Would I! It was a riot from the first read-through. It was called 'The Girls of the old Brigade' and we were two tram-conductresses in the uniform of the first world war, who emerged from retirement to do their bit in the second holocaust. Nan Scott, the knowing one of the pair, was a tall vigorous blonde with a fine physique, long hair which she wore in a little knot at the nape of her neck, and a Cicely Courtneidge attack. I played the little naïve one, to whom she was showing the ropes, and we sang a catchy little song to open and close the act, and made our exit after a snappy tap dance, with me leaping into Nan's arms and being carried off.

We borrowed first world-war uniforms from Glasgow Corporation, with the old cheese-cutter hats, and I may say these clothes were borrowed dozens of times by us during the course of the war, for our 'Girls of the Old Brigade' was played by us all over Scotland. And it was thanks to that sure-fire duet that I had the good fortune to tread the boards with the great Sir Harry Lauder. There was no entertainment at all on Sundays, and it was decided that to keep up the morale, the Kings Theatre would open experimentally for a single Sunday evening, and put on a variety show with all the stars they could rope in. As there was no certainty at any time that bombs wouldn't disrupt communications, and London artists might find themselves miles from the Kings at the right moment, local acts were drafted in, and Nan and I were asked to appear in our Tramcar number.

I was in a fever of nerves that the theatre would be empty, for no advertising was allowed in case the enemy would get wind of the fact that hundreds of soldiers would be under one roof, and would treacherously drop a bomb on us. I kept pestering Nan, 'But how will anybody *know* there's a show on?' I couldn't see how they could possibly guess, when there had never been such an entertainment before. In my youthful ignorance, I didn't realize that in entertainment-starved Glasgow, the word would get round as though the Fiery Cross had been employed to carry the news to all.

We didn't know who would definitely be on the bill, because again, for safety's sake, we hadn't been told and we only found out when we turned up for Sunday morning's band call. This time I rejoiced in the knowledge that we had play-on, play-off music, just like the real turns, and with all the nonchalance acquired after a week's experience at the Lyric, we bade the orchestra speed up or slow down just where we wanted such change of tempo. Somebody whispered behind a cupped hand 'Sir Harry's on the bill tonight'. I stared in delighted surprise. 'Sir Harry Lauder?', I gasped, just to make sure there wasn't another Sir Harry, and I wasn't building up my hopes for somebody else. 'Who else?', said the informer.

The theatre was packed. The tom-toms had sounded all right. The audience were practically hanging from the chandeliers. I'd never performed for a troop show before, and the deep masculine buzz made the stomach turn over. Bernard Miles was on before us, with his wheel, and his country yokel character and went down well. The curtain rose again with our two chairs in position, and there was a roar of laughter when we pranced on, me up to Nan's elbow, marching in strict tempo towards the chairs, and sitting down right on the down-beat. The troops found us hilarious, and when we came off we hugged each other, starry-eyed. It was then the idea was born that we had an act which we could take anywhere. For the applause came from people who didn't know us, and we were being judged against really top variety acts. 'Molly my girl', laughed Nan, 'we've got an act, we have. Tell the man in the Corporation when you return the uniforms, that he must keep them in readiness for us whenever we want them.' He did too.

Our own turn safely over, we could wait in the wings to watch the great Sir Harry.

I saw a little old man being cossetted and protected by his niece Greta, from whom had come the strict command that none of us must attempt to speak to him for he was very frail, and needed all his strength for the show. He was so tottery, and so obviously dependent on Greta for support that I was dismayed. Would the real presence destroy the legend? I started to pray again. 'Oh please God, let the troops not give him the bird. Let them be kind to him. Let them not give him the bird.' What an idiot I.was, and how little I knew of true star quality. The moment he heard the opening music Sir Harry, like an old war-horse scenting battle, lifted his head, seized his curly walking stick, and jigged on to the stage. He was greeted by a roar which shook the chandeliers. 'I love a Lassie', was followed by 'Stop yer Ticklin' Jock', then on to 'I'm the saftest o' the family', 'Bell o' the Heather' and so right through a repertoire which we all knew and loved. It was electrifying. It was magnificent. And still the boys roared for more, and we in the wings clapped and stamped and cheered, proud to share this historic moment when we'd witnessed the miracle of an old man re-charged with the vigour of youth, and who was displaying for us all the artistry acquired through a lifetime's experience.

They wouldn't let him go. But Greta was watchful, and gave the signal that this was to be the last encore. She stood with chamois and cooling lotion to dab the perspiration from his face on each exit, and she knew the exact moment when enough was enough. The applause thundered round the roof, and under it a little old man tottered past those of us who stood applauding in the wings. A little man who now looked as though the mechanism had wound down but who, while the magic lasted, had given us a glimpse of greatness. I'd have loved to have spoken to him, but Greta shook her head imperceptibly and we let him go without a word. But I am sure he saw the love in our eyes as we applauded his passing, for he gave a little smile and a nod, before vanishing from our sight. 'Well', I said to myself, 'you might not have said a word to him, hen, but you can always say that you once trod the boards with Sir Harry Lauder, and that's something no' everybody can say!'

That was only the first of many shows we did for the troops. Moultrie and Ruby organized them, and we did shows under various titles, like 'Salute the Soldier' concerts, 'Prisoner of War' entertainments, 'Salute to the navy' shows. We ranged quite far afield, and when Stirlingshire seemed a good central base for our week-end activities, we stayed at Moultrie's lovely house in Blairlogie. His pre-war hobby had been buying and re-conditioning old cottages of charm, and selling them, but whatever his original intention had been regarding the Blairlogie house, the war effectively put a stop to thoughts of moving, and so we all enjoyed staying in this little jewel of a cottage. The feeling of being in real country was a benison in itself, after the dark pressures of Glasgow tenements, when the drone of bombers conjured thoughts of tons of masonry on top of us. In the country, the stars shone comfortingly and all that beautiful untenanted space was a solace to the mind.

But it was really quite a small house, although it seemed large to me after tenement life, and we all had to double up for sleeping accommodation, and I found myself one night with Madeleine Christie. I was snug as a bug, but at breakfast time she stared at me accusingly. 'I will never share a bed with that one again', she said, 'I've spent my married life training my husband never to put his feet near mine. I can't *bear* people's feet. And now, I've had the misery of pursuing feet chasing mine all night.'

I thought she was joking, and gave a shout of laughter at the thought of anybody worrying about a bed-mate seeking warm feet. I'd always done this with my grannie and my mother, and we were all used to coorying together for warmth. 'There's nothing to laugh about' she told me wrathfully, 'I was pursued to the edge of the bed, had to get up and walk round the other side, and had no sooner settled down than the whole thing started again'. I was practically in hysterics by this time, and everybody round the table thought it was a great joke, but not Madeleine, who was sleepless and cross.

I only appreciated how seriously she regarded my conduct when she refused to sleep in the same bed the next night, and preferred a mattress on the floor of the lounge! It was a terrible humiliation. I didn't mind so much about chasing her feet, for after all I was only in search of warmth, but that hadn't been my only crime. It seemed I had also snored. It was unfeminine and shame-making and the memory has haunted me to this day. It didn't affect my feelings towards Madeleine, who has been a dear friend down through the years, but it dejected me to feel I was still miles away from the sensitive lady-like susceptibilities shared by those posh office colleagues and by others nurtured in a more hot-house atmosphere than mine.

But I had a wee triumph when we visited a big military hospital. Madeleine was the acknowledged singer of the company, for although we all shared solos and choruses, hers was a lovely soaring soprano of a most pleasing quality. She sang ballads and good semi-classical pieces, and had little interest in or knowledge of the 'standards' of the day. So when, at the end of our show, we went round the corridors of the hospital and the boys in the wards were asked to shout out any requests, it was I with my snoring tonsils who knew all the words and music of the pops. The accoustics of the high corridors flattered my voice bewitchingly in my ears, and I belted out 'Paper Doll', 'If I had my Way', 'My Ideal', 'All Alone', and 'The White Cliffs of Dover'. And when I finished up with a soulful 'I haven't said thanks for that lovely week-end', I was met with gratifying whistles and cheers from the unseen lads in the wards.

Madeleine raised her eyebrows, and said, most generously, 'Well, I can see I'll just have to learn the words of that type of song if we are going to do more shows of this sort'. 'I'll teach you, Madeleine', I said eagerly, 'if you don't tell anybody I snored!'

7

Shortly after this troop concert, I was invited by Ronnie Munro to join the girls who sang on radio with his BBC dance orchestra. That really put a feather in my hat. Fancy me singing with a dance band! There was Janet Brown, who later became so well-known as an impressionist, Ann Rich, who also sang with the Locarno dance band and later was in ITMA, Edith Stevenson, and me. Ronnie and I sang all the duets popularized by Elsie Carlisle and Sam Brown, and I did solo swing versions of the Scottish songs. Ann and Edith sang the romantic ballads, and Janet and I did the comedy numbers.

Ronnie particularly cherished my deep hearty laugh, and wrote songs for me, where I did nothing but laugh in tune and to the rhythm of the music all the way through. It was the first time I realized how exhausting laughter could be. Really strong laughter is quite a violent assault on the diaphragm, and it also uses up a tremendous amount of oxygen. After some of those laughing sessions, I used to reel from the microphone, dizzy and spent. But everybody seemed to enjoy them, and I'd never have dreamed of saying anything was too much for me. It was all tremendous fun, and even if I had never learned to play the piano properly, those sixpenny lessons were now paying off, for I could at least read music, something absolutely essential for quickly learning new tunes. I could hardly have asked a band leader to translate the numbers into doh-ray-mees!

Meg Buchanan had a lovely old Scottish saying, 'A gaun fit's aye gettin',' and so it proved with me as far as working for the BBC was concerned. Somebody would spot me in the canteen and would be reminded that I was around, would ask for me for their next production, and soon I seemed to be working for everybody, from schools to the variety orchestra. All this was in addition to looking after a house and a job, for nobody at that time considered that mere radio work was helping to win the war, or indeed was work at all. And looking after a husband, which had once seemed a full-time occupation, was now taken on the wing as it were. We were all getting married.

Brother Willie was first from our house, and vanished into the bosom of his in-laws, who had a nice little house with a garden not too far from Springburn, and as his was a reserved occupation my mother had no worries about him being killed by 'thae blackguards of Germans'. She herself returned cheerfully to munition work, and was quite rejuvenated at finding herself in dungarees once more, and working with machinery. Like me, she hated the black-out, but she worked on nightshift quite frequently and preferred coming home in the light of morning, never giving it a thought that she was in much greater danger of being hit by bombs in the munitions' works than in the unwar-like tenement where she usually shared a shelter with the other neighbours.

While he waited for his call-up papers, Tommy decided to accept my offer to teach him shorthand, which we both felt would be a great asset to him as an embryo writer, and I also taught him to use the typewriter efficiently. He came out to our house on the other side of Glasgow for those lessons, for I was now married to my Sandy, and we had taken the enormous plunge of starting to buy a house of our own. Considering the state of our finances and the times we were sharing, it was a tremendous gamble, but I had lived in a tenement all my life, and I flatly refused to consider adding a wedding ring to that engagement one unless the offer included a house with a garden. I didn't care how small the house was, but it must have a place where I could grow things, and feel the soil between my fingers. I think I inherited this love of growing things from Grannie, whose skill with sick or wilting plants was the envy of our tenement neighbours, and who could prolong the life of cut flowers beyond all normal limits it seemed.

Our budget was as tight as a drum, and if we bought a bar of chocolate, then we had to walk into town for there was no extra for fares. I remember the very first meal I ever cooked cost a shilling. I had gone down to the local butcher intending to buy a nap bone and a half-pound of hough, to make soup and potted hough. The butcher, sensing I was a new customer, held up an enormous bone hanging with meat and said 'Sixpence to you, hen'. I gazed at it with a calculating eye. There was enough meat there to make the hough. I took it and bought no meat. Sixpence-worth of vegetables in the shop next door were more than enough to make a grand pot of broth, when added to the beautiful hough stock after the meat was cooked. That soup was the first course, and a shining mould of hough was the second, and few things have given me more pleasure than the sight of that mound of shimmering jellied meat achieved without even a hint of artificial aids like gelatine, and costing only the price of the gas which cooked it to that tender stage. For of course a bone like that would have cost sixpence anyway.

However I set an impossible precedent for the rest of our budgeting, because however economical I was in later years, my husband would say with a smile, 'Aye, but you've never come up to that first shilling meal!'

I was so keen on the idea of a garden, that before we even had a stick of furniture, I had obtained hedge cuttings from somebody in the office, and broom cuttings from my fiancé's colleague, and there we were with an empty house, digging away at the virgin soil and planting our little gifted treasures. I could see from the corner of my eye our future neighbours gazing at us in astonishment from upstairs windows, for most newlyweds scrubbed out the house before they thought of the garden. But I didn't care how eccentric they judged us. I was working in my very own garden – at last! The hedge drooped and perished but, undeterred, we planted another and it survived.

And what a boon that treasured garden was when vegetables became as scarce as hen's teeth as the war progressed. Neighbours used to come in and help themselves to the leeks, enormous beauties with thick white flesh as broad as a fair-sized wrist. They reasoned, quite rightly, that I'd never get through that lot by myself, for my husband was by this time in uniform, far away, and very pleased with the rows of golden wonders and fine onions he'd left to eke out my meagre rations. Black currants provided jam made with the precious sugar saved from my one ration book, and wallflowers filled the vases in spring, and graced the tables of neighbours when husbands came home on leave.

I planted fifty crocus bulbs in defiance of Hitler's bombers, and my proudest moments were when people stopped to admire the display. They were like a brilliant flag painted by nature, shouting defiance and proclaiming that this tight knot in the stomach wasn't fear. Few people had had the heart to plant bulbs during that awful autumn, so ours stood out and gladdened many hearts at that particular time when other gardens were bare. Never have a few shillings been better spent, even though I knew really I couldn't afford them.

The neighbour's little boys, toddlers, brought their little spades to 'help the lassie' dig for victory, because, as they told each other, she had nae a man at hame. One four-year-old, a Jehovah's Witness, sternly took me to task one Sunday for picking black currants, and refused to help the little team I'd gathered around me. I explained solemnly, controlling my amusement, that God had grown the currants, that it was a sin to waste anything in war-time, and that as I was out working during the weekdays, I must pick them when I had the time for such work and also the time to make them into nourishing jam. He listened with great seriousness, then left to consult his parents. He was back in a few minutes with a bowl, 'It's all right', he assured me, 'my mammy says God understands.'

Incidentally it was this same wee lad who ferociously crushed my one and only surviving anemone and scattered its petals to the wind. I was quite shattered. Surely the devil must have got into him. I gathered my little band of toddlers round me and put the culprit in the middle. I told him he had done a very naughty thing, for he had destroyed the pleasure for all of us in a beautiful flower, for a moment's destructive satisfaction. That now nobody could enjoy its beauty, and all the waiting for the moment of flowering had been in vain. I was fairly carried away by my sermon, and said that God meant his garden for all to enjoy, and that we were fighting the Germans to keep our homes safe and happy, and God had made the little anemone flourish to encourage me to be bright and happy. Now it was destroyed beyond all recovery. They all listened intently, and I finally forbade the vandal from playing in my garden for twenty-four hours. God banishing Adam couldn't have had a more powerful effect. I had to harden my heart when the little figure accepted the verdict with dignity and turned and walked slowly down the path, while the others returned to their play round the currant bed. But I felt he would never forget how hurtful it was to destroy living growing flowers meant for all to enjoy. And I know I was right. After a day had elapsed, he was back, with no hard feelings on either side, and when his dad came home on leave it was his mother who picked my flowers without permission! Not the boy. He had truly learned his lesson.

Even with a war on, the builders had managed to keep back a few essential men, mostly judged Grade C by the powers-that-be, to attend to the multitude of little repair jobs inevitable with any new estate. My mother never ceased to marvel at this arrangement. 'Fancy no' having to wait for the factor for a' thae wee jobs', she would say, 'and that smert wee man at yer beck and call'. The smart wee man she so much admired had a running battle with the foreman, for as well as all the official jobs he was employed to do, he earned an honest shilling on the side for all the countless tasks which only a man seemed able to tackle. What did newly-weds know about cracked cement, or stiff window fastenings, or a boiler which wouldn't heat the water?

On top of all this, he was always delighted to tell us how rotten the houses were. He hadn't built them. He'd just been called in when the damage was done. It was he who had alerted me to the unsafe state of the concrete slab at the foot of the front-door steps. He'd seen me working in the front garden, cast a furtive eye up and down the road to make sure the hated foreman wasn't lurking anywhere, then dropped his hammer with a hollow thud on the concrete. 'D'ye hear that?', he'd asked conversationally. 'Hear what?', I asked in bewilderment. I couldn't hear a thing except the wireless next door. 'Hollow', he spat, expertly, right into the centre of the lilac bush, 'absolutely hollow'. I was alarmed, and I could see the look of smug satisfaction in his eyes as I asked him what I ought to do about it. Again came the darting glance right and left I was to learn to know so well, 'If you keep your bl....., eh, your mooth shut, I'll get the stuff and make a right job of it for you'. This was followed by a scowl, 'But nane o' yer talking to the other neebors noo, if you don't want me to get the sack'. He was only 4 feet 8 inches or thereabouts from the top of his wee bald head to the toe-cap of his tackety boots, but his energy was so ferocious that I gladly swore utter silence, and crossed my heart and hoped to die to prove I would keep my word.

'That's a' right then', he said, and in due course the slab was strengthened.

That was only the first of the many 'side jobs' he did for me. For if I didn't find anything for him to do, he found it for himself. And he made sure I appreciated the quality of his craftsmanship, and didn't overlook the finer details which an ordinary woman couldn't be expected to observe unless an expert like himself pointed them out. 'See that red stuff ah've put roon' yer windaes?' he would ask, cocking a loving gaze towards the mess round the glass. 'Well, that'll keep oot a' the damp this winter. Dear stuff mind you, but there's naethin' tae beat it.' With a vice-like grip of my arm, he whispered hoarsely, 'I don't put it in every hoose, ah can tell you'. I had a feeling he liked me because I was so close to his own height. I'd hardly ever met anybody as small as myself, and I could appreciate his pleasure in finding somebody with whom he could literally see almost eye to eye.

But if I was a favourite, this didn't mean he was going to buoy me up with false hopes about the property. 'Rotten hooses thae', he would say pensively, gathering ammunition for another satisfying spit, 'I've been on many a dud job, but thae hooses . . .' When I found the spirit to argue back that the building society couldn't have thought so or they wouldn't have lent us so much money, and that anyway it wasn't very nice of him to condemn so heartily the bricks and mortar to which we'd pledged our financial future for the next twenty-five years, if we lived that long, he was all sweet reason. 'Whit else could youse dae?', he would say, throwing his arms wide in a dramatic gesture I couldn't have bettered myself on the stage. 'Youse canny get a Corporation hoose. And if you MUST have a modern hoose and a garden, well, youse have just got to pey oot braw saut for the trash they've put up for mugs like youse'.

Before I could stamp off in annoyance at being called a mug, he would launch into his adventures in the Kaiser's War, when he'd been in the Bantams and when, according to him, he'd sent the troops up the line wi' a guid hert because of the excellence of his cooking, and the unfailing supply of hot cups of tea at any hour of the day or night. It seemed he never slept. And the lads appreciated it.

He told me with great relish of his strength and his toughness.'Aye, there was wan time when ah wis the only man oot o' the hale regiment that hadnae the 'flu. And nae wunner they a' had it, staunin' in a' that water by the 'oor. Water up tae their oxters, so they had'. I smothered a smile, which I disguised as a cough, as I imagined that with a normal-size soldier this would have been about knee level. He would smile nostalgically, 'Aye ah wis in the Bantams. Wan o' the toughest regiments in France'.

I thought there was no such regiment, but when I asked my mother, she said that indeed there was, so maybe it was all true although I could hardly really believe he sent regiments of Bantams into battle, their innards lined with his special Yorkshire pudding.

But the best laugh he gave me was when he confided in me about his romance. This confidence was only exchanged after he'd done about a dozen little unofficial jobs, not one of which had reached the foreman's ears, so he felt he could trust me. He had been courting a widow for three years, it seemed, 'Seeing her regular, every Setturday night, takin' her tae the pictures, and staunin' her a fish supper'. He would never have spent such sums on any wumman unless he had been deadly serious, he told me. And I believed him. Anyway, one night arriving unexpectedly early, he had found a rival sitting in his favourite chair. The Jezebel had been deceiving him. Him! The pride of the Bantams! 'What did you do, Jock', I asked. 'Was there a fight?' I expected to hear he'd massacred the other man, for, after all, I'd listened to tales of his toughness for weeks. 'A fight?', he echoed incredulously. 'For a craitur' like yon? Not on your nelly'. 'But you must have done something, Jock', I protested. 'Dod, I just turned on ma heel and walked oot o' the hoose and doon the stair, and I never saw her again fae that day tae this.' I clapped my hands in delight. I could just see him do it too. He smiled at me loftily, 'Oh she wrote and tried to get me back'. The lilac bush quivered under the assault of another fierce jet of spittle.'Aye, she knew a good man when she saw him, but nothing doing! Once bitten, ye ken'.

In spite of my approval of the way he'd handled the whole affair, the memory seemed to infuriate him all over again and he included me in his contempt for the whole unstable silly sex. 'They're a' the same', he said bitterly. 'If they're no' cheatin' you, they're talkin' too much an' getting ye the sack'.

'I like that!', I said indignantly. 'You're just as big a blether as I am'. He gave me a prodigious wink and a dig in the ribs, and I wish I had known this was to be our last conversation, for I'd have managed a wee tin of tobacco for him somehow. 'They'll have been thinkin' you and me were winchin' wi' a' the cracks we've been havin', eh?' We both laughed in slight embarrassment at this almost personal witticism, the first he'd ever knowingly made, and I might have guessed then that the Grade C's had been called up, and he wouldn't be left on the estate on his own. He balanced his tool-bag on top of his workman's bunnet and walked leisurely up the road and vanished over the crest of the hill. Wee Jock, the only Bantam I had ever had the pleasure of knowing. I kept waiting and waiting for him to reappear during the following weeks but he never did. And when the foreman's little hut disappeared, I knew I'd seen the last of Jock. It was terrible to know that there was no spare man to whom I could turn if I was in trouble, for by this time practically all the husbands had gone, and those who were at home couldn't be expected to chase round after all the rest of us with problems on our hands.

I was very frightened of going into the house alone in the blackout, and this fear led me to the daftest adventure one night. It was very late, because I'd been at the BBC in a play which of course went out 'live', as everything did in those days. With London under constant bomb attack, we in Glasgow were liable at a moment's notice to be told to take over because the studios or the artists, or both, in the South were unable to go on the air. Working in the garden, I'd hear the 'phone ringing. The acquisition of the telephone was a great adventure, and a great expense out of my small salary, but it was an essential item of equipment for me living mostly on my own, and it also attracted BBC work because they could get me on the line. Often the call would be from Moultrie. 'Get here as quickly as possible', he would urge, 'we're on the air tonight'. I'd rush out of the house, and catch a tram to town and then to Botanic Gardens, and many times we went straight on to the mike without rehearsal, pages being handed to us as they left the roneo machine. No wonder I learned to be able to give a performance at first read-through. These skills were acquired figuratively under fire, the fire that was raging many miles south in London. On my way home on this particular night, it was pitch dark. Not a star to lighten the sky, and not a sound on the hill but my own footsteps. Every window blacked out, with not a chink of light to betray us to any cruising enemy 'planes. And then as I drew near to my own house, I could see a soft glow in the living room. I stopped dead outside the gate. What could be making such a peculiar light? The house was empty. Was it a burglar with a torch? In my rush out to the BBC I hadn't drawn the curtains, and in the surrounding blackness that small light looked menacing. I couldn't knock anybody up, and frighten the life out of them. What would I do? Suddenly I heard footsteps coming over the hill. Never giving a thought to the idea that the approaching stranger might be as menacing as the imagined one in the living room, or that I might be scaring him half to death, I rushed up to him and gasped, 'Oh will you come in with me, there's a light in my living room and I'm afraid it might be a burglar!'

It didn't dawn on me either that a grown man could be afraid, but his voice wasn't at all steady as he said,'I beg your pardon, madam, what did you say?' He was English. He clearly thought he had a nut case on his hands. So I repeated my question. We couldn't see each other's faces at all in the darkness, and if I'd met him in my porridge I'd never have recognized him again. What I *did* recognize was that he wasn't at all willing to enter a strange female's house at that time of night, and risk being bashed over the head by a burglar. And I had imagined *all* men were to be trusted to behave gallantly to a frightened female – except the Germans of course. Anyway,

I was getting impatient in spite of my fear, so I said crossly, 'Oh all right, you needn't come in, but stand by the door so that if I shout for help you can raise the alarm'. Would you believe it, he let me go in ahead of him, while he stood cravenly on the door mat. With panting heart I tiptoed cautiously through the tiny hall into the living room, and at once burst into relieved laughter. The small glow which had so scared me came from the radio! I had rushed out in such a hurry I'd forgotten to switch it off, and because I'd left the house in the daylight, the light in the cabinet hadn't shown itself.

At the sound of my laughter, the man turned and ran, without waiting to hear another word from me.

But it was a symptom of the nervous tension of the times that a little unexpected light could cause such a situation. I often wonder, though, if that man thought I was an abandoned female trying to lure him into her parlour! When I told my mother about it later, she was scandalized. 'My Goad, he might have been a murderer. If you werenae sae faur from ma work, I'd come oot and stay wi' you for a wee while, but I'd never manage the travelling. You'll just have to get a lodger.'

While I was turning this novel idea over in my mind, an army officer came to the door one evening and said he was looking for private accommodation for some of his men who wished to have their wives up to stay with them for a short spell. It would be good for morale, for the men were getting very bored. Had I any room which I would let? He was an English officer and all his men were from the Midlands or Wales. It was army policy to station men far from their own districts, to ensure that there would be no temptation to run home, so the Scots were stationed in the south, and the English in the north. Cautiously I said I didn't want permanent lodgers, but if it were only for a week or so, I would try it and see how we all got on with one another. He arranged for his sergeant and the sergeant's wife to move in the following Friday. Everything in the house was brand new, of course, and he was very flattering about the excellent accommodation I was offering, and regretted that the financial reward must be so small. £1 a week, to be precise, plus the cost of the coal used. £1 a week seemed a wee fortune to me, for they would be supplying their own food, doing their own housework, and I would be coming home to a warm house at night.

When I arrived home that first Friday night, the first thing I saw was a sheet of newspaper spread on the hall linoleum, and a man was sitting on the bottom step of the stairs taking off his boots 'not to make a mess', he told me. The boots were placed neatly on the newspaper, while he changed into slippers. That small incident illustrated my lodgers' attitude to everything. They were fanatically clean and tidy. I've never met a man so well-trained, or a wife so house-proud. In fact, much as I appreciated their careful regard for my possessions, I came to feel she was *too* house-proud. I'd been told by the salesman not to vacuum the new carpets too often, for fear of removing all the soft fluffy top pile too harshly, but the woman vacuumed them every single day, until I could swear I saw the under-threads before she'd been in the house a week. She was pale and thin and dark, and obviously taken aback that I was so young. I wished that I had been a bit older myself, so that I could have had the confidence to ask her to stop bashing our irreplaceable carpets so enthusiastically! This couple seemed almost elderly to me, but I imagine they were in their mid forties.

As there was only one of me, and two of them, I quickly came to feel that I was the interloper. I'd dash in from work, swallow my tea, and dash out again, whatever the weather. I didn't like to sit with them in the living-room, as I felt they only had two weeks together and they wouldn't want me there playing gooseberry. One night, as I skipped past the bathroom, I solved the mystery of the little piece of towelling I had noticed lying on the edge of the bath. I couldn't think what it was for, because I had proper cleaning things up there, but now all was revealed! The sergeant was using it to catch the drips from his elbows as he shaved! Was there no end to their carefulness? Fancy thinking of drops of water in a bathroom! I noticed too that they used old gloves when they brought in the coal, and not a thing was put down on the carpet without a paper being placed underneath. I realized much later that it was surely because they were childless and theirs had been a late marriage, that they could follow this pattern of perfection. No young life had ever disturbed the orderly neatness of their ways. At that time I thought it was because they were English, and old.

One pouring wet night as I retreated to the kitchen to allow them to enjoy their meal in privacy in the living room, the sergeant followed me, took me by the shoulders, and turned me towards the chair by the fire, very gently. 'Madam', he said, 'will you *please* sit down at your own fireside. You've never sat in a chair since the day we arrived. You won't bother us' I wasn't so sure when I glanced at his wife, who was silently serving the vegetables. But I was tired, and I sat down and gratefully stretched my toes to the blazing fire. Coal was strictly rationed, and in very short supply, and we could only have a fire in the evening, but oh it was pleasant to have it glowing strongly so early, because somebody was there to light it in good time for us all to enjoy its comforting cheer with our meal.

I almost fell into a doze as I sat quietly there, for it was the first time for weeks it seemed that I had actually taken time to relax, and afterwards while the wife cleared the table and washed the dishes, the first time I think she had done this task unaided, the sergeant knelt on the hearthrug and showed me all their family photographs. Their little house and garden, his folks and her folks, holiday groups, and a small snap of their wedding taken outside the church. It was then that I saw they hadn't been married very young, and it was also then that I learned they had had no children. Not only was I relaxed, and rather touched that this serious man was so enjoying showing me his home background, but for the first time his face had lost the look of pathetic anxiety it usually wore. Suddenly his wife's voice cut across his story of his best man, 'Will you please go out and fetch some coal', and as he rose obediently she added 'You've been talking to her for half-an-hour'. There wasn't the slightest reason for it, but I felt guilty. In my own house. Looking at snaps. So I rose and said with as casual a tone as I could muster, 'Oh is that the time? I'm due at my mother's soon. I'd better get my skates on.' I avoided the sergeant's eye as we passed each other in the hall, but I knew these were the one and only lodgers I'd take under my roof. I couldn't endure such an atmosphere, and this if you please on top of not feeling free to sit at my own fireside when I felt like it.

When the army officer came back again to see if I would take another lot, I was pleasant (I hope!) but firm. Impossible, I said. They were extremely charming, the couple he'd sent, and it was probably my fault that I felt like the interloper, but anyway my husband was probably coming home on leave and we wouldn't want strangers around. This wasn't exactly true, but it was as plausible an excuse as I could produce without hurting anybody's feelings and it was strong enough to save me from being talked into something I was determined not to do.

It was after they left that I had my nightmare. Because of my claustrophobia, before I went to sleep I always wound up the thick tarred paper which was my black-out in the bedroom, so that only the curtains and the open window were between me and the night air. And before I closed my eyes I always repeated, in case sirens went in the night and I'd switch on the light before remembering I had no black-out in place, 'Don't switch on the light if the sirens go. Don't switch on the light. Attend to the black-out first. Attend to the black-out first'. So that I know it wasn't a nightmare at all, and it all actually happened. How else can my lack of fear be explained, I who was terrified if so much as a mouse scampered across the kitchen in the dark.

I had put out the light, wound up the black-out paper, and realized with pleasure, half-mixed with fear, that it was a bright moonlight night. I loved the clear washed light it shed over the countryside, but I also knew the bombers liked it too, for it lit up their targets, and moonlight and sirens had come to be synonymous.

I fell asleep almost at once, I think, and when I wakened it was because something had broken into my sleep. I looked towards the curtains moving slightly in the night breeze, and without the slightest fear, but with intense interest, I saw the figure of a man appear through the curtains, pause on the ledge for a second, and swing into the room. He was smoking a cigarette and I could see the drift of the smoke in the moonlight, and smell the tobacco. I propped myself on my elbow, and my heart gave a great bound of pleasure, for I saw that the figure was that of Leslie Howard. Now one of my strongest reasons for ever wishing to become a film star was to meet Leslie Howard. He was my idol, gentle and cultured, a marvellous actor in my opinion, and all the films in which he appeared were the sort of stories I adored.

He came towards the bed, sat down on the edge, and gazed into the moonlight with the dreamy abstraction I'd observed so often in his films. He was so close to my vision that I could see the tweed of his jacket, every thread of it magnified at such close range, and the buttons on the sleeve almost brushed my nose. Not a word was spoken. This trance-like stillness must have lasted for about five minutes, and then with a sigh he rose, moved towards the window again, swung his legs over the ledge, and vanished. I calmly accepted this feat of acrobatics, for my bedroom was about twenty feet from the ground and, strangely comforted and honoured by a visit from my favourite actor, I fell asleep again.

In the morning, the wonder of the visit was still with me. When I opened the back door, my neighbour caught sight of me. She was reading a newspaper. 'Oh isn't it awful, Molly', she said, 'Leslie Howard has been shot down in a 'plane coming from Lisbon'. It appeared that enemy intelligence had supposed Winston Churchill was on that 'plane, although there were others who said that Leslie Howard himself worked for Army Intelligence and was quite a prize for them, even if they hadn't got Churchill.

I have absolutely no explanation as to why this visitation happened to me. But I am as sure that it did happen as I am of knowing that we won the war. And I never forgave the Germans for robbing me of my chance to meet him in everyday life. I did meet his sister in the casting studios much much later, but I didn't like to tell her of this extraordinary thing which had happened, because I felt it would be tactless to let her know he had chosen to appear to me who hadn't even met him, and not to his own family who loved him.

Apart from the black-out and the air raids, the most frightening one of which was the intensive bombing of the Clydeside shipyards and Clydebank itself, when the sky was ringed with fire and which I spent huddled in brother Willie's shelter in

Robroyston with his family, the worst thing which happened to me was having to go into hospital. I had a blood disorder which required hospital treatment, and the whole thing was a nightmare, from being carried downstairs to the waiting ambulance to the weeks of near-starvation and sleeplessness.

I had never been accustomed to enormous meals at any time, but in hospital I cried from hunger. The food was so tasteless, and half cold when we received it, that my stomach rejected it. I longed for something tasty, and one night the nurses promised they'd share their midnight feast with me. It was to be black pudding, fried, with a wee potato to eke it out. I drooled over it all during the visiting hour, and my mouth watered in anticipation as the smell drifted from their little kitchen through the ward. I waited and waited, not liking to mention it in case anybody else heard me and would want to share the feast too. Ambulances arrived, feet flew up and down the ward, and at length all quietened down. When a nurse came to take my temperature, I whispered, 'Where's my black pudding?' She stared at me in dismay. 'Oh we forgot all about you', she said. 'We had an emergency, and we've eaten it all.'

I turned my face from her, stifling an anguished cry of disappointment, and cried myself to sleep, my stomach gnawed with hunger, emptier than ever before, because it had expected the delight of fried black pudding. It was a bitter moment, not least because mingled with my empty disappointment was shame for my childish tears.

The nurses obviously thought I was a cough drop. This was because I had answered the matron back, something nobody else dared to do. She was a tiny, black-haired woman with a face of stone, who strode swiftly through the wards each morning and evening, her one concern apparently being to check that all the beds were in perfect line. I used to tell the nurses that if we were a row of corpses, she'd never have noticed, so long as all beds presented a symmetrical picture.

After the episode of the black pudding, I abandoned thoughts of help from the hospital kitchen, and begged my main-law to bring me in a wee pie-dish with a morsel of steak buried in mashed potatoes and turnip. When she smuggled it to me, I persuaded a nurse to heat it on top of the kitchen boiler. As I lay there, wearing a smile of happy anticipation for the feast to come, the matron swept in like an avenging angel. She stood dead centre of the ward and called out in icy tones, 'WHO has dared to bring in food, and asked that it be heated on OUR hospital boiler?' Anybody would have thought it had been a bomb which had been brought in, from her manner. I sat up. Shades of Oliver Twist, I thought. In spite of my quivering fear that the wee pie-dish would be swept from my lips as had been the black pudding, I faced her bravely, 'I dared', I said. She stared at me, then came up to the bed, 'And what do you suppose would happen if everyone did such a thing?', she asked. 'The hospital would be in chaos'. This roused me to a biting defence. 'I don't suppose it would occur to anyone else to do such a thing', I replied in tones as icy as her own, 'and I cannot really see what the fuss is about. I find the food abominable, and I am starving. The food is mine, and I demand to be allowed to eat it.' There was a frozen silence. Everybody was terrified of this wee dragon. Our eyes met and locked. 'Very well', she said at last, 'for this once only. But don't attempt to do it again'. I promised nothing, but I knew I wouldn't get away with a second time, although I hadn't really realized I had done anything so dreadful. But the wee pie-dish filled with home cooking was worth the battle. It was delicious. I savoured every tasty mouthful, and at that moment wouldn't have exchanged it for a mixed grill from the Royal Restaurant, not if the chef had brought it to me with his own hands.

My next clash with the matron came during the night, when I had to rise to go to the toilet. I wasn't supposed to do this, but I avoided bed-pans whenever possible. We only had a tiny night light to illuminate the ward, and because of my phobia about cats and my fear that the ward cat might be prowling around in search of scraps, lifted my long nightdress in one hand, and held out my other hand in front of me in readiness to shoo it away if it came within purring distance. All the nightdresses were the same size, and it depended on the shape and size inside as to whether it was tight or loose, long or short. Mine was long by a good six inches. I must have looked like a sleep-walker, with my hair streaming down my shoulders, my eyes fixed fearfully for a prowling cat, hand stretched in front of me, when the doors of the ward were flung open and in walked the matron with a doctor and the registrar. They stopped dead in their tracks, speechless at first, no doubt afraid to waken what they imagined to be a sleep-walker. 'Good evening', I said serenely, hoping to carry it off by sheer calm acceptance of the situation. The matron came to life. 'Get back to bed immediately', she ordered. 'You have no right to be up'. 'I'm on my way to the toilet', I said, 'and I might as well carry on now. It will be quicker than calling a nurse.' And I did. She was furious, and I had a spasm of sympathy for her that I had been so disobedient in the presence of her two male colleagues.

The only time I saw her smile was when she was in the wee cubby-hole in the ward one morning and the light failed. 'Now I see through a glass darkly', I intoned. She lifted her head in quick surprise, and a smile twitched her lips. 'You're well in noo', hissed a nurse out of the side of her mouth when she passed my bed. 'She's awfu' good-livin', and you're the first person she's ever met in here who kens her bible'.

Everything is mixed with mercy. I learned one valuable lesson in that hospital which was to serve me in good stead in tricky situations in the future. It was, that if you say anything with sufficient authority, people will believe you. The soldiers used to come round the ward to move the beds when the floors had to be polished, and this sudden lifting movement always made me sick. No amount of pleading to be left in peace had any effect. So I worked out a plan.

Next time, two new recruits appeared and the moment they laid hands on my bed I said firmly 'My bed must not be moved. It stays where it is'. They left it alone. They assumed, as I knew they would, that the order had come from the doctor. And the bed was never moved again all the time I was in hospital. The maids just polished round it, and nobody knew the difference. Except me. On polishing days my breakfast now remained where it was intended to stay, in my stomach.

After that success, I used the same voice of implied authority for everything which I knew upset me. I lay flat, undisturbed by queasiness, when all the ward had to sit bolt upright after lunch. I ate dry bread instead of being forced to accept the oily war-time margarine, and I knew the keenest sense of victory when I won the right to keep my rationed butter in my locker, ready to smear on the waxy potatoes to make them more palatable. It was a heady success, and helped to make me well.

8

When I came out of hospital, although I only had one ration book, I was deliriously happy to be able to buy food of my own choosing once more. All the economies I'd learned in childhood from Grannie served me in good stead now, and I could make tasty dishes from the scraps which served as our permitted food allowances. My brother-in-law flatteringly said I was the only person he knew who could make dried egg powder taste something like the real thing, instead of the usual sickening flavour of metal polish. I simply mixed the stuff with milk and seasonings, but blended it with great care, and added the optimism I usually brought to my gardening efforts, and the results were happily palatable.

I used packet soups, like everyone else, but I added rich bone stock to transform them into a tasty and nourishing brew. This passion for bone stock brought my ma-in-law's wrath upon my innocent head, though. My kitchen tended to look like a laboratory, with pots of different sizes full of bones and vegetables which were carefully brought to boiling point daily, all ready for adding their nourishing strength to the basic powders and packet foods which formed such a large part of our war-time diet.

Naturally, when I was whisked off to hospital, the last thought in my mind was of stock-pots, and everyone else was too upset even to think of food, or of checking on my kitchen. Consequently, when my poor ma-in-law visited the house about three weeks later to collect some towels and other items for me, she was nearly knocked flat on her back with the stench of sour and mouldering liquids bubbling in nauseating gassy decay. She was furious. Her normal gentle manner was transformed. I might have prepared the trap deliberately to poison her, from her angry reaction. She banged the towels down on my hospital bed. 'A kitchen fu' o' stinkin' soup', she fumed. 'It was enough to have given me the jaundice'. Every time I tried to explain, 'But ma, how was I to *know* I was going to have to go to hospital', I'd burst into helpless laughter. Which infuriated her all the more. Other people's anger always makes me laugh. Giggling helplessly, I tried to tell her she was being unjust, for nobody enjoyed my soups and stews more than she did, and the secret of their goodness was in the now despised stocks.

She and I were the perfect examples of the wise and foolish virgins. I was always hoarding a wee something for another day. I used to tell her she would turn in her grave if a bomb dared to get her while she had a tin of beans in the larder. She had never been known to keep a single thing for a rainy day. She hated the thought of anything going to waste, so she ate it at once to make sure of it. She was a darling, and I loved her, and it was typical of her large-hearted generosity that she couldn't keep a thing back for what might be a hungrier moment. With ma the time was now. She simply couldn't understand my fears of 'coming to want' and my being so much against eating everything on the ration book at once. I *had* to know there was something left in the larder. I incensed her again, I'm afraid, when I refused to bow to authority and accept what they thought I ought to have for my rations one month. There was a dearth of lean bacon, and an abundance of fat, so the powers-that-be decided that every family must take 2oz. of fat with their ration. This was all right for a family with several books, but I only had one book and 2 oz. of fat represented half my allowance. With infinite patience and with what I saw as clear logic I tried to explain to the grocer that with four books, 2oz. of fat was only one-eighth of the allowance, but that with my one book 2oz. was one-half, and that a single slice of fat with my lean would be just. He kept repeating stubbornly, 'You must take 2oz. That's a Government order'. Food was getting so short by this time that nobody in their right mind refused anything, but I suddenly felt the time had come to show the strength of my determination, and to demonstrate once and for all that we still had a choice. Greed and hunger weren't going to be my masters. There was a principle at stake. I heard myself saying, 'Oh no I need not take 2 oz. of fat, whatever you or the Government says. I can choose to take nothing'. And I walked out of the shop triumphant, leaving a gaping grocer and a group of murmuring women to shake their heads over my folly.

My ma-in-law was outraged when she heard of it. 'You should have taken it and given it to me', she said. Maybe I should, but the sight of that grocer's face was worth the gesture. I showed the same royal disdain the month 'they' decided we had to take one pound of rhubarb jam with our ration. Again this meant my entire month's allowance had to be spent on this unpalatable mixture. Home-made rhubarb jam is one thing, the war-time concoction was a waste of my tiny resources. Again the unfairness of such sweeping decisions overcame hunger. With four books, three pounds of varied preserves were possible, and the 1 lb of rhubarb was merely a fourth of the ration. With me it was 100 per cent. It wasn't fair. I waited until the grocer brought it out from the shelf and started to tear out my jam coupon from my book. 'Wait', I raised an imperious hand. 'I don't want my jam ration this month. I'll wait till next month and have two pounds.' This manoeuvre wasn't really allowed, but the grocer was now becoming nervous that I'd simply vanish down a drain from sheer cussedness in my fight for fairness, for he knew I'd been in hospital and my thinness alarmed him. Or maybe he was just tired and couldn't be bothered arguing. And that month's abstinence was gloriously rewarded for the next month there was a shipment of tinned jam from Australia, apricot and pineapple, and great was my rejoicing when I carried that treasure home. The tins only came in 2lb sizes and if I hadn't spurned the rhubarb, I'd never have qualified for one. This tiny victory fairly put new heart into me, and I knew I must be well on the way to good health when my fighting spirit was returning so vigorously.

I was glad to be able to share that jam with my ma-in-law for she had a particularly sweet tooth, so sweet indeed that if I had taken it into my head to have refused sugar, for whatever reason, I think she would have shown me the door! She used to put sweeties in her tea as a last desperate resort when there wasn't another grain to be scraped out of the sugar poke. We were so used to sharing what little we had with each other, that I was astounded when I went to Nan Scott's house one day to rehearse our Girls of the Old Brigade act for a special concert, and found that she, her husband and sister all had little separate butter plates and sugar bowls. Because I was Nan's visitor, I shared her rations, and when I inadvertently took a wee piece of butter from her sister's plate during the meal, there was such a howl of correction from all of them that I hastily put it back. I couldn't see our family accepting such strict rules at the table, for if one of us didn't take sugar, it was a piece of luck for the others that they got a spoonful more, and visitors shared the lot.

However, this determination to enjoy their entitlements gave me an idea. The one ration I really hated to eat was the war-time margarine. I hadn't tasted bread and butter as a regular part of my diet till I was thirteen years old, but now I loved it, and I didn't mind how thinly it had to be spread so long as it was butter I was enjoying. I knew I could make my two ounces last a week if I kept it solely for my own use so, spurred on by the Scott household's example, I decided that from henceforth my precious 2 oz. was sacrosanct. Everything else I shared, and shared gladly, but my butter was strictly for greasing my own wheels! *What* a difference this made to my attitude towards friends who enjoyed the orgy of devouring their butter ration in one fell swoop. They were now welcome to indulge their taste in this abandoned way without a hint of criticism from me, for when they visited me they ate margarine, and I no longer had to feel resentful watching them devour my butter as well as their own. Fairness was all!

Everybody in war-time had her own particular shortage which was intolerable. With some it was sugar, like my ma-in-law, with others tea, while some people felt a constant craving for bananas and oranges. With my little niece it was what she called 'shell eggs'. To watch her scoop out the contents of a boiled egg was to be reminded of the 'Hums of Pooh' for she hummed joyously as she extracted each spoonful, and only stopped singing long enough to swallow the delicious mouthfuls.

One week-end I told her grannie I would call for Maureen and bring her back to spend Saturday night and Sunday with me, just for a wee change. Travelling with her on the tramcar to my house, we found the lower deck packed and we had to go upstairs. It was a Saturday afternoon, and the entire upper deck seemed to be filled with men, for there were still football matches being played at selected pitches, and they were all obviously on their way to watch the game. Maureen couldn't sit still on my knee, so excited was she to be travelling away from home, and she stood leaning against the far door of the tramcar facing everyone. She carried a string bag which clearly revealed a bottle of a sticky fruit drink, and another which held her milk ration, for she was barely three. 'By jings, hen', said a large man surveying the bag, 'I see you've got yer boatles wi' ye. That's no' a wee hauf ye've goat there, is it?' Maureen pressed her lips together, and shook her head. Then in a burst of confidence she announced to the top deck, 'I'm sleeping with my Auntie Molly tonight, and I'm having a shell egg for my breakfast'. There was a moment's silence, then a roar of laughter as an Irish voice said reflectively, 'Begod, I could be doin' wi' both!'

Maureen's face flushed with bewilderment at the laughter, and I bent my crimson face and prayed for the floor to open up and swallow me. But even in the midst of my embarrassment, a corner of my mind appreciated that it was as neat an example of witty repartee as I was likely to hear in a twelve-month. The whole atmosphere had lightened on that top deck, and if Maureen's innocent remark had sent every man jack of them off to their match with twinkling eyes, then my blushes were a small price to pay. Laughter was in pretty short supply just then.

I certainly found it hard to laugh when I had to turn down a chance to sign with the BBC concert orchestra. They were putting on a special show, and wanted me to do some of my quick-tempo Scottish numbers, but my brother Willie had seen me in hospital, decided it was far too much of a strain just then when I wasn't fully recovered, and threatened to ring them himself if I was mad enough to accept. I was quite impressed by this forceful attitude from easy-going Willie, who knew nothing of show business, and so I meekly bowed to his decision. But secretly I felt I had burned my boats, and the BBC would never ask me to do anything again. Never.

But I was wrong. Shortly afterwards Moultrie rang and asked if I would come to the BBC one Saturday afternoon to meet some film people from London. Film people! Magic words to me. I'd always longed to work in films. What could it be? Over tea in the canteen I learned from the youngish couple to whom I'd been introduced that they were starting a Government sponsored documentary film on the life of a young war wife whose husband was fighting overseas, leaving her to work in a factory, to live in overcrowded digs, and who was expecting a baby. The story was meant to illustrate the harsh facts of everyday living in war conditions, as well as the young wife's ignorance as to how long she could safely continue working. Then would come the birth of the baby in the hygienic conditions of a hospital, and subsequent transfer to dirty tenement digs. The film people accepted Moultrie's recommendation that I could act, and they found my looks just what they wanted. It was all to be shot in two weeks and I was given time off work because it was a Government effort. I was to be a film actress! Not on a glamorous set with Leslie Howard. Up a close, and in a house filled with dirty kids. But a film actress all the same.

When I arrived on the first morning at the empty two room and kitchen tenement we'd been lent for the picture, I was terrified to find that it required about a dozen men to shoot the film. And I had never done a film in my life. I would have to learn it all in front of this critical, technical audience. There were men on the lighting, on the camera itself, on the sound boom, men to haul the camera back and forth, one to load it with film, men to move furniture and props around, to instal the cooker from one part of the kitchen to another as the angles changed, and even a man to make the tea. The simplest action became fraught with tension. Even lighting a match and applying it to the gas stove became unnatural, I shook so much. We rehearsed each short 'take' and then shot it. At the end of the first day the director took me aside. 'Molly', she said, 'in rehearsal you're marvellous'. (I wasn't, but she had to say something encouraging to stop me bursting into tears), 'But when it comes to a 'take' you stiffen up and all the naturalness goes. What can we do to help?'

I was mortified that I was doing so badly something I had always wanted to do. 'Well', I blurted out at last, 'I'm so frightened I'll make a.mistake, and waste all that expensive film, and there's the wages for all those men having to be paid if I don't do it right the first time'. She laughed in genuine amusement. 'Good God', she said, 'is that all? Look Molly, *they* will make mistakes too. They'll underestimate the amount of film for a particular shot, and you'll have to do it again. They'll ruin your best shot because the sound boom will come into vision. They'll do a dozen silly things because we're all human, and in filming nobody expects you to get it right the first time. This isn't Shakespeare, it's a piddling little documentary, which we must do as well as we can, but it won't lose the war if we spend a few bob extra on it.'

We had stopped for the day, and when she said goodnight she said, 'Now tomorrow I want you to forget the camera, and just be your own natural self.'

Next morning we hadn't been going half an hour when the camera ran out of film. The assistant had under-estimated the length of the shot. I was charmed. The director had been speaking the truth then, and not just saying those things to comfort me. I never from that moment gave the camera another thought. I let them get on with their part of the job, and I got on with mine, and the whole day's shooting apparently showed such a staggering improvement that she re-shot the first day's work, and it was all sheer fun from that moment on.

It wasn't much fun for the rest of the tenants living up that close though. They were livid that their rather posh building was playing the part of a slum for any film, and they were certainly not putting up with the annoyance of lengths of cable running up and down the stairs like snakes, although they had been told this was necessary to provide lighting from our own generator. They also had strong objections to the crowds of men and actors clattering up and down the stairs all day long, starting at the usual unearthly film time of 7 A.M. When we arrived on the third day, a large policeman barred our way, brought in by the tenants. My heart turned over in dismay, for

I was sure my film career had come to an untimely end. However, the director smilingly produced our authority, a buff form imposingly stamped by a government official that we were part of the war effort, and the tenement rebellion was at an end.

We had a real slum mother and her six children for the tenement scenes, for hers was supposed to be the house to which I returned after the birth of my baby. Their ages ranged from about eighteen months to eight years, and they were enchanted to find themselves in a house which contained an unknown magic to them, an inside toilet. Every time we went to shoot a scene, we had to rescue one or more of the children from the lavatory, where their favourite entertainment was pulling the chain. The noise was continuous, like a miniature Niagara, and the sound boom couldn't go into action until the last gurgle had been silenced. The mother of this brood was dazed with her luck at not only earning money for all of them, but in having their food provided. This was a 'perk' we all enjoyed. To be free from the nagging planning of our meagre rations was a bonus to be prized above the modest pay packet. Special arrangements for our catering were possible because we were working 'on location'. We had hot doughnuts and tea mid-morning. Meat and vegetables and a sweet were brought in containers at lunch time, and we stopped for more tea and buns around half-past-three. Those children visibly filled out during the week we worked in that tenement. The mother gave me my most hilarious moment when she told me of her husband's behaviour when he had been home on leave. She had left him to look after the six of them while she had the bliss of a night out at the pictures with her sister. Just to get away from the house for a night had become a craving, for of course she couldn't leave them when he was away. On her return from the pictures, she found all six children sitting up in bed, three at the top and three at the bottom, each smoking a half-cigarette. Her husband groaned at sight of her, 'My heavens', he said, 'I'd rather fight the Germans ony day than look efter this mob'. 'Smoking, Mrs Clark', I gasped, 'the baby too'. 'The hale six o' them', she assured me. 'What did you do?', I asked curiously, assuming that she would be terrified by the thought of them setting fire to the bed, or ruining their health at such a tender age. 'I just tellt him that if he wis teachin' the weans tae smoke, then he would dampt well pey fur their cigarettes'. That was all it had meant to her. An expensive habit. But I suppose when you live in a condemned house, with water running down the walls, on the tiniest of allowances, everything has to be measured in terms of money. And in spite of poverty, she was a large placid happy woman, and I rejoiced with her at the sight of those children tucking into all that good food, provided so unexpectedly because of a Government film.

On the Sunday we were filming at the steam wash-house near Gallowgate. At last I was really going to see the inside of 'the steamie', whose interior had only been glimpsed when I was a wee girl visiting the swimming baths and the slipper baths in Springburn.

Again it was a 7 A.M. start, and the wifies who had been recruited were thrilled to be allowed to do their washings free of charge, to feel they were elevated to the glamorous world of films, and to be paid £1 each for their day's work into the bargain. They smiled self-consciously as they thrust clothes into tubs, and later lifted dripping bundles with strong graceful movements from one water to the next, finally gliding in a smooth swooping movement across the line of the camera, their baskets overflowing with clean sweet-smelling clothes.

They had left husbands at home with the children. They had merely been told by the casting director that they were just to do their washing in the ordinary way. As this was something they could normally accomplish in an hour or so, they had assured their husbands they would be home in good time for lunch. They'd get their washing done buckshee, and £1 for their trouble! It was money for old rope! That was what they thought!

Lunch-time came and went. Tea-time came and went. And still the director hadn't managed to get the shots she wanted for the 'steamie' sequence. Once more the wifies had to swallow their irritation, and put the clean clothes into the water and lift them out again. And again. And again. I could see how this offended their housewifely pride, and that for two pins they'd have thrown the ten-times-over washed clothes in the director's face. I think they would really have mutinied if they hadn't seen that the same thing was happening to me, and that I was having to do several shots over and over again until the director was satisfied it was perfect. One of the women said to me wonderingly, as snow was being brushed off my hair for the sixth time, 'My Goad, dae ye earn a livin' at this? I'd rether scrub flairs, so ah wid'. Another said, 'Ma man'll knock the stuffin' oot o' me. Ah've been oot the hoose since hauf-past-six this mornin' an' ah've left him wi' seven weans. God knows whit he's gi'ed them tae eat'. Disillusionment was complete. Weariness filled their eyes and slowed their movements. The clothes felt like lead as they lifted and rinsed them once more. '£1', one of them muttered, 'Ah widnae dae this again if they peyed us in diamonds'. Who indeed would be a film actress, unless she were truly star-struck?

But in spite of the hard work, there was unexpected cosseting which was very much to my taste. As a rule, I had to make my own way everywhere by unreliable tram or bus, and in wartime it was nothing to have to stand for over half-an-hour in freezing cold. So to me, it was truly privileged comfort to be brought back by special coach from all locations, with never a thought of queueing. At the end of each day I was so happy that it had gone well and that I was at last getting the hang of the technique, I sang all the way. I did impersonations of Barbara Mullen singing 'Eileen Og' and 'I know where I'm going' for the especial delight of the Irish director, who found them 'twee' and amusing. But when I at last got into the house, I was so tired I could hardly find the energy to make the tea. Rising at 6 A.M. and working through to at least 6 P.M. seven days a week was a punishing routine, especially when it was all so new to me. And although we were being fed on location, fresh fruit or vegetables were practically unknown at this stage of the war, and there were few energy-producing vitamins in anyone's diet.

And then, just when the finished film had been taken to London for cutting and editing, I came home from work one night and my husband was sitting in the living room. He took one look at my thinness and my pallor, and as he dried my tears of surprise and relief at the sight of him all safe and sound, he said slowly, 'Aye, it's time somebody was here to look after you.'

I hadn't realized how much being independent and facing all fears alone had taken the stuffing out of me, and oh it was nice having the one I needed most to lean on for a wee while.

It was for a very wee while, as it turned out, for this was embarkation leave. At that time, all troops bound for foreign-shores were assumed to be going to the dreaded jungles of Burma.To fool the enemy intelligence, every departing service-man seemed to be issued with tropical kit, so we all feared the worst. Sure enough, my husband was no exception, and we both felt it was surely Burma for him. He had to go to Blackpool for some more training, and to be issued with his overseas kit, and I vowed I'd manage a week-end there somehow, to wave him off. We were all inspired by the example of Vera Lynn, the sweetheart of the Forces, who sang so bravely, 'Wish me luck as you wave me goodbye'.

We had worked out a little code to fool any enemy spies who might tap our telephone line. When he knew it was his final week-end before embarkation, he would telephone and ask if I fancied some shell-fish, and I'd know that was the week-end of parting. I didn't dare tell my ma-in-law of this plan, for even if the artist Fougasse drew his fingers to the bone with cartoons of Hitler and his minions hiding under train seats, or under beds, or up in railway racks, or even in left luggage shelves listening to our every careless word, ma refused to believe that the woman up the stair could be a spy, or for that matter the man in the Co-operative, and she had to say *something* to them when they asked where her son was. Dear innocent ma couldn't accept that although neighbours might be entirely innocent, a casual remark could travel far and endanger a whole ship. Or a whole battalion. I on the other hand believed anything was possible, for hadn't Hitler's deputy, Rudolph Hess, landed almost at the end of our street and been taken to our very own local police station? If they could find Giffnock, there was no knowing where else they might be lurking. So I was very careful, and I told nobody, not even my boss, that I was bound for Blackpool for the week-end.

It was bitterly cold there, and my heart felt numb as I

476

watched platoons of men in Air Force uniform drilling and marching, my own loved one just a blue blur seen through watery eyes. Although it was winter, the fairground remained open, and we sat in empty roller-coasters and pretended we were having a marvellous, unexpected winter holiday. Those stomach-jolting entertainments usually terrified me, but when all was fear, what did one more matter?

We ate shell-fish in vinegar, holding the little plates in blue fingers at wayside stalls. And that night, when we wakened with the queasy sensation that the house was rocking, we thought it was the shell-fish, or a too vivid dream of the roller-coaster. But it was none of those things. It was a small earthquake, the first Blackpool had experienced in its history. Amidst so much that was strange and unreal, this was just one more item, and we wondered if there would be any future for us when we would be able to talk about our earthquake, or if Burma would be the end of everything.

On the train going home to Glasgow, I began to feel ill. Surely emotion couldn't have such a physical reaction, I thought. I had to change trains and, standing on the darkened platform, I longed to find the courage to go into the buffet and ask for whisky or brandy. But I lacked the sophistication to go in alone, in December, to ask with a Scottish accent for such strong drink. Instinct told me spirits would be the only thing which would stop this shivering pain that gripped me. Years of Rechabite teaching held my feet in a vice on the platform, but when perspiration started to trickle down my arms in an icy stream, I broke loose and tottered into the station bar – only to find that the hours were wrong and they couldn't serve me. Maybe God and the Rechabites were fighting the demon drink and protecting me from myself.

I was thankful only the dimmest blue light illuminated the railway carriage, for I staggered back and forth to the toilet a dozen times between Blackpool and Glasgow. I was ashamed and felt the other passengers must imagine I was drunk. Somehow I managed to reach home, having to get off the tramcar more than once to be sick, but at last I reached the blessed sanctuary of my own bed, and fell instantly into an exhausted stupor. It was shell-fish poisoning, the doctor said, and gave me a line to get extra milk to help build me up.

Nobody had time to be ill in war-time, and I was glad I had a 'Down at the Mains' broadcast for Hogmanay, to keep my mind off thoughts of convoys and submarines, and men floundering in icy waters. I played the wee servant, Teenie Tawse, in this radio series, with Grace McChlery playing the farmer's wife and Willie Joss a pawky old buffer called Old Cairnallochie, and our signature tune was lively 'Dashing White Sergeant'. On this particular broadcast, we had to sing 'A Guid New Year', and each time in rehearsal when we came to the second verse, and the words 'And may ye ne'er ha'e cause tae mourn, or shed a bitter tear', thoughts of my husband and a Burma grave swept over me and I burst into floods of tears. I was determined to overcome this shaming weakness, but when we came to the actual broadcast, Grace McChlery took me gently by the arm, and opened the door leading out of the studio. 'Molly', she said, 'don't try. Just stand outside till it's finished, or you'll have us all in tears'.

The shell-fish poisoning must have robbed me of my strength, for I did as I was bid, and stood on the other side of the door, gazing through the little glass panel at them all singing round the microphone, tears streaming down my cheeks. When the song was over, I dried my eyes and went back and finished the scene.

When the first air-mail letter came it wasn't from Burma after all. It was from the Middle East. Those sun-hats and that tropical equipment had been a cheat-the-Germans subterfuge right enough. When the first glorious feeling of relief had subsided, I felt mad at the Government for having given us all that heart-stopping worry unnecessarily, and then I slowly had to admit the wisdom behind such planning. For although I was now beginning to believe I had some qualifications for calling myself an actress, I knew that if a spy had been keeping an eye on me during that time of strain and worry, no histrionics of mine could have been so convincing to an onlooker as was my genuinely haggard appearance between the Blackpool farewell and the arrival of that beautiful air-mail letter.

My ma-in-law had been very hurt by my keeping Sandy's

departure a secret until he was well and truly on the eve of arrival at his destination, so I now told her he was in the Middle East but kept the exact location deliberately vague. I still felt that Glasgow was hotching with spies, and I brushed up my German at conversation classes, so that I would be wise to their every utterance if ever their path crossed mine.

With my mind relieved that my husband wasn't destined to perish in Burma, I could enjoy all my BBC work again. Gordon Jackson became a great chum, although he was a nightmare to work with because of his tendency to giggle. I remember when we were doing Bridie's 'The Tragic Muse', where he and I were playing the young lovers, and there was a line of Meg Buchanan's where she had to react to finding a body in her bath. Instead of horror, she had to bemoan the fate of her bath, and in a strident tone she wailed, 'Ma bath! Ma bath! Ma GOOD bath!'. Gordon stood opposite me at the microphone, and as soon as Meg howled out this line, his eyes caught mine and he burst out laughing, setting me off too. It was a very dramatic moment in the play and the producer was furious. He bade Gordon to stand where he couldn't see my face, for it was to be a live broadcast, as were they all in those days, and he didn't want the atmosphere of the play ruined at the actual performance. Gordon obediently stood close behind me, to be ready for our dialogue, and when we reached the dreaded line from Meg, he laughed so hard that his stomach beat against my back like a drum tattoo, and I could hardly get a word out through my suppressed laughter. When we came off the air, Gordon gasped, 'Oh I hope the public thought it was emotion which made our voices shake'. They did too. I know they did, because many people told me that our terror was most convincing, because our voices trembled so uncontrollably! But I came to dread working with Gordon after that, because once the pattern of laughter has been set, it becomes increasingly difficult to control.

I remember another time when he was sent out of the studio for giggling, and he sat in the control room till he was wanted for his scenes. When he came back for a scene with me, he was determined not to meet my eye in case an accidental glance would set us both off, so he did something we never normally did – he took his eyes right off the script and gazed into space. I finished my speech. Silence from Gordon. I looked up in alarm, and saw he was dreaming. I kicked him savagely on his shin-bone, and with a start he came back to the play and found his line. But in taking my own eyes off my script, I'd now lost my place! My heart skittered with fright. Wildly my eyes flew up and down the page, and just in the nick of time, as he uttered his final word, I found my next speech. That taught me a lesson. Never again would I lift my eyes from the script, not if every actor at the mike dropped dead in front of me.

And by jove, one of them very nearly did drop dead, thanks to a too realistic sound effect while we were playing 'Kidnapped'. The old chap playing Ebenezer was supposed to be having his breakfast porridge when I, playing the boy, came in to impart some vital news. To get the right effect, our producer had had a thin sort of gruel made up, which Ebenezer supped and smacked right through his next speech. Some of this gruel went down the wrong way, and he stood there choking, and uttering strangled whistling noises, fighting for breath. As he was a very experienced elderly actor, I just thought it was wonderfully realistic acting. Only when he rushed from the studio at the end of his speech, and I could see him through the glass of the control room being thumped on the back, tears streaming down his cheeks as he fought to get his breath back, did I realize it hadn't been acting at all, but a near tragedy. Again this was a live broadcast, and the listeners must have been most impressed with the quality of that choking scene!

I had never heard the army advice 'Never volunteer'. So it was my own fault when, during the rehearsal of a play, where one of the actresses had to play a consumptive, I found I had jumped right into it with both flat feet. I had piped up and said to Moultrie Kelsall, our producer, 'That's not a consumptive cough'. This was in no spirit of criticism of the actress, but because I couldn't bear inaccuracy. I knew full well and everybody in Springburn knew only too well the authentic cough, for TB at that time was very common.

Moultrie laid down his script and raised his eyebrows. 'Oh?', he said, 'Perhaps you'd like to let us all hear what *is* a consumptive cough'. I gave the little dry rattle which I knew so well. He pursed his lips reflectively, 'Well, since you can vouch for it, perhaps you'd like to do it throughout the play?'

It was ghastly. I had my own performance to do, we were at the mike for an hour, and I never sat down. I had to mark every blessed cough on my script, timing it to the other actress's lines, and then clear my throat and get into the character for my own part. At the end of the performance, Moultrie gave me a sly smile, 'Very nice, dear. Very nice'. I smiled weakly back, my throat raw, reeling from nervous concentration. That would teach me not to open my big mouth in future. But it was characteristic of Moultrie that he trusted my judgement about the accuracy of the cough, and that he knew I could be relied upon to fit the coughing to the lines. He was a great man for stretching the talents of any performer, and we all did broadcasts and stage shows for him which extended our range in ways of which we never dreamed we were capable.

By this time, I was well established in my second regular radio series, which was to become a great joy to me and which was to make me a real 'name' in Glasgow, and in Scotland. Helen Pryde, also from Springburn by the way, had devised the authentic Glasgow family called 'The McFlannels', which I've mentioned earlier in this book. Mrs McLeather, my original part, had been quietly dropped, to my delight, and I was now that wee Glesca Keelie, Ivy McTweed, and Ivy made an enjoyable contrast to the wee douce Teenie of 'Down at the Mains', which I was still playing. I felt I knew everything about Ivy, from the top of her frizzy perm to the peerie heels of her dance shoes, and I devised a sort of basic gallus laugh for her, which apparently was so true to life that I was unable to convince a man met on a journey from London to Glasgow that I hadn't based it on the neighbour round the corner from his house in Rutherglen. 'But you *must* have copied Sadie McPherson's laugh', he kept saying, 'fur the hale close recognized it the minute you did it. It wisnae just me'. He refused to believe I'd never even heard of Sadie McPherson, much less her laugh, for he was quite certain nobody, but nobody, could have copied such an individual laugh so accurately.

Ivy wasn't the only one with an identifying laugh. She had a bosom pal, 'Giggling Bella', who never uttered a single word

481

during the eleven years the series ran. She brilliantly varied those giggles to sound admiring, frightened, awed, daring or flirty, as the stories demanded, and she was beautifully played by Effie Morrison, later to reach world recognition as Mistress Niven of 'Doctor Finlay's Case-book'.

I was now doing so much radio that there was scarcely an evening or a week-end I wasn't out rehearsing, and my fellow-actors and actresses had become real friends and were great company.

Between times there were the concerts, and I even took part in one from the war factory where I now worked in the typing pool as my part of the war effort. They were glad of my speeds, and it was within walking distance of my home – a great boon. I had always used trains, or buses or trams to get to work, but with unreliable schedules, and black-out it was now bliss to have my timekeeping controlled by my own fleetness of foot. One of the older colleagues used to shake her head when she saw me racing up and down the hill, 'It's not *good* for you to rush about like that', she would say. 'You should allow yourself five extra minutes and go at an even pace.' But I just laughed. At that time I must surely have had the heart and stamina of a long distance runner, and a slow pace was something which simply didn't apply to me.

I taught my big friend Mary the words and music of 'Girls of the Old Brigade', and I borrowed the tramway uniforms, for my colleague Mary was near enough the height and build of Nan Scott, my stage partner. We had allowed it to be whispered throughout the factory, via the office boys, that we were doing a very classical number, and we knew the men and women from the benches where the bombs were made were prepared to be bored to tears. We were from 'upstairs in the office' and in their view we were the posh side of war effort. So they swallowed our propaganda, hook, line and sinker. When they saw us march in wearing the uniforms of the first world-war conductresses, they couldn't believe their eyes. There was a yell of delighted laughter, and we brought the house down when we went into our broad Glasgow patter. They couldn't believe 'thae yins in the oaffice' had it in them! Mary and I enjoyed their smiles and friendship for the duration of the war after that appearance. And my popularity with the management was sealed when I made up a slogan in the 'War Effort Contest', with the winning sentence, 'NO VIC.ORY WITH AN ABSEN-TEE'. This was painted on the factory walls in letters of vivid blue thereafter. But I never got my prize money.

9

I so despised that rich management for gypping me out of my
£5 prize for my slogan, especially when they used it right till
the end of the war, that I simply cocked a snook at them and
became an Absen-tee myself when I got the chance of an
interview with John Mills for a part in a new play he was
touring, written by his wife. Strangely enough, I had been
recommended to John Mills by Leslie Howard's sister Irene,
who was casting director for the famous MGM studios and *she*
had heard of me through the film director who had done the
little documentary picture up at that posh close in Glasgow.
Apparently the Americans had been delighted with the picture.
It was the first time they had been shown anything of the
working-class side of Britain. Previously their mental picture of
our country had been of Royalty, old lace and polished silver,
of country house parties and riding to hounds. They were
enchanted to find we had an earthier side, and declared that
the film owed everything to the sincerity of the young couple
playing the husband and wife. It was an odd sidelight to me
that I never even clapped eyes on my 'husband' during the
entire film. He was supposed to be a soldier, of course, and all
his scenes were shot on active service. When I did meet him
after the war, he had to introduce himself to me, and now I see
him practically every time I visit the STV studios in Glasgow,
where he works, and we share nostalgic memories of our
'starring' roles in our very first film.

When I received the telegram from Irene Howard asking me
to ring her at MGM studios, my heart gave a hop, skip and a
jump of excitement. What could it be? Was I going to star in a
first-feature film? How had she heard of me? It was my lunch-
hour so I flew to the telephone, only to discover she wasn't

there. I had to cool my heels until I had finished at half-past-five, for, short of my house going on fire, I hadn't a hope of being given permission to use the office telephone. After work, I raced up the road to the house, got through to the studios and she told me that John Mills wished to re-cast a real Scottish character for his new play. It was an oldish part, a woman of sixty-plus in fact, but she was sure that it would be useful for me to be seen and that if he liked me otherwise, make-up and costume would do the rest. He was in Leeds, and I was to present myself to his hotel at tea-time the next day, and watch the performance that night. The next day was Friday. How was I to get the time off? Not for a moment did I dream of missing the interview. War-time or no, I was determined to see John Mills in person. It was only the carrying out of my plan which exercised me.

I knew it wasn't the slightest bit of good asking off, because we had had a high old drama only a few months back when one of the lads in the office had asked the boss if he could go home to Liverpool for the week-end, as his fiancée was very ill. He had been refused permission, but he went just the same, and when he came back to the office on the Monday morning he wasn't even allowed to take his coat off. He had been handed his cards, and shown the door. This in spite of the fact that we were desperately short of young men of this lad's experience in accountancy. We had counted ourselves lucky to have him, and blessed his flat feet which had kept him out of the forces.

When I came into the main office that morning, after taking some notes from the boss, I found the place in a ferment. Everybody was denouncing the boss, 'As if dogs widnae lick his blood', as my grannie would have said. As I approached the group crowded round the centre desk, I heard wild words of 'all coming out on strike' to show our solidarity with young Len. 'What do you think, Molly?', they asked me. 'You've just seen that old devil, has he said onything?'

I told them, quite truthfully, that he had said nothing to me but that I thought they had no justification for coming out on strike. They stared at me, furious that I didn't agree with them. Patiently, working it out in my mind as I spoke, I said that if Len had simply taken French leave and gone to Liverpool, and returned on Monday morning with the story that he had a chill, even if the boss hadn't believed a word of it and had suspected a bit of skiving, without proof he could have done nothing. But because we all knew that Len had *asked* and been refused, and had openly defied the boss's authority, then there was no alternative but to make an example of him and dismiss him. It was cruel, I agreed, but in war-time conditions above all, it was absolutely essential that the man at the head of the affairs should be seen to have authority and to have his decisions respected and obeyed. There was silence for a moment or two. 'She's right', one of the older men said, 'Len was a bloody fool. He should never have asked'. As they drifted back to their desks, the boss, who had opened his door during the latter part of the discussion, rang for me. When I entered, feeling quite a heroine for having saved the factory from a strike, which might have left those hellish Japs free to wreak more evil upon us (we were making bombs for use against Japan), I was stunned when the boss informed me that I was far too dangerous a personality to be tolerated, and had far too much influence over the others, and that for me to encourage a strike in war-time was treason! I could feel myself almost suffocating with righteous indignation. 'Encourage a strike!', I cried dramatically, 'I have just averted one, and it was precisely because I knew your authority must be upheld, rightly or wrongly, that I told them they had no justification for coming out'. For good measure, I added cuttingly, for I was well away by this time and had forgotten he was the boss, who could easily sack me, 'Poor Len was a fool. He should never have asked you. But having asked you and then defied you, you had to sack him'.

There was a silence, while my heart thumped, and common-sense returned and I waited to be told to collect my cards. The boss coughed. 'I see', was all he said. 'I'll want these notes typed by lunch-time', and he returned to his desk without another word. Not even an apology for having misjudged me. We had been standing facing one another like boxers, and I found my legs trembling when I went back into the main office.

So, with that experience to guide my actions, plus the memory of having been robbed of my fiver for my slogan, I made my plans. As soon as I'd swallowed my tea, I rushed up to Springburn, a forty-five minutes' journey by tramcar, and I plotted with my ma-in-law. She would ring the office next morning and say that I had been up all night with diarrhoea (there was a lot of it about, with all the queer food we were eating), and she would tell them that I would be back on Monday if I felt better. I couldn't ask my own mother, for not only was she unused to the telephone with her deafness, but she didn't go home from her work at the munitions factory during the day and would have had no access to a telephone anyway.

Later, my friend Mary told me when ma had rung to pass on the news of my unreliable innards, the boss had tut-tutted angrily and had said, 'That mother-in-law of hers simply spoils her. She's as strong as a horse, really'. Mary had been let into the secret, for she would have to tackle my work as well as her own, and she told me she had had a job to stop laughing at the boss's reaction.

With the factory deception safely arranged, I packed a bag, remembering to include the solitary pair of sheer silk stockings that brother-in-law Jimmy had managed to buy for me in France before the Germans swept through, laid out my one and only decent suit, a green Shetland tweed that my husband had bought for me before he left for the Middle East, and set the alarm for the morning. I always kept a few pounds in the house to cover emergencies, so I had enough for my train fare.

Next afternoon, when I arrived at the hotel in Leeds, I went straight to the ladies' room and took off the thick lisle stockings which we all wore at that stage of the war. I took the fine dark silk ones, so prudently saved for just this sort of occasion, it seemed, and started to pull one over my toes, scarcely daring to breathe in case a ragged nail might catch a thread and cause a ladder to mar its perfection. Suddenly I was aware of a rustle of movement around me. I had been too absorbed and excited to notice anyone else in the ladies' room. But they had noticed me, and I looked up to find a circle of faces gazing with awe at the fine silk I was pulling over my knee. 'Where did you get them?', one lady breathed, looking down sadly at her own clumsy stockings. I started to tell them that my brother-in-law had brought them from France, but they weren't listening.

They stood as though mesmerized by my legs. They seemed to sigh in unison, and one of them vowed that when the war was over the first thing she was going to buy was a pair of the sheerest silk stockings she could find. As they drifted away, I heard one lady say to her friend, 'Do you know, I had actually forgotten our legs could ever look like that'. So had I, and as I gazed at my reflection in the mirror, I decided that even if John Mills disliked every other thing about me, he couldn't but be impressed by the elegance of such expensive-looking silk-clad legs.

When I went into the tea lounge, I recognized him at once. I was so excited to be greeted by the famous John Mills that I forgot to be nervous or self-conscious. I even forgot my silk stockings. I was surprised to find him such a finely-drawn man, with small bones, a slim build, and a pale look of tension which vanished the moment he smiled. When he did so, his entire face lit up, the eyes, the mouth, and one felt he was basically a witty, humorous man, but that the strains of touring theatre in war-time were perhaps beginning to tell. He was dismayed to find me so young, and found the same resemblance to Janet Gaynor in my appearance that newspapers had remarked, and which at that time was the nickname the children in Glasgow gave to me. He described the plot of the play, and said that while he would be delighted to re-cast the part with a real Scot, he felt it would be a great pity if somebody so young as I was (he also said 'and so pretty' if I am going to speak the whole truth!) made her début in London in a part which was really for an elderly woman. I would be able to judge for myself when I saw the play that evening, but he added 'You'd be type-cast for good, Molly. Managements would only remember you as they first saw you, and it would really be better to wait to appear in something much nearer your own age'. I liked his assumption that it was only a matter of time before I appeared in London!

Over a delicious tea of toast and tea-cakes he told me what a perfectionist his wife was as a writer, and how often he had had to rescue her work when she chucked it out in disgust. I blushed when he confided, without a trace of self-consciousness, that once she'd actually thrown a play down the lavatory. And he'd fished it out! We didn't talk like that about lavatories in Springburn. He knew how good her work was, but she was never satisfied – a true sign of talent. I could see he adored her.

I heard all about his early days, of trying to pretend he liked office work, and of his struggles to break into the theatre and films, and I listened with my mouth open, drinking in every word and wishing he didn't have a play to do, so that I could have gone on listening to such confidences, straight from the fountainhead, for the rest of the evening.

Still there *was* the play to see, and I had a 'house' seat in the stalls, four rows from the front, free of charge. I found the play thoroughly absorbing, and very strong melodrama. As well as John Mills, the cast included Elspeth March (then the wife of Stewart Granger), and Elwyn Brook-Jones. In spite of my concentration on the part I was being considered for, I soon forgot to watch out for her entrance, so dramatic were all the twists and turns of the plot. When she did eventually make her appearance, I was terribly tempted. She was an old Scottish nannie, fey and spry, with an agile turn of speed on her entrances and exits, and although the part was smallish, it was important to the plot. But oh, could I endure to cram my hair under a wee tight grey wig for every performance, and sit till the third act before I opened my mouth? And did I want to go on playing elderly wifies before I'd even been seen as a young one in London? John Mills' words about type-casting had given me pause, for this was something I had never had to consider in Scotland, where I played anything and everything from schoolboys to grannies.

Afterwards, I was invited to join the party at dinner in the hotel dining room. Not only were the play's principals there, but Florence Desmond had been included, as she was starring at the nearby variety playhouse. I was nearly swooning with excitement at eating in such starry company. I devoured every word they uttered, as though wisdom had been brought down with the tablets from on high. After all, I was with the crême-de-la-crême. These people had all 'arrived'. They were household names. Their world was the world of show business, and I could learn much if I kept my mouth shut and my ears open.

I was specially interested in the theories of Florence Desmond, although I had enough sense not to mention that I also did impersonations. I could recognize a member of the first league when I saw one! And I knew I was in the third division. She was of the opinion that one should only work with the best. Some variety people, she said, liked to be the big frog in the small pond, and to top a bill of mediocre players, because they thought that by doing so they'd shine all the brighter. 'And don't they?', I ventured to ask. 'No honey', she said. (Honey! What a nice thing to call me!). 'All that happens is that the audience goes out at the end of the show and says "Well, that was a lousy bill". They *don't* say, "That was a lousy bill, but Joe Doaks was all right". What they go out with is an impression of second-rate entertainment and that goes for every act on the bill'.

'Now', warming to her theme, 'if *all* the acts are first-class, not only does the quality rub off so that everybody gives absolutely top performances, but the audience goes out saying, "That was a *marvellous* show. Not a dud act among them", and every name on that bill shares in their memories the magic of a great night out, when nothing disappointed.'

I suppose it was just another way of expressing Shaw's advice, 'Never associate with failures', but I was most impressed with her clever reasoning, and I never forgot it. Later, when I went into the real West End theatre, I found that managements knew this truth too, for few successes included also-rans in the cast-list.

Before we parted for the night, John Mills said to me, 'Well the part is yours if you want it, Molly. How do you feel about it?' When I had left Glasgow, it had never crossed my mind that the choice would be up to me. If anybody had suggested that I would be offered a chance to appear in the West End of London and would have hesitated for an instant about saying 'yes', I'd have laughed in his face. Now I was all mixed up. The seeds of indecision had been sown with all this talk of typecasting. What was I to do? My stomach whizzed with nerves. Suddenly, inspiration came, and I saw my way out of this dilemma. I would just throw it back to him again. After all, he knew far more about show business than I did.

'What would be your advice?', I said. 'What would you do if you were in my place?' He looked at me very thoughtfully, and I held my breath. My life could easily turn completely upside down, depending on what he said next. 'I'm speaking against my own interests in saying this', he said at last, very slowly, 'for I know you could play this part standing on your head, and I badly want to re-cast it, but for the sake of your future, I would advise you to wait'. I didn't know whether to be glad or sorry. He patted my shoulder, 'Wait for the right part, wait till you can be seen as the lively young person you are. Don't let London's first sight of you be in the disguise of an old woman. That's my advice'.

I took it.

On my way to my bedroom I passed the beautiful Elspeth March and she was speaking on the corridor telephone to her husband. I was fascinated to hear her call him 'Jimmy'. Fancy me hearing Stewart Granger's wife chatting to him, and using his private name, and giving me a friendly wave as I passed as though we were chums. And fancy me having been allowed to choose whether or not I'd accept a stage part! A London career did honestly seem a little nearer now. I had been accepted into the acting scene by professional actors, without anybody turning a hair or thinking it in the least odd that I should be one of them. The entire marvellous day and evening had been like a dream. And wouldn't my mother be thrilled to hear I'd actually sat at the same table as Florence Desmond, Elspeth March and John Mills and indulged in show-biz chat as we passed the chips round? I could hardly wait to get home to tell her all about it.

I'd have to calm down, though, before I returned to the office on Monday morning, and try to look suitably peelie-wallie to convince the boss that I truly had been under the weather. This would be a very good acting test for me, to have to save all my news for the evening, when I'd invite Mary home for tea and would reward her co-operation by telling her chapter and verse everything that had happened since we had parted on Thursday. Was it only Thursday? It seemed weeks since the diarrhoea plot had been hatched.

But when I did get to the office on Monday, I found that Mary had been laid low by asthma, that scourge which felled her with sickening regularity and which prevented her from adding so much as a pound to her slender frame. So there was no need to do any acting to prove my integrity, for it was all hands to the pumps to get through the work, and nobody was paying the slightest attention to my looks, healthy or otherwise.

By the end of the week, I was well and truly punished for my pretended illness, for half the office were down with various complaints, from gastric upsets to bronchitis, and I hadn't a minute to breathe. It was wages week too, and the wee old-fashioned accounts' clerk, whose thin legs and shallow complexion made her the butt of the office boys' jokes, was frantic that she wouldn't be able to meet her deadline and balance cash, books and Income Tax deductions in readiness for the Friday pay-out. Filled with euphoria at having dined with John Mills and Florence Desmond, and feeling I owed the company extra time anyway, I nobly volunteered to come in at 8 A.M. on Thursday morning and help wee Miss Turpentine to get through the work. Her sharp little face filled with gratitude, and I went to bed early to make sure of being fresh as a daisy when the alarm went off.

Next morning as I slowly drifted to an awareness of the day, I decided I must have had a really refreshing sleep for I was awake before the alarm went. Mmmm, I reflected as I snuggled luxuriantly into the warmth of the pillow, how lovely not to be jerked to my feet by the whine of that penetrating electric buzzer. Then I became aware of another sound, that of the murmur of neighbours' voices on the pavement outside. Apprehension gripped my stomach. 'What time was it, when they could stand chatting in such a leisurely manner? It must be after breakfast time!' I leaped from the bed. It was broad daylight. There had been a power cut, and the alarm had stopped at 4 A.M. I rushed downstairs and found it was twenty-five-past eleven!!! And I had promised that fraught wee soul that I'd be in at 8 A.M.

I threw on my clothes, and didn't even stop to make a cup of tea, but ran all the way to the factory, and I was so distraught that the aloof glare which Miss Turpentine turned on me changed at once to a touching concern. I shouldn't have run like that, she told me, it was enough to make me drop dead. 'I knew something must have happened', she assured me, 'I knew it, because you are utterly reliable'. I had missed the coffee break, and didn't even have the comfort of a hot drink to see me through till lunch time, but my heart was singing with that heart-warming testimonial. How my grannie would have rejoiced to hear such words spoken of me. I had been taught that loyal service wasn't to be measured by the pay packet, and as I was only earning £3 7s. a week, it certainly wasn't for the financial rewards that I felt it necessary to give unstinted service. But I had given my word, and I had a Saturday morning to repay, and I was helping to win the war after all.

After that, Miss Turpentine and I exchanged many a confidence, and when Mary returned to work we often made a threesome when we went for our canteen lunch. She was full of good works, a regular church attender, delivered the church pamphlets, and cared for an aged parent, and she sent Mary and me into hysterics when she unexpectedly decided that she was so fed up trying to get fixed up with a single room for her holidays at sea-side hotels, she was considering spending a fortnight at a nudist camp! If she had told us she was contemplating living in sin with the boss for a fortnight, we wouldn't have found it more incongruous. It was such an original, as well as such an outrageous idea coming from a docile little spinster like her, that it fairly took our breath away. She sent for brochures, and we laughed ourselves into a state of hiccups at the idea of being served tea by a maid quite starkers. Imagination ran riot when we thought of Miss Turpentine leaping about playing table tennis, wearing nothing but a pair of tennis shoes, and we dreamed up hilarious situations where we saw her passing the vicar on the stair and uttering a cool 'Good morning', with not a stitch of clothing between them. Altogether it was the best laugh we'd had since the factory concert, and although we had intended to keep it to ourselves, the news soon swept the factory, and wee Miss Turpentine received many a thoughtful glance for quite a long time afterwards.

Alas, though, the pamphlets unnerved her, and she ended up having a fortnight at a very ordinary boarding house at Rothesay. It was such a pity. We felt quite defrauded that we weren't to hear unabridged tales from a nudist camp after all.

For my own holiday, I decided to take my mother down to

Arran to a little cottage owned by my hairdresser. There were no mod cons whatsoever, and it was a wonderful contrast to the tenement life of the black-out in Glasgow, so that for once the war seemed very far away. We went to the stream for water for our cooking and washing, and we built our fire in a huge kitchen range, with wood gathered nearby, topped up with the precious coal ration which was stacked behind the cottage. We felt we were really in the wide open spaces when an inquisitive horse, ecstatic at finding company, galloped round and round the place, and even poked his nose right inside the kitchen where we were having our breakfast. We leaped up in alarm, but we soon grew used to him as he daily popped his head round the door to see how we were getting on, and we actually found courage to smack him on the rump to get him out of the way when we came out with a bucket for water. Who would have believed that my mother and I, both terrified of cats, could grow so chummy with a huge creature like a horse? We felt those women pioneers of the West in their covered wagons, had nothing on us.

But it wasn't long before we met our Waterloo. One lovely sunny afternoon, as we crossed the open field which formed our right of way to the shore, our path was blocked by an enormous bull. We were transfixed with terror. Struggling with my fear was indignation that the farmer had allowed such a dangerous animal into this field, when he knew it was a recognized right to cross it to reach the sea. Trembling with fright, and pushing my mother in front of me, I dashed for the gate, beating the bull to it by a short head.

All to soon it was time for me to return to the job in the office of the factory, but my mother had a few days left, and I urged her to stay on in the cottage, and to make the most of the blessed respite from the fear of air raids among the tenements of Glasgow, and the suffocating feeling of the black-out. It was dark in the country too, of course, but it was a more comforting darkness. One could believe God was on our side in the vastness of that sky, and was keeping a watch over us.

When I reached home, I found a most welcome parcel, handed in by my neighbour. It had been left by some Americans who had seen me in the Lyric Revue and who received my address from the Pantheon Club and had posted it on to me. When I opened it, I found bars of chocolate, packets of cigarettes, some peanuts and chewing gum. 'Corn in Egypt' as my dear ma-in-law would have said. It was the one and only time I had a food parcel, and so thrilling to know it came from American 'fans'.

Knowing my mother's sweet tooth, and being only too aware how lonely she would find it on her own in Arran, I at once made up a little parcel with a selection of the American goodies, ran down to the Post Office and got it off on my way to work next morning. My mother told me later that she had been out for a wee walk and when she was climbing the hill to the cottage she had been saying to herself, 'My, I could go a wee sweetie', but she hadn't even any coupons left to enable her to buy any, nor for that matter was there a sweetie shop within miles. Once indoors, she had sat down by the window, pondering what she should have for lunch when her eye fell on my parcel. She'd left the window up about six inches, and the postman had apparently pushed the little box through.

She had stared at it, and said aloud, 'Noo, where did that come frae?', gazing all round to look for some human agent. Or even a wee fairy. She couldn't believe her eyes when she opened it and realized it had come from me, for I had only left her a bare forty-eight hours earlier. 'Manna from heaven', she declared, 'I don't know when I enjoyed onything mair'.

As the sage has it, he gives twice who gives quickly, and I rejoiced that this small gift had given her such pleasure. We both talked of that simple little holiday for years afterwards, and when she was in a low mood I had only to mention our meeting with the bull to send her into reminiscent giggles, and set her eyes sparkling with remembered delight over the boon of that coupon-free chocolate.

Such small pleasures became remembered landmarks of joy in war time. Anything at all which raised a smile was doubly welcome at that time and my mother always gave me a slightly scandalized giggle by her total inability to recognize that the word 'bum' might be considered vulgar in polite society. In company, when she was in a particularly chirpy mood, she was wont to burst into the wee song,

495

> 'There wis a wee lassie
> She cam' frae Camlachie,
> She hurtit her bum on a wee chucky stane.
> A sojer was passin',
> An' filled wi' compassion,
> He lifted her up an' he carried her hame.'

It was the comical words which amused her, and the jaunty tune, and it didn't dawn on her that the laughter which always greeted this ditty was due to her unselfconscious use of the coarse word for bottom.

Another one which tickled her, because she loved the word 'spiflicate', and which was mercifully free from any suspicion of vulgarity was,

> 'Jean, ses I, ye're lookin' smert,
> Could ye spiflicate an aipple tert?
> Noo her wee nose was lookin wat,
> So ah handed her ma hanky.
> Too-ra-loo-ra-loo-ra-loo,
> They're wantin' monkeys in the zoo,
> If ah wis you, ah'd go the noo,
> An' get a seet-u-a-tion.'

It was quite something to watch my mother leaping into her dungarees before setting out for her job in munitions, warbling this infectious song as she snatched up pieces, hankie and key, with a last look at the black-out before she ran down the stairs to go on the night-shift. I saw all this on the occasions when I went over to spend the odd night with her, and I marvelled at how enthusiastically she was throwing herself into the war effort. She adored Churchill, as I did, and although she couldn't hear his words clearly on the radio, for she was very dull of hearing, she could catch the low rumble of his voice and the defiance which ran like a clarion call through every word, and she'd say, with an admiring grin 'The British bulldog. My Goad, he pits new hert into ye.' She despised Lord Haw-Haw and his lying propaganda and got mad at anybody who quoted him, and as for 'that blaggard Hitler', she and the woman next door took him down a peg by referring to him always as 'Hilter.'

Auntie Tassie had a more childish sense of humour, and I could always send her into chortles of delight, by my fast variety style patter, cultivated for her amusement. She would choke over her tea, as I stood up and rattled off like an old-time comic.

> 'Ah gi'ed her ice cream,
> An' she aye screamed fur mair'.

> 'A gi'ed her macaroni,
> An' it didnae mak' 'er ony better'.

> 'Ah gi'ed her satinettes,
> An' she sat an' ett them a' hersel'.'

She was quite sure I was every bit as good as Dave Willis. We all loved Dave, whose song about the 'Nicest lookin' warden in the ARP' had the whole audience joining him in the chorus and yelling out 'An aireyplane, an aireyplane, away 'way up a kye.' He must have sung this ditty a thousand times by the time I worked with him in a BBC programme, where Ian Sadler and I were doing all the voices in a potted pantomime, and I was astounded that Dave had to have the words chalked up on a board in case microphone nerves would make him forget them. It was a revelation to me that somebody who could hold a packed theatre in the hollow of his hands, without a cue to help him, could find a studio mike such a nervous ordeal. I was very thrilled to meet him, and could scarcely believe that this quite modest little man was the same dynamo who raced on to the stage of the Theatre Royal dressed in shorts, and sent us into uproar with his 'Whit dae ye think o' the legs? Ah tossed a sparra fur them!' Typical Glasgow humour, which I loved, and which could be found in the trams and on the streets, Hitler or no Hitler. I remember one day I happened to be waiting at the tram stop when a dozen cleaners streamed up from the factory at the end of their day's stint. They were marching in a sort of congo line, each with a hand on the shoulder of the wifie in front. As they marched in a sort of jazzing rhythm they sang,

> 'Fares please, fares please,
> You'll always hear me say,
> As I go up and down

The tramcar every day.
Oh Ah work fur the Corporation,
You'll know me by ma dress.
Ah'm Lizzie MacDougall,
Fae Auchenshuggle,
The Caur con-duc-ter-ess.'

I burst out laughing. It was pure comedy. A hilarious example
of Glasgow sturdy humour at its best. As they drew up to the
stop, another of their colleagues joined them. 'Aye', said she,
'youse urr ferrly gaun yer Acme wringer the day!', I'd never
heard the rhyming slang for 'Gaun yer dinger' before or, as the
English would say, going at a tremendous lick, and I giggled all
the way into Argyle Street. My heart expanded in a great wave
of love for those women. The salt of the earth. Hitler might as
well throw up the sponge. He'd never defeat people like that.

I was still laughing when I went into the BBC and Moultrie
was greatly entertained when I told him of the incident. But he
had most exciting news for me. Alastair Sim, and J.M. Bridie
the playwright were in the building, and they wanted to see
me, to consider me for a part in a new Bridie play 'It depends
what you mean', which was to be put on in the West End of
London after a short tour. We met in the canteen, and over a
cup of tea they told me the story of the play, which derived its
title from a popular radio brains trust programme in which one
of the contestants, Professor Joad, always replied to the simplest question with the words, 'It depends on what you mean
by...'

Alastair Sim took one look at me and turned with a huge
beaming smile to Bridie, 'Jessie!', he said, 'She's perfect.'

It was arranged that I would go down to London at a date to
be advised later, armed with all the necessary documents to
enable me to do the play. For of course I was subject to war
regulations, and with my high speeds couldn't just jump out of
the war factory into a theatre without a great deal of negotia-
tion. My stomach was doing its familiar somersault, a mixture
of fears that the Ministry would never release me, joy that
Bridie and Sim had both liked me, excitement that at last I was
to appear on a West End stage and, above all, terror at having
to go to London which was under constant bomb attack. Then

498

when my excitement died down, I was filled with a gloomy certainty that I'd *never* be allowed to leave my job for anything so frivolous as a play.

I was completely ignorant of the fact that the theatre was considered a great contribution to the war effort as a morale-booster, and I didn't believe Sim and Bridie, those impractical theatre people, that there would be no difficulty in getting away. But they were right. In a matter of weeks, I obtained my release papers. Shortly afterwards, I had a letter from Alastair Sim's London Agents asking me to present myself at their office the following Tuesday, when I would sign on the dotted line. I would then return to Glasgow, there to await the exact date on which rehearsals were due to start. It might be a few weeks before everything was tied up, but in the meantime a day in London would be useful for signing the contracts and having a read-through of my part with Mr Sim.

I was able to have a day from the holidays which were due to me, so no deception of the boss was necessary this time, thank goodness, and there was no difficulty getting a sleeper on the London train. It was out of the question to think of sitting up all night, for I had a busy day ahead of me, and I had enough sense to know that the saving of the sleeper charge would be false economy on such an important occasion. As I climbed into my berth, I prayed that no spiteful German bomber would score a direct hit on the train, for I was at last on my way. To London. To the theatre capital. There were six of us, three a side on the sleeper shelves of the third-class compartment, and I didn't care what sort of exploits the others were up to, none of them, I was absolutely certain, was bound for an adventure a quarter as exciting as mine. I longed to share my secret with them, but prudence bade me hold my tongue in case speaking of it would put a jinx on my chances. So I lay quietly and dreamed of the future as we rattled through the uneasy darkness towards my goal.

10

I was far too early for my 10 A.M. appointment with the agent, so I decided to walk from Euston towards the West End and find some breakfast in any Lyons' cafe which happened to be open. I hadn't seen much bomb damage at this time, and was quite unprepared for the effect it would have on me. My heart turned over at the sight of bomb-shattered buildings, at the broken glass and boarded up windows, and, above all, at the sight of the indomitable Londoners, many bandaged, many more wearily emerging from underground shelters with their blankets, but all showing obvious satisfaction at the sight of so many familiar landmarks still standing. I was impressed and humbled by their courage, as I watched their eyes rest on the tall buildings, but I grew so nervous at the prospect of being buried underneath tons of solid stone, that my heart skittered into my mouth at the first sound of a 'plane. They, more used to the scene than I, never even glanced towards the sky, and during that long day came to learn that only the sound of the sirens would stop them in their tracks to look for shelter.

Lyons was packed with people who had been sheltering all night and were now on their way to work, several wardens either going on duty or coming off their night watch, and a smattering of the elderly who looked almost too tired to eat. What was I doing thinking so selfishly of a career when these people were in the front line, facing the nightly horror of air raids, asking only to live to enjoy a future free from Nazi tyranny. I could scarcely meet their eyes as I ate my toast and drank my tea, and afterwards I felt that looking at shop windows would be tantamount to dancing at a funeral, so I went down into the underground and sat and gazed at the advertisements along the tube wall and sniffed the hot dusty, human smell which for ever afterwards spelt London to me.

A light rain was falling when I came into the street an hour later, and I checked the agent's address with a helpful London policeman, who didn't seem a bit surprised to find a Glasgow lassie in Piccadilly in wartime, although he did register great pleasure in my accent.'You didn't bring a haggis with you then?', he enquired, with a friendly wink, and I felt cheered and uplifted as I nipped through a short cut which would take me to the offices I sought. I peeped cautiously round the door marked 'enquiries', and saw a girl sitting tapping away at a typewriter, and a few people sitting around in chairs, obviously waiting to be seen. Were they all actors, I wondered? Would they think I was an actress too, or would they see right through me and recognize that I had never set foot on a stage as a bona fide professional? I was so self-conscious that it was several minutes before I realized that they were quite uninterested in me. Their eyes were riveted on the girl, and their ears on the inter-com telephone which summoned the lucky one to the inner chamber. I had given my name to the girl, and in about five minutes the inter-com chattered and she jerked her head towards a door, 'In there, Miss Weir', she said. 'You will be seen now'.

The agent looked me over, glanced at the script on his desk before passing it to me, nodded approvingly, and asked me to sign the various papers he had ready. He had obtained confirmation of my release from industry. There had been no trouble. I was now to go along to Alastair Sim's flat to read the play with him, and we would meet again when I joined the company for rehearsals in a week or so. He also said that there would be three months' tour round the number one dates before opening in London. I had no idea what number one dates were, and wouldn't have cared anyway whatever they had turned out to be. If they pleased Alastair Sim and J.M. Bridie, then they were good enough for me. But the thought of rehearsing in a London which was the target of almost nightly air bombardment made me shiver. Still, if other people could do it, then so could I.

I didn't feel quite so bravely defiant later that afternoon

when I allowed myself a stroll round Selfridges while waiting
for the clock to creep round to my three o'clock appointment
with Mr Sim. Suddenly, all the sirens in the capital started up
their stomach-turning wailing. Posters all over the shop
announced, 'In the event of a warning, remain where you are.
Then make your way to the shelters, following the signs'. I did
as everyone else did, and stood motionless, while my eyes
searched for the arrowed signs which would lead us to the
shelters if necessary.

My legs trembled beneath me as I gazed at what seemed to
be acres of plate glass and mirrors. If any of those bombs had
Selfridges' name written on it, we would be cut to ribbons, and
would surely have enough stone masonry on top of us to build
a small town.

I felt sick. But I wasn't going to show fear in a shop filled
with English people. Before we could take a step towards
safety, we were frozen in our tracks by the unmistakable whistle
of a bomb plunging towards its target. I had never been in a
day-time raid, and I had never heard anything so terrifying as
the whistling intensity of this unseen enemy. My heart filled
with wonder and admiration of the long-suffering Londoners as
I watched the eyes of shoppers and assistants, schooled to a
stony stoicism. I had time to observe all this, even as I
wondered whether I should dive to the floor, or make a run for
the shelter. There was a 'cccrrump' in the distance, and a long
sigh from all of us as we were released from this waking
nightmare. It was all over in seconds, but it had seemed like an
eternity.

But what terrible morality war induces, I thought, when we
could be so glad that the bomb hadn't had our name on it, and
show so little sorrow for the target which it had found. I learned
later that it had fallen on buildings in Park Lane, not very far
from Selfridges, and I prayed that casualties had been few. All
the way to Alastair Sim's flat, I pitted my wits against what the
fates had in store for me from enemy 'planes. For five minutes
I'd run tucked in as tightly as possible to the walls of the high
buildings. For the next few minutes I'd move out to the centre
of the pavement, and then right out on to the kerb itself,
risking splashes on my good thin lisle stockings from the traffic
swishing past so close to my legs. The sirens went twice while I

played this game, but I heard nothing, neither explosion nor 'plane so they may have been false alarms, and I was a nervous wreck by the time I fell in at the door of that quiet comfortably furnished dwelling. I was very ashamed to be so fearful of my own safety when so many appeared able to take it in their stride, and, looking back, I wonder how on earth I managed to give any sort of comedy reading in such a state of jitters. However, the sight of the famous comedian in his own lounge soon knocked every other thought out of my head, and after I'd taken off my hat, at his request, we plunged into scene after scene of the play. I was a wee bit disappointed at having to remove my best hat, which I thought made me look more actressy, but he seemed well pleased with my appearance without it, and with my fly-away fluffy hair which I wore in page-boy style at that time. He prowled about the room as we read, hunching his shoulders, and arching his eyebrows in the way I'd seen him do so many times on the stage and in films, and once he let out a chortle of satisfaction, as a huge smile lit his face. 'Do that again', he commanded. I read the line once more, and did the deprecating little gesture I had found confidence to include. Again the chortle. 'Now *that was pure comedy!*' he said. 'Yes, you're Jessie all right'.

I think we had some tea together before I left, but everything faded into the background against the blazing joy I felt in his approval of me as a comedienne. To have my idea of comedy endorsed by Alastair Sim was truly a joy devoutly to be wished. I hugged myself with delight as I raced back towards Oxford Street, not bothering this time where I walked. I felt that neither bomb nor disaster would have the cheek to touch me now. I laid the play on the table in Lyons during my modest meal, and started to learn my scenes there and then. A lady and her husband were sitting opposite, and she seemed very interested in my absorbed mouthings as I went over the speeches. At last, unable to contain her curiosity any longer, she asked me what I was doing, and, now that I had the part, I felt I could risk jinxes, and I told her the whole story. She was quite elated, and declared she was an avid theatregoer, and one day when I had 'made it' she would write and remind me that we had met when all was before me. She kept her word.

For, years later, I had a letter from her and she told me she had kept every cutting about me she'd come across in newspapers and magazines, and she felt I was her very own discovery.

But maybe I shouldn't have told her after all, for jinxes are not to be trifled with.

When I went back to the office, I told the boss that I would work there till I was wanted to begin rehearsals in London. At home, I hauled the cabin trunk from underneath the bed, and started putting in my few possessions. My typewriter had to go with me, of course, for wherever I went I liked to jot my ideas down on paper, and I also wrote long detailed letters to the Middle East, letting Sandy know exactly what I was getting up to. I learned later that the boys in the squadron dubbed my love-letters 'Sandy's DRO'S' (Daily Routine Orders), because in their length and neat typing they resembled the routine orders pinned to their notice board daily. The joke had come about because one day as Sandy was devouring one of my long epistles, several of the boys started reading over his shoulder, thinking he was studying the daily orders before pinning them up. When he indignantly shooed them away, they laughed and apologized and one of the lads said he'd never seen a letter from home which so resembled official orders. From that moment, when my letters were handed out they were 'Sandy's DRO'S.'

Apart from my engagement ring, my typewriter was my most prized possession. I was still writing little pieces for the newspapers and magazines, and I could pour out my heart in long letters to Sandy. Each of us had different highly treasured things which we dreaded would be destroyed by German bombs. Mine was the typewriter. The old lady at the back told me that hers were her false teeth. She took them out and put them in the gas oven every night before she went to bed, using it as a safe. She clearly shared wee Bantam Jock's opinion of the quality of the houses, for she gave it as her opinion that the cooker would stand up to the worst weight which was likely to fall on it. 'Och', she would say, with a disparaging look round, 'there's nae a beam in this hoose that would fell ye. Naw, naw, ma teeth are safe in the oven. They're the only thing I care aboot, for whit would ah dae without them? No' only would ah look a sicht, but ah'd sterve tae death into the bargain'.

So, in preparing for the move to London, transporting my typewriter safely gave me a lot of thought. Eventually I managed to get a stout wooden box, specially made for the job, which had securing bolts which would keep the machine rigid during the journey. Next I spread the bottom of the cabin trunk with packets of foolscap and quarto paper, a box of carbons, and two new typewriter ribbons. My old school pencil-case, an old treasure which I'd hung on to, held cleaning brushes, cleaning oil, rubber, pen and pencils and paper clips. Lastly a duster, and some envelopes completed my office equipment and I wouldn't have parted with any of them for gold. They were far more important to me than clothes, for they gave me something no mere garment would provide – contentment and a release for my imagination.

I couldn't quite believe it, but it was to be my last day in the office. The summons had come from London, and I was leaving Glasgow on the overnight train, ready to start rehearsals in the morning. I had no idea where I was going to stay, and had some vague idea of presenting myself at the YWCA and sleeping there for a few nights until I got myself sorted out. The cabin trunk was packed and I had an empty box in readiness to take the rest of my rations when I'd eaten my final meal that evening. The few men still left in the factory office drifted in to say goodbye to me during their coffee break, and one of them from the drawing office left a sheet of statistics for me to type. I soon rattled through this little job, and took it along to him for checking.

As I skipped along the narrow corridor, which ran like a balcony from one end of the factory to the other, the Tannoy sprang into life, and the voice of Eisenhower stopped me dead in my tracks. General Eisenhower himself! The commander of the Allied Expeditionary Force! What terrible news was he giving us? We had had too much bad news to be sanguine that anything good was going to be told to us at this hour in the forenoon. The Russians had been growing more and more dour about our apparent slowness in wishing to mount the Second Front and relieve the pressure on them. Bickering had been added to slaughter and we were all tired and hungry. At first my ears wouldn't take in the words that the General was saying. I shook my head and listened hard. He was repeating it all, thank goodness. 'Today the Allied Expeditionary Force has landed in France'. I didn't hear the rest. The Second Front had started! And I was leaving for London that night. All hell would be let loose on the capital, I thought, for the Germans would never take invasion lying down. They'd go for the capital.

Everybody had rushed out on to the corridor, and we gazed at one another with eyes which were a mixture of fear and elation. This was the moment we'd been waiting for, for how many years? How would it all end? This was the beginning of the end all right, and there would be no holds barred by anyone. What was in store for us?

When I went home at lunch time a telegram was lying behind the door. My neighbour had given her signature and put it through. It was from the theatre management. 'Delay departure for London. Second Front opened. No one knows what is going to happen now. All transport strictly controlled for emergency journeys only. Await later instructions.'

I tried to tell myself it was merely postponement, not cancellation, but that part of my stomach which knows the truth long before my head does, felt hideously hollow. If I had been older, and bolder, and more like Scarlett O'Hara to whom the office wags compared me, I might have ignored the telegram and gone just the same. I could have pretended it had never arrived. But I had not the sophistication for such deception. Truth and obedience were instinctive to me, and so I swallowed my bitter disappointment, and sent off a telegram in reply, 'Message received and understood. Will await instructions as to when I shall join you.'

The trunk went back under the bed. The typewriter was removed from its wooden shroud and, to my boss's delight, I remained at my war job in the factory.

I wrote to Alastair Sim asking when they visualized starting rehearsals. His reply was vague. I wrote to the agent and the management, refusing to listen to the foreboding rumblings from my most knowledgeable stomach. It was only a natural delay, I told myself. If I was right for Jessie before the Second Front, then I was surely just as right a matter of weeks later. It wasn't as if *years* had elapsed, and I was too old for the part or anything. The thought brought me up with a jolt. Up till now, I had always been too young for anything, but I forced myself to realize that one day it would be the other way round. Och I was getting morbid, I'd be hearing from them any minute now, saying the magic word 'Come'.

I did hear. They told me, so tactfully and with such charm, that with the war situation they couldn't take the risk of bringing me all the way from Glasgow, involving leaving my home and finding digs, and that all things considered they had decided it was wiser to engage an actress who lived in the London area and who, if things went wrong, would be able to return to her family. And as though it were an afterthought, would I please return the book of the play as I would now no longer require this.

I didn't cry. I wanted to, but I didn't. Instead I shook my fist at the sky, denounced that blackguard Hitler, topped up the pepper pot in case any dastardly German paratrooper would have the nerve to drop in our garden, parcelled the play and took it down to the Post Office. As I watched it plop into the pillar box, I shook my head, angry at the tears which threatened to spill over, and found comfort in the knowledge that this had been my second chance to go to London. First John Mills. Then Alastair Sim. Surely the third time would be lucky. For now I truly did believe it was only a question of time. How many Glasgow girls had had one chance, much less two? Och the second front was far more important than any piddling little play. My time would come.

We had had enough drama to fill a dozen lives, it seemed. The retreat from Dunkirk, which had been turned into a victory by the use of all the hundreds of little boats which had turned themselves into an Armada to rescue our troops from the pursuing enemy. My brother-in-law Jimmy had volunteered for the later Cherbourg rescue operation, when the Germans had been so closely at their heels that if they had misread a map and taken a wrong street turning, they'd have been cut off. He had arrived home in the middle of the night, filthy, dropping with weariness, and when I quietly let him in, he just patted my shoulder, staggered through to the bed which ma had prepared on the floor in case he got back, and was asleep in seconds.

Next morning, as ma collected his grimy clothes for washing and cleaning, he hushed us with the drama of the tired race they'd had for the train the previous night. An officer had stopped them, observed their dishevelled state with disgust, and rapped out to Jimmy's pal, 'Where's your cap?' Wearily the lad had straightened his shoulders and replied, 'I left it at Cherbourg, sir'. The officer had coughed, then given a magnificent salute. 'Carry on', he said. As they stumbled towards the train, his voice had followed them, 'But get a replacement cap as soon as possible.'

He later thrilled us with his tales of the military operation, and of how his sergeant had become a hero in the eyes of the men when he had drawn not one gun, but two, on the Guards' officer who had attempted with his platoon to crash the queue waiting for the rescue ships. This little sergeant was having none of it. The pier was mined, and bombers flew overhead, and they were all in imminent danger of being blown sky-high if anything had landed on the pier where they stood. Jimmy and his fellow soldiers had been waiting for an hour or so when the Guards appeared.

'Get back', ordered the wee sergeant, and drew one gun on the officer. Jimmy said that the officer, towering above the sergeant, ignored the order and continued marching his platoon forward. 'Back', repeated the sergeant in a voice of thunder, drawing another gun. The men stood completely silent, hardly able to believe their eyes and ears. The officer halted. Stared in shocked amazement at the two guns, then ordered his men to the rear of the queue, and stated for all to hear that it was his considered opinion that the sergeant had gone mad, and he would be reported to the appropriate quarters.

Jimmy's crowd cheered, and a wag among them shouted, 'Noo a' get yer tuppences ready, fur yer pier dues!' From that moment onwards, the little sergeant was 'Two-gun Tony' and the men were wax in his hands. But my own salute went to the lad who had had the wit to shout out the command about the pier dues. Anybody who could find comedy in the grimness of such a situation filled me with admiration.

Later, when the Americans, the Russians and the British were pressing towards Berlin, the succinct vulgarity of General Patton is among my treasured war laughs. The whole world waited to know who would reach Germany first, and reach its heart. A telegram was received at the White House, which merely said, 'Peed in the Rhine today – Patton'. Not a word more. There were some who deplored such unofficial language. Not me. It had the lusty humour of Rabbie himself, in my opinion, and it said everything.

And all at once, almost before we realized it, the first danger was over and we could cautiously allow ourselves a little light in the highways and byeways. For me, this was the end of fear. Oh the sheer bliss of walking through the streets in this period of 'dim-out'. No more claustrophobic gloom. No more suffocating darkness on those nights when no star shone to guide our footsteps. The authorities might call this lighting dim, but for me it was as radiant as the joy which flooded my heart and soul. Victory was in sight, and soon it came, in Europe.

I have never in my life, before or since, felt the utter ecstasy of VE night. We all headed for George Square after our day's work at the factory had ended, and we sang our hearts out. Mary and I were the factory harmony duet and we fairly 'gave it laldy', as the Glaswegians have it. We sang 'For me and my gal', 'Let the rest of the world go by', 'It's a long, long trail a-winding', 'The white cliffs of Dover', 'Danny Boy', everything we could think of, and of course 'Auld Lang Syne' a dozen times or more. The square was packed. We danced eightsome reels, making a space somehow for our figure eights and our birling. We hooched and we cheered. The lid was blown off the damped-down furnaces of fear, and we were drunk with relief that we had lived to enjoy our victory. It was years since we had felt such energy charging our batteries. It was Christmas, Hogmanay and Ne'erday all rolled into one, and the Fair thrown in for good measure. It was a spontaneous hymn of gladness and praise. The air was charged with loving kindness. It truly felt that night, that Rabbie's words might yet come true, that 'man to man the world ower, shall brothers be for a' that'. But before that could happen, the war had still to be won in Japan.

Mary and I were on holiday in Dunoon when the bomb went off in Hiroshima. The factory had shut down for a fortnight, for now that the war with Germany was over, the work force was gradually being whittled down, and we had our holiday together in an excellent boarding house, and were blessed with glorious sunshine every day. When the radio told us that the atom bomb had been dropped, we shivered as though an icy blast had cut through the warmth of the day. I remember Mary went white as a sheet and her eyes widened with horror. 'Oh Molly', she gasped. 'Oh Molly. They shouldn't have done it'.

I remained silent, although I felt sick. I remembered those Japanese soldiers who had so brutally massacred the Australians, roasting them alive in their quarters. I remembered the slave conditions of the building of the Burma Road. I remembered those suicide pilots. 'Mary', I said at last, trembling as I spoke the words, 'if it shortens this war and brings it to an end before we dare hope for such a thing, it will have been worth it'.

It was a terrible thing I was approving. But after years of nightmare slaughter, I honestly believed that anything which would end hostilities had to be tried. And this surely was the ultimate horror.

Strangely enough, it was Mary, who had been so distraught by the news of Hiroshima, who lost her sympathy for the Japanese after she met and married a splendid soldier who had been their prisoner for two long hellish years. He was recovering from prison brutalities when she met him, and when she saw photographs of three shrivelled creatures like witches, taken at the camp, she wept. She had thought they were three old crones and they were her fine soldier and his companions under Japanese conditions.

Now it was I who shivered at my acceptance of this obscene weapon, although I believed then, and still do, that by its very nature it would put an end to wars on a global scale.

And the bomb did shorten the war. We were soon rejoicing in VJ night(Victory in Japan), but it wasn't the joyous outpouring that VE night had been. The horror of Hiroshima brooded over us all. We took our pleasures more soberly on this occasion, although we were filled with a deep thankfulness that at last it was all over.

Shortly afterwards we began to make an inventory at the factory of all the goods which the Government would now wish to sell to other industries. I had never before been part of anything which had outlived its usefulness, and although the relief that we were at peace ran like a thread of pure gold through every minute of the day, it was at the same time sad to go to the empty factory each morning, where 'Music while you work' still echoed through the stillness of huge buildings, where not a footstep could now be heard. Indeed this music sounded so ghostly in the reverberating empty workshops that I was compelled to ring up the source of it one day and beg to have it shut off. 'Oh ah thought it wid cheer you up, hen', a warm Glasgow voice said in surprise, 'I knew youse yins in the oaffice were the only wans in the building'. 'We are', I informed the voice, 'but that music is driving me mad. It's like a wake. And anyway, I can't hear the telephone because of the echoes'. So it was turned off. And I got back to my marathon task of listing every last nut and screw and bolt, pages and pages of them to be typed on enormous sheets of lined paper which fitted together finally, and made up a book for distribution to the interested Government departments.

Then the boys began to be repatriated, and all Glasgow threw itself into the jollifications. Tenement streets were bedecked with coloured paper streamers saved from pre-war Christmasses, and huge placards were strung across from opposite windows bearing the proud words, 'Welcome hame Jimmy, after four years fighting the Germans'. Or, 'Welcome hame Tommy, after two years as a prisoner of war.' But my favourite placard bore the words, with typical Glasgow humour, 'Welcome hame Maggie, after two hours in a tottie queue'.

For of course we still had rationing. And for the backcourt parties to celebrate the warrior's return, everybody pitched in with their coupons which were absolutely necessary if the feasting were to include tins of beans, and tins of Spam, that lease-lent American meat roll which had enlivened our frugal

511

wartime diet, tins of tomatoes, and indeed anything at all which could be scraped together to make a party.

The entire street was invited to each party. Tables were set up in backcourts, and sometimes even in the front streets if they could be cordoned off from traffic, and there was dancing to the music of an accordion, and singing, and old feuds were forgotten, and every heart filled with rejoicing because long-absent sons and husbands were home among their own folk at last.

At these parties shyness was forgotten and maiden aunts or grannies were persuaded to sing faintly daring songs parodying hymns, and I won't easily forget the memory of Auntie Jenny standing with sparkling eyes, waiting to be struck dead for her blasphemy, belting out:

> 'Oh for a man, Oh for a man
> Oh for a man-sion in the sky!'.

She was quickly followed by her sister Mary, who had the company in stitches with her story of the conceited lady who wore a new hat to church, and was delighted when the whole congregation seemed so impressed that they stood up and sang what sounded to her like, 'Glory, Glory, ah hardly knew ye!' This tale was a great success and fell into family folk-lore, so that 'Glory, Glory, ah hardly knew ye' was the theme song whenever a relative appeared in anything new. I even found myself singing it in church instead of the correct words 'Glory, Glory Hallelujah'.

It was a marvellous time of innocent enjoyment and, unlike the Sunday School picnics or the Fatherless children's treats which only took place once a year, these exciting welcome-home parties seemed to take place somewhere in Glasgow almost every night in the week. From the top of tramcars I would gaze down on side streets as gay and lively as scenes of the Mardi Gras from the pictures. Over the tops of wash-houses I would catch sight of coloured streamers, and even the occasional balloon prudently hoarded for just such a day. And always people, laughing and happy, glad to be alive together, not wanting anything more just then but to savour the taste of it, and discover their feelings towards one another all over again. Glasgow was en fête, a happy city, and it reminded me of the description in the hymn of the streets of the New Jerusalem filled with the sound of happy voices. It was a good time to be alive.

Our BBC revue was in great demand at 'Salute the soldier concerts' again, and 'Soldiers' Parcels' concerts, for of course many of the boys were still overseas and although they were now in no danger we still had to look after them and not have them feel they were being forgotten. So we travelled to little village halls, and to big concert buildings, and we did our 'Girls of the Old Brigade' song and dance routine times without number. I also donned a hoarded black net and lace evening dress for two ship's concerts we did at Dunoon, first for the naval ratings and then for their officers, and impersonated Dietrich herself in the seductive number 'Falling in Love again'. I felt a real femme fatale when sailor after sailor came up to me afterwards and said he had believed I was singing just for him! My word, they must have been starved of feminine society right enough if I could hypnotize them so easily!

We updated our 'Down at the Mains' stories for radio, and I was to be 'married off' to Jock Tamson, my lad who had returned safely from the war. We were reflecting the world situation in our little farm dramas, and so I, as Teenie, had a lovely reunion with Jock written for me. I was so filled with innocent romance at the thought of all the other reunions which must be taking place all over Britain that I gave this scene all I'd got. I sighed softly, I paused for long moments, I murmured huskily, and in fact painted such a fearful picture in the minds of those in the control room that Auntie Kathleen burst through the door, horrified at what my silences implied, and told me to speed the whole thing up and be *far* more matter of fact. So much for romance. But it was a lesson all the same, that more can be suggested by what you don't say, than by any amount of spicy conversation. Strangely enough, when I later came to London and visited Children's Hour, it was this episode of 'Down at the Mains' they remembered, so I must have kept enough ginger in the scene after all!

The Pantheon decided to put on 'WILD VIOLETS' as their first peace-time production, and I was afire to play the part of the French schoolmistress. We were to be produced this time by a new man, and the usual auditions were held in early autumn. This time I didn't worry about how much or how little singing there might be for me with this part, because I felt I was so right in every other way I'd take the warbling in my stride. The first part I had played with any success in Glasgow had been that of a French girl. The critics had found my height and type dead right, and my broken accent convincing. Added to this, I normally used my hands and arms so instinctively to illustrate my speech that it used to be said I'd be struck dumb if my hands were tied behind my back. So, naturally, in my zeal to play this part I couldn't see how they could possibly find anyone else who could interpret it as entertainingly and as faithfully as I could.

I was wrong, of course. Enthusiasm doesn't always mean success. After three auditions – *three*, when I'd never had to do more than one – I was informed they didn't think I was tall enough. I didn't believe a word of it. They could see my height at the first audition, couldn't they? They surely didn't expect me to grow during the course of three auditions? It was the end of college days all over again, when I was either too wee or too young for the jobs I wanted to do.

I just couldn't understand it, particularly as I was now established as a reliable comedienne, and even had a little bit of a name. Rightly or wrongly I became convinced, as I chewed over the matter in my mind, that the new man had had somebody else in mind all the time. He had merely been going through the motions so that fair play would be seen to be done.

He did me a good turn really. For months I had been torn with indecision as to whether or not I ought to have a shot at London before my husband returned from the Middle East. I knew if I waited until he returned, I'd never want to rush off in pursuit of a stage career, and yet I did want to see what would happen if I tried. I had twice been given the chance to go into West End plays. I couldn't risk waiting until somebody came in search of me a third time. I was swayed this way and that, until disappointment over the loss of this coveted part made up my mind for me. I'd found the necessary spur.

I began to make plans. I looked at my Post Office Savings

Book and decided I could back myself to the extent of fifty pounds. I would go to London and stay there as long as my money lasted, and if I had no luck, then I would come home. It was a £50 win or lose bet. The factory job would come to a natural end in a few weeks' time, and I would pack and go south to the city of theatres and films as soon as I'd collected my last pay. I had no idea where I was going to stay. I just knew I was going.

11

I was amazed at the interest everybody took when I told them I was London bound. You would have thought I was going to take on the German army single-handed from the way they carried on. Where would I stay? I said, quite truthfully, that I didn't know but the YWCA were bound to give me a bed for a couple of nights at least. I was a member of that excellent organization in Glasgow, and felt confident their London branch wouldn't let me down. And I knew that I would be allowed the freedom of their kitchens, so I wasn't likely to starve. It was vital for me to conserve my small financial resources and I mustn't waste a penny on unnecessary luxuries.

I didn't have the name of a single theatrical agent, apart from the one who had seen me for the Alastair Sim play, but I wrote to the BBC telling them that I was coming. I sent letters both to Broadcasting House and to Aeolian Hall where the light entertainment shows were handled. It really wasn't broadcasting I was after, for I could get plenty of that in Glasgow. It was theatre and films which lured me. But I knew I might be glad of the chance to earn a few broadcasting fees while I waited for my big chance.

I hauled out the trunk from under the bed once more, and this time I knew it wouldn't be opened until I reached London. There wasn't much time wasted on indecision as to which clothes I should take. After years of clothes rationing, my only respectable garments, both for underwear, and outerwear were few and far between. The lovely mossy green Shetland tweed suit which Sandy had bought for me in Frasers before he left for the Middle East was easily the best thing in my wardrobe. It would definitely be my 'audition' and 'interview' outfit.

The short mole jacket from Karters which had been my

wedding present would go on top of the suit if the weather was cold, but I had a vague feeling London must be far warmer than Glasgow because it was hundreds and hundreds of miles further south. I was to learn the hard way, during two Siberian winters, that this naïve trust in southern weather couldn't have been more misplaced, and I was to rue all the thick old woollies I'd left behind in damp muggy old Glasgow.

My shabby red coat would do for travelling in, and for knockabout wear in London. A spare skirt, my hand-knitted dress, some jerseys, a blouse, my two pairs of shoes, my raincoat, an umbrella, my short rubber bootees for really wet weather, one or two nightdresses, my fluffy dressing gown made for my trousseaux by dear Mrs Campbell, my slippers, spare stockings, that was the lot. There was plenty of room in the trunk for the carbons and notepaper. The wooden box with my typewriter safely bolted down, would go separately, specially labelled to ensure careful handling, and I'd pack the left-over food rations in a cardboard box which would sit inside the top inner lid of the trunk, to give me a good start before I had to seek out the nearest Ministry of Food office to change my registration with grocer and milkman and butcher.

I had written to my husband to tell him of my plans, of course, and he gave me his blessing. Well, actually what he said was, 'Go ahead and get it out of your system, for you'll never settle down otherwise.' He was more interested in describing how I was to shut off the water system after draining the tank, and in reminding me to turn off the gas at the main and the electricity. It was December 1945, and I didn't know when I'd be back.

A neighbour round the corner told her English sister-in-law about my proposed departure when she was up in Glasgow for a family wedding. A Londoner herself, this good soul was horrified at my even contemplating arriving at the capital without a place to lay my head. She was certain I would be robbed, possibly murdered, or worse, if I didn't have someone to keep an eye on me, and she insisted on ringing a widowed sister who lived at Sudbury to see if she could provide accommodation. She brushed aside objections that I couldn't afford full board, and only wanted a bed, for she was sure I'd starve

517

myself just to make my money last as long as possible. Her sister would make sure I ate, she informed me, and that was that. Her niece would meet me at Euston and take me out to Sudbury, and she could now sleep safely in her bed at night knowing I wasn't going to be alone in a wicked place like London.

My heart sank at the idea of eating landlady's meals and at having to be back at set times, for although I hadn't the slightest idea where Sudbury was, I knew it wasn't the West End of London and I guessed it would be miles away and it would take me ages to get back and forth to appointments. My mother, however, was delighted. 'You're that heidstrong', she had kept saying when I told her I was having a shot at London. 'Whit'll Sandy say to you gwan away doon there among the English'. If it had been the cannibals she was describing, her tone couldn't have been more critical. 'He knows', I told her patiently. 'He approves.' She gave me a shrewd look. 'Aye, that's whit *you* say', she said, 'but I'm sure he just knows fine he's nae option, him being so faur away. You've a sin tae answer for, so you have.' Now all was smiles because I was to be in the care of a respectable woman, obviously a right nice buddy at that, when she had a sister who went to the bother of telephoning all the way to London just to make sure I would be looked after. 'Aye she'll see ye get yer meat', she said happily, 'an' I'll know where you are.' My ma-in-law knew London well from her young days, for she had actually worked there, in the nurseries of the great families, and she kept nodding her head sagely and telling me with great solemnity, 'Aye, London can be the loneliest place in the world'. I didn't really believe her, for I was used to the easy friendliness of Glasgow, and how could anybody be lonely in such a big place as London, with millions and millions of folk there. I thought she was just trying to talk me out of going, but time was to prove her absolutely right.

I caught the ten o'clock in the morning train for Euston, so nobody came to see me off. My mother was working, and the others were busy. I had sent off the trunk and the typewriter by Advance Luggage carrier, and both should be at Sudbury when I arrived. The journey passed in a dream. I remember a sick feeling at the pit of my stomach, a mixture of excitement at the thought of what may lie ahead, and apprehension that I had taken an irrevocable step. I kept checking my Post Office book and trying to work out how long my money would last, an impossible task really, for I had no clear idea of what fares or anything else cost. I knew that for everyday living I would look at prices with an entirely different eye compared with my reactions when I was only down for a brief day.

It was foggy when the train arrived at Euston – over an hour late – but the good niece Doris was waiting for me, and she recognized me from her aunt's description and from my red coat. We travelled in the underground for over half-an-hour, to my dismay, for I realized this lengthy journey was going to be an obstacle if I were making last-minute appointments. Worse, it cost whole tenpence. This compared to Glasgow's maximum fare of tuppence-ha'penny, was a fortune and would soon knock a hole in my bank book. But I didn't let Doris see any of this unease and chattered non-stop to her, just the way I did at home. I didn't realize that Londoners didn't speak in trains, and couldn't understand why they all seemed to be listening to me and to have nothing to say to each other. Doris told me long afterwards that she'd never seen such a stunned carriage in her life, for she was sure that to a man they'd not heard such a ceaseless flow of entertaining talk for years. I was glad she said 'entertaining', but I had a feeling she was just trying to be tactful, and was letting me know that this wasn't correct behaviour in public transport in this part of the world. Later observation confirmed me in this, and much later, when my husband came to live in the south, he travelled for twenty years in the train without anyone so much as opening his mouth to him.

Mrs Horton, my landlady, was a nice gentle soul, whom I took to be in her late forties. The house had a little garden, to my delight, and I had a small but pretty upstairs bedroom which was almost filled with my cabin trunk and my huge typewriter box. She had an enormous meal waiting for me which, in my tired and excited state, I was quite unable to manage. 'Mrs Horton', I gasped, 'you must have spent all your food coupons and I'll never be able to eat all this. I'm not used to such big meals.' Having had only one ration book for years, my appetite had dwindled to that of a bird. She brushed my objections aside and insisted I took every drop of soup, ate as much Shepherd's pie as possible, and finished off with a decent helping of her special bread and butter pudding, made with a real egg. All this at past eight o'clock at night, when I was used to having my dinner in the middle of the day, with just a tasty wee snack at six o'clock and a cup of tea at bed-time. English ways I was to learn, were very different. They dined in the evening, and had a light lunch in the middle of the day. How long would my stomach take, I wondered, to adapt itself to this altered regime?

Next day being Saturday, with all the London offices shut for the week-end, gave me plenty of time to attend to unpacking my trunk and filling drawers and wardrobe with my belongings. This done, I borrowed a screwdriver to release my precious typewriter from its restraining bolts, and as soon as the machine was in its place on the table, I began to feel quite at home, and I immediately sat down and typed out a letter to my husband, telling him all my news and describing my digs in minute detail.

In the middle of this, Mrs Horton called me down for coffee. I had been afraid I might be a bit of a nuisance, for she wasn't really used to lodgers, but she seemed genuinely glad to have me in the house. Her twin daughters were both away in the forces, she told me, and she missed their company so much since she had lost her husband. My heart grew lighter with every word she uttered, for I could see she really was pleased to have me there to fill at least one vacant chair.

We went for a walk in the afternoon, and she showed me the local shops, and the Food Office where I'd have to register on Monday to enable me to use my food coupons in the district. I was amazed to find that it didn't feel like London at all. Apart from the English accents, it was more like Thornliebank, or Springburn, with small shops and little houses and not a tall building anywhere in sight. And of course, when I really thought about it, it wasn't London. It was suburbia. It was nice, and it felt comfortingly familiar, but it was a far cry from the world of show business, and I felt in my bones that it was too far from the sounds and smells of theatreland to keep me there very long.

On Sunday, when we sat chatting, I was astonished when Mrs Horton confided that she was glad it wouldn't be long till she received her pension, for then she would be able to make ends meet without any trouble. 'Your pension!', I exclaimed. 'But how old are you then? I thought you were just forty-something'. She smiled, and passed a hand over her dark hair which hadn't even a single silver thread that I could see. When she told me she was in fact coming up for her sixty-fifth birthday, I looked so disbelieving that she burst out laughing. 'Its true', she said, 'I'll show you my birth certificate if you like'. I looked into her face intently, not troubling to make my study discreet or polite. She was a plain, simple, woman and it was absolutely clear that it wasn't cosmetics or special effort on her part which contributed to this appearance of youthfulness. She simply looked an ordinary woman of forty-plus.

I shook my head in bewilderment, and seeing that I was so bemused, she told me a fascinating story which explained this phenomenon It appeared that she and her sister hadn't aged at all in looks since they were around forty. They'd just accepted it as a piece of luck, which they scarcely even noticed. However, one day her sister had slipped in the street and fallen, breaking an ankle, and was taken by ambulance to a large London hospital nearby. When they took particulars and learned her age, they reacted just as I had to Mrs Horton's age. So much so, that they asked if they could do a series of tests on her, to check whether or not her physique matched her appearance. She had no objection, so they did blood tests, bone X-rays, skin examination, heart machine, the lot.

Some time later when she went back to have the plaster removed from her ankle, they told her, with some excitement, the result of their tests. It seemed there was a rare Polynesian strain in her physical heritage, and this would slow up the ageing process to a degree which meant she would never look really old unless she lived until she was well over a hundred. I gasped. 'Just like the people in James Hilton's *Lost Horizon*,' I said. 'They had the secret of perpetual youth, but only so long as they remained in the Valley'. 'A bit like that', she agreed, 'except that of course we're not affected by geography at all'.

What would affect their descendants though, was dilution of

the strain through marriage, so her daughters wouldn't be quite so lucky, and *their* children would be a little less so, until after some generations there wouldn't be such a noticeable difference in the ageing pattern from the rest of us.

'Oh', I said enviously, 'what a marvellous inheritance for a woman to have, especially if she were an actress'. But she just laughed. She was so used to the miracle, she took it for granted. As it happened her daughters arrived home on leave while I was with her, and if I hadn't known they were in their late twenties, I'd have sworn they were seventeen. Both beauties too, and much more aware than their mother that their looks would endure, untouched by the unkind finger of time, into middle age.

We had great talks together, and I decided that if the south was going to provide such unusual types, I was very glad I'd come. I'd have had to have looked far enough in Glasgow before I'd have found anybody possessing a Polynesian elixir of youth in her bloodstream! Suddenly, home seemed very far away.

On Monday I had an appointment at the BBC with Jo Plummer, a Children's Hour producer. To my surprise, she seemed to know me, and greeted me as 'Teenie' of 'Down at the Mains'. I hadn't realized London took any of our Children's Hour programmes, and so knew some of our names quite well. The very last thing I had expected in London BBC was that Molly Weir would mean anything to anybody. The blood rushed to my cheeks with pleasure, and the cold nervous knot in my stomach melted under the warmth of her friendliness. Although we were from entirely different backgrounds, we were on the same wavelength right away. She was a tall cool young lady, with a ready smile, and clearly out of one of the very top drawers. I learned later she was an honours graduate of Cambridge University, and at one point in her career had assisted the Poet Laureate, John Masefield. She was by far the youngest of the producers in that department, of whom the others were May Jenkin (Auntie May), and David Davis of the gentle voice and brilliant musical talent. I was to come to know all three very well indeed.

As I was leaving Jo's office, she advised me to have lunch in the canteen, which I would find was cheap and good, and she assured me she would get in touch the moment she had anything to offer. I believed her. I followed her advice about eating in the canteen, where I had the great good luck to run into Jimmy McKechnie and Joy Adamson, both from Glasgow, and with both of whom I'd worked in the Glasgow studios. It was marvellous to meet them just then when I felt so far from home, and right at the beginning of the adventure, and to know that I might run into them at any time in the future, for they had both settled in London and worked a great deal for the BBC. I coaxed from them, and from others who joined us round the table, the names of various agents to whom I might apply if I had no luck with the one who'd seen me for the Alastair Sim play. At first, nobody could think of a single possible name, but I took out my diary and sat with pen poised until they were forced to rack their brains, and soon I had a dozen names, and a purpose for being where I was.

The lady assistant in the big Agency who had cast me for the Alastair Sim play during the war was very disparaging about my accent. 'You'll never do anything in London', she said with a sniff, 'unless you lose that accent'. What did she mean, when there she was, sitting behind a large desk, successfully employed in a top agent's office, and with a voice not very much less Scots than my own! Telling ME to adopt the accents of the Sassenach! I hadn't the guile to hide my feelings, and I was much too inexperienced to know that an unemployed actress doesn't tell the truth to one who holds a position of power in an important agency. 'I have no intention of losing my accent', I said, 'and I notice you haven't been too successful in losing yours'.

I should never have said such a thing, of course, for she may have thought it was good advice she was giving me, but I couldn't bear what seemed to me such disloyal criticism of her own tongue.

It goes without saying that I never got a single job from that agency, or even another appointment!

Apart from that lapsed patriot though, I found it surprisingly easy to make appointments to see people. And, unlike her, everyone else embarrassed me by being almost too free with their admiration for my voice, so that I became very self-conscious about it and started speaking in whispers again, just as I had at school. As I left each interview, I was given another name to try, until I had pages and pages of names in my little diary, and I flew up and down Charing Cross Road and Shaftesbury Avenue like a yo-yo. I learned that I could use the BBC canteen any time, because of the work I had done for them in Glasgow, and as soon as I knew this, I stopped trying to go back to Sudbury for lunch. I could get a meal in the canteen for tenpence instead of spending it on fares, and that left all the more time for seeking work.

I felt I'd been away from home for weeks, but it was in fact only nine days when Doris, the girl who'd met me at Euston, invited me to go over to see her great friend at Clapham Common on the Sunday. We were invited for tea, and Doris would call for me at Sudbury about four o'clock.

On the way to Clapham, Doris asked me how I liked living with her aunt. I said, quite truthfully, that I liked Mrs Horton very much, but that I was worried about the high cost of fares and the expense of having to take full board. I realized it wasn't really pricey, but it was too much for me, and I needed to be free of domestic ties, for I fretted when appointments prevented my getting back punctually for the meals she had ready waiting for me. I hadn't really come to London to be cosy, but to be ready and accessible for theatrical opportunities, and ideally I should be nearer London. Doris was very understanding, but doubted whether it would be very easy to get a furnished room cheaper, because the nearer one got to London, the more digs cost.

When we turned off the main street into the Close in Clapham where Doris's friend lived, I immediately felt a great sense of belonging, and I knew that this was a good place for me. Everything, for the first time, felt just right, in spite of drifting fog which stung nose and eyes. Although the railings had gone to help the war effort, the gardens in the middle of the square were pleasant and well cared for. The pillared houses were tall and gracious, and had once been the homes of rich Londoners, although they were now fallen upon more stringent days, and were sub-divided among many tenants. The one we were visiting had once been the town house of Sir Godfrey Tearle, I was told.

A flight of steps led to an imposing front door, and a light to the left at street level showed there was a basement flat. I'd read about such places in Sherlock Holmes, but this was my first sight of one. It was a very large house, and the hall seemed vast in the dim light when Doris's friend Lois softly opened the door. A staircase went twisting round and round to the top of the house, and on the third floor, at the very top, Lois had her room. The minute I walked in, I fell in love with it. Not because it was furnished with any great beauty or skill – it was after all just after the war and it was a rented room. But it was *huge*, to my eyes, with a high lofty ceiling, large windows, and a gas fire which blazed cheerfulness from every pulsing jet. A kettle hummed on a gas ring, and beside it stood a trolley with tea things and a plate of buttered toast.

Lois was a civil servant. She worked in the Post Office behind the scenes, a gentle creature (my mother would have approved!), with soft brown eyes, dark red hair, and a shy smile. She seemed surprised by my enthusiasm for her room, and amused when I darted about exclaiming over its appointments. 'A gas ring for cooking', I said. 'Great'. 'A shilling in the meter slot – oh what a good idea, for then you've no bills'. Oh, what would I give for just such a room, where I could come and go as I pleased and cook as little or as much as I wanted, with no time-tables except those of my own making. And all this in a district which felt and smelt like the real London I'd come to find.

I looked imploringly at Doris, hoping she would get round to the subject of accommodation, and at last she understood and wondered if Lois knew if there was a room vacant in the house. 'Yes', said Lois, 'I think there might be, for there was a couple next door and Mrs Parker doesn't really like men in the house, and would prefer a woman to share the landing with me'.

I had noticed a little sink outside on the landing and only now realized this was the sole source of water for Lois and the room next door, and that dishwater and washing water would have to be got there. I could quite see it might be embarrassing having a man so close by, especially if tenants were running about in old dressing gowns in the morning. I jumped up in my excitement at the mere possibility of my getting the room on the same landing with this nice quiet girl. 'Can I ask the lady now?', I said, dropping my toast back on the plate and making for the door. Lois decided that wouldn't do. It would be better if she went down and asked Mrs P. to come up and show me the room. She was particular, and only took recommended lodgers.

I had to contain myself till we had finished tea and washed up the dishes in the little sink, and then Mrs P. was brought up to be introduced. She was a plump elderly lady, with swept back black hair, smallish dark eyes, round rosy cheeks, and a habit of rubbing her plump hands together as we talked. We went inside the vacated room, which was now festooned with ladders and buckets of distemper. The walls were a cold grey and the woodwork a sooty black, but I didn't mind the funereal colours. The ceiling was lofty, just like Lois's, the room was large, and there was a broad ledge outside the barred windows which reminded me of a castle battlement. This must have been the nursery when the house had had one single family living there, and the bars were to keep the children safe. I thought of Peter Pan. There was more than just a gas ring in this room, I noted with a start of pleasure. There was also a tiny tin oven, with another little ring on top, besides the usual one on the hearth like Lois's. By jove, I would be able to cook a whole dinner here!

I tried to damp down my enthusiasm in case Mrs P., like my mother, preferred people with gentle ways and might think I was too wild. But she could see I liked the room. 'If I get it when can I move in?', I asked her, trying to keep the eagerness out of my voice. 'Well', she said, 'the painter won't be finished till next week-end, but you could come the following Monday if you like'. 'How much was the rent?' She hesitated, and I saw as clearly as daylight that she was going to jack it up for the new tenant. I later learned that I was right! However, it was barely £1 a week, and with the shillings for the meter under my own control, I could keep my expenses down. There would be no fuel bills, whose hidden totals could strike a lethal blow at my capital. It was less than half my Sudbury digs, and although

I would now be catering for myself, I knew how economical I could be. And of course, the fares to the West End were half those from Sudbury. It was corn in Egypt! It was mine! I hugged myself with delight. Who could have guessed that a simple invitation to Sunday tea would end in my future digs being settled for the rest of the time I stayed in London on my own? Such small encounters shape our ways. My stomach, always the barometer of events, told me I had made a wise decision, and I had no cause to doubt its accuracy.

I was so glad that Mrs Horton didn't mind my moving to Clapham. But she seemed to understand that I had to be nearer my goal, and she wouldn't be alone for long, for she'd had news that one of her daughters would be getting demobbed in a matter of weeks. Everything fitted, and nobody was hurt. We parted the best of friends, and I'll always be grateful to her for sharing her home with me, a stranger, and for making my first week or so in the south so comfortable and happy, a true home from home.

It was a real pea-souper when I arrived at Clapham, and I was thankful I'd sent the luggage on by road haulage, and I hadn't made the move by taxi as my landlady had suggested, for it would have cost a fortune to have crawled from Sudbury through fog-shrouded streets. I'd travelled by underground, which was not only cheaper but infinitely quicker and safer on such a night. I rang the bell. Not a sound came from inside the house. Surely Mrs Parker hadn't gone out? Who else would hear the door-bell if she wasn't in? Where would I go if there wasn't a reply? Maybe she had changed her mind and had let the room to somebody else! My heart was thumping as I pressed the bell a second time, and kept my finger on the button. It was all I could do to stop myself battering at the door with my fists, for now that the sound of my footsteps had ceased, the fog had blotted out all other human noises. A hooter sounded mournfully in the distance. I was alone in London.

I hadn't realized my finger was still pressing the bell until I heard a high Scottish voice calling from somewhere inside the house, 'Hold the line. Hold the line. I'm coming'. Oh thank goodness, somebody was in. The door opened, and a tallish, spare, elderly lady with a fine head of silver wavy hair addressed me in a voice which was a mixture of welcome and irritation, 'Come away in, lassie', she said, 'don't stand there on the doorstep letting a' the fog in'. With an imperious arm she drew me inside and shut the door. 'They're a' oot'. As I moved to follow her upstairs, she turned, 'Noo, tak' yer time. I'm two stairs up, in the room underneath yours, and it's no a race we're having. You'll come in to me first. The kettle's on. I was just having a cup of tea'.

Much much later I was to learn that she was only exaggerating the homely tongue of our native land to make me feel at home. Born in Aberdeen, her knowledge of English was encyclopaedic, and when required her accent was impeccable, but she had the right words for a frightened newcomer, which was how I had struck her with my white face and startled eyes when she had opened the door.

Her disdain for polite nothings warmed my heart. It was my grannie all over again, keeping me right. Instinctively I felt we were going to be true friends, and twenty years of basking in the warmth of her affection amply confirmed that first impression. But just then as I followed her upstairs, slowing my pace to please her, I was aware only that I must curb my impatience to see my own room and spend a little time with this kind creature who was making me so welcome.

The bitter fog had seeped into the house, and the first thing in her room which greeted me was her roaring gas fire, turned up to its fullest, with no thought for greedy meters. In front of it stood a wee steel 'winter' such as we had used in Springburn for keeping food warm, and a plate of toast was being kept hot in the reflected heat from the glowing fire. A kettle sang on a gas ring, and in minutes I was sipping a steaming cup of tea, and having toast piled on my plate, 'Tak' it noo', she said, 'it's newly made. And It's REAL butter'. To lavish the butter ration on toast was no small sacrifice, and I knew it, but once she had made her point and made sure that I appreciated what it was that I was eating, she would have no thanks.

She was astonished to learn that I had only been in London a matter of weeks. When Mrs P. had called up to her, 'Oh Miss Chree, if Miss Weir comes, perhaps you'll let her in', she had assumed I was a Londoner, and knew my way about. She shook her head and wondered what I would have done if she herself had had to be out and I'd had a shut door on such a night. I discovered that it was only a matter of luck that she had been in the house, because she was a housekeeper and they were up to their eyes with Christmas preparations, and she had merely come home for the night to collect a few things she needed over the Festive Season. 'I always keep on my room', she said fixing me with a fierce blue eye, 'because that preserves my independence. Once you accept an employer's roof over your head, you're done for if you want to make a change, for it gives them too strong a hold on you.' Wise words which impressed me very much, and which increased my respect for this vigorous, clear-thinking new neighbour. As she spoke, I was glancing round this precious room whose possession enabled her to choose whom she would serve, and for how long. It was chaos with the lid off! Drawers had been pulled out, stood upright like cupboards, and were used as book-shelves. Papers were heaped everywhere. Clothes lay in bundles, where they'd been removed from the drawers – it was clear Miss Chree preferred literature to mere dress. An upturned drawer with a cushion on it served as a stool. Another with a cloth spread over it was my table. The only colour on the walls (distempered grey, like mine, I noted) was given by two large photographs cut from newspapers. The one over the mantelpiece was of General Smuts, and facing him from the opposite wall was Winston Churchill. I was not only to learn in the months which followed, that they were her heroes, true champions of the right in her opinion, but she could quote extensively the main episodes in both brilliant lives.

On the bed a beautiful faded Paisley shawl was folded, and when she saw me looking at it her blue eyes softened and she told me it had belonged 'to mother'. It was touching to hear an elderly lady refer like this to her parent, as 'mother', without the more usual 'my' we used in Glasgow, and I could sense what a strength this lovingly mentioned parent must have been to the family.

The whole place looked as though a storm had blown through it, leaving disorder in its wake. Everything was clean, but there was a sort of 'playing at houses' atmosphere, because nothing, apart from the bed, was being used for the purpose for which it was intended. But somehow, it all added up to a cosy, lively, welcoming refuge. As I watched her move back and forth with milk-jug and plates, and listened to her soft Aberdeen accent, I found I was smiling in sheer pleasure at having found such a glorious eccentric living in such close proximity. As somewhat of an eccentric myself, I was right on her wavelength, and although she was being very casual I could see from the sparkle in her eye and the flush on her elegantly thin face that she knew it too.

When our friendship strengthened and developed, I was trusted with the crisis which had brought this fine, well-educated Scot to London. She had been secretary to an old-established firm of whisky blenders in her native Aberdeen, and her description of the serious art of blending was a poem in itself. The owner was a gentleman of the old school, greatly esteemed by everybody, by none more than Miss Chree who knew quality when she met it.

Everything had gone like clock-work, all tasks properly accomplished in their due season, owner and workers in perfect harmony, and a quiet sense of service and mutual respect graced all their activities.

And then, one terrible afternoon the long arm of the law stretched out and plucked from their midst their chief accountant. He had been systematically cooking the books, and because of the very nature of the trust reposed in everyone in that happy firm, his fraud had gone undetected. Until that moment. Inquiries had been started by creditors and now, when the firm was on the verge of bankruptcy, was the moment of truth.

The disgrace was numbing, and the whole staff grieved that the owner should have been betrayed by one of them, for it was very clear that he had known nothing of what was going on. But he blamed himself, knowing he should have been more watchful and not made it possible for his accountant to have been tempted by easy money.

He felt the disgrace of the loss of the firm's good name keenly, and on top of that he felt guilt that he could have let it happen, and when he had made all arrangements for debts to be cleared, he tidied his desk, went home, locked his bedroom door and cut his throat.

When they came to tell them the news at the office, Miss Chree had been so shocked and so bereft by the terrible thing which had happened that she walked from the office without a word, caught a tram home, packed a bag, and sat in the station until the overnight train was due to leave for London. She never returned.

And because this grief was almost too much to bear, as she travelled south she' decided that never again would she allow herself to become attached to any one employer or situation. She would become a rolling stone. She wanted a changed life, with nothing to remind her of the old. As the train rattled through the night, she forced herself to assess what talents she had for earning a living in the vast unknown city of London. She had chosen London because she could disappear there, with no curious eyes to give her a second glance. She would never be a secretary again. It had to be a complete break with the past. She was intelligent and well-educated and as she mentally surveyed the needs of employers, it came to her with a flash of truth that wealthy houses required domestics. They would always be in demand. She had had the good home training of most Scots girls of her generation and she knew she could fulfil this role. That would be her future. She was so certain that she had found the right solution to her problems that she slept for the rest of the journey.

Like me, she knew of the YWCA, and as a trained secretary she knew where to look to find domestic agencies, so she registered with one which specialized in 'temporaries', and which dealt with the best families. She had a great love of the fine things created by craftsmen. Beautiful furniture, precious antiques, paintings, old silver. She would care for the possessions but wouldn't become attached to the families, for she wouldn't stay with any one family long enough to be hurt. She didn't need to earn a great deal to find peace of mind. She offered herself as a housekeeper with a knowledge of cooking.

By the time I met her, she had seen many of the kitchens of the aristocracy, and had also cooked for Royalty. Her account of this, when they had no soup ladle and she had to transfer soup from pot to serving bowls with a handle-less cup was hilarious. She had even been rung up by Buckingham Palace one evening, when they wished to know if the Duke of Windsor was with her employer! Her knowledge of antiques had made such strides that she had been asked to catalogue the priceless treasures of one of our noble Lords when he had moved house. And of course, trained in an age which scorned typewriters, her handwriting was copperplate, and each item of his Lord-ship's household carried a label in her lovely handwriting, so that locating a particular item in storage was reduced to simplicity itself.

She was honest as the day, and had a rakish elegance which lifted her well above the normal run of domestics. She must have been worth her weight in rubies to any employer lucky enough to acquire her services. But these rich people all had one thing in common. They hated to pay decent wages. And my dear Miss Chree never earned more than £3 10s. a week, plus her food, in all the years she lived in the Capital. But she had a soul above money. She had a marvellous life. She fell in love with London at first sight and never failed to rejoice in the richness of the passing scene. She taught me to appreciate its markets, its fascinating back streets, and its riches in a way which would have been impossible for me to do in the company of any of the acting fraternity.

But all that lay ahead. Now as we chatted, the voice of Mrs Parker soared upstairs, and soon she was panting up to show me how to manage the gas meter and to give me my rent book.

12

I loved my room from the very start. Other eyes might have seen only the assortment of second-hand furniture. The easy chair with the stuffing bursting out of its bottom seams, the small rickety table for my meals, the narrow bed with its lumpy mattress, the drunken gas fire with its missing fitments, but to me the place had the very savour of theatrical digs.

It was large and dignified, with lofty proportions, and when I saw it for the first time in daylight I was thrilled to find I was looking right over the roofs of London and could actually see the Tower of London itself. It was as romantic as René Clair's film, except that my exciting rooftop view was not of Paris, but of London.

I gazed round me with calculating eyes and saw where I could put extra hooks for my clothes, which I could later cover with an attractive curtain. (Miss Chree's introduction to the street markets provided a great source for such bargains.) I'd look out for a new steady table to hold my typewriter, and eventually I'd coax the landlady to allow me to buy a bigger bed and better mattress so that I could have my mother down to stay for a few nights. She'd never been to London in her life, in fact she'd never crossed the border, and it might calm her suspicions that I was living in squalor if she could see it all for herself. The little tin oven and the extra gas ring had already met with my full approval, and I was so busy planning future feasts in my head that I didn't take in a word of the landlady's instructions about the shilling-in-the-slot meter, and only vaguely heard her tell me to be sure to have a good stock of coins. I was to be sure to ask for shillings when I received change in the shops, for they were very scarce.

I wasn't used to the world of bed-sitters, and shilling meters, but it didn't take long to find out that all Clapham hoarded their shillings for this purpose, so that trying to get these precious coins in change was like expecting to find a sovereign in the gutter.

As well as shillings for the meter, I had to make sure of sixpences for 'toll' telephone calls, and pennies for local calls. I'd never heard of a 'toll' call, and discovered this wasn't quite so distant as a trunk call, but beyond the range of a local one, and that *all* the film studios involved toll charges. I'd be asked to ring a film casting director at eleven A.M. I would do so. 'Oh', an airy unconcerned voice would say, 'I'm afraid he hasn't come in yet. Could you ring about twelve?'. At twelve, another precious sixpence from my dwindling capital would be fed into the box's greedy mouth, and I'd be told, 'Sorry, he isn't coming in today after all. Try again tomorrow if you like'. What with finding sixpences, queueing for a cubicle, hanging about until the agreed hour to ring again, I determined that the first thing I was going to do when I got a job was to have a telephone installed in my room. It was impossible in such early post-war days to have a telephone at all unless the wiring had been previously done in the house for a former user and where, for some reason, only the instrument itself had been removed. One day when I had been wailing about running back and forth to the Post Office, up and down three flights of stairs to my room, to make appointments with those elusive film people, and had vowed that I'd get a telephone in the room or die in the attempt, Lois, the girl next door told me my room was already wired for one. I jumped with excitement. Only essential workers had been allowed telephones in the war, and the nurse who had earlier occupied my room came into that category, but when she had been drafted elsewhere the landlady had had the instrument removed, as she didn't wish to pay for it, and was afraid a future tenant wouldn't have taken it over. I gnashed my teeth in vexation. Oh *why* couldn't she have left it! Fancy anybody in a rooming house not realizing the usefulness of a telephone!

Lois, who was in the Post Office herself you may remember, brought home forms which I could fill in, for she said it would take ages before I'd get to the top of the queue, and if I couldn't afford to have the 'phone connected when the time came, I could always say so. Nothing would be lost. I felt it was an act of faith in my future, so I applied for my telephone, and then prayed every night that I would have a job before the Post Office reached my name.

It was marvellous though to find that the tube only took twenty minutes to get me right to the heart of the West End at a cost of sixpence. I saw every agent I could coax into giving me an appointment, and I enjoyed chats and cups of tea, and told them everything I'd done in radio and on the stage, left a note of name and address, regretted I was sorry I had no telephone, then whizzed on to the next appointment. I went to see the Light Entertainment people at Aeolian Hall, the BBC headquarters for this side of the business in Bond Street, whose name I had from Moultrie. I had sent him into shouts of laughter over the telephone in Glasgow when I first heard this unfamiliar name and thought he was recommending me to go to see a lady called 'Oley Anne Hall'! He couldn't believe I'd never heard of the place. Leslie Bridgmont saw me there, and was so friendly that I told him of my gaffe over Miss Oley Anne Hall, and laughed, gave me a delicious cup of coffee, and said he'd certainly remember me. I was so elated after this appointment that although I still had no prospects of any sort of job, I was grinning from ear to ear as I cut through to Regent Street, and an American soldier pressed a packet of cigarettes into my hand and said I must have them, as mine was the happiest face he had seen since coming to London! I couldn't wipe the smile off my face like lightning, or he'd think I was a bit dotted. Gosh, I'd have to be careful, or folk would think I was like the poor daft lassie who used to rush down Buchanan Street in wild spurts of speed, alternately laughing and scowling, a long hat-pin at the ready to repel any masculine assaults. The American refused to take back his cigarettes, gazed long and earnestly into my eyes as he repeated he would never forget my laughing face, shook my hand and went on his way.

My next appointment was with a film director, again introduced by the always helpful Moultrie, but as this man preferred to see me at his flat, I was terrified. Everybody knew that film directors were the wolves of show business. All the movie magazines had told us so for years. What would I do if he attacked me? I had no experience in such matters, and I hadn't even a long hat pin. I walked up and down on the pavement outside the block of flats for a good five minutes before I could summon courage to press the bell and, once inside, I wouldn't remove so much as a glove although the room was like an oven. It turned out he was pleased to see me because I had worked with his wife on radio in Glasgow, and he wanted to hear all about her. In case this was merely to lull my suspicions, I still kept my gloves on, and I was so nervous that any impression I created must only have been off-putting. Anyway I never worked for this man, but it had been quite interesting in a way, seeing the inside of a posh London flat. It had also been the first flat where the occupant spoke through a little tube which ended in an ear-piece at the door, and when one pressed the bell and gave a name, a mysterious force allowed the door to be pushed open. What a good idea, I thought. It was a pity we hadn't such an arrangement in Clapham, for I couldn't count the number of times I had had to race down three flights of stairs to answer the door, usually to take in a parcel for somebody else, or let the meter man have the keys, or take delivery of the laundry. Everybody else was out working during normal hours, and I often had the house entirely to myself.

My landlady was an ardent Catholic, and as we were getting close to Christmas, she was in constant attendance at the church round the corner. I seldom saw her, but when I did, she fascinated me. Less experienced mortals may have gasped in admiration at the sight of Fanny Craddock performing cookery chores clad in stunning dinner gown, but this came as no revelation to me, because my Mrs Parker brought the same assured approach to all her household tasks. She was always dressed for the church rather than the kitchen.

In her cubby hole of a scullery I would catch glimpses of her clad in rich blacks, the materials varying from heavy silk to gleaming velvet, even occasionally trimmed with fur, and on her head she almost always wore an elegant toque. Thus attired she might be baking scones, cleaning the oven, or making her stately way towards the door to clean the front steps. For this last task she had the fanciful notion of using a vegetable pot instead of a basin, and her brush might once have served to apply the shaving lather to a departed lodger's beard. I had a notion that she preferred this tiny brush and pot to the more usual cleaning equipment in case a passing priest caught sight of her, and could be allowed to assume she was feeding a needy stray animal. But this mis-use of the vegetable pot filled Miss Chree with horror, and we both felt secretly rather glad we catered for ourselves.

When my mother eventually came down to visit me, she was stunned to find such a regally clad lady performing household tasks without so much as an apron to protect her finery, and declared, 'My Goad, she must be an auld theatrical'. When I laughed, she said, 'I'll bet ye onything ye like that ah'm right. She'll hiv been used tae playin' the part o' a Duchess who has seen better days'.

This was nearer the truth than we could have supposed, for I subsequently learned that Mrs Parker had indeed 'trod the boards' in her younger days, but alas had got no further than the chorus. But there was no doubt she exuded an air of grease-paint.

Although she had a theatrical background, she was extremely modest and would pull her dressing gown tightly round her ample curves if I happened to be passing as she was coming from the bathroom in a cloud of steam, after her bath. I had been warned that I must always knock before I entered her room if I wanted anything. She had told me, frowning with distaste at the mere recollection, that on holiday in Italy a waiter had entered her bedroom without tapping the door. She had been stark naked and was about to don her corset. 'What did you do?', I asked, waiting for some terrible revelation of screams, or attempted seduction, or fainting clean away with horror. 'I just turned my back on the beast', she replied, closing her eyes with a shudder. I had to sneeze and pretend to cough to stifle the laughter which threatened to explode from me. She clearly hadn't the slightest idea that a susceptible Italian might have found the sight of her plump bottom quite as alluring as those parts she was at such pains to keep hidden from his gaze. In all our future conversations I had a terrible job keeping that mental picture from flashing before my eyes, for she had a very serious turn of mind and was extremely suspicious of misplaced levity.

One day when I left the BBC canteen and stood wondering who else I could ring, it occurred to me that I had been in London for nearly three weeks and I hadn't yet seen the Thames. It was a grey gritty day, and although all Britain might be getting ready to celebrate Christmas, the Festive Season for me meant only that all the offices would be shutting down and I would have nobody to approach in my search for work. Things were already slowing down, so I might as well have a look at the Thames. But how did I get to it, I wondered. I was at Oxford Circus, and I approached a policeman. 'Could you direct me to the river?', I asked solemnly, not realizing the impact of my words. The policeman gazed down at me and smiled. 'What's the matter, Jock?', he asked. 'Too far from Bonnie Scotland, are you?' When I shook my head, he said, 'Not thinking of chucking yourself in then, eh?' For the first time since I had arrived in London, I really burst out laughing. The very idea! 'No, no', I assured him. 'It's just that I've been here for weeks and it's high time I saw the Thames to see how it compares with the Clyde. How do I get there?'

Following his directions, I found myself passing the end of Downing Street. Could that wee street really be where the Prime Minister lived? And there was the centre of all the crime-busting brains and the place mentioned in all the detective stories, New Scotland Yard. Somehow the Cenotaph seemed much smaller than when one saw it in the news-reels, but it was a most impressive street, and the buildings were beautiful. And then, before me, was the whole magnificent façade of the Houses of Parliament. What had I been doing all this time, neglecting such historical landmarks. I leaned over the parapet and gazed at the murky swirling waters. Lights were beginning to pierce the twilight, and the Embankment looked romantic and very beautiful. Across the river, the skyline showed a fretwork of exquisite architecture. There was no doubt it was a wonderful city. Oh I hoped my fifty pounds would last long enough to let me explore it to the full before I had to go home, which I would have to do very soon if I didn't get a job.

I hadn't intended going home for Christmas, which wasn't

celebrated to any great extent in Scotland, but when I discovered that practically everything in London would be closing down not for the single day I had supposed, but for nearly a week, I agreed with my landlady that I'd probably be better off at home. Lois was going away to friends. Miss Chree, whom I hadn't seen at all since she had welcomed me to the house, was obviously busy with her employers, and I didn't know anybody else in the place. I looked at my bank book. It would cost me nearly £4 to go home (I had a concession ticket as the wife of a serving man), but maybe it would be a good idea to pop back, check that the water and our house were all right, and see my mother and my in-laws. Yes I'd go, while I still had enough money to come back to London again. My mother's letter next morning confirmed my decision, 'Don't stay down there by yourself for Hogmanay', she wrote, 'Come home for a wee while'.

I caught the 10 A.M. train from Euston, and as I opened the front door of the house in Glasgow the telephone was ringing. it was the BBC in London. Aeolian Hall to be precise, from Leslie Bridgmont's office. He had kept his word and he hadn't forgotten me, but oh if only he'd thought of it twenty-four hours earlier he'd have saved me such a lot of time and precious cash. They wanted me the next day to play the part of a wee boy in a comedy sketch, and to join in some of the concerted items with the orchestra. Dorothy Carless was the soloist, and the variety orchestra would be featured. Was I free to do it? I was tired and hungry after my journey, but it was my very first offer from a London producer. I couldn't say no. 'Yes, I'll be there', I said. 'What time do you want me in the morning?'

Long long afterwards when she heard this story, Grace McChlery said that that was the moment when she knew I would make a success of my life in London. 'With the strength and determination to say yes, and to be able to turn round and go straight back to London', she told me, 'you were bound to succeed.'

My neighbour thought I was mad, but lent me a kettle of water to make myself some tea to save the bother of filling up the water tank all over again. I took a quick run up to Springburn to break the news to my mother that I had to go back to London right away, but would be home for Hogmanay. She was aghast at the expense and even more so at the thought of the journey, and she cast her eyes upwards, 'My Goad, you must be ambitious,' she said. 'Can ye no' juist tell them you canny come till efter the New Year?' As if the BBC planned their programmes round my convenience! I laughed and shook my head. 'It's all right, Mother', I told her, 'I'm lucky to have my room to go back to. I'll be home the day after tomorrow'.

So that was how my first broadcast from Aeolian Hall came about. I was thrilled to meet Dorothy Carless of the velvet voice, who surprised me by being tall and blonde, when I'd thought of her as being small and dark. She obviously had the sort of voice which conveyed that impression, because when I said impulsively that I had pictured her entirely differently, she said wearily that everybody told her so. She must have been fed up listening to this remark, as I was later to be myself when people met me who'd only heard me on the air and told me they'd imagined me to be a big fat wifie!

It was most exciting finding myself singing with her and the others rousing Christmas choruses, backed by musicians to whom transposing, re-arranging and brilliant improvisation were child's play. One knew that however one faltered, they would be there to sustain and cover up, and I may say I've found this impressive musical talent in every BBC orchestra with whom it's been my good fortune to work. I have never taken such expertise for granted, and they always seemed highly amused by my open admiration of their talents. I think they were pleased though, for it's always nice to be told you're good, even in the rarefied atmosphere of top entertainment, where you've just *got* to be extra special to have reached that height. It's no accident that musicians are among my best friends in London. As a sixpenny pupil, I know how much hard work has gone into putting them in the top rank!

This was my first engagement as a London artist, and of course as I was supposed to be resident in the capital it was just my bad luck that I had been in Glasgow when the booking came through. So my first fee went to British Railways, for the amount I was paid almost exactly matched my fare, to a penny. But I was creating goodwill and I could now say I'd worked for

London BBC. After all, you had to invest before you could expect a return. I couldn't expect to show a profit as well, not at this early stage.

So I returned to Glasgow with a light heart to match my pocket, and it was great to be home for Hogmanay. I stayed in Springburn and went first-footing, and nobody seemed particularly interested in my activities in London, which was just as well for I wasn't exactly setting the Thames on fire. It was all too remote for them to comprehend, and they were far more absorbed in knowing who was getting home from the camps abroad, who was likely to be demobbed soon, who was getting engaged or married and, above all, in pitting their wits against food and clothing shortages.

We were still strictly rationed, and the big fruit cake that year was once more heavily fortified with grated carrot and a dollop of stout to make up for the other missing ingredients. But there were promises of whiter flour any month now, promises which had us agog with anticipation, for we all longed for the taste of a slice of really white bread, and a sponge cake of feather-light quality. I normally preferred brown bread, but after years of grey dough found myself yearning for the luxury of a piece on jeely with soft white bread as its base.

The whole of Glasgow seemed to be stuffed up with colds and catarrh, and when I returned to London after New Year it was with a heavy stupefying cold which blotted out all sense of taste and smell. The train sleeper was freezing, and every muscle ached from trying to hold myself in a warm position once I'd found it. When I reached Clapham, I crept upstairs to my top-floor room, filled a hot-water bottle, didn't even trouble to make myself a cup of tea, but quickly undressed and fell into bed. I was awakened by the sound of the landlady's voice, growing stronger from each landing as she panted up the stairs. 'Miss Weir, Miss Weir', she gasped. 'A telegram for you'. I swung my legs over the side of the bed. My head felt about the size of a football and buzzed like a bike of bees. I felt terrible. There was a strange wobbly sensation in my legs, and I thought I might be going to be sick. Suddenly, the thickness in my head cleared, the way it sometimes does when one has a cold, and I heard a curious hissing sound coming from somewhere. What could it be? As I looked feebly round the room, my eye fell on the tap of the gas fire. It was turned full on and it wasn't lit. I had put a shilling in the meter when I came in and boiled the kettle for my bottle, so the gas must have been hissing into the room ever since. Naturally, because of my cold I had neither heard it nor smelt it. I staggered forward and twisted the tap closed, and then threw open the window and gulped in the fresh air to try to clear my head. Mrs Parker came in and handed me a telegram. It said 'Can you come to the Globe Theatre 10.30 this morning re part in play', and it was signed by H. M. Tennent, one of London's biggest managements.

Although it was now after nine o'clock, I went back to bed to consider the situation. My stomach swung uneasily between excitement at the telegram's news, and terror that I might have been gassed as I slept if Tennents hadn't been so extravagant as to wire me. For my landlady wouldn't have climbed three flights of stairs for a mere letter. But how had the gas fire tap turned itself on? I knew I hadn't done it, because I never spent precious shillings on the fire when I was in bed. I learned later that my landlady had done a little tidying while I was away and had lit the fire to keep herself warm. When the shilling had run out, she hadn't bothered to put another one in, and when she left the room later she had forgotten to turn off the tap. So of course the tap had still been open when I put in my shilling in the morning. It was a most dangerous practice, and my near escape taught me to check the taps every time I came back to my room.

Having considered the situation from all angles, I could now turn my attention to the staggering news in the telegram. But first I must have a cup of tea. It dawned on me I had had nothing to eat or drink since my supper in Glasgow the night before. Was it only the night before? Already it seemed a lifetime away. I jumped up and put the kettle on, then popped back to bed while it boiled, and savoured the full delight of having been invited to attend H.M. Tennent's pleasure at The Globe. What play could it be for? What stars would be in it? Oh what did it matter who was in it, so long as I was being considered for it too. I'd wear my one and only green suit, and I'd get a bottle of Vick on the way to the theatre, to try to clear my head. The room was now perishing because of the wide-open window, but I had to make sure every trace of gas escaped, so I had breakfast sitting up in bed with my dressing gown on to keep warm.

As my head got a bit clearer, I began to wonder how on earth Tennents had ever heard of me. I hadn't gone to see anyone there. Could it be a mistake? I seized the telegram and examined every word of it again. No, it was addressed to Molly Weir. It was me all right. Oh thank goodness I lived so near the West End. It would only take a little over half-an-hour from door to door, so I had time to give myself a thorough wash, and brush my hair, *and* my suit, to achieve as neat and pleasing an appearance as possible.

They were all rehearsing when I presented myself at the stage door, and a young man handed me a script and told me to study the part of Bertha. I found a corner back-stage and plunged into frantic study of the lines I was to speak for the audition. I took no notice of anything else that was going on, until the same young man beckoned to me to come on stage where the producer was now ready for me. It was the famous Richard Bird, known to all theatreland as 'Dicky Bird'. He explained that they had several people to see so couldn't give an immediate decision about the part, but they'd like to hear me read for it. It was that of an ex-ATS girl who performs all her duties as a maid at the double because of her wartime training, and nearly drives her employer mad because she *will* salute each time she is given an order. 'Will I do it in Scots?', I asked seriously. There was a muffled snort of laughter from the unseen figures in the stalls. 'Nacherally', said Dicky Bird, in mock imitation of my accent, and I blushed with embarrassment. I was so accustomed to using a variety of dialects for the BBC and the amateur productions in Glasgow that the first thing we established was the accent, and it didn't dawn on me that nobody in London would think of me other than as a Scot with the heather growing out of her ears, capable only of speaking with the broadest of Scottish accents.

As soon as I'd said the first line, Dicky Bird's face lost its detached look, and by the end of the scene there were encouraging little chuckles from the darkness out front. I closed the book and handed it back to the young man who hovered in the wings, for I knew they had other people to see. To my surprise, Dicky Bird said 'Don't go. Just sit down there for a moment', and he motioned me to a chair in the wings. I heard a murmured conversation and then, unbelievably, Dicky Bird's voice said, 'Well the part is yours, Miss Weir. Go with Bob up to the office and sign your contract and come right back to resume rehearsals'. I stared at him. What about the other people they had to see? He patted my shoulder and told Bob to take me to the offices, and bring me back as soon as possible for there was a lot to do. As the lift took us upwards, I heard the tinkle of cups and knew the coffee break was over, and that by the next meal-break, I would be one of the company.

Bob ushered me into an outer office, then I was shown into the holy of holies, and found myself facing one of Binkie Beaumont's minions, Beaumont himself being the great white chief who ran Tennents. Even I had heard of him via the press. I wasn't to see him in person until the dress rehearsal as it turned out. They offered me ten pounds per week, which seemed a small fortune, told me there would be a three months' number one tour (number one again – it must mean something special!), and then the play would open in London. I was to sign where indicated, and could ascertain all other relevant details at my leisure. I signed eagerly, dying to get down to the stage again to see my fellow-actors who, up till now, had been invisible.

Two people were working on a scene on stage, and Dicky Bird faced them from a chair propped securely behind the footlights which were of course not lit. There was just a smallish amount of illumination, it seemed to me, but it all smelt wonderful. The same smell which I knew from the Empire, the Theatre Royal and the Kings in Glasgow. London theatres didn't smell a bit different. I felt quite at home. An elderly chap sat mouthing his lines behind the scenery, clad to the ears in a heavy overcoat, and a young couple nearby were going through their scene in whispers. A beautiful red-haired lady sat with closed eyes, her hand steadily moving from line to line as she went down the page memorizing her dialogue. I stared at all of them. My first close contact with real actors and actresses.

We broke for lunch before my scene came up, and when I

asked the youngest-looking where they went, she said 'Oh *we* go to so-and-sos, but I expect it would be rather expensive for you.' I bit my lip, and forced a smile, 'Oh it doesn't matter', I said, 'I want to do some shopping anyway', and I flew out of the stage door, determined to let nothing spoil my moment of triumph at having landed a part in a West End play. I danced up Shaftesbury Avenue and I wanted to stop everyone and say 'I'm an actress. I'm rehearsing at the Globe Theatre. I'm going to be in London's West End. And I'm not nearly through my fifty pounds yet'. But instead I found myself in Soho, in front of a mouth-watering window filled with French pâtisserie. I hadn't seen such rich-looking cakes for years. In fact I doubted if I'd ever seen such creamy concoctions. I went in. And to celebrate my first theatre part, in the perishing month of January, I had a cup of coffee, two French cakes, and an ice cream. I blanched when I saw the bill, but recovered immediately. It had been worth it. It had nothing to do with practical everyday eating, and I would remember that lunch all my life.

In the afternoon I was introduced to the rest of the cast. The elderly gentleman was A. E. Matthews, whom I was to know later as beloved Matty, that glorious eccentric recognized by everyone in theatreland as a law unto himself. The others were Marjorie Fielding, a delightful lady who gave me great help, Ronnie Ward whose style afforded me much amusement, Denis Goacher and Barbara White, Charles Cameron (later to be a stalwart of the Whitehall farces with Brian Rix), Jean St Clair who understudied me as well as playing the overgrown schoolgirl, and the beautiful red-haired Ambrosine Phillpots.

I found Barbara White enchantingly lovely, and I never understood why she didn't go right to the top with those looks especially in films. But she was engaged to Kieron Moore, who was quite an eyeful himself, and they made a stunning couple. Kieron was playing in a theatre which had Mondays off, and we were to see much of him on our tour, as he tore all over Britain on Mondays to spend a few hours with his beloved Barbara. When they married, she retired from the bright lights and concentrated on having babies and creating a happy home. I hope Kieron appreciates it was I who taught Barbara to iron during our laundry sessions in the wardrobe between matinée and evening performances. Barbara was astounded by the speed with which I tore through such chores, not realizing possibly that the work might have been more professional if I had taken more time, but she was all for learning my method, so I passed on my hit-and-run technique!

The young man who had looked after me at the audition was called Bob, and he was stage manager as well as understudy to Denis Goacher and Ronnie Ward. We even had an Assistant Stage Manager, so that in the event of illness all eventualities were covered. This was a luxury unknown to me in Glasgow. Fancy even the stage manager having an understudy! Later two other understudies were engaged to 'cover' Marjorie, Barbara and Ambrosine, but they didn't join us until the last week of rehearsals.

It was ages before I discovered how the management had come to hear of my existence. It appeared that the part of Bertha had already been cast, but the comedienne who had been engaged had received a better offer and had accepted it. She had simply walked out and left the company after two or three days' rehearsals. It was quite a tricky part. It wasn't big enough to tempt an established comedienne, which the other girl was, so although they were furious that she had let them down, they couldn't really blame her. Yet it was too important to trust to an unknown inexperienced beginner. Time was pressing, and while they were deliberating as to whether or not they should bring back one of their contract players who was on tour with another play, Dicky Bird met the director who had made that first film with me in Glasgow. That was a lucky meeting for me. When he had asked, half-joking if she had a good young comedienne up her sleeve, she told him about the film and flatteringly added that although I had finely played a down-trodden little creature for her, it was right against my true type and I had had them all in stitches in the bus coming back each day from location. She obligingly boosted my chances further by telling him that both John Mills and Alastair Sim had liked my work, and that I was an established BBC artist!

So Dicky took her word for it and decided it might be a good idea to have a look at me at least, for at this stage there just wasn't time to hold general auditions all over again. By telling me they had others to see, they had just been paving the way for a polite 'we'll let you know' if I hadn't been any good. If I was any good, I was in. It was a fantastic coincidence that Dicky and Budge should have met while her memory of my work was still fresh, and lucky beyond my wildest hopes that the part should have been one where my accent was not only acceptable but actually enhanced the comedy.

The rehearsals were enthralling, and at the same time they sufficiently resembled the work I'd done in Glasgow to make me feel at home. The main differences were that with stars in the cast, with their own ideas, the finer points were the subject of intense discussion and mutual agreement, and various ways of interpretation were tried before the final style was set. As for me, I just did as I was told which, as I was a Scot with 'foreign' intonation of my own, was surprisingly little. Apart from being shown my 'moves', I was left to get on with it, and luckily everyone seemed to find my peculiar voice rhythms amusing. There wasn't much time for us to get to know one another, for we were all intent on learning lines and in getting the play into shape before the opening night in Edinburgh, which was to take place two and a half weeks after the arrival of that fateful telegram

We had dress fittings and last minute alterations in Tennent's own wardrobe before the clothes were packed into their baskets ready for the train to Scotland.

I used to love to visit the wardrobe right at the top of the theatre, and watch the scurry and bustle which took place when they were getting a play ready for the road. A whole team of girls busied themselves pressing beautiful clothes, hanging them up to air and leaving them perfect, ready for the next pair of hands to insulate them with layers and layers of tissue paper and pack them into the yawning mouths of enormous wicker baskets. Hats and gloves and undies stood in neat piles, and handbags by the side, with every item checked to see that it matched the entire outfit.

It was just like being behind the scenes at a top sewing establishment.

When they weren't packing clothes for a tour, they sat busily sewing, altering, repairing, and sometimes re-making dresses which lent themselves to adaptation for another show. And I enjoyed to the hilt the sight of well-known actors and actresses being fitted with their wardrobes for their latest play. And some of them were very well-known stars indeed, for Tennents always had several plays running in the West End at the same time, as well as many on the road, and they used the top talents in all of them.

And when I'd examined all the dresses and the lovely materials, I stood entranced before the rows of new shoes waiting to accompany each outfit.

To my delight, after years of pinching and scraping to acquire respectable shoes and stockings to set off my carefully-hoarded best clothes, I was allowed a split new pair of black lacing shoes, and two pairs of fine black lisle stockings for my part of the maid. The shoes would have to be handed back at the end of the play of course, to go into Tennent's general store, but the stockings were mine for keeps. What a bonus! And I didn't even have to go hunting for my small size three shoe. The wardrobe mistress did this for me, and only took me along at the last minute to check that size and fitting were right. Gosh, it was like having a lady's maid.

Three days before leaving for the north and the opening night, the Post Office, with an unexpected burst of speed, informed me that I could have the telephone installed any time I wished. What luck. I'd be able to ring the landlady if I were to manage home any week-end, and I could rejoice in the knowledge that when the tour finished I'd have no more chasing for pennies and sixpences for I'd have my very own telephone at my command. It was a bit of an expense before I'd even started earning regularly, but I could just about manage the installation charges, and I would have a pay coming in every week for ages and ages. It would be well worth a bit of scrimping now.

Luckily I arrived home early from rehearsal when the engineers were in the house, for to my indignation I found that my landlady was calmly instructing them to instal it in the hall and to make it a coin box. What cheek! When I had been the one to apply for the instrument, and when I would be the one who would be expected to pay for its rental. Worst of all, I would be back to square one, hoarding coins, waiting my turn in the queue, the only advantage being that of merely descending three flights of stairs instead of having to dress and go round the corner to the Post Office. Plus of course the privilege of paying for the installation.

I could feel the sense of outrage rising and threatening to choke me. Injustice always brings on feelings of claustrophobia, I don't know why. But I made myself speak reasonably and calmly. I didn't want to find my things in the street before I even left for Edinburgh.

'Oh, do you want it in the hall, Mrs Parker?', I asked, all innocent surprise, 'For use of the whole house?' She fluttered her hands and didn't meet my eyes. 'Yes, I thought it would be better here', she said, 'and then we could all use it'.

I swallowed, but managed a reasonable, frowning expression as though I were considering the matter. 'Well', I said, 'you do realize of course that a coin box is a higher rental, and that it will be the house telephone and not mine, but of course I don't mind since you will be paying for it'.

There was complete silence. I gazed dreamily at the ceiling. She rubbed her hands and looked at the engineers. They swung their boxes and said at last impatiently, 'Well, where do you want it, missus, we haven't got all day'. They looked at Mrs Parker and then at me, wondering what on earth it was all about. 'Do you want to take it over, Mrs Parker?', I asked. 'No', she answered, and disappeared into the scullery without another word.

'Follow me', I told the engineers.

My goodness but I was getting devious, I thought. We both knew, the landlady and I, that an attempt at a little bit of sharp practice had been foiled, yet not a harsh word had been spoken which would have been difficult to overlook living under the same roof. And before I left for Edinburgh, I told her that I would leave my door unlocked so that if anyone wished to use the telephone they were most welcome, and they could also give my number to any important personal or business contacts, so that everyone in the house could share my good luck in this way. After all I had the boon of having the telephone right beside my bed and didn't even have to put my clothes on to answer it.

I left a wee saucer for money for outgoing calls, and the other tenants seemed highly delighted with this arrangement.

I knew I was fortunate to be living in a house of such irreproachable honesty that I could leave everything behind an unlocked door. The use of my telephone was a very small thank you to such trustworthy neighbours.

13

When we all met in the morning at Kings Cross Station at the start of the tour, and found our reserved compartments, I felt it was just like Priestley's 'Good Companions'. I was very excited about the whole thing, and considered it was a terrific bonus to have my fares paid to places I'd never seen before, because, apart from London, the rest of England was virtually unknown to me.

I wondered what my Edinburgh digs would be like. I'd never lived in theatrical digs, and was amazed to discover that Equity, the Actors' Trade Union, supplied a booklet of addresses for every single town and city which boasted theatres. There were dozens and dozens of names, far more than the holiday lists in the *Evening Times* which we used to study with such passion when we were looking for a house for our Fair holidays. And this theatrical letting went on all the year round. My goodness, it must be an industry in itself, I thought.

The lower-paid members of the company pored over the addresses, mostly in ignorance of where any of the lodgings were situated in relation to the theatre or whether or not they might be in slum districts. But we were kept on the right track by the troupers who had toured the theatres for years, and warned which ones not to touch with a barge pole, and which ones were truly home from home. Because I had a typewriter, I did most of the writing, and we shared out the favourable replies between us, and before we left London I felt thankful and assured that I would have a place to rest my head in every town or city the play visited. Before the end of the tour though, I was to regret having planned my life quite so far ahead.

The company had been very surprised that I couldn't pass on any recommendations about good Glasgow digs, but because it was my home town I hadn't the faintest idea where 'theatricals' lived. With my own home and other relatives there, I had never had to think of such a thing. However, I could keep them right about the good districts to choose, and the Equity booklet had a list of excellent ones around Hill Street and the Charing Cross area, handy for getting to and from the theatre, and dead centre of the good shopping area. There was some curiosity about where I lived, but the moment they discovered it was half-an-hour's journey by tramcar, they lost interest. Actors, like railwaymen and shipyard workers, like to live on top of the job, especially when touring.

My Edinburgh digs were in a dingy tenement round the corner from the theatre, and the house resounded with the tread of heavy tackety boots as the sons tramped in and out for their meals. She was a very nice friendly body though, my landlady, my very first 'pro' landlady, and I was far too excited about the play to bother about cooking smells or the aroma of drying dungarees. I was longing to see the 'set' in position and rushed round to see the theatre the moment I'd unpacked. I knew the props and the scenery had gone ahead, and that the men would have been building it all day to have it ready for our first run-through that evening. It was fascinating to find 'my' drawing room, where I made my first entrance, so beautifully realized with walls, doors and windows, and handsome furniture, and when I'd finished admiring the rich effect I tried the window fastenings and the door handles to make sure they worked properly, before going in search of my silver tray and the other props I'd require during the course of the play. It's a good maxim always to check everything you will use in a performance, from doors to teacups, and then you will avoid nightmares during the actual performance.

In contrast to the brilliance of the lighting when audiences are expected, theatres, when occupied only by actors, are dimly lit places with great pools of darkness where single bulbs send little radiance. It's always exciting for the actor, but the magic only begins when the audience arrives.

I had time to walk back to my digs for a welcome pot of tea and some toast, and when I went back to the theatre, the stage was transformed, brilliantly lit, with the electricians going through their paces in readiness for our first rehearsal. We all seemed to have the jittery feeling which comes from knowing time is running out, and that all the weeks of rehearsal will soon be put to the test in front of a critical audience. The real furniture always seems different, and the props unfamiliar, and inexplicable 'dries' become commonplace. But Dicky Bird was encouragingly happy, and when tiredness threatened to engulf us all in a brittle edginess he said, 'That'll do for tonight. Ten o'clock in the morning, please, for full dress rehearsal'.

As I lay in that unfamiliar bed in that Edinburgh tenement, I was surrounded by the familiar tenement noises I had known since childhood. The footfalls overhead, the bang on the wall, the pulley noises from downstairs, and the sound of front door keys being turned in locks. It was like being back in Springburn again. But oh I was glad it wasn't Springburn, for that would have meant Glasgow, and I didn't feel quite courageous enough to be judged by my very own fellow-Glaswegians on my very first performance with a company of professional actors and actresses. Auld Reekie didn't know I'd gone to London to seek fame and fortune, and I would be of no particular interest to them, thank goodness. They would be watching the stars, not studying me looking for signs of anything special, and I could concentrate on doing my very best to make the most of the author's lines without being too palsied with terror, as I would have been had I been facing a Glasgow audience on opening night.

The dress rehearsal went in fits and starts, as dress rehearsals usually do, until it seemed impossible that we'd ever get through the play in the usual two and a half hours which normally saw the unfolding and solution of all such tales. It went on for *hours,* with unsuspected snags cropping up all the time. Doors opened the wrong way for certain comedy entrances. The sofa was too bulky for swift manoeuvring at a particular point. The tray was too large to get through the French windows. Even the clothes developed a temperament of their own, and buttons mysteriously appeared in the wrong places, or seams twisted, and hems dipped confusingly. The wardrobe mistress pattered back and forth with needle and thread and scissors, and the iron was on the go all day long.

Carpenters hammered, and removed screws, and changed fitments round to suit us. We had one clear run-through of the play from start to finish, and it felt quite lifeless. Our hearts were in our boots when we broke for tea.

My dressing room was right at the top of the theatre, and I was sharing with Jean St Clair, the big Irish girl with the droll looks, and with Caroline, one of the understudies. Jean had a great sense of humour, and as she didn't appear until the very last moments of the play, decided it was far too early for her to be nervous, and so reeled off a non-stop flow of Irish jokes which had me giggling and spluttering with laughter in spite of my own tremors. Once made up and into my maid's uniform, I felt more like Bertha, the ex-ATS tear-away maid, and the neatness and sparkling cleanliness of the outfit appealed to me. Wherever else I fell down, at least I looked right.

By this time, back-stage fairly pulsed with excitement and we all raced around, wishing each other good luck. However strong is the faith of actors in the play, the author, the management and their own hard work, they know they also need a big helping of the final ingredient, luck to fuse memory, talent and vitality into that special something which spells success. The overture ended. It was curtain up, and on with the show. The laughs came surely and steadily, and I got a roar on one exit line, and a round of applause on another. It was so unexpected, I nearly dried up, and Bob, never taking his eyes from the 'book' where he was on 'cue' duty in the wings, whispered 'Good girl, you're doing fine', as I ran past him for the prop table, to pick up a duster for my next entrance.

In the third act, I had an entrance where it was vital that Matty didn't finish the last sentence of his speech, or it would give the whole plot away. I had to enter carrying my silver tray laden with tea things, and as it felt as though it weighed a ton, and they knew it was very heavy for me, I was ordered not to pick it up from the prop table until the very last moment, so that I could carry it on with sure strong steady arms, without a wobble anywhere. On that first night, long before the plot line was due, I decided to try out the weight of the laden tray once more and I poised myself behind the door to estimate yet again just how much space I'd require to sail smoothly through at the correct moment. This ritual was merely for my own peace of mind, and I was just about to relieve my arms of the dead-weight of the tray when, to my horror, I heard Matty start the vital line *miles* too soon. I hadn't a second to collect my thoughts, much less think of my lines. I wrenched the door open and catapulted on stage, dishes, cakes, bread and milk clattering like castanets. Ronnie Ward gave a snort of laughter, Marjorie Fielding an approving nod, and Matty merely smiled amiably. For a frozen moment my lines vanished, and then as my heart turned over with fright, I found my mouth was opening and shutting and the rehearsed words were coming out.

At the end of the scene, I tottered off the stage like a limp rag. Oh gosh, I hoped I'd never have to go through that nightmare again. But I had. Every single performance! I can say, with my hand on my heart, that I never had a correct cue from Matty in that scene during the entire tour. I used to stand poised outside that door, frantically trying to guess where he'd put the line this time, and indeed how he would phrase it, for he said something quite different at each performance. The cast took bets as to whether or not he would beat me to it! It was agonizing and I ought to have felt like strangling him for making me go through this ordeal eight times a week. But somehow one forgave Matty everything, for the colour, the extravagance and genuine eccentricity of his style in a largely disciplined back-stage world.

The first member of the family to see me as a real actress was my brother-in-law Jimmy. I found him standing in the doorway of my digs one afternoon when I came in for tea. He was home on demobilization leave, had learned that I was acting in Edinburgh and had decided to come through to see the play. I was delighted to see him, for he and my husband shared the same rich vein of wit, and I applauded his good sense in finding my address from the stage door. Come to think of it, anybody who could find his way out of Cherbourg with the enemy at his heels, not to mention other wartime hazards, wasn't going to be stumped merely because he had no address for me in his pocket-book. He would have to stay in Edinburgh for the night, because the last Glasgow train left before our final curtain, and he wondered if there was a spare bed in my digs. My landlady, with all those sons, took his request in her stride. Yes, of course he could stay there, if he didn't mind sharing a bed with one of the boys. This presented no problem to Jimmy, who had had to find his rest where he could during five years of warfare. It was a concealed bed, behind a door in the lobby, but he would find it comfortable, she assured him, and he need only pay for his breakfast. The bed would be her present to a serving soldier, seeing all her boys had been safely at home, some too young to serve, and the others in reserved occupations.

I had had very good notices from the Edinburgh press but none meant so much as Jimmy's assessment, for I had a great respect for his sense of fun and his lively appreciation of the humour of any situation. I felt as though I had won an Oscar when he told me afterwards that for him the funniest moment in the play was when I tiptoed through the French windows bearing my silver tray (a short cut I had been forbidden to use), caught Matty's warning eye indicating that his wife Marjorie was in the room, and tiptoed cautiously out again without opening my mouth. I had particularly enjoyed working out this little piece of mimed comedy, and I was thrilled to feel it had come over as I intended, to one member of the audience at least. Dear Jimmy, I don't suppose he ever knew how much his compliment meant to me, but at the start of my professional stage career it was of greater encouragement than I could have put into words.

With an all-English company, I was like Ruth among the alien corn, and I really had no one in whom I could confide or with whom I could discuss anything. Jimmy's unexpected visit provided a marvellous opportunity to discuss the whole play, chapter and verse, over supper and it was great to be able to sit up chatting non-stop and know that every word would be understood, with no translation required for English ears.

The play had a fairly cool reception in Glasgow, although again my own performance met with some approval. I was vexed that we hadn't set Glasgow on fire with our drawing-room thriller-comedy, but very thankful that no brickbats had been thrown at me. It would have been too awful to have returned with a London company, looking like a fish out of water. But cool reception or no, all my neighbours had booked for the Saturday night, and were throwing a farewell party for me afterwards. That Saturday performance found me shaking with a horrible sort of terror, which chilled instead of making me fevered, which sent my teeth chattering and a cold perspiration to trickle down my arms.

At least I thought it was fear which produced these nightmarish sensations, but at the party afterwards, held in my neighbour's house next door, everything began to swim before my eyes and I had a sensation of floating. I knew without doubt that this wasn't nerves. It was my old enemy, 'flu. As my temperature rose and sweat began to trickle down my face, one of the husbands said decisively, 'Well, there's one thing certain, you can't go to Newcastle with the company tomorrow. It's bed for you for the next few days'.

I stared at him as though he'd gone out of his mind. 'Not go to Newcastle!', I said, 'I *must*. The understudies don't know their parts yet. And anyway, I couldn't stay here knowing they'd gone without me. They might not have me back.'

Imagine him thinking *anything* short of death would prevent my travelling to my next lot of digs the following morning. I might drop dead on the station platform, but I was going.

On Sunday morning I staggered about emptying the water tank and making sure everything was left neat and tidy and safe, before setting off with chattering teeth for the station.

In Newcastle, three of us had booked in at a guest house recommended by an actor friend, and I will never forget the kindness of that compassionate landlord and his wife. She took one look at my face, packed me off to bed in my room on the third floor and told me to stay there, and tea would be brought up to me. 'It's too far to carry it', I protested feebly, I'll get up if you give me a call'. They would have none of it. 'I'll bring it up', said the landlord, 'so you'll stay in bed when you're told.' Oh the bliss of that welcoming mattress. I sank down into a deep fevered sleep, only swimming back to a hazy consciousness when a tap on the door told me it was time for afternoon tea. I drained the teapot with greedy thirst, but I had no appetite for the scones or the biscuits which had been left on the tray. Supper (as they called their high-tea-cum-dinner) was at 7.30 on Sundays, and when I crept into the dining room these kind proprietors were dismayed that I'd dressed and come down for it. Why hadn't I stayed in bed? Gosh, I thought, it was bad enough the man having carried up a tea-tray, I wasn't going to have him carting a whole dinner up three flights of stairs. What would my grannie have said? She would have despised such weak behaviour. And anyway, they hadn't mentioned serving dinner in my room and I never dreamt guest-houses would have thought of doing such a thing.

I stayed in bed most of Monday, only visiting the theatre after breakfast to see if there was any mail and checking where my dressing room was, and how the scenery fitted the new stage. It was to become a great thrill looking for mail on the green baize board behind each stage door, or sometimes in little pigeon holes in the stage-door-keeper's office. I really felt the complete actress when I'd enquire with studied casualness, 'Any mail for me, George?' (they all seemed to be called George), and if a letter was handed over addressed to me c/o whatever theatre we were appearing in that week, I felt part of the very fabric of show business.

On this Monday morning there was nothing and I crawled thankfully back to the guest house and bed, very relieved that I was having full board this week and there would be no need to do battle with the local shops for my groceries. During the tour I was to find that we never arrived at any town at the right time for anything. Eggs had been delivered last week and their allocation had gone so none for strolling players. Tinned fruit wasn't expected till next week, so our coupons couldn't be used for that covetable item to add zest to our diet. When we demanded onions, because we'd read in the papers that this area were having their quota this very day, they smiled and said that alas they'd had theirs much earlier in the month, and couldn't expect any more supplies till the following allocation. We'd be half-way to London by then, of course.

I remember in one town I took a great notion for parsnips. My landlady had incautiously told me she thought there might still be one or two around, as she'd managed to buy some at the weekend. Any fresh vegetables were as manna from heaven and I wouldn't rest until I'd found some for myself. I went into every single greengrocers in the neighbourhood, and in the end victory was mine. The last one in a row of grimy little shops yielded up almost a pound.

I rushed back with them, gave the landlady instructions to cook only one with my stew, and drooled all afternoon at the thought of having this delicious vegetable stretched over at least three meals to add savour to my dinners. When I sat down to dinner later that night, I was astounded to find that my fellow-actor, Charles Cameron, was sitting before a plate containing a liberal helping of parsnips. 'Oh did you manage to get some too, Charles?' I said innocently, for I knew he hated shopping and I was quite interested to know how he had tracked them down. I never even began to suspect the truth. 'Oh no, Molly,' he said, seizing a forkful as he spoke, 'they're yours. I just told the landlady to cook them all. I knew you wouldn't mind, and I can always get some more for you tomorrow.'

When I could find my voice, I nearly shattered the dishes with my roar. 'You *can't* get me more tomorrow, Charles Cameron', I yelled, 'for there *aren't* any more to get. How *dare* you take food without knowing whether or not you could repay it'. He was staring at me, open-mouthed, obviously baffled by my rage. I then turned on the hapless landlady, 'And *you* had *no right* to give that man my parsnips.' And I turned and walked out of the room, my food uneaten. Charles was tall and handsome and I could imagine how persuasive he had been, but I was unforgiving. I had to come back and eat my dinner of course, for I was hungry, but I waited until he had finished. I couldn't have swallowed a mouthful with him in the room – it would have choked me.

Food, after years of scarcity and rationing, assumed an almost unbelievable importance to us at that time, so much so that I have to confess that I don't remember a thing about Charles's performance in the play. I only remember that he stole my parsnips. When I met him years later and recalled his name the instant I saw him, he was flattered and surprised at my being able to put a name to him so quickly (actors are notoriously forgetful of each other's real names). I had the grace not to tell him that his name and face were riveted in my memory for ever, and meant only one thing to me, that his soft words to the landlady had buttered MY parsnips!

I managed to get through the week at Newcastle by staying in bed most days and just getting up to go to the theatre at night. Although there was one terrible day when I decided a breath of sea air might just be the thing to get some energy into my aching bones, and I nearly didn't have strength to get back to the guest house, much less to the Theatre Royal. Somebody had told me we were only a bus ride from Whitley Bay, and as I've always been mad about the seaside and convinced salt air would cure anything from ingrowing toenails to galloping dandruff, nothing would do but that I'd make for the miles of sands as soon as I'd swallowed my lunch. It was the first time I'd had any real exercise since I'd caught the 'flu virus, and I had no idea of the bracing strength of those wintry winds, or of how weak I was. I set off at a fine pace across the sands, gulping down great draughts of sea air, but, to my dismay, instead of bounding along with greater and greater vitality after all this beautiful ozone, my head spun with dizziness, my legs wobbled like a jelly and, worst of all, I couldn't draw a breath. What was the matter with me? There wasn't a soul within miles – nothing but sea birds and me. Thankfully my eye caught a little beach hut and I struggled towards it, collapsed on to the beach, and fought to get my breath back. I sounded like Grannie in one of her bad doses of bronchitis. I wheezed like an old gramophone. I had gone too far to go back the way I'd come, and there was a staggeringly long way to go yet before I could catch any sort of transport. I grew so scared, I wouldn't allow myself to rest as long as I felt I ought, but set off in a zig-zag motion towards the end of the beach and, I hoped, the route to the buses. I kept turning my back to avoid being choked by the wind, and it seemed to take hours before I reached the path which eventually led me to a bus, and home. When I got to my room, I threw myself down on the bed, and I felt so weak that I didn't know how I was ever going to summon enough energy to walk downstairs for tea, much less do a show that night. I felt that this was what it must feel like to be drunk. And in a sense I suppose I was. Drunk with far too strong air gulped into 'flu-weakened blood and lungs.

Eventually I made myself swing my legs to the floor to see if I could stand upright. I could. I determined to say nothing to anybody, so that if they behaved normally towards me, expecting nothing unusual in my performance or manner, then I might just get through the evening. Luckily Jean St Clair was in sparkling form throughout tea, so my quietness went unnoticed, particularly as she and one of the understudies started arguing as to which of them had left the bathroom in a mess, with towels on the floor. They made such a row that I could rise from the table with a casual 'See you later. I've my apron to check with wardrobe', and make my way to the theatre without them. I needed all my precious energy for the performance. At a chemists I picked up some glucose, which the man behind the counter recommended as a first-class energy-giver after too much exertion. Thanks to its help, and to keeping my own counsel, the final curtain saw me still in one piece, with nobody suspecting how near I had come to missing the performance. That afternoon taught me one valuable lesson – that you can have too much of a good thing, especially if that good thing is strong pure sea air when the body is weak.

I learned too, the truth behind Lady Churchill's precept, 'Never enlarge upon your difficulties except to tried and trusted friends.' For if people don't know you are in difficulties, they won't undermine your struggle by too much sympathy which can sap the will.

After Newcastle, we were to visit Sheffield, Manchester, Northampton, Nottingham, Blackpool, Liverpool, Cardiff, Swansea, Leeds, Birmingham, Cambridge, Bournemouth and Brighton. These were all Number One dates. I was delighted by the prospect of seeing so many new places, for with my husband overseas and no home responsibilities while I was chasing a career, I was footloose and fancy free. But those who had left comfortable homes, and in some cases husbands, wives or families, weren't so pleased to be touring. I soon saw why. It was too soon after the war for travel to be anything but a penance. There was no new rolling stock on the railways, the trains had little or no heating, and Sunday travel took hours over the normal timetables. 'Actors and fish always travel on Sundays', Reggie Gosse our manager would say with his genial smile. The other manager, Ossie Wilson, always made me laugh because of his firm determination *not* to share his train beer. There were no buffet cars and hardly any food or drink of any kind to be had on station platforms. When we'd assemble on Sunday mornings he would call out in ringing tones, 'I hope anyone who wants beer has made proper provision, for I do *not* share my train beer with anyone. Is that clear? Good.' Nobody could now expect misplaced charity from him, or have any hope of softening his heart by pleading sudden thirst.

I was most impressed by Ossie's courage in warning off moochers like this, and I applauded his attitude. I remembered only too well my own irritation with those foolish Virgins who came on our Guide outings without a bit of food to cook, well content to take advantage of the wise provisioning of more obedient girls. Now if only I had had Ossie's courage and strength of character, I might just have taught such improvident girls a lesson which would have served them in good stead all their lives.

Although practically everyone bought Sunday papers to while away the hours spent on freezing journeys on those terrible trains, once we'd read each other's horoscopes, Matty wouldn't let us read a word. He'd fling his arms wide and knock the papers away from us as we attempted to digest the news. 'You don't want to bother with that rubbish', he would roar. 'It's been the same for the last sixty years and it won't be any better in the next sixty – let's talk and keep ourselves warm.' (When I first saw him I thought Matty was about sixty years old, and I was absolutely amazed to learn that he was actually seventy-six.) On those train journeys he would keep us so enthralled that we almost forgot our numb toes and fingers as we listened to tales of Sir Gerald du Maurier, and of the horse which Sir Gerald had taught to stop outside Harrods while he went in to do his shopping. On one occasion he had lent it to a distinguished Parliamentarian whose own horse had gone lame, and when the Hon. gent had finished his ride in the park and reached Harrods on his way to the stables, the animal had stopped dead in its tracks and absolutely refused to budge. It was deaf to command or prod, and by the time the beast decided shopping time was over, a small crowd had gathered round the scarlet-faced rider wondering what the famous man was doing sitting outside Harrods as though on traffic duty.

But the tale of du Maurier which shook me to the core, new recruit that I was, was of the night he and Matty stood in the wings waiting for their entrance in a new play, and, to while away the time, started discussing a play they had both been in some years earlier. When they eventually walked on to the stage, they did a whole scene from the *first* play. 'But Matty', I said aghast, 'weren't the audience all mixed up?' 'Not they', he roared. 'Never noticed a damn thing'. Then he added as an afterthought, 'It was a far better play anyway!'

He told me that Gladys Cooper at seventeen was the prettiest thing he had ever seen in his life. 'With the possible exception of Ellaline Terris', he added. 'There was another beauty'. In this first play of Gladys Cooper, in which he was starring of course, he told me that for her first appearance on stage she was seated on a sort of cushion, like little Miss Muffet, and when the curtain rose she was discovered there. 'The curtain rose', Matty told me. 'There was one long intake of breath, and then the whole audience broke into spontaneous applause.' He added that it was the only time in all his long career that he knew of such an instinctive tribute to sheer beauty.

'Och Matty', I said to him during one of those journeys (this was before he wrote his biography). 'You should get it all written down, for you have so many memories that nobody else shares'. 'Tried it once, young Molly', he said. 'They sent a damn girl with a notebook who sat and gazed at me waiting for me to talk – couldn't think of a damn thing, so *that* was no good'. I believed him. He needed the stimulus of fellow actors before he could let himself go.

These cold journeys took their toll of the company's health, and there always seemed to be somebody who was coughing or sneezing, and terrified of losing his voice. Matty was hit like the rest of us lesser mortals and he went into very bad bronchitis.

We always had a theatre doctor allocated to us in each town for, like cricketers, actors are notoriously accident prone, and, like the Chinese, when it's a case of 'no work no pay' the show must go on! The theatre doctor prescribed one dessertspoonful of a strong chlorodyne mixture for Matty, three times a day after meals. He loathed the stuff and one day, whether by accident or design, he forgot to take the medicine as prescribed. He may even have decided to get the whole nastiness over at one fell swoop, for he took all three dessertspoonfuls after his light pre-theatre meal. This concentration of chlorodyne was far too much for him in what was almost a lethal dose, and as he returned to his dressing room at the end of act two, he collapsed in the corridor outside my dressing room. Everybody thought he had died, for the sound of his crashing down brought us all into the corridor. To my amazement, the others retreated in fright, but I hadn't been a Girl Guide for nothing. I flew to his dressing room, found towels and soaked them in water, grabbed a cushion to put under his feet, and loosened his collar. The understudy meantime was dressing with frantic speed, to be ready for the third act, which was due to start within a few minutes.

As I dabbed his forehead and wrists with the wet towels, Matty gradually recovered consciousness. The manager appeared and told him not to worry, everything was under control, the understudy was ready to take over. 'What' roared the now recovered Matty, whom I was helping to his room. 'Understudy he damned! I've never missed a performance in sixty years, and I'm not going to start now!' And go on he did, in spite of lips as blue as Stephen's ink, and sublimely ignoring the fact that the rest of us were nervous wrecks wondering if he was going to die on stage. He was so groggy that he had to sit down for the entire third act, all the rehearsed moves thrown out of the window, and we had all to adjust our moves by instinct to accommodate this new position. We ducked round him behind the sofa, said a line and then drifted towards him, pussy-footed round one another until we nearly had hysterics, but we ended the play as written, and the audience wasn't a bit the wiser.

Next morning, because I felt that an old man like him needed it far more than I did, I took my solitary egg, my ration for the month, round to his digs. 'Now eat it all', I commanded him, 'you need the nourishment an egg can give after that carry-on last night. We don't want to go through all *that* again.' He seemed very amused, and promised to eat everything but the shell. The following forenoon he appeared at the door of my digs with a slice of ham between two slices of dry bread. There wasn't even a paper round the 'piece', and I may say his hands were none too clean. 'Here y'are, my girl', he said, thrusting his offering into my hand. 'A slice of good Belfast ham in exchange for your egg.' Then he looked round the tiny hallway with a conspiratorial air and whispered in my ear, 'How much do you pay for these digs?' '£2. 12s. 6d. A week with attendance. Why?' 'Ha!', he snorted, 'I *thought* that old devil next door was overcharging me, I'm paying £2 15s.'. I shouted with laughter. It was the most unlikely conversation between the star of the show, on top salary, and the youngest member of the company earning rock-bottom wages.

They tried to persuade him to go to an hotel after his collapse. 'Not me', he told me on our way home in the tramcar to our digs alongside each other, 'can't stand the damn places. Vacuum cleaners roaring away at six in the morning and pipes rattling and wheezing all night with all those damn fools having baths.' He was right too. In hotels, actors have to fit in with the rules of the establishment, and must eat and sleep according to the staff's convenience. In theatrical digs, the household revolves round the time-tables of the actors, and the good pro. digs are a home from home.

During one of our tram journeys together, Matty startled a conductor of whom he had asked the time. As the chap started to undo his muffler and fumble about inside an inner pocket to find his old-style watch, Matty fumed impatiently. 'Oh don't strip to the bone, young fella – the nearest hour will do.' He was without doubt a coughdrop, and every outing with him ended up in the rout of those more accustomed to douce obedient citizens. In one town a delivery of melons coincided with our arrival, and Matty decided his wife and sons in London must share this good fortune. He made up an enormous parcel which we both took along to the Post Office, as I wanted some stamps there anyway. When it was weighed, the parcel was too heavy for the permitted maximum. Matty opened the whole thing up and instead of extracting a whole melon, proceeded to reduce the weight slice by slice, which he ate, standing there at the counter! The parcel went on and off the scale as each slice was consumed, and by the time the correct weight was achieved, the Post Office was in an uproar. If they remembered that scene, I'm sure none of those present that day would have been a whit surprised when, in later years, Matty took on the whole Town Council, and posted himself outside in the street, on guard, to prevent their removing the gas lamp which stood outside his house and which he loved. He was a law unto himself, and lovely with it. He posed a terrible threat to those who expected utter conformity to orthodox behaviour, but he was an inspiration to all eccentrics, and embryo eccentrics like me.

He gave me a great demonstration of how an audience can imagine they are seeing something which is not there at all.

Because he lived at Bushey, and wanted to get the earliest possible train home after the show, he started preparing for the homeward journey at the end of the first act of any play in which he was appearing. I saw him do it with ours, and his theories were proved to work. 'Once the audience has accepted the picture of you at the start, young Molly', he said, 'they retain that impression throughout the play, so long as any changes you make are steady and gradual and normal'. So after act one, he used to begin the gentle removal of his stage make-up. Any shading was wiped off first. After his next exit, the eyebrow line was thinned. Then a little greasepaint. And so on. Until by act three his face was cleaned, ready for the street, and nobody had noticed a scrap of difference. They had indeed retained the impression he had created in act one, and this had sustained belief throughout all the gradual removal of the make-up which had created the original picture.

He had a pair of 'going-home' trousers, which he wore for the last scene of every play, whatever the period, and quite irrespective of the type of jacket, robe or waistcoat which appeared above. They were a brownish tweed, and again because of the roguish confidence with which he did everything on stage nobody noticed when this trouser-swopping took place. I proved this for myself when, years later, my husband and I went to see a play starring Matty and Mary Jerrold. I didn't say a word about Matty's strategy, and just waited to see if my husband would notice anything. Up till the final scene, Matty had been in evening trousers, with a short dressing gown on top. The moment he came in for that scene, sure enough, there were the 'going-home' trousers under the silk dressing gown. When I whispered the secret to my husband during the curtain calls, he could hardly believe he hadn't spotted the change. Especially from evening trousers to tweeds. But he hadn't. *Nor* had he noticed that when the hypnotic Matty took his final curtain, his face was naked of the make-up he had worn when the curtain rose. A magic personality, without a doubt, who knew every trick of the trade.

He was a great character. I felt greatly privileged to work with him. Everybody loved him. Even British Rail responded to his eccentric reasoning. He had read somewhere that so long as the wheels of a train are turning, it is technically in motion, so on homeward journeys he actually persuaded drivers to slow down almost to a halt as they reached Watford, the wheels barely turning, so that he could throw his luggage on to the platform and leap out after it. This saved the nuisance of having to go all the way to London, and back again to Bushey. Of all Matty's tricks, I think this was the one which impressed me most. I've never been able myself to persuade train drivers to this point of view, and every time my train roars through Watford without stopping, I think of Matty.

14

Each town we visited offered fresh surprises, and I was enchanted to discover that although Sheffield gave me the most uncomfortable digs of the tour, the countryside outside the grimy centre was well worth exploring. The weather was crisp and sparkling, and I found two soul-mates in Marjorie Fielding's understudy, and the Welsh Assistant Stage Manager, Eirig. We roamed the hills and dales during the day, and one red-letter afternoon we found a welcoming hillside Inn which offered fresh country eggs for tea, without asking for a single food coupon in exchange. Manna from Heaven indeed, which left a lasting impression on my mind, and erased everything else I may have felt about the industrial north.

But the landlady resembled a character from Dickens. She was so short-sighted that she never even noticed the sooty oily smuts which drifted on to the food she brought in to us, and worse, the scattered hairs from her brindled coiffure, which I daren't pick out from the stews or spaghettis, for she stood and toasted herself at the gas fire while we ate our suppers. Imagination of what her kitchen must be like threatened to choke me even more than the hairy food, but I had to make a show of getting it down because she thought she was being so good to us.

Her taste in pictures was macabre, to say the least. My bedroom walls were adorned with paintings of rats, peeping round the corners of barns, squaring up to one another like boxers, rolling eggs with their feet. Before I went to sleep, I had to turn the pictures to the wall, shuddering as my eyes came so close to the horrid painted vermin, or I'd have had even worse nightmares than I suffered during that awful week in such unsavoury digs.

Bob, one of the stage managers, also stayed at those digs and although he laughed at my fussiness over the hairs and the smuts in the food, he was scared enough of her not to knock her up when he arrived home after midnight, preferring to throw stones at my window to bring me down to open the door for him. We were each allowed a key, but the door was bolted at midnight and no excuses were accepted.

Actually the reason why Bob was so late that night was because he had gone to see a late performance of 'Lost Week-End', that marvellous film about a dipsomaniac which was supposed to serve as an unforgettable lesson to all heavy drinkers. Bob, in the words of the true Glaswegian, liked a good bucket, and when I said primly that I hoped the film had taught him the error of his ways – (I was mad at being wakened out of my hard-won sleep under the picture of the rats) – he said he had been so shattered he had had to find a club, and calm his fears with a few whiskys!

It was at Blackpool that I started my love affair with seaside resorts out of season. The miles of wide bare sands, the clean-washed look of the town devoid of trippers and candy floss, the friendliness of shops which had time for me. All this made a strong appeal and taught me there is much charm to be found in a resort when it is not wearing its holiday face. So much so, that I have deliberately sought such conditions ever since. Never again for me high season holidays and crammed beaches.

During one of the Sunday train calls, Reggie Gosse told us we might have to extend the tour for a week or so because London was enjoying a theatre boom. The entertainment-starved demobbed soldiers were packing the theatres, and managements couldn't be expected to take off plays which were playing to full houses. There were one or two grumbles, but in the end everybody accepted the logic of the situation, for it was felt we had a good play on our hands which could easily run for a year in London. I, in my ignorance of the vast passing population which went through London, couldn't imagine how there could be enough people to attend a theatre eight times a week for twelve whole months, but the others said a year and I took their word for it.

During the tour, a steady flow of air letters from my husband in the Middle East followed me from theatre to theatre. We both longed for the day of his release from the Air Force, but hadn't the least idea when his class would be sent home. And then, in Liverpool, there on the green baize board was the letter I had been waiting for. He would be home any day. His section were due to arrive in England some time during the week beginning 19th March. That was this week! As soon as his papers had been cleared, he would join me.

My heart turned a dozen somersaults of delight. It had been over two years since I had seen him. And here I was, meeting him as an actress. It was going to be *marvellous*. And then I had a sudden thought. What about my digs, so carefully and prudently booked for a lone female? Would my landladies be able to change my booking to a double room? Would they even believe he was my husband? Or would they, as the more ribald members of the company suggested, imagine I had found myself one of the 'Brylcreem boys', (the nickname for Air Force lads), and was taking him under my wing for the rest of the tour? I wished they hadn't sown that seed in my mind, for now I was in an agony of embarrassment as I wrote to the landladies, and I tried to sound honest and respectable so that there couldn't be the slightest doubt that I was speaking the truth and sought space for a newly-returned husband.

Each day I looked for the telegram which would tell me he was in England. But none came. And then on the Friday night, as I came off stage after my first entrance in the second act, there he was standing in the wings. My Sandy. In uniform. He looked tanned and splendid. He held me at arm's length. 'My, you're awfu' wee', were his first romantic words. 'You're no' very big yourself', I retorted, and, on shaking legs, went on to make my next entrance. So his first sight of me after all that time apart was in full stage make-up, dressed in cap and apron as Bertha.

The cast were thrilled to the marrow that the romance of our reunion had taken place before their very eyes, and the ladies all insisted on contributing their most glamorous nighties and undies to form my borrowed trousseaux. They guessed, quite rightly, that my own were nothing to write home about after years as a low earner, with little cash and fewer coupons to spend on fripperies. I didn't really want to take their things, but they seemed so hurt by my attempts at refusal that I weakly accepted everything. I was terrified at the mere thought of washing such delicate and expensive finery before handing it back, for I knew full well that if I spoilt anything it was quite irreplaceable. They were pre-war silks and crêpe-de-chines, their treasures, which they were lending, and nothing like that could be bought anywhere in England just then. As it turned out, only one ghastly nightie refused to be tamed and remained creased and sad however much I ironed it, but nobody seemed to mind. I'd have been mad at getting my best goonie back in such a poorly-ironed state. No wonder they say 'toffs are careless'.

Temporarily free of all responsibility, my husband was able to enjoy the hilarious turn his life had taken. He sometimes shook his head, with a bemused air, and said he couldn't imagine anything which provided a greater contrast to conditions in the Middle East with the RAF, than finding himself touring with a company of 'theatricals'. He too found the whole set-up very reminiscent of Priestley's 'Good Companions', just as I had. Especially the theatrical digs. When we'd arrive at a new address, we'd pretend we were a double act. We would stand on the door-mat side by side, strike a pose, throw our arms towards the heavens and announce to the closed door, 'We are the Flying Scots'. We'd then dissolve in laughter at our own clowning. Sometimes, to our confusion and dismay, a soft-footed landlady would throw the door open as we were going through this pantomime, and we'd swiftly transform ourselves into meek, well-behaved quiet tenants in case she'd think she was dealing with a couple of lunatics and shut the door in our face.

Spring came very early that year, and after the bitter winter, and years of war, this first peace-time awakening melted the heart. Sandy revelled in the soft beauty of the Welsh and English countryside after the harsh light and parching heat of the Middle East, and the tour turned into a long glorious holiday. During long enchanted days we wandered along the sea-shores, or climbed the hills, and we remembered a hundred things we had to say about the time we had been apart. Letters cannot say it all. It was all quite, quite perfect. Even the landladies managed to greet us with smiling faces, in spite of having had to re-arrange accommodation to suit us, and with our Scottish voices had no doubt at all that we were legitimately Mister and Missus!

The weather grew balmier, and Cambridge in May was a dream. No wonder so many romantic tales had been woven around the River Cam, and the punts, and the lush meadows. After the industrial north, this was fairyland. There was blossom on the bough, and the trees unfolded delicate foliage to delight our senses. The little chintz and mahogany furnished parlour put at our disposal by a charming landlady couldn't fit into the category of 'digs' by the wildest stretch of imagination. It was a picture-book setting, and we loved every minute of that week in Cambridge. And if we loved Cambridge, Cambridge loved us. The undergraduates roared their approval of the play and we came off flushed with success after each performance. We had had every last roughness polished during the tour, and we all felt we were ready for London.

Cambridge was to be a week of decision for all of us. It was in the little chintz parlour that my husband picked up the book which made him decide he would study for the qualification of shipbroker when he returned to Scotland. He had always been in shipping, but knew that after the break caused by the war he would take a little time to pick up the threads of his job. This then would be the right moment to expand his knowledge and help his prospects.

It was in the theatre, after Friday pay-call, that we actors faced our moment of decision. We had been asked to remain for a few moments as the manager had something to say. We were within a week of the London opening, and nobody wanted to voice the foreboding we all felt, that we were going to be asked to continue the tour. But instinct was right. It was put to us that the situation continued of too many good plays chasing too few theatres. Try as it might, the management simply hadn't been able to spot a single play which looked like tottering to a close. We were asked to consider extending the tour by another month, by which time conditions might be more favourable for us coming into London.

I would gladly have agreed to go on with the tour. Sandy was still on demobilization leave, and we were thoroughly enjoying ourselves, for we felt this was as good a way of spending it as any other. In fact it was such an original way of spending his leave that we couldn't quite get over it. Once the play opened in London, there was no knowing when we would have any length of time together, for I would be there for the duration of the run and he would be returning to an empty house without me. So an extended tour suited us very well.

Alas, the stars were growing impatient. Other offers were coming in, and above all they were anxious to go home to rejoin their families. Even more so than today, it was star names which sold plays and drew audiences, so when they said they preferred to finish the engagement at the end of the following week in Brighton, it was the final curtain for all of us. It hadn't occurred to me that their refusal to tour would mean the end of the play. But it did.

Before we said goodbye, Marjorie Fielding sent for me. 'It's such a pity for your sake, we're not having a London opening', she said. 'This would have established you in London as a real comedienne. That part is yours and no-one else's'. At the time I took this with a pinch of salt, although I thought it was very nice of her to bother telling me such a thing, but in the light of later experience I've come to believe she may have been right. Theatregoers and managements would have seen me in my own style of comedy, in a strong part, playing my own age, and yet a part not taxing in a way which would have brought out the hatchets if I'd fallen short of expectations. I believe I could have made steady progress from there. I've often thought that if 'A Play for Ronnie' had opened in London as planned, my future would have been found in the theatre and not in the other media.

But it was not to be.

Our fates are hinged on many contingencies and my footsteps were turned in quite different directions for the strangest of reasons, simply because the theatre was doing too well. The post-war boom brought my short stage career to a sudden halt when continuity was essential.

Marjorie Fielding said something else to me which I have

never forgotten. 'If you stay in this profession, Molly', she said, 'and I believe that you will, you'll surely find that you either have no work at all, or you'll get three offers all at once, all clashing. You will only be able to do one. So sit down, look at them from all angles, and decide in the light of your knowledge *at that time* what is best for you to do. Having made your decision, forget the other two. If you don't, you'll become embittered by the memory of bad decisions, which only seem bad because of *later* knowledge. And you'll become an old woman before your time. Never waste time looking back regretting jobs you didn't accept.'

I didn't realize then how hard it was going to be to follow this excellent advice, but time has proved how right this wise lady was. Because she foresaw so clearly how things would be, I've tried to profit from her kind words of wisdom, although not always with conspicuous success. The hardest thing in show business is to refrain from saying, 'Och if only I'd taken the other one'. Whenever I'm tempted into this profitless folly, Majorie's words appear before me in letters of fire, and I bless the thoughtfulness which prompted a leading lady of the theatre to pass on the fruits of her experience to a raw recruit.

The tour ended at Brighton and we were all brought back to London, where we disbanded, and although we had all lived so closely together for fourteen weeks, there were some of that company whom I never met again. I found that very sad. Sandy and I spent a few days in London, sight-seeing in the day time and squashing uncomfortably into the lumpy single bed at Clapham at night. We couldn't make up our minds whether our future was to be in London or Glasgow. I had had excellent notices in every town we had played, and Sandy felt it would be only fair to let me try to consolidate this success while he was busy studying and settling into civilian life in Glasgow. To allow me to do this, I should keep on the London flat for another six months at least and see what would follow 'A Play for Ronnie'. I wouldn't stay in London all the time, of course, but pop back and forth as events dictated, and Sandy preferred the idea of my having a settled base in Clapham rather than seeking odd digs from time to time.

With that decision taken, the rent was paid, and we headed for home, back to Scotland, together.

Oh it was lovely to see all the husbands back home again, and the look of strain fade from the faces of the young wives now that they could pass the reins of responsibility to a stronger pair of hands. The children were so proud of their returned daddies, and the whole avenue radiated pure happiness. Everybody was in demand, as babysitters were at a premium, for all wanted to go on the town to celebrate their release.

I hardly dared breathe a word to anybody that I wasn't home for good, for it seemed the basest ingratitude to welcome a safely returned husband, only to abandon him to an empty house. My mother and my ma-in-law both thought I was out of my mind, and that Sandy was worse for letting me go. 'Whit in the name o' Goad dae ye want to go away doon there again for?', my mother demanded. 'Ah thought ye'd be glad tae get hame tae yer ain hoose, and look efter Sandy.'

But we knew what we were doing, and Sandy thought he would quite enjoy coming to London when I didn't come north. I left him my easiest recipes, with all the instructions written in shorthand, so it was a splendid opportunity for him to refresh his memory of his shorthand studies at the same time. Nothing like hunger for sharpening the brain, and he'd have to transcribe those outlines before he could unravel the cooking secrets. I may say that many a dish was left at a vital moment while he dashed to the telephone and checked with me the meaning of a forgotten outline!

Some weekends he came down to see me, and at others I went up to join him, and we didn't realize we were setting a pattern we were to follow for many a long day. I can never understand why the Railways run at a loss, for I am confident that the money we have spent in fares over the years, merely to be together, would have been enough to make any dubious line solvent.

In London I made the usual appointments to see agents, and producers, and this time I extended my range beyond theatre and films to TV but nothing much was happening. If I thought I had created a tiny ripple among the critics in the provinces, not a whisper of my performance had reached the ears of anyone in London.

As always when things reach stalemate, I turned my thoughts to studying again. I would take singing and dancing lessons. Where could I find better coaching than in the capital? I found my mentors in the most casual way. A girl met in the canteen gave me the name of her singing teacher, while another met in an agent's waiting room passed on the name of her dancing coach. I didn't check whether or not they were first-class. It was enough to have a name or a telephone number I could contact.

The dancing teacher was a charlatan of the first order. It was Mr Torrance of the piano lessons all over again*, that rascal who had used my piano-time to retreat behind a newspaper and who taught me nothing, while taking my mother's hard-earned cash.

This 'dancing master' asked me to show him what I knew of dance routines, seemed delighted with my execution of the 'time step' which my mother always referred to as the 'clog wallop', directed me to the barre, showed me how to do a few exercises, and vanished into the back premises, never to reappear until the hour was up, when he collected his fee and shut the door behind me.

I went once a week, continually waiting for the moment to arrive when I would be shown some exciting new dance routines. The London weather grew hotter and hotter, and perspiration poured from me as I exercised like a dervish at the barre, while my dancing master remained serene and cool, having moved not a muscle during the entire lesson.

I don't know how long I would have tolerated this behaviour, but one day when I ventured to put my head round the door leading to the back premises, nerving myself to ask when I was going to learn some routines, I heard him 'phoning in a bet to his bookmaker. The ingrate was taking my money, doing nothing to assist me to become another Vera Ellen, and putting my fee on horses! That was the end. I handed him my fee at the end of the lesson – and it was every penny of half a guinea – shook hands with him, and told him I was off home for a

---

* BEST FOOT FORWARD

holiday. I never saw him again. Nor did I ever see the girl who had given me his name. Perhaps they were in league to rob the innocent!

The singing teacher, however, was a great find. I went to his office in a music publisher's building off Charing Cross Road, where all the musicians hung about, and we practised scales, and ran through the many excellent numbers he found for me from the current revues and musical shows. This was the great age of the revue, and the numbers were both witty and tuneful and great fun to interpret. I went to this splendid coach off and on for years afterwards, and we became good friends. It was typical of the London scene though, that we had no idea where each other lived, and after I'd been going into London for several weeks for my lessons, I asked him one night if I might have his home telephone number as it might be necessary for me to cancel my next lesson and I'd only know the evening before. When he gave this to me, I looked up in great surprise. 'Macaulay?', I said, 'That's my exchange. Where do you live?' 'In Clapham', he answered. Not only in Clapham, would you believe it, but two doors away from my room! And I'd been spending money on fares all that time when all I needed to do was walk ten yards! After that I always went to his rooms and we rehearsed there, at no travelling expense for me, and a great convenience for both of us.

Everybody seemed to be going on holiday. London was a steaming cauldron. I'd never known such heat. The grass in the parks was scorched brown, something I didn't know was possible. I'd certainly never seen it happen in Scotland. It grew airless and humid as day followed day, and my room at the top of the house caught and held the heat, and it was like the blast from an oven when I opened the door. Miss Chree seemed never to be there, and Lois was with her friends. Even the landlady had gone to ground, and the rent book was pushed under my door without benefit of a friendly word. Everyone seemed to have her own fish to fry.

Suddenly it seemed the height of folly to be wandering around London on my own when nobody showed the slightest interest in employing me. Neither in films, theatre, or TV was anything promised for the immediate future. I'd done everything I could. I'd go home for a while, and try again after the holidays.

But before I went, I'd just see what radio had to offer. I hadn't really tried very hard for radio work, feeling that I could always get such engagements in Glasgow. I wasn't in London for BBC work. I saw London as the mecca of theatre, films and television, not radio. But there was one radio show which could only be done from London. And it was the best show of all. There could be no harm in having a crack at it before I went home. I would try for ITMA.

I was quite ignorant of the mainsprings of this immortal show, which had sustained and gladdened the hearts and minds of all Britain during the war, and which had also been listened to by partisans on many illegally-used sets in enemy controlled territory. I only knew that it starred Tommy Handley, and that it was written by Ted Kavanagh. Beyond this, I knew nothing. I hadn't the faintest idea as to the whereabouts of Kavanagh's office, and indeed I only knew he was the writer because I met him with Tommy one day in Aeolian Hall when they were having lunch. The first time I had seen them there, I had gazed long and intently at Tommy's famous face, but had been far too shy to dream of going over and speaking to him. When I told my landlady, with great excitement, that I had actually been in the same canteen with 'that man' and a big red-haired chap, she was contemptuous of my lack of gumption in not seizing my opportunity to have a word with him. 'Next time,' she said, 'that is, if you're lucky enough to *have* a next time, go over and speak. You can't expect them to know who you are. But everybody knows who Handley and Kavanagh are. It's up to you to introduce yourself'.

Sure enough, my luck was in, for on my next visit to Aeolian Hall where I had an appointment with Ronnie Waldman, there they were again sitting at lunch, Tommy Handley and the same plump red-haired man. The BBC canteen in those days was a very democratic place, where the famous and the unknown queued up together for meals.

I waited until they were sipping their coffee, then, with beating heart, approached them. I think I really only found the courage to do so because I couldn't have faced my landlady if I had had to confess that I had seen them again and hadn't spoken. I hadn't the least idea what I was going to say, and when they looked up to see who had stopped by their table, I found myself murmuring something about how wonderful it was to see Tommy in person, having listened to him all during the war. I told them how much the people in Scotland enjoyed the programme, and how we marvelled at the topicality of the scripts. Tommy laughed and said, 'Well, this is Ted Kavanagh. He writes the words. I just say them'. As I shook hands with Ted, I said, 'I'm Molly Weir', remembering my landlady's advice to introduce myself. He at once asked, 'Do you know what a tattie bogle is?' 'Yes', I answered, a bit surprised by the question. 'It's a scarecrow'. They both laughed, I said cheerio, and that was that.

So I was able to tell my landlady that I'd had the spunk to talk to them, and that Ted Kavanagh had revealed as I walked away that he had heard me in Down at the Mains. That was almost as hard for me to take in as it was to realize that I'd had the cheek to speak to them at all.

So, I thought, before I go back to Glasgow I'll try to see this Ted Kavanagh again, just in case there might some time be something in the show for a Scot. You never knew your luck.

As I stood at Piccadilly Circus, wondering if I could be bothered in all this heat to go back to Aeolian Hall to try to find out the address of the Kavanagh office, I saw coming towards me one of my Glasgow radio friends, Ian Sadler. 'Ian', I called, 'have you any idea where Ted Kavanagh's office is?' 'Down there', he said, and turned me round to face the street running down the Circus to the Mall. And he gave me the number. Ian smiled and said that I must be the only aspiring actress in London who didn't know that address. I was almost within spitting distance of it, without being aware that I was.

When I asked the girl at the desk if I could see Mr Kavanagh, she threw me a glance in which she blended scorn for my nerve and pity for my ignorance. 'Mr Kavanagh', she said, as if I had enquired for God Himself, which in a way I suppose I had. 'You can't see Mr Kavanagh without an appointment, and in any case he is at a meeting and cannot be disturbed.'

At that psychological moment, the door to an inner office

opened and Ted Kavanagh came out carrying a sheaf of papers. He had heard my voice apparently, for he stopped. 'Are you in London nowadays, Molly?', he asked. My goodness, I thought, he must have a phenomenal memory for faces and names. He'd only met me once. 'More or less', I answered cautiously. I didn't want to tell a lie. I had a room in London, but I was on my way home after all, so 'more or less' seemed reasonably accurate.

'Wait a minute', he said, and disappeared into his office. What was I having to wait for, I wondered? The girl looked at me with dawning respect. Clearly I wasn't so insignificant as I looked.

A few minutes later he appeared again, handed me some scripts and said, 'Ring Francis Worsley at Aeolian Hall and make an appointment to go to see him tomorrow. We're holding auditions for new voices for ITMA all day'.

My mouth fell open. I clutched the scripts he'd given me to my beating heart. It was unbelievable. It was one of those show business coincidences which sound too fantastic to be true. Without so much as a whisper from the grape-vine, of which I wasn't a part anyway, and in complete ignorance of any future plans they had for the show, I had innocently gone into Kavanagh's office at the precise moment when a complete re-shuffle of the cast was to take place. Plans had been made to introduce a post-war freshness to ITMA by the introduction of anything up to four new voices, and thanks to my shot in the dark, I now had a chance to try for one of those voices.

If I hadn't been in Piccadilly Circus on that day and at that time, and if I hadn't met Ian Sadler, or had decided to postpone action till a later date, or indeed if Ted Kavanagh hadn't come into the outer office when he did, I would have missed my opportunity, for there was only the next day for the final auditions. Tommy was off on holiday immediately afterwards.

One day later would have been too late.

Five minutes either way could have been too late.

When I rang Aeolian Hall, I asked for Miss Frances Worsley and I heard a suppressed giggle at the other end of the telephone. I seemed fated to bestow the wrong sex on everything connected with the Bond Street premises of the BBC.

What with Miss Oley Anne Hall, and now Frances for Mr Francis Worsley who, I now learned, was only the producer of the whole show! He was the third of the great triumvirate, the creators of ITMA. Tommy Handley, Ted Kavanagh and Francis Worsley. Kavanagh had rung him confirming that I had been given scripts. Now I was told to be at the studios at eleven A.M. next morning. I was to have a look at the scripts, and also bring along any other material I had which would demonstrate any comedy talent which might be useful.

I flew home and rushed immediately into the landlady's cubby-hole, to tell her my exciting news. She was quite sure it was because she had encouraged me to speak to them that they had given me this chance. I didn't want to rob her of her triumph by mentioning that Kavanagh hadn't exactly been out combing the streets looking for me, and had probably forgotten all about that brief encounter over the coffee cups until he saw me in his office.

I decided I must be fully rested for the auditions next day, so after tea I undressed, threw open the window to make the room as cool as possible, and studied the scripts I'd been given until I could have said them backwards. I tried out every accent, with every permutation of tone and vocal range I knew. I sounded flat as a pancake. I wasn't within miles of the sparkling attack I'd enjoyed listening to in past ITMAs. Och I hadn't a hope. I leaped from the bed and rummaged through my songs and old scripts. Maybe if they had time to listen to me doing 'Please Captain I've swallowed my Whistle', and my imitations of Dietrich and Francis Day, I'd make a better impression. I'd take them with me, just in case.

I tossed and turned all night, and felt as limp as a rag next morning. It was a morning of shimmering heat again, and when I presented myself at Aeolian Hall and was shown into the studio, I was astounded to find Tommy Handley himself at the microphone. 'Oh', I said, my voice squeaking with surprise. 'Have I to read with you?' Somehow I had never imagined Tommy would read with everyone. I thought he would be saved to read with the winners. 'Who else did you think you'd be reading with?', he said with a chuckle, and I blushed for my ignorance. Of course, when I thought about it, they'd have to hear each voice with Tommy's for how else could they judge how it would sound against that inimitable style?

Somebody called from the control room and told me to start with script number three.

We went through them all, Tommy and I, and he was kindness itself. He made me feel I was giving a good performance, calmed the worst of my fears by laughing in all the right places, and turned the whole thing into as happy an occasion as it could be, considering my heart was beating like a drum at a military tattoo. I realized that not only was I getting a great chance, but I was also being given every assistance to make the most of it. I knew that whether I succeeded or whether I failed, 'that man' was going to be right up there in my personal gallery of the 'greats' of show business, not just because he was the brightest star in radio, but because he was a kind, gentle man, with time to be generous to an unknown performer who was consumed with nerves.

While I went through my own comedy material, Tommy left the studio to join the others in the control room, and I turned my back to the glass panel because I couldn't bear to watch their reactions to my comedy numbers. When I had finished, the pianist gave me an encouraging wink. Then there was silence.

'Thank you, Miss Weir. We'll be in touch if we want you.'

As I walked through the corridor, Ted Kavanagh barred my way. 'Where can we contact you when we've made our decision', he asked. I gave him my Clapham number. When I ventured to ask if it would be all right if I went on holiday, he patted my shoulder. 'Of course', he said. 'So long as we have your London number. We won't come to any decision for at least six weeks'.

And then I was in the street.

This time my stomach told me nothing. I had no inner advance warning to prepare me for success or failure.

I would just have to wait and see.

15

If Sandy found theatrical touring was a bewildering contrast to his life in the RAF, my life as a Glasgow housewife was almost equally strange compared with my existence in my bed-sitter in London. I felt as though I were two different people. In Clapham I was perfectly capable of staying in bed till ten o'clock in the morning, then dressing to the nines and sallying forth to involve myself with interviews and engagements all day, not returning to my room till around eight o'clock in the evening. The idea of housework scarcely entered my head, and my personal shopping and laundry were taken care of almost on the wing, as it were.

In London, all entertaining was done in tearooms. Nobody ever invited you to their house. You met in canteens or in Joe Lyons, and you sat for hours over a cup of coffee and, if you were lucky, a sandwich. I was one of the few actresses who did any cooking, and even I had now reduced my culinary adventures to eggs and cheese and the odd pot of soup. This wasn't because I had gone off cooking or eating, but because of the ghastly shock I had in the tube one day when I became very conscious of a very strong smell of fat nearby. I gave surreptitious little sniffs to right and left of me, wondering if anybody was carrying cooked food in their brief-cases. No, they were all very correct business types. It clearly wasn't any of them. And then a horrible suspicion dawned. Could it be my own clothes which were sending off the fatty fumes? It could, and was.

All those chops and joints of meat I'd cooked in my little tin oven had wafted their greasy vapours into the soft wool of my suit, and of course the moment one went into a warm humid atmosphere the vapours were released. I hadn't realized that when clothes are merely concealed behind a curtain they're not protected from cooking smells, for I had never before, not even in Springburn, had my best clothes hanging where the food was cooked.

Everything had to go to the cleaners.

And that was the end of the frying sessions in Clapham.

Now that I was back in Glasgow with a man to feed, a house to look after, and droves of visitors and relatives coming out and in, the bachelor girl existence I'd led in London seemed like a dream.

As soon as I heard the children's voices in the morning from neighbouring gardens, I was out of bed, and busy from then till bedtime. I hadn't remembered how dirty a house became when people were living fully in it every day, or how many clothes two people soiled. I was forever washing and polishing, taking down curtains and putting them up again, dusting, making beds and lighting fires.

All the family were delighted to think I'd shaken the dust of London from my feet so soon. They knew nothing of the ITMA audition. I had been sworn to utter secrecy by the BBC because they wanted no hint of their plans to leak out to the press until they were ready. Sandy was the only one I was permitted to tell. We had talked round and round the difficulties of our situation if I actually did get this part, for as the show went out live each week it meant I'd have to be in London. Sandy had now started with his old shipping company again in Glasgow. How on earth would it all turn out?

Then we decided we were mad planning so far ahead. It was most unlikely anyway that I'd be offered ITMA for I didn't think I had impressed them very much. We agreed to put it right out of our minds and enjoy ourselves and make the most of this glorious summer weather.

I plunged into the Glasgow life-style with zest. Nobody here entertained in tearooms. Visitors were entertained at home and the whole place had to be gone over again, from top to bottom, to make it all quite perfect. Not that anybody would have criticized, but that was the custom and I conformed like everyone else. I baked cakes and shortbread for our visitors and the relatives, scones and pancakes, fruit bread and pies, and revelled in the luxury of two ration books. It was the double coupons for the tinned food which were the nicest bonus, and one could indulge in all sorts of little luxuries not possible with one lot of coupons.

Nothing was any trouble. Once I even made doughnuts for eight people, going like a dervish over the boiling fat, and serving them sizzling hot from the pan. If I'd been on piecework in a bakery, I couldn't have worked faster, or looked greasier than I did at the end of this session. But nobody in Glasgow pretended there was a cook hidden in the kitchen, and nobody minded my scorched shining face, least of all me. Only London agents paid attention to looks. Glasgow visitors were much more interested in what was provided for their stomachs, and I was delighted to please them.

I did go over the score on one terrible occasion, though, when the local shop had a delivery of ground almonds, a luxury item nobody had seen for years. I decided a little touch of Cordon Bleu artistry wouldn't come amiss, and attempted to make chocolate-almond petits-fours of pâtisserie-like richness. I ignored the expense, as I concentrated on getting the squashy mess into my forcing bag, determined to turn out professionally shaped squiggles and crescents. 'Squeeze steadily but firmly' the instructions said. I did so, and the whole chocolate mixture exploded like buckshot from the other end of the bag, and hit the cooker, the tiled walls behind it, shot up my arms and into my face, and as I ducked, sent the last lot over the kitchen door. Tears pouring down my cheeks at the thought of all those expensive ingredients wasted, I choked at the sight of the chaos all round. But even as I sniffled and gulped, my brain was recovering from the shock and a solution was emerging. The house was practically new. The place as clean as a whistle. I shut my mind to the full implications of what I was doing, and scraped the lot off, and salvaged a respectably sized bowlful from the cooker and walls and a small cupful from my arms and face. I was thankful I worked with clean hands and didn't use make-up on my face in the kitchen! I shaped the chocolate mess into little circles with my fingers, and put them into the oven and prayed for a miracle.

I didn't say a word of this to anyone. Not even to Sandy. At least not until afterwards. He'd commented on them before the visitors arrived, mark you, and said he'd never seen such oddly shaped things before. 'All hand-made pâtisserie is irregularly shaped', I said firmly. 'That's the authentic touch'.

The visitors drooled over them. They were crisp on the outside and gooey in the centre, and they tasted delicious. I watched cautiously before I ventured to try one myself. I realized the visitors weren't just being polite. My chocolate disasters *were* really scrumptious. If there was anything in them which shouldn't have been there, it was either killed in the cooking or disguised in the richness of the mixture. Anyway, nobody was poisoned. But I never made them again. Not even to this day.

I loved the long light evenings, for in London it grows dark so much earlier than in Scotland, and many a stroll we took at midnight round quiet streets, when fingers of light still caressed the sky.

There was a great happiness in just being together without fear. No air-raids. No black-out. No dangerous separation. The simplest pleasures were a matter of rejoicing. Coming into the house and being able to switch on a light without having to think of enemy bombers. Street lamps which could lawfully illuminate our path when it grew dark. Two eggs in one week when there had only been one the previous week. A delivery of skins which inspired our butcher to make mouth-watering sausages, with real meat, and more than a hint of pre-war goodness. An extra half-pint of milk. Enough coupons to buy a pair of summer shoes. Life was very good.

Such was my euphoria that it was fairly easy to forget the world of show business, and that somewhere away at the back of my mind there was a question waiting to be answered. Would I be hearing from Aeolian Hall one of these days, or had it all been settled, and would the nearest I would ever get to ITMA's history be as one of those who had been asked to attend an audition? Oh well, if that were all it was to be, it was more than a lot of people could say.

We hadn't thought Sandy would get another holiday, since he hadn't rejoined his firm until late spring, but they were very fair and said returning servicemen couldn't be penalized because of the timing of their demobilization, and they put his name on the holiday list with the others.

This was a marvellous and unexpected bonus and we decided we'd go mad and go to a really classy resort, and book in at an hotel instead of our usual modest guest house or digs. We've always loved islands, and this time we chose the Isle of Man, a resort which holds great glamour for Glaswegians. From our youth we'd heard colourful tales of wild goings-on at Douglas, but we ourselves preferred the quieter elegant appeal of Port Erin and we managed to book in at a tasteful looking hotel for a fortnight.

It was a glorious holiday from start to finish.

We found the island enchantingly beautiful; when young people describe holiday resorts, they seldom dwell on scenic beauty, and so the sheer loveliness of the Isle of Man came as a great surprise. We would race down the close-cropped turf and gaze on the Calf of Man, letting our eyes search the wide horizon, and rejoicing in the emptiness of sea and sky. We watched fishermen handle huge crabs, and wondered wistfully why the people in our hotel kitchen had no thought of purchasing such beauties for the guests. For it was an undeniable fact that although it was an hotel, and not one of your drab guest houses, the food was decidedly on the skimpy side. So much so, that I couldn't help thinking we should have fared much better if we had just taken a wee house and had spent our money on all the plentiful food which we could see in local shops, but which never seemed to find its way on to our plates. Baskets of eggs filled the windows of the local dairies, and all we had for breakfast was one tiny kipper apiece. It was such a shame, and we were so hungry with all that sea air. I wanted to buy eggs and ask the kitchen to cook them for us, but my husband was aghast at the mere idea.

But if we were critical of the food, we had no such reservations about the company. They were a great crowd, with quite as many English as Scots among them, and we had no difficulty in identifying with all of them. We went bathing, a dozen or more of us, laughing and gasping in sparkling seas, and we became children again as we scampered across miles of golden sands and tossed a huge painted ball to one another. The sun shone from cloudless skies, and we grew tanned, and so filled with energy we felt we could have run right round the island on our own two feet. All the weariness and tensions of war-time finally vanished like morning mists in these blissfully sunlit, health-giving days.

There was a heady excitement for us in savouring all the pleasures of this first post-war holiday together, and everything combined to invest our stay in Port Erin with an unforgettable magic. And we weren't the only ones who felt like this. For of course it was the first post-war holiday for all of us. I was astounded when we all went to say goodbye one evening to a young couple who would be leaving very early next morning. They were one of our bathing crowd, and as we chorused our 'Cheerios', the young wife dissolved in floods of tears. I had never thought an adult could cry for something so slight as the end of a holiday. But perhaps she knew it wasn't just the end of an ordinary holiday. It was the end of the world's honeymoon, when it was enough just to be alive and safe and together. We asked for little more just then. I never forgot that young wife, and I truly hoped that she would find nothing worse in the future to make her cry more sorrowful tears.

For us, something else was to make this holiday even more memorable.

One night, in the middle of dinner, a waitress beckoned me to the door. 'You're wanted on the telephone', she said. 'It's a call from London'.

Sandy and I looked at one another, and I found that my legs were shaking as I crossed the room. I stared at the telephone and couldn't find the courage to pick up the receiver. Thoughts flew through my head like the buzzing of bees, and my mouth went dry. Was it the ITMA office? Would they ring me just to tell me they didn't want me? How had they found my holiday number? Maybe it wasn't Aeolian Hall at all. Maybe it was only my landlady speaking from my own telephone in Clapham. She, after all, had my Port Erin number. No. It *must* be ITMA. They would have obtained the number from my landlady if they were anxious to find me. But if they were as anxious as all that, then it *must* be to tell me they wanted me. But hadn't they said they would let me know one way or the other? I found I couldn't remember whether or not that was what they had said. I felt sick. I hadn't realized I could find the possibility of disappointing news so calamitous. Had I then secretly expected success? I didn't know I had. But if indeed this call was to put an end to any hopes I had cherished, then I must just nerve myself to face rejection and never let them see how much I cared. I remembered with sudden vividness Grannie's scorn for showing my disappointment too openly when I hadn't been included in the back-court concert, and it was like a bracing dash of cold water.

I picked up the receiver.

'Francis Worsley here', the voice said. 'Is that you, Molly? Good. We want you for ITMA.' I let my breath go in a long half-crying gasp. 'The show comes back on the air in September, but we'll give you all the details later about actual dates and rehearsals. I just thought you'd like to know you're to be with us'. I gave a shout of delight, which I stifled at once, for I thought it was all still to be a secret and I was afraid somebody might overhear. The telephone was out in the open hallway, not even in a booth. I forced myself to reduce my excited responses to a whisper until Francis said, 'This is a very bad line, I can hardly hear you'. When I told him why I was whispering, he laughed, 'Oh that's all right, Molly', he said. 'You can tell anyone you wish now. The papers have been informed, and the news will break tomorrow morning with the early editions'.

I laid down the receiver. A thousand emotions exploded inside me like fire-crackers.

When I went back to the dining room and looked at the clock, I could hardly believe that less than five minutes had elapsed since I had left it. Five minutes which changed my whole future. My husband took one look at my face and laid down his knife and fork. 'What was it', he asked, taking my hand. 'I'm in ITMA', I said. 'They want me for ITMA'.

And all at once the whole dining room knew, and, unbelievably, everybody was standing up and cheering. If they had heard I was to be crowned by Royalty, they couldn't have been more thrilled and excited. ITMA had always been more of an English taste than a Scots one, but I had had no idea of the strength of English feeling about this show until I saw the reaction of the quite considerable English crowd at that hotel. For a Scottish crowd to have shown such enthusiasm, I think I'd have to have scored the winning goal for Rangers!

Everybody was speaking at once. They were all congratulating one another that they had *actually* been right *there*, in the room, when the news had broken. This would be something to tell their folks when they went home. Fancy, they had actually heard about it before it had even got into the newspapers.

Sandy and I were quite stunned by their enthusiasm. We'd never expected anything like this. We knew it was important for us, but we hadn't thought it would be of such riveting importance to an entire holiday hotel. It was a slight foretaste of what was to come much later in London.

Even the Management went mad. A party was arranged there and then, and for once they forgot their frugal attitude and we had a buffet which they couldn't have bettered if they had had a week to prepare for it. Nothing was held back for later hunger. The fatted calf was well and truly killed.

We danced and we sang, and I recited and did all my impersonations. The children were allowed to stay up just this once, and we played games and roared through 'The Grand Old Duke of York' and Musical Chairs and other party games for their benefit.

When at last we crept away to bed in the wee sma' hours I had no voice. Excitement and all that yelling had robbed my vocal chords of all sound.

But it didn't matter.

Nothing mattered.

It was less than twelve months since I had left Glasgow with fifty pounds in my Post Office book to seek fame and fortune in London.

My gamble had paid off.

I had been in a play put on by one of London's top West End managements. I had broadcast from London.

Now I was the newest recruit in the greatest radio show anyone had known, a show which would take its place in the history of the second world war as surely as the air battles over London. And although the war was over, I would become part of that history.

One toe was now placed securely on the ladder.